Christian Light Literature Series

Perspectives of Life in Literature

A Christian Literature textbook

Compilers:
John D. Martin
Lucy A. Martin
Lester E. Showalter

Editorial Committee:
Keith Crider
James Hershberger
Robert Wilson

Artist: Mary Beth Bentz
(except as otherwise acknowleged)

CHRISTIAN LIGHT PUBLICATIONS, INC.

Harrisonburg, Virginia 22801-1212

ISBN: 0-87813-927-3
Lithographed in U.S.A.
Christian Light Publications, Harrisonburg, Virginia 22801-1212

Contents

Introduction   ix

UNIT 1: THE SHORT STORY—
FOR THE CHRIST-FILLED LIFE   1

Introduction   1
Mama and the Garfield Boys   Lewis Grizzard   3
The Horse   Marian Hurd McNeely   11
Second Chance   Robert J. Baker   22

   SYMBOLISM   32
Shago   James Pooler   35
A Spark Neglected   Leo Tolstoy   43
Cache of Honor   John F. Hayes   55

   TONE   64
The Mote and the Beam   Robert J. Baker   67
Where Love Is, There Is God Also   Leo Tolstoy   74
Whom Shall I Fear?   Joseph Stoll   86

   UNITY   98
The Great Stone Face   Nathaniel Hawthorne   100
The Doctor of Afternoon Arm   Norman Duncan   118
Too Dark   Ruth Kurtz Hobbs   132

UNIT 2: POETRY—
FOR THE JOYOUS LIFE   144

Introduction   145
Pippa's Song   Robert Browning   145

Sheer Joy   Ralph Spaulding Cushman   150
A Psalm of Life   Henry Wadsworth Longfellow 152
The Pilgrim   John Bunyan   155

POEMS OF A FEATHER—
KINDS OF POETRY   157

Blank Verse   158
The Man With the Hoe   Edwin Markham   159

Rhymed and Bound Verse   162
The Jericho Road   Edwin McNeill Poteat   162

Free Verse   164
Lament   Evangeline Paterson   165

THE ANATOMY OF A POEM—
FOUR POETIC FORMS   168

The Acrostic   168
Infinity   Viola Jacobson Berg   169

The Triolet   169
The Triolet   Lester E. Showalter   169
The Bible   Lester E. Showalter   170
A Key to Happiness   Lester E. Showalter   170
Winter's Coming   Faustina Martin Garber   171
Spring   Lester E. Showalter   171

The Sonnet   172
Lord, What a Change   Richard Chenevix Trench   173
O God, I Love Thee   Nadejda de Braganca   175
Forgiveness   John Greenleaf Whittier   176

Hebrew Poetry   177
Psalm 1   The Bible   182
Psalm 43   The Bible   183
Psalm 66   The Bible   184
Psalm 119:9-16   The Bible   186
Psalm 126   The Bible   188

THE HABITAT OF A POEM— FOUR PURPOSES FOR A POEM 190

George Wagner	John Overholt, translator	191
The Fool's Prayer	Edward Rowland Sill	194
The Battle of Blenheim	Robert Southey	196
A Fable	Ralph Waldo Emerson	199
Prayer Answered by Crosses	*Brethren Hymnbook*	200
The Merchant of Venice	William Shakespeare	204
Macbeth	William Shakespeare	205
Julius Caesar	William Shakespeare	207
What Is So Rare as a Day in June?	James Russell Lowell	208
The Spacious Firmament	Joseph Addison	210
Apostrophe to the Ocean	George Gordon Byron	212
Elegy Written in a Country Churchyard	Thomas Gray	215
Bad Times	Joseph Beaumont	223
Building	Author Unknown	224
The Poet	William Cullen Bryant	225

A FLOCK OF POEMS—POEMS TO PONDER 228

Joy for the Mounting Character 229

Victory in Defeat	Edwin Markham	229
Conscience and Remorse	Paul Laurence Dunbar	230
No Enemies	Charles Mackay	231
Betrayal	Hester H. Cholmondeley	232

Joy for the Caged Spirit 234

Blind But Happy	Fanny Crosby	234
On His Blindness	John Milton	236
Sympathy	Paul Laurence Dunbar	238
A Little Bird I Am	Madame Guyon	239

Joy in the Heights With Christ 241

The Crystal Christ	Sidney Lanier	241
The Boat	George Macdonald	243
Calvary	Edwin Arlington Robinson	244
Good Friday	Christina Rossetti	246

Joy on the Plains With Others   247

Bigot   Eleanor Slater   248

Conventionality   Eloise Hackett   249

Mending Wall   Robert Frost   250

Thy Brother   Theodore Chickering Williams   252

UNIT 3: BIOGRAPHY—

FOR THE EXEMPLARY LIFE   256

Introduction   257

Menno Simons, 1496–1561   John C. Wenger   260

Grace Abounding to the Chief of Sinners   John Bunyan   268

   Preconversion Experiences   269

   Postconversion Experiences   275

   Preaching Experiences   277

   Prison Experience   280

True . . . Till Death—

   The Story of Clayton Kratz   Clarence Y. Fretz   286

   From Childhood to Manhood   287

   Kratz Answers the Call   293

   Calm in the Face of Terror   299

   To Serve and to Suffer   305

William Carey, 1761-1834   F. Deaville Walker   312

   Moulton and the Missionary Call   312

   The Formation of the Baptist Missionary Society   318

   Converts, Trials, and Progress   323

UNIT 4: REFLECTIONS—

FOR THE VICTORIOUS LIFE   330

Introduction   331

REFLECTIONS ON DISCIPLINE   333

Discipline   William MacDonald   334

The Chariots of God   Hannah Whitall Smith   339

The Discipline of Deformity   V. Raymond Edman   347

REFLECTIONS ON AMBITION   353

Acres of Diamonds   Russell H. Conwell   354

The Man Who Planted Hope and
     Grew Happiness   Jean Giono   361

RMS Titanic   Hanson Baldwin   370

Top Man   James Ramsey Ullman   383

REFLECTIONS OF FAITHFUL CHRISTIANS   399

Diary of David Brainerd   David Brainerd   400

Letters of Hermann Stohr   Hermann Stohr   407

Though He Slay Me   E. J. Swalm   413

REFLECTIONS OF BIBLE CHARACTERS   423

Last Night of Sodom   Daniel March   424

The Self-made Fool—Saul   Clovis G. Chappell   435

Ruth, the Moabitess   The Bible   445

UNIT 5: ALLEGORY—

FOR THE FRUITFUL LIFE   454

Introduction   455

The Parable of the Ten Virgins   Matthew 25:1-13   459

Wheelbarrows   Don Kraybill   463

A Plea for Fishing   John M. Drescher   467

The Pilgrim's Progress   John Bunyan   472

     Chapter 1: Christian Begins His Journey   474

     Chapter 2: Christian Falls in the Slough of Despond   479

     Chapter 3: Christian Meets Mr. Worldly Wiseman   483

     Chapter 4: Christian Passes Through the Wicket Gate   488

     Chapter 5: Christian Visits the Interpreter's House   491

     Chapter 6: Christian Reaches the Cross   498

     Chapter 7: Christian Climbs the Hill Difficulty   502

Chapter 8: Christian Visits Palace Beautiful   506

Chapter 9: Christian Battles with Apollyon in the Valley of Humiliation   514

Chapter 10: Christian Passes Through the Valley of the Shadow   518

Chapter 11: Christian Meets Faithful   523

Chapter 13: Christian and Faithful Meet Talkative   529

Chapter 13: Christian and Faithful Enter the Town of Vanity   536

Chapter 14: Hopeful Joins Christian   546

Chapter 15: Christian and Hopeful Meet Giant Despair at Doubting Castle   554

Chapter 16: Christian and Hopeful Pass Through the Delectable Mountains   560

Chapter 17: Christian and Hopeful Reach the Enchanted Ground   563

Chapter 18: Christian and Hopeful Attempt to Help Ignorance   571

Chapter 19: Christian and Hopeful Enter the Land of Beulah and Cross the River   577

Chapter 20: Christian and Hopeful Reach Zion   581

The Celestial Railroad   Nathaniel Hawthorne   585

     Part 1   586

     Part 2   591

     Part 3   597

Index of Authors, Titles, and First Lines of Poetry   605

Index of Literary Terms   607

Index of Biblical References   608

Acknowledgments   610

116 stories

INTRODUCTION

The study of literature can be approached in several ways. Literature can be arranged in order of time, with the oldest writing first and the later compositions last. The literature of the Bible is somewhat arranged in this way with Genesis first and Revelation last.

Literature can also be grouped according to country or author. English literature, African literature, American literature, and Japanese literature are divisions of literature by country. A text that groups literature by writers such as John Bunyan, Robert Frost, or Menno Simons would be an example of an approach according to author.

This text uses yet two other methods of grouping literature. Most of the literary selections in this book are grouped according to form. The first unit is a group of short stories, followed by a unit of poetry, and then a unit of biography. The fifth unit is made up of allegories.

The fourth unit does not focus on a specific form of literature. In fact, you will find a wide spectrum of forms, ranging from formal essays to informal letters and even part of a diary. Many of the selections are excerpts from full-length books, including one from the Book of books, the Bible. But in spite of all this variety, you will find a very definite similarity of subject. This is the second grouping method used in this book, the thematic approach. Here the selections center around one theme or subject, life. In this fourth unit you will discover the secret to the successes or failures of men who lived from Lot's day to our own.

This does not mean, however, that there is no thematic grouping throughout Units 1, 2, 3, and 5. The basic theme of *life* unifies this entire textbook. Also within these other units you will find subgroupings according to theme. Specifically Units 1 and 2 follow this pattern. While there are no such groupings in Units 3 and 5, be alert for similarity of subject.

The thematic approach to literature focuses on the message, which, after all, is the most important aspect of any literature. No matter how excellent the form, if the content is not worthwhile, the literature is not of good quality. The compilers of this textbook have attempted to choose selections with both excellent content *and* excellent form.

As mentioned earlier, you will study several selections from the Bible interspersed among the selections which are not from the Scriptures. As you study, keep in mind that the Bible is the inspired Word of God. Therefore, what the Bible tells us is infallible and without error. In contrast, the uninspired writings of men may contain error and always need to be evaluated carefully according to the Word.

As you read these selections about life, compare them first to Jesus, who lived the one "true life," and who must be the pattern for every other worthwhile life. Then apply the lessons you learn to your own life. The best reason for studying literature is to find, in the lives and writings of others, patterns to help our lives conform more nearly to the life of "him that is true" (1 John 5:20).

UNIT 1

The Short Story

for the Christ-filled Life

Like most people, you probably think stories make the best reading. What makes stories so popular? Is it that stories are simple, easy reading? Or do they help people escape from the routine of real life?

To be sure, some unworthy stories are written simply to entertain, or to provide an escape into fantasyland. But good stories, like the kind that Jesus told, demand deep thinking. They certainly are not a flight from reality. In fact, you may be surprised to learn that well-written stories can be just as realistic as any other kind of writing.

Here are two descriptions of the same event. The first one is a factual report:

Andy Gates lost his pet dog in the river. The dog had attacked an otter pup and was pulled under the water by the pup's male parent and drowned.

Now read the story version:

Standing up to his chest in the water, Andy Gates stared in helpless anguish at the spot where the dog had gone down. He saw the bubbles burst to the surface, and a short time later, a swirl far out where the otter breached for air as it followed its mate and the pup. At first he couldn't believe that the dog wouldn't come up again. But time passed and realization finally came upon him; he dropped the branch he was holding, and clenched his fists as his blue eyes filled with tears. The world about him was suddenly a new and terrible place.

The report gives the facts. But it views all of the happenings from the outside. Andy's response to his loss is perhaps more important to us than the facts about the dog's death. But a factual report cannot give this most vital aspect of the incident.

The story, however, takes you inside the heart and mind of Andy. You feel his reactions to the loss of his dog. His thoughts become yours, and you gain a fresh understanding of experiences like Andy's that you may sometime need to face.

As you can see, life is far more than facts, no matter how accurately they are reported. Indeed, a fact may often have little meaning until we see how it relates to other facts.

A report, for instance, may tell us that a man died of cancer and that his wife died suddenly a month later. We could suppose that the first death had something to do with the second. But any relationship between these facts would be hidden. A story, though, could show us the wife's inner life as she wasted away with grief.

Behind the facts, then, lie the true meanings of life. But to get these meanings, someone must interpret the facts. This interpretation must consider the feelings and thoughts of people as much as the facts themselves. Yet this is what pure factual reporting cannot do because feelings and thoughts cannot be considered by a reporter of facts. That is why the factual article cannot portray the fullness of life as a story can.

Now you can understand why people are fascinated by stories. People have a strong, God-given urge to enter into life itself and interpret its happenings. Stories help them to interpret life. God wants His people to do just this. He says, "With all thy getting, get understanding [meaning, *interpretation*]" (Proverbs 4:7).

How do story writers take you behind the facts? How do they lead you to interpret the meaning of life? The story writer takes you inside a life experience by weaving four story elements together: theme, character, plot, and setting. Using these elements, he directs your imagination so that you can sense thoughts, feelings, and actions all working together. As you enter into the life experience the writer has arranged, you discover its meaning for yourself.

In the first three stories of this unit will learn how theme, character, and plot interact in a story. Then in the remaining stories of this unit you will explore three aspects involved in the setting of a story.

Mama and the Garfield Boys

by Lewis Grizzard

Is every person a diamond in the rough? Can everyone become a shining gem if polished enough? With some people it appears hopeless. It seems no amount of chiseling and polishing can perfect their ugly, sharp edges. They apparently are solid chunks of meanness. But the love of Christ, patiently and repeatedly applied, can coax a luster from the most hopeless, unlovely person. This was the unforgettable lesson which Mama taught her son.

Defining for Comprehension	Choose the word or phrase below which best defines each word at the left as it is used in the story.		
1. **suspended**	a. surprised	b. reprimanded	c. temporarily denied a privilege
2. **headlock**	a. wrestling hold	b. stagnation	c. security measure
3. **groveling**	a. complaining	b. digging	c. acting in a low, pleading manner
4. **pummel**	a. to ridicule	b. to beat	c. to question
5. **profound**	a. restored	b. famous	c. impressive
6. **beck**	a. summons	b. pleasure	c. nuisance

Mama and the Garfield Boys

What I recall most vividly about my first day at the school in Moreland, Georgia, where my mama taught was that, as my teacher, Mrs. Bowers, welcomed us to second grade, the Garfield brothers set off a small bomb on a window ledge.

The bomb blew out several windows and sent Mrs. Bowers screaming to the principal's office. Mr. Killingsworth **suspended** the Garfields for a week, which is what they wanted and why they set off the bomb. Frankie Garfield was ten and David nine, and both had failed first grade several times.

Having your mother as a member of your school's faculty had its advantages. I could go by her room on my way home and ask for a few coins to spend on treats at Cureton and Cole's store. My friends and I would sit outside and eat our candy and hope we could finish before the Garfield brothers showed up and took it away.

I managed to stay unmarked by the Garfield brothers, other than a few punches to my arms and the day Frankie got me in a **headlock** and rammed my head into a pole. But Frankie had just been teasing around. When he was serious about hurting someone, he didn't let him go until he was bleeding and **groveling** for mercy.

In the fifth grade, I finally got mine. I was biking my way to Cureton and Cole's. At the end of the narrow path was a deep ditch that forced a hard left turn. The problem arose when Frankie Garfield ran up behind me. "Get that bike out of the way. I'm in a hurry," Frankie demanded.

The moment I slowed to make the turn, Frankie lifted the back of my bike and flipped it, with me astride, into the ditch.

I landed headfirst, and my bike landed on top of me. After seeing my nose bloodied, my face scratched and a giant knot on my forehead, Frankie figured the job was done and proceeded to the store to detach children from their candy bars.

I rode my bike home as fast as I could. I looked like I'd been in an ax fight and finished fourth. I tried to wash away as much mud and blood as I could and even tried to press the knot on my head flat. That didn't work.

My fear was this: Mama would see me in this condition and force the truth out of me that I had fallen victim to a Garfield. She would tell the principal, who would suspend Frankie. That would delight him, but he would also be angry that I had tattled on him. He would **pummel** me. On top of that, he would probably tell his brother, David, who would also take his turn at bruising my person.

I avoided Mama until dinner time. "What happened to your face?" she asked. "How did you get that knot on your head?"

"Bicycle accident," I said. "I was riding down the path and fell into the ditch."

"It was one of those Garfields, wasn't it?" Mama said. How did she always know those things? Still, I stuck to my story.

"Did one of those boys hit you?" she asked.

"No, ma'am," I said. Well, he didn't hit me.

"You've been down that path hundreds of times. Now you tell me what really happened."

I told her.

"I'll see Frankie Garfield in the principal's office in the morning," she said. "I'm tired of those boys bullying you children around."

Just as I thought.

"Mama," I started, "please don't tell Mr. Killingsworth. He'll call Frankie in and then Frankie will beat me up again, this time worse."

She looked thoughtful. "Okay, but I'm going to have a talk with Frankie myself."

When school was over, I took another route home and hid under my bed. Forty-five minutes later, I heard Mama come in the house and call me. "I'm under the bed, Mama," I said.

"Well, come out from under there," she said. "Frankie Garfield isn't going to hurt you."

Mama had called the sheriff. That's what had to have happened. Frankie and his brother had been taken to jail.

"Come into the living room and sit down," Mama said. She had something to tell me.

"Before I talked to Frankie," she said, "I

pulled his records. Do you know his daddy is dead and they don't know where his mama is? His aunt is raising those boys alone. I talked to the other teachers and they said his mama used to beat Frankie and his brother. They simply haven't known much love, and they don't have spending money like you. All they know is that they have to fight for everything they get. I really feel sorry for them."

This wasn't exactly what I had expected.

"Do you know what I did?" Mama asked.

I had the feeling that whatever it was she had done, it hadn't involved the sheriff.

"I had Frankie come down to my room during recess and asked if he would help me put up the blocks and crayons from the morning. I told him if he did, I'd give him a quarter, and he and his brother could spend it however they wanted. He was as nice and cooperative as could be. So I told him if he would come back and help me tomorrow, I'd take him and his brother and you to the park Saturday."

Obviously the ditch incident of the previous day had damaged my hearing. Me going to the park with the Garfields? Me, alone with them in a tree-shadowed park?

"I'm not going," I said.

"Yes, you are," Mama said. "The Bible tells us, 'Love your enemies.'"

"The Bible also says, 'Thou shalt not kill.'"

"Those boys just need some love and attention," Mama replied.

Saturday morning, we drove to where the Garfield brothers lived. A woman appeared on the front porch in a tattered housecoat. Mama got out of the car. I stayed put. I heard the Garfields' Aunt Pearl say to Mama, "I shore do appreciate you doing this for the boys. I ain't got no car to take 'em nowhere."

Mama said, "Frankie worked hard for me last week at school, and I know David is going to help me, too."

Frankie and David got into the back seat. They were wearing old clothes, but clean and fairly wrinkle-free. Both had their hair combed. I've never seen a Garfield look anything like that before.

As we drove away, Mama said, "Son,

About the Author

Lewis Grizzard (1946-1993) was born in Fort Benning, Georgia, to poor parents. Because his father served in the military and separated from Grizzard's mother, Grizzard was raised largely by grandparents. After graduating from the University of Georgia, he became a syndicated columnist and published seven best-selling books. In 1993, while waiting for a heart transplant, Grizzard died of heart failure.

Frankie's got something he wants to say to you." I sensed a certain embarrassment on his part, almost a shyness. Was this the same Frankie Garfield? He mumbled something I couldn't understand.

"Speak up," Mama said to him.

Still unable to meet my eyes, he said, "I'm sorry I threw you and your bicycle in the ditch."

I couldn't believe what I was hearing. Frankie Garfield apologizing to me?

"And what else, Frankie?" Mama asked.

"I promise not to hurt anybody at school again," he said.

"What do you say?" she asked me. I was too stunned to say anything.

Mama finally said, "Tell Frankie you appreciate his apology."

"I appreciate your apology," I said to the front window. We rode to town in silence.

When Mama pulled into the park, my eyes said to her, "Please don't make me get out of this car."

"Go ahead," she said. "Everything will be okay."

When Mama picked us up, Frankie and David began to recount their adventures in the park.

After we pulled into their driveway, Frankie came to Mama's side of the car and said, "Mrs. Christine, do you need me to help you Monday?"

"I'll see you at school and let you know," she said. "Now, go tell your Aunt Pearl about the park." Mama smiled as we drove away.

The Garfields never bothered anybody very much after that. And the three of us went back to the park a few more times. We never became close friends or anything like that. But Mama's kindness toward them obviously had a **profound** effect.

They were always at her **beck** and call. They cleaned her blackboard and took the erasers out and dusted them. They watered the plants and found a special pleasure in feeding the fish Mama had in a small aquarium.

Mama had the thing some teachers develop, the idea that the students were her children, too.

She taught me a lot, my Mama.

Testing for Understanding

1. The main character first learned about the Garfield boys
   a. during his first year of school.
   b. in second grade.
   c. at Cureton and Cole's store.
   d. in fifth grade.

2. Suspension failed to correct the Garfields because
   a. Mr. Killingsworth did not care about them.
   b. they had been suspended often before.
   c. they enjoyed missing school.
   d. they were beyond hope of correction.

3. The fifth-grade incident with Frankie Garfield was
   a. as much the main character's fault as Frankie's.
   b. the first the boy had ever been mistreated by the Garfields.
   c. the last of repeated similar encounters between the main character and the Garfields.
   d. the first serious encounter the main character had with the Garfields.

4. The main character didn't want his mother to know that Frankie had flipped his bike because
   a. he was embarrassed.
   b. she would scold him for getting caught.
   c. he was trying to keep Frankie out of trouble.
   d. he feared he would be hurt worse by Frankie if he told on him.

5. Mama's secondary response to Frankie's actions show that she recognized that
   a. drastic punishment would be necessary to correct the Garfields.
   b. she needed to shelter her son from the Garfields.
   c. behind every misdeed lies a cause.
   d. "Idleness is the devil's workshop."

6. In asking Frankie to apologize to her son, Mama proved that
   a. she was as tough with her students as with her son.
   b. she was overprotective of her son.
   c. she believed that everyone must take responsibility for his own actions.
   d. grown-ups are frequently too demanding of children.

7. Mama's reason for taking her son with the Garfields to the park was
   a. to bring them to a measure of reconciliation.
   b. to reward the Garfields for helping her throughout the week.
   c. to occupy their time profitably.
   d. to prove her love to them.

8. In the car ride to the park, the main character's response to the Garfields was one of
   a. wholehearted forgiveness.
   b. heroic effort to be friendly.
   c. fear and disbelief.
   d. suppressed hatred and unforgiveness.

9. The chief reason for Mama's success with the Garfields was that
   a. they were afraid of her stern discipline.
   b. she had taught them to enjoy doing favors for other people.
   c. they wanted the money which she gave them for helping her.
   d. they wanted to please her because she had shown them that she cared about them.

10. Mama's success with students in general could best be defined as
    a. firm love.
    b. unyielding sternness.
    c. lavish affection.
    d. permissiveness.

 *Reading for Understanding*

1. *After seeing my nose bloodied, my face scratched and a giant knot on my forehead, Frankie figured the job was done and proceeded to the store to detach children from their candy bars.*
   Frankie
   a. cared more about candy than about losing friends.
   b. had no consideration for others.
   c. left the scene of the accident to avoid blame.
   d. had flipped the boy's bike to get his candy bar.

2. *"You've been down that path hundreds of times. Now you tell me what really happened."*
   Mama meant that
   a. her son often tried to fool her with stories like this.
   b. her son had often been hurt by the Garfields.
   c. her son knew the narrow path on which he was bicycling too well to have simply fallen off.
   d. no one should have objected to her son riding down this path.

3. *When school was over, I took another route home and hid under my bed.*
   The boy took another route
   a. to avoid meeting his mother.
   b. to reach home sooner.
   c. to get his mind off his trouble.
   d. to avoid meeting the Garfields.

4. *Me going to the park with the Garfields? Me, alone with them in a tree-shadowed park?*
   The boy is
   a. astounded that his mother is permitting him to spend time alone with the Garfields.
   b. pleased at the prospect of going to the park.
   c. distrustful and afraid of the Garfields.
   d. asking his mother to repeat what he did not quite understand because of his damaged hearing.

5. *"Yes, you are," Mama said. "The Bible tells us, 'Love your enemies.'"*
   "The Bible also says, 'Thou shalt not kill.'"
   This conversation shows that
   a. Mama feels that for her son to refuse to go along to the park out of hate for the Garfields would be as wrong as killing.
   b. the main character feels he is not obligated to keep the command to love his enemies when the Garfields don't follow the Bible.
   c. the main character fears that the Garfields may kill his mother if he goes along to the park.
   d. the main character is saying that only the Bible command is keeping him from taking revenge on the Garfields.

 **Meditating for Meaning**

1. This story shows that no one is "born to be mean." Rather something in the mean-acting person's background or present environment has contributed to this trend in his life.
   a. What facts about the Garfield brothers' background did Mama learn from their records?
   b. What additional fact did she learn from other teachers?
   c. From these facts what two conclusions did Mama draw as reasons for the Garfields' misbehavior?
   d. Which of these two reasons was their most basic problem?
   e. What other things did they likely lack because of this basic need?

2. This story points out the difference between effective and ineffective methods of dealing with such troublemakers.
   a. How did the principal handle the bomb incident?
   b. What did the boy predict would happen if the school authorities were involved in the bicycle incident?
   c. What did Mama's talk with Frankie consist of?
   d. Why was this effective while earlier discipline had failed?
   e. What aspect of Frankie's question to Mrs. Christine near the end of the story shows a specific lack in his life which Mama filled?

3. A confused concept of God's love has led modern child training to disaster. Many people think God is too loving to punish His children.
   a. While God is unwilling that any should perish, what other attribute of His makes it necessary that He punish men?
   b. Find and write a Bible verse from Revelation 3 which disproves this false concept of God's love.
   c. Although Mama did not physically punish the Garfields, prove that Mama did not believe in love without firmness.
   d. Explain how love without firmness is really not love.

4. There are two qualities of love.
   a. What low quality of love did Jesus condemn in the publicans in Matthew 5:46, 47?
   b. What higher quality of love, which Jesus was teaching in earlier verses of Matthew 5, did Mama teach her son?
   c. What characteristics of this love make it high quality?

 *Looking for Literary Technique*

Every good story reflects some truth about life. This truth is the story's **theme**. The theme is a basic principle which emerges from the conflict of the story.

Running through the story of the Good Samaritan is the theme, "a neighbor helps anyone in need." Other stories have centered around such vital themes as, "sin doesn't pay," "wealth doesn't bring happiness," "acting responsibly is more important than having talent," or "selfishness eventually causes someone pain."

We state a story's theme as a generality that does not include the characters from the story. A good theme can be taught by many different stories.

You will find hints about the story's theme near the beginning of a story, sometimes even in the title. In the unfolding conflict, this idea about life will be tested. As the conflict climaxes, the theme will stand out in the clear light of seasoned experience. Therefore, you will often find the plainest statement of the theme near the end of a story.

In the story you have just read, the boy's idea about life was under test as he came into conflict with the Garfield boys. As this conflict climaxed, Mama showed her son true ideas about life through her seasoned experience. This lesson which Mama taught her son is the theme of the story.

1. Mama stated the basis for the theme of the story by quoting a Bible verse to her son. Find and copy this verse with its Bible reference.

2. Now state the entire theme in your own words. Keep it to one short sentence. Be sure to state it in generalities. Do not include names of the characters from this story.

Writing for Skill

The story by Lewis Grizzard which you have just read is condensed from a longer writing called "Don't Forget to Call Your Mama . . . I Wish I Could Call Mine." As people grow older they often come to realize the value of what their mothers taught them and treasure such experiences. Write a story telling about an experience of yours in which your mother taught you an important life value. Work your theme into your story clearly without specifically stating it. A theme should be so obvious in the action of a story that the writer does not need to state it for his readers.

The Horse

by Marian Hurd McNeely

Few teenagers will admit it, but if they are not careful, they will find themselves craving the acceptance of their peers more than anything else. Do a bit of observing. You will see many of your friends doing things clearly unwise just to be part of the "in" group. When this happens, something is drastically askew with the "in" group as this story will clearly show.

Defining for Comprehension			

Choose the word or phrase below which best defines each word at the left as it is used in the story.

1. supplement	a. natural food	b. scene	c. special part
2. pigments	a. shadings	b. colors	c. expressions
3. gait	a. movement	b. walking manner	c. gesture
4. dusky	a. unpaved	b. uneven	c. dark-colored
5. reticent	a. reserved	b. shy	c. curious
6. perception	a. hearing	b. reply	c. insight
7. engrossing	a. time-consuming	b. difficult	c. absorbing

8. **deter**	a. hold back	b. keep up with	c. defeat
9. **spires**	a. tapered towers	b. stained glass windows	c. stars
10. **reconciled**	a. not caring	b. made agreeable	c. enthused
11. **warrant**	a. justify	b. help	c. catch
12. **garish**	a. coarse	b. dull	c. glaring
13. **becomingness**	a. incompleteness	b. suitability	c. extravagance
14. **august**	a. mature	b. dignified	c. sunny
15. **cobbled**	a. made roughly	b. pasted	c. spoiled

The Horse

Two months of the fall term of school had passed when Martha Edgewood of Sageville enrolled in the Dubuque High School. Martha was fifteen and looked as though she had been drawn for the color **supplement**, before the **pigments** were added. Eyes, hair, skin, and clothes were all of pale tan; her face was very plain; her **gait** awkward.

"It is unfortunate that you did not enroll at the beginning of the semester," said the principal as he helped her fill out her card of admission.

"Sir?" said Martha.

"Too bad you couldn't have started two months ago," said Mr. Edwards. "You've lost a big part of the term."

"Yes, sir," the girl looked very scared. "I wanted to, but I couldn't. I had to wait till after corn shucking. I don't know if my father'll leave me come now, but I'm making out to try it. He thinks I've got schooling enough."

"I think you've had enough to start the freshman year," said Mr. Edwards kindly. "Latin and algebra will be hard for the first few weeks, but we can help you make up lost work. You're sure you want the Latin course, not the commercial?" And he explained the difference.

"I want to have what'll help me to teach," said the girl. "If I can get a school quick, maybe my father'll be more willing to have me go to high school. But I've got to learn fast, for I'm so far back. I got to learn how to talk right while I'm studying other things. But I can. I learn quick. An' I like to work."

A faint flush mounted the girl's tan face, and she looked a little less plain.

"The report cards you brought from the Sageville School show that," said Mr. Edwards. "Where are you going to live, in town? Have you found a room?"

"Oh, I ain't goin' to live in Dubuque. I'm going home every night, but not noons, of course. I'll carry my noon lunch from home."

"Will they send for you every day?"

"No, sir, I'll walk it."

"But it's four miles."

"Yes, sir."

Mr. Edwards laid her enrollment card on his desk. "Well, best wishes to you. I'm sure you'll make good. The teachers will give you a start, and you'll make friends soon. I hope you won't be lonely."

But being lonely had not entered the girl's thoughts. Companionship was a secondary thing to the miracle that opened before her—the chance of learning. Perhaps it was for that reason, perhaps because she was confused, bewildered, and lost in the throngs of strange young people that she did not notice the looks of amusement on the sea of faces in the study hall as she went into Latin class.

"Oh, what is that?" quoted David Conroy to his desk neighbor, Naomi Hiltman.

"Something got loose on the farm," whispered back Naomi.

"She must have broken her halter. She looks exactly like a horse, doesn't she?" said David.

And she did. Long narrow face, flat nose, and patient eyes with half-drooped lids. The name was perfect, and it stuck. After that she was always "The Horse" to the girls and boys.

The road to Sageville was **dusky** and frozen into icy ruts, and the wind from the north slapped Martha's face as she made her way home after her first day at school. But it was neither cold nor fear of the dark road that quickened her steps. It was the thought of the chores and her brother Ben. Ben was two years younger, and cared for books and school as much as Martha. It was his pledge to do Martha's chores, as well as his own, that had wrung from their father the grudging consent that Martha should go in to Dubuque High School. "A turrible waste of money," old Ben had growled. "The more ye know, the more ye got to know." But he had finally given in to the pleadings of both children. Martha's joy had been tempered by the regret that young Ben was not to share in the schooling, but her brother had quickly put an end to expressions of sorrow. "My turn'll come later," he said stoutly. "An' the quicker you get to going, the easier it'll be for me."

Ben was waiting where the lane attached itself to the Sageville road, and Martha knew he had driven the cows home that way in order to meet her. She also knew that the casual "H'are ye?" meant a hundred questions from her **reticent** brother. And these unasked questions she answered all the way up to the barn—about the school, the lessons, the teachers, and her

course of study.

"How about the other students? Did you like any of them?" inquired Ben. "Didn't any of them come up and speak to you?"

"No." Nobody had, though she hadn't thought of the fact before.

"I think that was queer of them," commented Ben. "We wouldn't let a new child go all day alone at the Sageville School."

"I suppose they're all too busy," excused Martha.

"Maybe they expected you to speak first."

But Martha, remembering David Conroy's expression when she had made her first recitation and the amused look on Naomi's pretty face when she had filed into the wrong classroom, shook her head.

"I guess they're different from us at the Sageville School," she said. She hurried into the house, and changed her school costume for farm clothes before she came back to the barn to milk with Ben.

In the days that came after, Martha often remembered her own words. The school children *were* different. They didn't seem like children at all, but young men and women—all so sophisticated, so well-dressed, so good-looking, so well-informed. Except upon the subject of lessons. It was curious how little their intelligence seemed to count in their studies. Outside of the classroom, Martha envied them their ease, their grace, their familiarity with the things of life, but at the recitations she wondered at their lack of interest and was surprised at their stupidity. Martha had a good brain, quick **perception**, and a wonderful power of concentration. She absorbed her Latin, drank in her history, and devoured her English work. She was soon taking the second class work in algebra, carrying two classes of Latin, and leading the students of the freshman year.

"There's no beating that horse-girl," said David Conroy, who had always stood at the head of his class before.

Her power of concentration saved the Horse from many a hurt. Youth is the cruelest thing in the world and there was little effort to hide the sneer, the laugh, the uplifted brow from the victim. If Martha had not been buried so deep in her schoolwork, she must have noticed. But the teachers were kindly and appreciative, her work was **engrossing**, and she had little time to think of being lonely. Besides, the dream of her heart was being realized. Two years, besides this, would give her her diploma, and a chance to teach the Sageville School. Then Ben could have his opportunity. What was loneliness? Besides, they didn't mean to be unkind. They were different—that was all.

Naomi Hiltman and Martha were alone in the school library one morning, along about the first of May. Martha was looking up the word *Pali;* and as she put the encyclopedia back upon the shelf and left the room, Naomi took down the same volume. A sheet of paper fluttered to the floor. She picked it up, recognized Martha's curious, cramped handwriting, and read:

TO MY ALMA MATER

To thee, who made my youthful days
So bright, I offer thee my praise,
And in a hundred different ways
Endeavor to be worthy.

And where thy stately towers rise
So gold and gay against the skies,
The days of happiness I prize
No power can **deter** me.

Thou made'st my life a happy one
On my dark chambers turned the sun,
And life itself began to run
So I could see it.

Give me a chance myself to prove
A daughter worthy of thy love
Beneath thy **spires** that shine above
I vow I'll be it.

—Martha Edgewood

"The Horse a poet!" said Naomi to herself. The paper in her hand shook with her laughter. "What a find, what a find! Just the kind of poetry she *would* write. Oh, won't the girls enjoy this!"

At recess she showed it to David. "Whee, that's a gem. Has anyone else seen it?"

"I showed it to some of the girls. They almost laughed their heads off."

"I don't wonder. Say, let's ask her to read it before the Lit."

"She won't do it. She's too bashful."

"It won't do any harm to ask her. She's a member, and she's got to take part on the program before long. This would be a barrel of fun. Can't you see how she'd look—reading poetry."

"I surely can't imagine her reading any worse poetry than this."

"Well, ask her then. You're on the program committee. It will be the best entertainment we've had this semester."

So Naomi had asked Martha. She returned the lost poem to her, told her where she had found it, and invited her to read it at the next meeting of the Literary Society. To her surprise Martha agreed. She blushed a dull, painful red that showed even through her thick tan skin, but she accepted.

"As if it were an honor," Naomi said to Ruth Bradford later.

"I don't think it's a kind thing to do," said Ruth with a decided ring in her usually gentle voice.

"Why not? She'll never know that we're making fun of her."

"But *you'll* know it, and because she doesn't is just why it's mean. I'm sorry for the poor girl. She seems so forlorn."

"Why don't you adopt her then?"

"I do talk to her when I get a chance, but she is about the schoolhouse so little that I seldom see her. When I do talk to her, she seems pleased, even if she does act scared of me. It's just wicked that we don't *make* girls like that come out of their shells."

"She'll walk out of hers all right when she reads that ode. It's full of spires, and prayers, and vows, and heights. She'll have to undress her soul to read it."

"I think it's mean," said Ruth again.

"Why, if she doesn't know it?"

"Perhaps she will," said Ruth. "She's no fool."

Martha's rough shoes flew over the dandelion-bordered Sageville road that afternoon. The long walks to and from school were a pleasure these sunshiny spring days. The term was almost over, and Martha meant to make up an extra class at home, between canning and cooking, that summer. The year had been a lovely one. She didn't mind the summer of work with the thought of the fall that was ahead. And even her father had seemed **reconciled** to the thought of her going back, and interested in the school reports she brought home. She had not made friends, and she did miss companionship. But perhaps it was just as well that the girls didn't notice her loneliness; she would have nothing to offer them if they did come. The education was what she went for; and that, in itself, was enough. She wouldn't let herself wish for anything more.

But surely it was all right for her to be glad of this first bit of human attention, to be flattered by Naomi's invitation, and by her appreciation of the poem. The prettiest and best-dressed girl in the school had asked her to read it—it was pleasant to have it so. Her lonely heart sang.

"What's the matter with *you*?" asked her brother as they met in the chicken yard in the early twilight.

"Oh, Ben, I've been asked to read before the Literary Society next week." She couldn't even tell him what she was to read. Not even Ben knew that she wrote poetry.

Her brother eyed her heightened color curiously. Girls were queer to *care* so much for a thing of that kind.

"Glad of it. Know you'll do fine," he said encouragingly.

After the milking was finished, the dishes washed, and the milk pans scalded, Martha climbed the little ladder that led to the attic loft. She pulled a big box in front of the one tiny window, and carefully laid out, one by one, a pile of old clothes. Down at the bottom of the chest was the dress that had been her mother's best. It was a bright green, selected by old Ben, and worn only because there was no money to substitute a less trying color. It had lain there the two years since her mother's death, no occasion seeming to **warrant** its making over. But the time for it seemed at last to have come.

She soberly put the other things back into the box, pushed it under the eaves, and went downstairs. A brand-new 35-cent paper pattern lay on the bed in her room, the first new pattern she had ever owned. She had bought it for a dozen eggs from her own lame hen.

Ripping the dress took two good hours of work; it took another hour to plan how to cut the pattern from the limited material; still another hour to piece together scraps enough to eke out the gown. But when she went to bed at midnight, the dress was cut out, pinned together, and ready to start.

Three days of that week were devoted to preparations for the coming program. She revised her poem and committed it to memory as she went back and forth from country to town to country. A new light was in her face and a new confidence was in her manner. She had been noticed at last. They *had* cared, in spite of that coolness. That had been just the city way. The high-school pupils were her friends; they had *asked* her for this. It was only a beginning, but where might it not end?

After nightfall came, she was less confident and happy, for it was then she worked upon the gown she was to wear. The green cloth was very **garish**, and Martha had misgivings about its **becomingness.** She knew nothing about dressmaking, and her rough hands held the needle clumsily. The sleeves certainly had a peculiar look, and though Ben goodnaturedly tried to "hang" the skirt for her, the hem was as uneven as her father's temper. Still, she had done her best, material and making were the best she could command, and fortunately there was no mirror at the Sageville house large enough to tell her how it looked. She asked her father for enough money to buy lace for the collar and cuffs, sewed it in with neat, painstaking stitches, and wore the dress to school on the morning of the great day. At noon she spread her handkerchief daintily over the vivid green that not a crumb might drop thereon.

The Literary Society was the largest school organization, and even the **august** seniors were members. David Conroy, as chairman of the meeting, announced the program to the audience in the large assembly room.

"*To My Alma Mater*. An original poem by Miss Martha Edgewood."

Martha shrank within herself at the words. How could she ever dare to face that audience of older boys and girls, all so unconscious of themselves, so intelligent, so sophisticated. Could she offer anything to them? She had never thought much of that poem—it was merely the overflow from a grateful heart, put into rhyming form because the words had happened to come that way. Yet Naomi had said it was fine—Naomi the popular and beautiful—and she must know. Moreover, Naomi had asked her, as a personal favor, to do this. It was a symbol of friendship. She must not fail her. And the green dress was new. She mounted the stage.

There was a dead hush over the room—almost a gasp, as the awfulness of that green dress burst upon the audience. A dress that never was before, on land or sea—a misguided dress, a dress that was **cobbled**, not sewed. The skirt rippled like waves above her shabby shoes, the vivid green turned her skin to leather, the old-fashioned shell pin held the fullness in exactly the wrong place.

She began the verses timidly, with a tone of apology for each line. She was right, it *was* too poor to offer such an audience. How had she dared? But as she went on she warmed to her subject, and forgot the sea of faces before her.

> *And life itself began to run*
> *So I could see it.*

Poor poetry, but the words were true. School had done that for her.

Her voice lost its fear:

> *Give me a chance myself to prove*
> *A daughter worthy of thy love*
> *Beneath thy spires that shine above*
> *I vow I'll be it.*

There was a wild burst of applause. The room shook. At the chairman's desk she saw David Conroy pounding his hands together, and all the pupils—those who had never noticed her in the months of school life—were applauding enthusiastically. Some of the boys were even stamping their feet. She knew she could never face the room and its wild approval, and she fled across the stage into the

About the Author

Marian Hurd McNeely (1877-1930) the daughter of a lawyer, was born and raised in Dubuque, Iowa. After leaving school, Miss Hurd worked for a newspaper publisher. Together with another author she published her first book at the age of 27. Five years later she married Lee McNeely. For two years they homesteaded on the Rosebud Indian Reservation in South Dakota and then returned to Dubuque where the McNeelys raised four children. At the age of 51 Mrs. McNeely resumed her writing and wrote numerous books for girls, including *Jumping-off Place*, the first book of which she was sole author.

dressing room. She pressed her cold hands upon her hot cheeks, and smiled to herself for the very joy of living.

And then she heard—from the assembly room a burst of laughter that deepened into a roar. The room rocked. There was no mistaking the derision. Oh, Youth is cruel.

Martha understood. Her color slowly turned from scarlet back to tan. She did not cry, but something stiffened within her—stiffened and then broke. It was something she never got back again.

The study hall was deserted when Martha crept back to her desk after the meeting was over. She took out her Latin grammar, her algebra, all her textbooks, added her paper, her notebooks, and her pencils, and tied them into a neat bundle. One of the Latin teachers passed along the aisle.

"Are you going to do that much studying tonight?"

"No'm. I'm leaving. I can't come back any more."

"Why, that's a shame, when you're doing such fine work," said Miss Rountree pleasantly. "Your teachers all say you're such a good student. Are you sure you can't come back?"

"No, I can't come back," said Martha, "but my brother Ben will come. He's smarter than I am."

Testing for Understanding

1. The thing that seemed most against Martha was her
   a. country ways.　　　b. shyness.　　　c. insensitivity.　　　d. appearance.

2. Martha chose Latin rather than the commercial course because
   a. it would be shorter and she could begin teaching sooner.
   b. it was more challenging.
   c. it would be more applicable to the career she planned to pursue.
   d. it would cost less and be more acceptable to her father.

3. Martha was very sensitive about her
   a. poor grammar.
   b. brother's acceptance at Dubuque High School later.
   c. face.
   d. grades.

4. Martha believed the students responded to her as they did because
   a. their background was different.
   b. they envied her excellence in learning.
   c. she was too shy to speak first.
   d. her work showed up their stupidity.

5. The difference between Martha and the other students in their schoolwork was a matter of
   a. previous schooling.　　　b. culture.　　　c. purpose.　　　d. intelligence.

6. Martha's attitude toward the other high school students was one of
   a. jealousy.　　　b. complete awe.　　　c. mixed admiration.　　　d. deliberate rejection.

7. All of the following helped Martha to accept the lack of friendship except
   a. she was intent on her lessons.
   b. her teachers were kind to her.
   c. she didn't believe that the students intended to hurt her.
   d. she did not possess any of the social needs of other high schoolers.

8. Ruth Bradford believed it was mean to
   a. know something that someone else didn't.
   b. take advantage of someone's intelligence.
   c. secretly plan a joke on someone.
   d. neglect a shy person.

9. When the Literary Society burst into wild applause, they were
   a. only observing tradition.　　　c. finally accepting Martha.
   b. really making fun of Martha.　　　d. trying to be courteous to her face.

10. When the author says, "Youth is cruel," she means that they
    a. take friendships lightly and break them easily.
    b. are proud.
    c. seek their own enjoyment without considering how it hurts others.
    d. diligently seek opportunities to hurt others.

Reading for Understanding

1. *"It is unfortunate that you did not enroll at the beginning of the semester," said the principal as he helped her fill out her card of admission.*
    "Sir?" said Martha.
    "Too bad you couldn't have started two months ago," said Mr. Edwards.
    Martha probably said "sir" because she
    a. didn't understand the principal's words.
    b. wanted to voice her respect.
    c. saw no problem in starting school late.
    d. thought the principal was displeased with her.

2. *"There's no beating that horse-girl," said David Conroy, who had always stood at the head of his class before.*
    David Conroy's attitude here toward Martha was one of
    a. jealousy.   c. grudging admiration.
    b. spite.   d. ridicule.

3. *The dream of her heart was being realized. Two years, besides this, would give her her diploma and a chance to teach the Sageville School.*
    Martha was planning to finish high school studies
    a. in three years.   c. at another school.
    b. in half the usual time.   d. with her classmates.

4. *And where thy stately towers rise*
    So gold and gay against the skies,
    The days of happiness I prize
    No power can deter me.
    By this last line, Martha was saying
    a. school had enabled her to meet any challenge in life.
    b. she would not fail to win the literary prize.
    c. nothing could keep her from enjoying school.
    d. the unfriendly students dampened her happiness.

5. *"This would be a barrel of fun. Can't you see how she'd look—reading poetry!"*
    David Conroy's comment suggests that the chief entertainment of Martha's reading poetry would be
    a. the presence of someone so unattractive on stage.
    b. the contrast produced by such a homely person reading poetry.
    c. such poor poetry being written by someone so intelligent.
    d. Martha's embarrassment caused by poor reading of poetry.

Meditating for Meaning

1. From the world's viewpoint, Martha had a number of strikes against her.
   a. Give five of them.
   b. Study Romans 8:28, 29 and Psalm 34:10b. For each of the three verses, summarize the truth which it expresses about circumstances such as Martha's.
   c. List several good characteristics that poverty and sorrow had developed in Martha.
   d. Martha saw the other students as "so sophisticated, so well-dressed, so good-looking." How had these "advantages" affected their characters?

2. Martha kept reassuring herself that the students didn't mean to be unkind.
   a. Since it is true that a person can be unkind without meaning to be so, it then follows that a person will not likely be kind unless he _____ .
   b. Ruth Bradford had a different spirit than the other students, and yet even someone like her often proves unkind. What should she have done?
   c. Why didn't she do it?

3. Many students have been treated like Martha, even in Christian schools. But you should see how God views such situations.
   a. According to Leviticus 19:34, God anticipated the common tendency to mistreat _____ .
   b. What is the reason for this tendency?
   c. What does God command us to do when a "Martha" comes among us?
   d. Study Deuteronomy 27:19. Explain what will happen if this command is disobeyed.
   e. What does Proverbs 17:5 say the students were actually doing in their treatment of Martha?

4. The title of this story is more than a name the students gave to Martha. It emphasizes the truth that when we treat anyone with less respect than a human being should have, we actually are regarding that person on a level with _____ .

5. Observe how the author used the setting to reinforce your impressions of Martha's experience.
   a. Contrast the setting in which Martha walked home from school the first day with the setting of the same Sageville Road the evening after she was asked to read her poem before the literary society.
   b. How does the setting in each case reflect the action of the story at that time?

6. Study Martha's poem. Its title "Alma Mater" literally means "fostering mother."
   a. Who was the "fostering mother" to whom she addressed her poem?
   b. Why would Martha's home circumstances have made the name "Alma Mater" hold special meaning for Martha?
   c. How does the name prove to be ironic, or the opposite of what it was supposed to mean?
   d. In writing the last two lines of stanza 2, did Martha understand herself? Explain.

7. Irony is the difference between the appearance and the reality of a situation. Notice the irony in these lines:
   a. Martha said to her school, *Give me a chance myself to prove/ A daughter worthy of thy love.* How was this request answered?
   b. "...Naomi had asked her, as a personal favor, to do this. It was a symbol of friendship." Actually, what was behind this request?

8. Martha said Ben was smarter than she.
   a. In what way is that true?
   b. Do you think he will have an easier time than his sister did? Explain your answer.

Looking for Literary Technique

Readers are quickly attracted to the action in a short story. But action is not the most basic element. The people in the story produce the action. Their characters determine what course the story action will take.

Think of the story of Joseph in Egypt. You recall how he fled from Potiphar's wife. Suppose the main character of this story had been Samson instead of Joseph. How different the story action would have been. Since character development and action work so closely together, you can pick up clues to character by observing what people do. The only thing a writer usually gives *directly* is the action. He handles character *indirectly*, using the action to reveal the emotions and ideas he wants you to get. Character, then, is best implied by the action, not told directly.

This method of handling character makes a story true to life. In life we understand people best by what they do, not by what is said about them. Grown-ups differ in this from children. Children often need to be told the motive behind the action or they will miss the meaning of the story.

Notice how character must be treated directly in this story for a first-grade reader:

> Cain did not love God. He did not love Abel. Because he did not love God, he did bad things. First, he did not obey God. Then he was angry. He was not sorry when God talked to him. He killed Abel and then he told a lie, so God punished him.

God knew that the mature reader would be more convinced by an indirect treatment of character, so He told the story this way:

> And in process of time it came to pass, that Cain brought of the fruit of the ground an offering unto the LORD. And Abel, he also brought of the firstlings of his flock and of the fat thereof. And the LORD had respect unto Abel and to his offering: But unto Cain and to his offering he had not respect. And Cain was very wroth, and his countenance fell . . . . And Cain talked with Abel his brother: and it came to pass, when they were in the field, that Cain rose up against Abel his brother, and slew him. And the LORD said unto Cain, Where is Abel thy brother? And he said, I know not: Am I my brother's keeper? (Genesis 4:3-5, 8, 9).

The Bible does not tell us that Cain didn't love God. But his actions clearly show that he had no interest in pleasing his Maker. We are not told that Cain lacked sorrow for his sin. The Bible account expects you to see Cain's character in his actions.

Actions not only expose character; they also affect character and help to shape it as the story moves along. Judas, for instance, apparently started out pilfering small change from the bag he carried for the disciples. The Bible story tells us "He was a thief, and had the bag, and bare what was put therein." These small, dishonest actions helped to mold Judas into the treacherous betrayer he became.

The life of Judas shows how actions help to mold character in a certain direction. His actions did not turn his character around for the better. Only a drastic action, such as repentance, would reverse the character-shaping process. Day-to-day actions reinforce small changes in character that are consistent and predictable. We can expect to observe this same process in a good story.

A good author describes his main characters three-dimensionally. First, he describes their outer traits such as the color of the hair, sound of voice, and type of clothing. Secondly, he uses these details to reveal and support their inner traits. For instance a deep, firm voice may reveal determination. An untied shoe may reveal carelessness. Thirdly, he describes their environment, which accents their inner and outer traits. Perhaps he shows a selfish person living in a luxurious mansion.

1. Copy some lines that indirectly reveal the character of some person in the story you have just read. These lines should tell something the character said or did. Tell what characteristic this reveals in the person.

2. Make three columns on your paper with the headings: "outer traits," "inner traits," and "environment." Find all the details you can about the main character, Martha, and fit them into these columns.

Choose a Bible character and make a list of his outer traits, inner traits, and details of environment. Then write several paragraphs, describing this character in action. Remember to reveal his inner traits indirectly by what he does, what he says, and the way he appears. Stick as closely to the Bible account as possible, but you will need to add other details to fully describe your character. A Bible dictionary will help you with outer traits and environment. You may wish to choose one of the following:

Job, when told of his calamities

Rebekah drawing water for her father's camels

the little Syrian maid

the lad who shared his lunch

Paul's nephew (his sister's son)

Second Chance

by Robert J. Baker

Have you ever heard someone say, "I'd give anything to . . . see the Pacific Ocean," or ". . . hit home runs like John," or ". . . know why this chainsaw won't run"? Obviously these are exaggerations, yet people sometimes pay outrageous prices to get what they want. One man paid nearly six thousand dollars for an ornately-carved antique wooden cane. Apparently he considered it worth the price. Esau exchanged his birthright for one dish of pottage. The price we are willing to pay for an item depends on the value we place on it. We should question ourselves in this regard: Is what I want worth the price I will need to pay for it? What is most important? Too late the boy in this story discovered the answers to these questions. Students in Christian schools may face trials and decisions similar to his.

Defining for Comprehension	Choose the word or phrase below which best defines each word at the left as it is used in the story.		
1. bungled	a. fell noisily	b. became angry	c. made a foolish error
2. optometry	a. eye surgery	b. prescribing eyeglasses	c. making eyeglasses
3. density	a. magnetism	b. mass per volume of a material	c. chemical composition
4. parrot	a. paint brightly	b. mimic; copy	c. show off
5. eligible	a. qualified	b. logical	c. easy to read

6. hefted	a. supported	b. hindered	c. lifted to check weight
7. savagely	a. fiercely	b. sparingly	c. wisely
8. data	a. argument	b. information	c. setting
9. scruples	a. principles	b. funds	c. opinions
10. interlude	a. introduction	b. exercises	c. interval
11. wax	a. become	b. grow less	c. compare
12. dramatic	a. sad	b. emotional	c. definite

Second Chance

I had reason to be worried. The lab period for Physics 12 at Blareton High was half over and I was scared that my lab partner, Jim Denton, and I had **bungled** the experiment. And I couldn't afford to fail on another experiment. My last lab sheet came back with a crisp note penciled on the margin by Mr. Riley to the effect that I, Bill Davis, should get on the ball. Our results on that last experiment went just beyond the margin of error that is allowed. Resulting grade? Please don't embarrass me by asking. I'm no brain but I can do better than that. I have to do better than that. I have to pull a good grade in this course. I need at least a B to enter **optometry** school. They don't want any failures prescribing glasses.

So I am sweating it out, this physics experiment. It looked simple. We came into the lab this morning and Mr. Riley distributed to each table a little piece of metal in the shape of some geometrical solid like a sphere or cone. Jim and I happened to draw a cylinder, silvery and light. We both thought it was aluminum. Our job was to find its **density**. It shouldn't have been tough. But things weren't working out.

We checked the weight on the triple beam balance twice. And we checked the volume by both actual measurement and water displacement. But when we worked out the density, it just didn't seem right. That cylinder had to be aluminum. Anyone could see that. Reference books in the lab gave us the density of aluminum. A cubic centimeter of it should have a weight of 2.7 grams. Our density figures kept coming out 1.74 grams per cubic centimeter. That was off too far to suit Mr. Riley. He's a perfectionist.

Even now I could feel his eyes focusing on our table. He probably knew we were in a sweat and was interested in seeing how we solved our problem. He gives you the beginning information, but he wants you to dig things out yourself. Physics is tough and so is Mr. Riley. Is he good? Say, he knows his physics from A to Z. He doesn't **parrot** the text—he teaches physics. You learn it. He's tops. But he's tough, real tough.

Mr. Riley moved over to the window side of the room and leaned against the sill, scanning the room with radar sweeps. Jim and I looked at one another. Somewhere we had made a mistake on this experiment. I saw the look of desperation grow in Jim's eyes. His prospects were worse than mine. He's a borderline case, just barely staying **eligible** for football and that's all. And athletics is Jim's life. Maybe a D wouldn't satisfy me, but it would him.

Suddenly the public-address box on the wall came alive and we heard Miss Sands' voice from the principal's office say, "Mr. Riley, could you come to the office, please? There is a long distance call for you from Chicago."

Mr. Riley looked over the lab class, and we looked over Mr. Riley. We saw his neat gray lab coat that seemed to match his crew cut gray hair. We saw his "quarterback" eyes that took in the opposing team without missing a thing, the thin lips that seldom smiled. Some of the fellows called him Mr. Neversmile behind his back. Those lips opened slightly and we heard him address the P.A. box on the wall with, "Thank you, Miss Sands. I'll be there in a moment."

His eyes swept us again. "Continue your laboratory work. If I am not back before the period ends, place your papers in the box on my desk marked 'In.' I will return them to you tomorrow." With that he was gone.

Jim waited a moment and then muttered, "I'm going to check with McGary and Elliot. Mr. Riley gave them a cylinder just like ours." He grabbed his lab sheet and moved rapidly over to the next row of tables.

I just sat there. Was I worried? Sure I was worried, plenty worried.

Jim talked to Elliot and McGary. He **hefted** their cylinder, picked up their *vernier calipers*[1] and quickly checked the diameter and length of it. He copied some material from their lab sheet to his. Then he hurried back to our table.

His voice was excited. "Their cylinder measures the same as ours. It's just like ours. Here's the weight they got and look at the difference."

I did look. Their weight was several grams more than ours. I quickly divided the volume of the cylinder into the weight Jim had brought back from Table 4. It hit the density of aluminum on the button.

Jim was in a hurry. He kept glancing at the door. "Something must be wrong with our balance. Copy this stuff down on your lab report. Riley will never know the difference."

He shoved the copied material over to me.

I found myself saying, "But we can't use these figures. They're not ours. Maybe ours isn't aluminum. Maybe he put it in to fool us. You know Mr. Riley."

There was something else I wanted to tell Jim, but I couldn't find the words. I wanted to tell him that as a Christian I couldn't do this. Two years ago I found the Lord. I've been trying to live for Him ever since. Something about this deal didn't ring true. I wanted to tell Jim that a Christian has to avoid the very appearance of evil. I wanted to tell him, but I didn't.

How often I've heard Mr. Riley say, "I expect you to be honest in all of your work. I have no room in my physics class for the student who is crooked, who is dishonest. A scientist has to be accurate, reliable. Every time you sign that lab sheet it means that the results are the product of your and your partner's experimentation. Remember that."

I was remembering it. But Jim was watching me and I heard him whisper **savagely**. "Are you crazy? Get that **data** down. Our lab data sheets have to agree and I'm not going to risk my eligibility against your Sunday school **scruples.** Get going."

So I got going. I put down the data that Jim had brought back from the other table. I signed my name. I told myself, "I guess it's one of those things you can't help. It's not our fault if our balance is off so we can't weigh accurately." But inside I knew that there was something wrong.

When the bell rang, Mr. Riley still wasn't back from the office. We filed the lab sheets as he had told us to do.

All day long I lived with that experiment. I had sweated over the problem in the lab, but now I sweated over the solution. As a Christian I had done wrong. But there was no way out. A person couldn't just walk into Mr. Riley's room and tell him about that. He'd fire you from Physics 12 so fast that you wouldn't see the door as you left. Mr. Riley was tough, as hard as nails. He wouldn't have any mercy. And I didn't deserve any.

---

1. vernier calipers. A precision measuring device consisting of a sliding scale with two arms.

Still a fellow has to live with himself. My last period of the day, English Lit, was impossible. It was a nightmare. I couldn't begin to keep my mind on the subject. All I could think of was Physics 12, thief, liar, Riley, failure. That's what would happen. Mr. Riley would drop me from that course like a hot potato. It would mean an "Incomplete," a lost credit. I could see the handwriting on the wall. But I had to face it. I had to see Mr. Riley.

Five minutes after the last bell had sounded, I found myself in the physics room. Mr. Riley was at his desk grading some test papers. He was busy but he took time out for me.

I made a clean break of it. He sat there, leaning back a bit on his chair, looking right through me with the coldest kind of a stare. He had one question: "Why did you come in here and tell me about this?"

I didn't know if he would understand, but I was fed up with the untruth from this morning. So I told him, "Because I'm a Christian. I'm sorry for what I did this morning. I had to make it right."

I don't believe that Mr. Riley had taken his eyes off me while I was standing there, knees shaking, blurting out my story, giving him my reason for doing what I did. Finally he handed me a stack of lab sheets and said, "Find yours from this morning. I've already graded them."

Mine was near the top. The grade on it an F. I read what was written beside the grade: "You could not possibly have gotten this data from the material you were supposed to have worked with this morning. How do you explain that?"

I hung my head. For an attempt at a higher grade in physics I had shot both my Christian testimony and physics grade full of holes.

In a voice that must have been a hundred or so degrees below zero on the centigrade scale I listened to Mr. Riley say, "I know that the data you presented on your lab sheet was not your own. The cylinder I gave you was magnesium with a density of 1.74 grams per cubic centimeter. You took your information from Table 4. They had a cylinder also, volume the same as yours, only the one they had was of aluminum. I wasn't asleep when I handed out

About the Author

Robert J. Baker (b. 1920) born in Goshen, Indiana, began writing when he was in high school. After studying at Goshen College, Indiana University, and Michigan State University, he taught school at Elkhart, Indiana, raising bees as a sideline. He also served as chief pharmacist's mate in the U.S. Navy from 1942-1946. His books show spiritual insight. *Second Chance* is a book of short stories for young people, which includes the story "Second Chance."

that lab material. I knew exactly who had what."

I just stood there, a high school senior that called himself a Christian, sick inside because I had compromised and acted as if something which was wrong was right. The only thing I could say was, "I'm sorry, Sir. I'm terribly sorry."

There was a miserable **interlude** of silence. Then I heard that cold, brittle voice chop out the words, "Being sorry is not enough. You get yourself in here tomorrow morning at 7:00 sharp. Do you hear me, 7:00 sharp? I'll give you another unknown on which to run a density check. This time you'll do it yourself. Do you understand that?" The words had cracked out like pistol shots.

I looked up, half shocked. "You mean I stay in physics? I get another chance?"

Mr. Riley had the faintest excuse of a smile on his face, a face that suddenly looked kind, understanding. He told me, "You gave yourself another chance. I can still use someone in physics who has the courage to straighten out a wrong."

I was so happy I could have shouted. But I didn't. I just said, "Thanks, Mr. Riley. I'll be here at 7:00 sharp. This time you can count on me. Thanks. Thanks a million."

Again there was that trace of a smile as he said, "All right now, Davis, let's not **wax dramatic**. That's all."

I almost ran out of the room. I felt like

singing. I felt clean inside and out. In English Lit I had gotten God's forgiveness. Now I had the same from Mr. Riley. I went down the wide stairway toward the main floor. At the landing turn I stopped and stared out the full wall window at the green lawn that stretched out from the front of Blareton High. I looked up at the blue sky and said softly, so very softly on the empty stair landing, "Thank You, God, for a second chance."

Then it seemed God smiled at me and I smiled at the whole world. I might get a black eye from Jim Denton when he found out what I had done, but I still would be able to smile. When you know you've done right, the world looks good even if you have to view it through a pair of black eyes.

Testing for Understanding

1. Judging by Bill's concern over the grade he would receive on this experiment we can conclude that he
   a. barely passed on the last experiment.
   b. received an F on the last experiment.
   c. would fail the course if he failed on another experiment.
   d. has not been making the needed B average in the course.

2. The boys' confusion on this experiment was due to
   a. inaccurate calculations.
   b. hasty, inaccurate measurement.
   c. a faulty balance.
   d. attempting to force the facts to fit surface appearance.

3. All of the following prove that Mr. Riley was a good teacher except
   a. he taught more than the textbook.
   b. he expected his students to find their own information with minimal coaching.
   c. he knew exactly what sample he had given to each table.
   d. he seldom smiled.

4. When Mr. Riley looked over the lab class before going to the office he was probably
   a. expressing his suspicion of them.
   b. checking to see how nearly finished they were.
   c. trying to decide whether he should leave the class unsupervised.
   d. conveying to them that they were on their honor and he expected them to live up to it.

5. Density is found by
   a. dividing the weight of a material by its volume.
   b. dividing the volume of a material by its weight.
   c. measuring the amount of water displaced by a material.
   d. multiplying the weight of a material by its volume.

6. Mr. Riley could best be described as
   a. cold and impersonal.
   b. delighting in students' frustrations.
   c. merciless and unreasonable.
   d. firm and exacting.

7. The boys could have known that their metal was not aluminum if they could have
   a. consulted the dictionary.
   b. weighed both metal samples on the same balance.
   c. asked Mr. Riley.
   d. compared the measurements of both metal samples.

8. The factor that finally convinced Bill to cheat was
   a. fear of failing.
   b. realizing that their balance was faulty.
   c. nearness of the end of class.
   d. pressure from Jim.

9. The turning point in Bill's experience came when
   a. he confessed to Mr. Riley that he had cheated.
   b. he realized that peace was more important than passing Physics 12.
   c. he walked into the physics room after school.
   d. Mr. Riley offered him a second chance.

10. Most likely Jim Denton
    a. needed to do another density check.
    b. hit Bill in the eye when he discovered that Bill had told.
    c. was dropped from Physics 12.
    d. continued Physics 12 but failed the course.

 *Reading for Understanding*

1. *So I am sweating it out, this physics experiment.*

   From the wording we gather that
   a. the atmosphere in the physics room was hot and stuffy.
   b. the physics experiment required the use of heat.
   c. the physics experiment had become unpleasantly difficult and required perseverance.
   d. the boys had failed on earlier experiments because they gave up before they were finished.

2. *. . . Mr. Riley distributed to each table a little piece of metal in the shape of some geometrical solid like a sphere or cone. Jim and I happened to draw a cylinder, silvery and light.*

   Apparently
   a. the experiment included making a pencil sketch of the metal sample.
   b. the students were allowed to choose their metal sample.
   c. Mr. Riley gave out the samples at his own discretion.
   d. the students were allowed to choose at what table they worked.

3. *Jim was in a hurry. He kept glancing at the door.*

   From Jim's actions we know that
   a. he knew that this cheating was considered wrong.
   b. he was eager to leave the physics lab.
   c. the boys were being timed on their experiment.
   d. he was tired of the experiment.

4. *As a Christian I had done wrong. But there was no way out. A person couldn't just walk into Mr. Riley's room and tell him about that. He'd fire you from Physics 12 so fast that you wouldn't see the door as you left.*

    From Bill's thoughts we can conclude that

    a. there was no solution to his problem.

    b. no one dared step into Mr. Riley's room unless he had been summoned.

    c. he was still more concerned about consequences than about a clear conscience.

    d. he was concerned about what Jim would say if he told.

5. *He sat there leaning back a bit on his chair, looking right through me with the coldest kind of a stare. He had one question: "Why did you come in here and tell me about this?"*

    From Mr. Riley's question we know that

    a. he thought Bill's sensitive conscience was ridiculous.

    b. Bill's confession spoiled the delight of catching him in the act of cheating.

    c. he wanted Bill to know that he had no intention of extending any mercy to him.

    d. he wanted to know why Bill came and confessed.

Meditating for Meaning

1. Appearance often fools people and leads them into trouble.

    a. Find three false assumptions based on appearance which the boys arrived at concerning their experiment. There are at least five.

    b. Explain how these false assumptions led them into trouble.

2. Often what appears to be success in the eyes of men is actually failure.

    a. What failure were the boys originally fearful of?

    b. What means did they use to try to avoid this failure?

    c. Explain how the boys' attempt at success defeated its own end.

    d. In other words, success is not truly success if we _____.

3. Jim, Mr. Riley, and Bill show three different levels of honesty.

    a. Find and copy Jim's statement which reveals what he felt was the only reason to be honest.

    b. Why did Jim think it was unnecessary to be honest in this situation?

    c. Bill remembered what Mr. Riley had said about honesty. On what basis did Mr. Riley feel it was necessary to be honest?

    d. Bill realized a higher reason to be honest. What was this?

4. Jim said, "I'm not going to risk my eligibility against your Sunday school scruples." This reveals what many people think about laws.

    a. What false concept did Jim have of the effect of law and conscience?

    b. Explain how his idea was proven wrong in this situation.

5. An improper fear can keep us from doing what we know we should do.

    a. What fear convinced Bill to put down the stolen data?

    b. What fear withheld him from confessing at first?

    c. What were both of these fears based on?

    d. Copy a verse from Proverbs 29 which proves that these are wrong fears.

    e. What right fear finally led Bill to confess?

6. Suppose Mr. Riley had refused Bill any mercy. Would Bill have failed or succeeded? Explain.

7. The last sentence partly states the theme of this story. State the theme in your own words.

Looking for Literary Technique

A story is character in action. In the action a conflict unfolds, usually between good and evil. An evil person may be in conflict with a good person, or a person may be battling good and evil within himself. In still another type of conflict, a character may be in a struggle with nature or his surroundings.

Frequently, all three types of conflict are going on at the same time in a story. Think of the account of Jacob when his sons came back from buying grain in Egypt. Jacob was in conflict with nature because of a famine. He clashed with his sons about Benjamin going to Egypt. At the same time he was torn between his fears for Benjamin and his duty to provide food for his family. Such a merging of conflict results in a rich story with deep meaning.

    1. Give an example of each of these three types of conflict from the story which you have just read—man versus man, man versus himself, and man versus nature or his surroundings.

The course of action in a story is called the *plot*. The plot of a story is built from one or more of the types of conflict which you just considered. Some stories have what is called a *complication plot*. Such a story begins with an opening problem or conflict.

    2. What was the opening problem in the story which you just read?

Throughout the story the conflict builds through a series of related crises or problems demanding decision and action. After each crisis there is a measure of resolution in which the character finds for his present problem some type of solution, whether good or bad.

    3. Besides the opening conflict, give several crises or problems demanding decision and action which faced Bill in the story you have just read. After each, tell how it was resolved.

Though a series of crises and resolutions take place throughout the story, the final climax and resolution do not come till the story's end. Here the main character faces the strongest test. Either he fails the test and weakens his character, or he passes the test and strengthens his character.

    4. Give the climax and resolution of the story which you just read.

The *complication plot* is diagrammed with an ascending jagged line.

Climax

Crisis 3

Crisis 2

Crisis 1

Ending

Opening problem

Some stories, however, move through a series of relating incidents that reveal character but do not build to a climax. These *loose plot* stories resemble the usual happenings of our lives. These are diagrammed with a simple incline.

Conclusion

Incident

Incident

Incident

Opening problem → Incident

A short story ordinarily does not cover a long period of time. It usually represents only one or two main characters living through one major episode of their lives.

    5. How long is the action of this story?

Because a short story must capture attention quickly and center it on one major experience, the writer usually plunges the reader into the story as near to the most important part of the action as possible.

The story you just read did not begin at the beginning of the physics experiment. Rather, the author brings in these earlier details by a *flashback* he has caught and focused your attention on the incident to be unfolded in this story.

    6. Copy the sentence where the flashback begins.

    7. Copy the sentence where the story jumps back to the present.

A flashback must be written well or it will confuse the reader. It must be clear that the story has dipped back in time. The point at which the flashback gives way again to the present must also be clear.

Writing for Skill

Choose an incident from your life when you had a major decision to make. Give that incident in a story, starting with the incident itself. After your episode is under way, write a flashback, giving some previous details that are necessary for an understanding of your story.

Setting

In the stories which you just read, you discovered how theme, character, and plot interact to create an interesting story. The same theme, the same type of character, and even sometimes the same basic plot appear in a number of stories, yet all of these stories are quite different. Each occurs at a time and place that has little in common with the others. We say that their *settings* are different. Each particular setting of a story stirs up its own special feeling in us.

Suppose a story has its setting in a dingy alley. The bleak and grimy surroundings will help you catch the depressed feelings of the story characters. You will be moved, not only by the ugly surroundings of the alley, but by a flood of things your mind has linked with such a setting: poverty, misery, immoral living, brutality, and the grinding struggle of people forced to live in such surroundings.

You can see how a well-chosen setting can reinforce the feelings and ideas in a story experience. Setting can also highlight character. The filthy alley almost invites some kind of sinful action. But if a sorely tempted character refuses to steal in such a setting, his victory is heightened by the contrast. Sometimes setting provides a contrast of another sort. As we have noted, the dingy alley leads us to expect some evil action. In the same way, a sunny meadow spangled with flowers and fringed with pines would suggest pleasant happenings. But suppose a boy fell out of a tree and died in such a setting. The irony of the situation would impress us with the uncertainties of life and inspire us to live soberly.

The setting of a story can affect a reader in still another way. In the dingy alley, picture a rose growing beneath one rare shaft of sunlight. Every day a young girl gives it devoted care, admiring its beauty and absorbing its purity. She goes on to achieve noble ideals in contrast to the other youths in the alley.

The rose may be interpreted as an influence that strengthened her noble character. But it can also be viewed as a symbol of her purity in squalid surroundings.

You will often find rich symbolism in the setting of a story. A buildup of trouble may coincide with the breaking of a storm. Stars in a dark night may stand for hope amid despair. A frill may symbolize ridiculous luxury. You should not try to see symbolic meaning in every detail of a story setting, but your search for deeper meaning in this element of the story will often be rewarded.

Short stories can be read with ease, but they, like life, can be interpreted only with diligent effort. As you learn to unlock the meaning behind the facts, you will be developing skill to interpret the experiences of real life.

 *Checking for Understanding*

You will find answers to the following questions from the ideas and literary techniques which you learned on pages 1 and 2 and in the three stories which you just studied.

1. What is the basic reason people are strongly attracted to stories?
2. Stories can be more realistic than factual reporting.
   a. How does a strict report of the facts tend to conceal reality?
   b. How does a story writer take you behind the facts?
3. Think about the basic elements of a short story: theme, character, and plot (action).
   a. Which element seems at first sight to be the most important?
   b. Why is it not the most basic element?
   c. Which element is handled directly?
   d. Which element is handled indirectly?
   e. Why is it handled indirectly?
4. What is a story theme?
5. Study the possible structures for the action in a short story.
   a. What is a complication plot?
   b. What is a loose plot?
6. Think about the functions of the story setting. List four effects the setting can produce in a story.

SYMBOLISM

Jesus declared, "Except ye eat the flesh of the Son of man, and drink his blood, ye have no life in you" (John 6:53).

"From that time many of his disciples went back, and walked no more with him" (John 6:66).

Did Jesus mean that His followers would need to be cannibals? Surely not. Yet His words literally understood left that horrible impression. What did He mean?

The day before, 5,000 men had eaten His miraculous supply of loaves and fishes. Now they came demanding an unbroken supply of such food. They wanted to use Christ's power for a lifetime of free food and physical ease.

The Master refused. His hearers had a deeper craving that He needed to satisfy. The loaves, He insisted, had merely symbolized the spiritual bread He could offer. But His hearers clung stubbornly to their material hopes.

Jesus needed to shatter their focus on physical things. So He used words that appeared ridiculous in the literal sense. Such language should have forced the people to look for a spiritual meaning. But many walked away probably shaking their heads. They failed to see spiritual reality behind the physical symbols.

Christ spiced much of His teaching with symbolism. He used fish to represent lost men. Fishermen and farmers stood for missionaries. Seed typified the Word with its hidden potential for life. A door symbolized opportunity, and sheep passing through that door stood for followers of the Shepherd who represented Christ Himself.

Christ saw truth symbolized everywhere, from the tiny mustard seed to large fields of waving grain. The opalescent pearl radiated symbolic truth for Him as well as the rustic lamp.

In His teaching, the material world opened the unseen world of reality. "For the things which are seen are temporal; but the things which are not seen are eternal" (2 Corinthians 4:18b). Rich truth opens to the person who sees the physical world as Jesus did. Notice how Job, by symbolism, peered deep into the plan of God.

In nature Job saw that "there is hope of a tree, if it be cut down, that it will sprout again.... Though the root thereof wax old in the earth, and the stock thereof die in the ground; yet through the scent of water it will bud, and bring forth boughs like a plant" (Job 14:7-9).

Nature clearly showed to Job a recurring cycle of death, decay, and renewed life. Then he looked at man, who died but didn't come to life again. Or did he! The truth of nature's symbolism began to burst upon him and he cried,

"If a man die, shall he live again" (Job 14:14a)?

Then fully convinced by the reality of the symbol, he replied,

"All the days of my appointed time will I wait, till my change come" (Job 14:14b).

Through symbolism in nature Job saw the resurrection of the human body centuries before God fully revealed it to man.

Job demonstrates symbolism in another striking way. His life itself is symbolic. When you hear someone say, "Caspar is having a real Job experience," you know something about what Caspar is going through.

Every life, like Job's, can be symbolic. We see this in the life of King David. Out of his own deep trouble, David once groaned, "My God, my God, why hast thou forsaken me?" (Psalm 22:1). That sob expresses the feeling of many people who have faced suffering in doing the will of the Father. It even echoed the feelings of Christ Himself as He confronted the necessary horror of Calvary.

In David's life, then, we see how a man's words and actions can symbolize reality far beyond his own small existence. Countless hearts in all ages have vibrated to the strains of "The Lord is my shepherd; I shall not want" (Psalm 23:1).

Your life, too, can be symbolic. As you let God control your life, parts of it will symbolize the experiences of other godly people in all ages.

As the old saying goes, "There's more to life than meets the eye." Much of this hidden meaning will expose itself to you if you learn to interpret the symbols around you and in your reading.

But symbols sometimes *seem* to make truth so obscure. Wouldn't plain, literal words make truth easier to understand?

Not necessarily. Like Jesus' hearers, we are so engrossed in this physical world that we tend to see only the narrow outlines of material reality. We need language that drives us to deeper levels of understanding.

Besides, symbolic interpretation is not as difficult as you might think. In fact, you've been reading symbolism for quite a few years already.

When you see a flashing red light, you stop or watch out for danger. A bit of thought will show you the advantage of the symbol. It conveys its message to a foreigner or child who can't read the word *danger*. But more importantly, the blood-like color of the symbol stirs feelings of concern that the word *danger* does not.

Or take the symbol of a white rose. The word *purity* can hardly say as much. White stirs feelings of cleanness and calls up other symbols of purity such as snow. White roses are rarer than the red ones as purity is rarer than lust. Instantly, the white rose calls to mind a wide range of past experiences with roses. Many of these experiences could not easily be put into words. Also, the symbolism makes three senses leap to the aid of thought: sight, touch, and smell. A whole page of words like *purity* could never say all that you think and feel about a white rose.

As you can see, the message of a symbol is often clearer, fuller, and more brief than direct words. With a symbol you truly get more with less.

No wonder Jesus filled His teachings with symbols, and we are not surprised to find a tapestry of symbols woven the whole way through the Bible. Ages of experience cluster around the symbol of the lamb. Even a child can catch some of the symbolism in a lion. How could direct words describe the devil as graphically as the dragon or serpent symbol? Think of the many symbolic meanings expressed by the vine in Scripture.

The next three stories rely heavily on symbolism to convey their meaning. You will find symbolism in their settings and objects.

As we have seen by the lives of Job and David, a character can be symbolic also. The mention of Judas calls up associations of treachery. The Samaritan who stopped to help has become a symbol of mercy.

Finally, you will find symbolism in some story incidents. Take the crossing of the Red Sea. You may have heard this incident compared to the conversion experience in a symbolic way.

When you begin to see the symbolic significance of settings, objects, persons, and incidents, you will begin to penetrate deeper realities. You will also be learning to see symbols in everyday things much as Christ did.

Checking for Understanding

1. What is symbolism?
2. Jesus used vivid symbolism in His parables.
   a. Why did He use this method of teaching?
   b. In contrast to seeing spiritual truth in physical things around them, how do most people view this world?
3. What did symbolism help Job to do?
4. What advantage does a symbol have over literal description?
5. What four things in a story may be symbolic?
6. Study the use of symbolism in Matthew 21:33-41.
   a. What does the vineyard symbolize? (See Isaiah 5:7, Jeremiah 2:21, and Hosea 10:1.)
   b. Who is symbolized by the "householder," the maker and owner of the vineyard?
   c. What do "husbandmen," caretakers of the vineyard, symbolize?
   d. Now, explain the things symbolized by each of these: hedge, far country, servants, son, slaying of the son.
   e. What truth was Jesus showing by this symbolic story?

Shago

by James Pooler

Some people cannot stand success. They let it go to their heads and drive their friends away. Others turn sour with the trials of life and wear a constant scowl. Pleasant things come their way, of course, but these are never good enough to lift the gloom. Shago shows us how to face both success and trial with a winsome outlook.

Defining for Comprehension

Choose the word or phrase below which best defines each word at the left as it is used in the story.

1. **bluff**	a. upright stone	b. bare plain	c. steep cliff
2. **sentinels**	a. guards	b. shadows	c. edges
3. **ebbing**	a. slow lengthening	b. cooling	c. flowing out
4. **summit**	a. pointed rock	b. top	c. high crevice
5. **hue**	a. darkness	b. cold	c. color

Shago

When the summer sun moves its heat a little low in the sky and there's a stir out of doors in the late afternoon's hush, I wonder if the Indian boys still gather under the **bluff**.

The bluff must be much the same. A gash of naked sand and stone upright for fifty feet and then the slope of green junipers and pines going to cover the top of the hill. And at the foot of the bluff the flat field where marsh and quack grass grow, fed by the waves that in storms reach up to the very foot of the bluff. And, toward the lake, all those huge rocks, too big for man to move and reasonless, stand in strange, silent rows for the waves to break on their outer **sentinels.**

That field was a fine one, with the high wind singing in the pines of the bluff overhead and the colder wind outdistancing the waves to come across the rocks and freshen us at our play. Always around us the steady roar of the waves breaking and their hiss as they ran up the slope of sand to die.

The Indian lads must still be there and I know the island boys are. There with the **ebbing** of day and before cows must be sought in their roaming, the lads must join in their game.

We used a ball hard-woven of fisher twine with a rock of rubber for its heart. It was a grand hard ball and our bats were good—they came polished off the Michigan shore, but some of us fancied the island ones, cut and honed of our own woods. Shawn Laferty owned the gloves which the catcher and the first baseman wore. And the bases were white driftwood.

Once we had a quarter ball which one of the resort men bought for us, but we played only a few innings before it got lopsided and sorry bits of wood and string flew from it, and we went back to our own wound ball.

It was Shago White-owl, who had a curve that would break your back, who wound the balls. Shago lived in Indian Town, though his mother once was of the Irish. Shago would take twine from the fishing shanties, and, with the old bits of hard rubber we carefully saved, wind a ball that was as round as any of the store kind.

When first I played, I remember Shago's pitching well. He was not much older than I, but had been playing longer, and already he was a pitcher for at least a few innings of every game. He had feathers for feet, a strong arm, and a sure eye. It always was Shago who was picked first if you won the choosing up.

The first time I ever came to bat, Shago was pitching. I was sick of heart and shaking and in great fear that I would make a fool of myself and the others would laugh. I still see Shago grinning there and whirling his arm like a windmill and the ball shooting at me and I making a helpless swing, a full ninny! And how I stood, decided to wait the next one out, and Shago blazing another past me and the umpire calling it a strike.

And I spit on my hands as the older boys did and glared out at Shago. I'll never know if it was accident, my skill, or the kindness of Shago, that I hit the next ball and got on base. For I remember Shago rolled on the sand and laughed and laughed and so did I—except I stood still on the base. I felt a man.

It would have done you who love boys good to see Shago. He was lean and sharp like a knife blade, and there seemed to be the glint of steel in his eyes. But his mouth was merry and was quicker to laugh or shout than any other. There was a strange madness on him, too.

I remember well the day that we had two men on the bases and Shago stopped his windup, pegged the ball to the catcher, and was away running fast to the foot of the bluff. He went up it like smoke up a chimney, only more quietly, and we saw him reach the **summit**, go swiftly along its edge, pounce, and hold up for us to see a young puppy, one of Pegh Mahone's brood, that might have tumbled down the bluff.

And again a day that the sun in strange complexion was dyeing all the sky and the hill and the rocks beside us, even our faces, with a grand blush, and Shago stopped the game. He would do it often when his side was way ahead by drawing back his arm and throwing the ball far over the catcher's head. It was what he did this evening and ran to a big rock right at the water's edge. We followed Shago up on the rock and sat beside him, perched like gulls. First he pointed out into the deep water where, just below the calm surface, you could see rocks big enough to farm, and then he pointed to the sun.

"A blood sun," he said.

"A red sunset, a fine day tomorrow," John Gallagher answered.

"You're wrong there," said Shago. "A blood sun." And our eyes followed his over the bluff and the world that had grown a strange **hue** and still.

"A bad sun," said Shago. "Any tug not in by midnight will end on rocks like those. The sun says so."

We all grew still and looked out at the mountain rocks in the lake. Many of us had fathers who were fishermen, and we had some dread of the lake. And we listened to the little waves patting the big rocks. Color was over everything. It was Shago who spoke first.

"We'll have to hurry for the cows," he said. "They'll be restless, and it will be no night to be out late looking for them."

We went together up over the bluff and searched for the cows in the fields and the woods to hurry them home with clods and sticks. There was little shouting that night, for a mood was on us, and when we'd eaten we went to the docks and in the early night counted the tugs. They were all home.

That night the winds quarreled and slammed water on the island from all sides. You could hear the boom of water and the scream of wind when you first awoke the next morning. There were no ball games, for the waves poured through the rocks, up to the foot of the bluff. Beyond, out in deep water where Shago had pointed, you could see between the rolling waves the heads of rocks four times the size of a tug. Big rocks which should not have been lifting their heads up into our world.

It was in my third year of playing there afternoons below the bluff that I saw something strange in Shago. He would squint long from the box before he threw the ball. It always came fast and with a sweep, but we were learning that if

we waited, often we got a walk. As the summer went, they came oftener. Shago, too, was losing his skill at the plate and not hitting as well.

With the next spring we knew. Shago's eyes were red, and his pitching was hard, fast, and with great curves that did not seem to find the plate. Once in a while Shago would steady and pitch and his side never would lose, but by September he was a bad pitcher, a poor hitter, and had taken to playing the fielders.

That winter, I remember, his mother bought him glasses from a man in *Charlevoix*[1] but because we laughed at him with the glint of glass on his dark face he only wore them going home.

The summer that came after found Shago early at the beach, but he no longer pitched. He pretended that he had no liking for that, and a custom grew up that whatever side took Shago always asked him if he would pitch. He would say "No," and would turn to go out into left field close to the bluff where the ball, if hit, never went far. His sight was such that he could not field well, and even when they would pitch easy to him he could not hit.

As fall came on, Shago, who had a pride to him, would come out late after the game had started, pretending he had been busy for his mother. He would sit with the little boys, who hoped to get into the game if we were a man short.

School came to an end for him, too. The teachers soon learning that sight was going from Shago, told his mother that she need not make him study any more, but to send him to school to listen. Shago went for a while, but after they asked him questions a couple of times to see if he were following the work, and he knew none of the answers, he would come no more. We saw him less and less. We found he had gone to work for one of the fishermen, clearing hooks, which took nimble fingers and which one might do with only a sense of touch.

It was early spring, and a few plucky crickets already had started their fiddling when Shago came slowly down the single street of St. James to stop in front of us. We stood in the light of the store where candy was sold and where we

___

1. Charlevoix (shär′ lə vói). A resort and fishing town in northern Michigan.

often met.

In Shago's hands there were five baseballs. They were wondrously tight in their winding and each as round as ever a baseball was. There never had been the like of such fine balls on the island.

"You'll be starting the game soon," said Shago. "So I got these ready."

We took them in our hands. We all told Shago how fine they were and thanked him. He stood curling his fingers around one wound so tightly you could not feel where strand lay next to strand.

"But aren't you going to bat one?" Shago asked. "I think they have a fine fly to them."

We stood helpless and looked from one to the other. Why were we so thick of head we could not have said we would go for a bat and

About the Author

James Pooler (b. 1903), the son of a fisherman, was born in Sheboygan, Wisconsin. Traveling with his father over the Great Lakes, he absorbed details for the setting of "Shago." Later he became a columnist for *Detroit Free Press* and taught journalism at the University of Detroit. He won the Pulitzer Prize for reporting.

so changed his thoughts to other things? But we stood there as helpless as once we were at bat when Shago was in fine form. It was Laferty who blurted it out.

"We can't, Shago," he said. It was night.

Testing for Understanding

1. Shago White-owl was
   a. a full-blooded Indian.
   b. not an Indian.
   c. partially Indian.
   d. fully Irish.

2. The setting for this story is the
   a. Pacific Coast.
   b. Atlantic Seaboard.
   c. Great Lakes region.
   d. Gulf Coast.

3. The boys played ball on the
   a. field at the foot of the bluff.
   b. gash of naked sand.
   c. green slope at the top of the bluff.
   d. beach.

4. Shago's most outstanding quality was his
   a. contagious good humor.
   b. determination.
   c. sharp skill.
   d. pride.

5. Shago responded
   a. better to success than to disappointment.
   b. equally well to both success and disappointment.
   c. better to disappointment than to success.
   d. to success with a bit of pride and to disappointment with a twinge of bitterness.

6. The first half of the story calls the most attention to Shago's
   a. bad temper.   b. eyes.   c. humor.   d. mouth.

7. In the incident about Pegh Mahone's puppy, Shago shows all of these traits except his
   a. keen vision.
   b. consideration for others.
   c. sense of humor.
   d. unpredictable nature.

8. Shago's blindness in this story is best symbolized by the
   a. bluff.   b. storm.   c. blood sun.   d. rocks.

9. Shago's character is best symbolized by the
   a. village.   b. storm.   c. blood sun.   d. rocks.

10. Shago made the balls at the end of the story as a
    a. gesture of friendship.
    b. sign of refusal to admit that he was blind.
    c. way of asking the boys if he could play ball with them.
    d. gift to win their sympathy.

 *Reading for Understanding*

1. *The bluff must be much the same. A gash of naked sand and stone upright for fifty feet and then the slope of green junipers and pines going to cover the top of the hill. And at the foot of the bluff the flat field where the marsh and quack grass grow.*
   The gash of naked sand
   a. ran along the crest of the bluff.
   b. formed a rocky beach beside the sea.
   c. helped to make up the face of the bluff.
   d. lay between the field and the bluff at its base.

2. *Shawn Laferty owned the gloves which the catcher and first baseman wore.*
   Shawn Laferty's gloves were most likely
   a. the only gloves the team had.   c. not borrowed like the rest were.
   b. expensive.   d. better than the other gloves the boys used.

3. *I'll never know if it was accident, my skill, or the kindness of Shago, that I hit the next ball and got on base. For I remember Shago rolled on the sand and laughed and laughed and so did I—except I stood still on the base. I felt a man.*
   Shago's actions probably mean that he
   a. was admiring the skill in the hit.   c. had helped the batter.
   b. was a good sport.   d. could cleverly hide his displeasure.

4. *Shago's eyes were red, and his pitching was hard, fast, and with great curves that did not seem to find the plate. Once in a while Shago would steady and pitch and his side never would lose.*
   Shago seldom slowed down with his pitching because
   a. that gave the other team a better chance to win.
   b. he enjoyed letting others win.
   c. the other players taunted him if he did not pitch hard and fast.
   d. it was hard for him to admit his weakness.

5. *He no longer pitched. He pretended that he had no liking for that, and a custom grew up that whatever side took Shago always asked him if he would pitch.*
   The custom grew up because
   a. giving Shago a chance would help his feelings.
   b. Shago was still a better pitcher than anyone else.
   c. the boys were afraid Shago might quit playing otherwise.
   d. they refused to believe that he was losing out.

Meditating for Meaning

1. Shago's character is symbolized at the beginning of this well-constructed story, then displayed in the narrative that follows.
   a. Study the setting given in the second paragraph. What part of this setting portrays the same qualities of character as Shago?
   b. Throughout the story, how does Shago show these same characteristics?

2. We see a rare combination of traits in Shago.
   a. List his personal characteristics and skills.
   b. What does the author mean when he says, "There seemed to be a glint of steel in his eyes"?
   c. What do you think the author means by the "strange madness on him"? Use an incident of the story to illustrate this trait.
   d. How do people often respond to someone with such a trait?
   e. Why?
   f. Study Shago's treatment of the author the first time he came to bat. How do his actions in this incident explain why the other boys admire and follow him in spite of the trait in Question 2c above?
   g. After reading 1 Kings 12:7, explain how this trait of character works.

3. The "blood sun" represents the turning point in the story.
   a. What will shortly happen to the sun?
   b. What does Shago predict from the sun?
   c. When does the color of the blood sun next appear in the story?
   d. Summarize your answers to a, b, and c. What future event does the blood-red sun symbolize?

4. Think about the violent storm.
   a. What storm occurs in Shago's experience?
   b. What does Shago point out that becomes more apparent in the storm?
   c. What does this feature symbolize earlier in the story?
   d. What effect does the storm in Shago's life have on him which is like the effect mentioned in 4b of the natural storm?
   e. Explain from Psalm 66:10, 11 how God uses adverse circumstances in our lives to refine our characters.

5. Follow the symbolism to the end of the story.
   a. During what season of the year did everything seem to come to an end for Shago?
   b. How does this season symbolize such events better than any other season?
   c. How was the last line of the story literally true?
   d. How was it symbolic?
   e. What might the fact that our last view of Shago is in "early spring" symbolize about Shago's response to his blindness in the future?

Looking for Literary Technique

The writer of "Shago" used several techniques to help you see and hear the things that were happening. These techniques added feeling to your understanding as you read.

To describe Shago climbing the bluff, the writer could have said, "With a few nimble steps Shago was up the bluff." This sentence would have been good, but less real to your eye than the words, "He went up it like smoke up a chimney, only more quietly."

This kind of comparison is called a **simile**. It helps you see Shago's movement by comparing it to something you have often seen. You know from experience how effortlessly smoke drifts upward, and of course, you have never heard it make a sound. The simile enabled you to live Shago's climb in your mind's eye.

Notice that the word *like* is used to introduce the comparison in this simile. Sometimes the word *as* serves the same purpose. The words *like* or *as* will be your clue as you look for similes.

1. Find one other simile in the story and explain what it helps you see and feel.

To help you see the action in "Shago," the writer also used an occasional **metaphor** such as this one: "He had feathers for feet."

You can see that a metaphor closely resembles a simile. The word *like* would have been added in the simile, and it would have read this way: "He had feet *like* feathers." Similes clearly tell you they are making a comparison by using *like* or *as*. The metaphor omits such comparative words and makes a direct statement that suggests a comparison.

2. Find one other metaphor in the story and explain what it helps you see and feel.

In describing the rocks at the beginning of the story, the author used a special kind of metaphor by calling the rocks sentinels. "And, toward the lake, all those huge rocks, too big for man to move and reasonless, stand in strange, silent rows for the waves to break on their outer sentinels." He actually makes the rocks seem like people by comparing them to watchmen. Such an implied figure of speech is called **personification**.

3. Find one other example of personification in this story and explain how the author has used it.

Writers sometimes use words like *zip*, *boom*, or *crash* to help you hear the action they are describing. The use of such words is called **onomatopoeia.** The onomatopoeia of a word like *plop* is very strong. The word *slip* has a weaker onomatopoeic effect, but it still stimulates the ears of the reader. If the writer says, "Glen *put* the paper into the drawer," the reader gets the meaning. But he gets meaning plus sound when he reads, "Glen *slipped* the paper into the drawer."

4. Find four onomatopoeic words in this story.

Write two sentences of your own that contain similes, two that contain metaphors, two that contain personification, and two that contain at least one onomatopoeic word apiece. Following are several suggestions of things you may want to describe in your sentences.

—dewy spider webs on a rosebush

—lightning bugs on a summer night

—the sound of dry oak leaves blown by the wind

—stage fright at leading your first song in public

—the sound of a harvester in a field of ripe corn

A Spark Neglected

by Leo Tolstoy

Ivan meant to set his neighbor straight. Instead, he set tragedy in motion for himself and many of his neighbors. Ivan needed to face up to the obvious truth that no man will straighten out his brother unless he is ready to first show him the right way by his own example.

Defining for Comprehension

Choose the word or phrase below which best defines each word at the left as it is used in the story.

1. **enmity**
   a. rivalry   b. hatred   c. misunderstanding

2. **petition**
   a. legal statement   b. official form   c. written request

3. **feud**
   a. wall   b. gossip   c. quarrel

4. **slandered**
   a. defamed   b. tormented   c. disliked

5. **malice**
   a. pride   b. spite   c. fury

6. **exile**
   a. banishment   b. punishment   c. confinement

7. **greenhorn**	a. youth	b. dunce	c. beginner
8. **roan**	a. reddish-brown	b. red speckled with white	c. cream-colored
9. **sullen**	a. deeply depressed	b. resentfully silent	c. faultfinding
10. **bereft**	a. robbed	b. confused	c. upset
11. **eaves**	a. overhanging edge	b. uppermost ridge	c. supporting framework
12. **injunction**	a. warning	b. request	c. court order

A Spark Neglected

There once lived in a village a peasant by the name of Ivan Shcherbakov. He lived well; he was the best worker in the village, and he had three sons, all of them able to work. The eldest was married, the second about to marry, and the third was a grown-up lad who was old enough to tend horses and was already beginning to plough. Ivan's wife was a clever woman and a good housekeeper. His daughter-in-law turned out to be a peaceable person and a good worker. There was no reason why Ivan should not have led a good life with his family. The only idle mouth to feed was his old, ailing father who had been lying on the *brick oven*[1] for seven years, sick with the asthma.

Ivan had plenty of everything: three horses and a colt, a cow and a yearling calf, and fifteen sheep. The women made the shoes and the clothes for the family and helped work in the fields; the men worked on their farms.

They always had enough grain to last until the next crop and sold enough oats to pay the taxes and meet all their other needs. An easy life, indeed, might Ivan have led with his children. But next door to him he had a neighbor. Gavrilo the Lame, Gordyey Ivanov's son. And there was an **enmity** between him and Ivan.

So long as old man Gordyey was alive, and Ivan's father ran the farm, the peasants lived in neighborly fashion. If the women needed a sieve or a vat, or the men had to get another axle or cart wheel for a time, they sent from one farm to another and helped each other out in a neighborly way. When a calf strayed into the threshing ground, they would just drive it out and only say: "Don't let it get in again, for the heap has not yet been put away." And in those days it was never thought of to hide anything of their neighbor's or lock it up in the threshing floor or in a shed, or to revile each other.

Thus they lived so long as the old men were alive. But when the young people began to farm, things went quite differently.

The whole thing began from a mere nothing. A hen of Ivan's daughter-in-law starting laying early, and the young woman began collecting the eggs for *Passion Week*.[2] Every day she went to the shed to pick up an egg from the wagon box. But one day when the young woman

---

1. brick oven: A heated brick chamber people sat or lay on to keep warm.
2. Passion Week: The second week before Easter when some churches commemorate the sufferings and death of Christ.

heard the hen cackle, she said to herself: "I have no time now, I must get the hut in order for the holiday; I will go there later to get it."

In the evening she went to the wagon box under the shed to fetch the egg, but it was not there. The young woman then went to ask her mother-in-law and her brothers-in-law whether they had taken it: but Taraska, her youngest brother-in-law, said: "Your hen laid an egg in the neighbor's yard, for she cackled there and flew back from that yard across the wicker fence."

So the young woman went to her neighbor's, and Gavrilo's mother came out to meet her. "What do you want, young woman?"

"Granny, my hen has been in your yard today," the young woman said, "did she not lay an egg there?"

"I have not set eyes on her. We have hens of our own, and they laid several hours ago. We have gathered our own eggs, and we have no need of other people's eggs. And we don't go looking for eggs in other people's yards, young woman."

The young woman was offended and said a word too much. Her neighbor answered back with two, and the women began to scold. Presently Ivan's wife came up carrying a pail of water. She stopped to take a hand in the matter. Gavrilo's wife rushed out and gave her neighbors the rough side of her tongue, regardless of what fact or what was fiction. She reminded them of things that had happened and mentioned things that had not happened at all. Then the tongue-lashing began. All shouted at once, trying to say two words at a time, and not choice words, either.

"You are such and such a one; you are a thief, a sneak; you are simply starving your poor old father-in-law; you are a tramp!"

"And you have worn my sieve to shreds, you everlasting borrower! And it's our shoulder yoke you are carrying your pails on. You just give back our yoke!"

They grabbed the yoke, spilt the water, tore off each other's kerchiefs and began to fight. At this moment Gavrilo drove up from the field and stopped to take his wife's part. Out rushed Ivan with his son and joined in with the rest. Ivan, being a sturdy peasant, scattered them all and yanked out a piece of Gavrilo's beard. People ran up to them to see what was the matter, and with difficulty they pulled the fighters apart.

That's the way it began.

Gavrilo wrapped the piece of his beard in a **petition** and went to the Township Court to enter a complaint.

"I did not raise a beard for pockmarked Ivan to pull it out."

In the meantime his wife went bragging to the neighbors that they would now get Ivan sentenced and sent to *Siberia*.[3] And so the **feud** began.

The old man on the oven tried from the first to persuade them to make peace, but the young people paid no attention to him. He said to them, "Children, you are doing a foolish thing. For a foolish thing you have started a feud. Think of it—the whole affair began from an egg. There is no great value in one egg. With God's aid there will be enough for all. Suppose your neighbor did say an unkind word—put it right; show her how to use better words. If there has been a fight—well, such things will happen. We are all sinful people. But go and make peace, and let there be an end to it! If you nurse your anger, it will only be worse as time goes on."

The young people did not heed the old man, for they thought that he did not understand the matter but was just babbling in old man's fashion. Ivan would not humble himself before his neighbor.

"I never pulled his beard," he said. "He jerked it out himself; but his son yanked off my shirt button and has torn my whole shirt—just look at it!"

Ivan, too, took the matter to court. The case was heard before a Justice of the Peace and in the Township Court. While they were busy suing each other, Gavrilo lost a coupling pin

---

3. Siberia: The extremely cold, remote area of northeastern Russia used as a place of exile for criminals.

out of his cart. The women in Gavrilo's house accused Ivan's son of having taken it.

"We saw him in the night," they said, "making his way under the window to the cart, and a neighbor says he saw him at the tavern, offering the pin to the tavern-keeper."

Again they started a suit. And at home not a day passed but that they quarreled, nay, even fought. The children, too, cursed one another—they learned this from their elders—and when the women happened to meet at the brook where they went to rinse the clothes, they did not so much strike the *beetles*[4] as let loose their tongues, and every word was a bad one.

At first the men just **slandered** one another, but later they began to steal things that lay about loose. And the women and the children followed their example. Their life grew worse and worse. Ivan Shcherbakov and Gavrilo the Lame kept suing one another in the Township Court and before the Justice of the Peace until all the judges were sick to death of their quarrels and tired of them. Now Gavrilo got Ivan to pay a fine, or he sent him to the lockup; then Ivan did the same to Gavrilo; and the more they did each other harm, the more furious they grew.

"Just wait, I will get even with you!" they said one to another.

Thus it went on for six years. Only the old man on the oven kept telling them again and again: "Think of it, my children, what you are doing! Drop all your accounts, stick to your work, don't show such **malice** toward others, and it will be better for you. The more the rage, the worse it will be."

But they paid no attention to the old man.

In the seventh year the matter went so far that Ivan's daughter-in-law at a wedding accused Gavrilo before people of having been caught stealing horses. Gavrilo, who was drunk at the time, flew into a rage and gave the woman such a blow that she was laid up for a week. Ivan rejoiced at this and at once set off to the prosecuting magistrate with a petition.

"Now," he thought, "I will get even with my neighbor; he shall not escape the penitentiary or **exile** to Siberia."

The magistrate did not accept the petition, for when they examined the woman, she was up and around and there were no marks upon her. So Ivan went to the Justice of the Peace, but the justice sent the case to the Township Court. Ivan bestirred himself in the township office, treated the clerk and the Elder of the District Court to a gallon of liquor, and got Gavrilo condemned to be flogged. The sentence was read to Gavrilo in the court.

The scribe read: "The Court has decreed that the peasant Gavrilo Gordyey shall receive twenty lashes with a birch rod at the township office."

Ivan listened to the decree and looked at Gavrilo, wondering how he would take it. Gavrilo became as pale as a sheet, turned round, and walked out into the hall. Ivan followed him out, meaning to go to his horse, when he heard Gavrilo say: "Very well, he will beat my back and it will burn, but something of his may burn worse than that."

When Ivan heard these words, he returned at once to the judges.

"Righteous judges! He threatens to set fire to my house. Listen, he said it in the presence of witnesses."

Gavrilo was called in.

"Is it true that you said so?"

"I said nothing. Flog me, if you wish. Evidently I must suffer for the truth, while he may do anything he pleases."

Gavrilo wanted to say something more, but his lips and his cheeks quivered. He turned away toward the wall. Even the judges were frightened by the looks of him.

"It would not be surprising," they thought, "if he actually did some harm to his neighbor or to himself."

Then an old judge said to them: "Listen here, my friends! You had better make peace with each other. Was it right of you, brother Gavrilo, to strike a woman? Happily God was merciful to you, but think what crime you might have committed! Was that right? Confess your guilt and beg his pardon, and he will forgive you. Then we shall change the decree."

Gavrilo would not listen to him. "I am fifty

---

4. beetles: Wooden mallets or clubs used to wash clothes.

years old less one," he said, "and I have a married son. I have not been beaten in all my life, and now pockmarked Ivan has brought me to being beaten with rods; and am I to beg his forgiveness? Well, he will . . . Ivan will remember me!"

Gavrilo's voice quivered and he could not talk. He turned around and went out.

It was seven miles from the township office to the village, so that it was quite late when Ivan reached home. He unhitched his horse, put it up for the night, and entered the hut. The room was empty. The women had already gone out to drive the cattle in, and the boys had not yet returned from the field. Ivan went in, sat down on a bench, and began to think. He recalled how the decision was announced to Gavrilo, how he grew pale and turned to the wall; and his heart was pinched. He thought of how he should feel if he were condemned to be flogged, and he felt sorry for Gavrilo. He heard the old man on the oven, coughing; then saw him turn over, let down his legs, and sit up. The old man dragged himself with difficulty up to the bench beside Ivan and coughed and coughed until his throat was cleared. Then leaning against the table he said: "Well, have they condemned him?"

Ivan said, "Yes, to twenty strokes with the rods."

The old man shook his head, "Ivan, you are not doing right. It's wrong, not only wrong to him, but to yourself. Well, will it make you feel easier if they flog him?"

"He will never do it again," said Ivan.

"Why not? In what way is he doing worse than you?"

"What, he has not harmed me?" exclaimed Ivan. "He might have killed the woman; and he now even threatens to set fire to my house. Well, shall I bow to him for it?"

The old man heaved a sigh and said: "You, Ivan, can walk and ride about the world, while I have to lie the year round on the oven; so that perhaps you think that you see everything and I nothing. But no, my son, it is not so. There is very little that you see, for malice has blinded your eyes. Another man's sins are before you, but your own are behind your back. You see his badness, but you do not see your own. Who was it pulled the hair out of his beard? Who was it overturned his rick when stacked? Who is dragging him to the courts? And yet you put all of the blame on him. You yourself live badly; that's why it is bad. Not thus did I live, and no such thing, my dear, did I teach you. Did I and the old man, his father, live this way? Do you call this living? It is a sin! You are a peasant, a head of a house. You will be responsible. What are you teaching your women and your children? To curse. The other day Taraska, that young **greenhorn**, cursed Aunt Arina, and his mother only laughed at him. Is that right, I ask you? Think of your soul. You say a word too much and I answer back with two; you strike a blow and I strike back twice. Is that right? No, no, my son, Christ taught us something quite different. If a harsh word is said to you—keep quiet, and let conscience smite him. That's what Christ has taught us. If they slap your face, turn the other cheek to them and say 'Here, strike it if I deserve it!' His own conscience will rebuke him. He will soften and will listen to you. That's what Christ has commanded us to do, my son. If any one has offended you, forgive him in godly fashion, and things will go better with you, and you will feel easier at heart."

Ivan kept silence.

"Listen, Ivan! Pay attention to me, an old man. Go and hitch the **roan** horse, drive straight to the office; quash there the whole business, and in the morning go to Gavrilo, make peace with him in godly fashion, and invite him to your house for tomorrow's holiday. Have the *samovar*[5] prepared and make an end to these sins so they may never happen again; then command the women and the children to live in peace."

Ivan heaved a sigh and thought, "What the old man says is true," and his heart melted. The only thing he did not know was how to begin to put matters right with his neighbor.

The old man, as though guessing what was

---

5. samovar (sa′ mə vär): A large urn used in Russia for serving tea.

in Ivan's mind, began once more, "Go, Ivan, do not put if off! Put out the fire at the start, for when it spreads, you cannot control it."

The old man was going to say more, but before he could do so, the women entered the room chattering like magpies. The news had already reached them about how Gavrilo had been sentenced to be flogged, and how he had threatened to set fire to the house. They had heard all about it and had again had a row in the pasture with the women of Gavrilo's house. They said that Gavrilo's daughter-in-law had threatened them with the examining magistrate. The magistrate, they said, was receiving gifts from Gavrilo. He would now upset the whole case, and the schoolmaster had already written another petition, to the Czar himself this time, about Ivan, mentioning all the affairs, about the coupling pin, and about the garden—and they said half of Ivan's homestead would be theirs soon. As Ivan listened to their talk his heart was chilled again, and he changed his mind about making peace with Gavrilo.

In a farmer's yard there is always plenty for the master to do. Ivan did not stop to talk with the women, but went out of the house to the threshing floor and the shed. Before he had fixed everything the sun had set, and the boys returned from the field, where they had been ploughing a double *tilth*[6] during the winter, in readiness for the spring corn. Ivan asked them about their work, helped them to put up the horses, and laid aside a broken horse collar for repairs. He was about to put some poles under the shed, when it grew too dark to see. So he left the poles until the morrow; and instead he threw some fodder down to the cattle, then opened the gate, let out the horses Taraska was to take to the night pasture, and again closed the gate and barred it.

"Now to supper and to bed," thought Ivan, going to the hut. By this time he had entirely forgotten about what his father had told him. But just as he took hold of the door handle and was about to enter the porch, he heard his neighbor on the other side of the wicker fence scolding someone in a hoarse voice.

"The devil take him!" Gavrilo was crying to someone. "He ought to be killed!"

These words made all the old anger toward his neighbor burst forth in Ivan. He stood awhile and listened to Gavrilo's scolding. Then Gavrilo grew quiet, and Ivan went into the hut.

Light was burning within. The young woman was sitting in the corner behind the spinning wheel; the good wife was getting supper ready; the eldest son was making straps for the *bast*[7] shoes, the second was at the table with a book, and Taraska was getting ready to go out to pasture the horses for the night.

Ivan was **sullen** and cross when he entered the room; he knocked the cat down from the bench, scolded the women because the vat was not in the right place, then sat down, frowning, to mend the horse collar. He could not forget Gavrilo's words, with which he had threatened him in court, and what he just had said about someone, speaking in a hoarse voice, "He ought to be killed."

The goodwife was bustling about to get Taraska something to eat. When the boy was through with his supper he put on his old sheepskin, took a piece of bread, and went out to drive the mares down the street. Ivan got up too and went out on the porch. It was pitch-dark outside and a wind had risen. He stepped down from the porch and helped his young son to get on a horse, shooed the colts after him, and then stood looking and listening while Taraska rode down the village, where he was joined by other lads with their horses. Ivan waited until they all rode out of hearing. As he stood there by the gate he could not get Gavrilo's words out of his head. "Something of yours may burn worse."

"He would not hesitate to do it," thought Ivan. "It is dry and a wind is blowing. He will come up somewhere at the back, set fire to the house, and go scot free, the villain! If I could but catch him in the act, he would not get away with it!"

This thought troubled Ivan so much that he did not go back to the porch, but walked straight out into the roadway, then round

---

6. tilth: Portion of tilled or cultivated land.
7. bast: Of fibrous material or cord.

behind the gates.

"I will examine the yard—who knows what he is up to."

Ivan walked softly down along the gate. He had just turned around the corner and looked up the fence, when it seemed to him that something stirred at the opposite end, as though it got up and sat down again. Ivan stopped—he listened and looked. Everything was quiet, only the wind rustled the leaves in the willow tree and crackled through the straw. It was pitch-dark, but when his eyes got used to the darkness, Ivan could see the far corner, the plough and the *penthouse*.[8] He stood and looked a while, but there was no one there.

"I must have seen wrong," thought Ivan, "but I will, nevertheless, go round," and he stole up softly along the shed. When he came to the corner, behold, something flashed by near the plough and disappeared again. Ivan felt as if struck to the heart, and he stopped. As he stopped he could see something flashing up, and he clearly saw a man with a cap on his head, squatting down with his back toward him, setting fire to a bunch of straw in his hands. Ivan's heart fluttered within him like a bird. Straining every nerve, he approached with great strides, hardly feeling his legs under him.

"Ah," thought Ivan, "now he won't escape! I'll catch him in the act!"

Before Ivan had walked another two lengths of the fence, a flame licked up in the straw of the penthouse and was climbing toward the roof, and there beneath it stood Gavrilo so that his whole figure could plainly be seen.

As a hawk swoops down on a lark, so Ivan rushed up against Gavrilo the Lame. "I will twist him up," he thought, "and he will not escape me."

But Gavrilo must have heard his steps, for he ran along the shed with as much speed as a hare.

"You will not get away," shouted Ivan, swooping down on him.

He was about to grab him by the collar, but Gavrilo got away from him, and then Ivan caught him by the skirt of his coat. The skirt tore off, and Ivan fell down.

Ivan jumped up.

"Help! Hold him!" and again he ran.

Meanwhile, Gavrilo had nearly reached his own yard, but Ivan caught up with him. He was just going to take hold of him, when something struck him a stunning blow, as though a stone had come down on his head. Gavrilo had picked up an oak post lying in the yard, and when Ivan ran up to him he hit him with all his might on the head.

Ivan staggered, sparks flew from his eyes, then all grew dark, and he fell down. When he came to his senses, Gavrilo was gone. It was as light as day, and from his yard something roared and crackled like an engine at work. Ivan turned round and saw that his back shed was all up in flames and the side shed was beginning to burn; the fire, the smoke, and the burning straw were being carried toward the hut.

"What is this? Friends!" cried Ivan, raising his hands, then striking them down on his thighs. "If I could only have pulled it out from the penthouse, and put it out! What is this? Friends!" he repeated. He wanted to shout, but he nearly strangled—he had no voice. He wanted to run, but his feet would not move—they tripped each other up. He tried to walk slowly, but he staggered, and he nearly strangled. He stood still again and drew breath; then started to walk. Before he reached the fire, the side shed was all ablaze, flames were leaping out of the hut, and it was impossible to get into the yard. People came running up, but nothing could be done. The neighbors dragged their own things out of their houses and drove the cattle out of their sheds. After Ivan's house, Gavrilo's caught fire; a rising wind carried the fire across the street. Half the village burned down. All they saved from Ivan's house was the old man who was pulled out; and the family jumped out in what clothes they had on. Everything else was burned except the horses in the pasture; the cattle were burned, the chickens on their roosts, the carts, the ploughs, the harrows, the women's chests with their

_____

8. penthouse: A shed.

clothes, the grain in the granary—everything was burned.

It burned for a long time, all night long. Ivan stood near his yard and kept looking at it and saying, "What is this? Friends! If I could just have pulled it out and put it out!"

When the ceiling in the hut fell down, Ivan rushed into the burning place, took hold of a brand, and tried to drag it out. The women saw him and began to call him back, but he pulled out one log and started for another, when he lost his footing and fell among the flames. Then his son rushed after him and dragged him out. Ivan had his hair and beard singed, his garments burned, his hands blistered, but he did not feel anything.

"His sorrow has **bereft** him of his senses," people said.

The fire died down, but Ivan was still standing there and saying, "Friends, what is this? If I could only have pulled it out."

In the morning the village elder sent his son to Ivan.

"Uncle Ivan," said the boy, "your father is dying, he has sent for you to bid you good-bye."

Ivan had forgotten all about his father and did not understand what they were saying to him. "What father?" he said. "Send for whom?"

"He has sent for you to bid you good-bye. He is dying in our house. Come, Uncle Ivan!" said the elder's son, pulling him by the arm. Ivan followed the boy.

When the old man was being carried out of the hut, some burning straw fell on him and burnt him badly. He had then been taken to the village elder's house in a distant part of the village, which the fire did not reach.

When Ivan came to his father, there were only the elder's wife and some little children lying on the oven. The rest were all at the fire. The old man was lying on a bench looking toward the door. When his son Ivan entered, he stirred a little. The old woman went up to him and said that his son had come. He asked to have him brought closer to him. Ivan went up, and then the old man said:

"What did I tell you, dear Ivan? Who has burned the village?"

"He, Father," said Ivan. "He—I caught him

About the Author

Leo Tolstoy (1828-1910), born near Moscow, Russia, was orphaned while young and raised by relatives. After attending Kazan University for three years, he continued studying on his own. He settled on a prosperous estate and established a school for peasant children, adapting his teaching to the individual child. At the age of forty-six Tolstoy sold all his lands and copyrights and sought happiness and closeness to God in a life of voluntary poverty as a self-sufficient vegetarian. His views opposing violence, smoking, drinking, and involvement in the world in general, appear in the legends and novels he wrote about peasant life. Perhaps most outstanding is his novel *War and Peace*.

in the act. With my own eyes I saw him put the fire into the **eaves**. If only I could have caught the burning bunch of straw and put it, nothing would have happened."

"Ivan," said the old man, "my death has come, and you, too, will die. Whose sin is it?"

Ivan stared at his father and kept silence; he could not say a word.

"Speak before God; whose sin is it? What did I tell you?"

It was only then that Ivan came to his senses and understood everything. Then he snuffled and said, "Mine, dear Father." And he fell on his knees before his father and wept, saying, "Forgive me, oh my father! I am guilty before you and before God."

"Glory be to thee, O Lord! Glory be to thee, O Lord!" the old man said, turning his eyes again toward his son.

"Ivan! Oh, Ivan!"

"What is it, my father?"

"What is to be done now?"

Ivan was weeping. "I do not know how we are to live now, Father!" he said.

The old man closed his eyes, moistened his lips a little as if to gather all his strength, and once more opened his eyes and said, "You will manage. So long as your life be with God, you will manage." The old man was silent awhile. Then he smiled and said: "Remember, Ivan, you must not tell who started the fire. Cover up another man's sin. Forgive, as God has commanded us to do."

And the old man heaved a sigh, stretched himself, and died.

Ivan did not tell on Gavrilo, and no one found out how the fire had been started.

And Ivan's heart was softened toward Gavrilo, and Gavrilo marveled at Ivan, because he did not tell anybody. At first Gavrilo was afraid of him, but later he got used to him. The men left off quarreling, and then their families left off also. While they rebuilt their houses, the two families lived under one roof. When the village was built again, with the farmhouses built farther apart, Ivan and Gavrilo again chose to be neighbors, living in the same block.

And Ivan and Gavrilo lived neighborly together, just as their fathers had lived. Ivan Shcherbakov remembered his father's **injunction** and God's command to put out the fire in the beginning. If a person did him some harm, he did not try to have his revenge on the man, but to mend matters; and if a person called him a bad name, he did not try to answer with worse words still, but to teach him not to speak badly.

In like manner he taught the womenfolk and his sons to do.

Thus Ivan Shcherbakov got on his feet again, and began to lead a more godly life, and prospered as he had never done before.

Testing for Understanding

1. Gavrilo especially deserved Ivan's kindness, because Gavrilo had
   a. no old father to advise him.
   b. a handicap.
   c. an ill-natured mother.
   d. no sons.

2. The first offense in the feud could be traced to
   a. Gavrilo's mother.
   b. a hen.
   c. Ivan.
   d. no one.

3. A person who apparently had been storing up accusations before the quarrel began was
   a. Gavrilo.
   b. Gavrilo's wife.
   c. Ivan.
   d. Taraska.

4. Ivan came the closest to repentance when
   a. Gavrilo was to be flogged.
   b. the coupling pin was stolen.
   c. his father first talked to him.
   d. he was threatened with exile to Siberia.

5. At the time of the fire, Ivan could have saved his property if he would have
   a. remained conscious.
   b. caught Gavrilo a bit sooner.
   c. let Gavrilo go.
   d. had friends to help him when he called.

6. Incidents in this story show that where people are fighting, you can also expect to find
   a. wealth.
   b. impurity.
   c. idolatry.
   d. lying.

7. The old man on the oven believed all of the following about quarrels except that
   a. when men accuse others they often have sin in their own lives.
   b. we should allow ill treatment to provoke us to good works.
   c. they may be based on nothing of importance.
   d. they never take place among Christians.

8. The detail for which there is no clear symbolism is the
   a. egg.   b. fire.   c. birch rod.   d. darkness.

9. Which was not a result of the feud?
   a. corruption of the innocent.   c. agreement within both families.
   b. work neglected.   d. physical violence.

10. Ivan's actions during the fire symbolize
    a. the insanity that sin may lead one to.   c. the renewed strength of a repentant sinner.
    b. broken relationships.   d. his conversion.

Reading for Understanding

1. *Gavrilo wanted to say something more, but his lips and his cheeks quivered. He turned away toward the wall. Even the judges were frightened by the looks of him.*
   Gavrilo's face showed
   a. deceit.   b. weeping.   c. anger.   d. mockery.

2. *"What, he has not harmed me?" exclaimed Ivan.*
   Ivan meant that
   a. Gavrilo had done him wrong.
   b. he was too big to be hurt by Gavrilo.
   c. Gavrilo had not harmed him.
   d. the wrong had not affected him personally.

3. *"He might have killed the woman; and he now even threatens to set fire to my house. Well, shall I bow to him for it?"*
   Ivan refused to ask Gavrilo's forgiveness at this point because he thought to do so would show
   a. strength.   b. regret.   c. weakness.   d. repentance.

4. *The magistrate, they said, was receiving gifts from Gavrilo. He would now upset the whole case, and the schoolmaster had already written another petition, to the Czar himself this time, about Ivan.*
   The schoolmaster seems to have been
   a. one of the few literate persons in the town.   c. related to Gavrilo.
   b. practicing law in addition to teaching.   d. used by both sides to write petitions.

5. *Gavrilo marveled at Ivan because he did not tell anybody. At first Gavrilo was afraid of him, but later he got used to him.*
   Gavrilo feared that Ivan was
   a. now better than he was.   c. unaware of who had set the fire.
   b. planning evil against him secretly.   d. not going to speak to him either.

Meditating for Meaning

1. This story centers around two neglected sparks.
   a. Describe both of them.
   b. Which spark was symbolic of the other and in what way?

2. Tolstoy describes the way relationships often break down.
   a. Did Taraska have undeniable proof that his sister-in-law's hen had laid an egg in the neighbor's yard? Explain your answer.
   b. What do Granny's first words reveal about her character?
   c. What do the words of Gavrilo's wife reveal about what was in her mind before this incident occurred?
   d. What do these observations and Proverbs 29:22 tell us about the real beginning of quarrels?
   e. What symbolic truths can you see in the fact that the feud began with an egg?
   f. What could be symbolic about the lost "coupling pin"?

3. How is the truth of Proverbs 26:20b shown in this story?

4. Notice Tolstoy's skillful characterization of Ivan's father.
   a. What impression do we get of him in the first paragraph?
   b. How does this characterization reflect the role he played in the feud until it came to an end?
   c. What changed their response to him, and what can we learn about peacemaking from this? (See 1 Peter 2:21.)

5. As the feud grew, the lives of all became worse and worse. As Ivan's father said, they were doing as much wrong to themselves as to each other. List at least five harmful things the feuders did to themselves throughout the story. One example would be the hateful attitudes which they encouraged in their children.

6. How did Ivan's father explain the truth of 1 John 2:11?

7. Search for truth in the final scenes.
   a. The fire took place at night. How was this symbolic?
   b. As the spark leaped into flame, the whole figure of Gavrilo could plainly be seen. How is this symbolic of what happened to both Ivan and Gavrilo in the story?
   c. What reality did Ivan's father help him to see as more important than getting even?
   d. He said that if Ivan would forgive, God would see that his needs were met. What did he say true forgiveness would do to prove itself?
   e. The making of peace did not put an end to all unkind words. How did they learn from Ivan's father to turn unkind words into opportunities?

Looking for Literary Technique

Since a short story covers only a few happenings in a brief span of time, the writer can give his characters only the most necessary description. He will describe the main characters the most completely because we need to understand them as fully as possible.

The other people in the story will be developed less since they play minor roles. We are shown only the things about the minor characters that will help us understand their part in the experience of the main character.

A writer can use five ways to describe a character in his story. The acrostic "CLART" can help you remember these five ways:

Conversation—what the character says
Looks—how the character appears
Actions—what the character does
Reputation—what others say about him
Thoughts—what the character is thinking

1. The author used all five of these ways to portray Ivan. Give an example of each from the story.

2. Give an example from the story for each of the four ways the author used to describe Gavrilo.

3. Which of these two characters is described more fully?

4. Why?

Writing for Skill

Choose a person in your experience who has an unforgettable personality. Take an incident that involved this person and write it as a story. Use as many of the five methods to describe the person as you can. In some short stories, the writer does not use all five methods. You will do well if you manage to use three or four of them in your rather short story.

Cache of Honor

by John F. Hayes

"Finders keepers; losers weepers." Those who have joyed over the spoils of others have parroted this timeworn saying for generations. But does that make it right? Jesus' formula for ordering priorities sounds just the opposite: "He that findeth his life shall lose it: and he that loseth his life for my sake shall find it" (Matthew 10:39). As you read this story, consider how the characters found life by being willing to lose it.

Defining for Comprehension

Choose the word or phrase below which best defines each word at the left as it is used in the story.

1. **cavalcade**	a. waterfall	b. procession	c. destruction
2. **treacherous**	a. unreliable	b. tiring	c. teacherlike
3. **floe**	a. stream	b. floating ice	c. disappearance
4. **gaunt**	a. ravenous	b. thin	c. stern
5. **cache**	a. money	b. snag	c. hidden store
6. **cairn**	a. campfire	b. iron kettle	c. stone landmark
7. **bleak**	a. windy	b. barren	c. sun-whitened
8. **ration**	a. use sparingly	b. abuse	c. reason
9. **lee**	a. shelter	b. meadow	c. dike

10. crag	a. shallow pond	b. jagged cliff	c. old horse
11. looming	a. turning dark	b. complaining	c. appearing larger
12. ample	a. easy	b. sufficient	c. miniature
13. hillock	a. small hill	b. old gun	c. young bull
14. asserted	a. varied	b. declared	c. interrupted
15. ravenous	a. angry	b. poisonous	c. very hungry
16. thongs	a. brambles	b. crowds	c. leather straps
17. inertia	a. ignorance	b. inactivity	c. sorrow
18. succumb	a. protect	b. call	c. be overcome
19. moderated	a. grew milder	b. judged	c. rearranged
20. pinnacle	a. award	b. restriction	c. highest point
21. crevasse	a. large sheet	b. dense under-growth	c. surface crack
22. haggard	a. lazy	b. worn	c. boastful
23. doggedly	a. crookedly	b. angrily	c. determinedly

Cache of Honor

Bitter cold settled over the frozen expanse of sea ice with biting fury, a silent fury that gnawed savagely at the little **cavalcade** crawling slowly across the **treacherous floe**. Christopher Farrell felt its sting as he plodded behind the weaving *komatik*[1]. The two men ahead of him hunched in the rising wind, and the **gaunt** huskies whined hungrily as they pawed for footing on the rough ice.

As Farrell glanced at the tired dogs, his lips tightened. They had eaten their last meal until they reached their **cache**. His mouth watered at the thought of the food he and his companions had stored so securely under a rocky **cairn** on the **bleak** coast just a few hours' travel away. They had been forced to **ration** their supplies, until only a bit of tea was left. For the last two lean days they had had only tea, strong and black, made over an Eskimo lamp in the **lee** of a hastily erected snow wall.

The gnawing hunger that drained their strength with every passing hour would soon be eased. The dogs would have their dried fish, and the men would feast on *bannocks*[2] and bacon.

The lead dog cast about between the jagged mounds of ice for the least difficult trail for the team to follow. Already Farrell could make out

---

1. komatik (kō ma′ tik): dogsled.
2. bannocks (ba′ nəks): unleavened griddlecakes.

the dim coast. Soon he would be able to see the tall sentinel **crag** at whose base lay their precious cache.

"Another three hours, Glen!" he shouted cheerfully. "Then we'll eat like kings!"

Glen Fraser, from his position immediately behind the komatik, wearily waved his answer. The Eskimo between the two white men nodded his head. "We hungry," he said. "Dogs starve. No travel far now. Storm come."

Farrell didn't answer. There was nothing to worry about, even though the twisting komatik did not carry a shred of food. Instead, it was lightly loaded with rare native work—beautiful carving, beaded garments, and queer weapons for the museum which had sent Farrell and his party on this lonely Arctic trek.

Eight weeks earlier they had left this very coast which was now **looming** ahead, and at the base of a tall, rocky landmark they had cached **ample** food to see them and their dogs safely to the nearest post, still hundreds of miles to the south.

Through wind-burned eyes he narrowly watched the men and dogs ahead of him. Their progress was painfully slow, and he knew that they must all have food soon. Only food could keep them on the trail much longer. It was late afternoon when he shouted to Mig-pik-huk, the Eskimo, to stop the team. The komatik crunched to a halt beside a tall mound of ice which towered thirty feet above their heads, pushed up in jagged chunks by the grinding floe.

"I'll check our position from this **hillock**," Farrell told his friend. "Our crag should be in sight."

He skirted the mound, not realizing until now how leaden his legs had become. The hillock sloped sharply at the rear. He laboured up its side, scrambling to his feet and brushing the snow from his deerskins as he reached the summit. He peered towards the coast where black rock showed through the snow in ugly patches. A chill fear clutched his heart as he stared unbelievingly across the tumbled ice.

The rolling hills stretched away in monotonous pattern. No tall crag could be seen. In mocking regularity the snow-covered rock melted into the cold horizon on either side. He brushed his fur mitts slowly across his eyes, as if his senses refused to believe the desolate picture that lay before him.

He glanced down at his companions who huddled together at the edge of the sled, and at the faithful dogs who lay exhausted on the ice, looking like carelessly thrown bits of fur on a white carpet. His eyes searched the coast hopelessly once more; then he turned and went slowly back down the slope. Farrell's face was grim as he told the others what he had seen.

They struggled to the shore before dark, but the tangled, unbroken hills still held no clue to the precious food they knew they must find. They decided to make camp, and Farrell and Glen Fraser numbly unhitched the dogs, while Mig-pik-huk probed with his big snow knife to find a suitable spot to build an igloo.

It was dark when the Eskimo fitted the key block of snow into the dome of their shelter. Outside, the roar of the cold wind filled the night with sound. The dogs lay in the lee of a snow wall, huddled in exhausted heaps. When Farrell last looked at them, only their ruffs could be seen above the drifts. They would be safe until morning, for the blanket of snow over them would keep them warm through the night.

When he crawled back through the porch of the igloo, Glen Fraser had the seal-oil lamp going, and over weak, hot tea they grimly weighed their chances of survival. Farrell's heart was cold as those chances narrowed to one thing alone—the finding of their cache. Mig-pik-huk listened gravely.

"No find food," the Eskimo put in. "We on wrong coast. We lost."

Farrell's eyes narrowed. "Our cache can't be far away," he **asserted**. "I've plotted our trip by the stars. I know I'm right. We'll—"

"Dog good," muttered Mig-pik-huk. "Maybe we have to eat dogs. Maybe we eat these." He pointed to his caribou-skin boots.

"I'll find that cache if it's the last thing I do!" said Farrell hoarsely.

Glen Fraser looked at him with a weak grin. "It may be the last thing you do, at that," he finished.

Naked in his caribou-skin sleeping bag, Farrell stared at the flickering flame of the *kudlik*[3]. Hour after hour his mind sought some explanation for the mistake in directions he had apparently made. He could find no answer. With growing hunger pushing all other thoughts aside, he finally fell into a fitful sleep.

Mig-pik-huk's shout brought him from troubled slumber to wide wakefulness. The native was at his elbow, shaking him. In a moment he had pulled on his deerskins and hurried outside. His heart sank at the sight.

Their komatik lay in scattered bits over the snow, while the huskies crouched around in defiant groups. He realized what had happened. Hunger was to blame. Hunger had dulled his senses last night, when he had allowed the dogs to sleep without being tied up. Hunger had overcome the exhaustion of the animals, too. In the darkness they had awakened, **ravenous** for food, and had attacked the frozen **thongs** of hide which held the komatik together. They had eaten the binding down to the last shred. The sled was useless.

He knew they would have to repair the komatik, if they were ever to reach even the nearest post in safety. With stumbling fingers they cut fresh thongs from the caribou skins on which they had slept. The knots blurred in front of Farrell's eyes as he worked. It was past mid-day when they finished. They hitched the dogs and once more started south.

Farrell felt sure their journey would be short. He had travelled the Arctic many times, and he knew that no living thing could long survive in such intense cold without food. As he walked he fought the drowsy **inertia** that crept through his body, dragging at his tired muscles, tearing at his will to keep going, coaxing him to the sleep to which he knew he must not **succumb**.

They covered less than ten miles that day. Glen Fraser's knees went from under him just as the Eskimo finished building the igloo that was to shelter them for the second night. Farrell forced hot tea between his companion's lips. His face was grim as he saw Mig-pik-huk relax in drowsy exhaustion on the snow-bench.

About the Author

John F. Hayes (b. 1904) a Canadian journalist and author of youth books, was born in Ontario to a merchant family. Hayes took 12 years of evening classes at the University of Toronto. He wrote for several Canadian publishing companies and was vice-president and general manager of Southam Press, Ltd. At the age of 57, Hayes retired due to ill health. His children's books have brought him numerous awards.

He realized now what had to be done. He lurched towards the door, wondering vaguely at his weakness. Outside, the dogs lay quiet in the snow. He was sure now that further travel with the heavy komatik was out of the question until they found food. He picked out the smallest of the animals....

In the early morning he arose quietly, pulled on his deerskins and went outside. The weather had **moderated**. Inside the igloo his companions lay in exhausted sleep. He was not quite so hungry now, and in his knapsack was a small portion of the remaining tea, and a few bits of frozen meat. In his mind was the determination to take one last desperate chance of saving himself, his two friends and his remaining dogs.

Setting a course down the coast, he plodded on through the Arctic morning, his snowshoes creaking sharply in the dry air, and his breath a swirling cloud around his head. All that day he pushed ahead seeking some sign of the high **pinnacle** that held their fate in its finding.

The sun was a slinking ball of light on the horizon when his tiring eyes startled his mind with what lay before them. A fresh trail led out towards the floe! His heart leaped with excitement as he fell on his knees and carefully examined the marks in the hard snow. They had been made by a komatik, lightly loaded and hauled by three dogs. He stumbled in his

---

3. kudlik: lamp used for heating and cooking when traveling.

haste as he swung north again, his eyes glued to the trail which led out over the barren floes from which he and his companions had so lately returned.

In the dusk he stopped, fishing in his parka for his flashlight which the heat of his body had kept from freezing.

On along the ever-sharpening trail he plodded. He was almost into the **crevasse** that blocked his path before he realized it was there, and in the tangled confusion of marks on the snow he pictured the tragedy that had befallen the man he was following—the suddenly opening crack in the treacherous ice, the plunging dogs, their frightened yelps silenced by the grinding floe.

With a sick heart Farrell stood up, throwing the glare of his powerful flashlight around him in the faint hope that the man might have survived. He moved warily along the crevasse, and was almost on top of a little igloo before he saw it, half buried in the drifts. A great shout sprang from his lips as he frantically crawled through the porch of the snow house.

His heart sank as he tumbled inside. An Eskimo sprawled on the snow bench. One look at the gaunt features told Farrell that the man was in far worse condition than he. The native's eyes were dull, narrow slits and his cheeks were sunken hollows. Farrell wasted no words. Over the kudlik he brewed his remaining tea, and there was no formality in their hasty meal of dog meat.

Life seeped back into the Eskimo's **haggard** face as Farrell spoke. "You talk English? You have no food? Where you go?"

The native's lips moved slowly. "Me on way to my village on floe-edge. Me not eat four days. Lose dogs last night. Only save knife off komatik. Me starve."

"I'm Farrell of the museum party," the white man explained. "We've lost our cache. It's somewhere around this part of the coast, at the foot of a high rock. We can't find it."

The native's eyes widened. Farrell's body tensed at the man's simple words. "Tall rock near point in ice? It fall in wind week ago. Me find your cache there yesterday. It not far back. Me. . ."

Farrell was on his feet, his hands on the Eskimo's shoulders, shaking him.

"You mean you found our food! Why—"

The native nodded. "Me find. It three hours back along trail."

"But, but—" Farrell groped for words. "You're starving! Why didn't you take some? Why—"

The round, honest eyes of the Eskimo peered into the excited face of the white man. "Me no touch," he said **doggedly**. "Not right to take food of men who travel on sea ice. Me know by marks it for men who come back."

For a moment Farrell didn't speak. He stood up, looking at the blank, white wall of the igloo, and when he faced the Eskimo again his eyes were shining. His voice was gentle as he spoke.

"Can you travel now, my friend?" he asked softly. "We must go back to the cache—the cache of honor," he added soberly. "There is plenty there for all of us."

The native nodded, not comprehending the white man's words. "Honor?" he questioned wonderingly. "Food there. Honor? What that?"

Farrell grinned. "Something you will never need to have explained," said the white man gravely. "Come along, now. I have a light that will show us the way."

Testing for Understanding

1. At the beginning of the story the party was traveling
   a. toward the sea.   c. south across a snowy plain.
   b. toward land.   d. over smooth ice.

2. Their greatest difficulty as they traveled was
   a. deep crevasses.   c. a fierce wind.
   b. severe cold.   d. extreme hunger.

3. The purpose of this expedition was to
   a. explore the geography of the Arctic.
   b. supply food for a remote settlement.
   c. secure native handcrafts for a museum.
   d. find more information about Eskimo ways of life.

4. The morning before he found the (second) Eskimo, Farrell was not as hungry because
   a. he was growing accustomed to hunger.
   b. he had found the cache.
   c. he was nearly frozen and didn't realize how hungry he was.
   d. he had killed a dog and eaten its meat.

5. Farrell found the Eskimo
   a. in the early morning.
   b. the same day that the dogs ate the sled thongs.
   c. in the crevasse.
   d. in the evening.

6. Farrell let out a great shout as he entered the Eskimo's igloo because
   a. he wondered if anyone was there.
   b. he wanted to waken the Eskimo.
   c. he was afraid the Eskimo had stolen their food.
   d. he was overjoyed to find the igloo because he thought he would find food.

7. The party's near starvation was due to
   a. an act of God.   c. the party's inexperience.
   b. Farrell's careless planning.   d. the severe cold and wind.

8. Farrell called the cache a "cache of honor" because
   a. it was the only thing that spared them from death.
   b. it was very honorable for the Eskimo to leave the cache untouched.
   c. the story of this cache would become famous.
   d. he honored the Eskimo by sharing it with him.

9. Farrell said the Eskimo would never need to have honor explained to him because
   a. he already knew its meaning.
   b. Eskimos find it difficult to understand American words and ideas.
   c. the Eskimo could not live much longer.
   d. he didn't want to take time to explain it now.

10. The Bible verse which best expresses the theme of this story is
    a. "Cast thy bread upon the waters: for thou shalt find it after many days."
    b. "As ye would that men should do to you, do ye also to them likewise."
    c. "Ask, and it shall be given you; seek and ye shall find."
    d. "Lay up for yourselves treasures in heaven, where neither moth nor rust doth corrupt."

 *Reading for Understanding*

1. *As Farrell glanced at the tired dogs, his lips tightened.*
    Farrell's lips tightened because
    a. he did not want to think of killing the dogs.
    b. he recognized that the dogs could not go much farther without food.
    c. he was trying to force down hunger.
    d. he realized that they had lost the cache.

2. *In mocking regularity the snow-covered rock melted into the cold horizon on either side.*
    The author uses the words "mocking regularity" because
    a. every inch of the landscape imitated every other inch.
    b. the absence of the tall rock with its cache of food gave the level landscape a cruel, taunting quality.
    c. it was almost amusing how smooth the landscape was.
    d. the landscape appeared to be the same but really wasn't.

3. *"Our cache can't be far away," he asserted. "I've plotted our trip by the stars. I know I'm right."*
    From this assertion we know that Farrell was
    a. overbearing.   c. superstitious.
    b. lost.   d. scientifically informed.

4. *Farrell felt sure their journey would be short. He had traveled the Arctic many times, and he knew that no living thing could long survive in such intense cold without food.*
    Farrell felt their journey would be short because
    a. he was sure they weren't very far from the cache.
    b. he thought they were near to death.
    c. he was confident of his skill in the Arctic.
    d. they would need to stop to eat very soon.

5. *Outside, the dogs lay quiet in the snow. He was sure now that further travel with the heavy komatik was out of the question until they found food.*
    Farrell recognized that further travel was out of the question because
    a. the sled was nearly worn out.
    b. he and the men were nearly exhausted.
    c. the dogs were too exhausted to pull the sled farther.
    d. if they traveled farther they would leave the region where the cache was.

Meditating for Meaning

1. Disappointment more easily turns to frustration under certain circumstances. Name one reason why the disappointment of not finding the cache was so severe.

2. God allows disappointments to happen for a reason. Hour after hour Farrell sought an explanation for the mistake he thought he had made but could find none.
   a. What was the actual reason that they could not find the cache?
   b. How did Farrell finally find the cache?
   c. Earlier, Farrell could find no answer for the lost cache. Considering the conclusion of the story, why do you think God allowed this disappointment?
   d. How did the Eskimo's tragedy of losing his dogs bring about good in the story?
   e. Find a verse from Romans, Chapter 8 which explains why God allows difficulties and disappointments in our lives.

3. Men often feel totally confident in themselves. They do not realize their need of others until they face difficulty. How does this story emphasize our need of others?

4. When we help others, we often bring good to ourselves. But Luke 6:34 says we should not do good to others only because we hope to receive from them.
   a. Give two incidents from the story of someone doing good for another without hoping to receive good in return.
   b. Explain what good each received in return.
   c. How was the experience of Farrell similar to that of the widow in 1 Kings 17?

5. Some men practice what is called "situational ethics." They say that it is acceptable under certain circumstances to do what is normally considered wrong.
   a. How could the Eskimo have practiced situational ethics in this story?
   b. Explain why it is wrong to practice situational ethics. (See 1 Samuel 15:22, Malachi 3:6, and Revelation 22:18, 19.)
   c. From the human viewpoint, which would have benefited the Eskimo more, to take the cache or leave it? Explain.
   d. How did the Eskimo actually receive a greater benefit by following the path of honor?

Looking for Literary Technique

Sometimes, early in a story, an author drops a hint of what will happen later. This is called **foreshadowing**.

1. What is the earliest hint or foreshadowing that they will not be able to find their cache?

2. Rather than spoiling the story, how does this foreshadowing add to the story?

At the end of the story, the author inserts a bit of symbolism when he says, "Come along, now. I have a light that will show us the way."

3. What literal light did Farrell have?

Because natural light provides guidance in a natural way, authors often use it to symbolize figurative or spiritual guidance.

4. What light shone in their experience which guided the Eskimo earlier and had become the means of them returning to the cache now?

Writing for Skill

Describe a time in your life when a seeming tragedy turned into a blessing to yourself and others or when blessing came to you because you refused to succumb to temptation. Include in it some foreshadowing to lead your reader and build suspense. Also include an object to symbolize the blessing which came to you. For instance, some object of beauty in the setting at the story's end, such as a sunset, could represent the peace which came to you by choosing right.

TONE

When Jesus spoke, people heard more than His words. The tones of His voice no doubt told them a lot about what He meant to say.

Today, as we read Jesus' words, we cannot hear the sound of His voice. Yet we can often catch the tone of what He said. His strong feelings come through in words such as these:

> Woe unto you, scribes and Pharisees, hypocrites! for ye devour widows' houses, and for a pretence make long prayer: therefore ye shall receive the greater damnation. Woe unto you, scribes and Pharisees, hypocrites! for ye compass sea and land to make one proselyte, and when he is made, ye make him twofold more the child of hell than yourselves.
>
> Woe unto you, ye blind guides, which say, Whosoever shall swear by the temple, it is nothing; but whosoever shall swear by the gold of the temple, he is a debtor! Ye fools and blind: for whether is greater, the gold, or the temple that sanctifieth the gold? (Matthew 23:14-17).

The words Jesus chose have much to do with the tone of condemnation in these verses. We can easily pick out the words that carry strong feelings: *woe, hypocrites, devour, pretense, damnation, hell, blind guides,* and *fools.*

From our experiences with these words in the past, we have linked definite impressions to each of these words. Now when the word is just mentioned, we instantly sense the ideas and feelings we have gathered from all those experiences.

Woe flashes a blended sentiment of tears and hopeless despair through our senses. *Devour* floods us with recollections of ugly greed and selfishness. The word *fool* is saturated with impressions of reckless self-will.

These impressions called up by a word are its *connotation*. Connotation gives us something more than the literal meaning of the word. Two words can mean the same thing but yet give us two very different feelings and impressions.

If a story says a boy was *slim,* we sense a connotation of the boy's trim appearance. But suppose it says the boy was *skinny*? Now we will have a connotation of his bony and gangling looks. *Slim* and *skinny* mean practically the same thing, but they carry opposite connotations.

Tone is the feeling created by the use of language in a story. When a writer uses enough words with the same connotations, his story will have a strong tone such as this:

> When the hearse backed up to a wooden sidewalk before a naked weather-beaten frame house, the same composite, ill-defined group that had stood upon the station siding was huddled about the gate. The front yard was an icy swamp, and a couple of warped planks, extending from the sidewalk to the door, made a sort of rickety footbridge. The gate hung on one hinge, and was opened wide with difficulty. Steavens, the young stranger, noticed that something black was tied to the knob of the front door.

The gloomy tone of this paragraph can be traced partly to the words *hearse, naked, weather-beaten, huddled, icy swamp, warped, rickety,* and *black.* These words are charged with sorrow, distortion, and pain in our memories. As such words are piled up in a description of a story's setting, our feelings go down, and we catch the same tone in the situation that the stranger did.

Language can be used in another way to produce a definite tone. Take this statement of Jesus: "Ye blind guides, which strain at a gnat and swallow a camel."

These words carry a tone of satire or ridicule for the dishonesty of the scribes and Pharisees. Jesus pictures the finicky Pharisee straining his tea. He wouldn't dare defile himself with a stray gnat! What is the next thing on his menu? A camel. The Pharisee turns from his untainted tea to gulp down the beast—humps, hoofs, fleas, and all.

We smile because the last act of the Pharisee is unexpectedly out of line with his fussy purity. Jesus has used *irony* to create a tone of humorous criticism. A writer is using irony when he shows us a happening that is the opposite from what we would expect. Irony can easily be used to produce a tone of satire.

Notice the use of irony in the following parable to produce a tone of ridicule:

The thistle that was in Lebanon sent to the cedar that was in Lebanon, saying, Give thy daughter to my son to wife: and there passed by a wild beast that was in Lebanon, and trode down the thistle (2 Kings 14:9).

As we see it, the thistle should have kept its place under the shadow of the towering cedar tree. But no, the overbearing midget made a bold request as disgusting as it was surprising. The sudden end of the presumptuous thistle is a second irony. With all its bravado, the thistle should have

been able at least to look out for itself. The ending adds a final touch to the unmistakable tone of satire.

Like all stories, this parable reveals character. But tone helps it reveal something more. Not only do we see the cocky nature of the thistle. We also see the writer's attitude toward the strutting little upstart.

The tone of a story always shows us the writer's own feelings about the situation he is unfolding. Writers are human beings with strong ideas about the things they see happening around them. In writing stories, they hope to make you feel as they do about life. The tone you feel as you read a story will give you a clue to what the writer himself thought about the happenings in his narrative.

Listen to the tone of Elijah's words to the prophets of Baal:

Cry aloud: for he is a god; either he is talking, or he is pursuing, or he is in a journey, or peradventure he sleepeth, and must be awaked (1 Kings 18:27).

Beneath Elijah's mocking words was a serious message. On the surface he was suggesting that their god was preoccupied, or tired out, or that he might not be able to run all his affairs and hear the puny pleas of man at the same time.

In reality, Elijah meant that the god they served was no god at all, but a phony. Elijah's tone was biting in its satire and conveyed the meaning clearly. Unfortunately Baal's prophets were so intent on proving Elijah wrong that they ignored his message, took his words literally, and began to slice themselves as they cried aloud.

We return to the New Testament and find that Jesus spoke with tones of deep feeling, especially when His followers missed the truth time after time.

Once, the disciples saw Him feed 5,000 men with a handful of bread; later they saw Him feed 4,000 men in the same way. Jesus then got into a ship and began to warn them about leaven. The disciples had forgotten the bread and they thought He was scolding them. Perhaps they misjudged the tone of Jesus' warning. But there could be no mistake about the tone of His reply:

> Perceive ye not yet, neither understand? Have ye your heart yet hardened? Having eyes, see ye not? And having ears, hear ye not? And do ye not remember? (Mark 8:17b, 18).

These rapid-fire questions reveal Jesus' tone of brokenhearted disappointment in His disciples, who still couldn't trust Him after two miraculous feedings.

As we have seen, the writers of the Bible expressed strong feelings about the issues of life. As we follow the Lord, we too, will be deeply moved by situations around us. Proper feelings can strengthen our wills in doing what is right. They can also help us teach the truth with meaning and power.

Biblical writers used connotative words, irony, and other language forms to give their words definite feeling. Their tone revealed their attitude about the happenings they wrote about.

In each of the following stories, the author's attitude is revealed by the tone of the language. As you read, let the tone tell you how the authors meant for you to understand what they said.

 ## Checking for Understanding

1. What is the tone of a story?
2. Why is it important for you to properly understand the tone of a story?
3. Study the two methods commonly used to influence the tone of a story.
   a. What is connotation?
   b. How is connotation used to give tone to writing?
   c. What is irony?
   d. What tone usually goes with irony?
4. Analyze the tone in each of the following passages of the Bible.
   a. What is the tone of Judges 9:8-15?
   b. Explain the method used to produce the tone in this story.
   c. Study Job 12:2 and explain the irony of Job's statement.

The Mote and the Beam

by Robert J. Baker

Danny was lost; and he knew it. The double jaws of cards and drink had clamped him tight. But Danny didn't climb into that vice alone. He had the "good" help of a "Christian" friend. Grieve for Danny as you read. But remember, Danny is not the only needy character in this story.

Defining for Comprehension

Choose the word or phrase below which best defines each word at the left as it is used in the story.

1. gingerly	a. cautiously	b. nimbly	c. submissively
2. proffered	a. sickly	b. offered	c. thrust out
3. tawdry	a. worn out	b. salvaged junk	c. tastelessly showy
4. squeamish	a. easily-sickened	b. ready to tattle	c. critical
5. amber	a. sparkling-clear	b. yellow-orange	c. foaming
6. caressed	a. picked	b. sorted through	c. touched lovingly
7. incoherently	a. illogically	b. bitterly	c. hard to hear

8. delve	a. wander aimlessly	b. plunge recklessly	c. search painstakingly
9. segments	a. separate pieces	b. living systems	c. selfish properties
10. inferring	a. suggesting	b. supposing	c. insisting
11. timely	a. one-time	b. practical	c. well-timed

The Mote and the Beam

I knew about what I would find. Lots of talk had been circulating about Danny. People told me it was my duty to go and see him, and I guess that was about the only reason for my going. My own philosophy was to let Danny alone. When a fellow sinks into the muck and persists in wallowing in it, I get disgusted. I believe in letting sleeping dogs lie.

Danny's name was on a mailbox at the foot of the stairway. I climbed **gingerly** up the twenty or thirty dirt-laden steps to the second floor of the cheap lodgings. Room 21 was at the end of the hall on my right. I brushed off my neat pin-striped suit and tapped on the door. I could hear someone shifting around inside, and then the door jerked open.

Danny stood there. We looked at each other. His face was stubbled with several days' growth of whiskers. Bloodshot eyes peered out from hollow, black caverns. He had a nervous twitch just below his left eye. The facial muscles in that area contracted rhythmically. The lips were spread slightly apart, revealing his even but tobacco-stained teeth.

I knew what he saw as he looked at me. My face was smooth, my shirt was white, my suit freshly cleaned and pressed, and my shoes were mirrored to perfection.

It took Danny but a moment to recognize me. Then he knew, and for a second his bloodshot eyes came to life as he stuck out his hand and said, "Well, well, what brings you *slumming*[1], old pal?"

I touched the **proffered** hand lightly and gave him a businesslike smile. "I wanted to see you, Danny, to talk with you if I may."

"Sure, sure, come in; the mansion is yours," and Danny stepped back with an air of mock grace.

It wasn't a mansion, just a single room. The shades were down and a naked bulb shed a dim glow about the room. There wasn't much to see—a narrow bed over in the corner, the usual dresser with cracked mirror, a small table, and several straight-backed chairs. Danny motioned me to a chair while he flopped himself on the bed.

"Things have changed, haven't they, Bob? A lot can happen in five years, can't it?" There was a harshness in Danny's voice, a harshness that fitted in with the surroundings. Not just a harshness, but coldness, too, was in that voice.

"Danny," I said, determined to get to the point, "what can we do to get you out of this mess?" I motioned around the room. There were the cheap, **tawdry** furnishings, the over-flowing ash trays, the deck of cards spread out on the table, and a half-emptied whiskey bottle on the dresser.

"You **squeamish**, Bob? You are slumming, aren't you? It must take a lot of nerve to visit an old buddy who's fast becoming the town drunk. Which reminds me, are you thirsty?"

Danny pulled himself off the bed and went

---

1. slumming. Visiting a slum due to curiosity or for amusement.

over to the dresser. He poured the **amber** liquid into a small tumbler. He fumbled around the dresser, muttering something about another glass.

"Danny, you know that I don't drink," I said stiffly. "Can't you leave it alone for a few minutes while we talk?"

"No, I can't," was the reply. "Whiskey is my friend—one of the few that I have. Whiskey and cards, they comfort me." Danny **caressed** the cards that lay on the table with one hand, and poured the liquid down his throat with the other. He set the empty glass down carefully, too carefully for a sober man, and gathered the cards in his hands. There they came alive. They rippled through his hands, ever moving, never seeming to stop. Gracefully he flipped them out on the table. He poured himself another drink.

"Danny, I'd like to help you. You need to get back on your feet. You're going down fast."

Danny straightened up in the chair. "I hear you teach a Sunday school class now over at the church. You're coming up fast, and I'm going down fast." He got a silly smirk on his face and chuckled as if it were a joke.

Of course, it wasn't a joke. It's no joke to sit and talk with a fellow who went to church with you five years before, but now is only a few bottles away from "the snakes." Yes, then we had been in the same Sunday school class. Now, we were worlds apart. That was quite evident. I felt helpless in this atmosphere; it was out of my field. We were very different. Why did people have to send me on a mission like this? I'll admit that once Danny and I had been very close; but that was five years ago.

By now Danny had lowered the level of the liquor in the bottle several inches. He wiped his lips with the back of his hand and looked at me. Then he started talking, rambling, almost **incoherently** at times.

"I've been doing lots of thinking, Bob—lots of it. I've been remembering, trying to figure out why I'm where I am and you're where you are today. Quite a contrast, isn't it? Bob, I've got it figured out. I know where it started. I believe I know where it'll end. Yes sir, I'm getting to be quite a psychologist. I **delve** into the past to explain the present. Or is that what the histo-

rian does? I don't know—it doesn't matter. You know though, don't you? You always knew the answers. You remember when we went to school together and you showed me that game where we pitched pennies at a crack in the sidewalk? The fellow that got the closest got to keep both pennies? I wondered about that. I kept asking you about it. I was always asking you stuff then—I guess because you were older and had been in church longer than I had. When I asked you if that was gambling, you said 'No.' You said that it was just a game. When I wanted to pitch for nickels you said 'No.' You said that it was gambling when you pitched for nickels. I never could figure out where to draw the line. You always knew. You had your life cut into little **segments**. You fenced in those little segments. You knew how big each piece was and how far it extended. You knew just how far you could go. I never did. I never knew where to draw the line. I thought if you could pitch for pennies, you could pitch for nickels. I never could figure that out."

I broke in coldly. "Danny, are you **inferring** that because of that silly little game, I'm to blame for your wretched condition? You don't know what you are saying. I'm afraid that you're drunk."

Danny had slumped over, his face on the table, but he pulled himself erect. His eyes could still flash. His flushed face got even redder. He pounded the table until the whiskey glass jumped over the edge and shattered on the floor. He fairly screamed at me. "You're pretty good, aren't you? You're pretty good! Who pushed you up here? You didn't come by yourself. Your kind never does. You're too good to come by yourself. You didn't come to help. You came to tell me what a bum I am. You don't have to tell me that, I know." With a violent motion he swept the table clear, cards and all. The cards fluttered about wildly, several landing at my feet. They lay there by chance, but I didn't like it anyway. I didn't like the way in which he had recalled the past. That was over with now, and best forgotten.

I didn't seem to be able to help Danny, so I left. When I closed the door he was standing there, looking stupidly at the cards which had lain at my feet.

I told my pastor all about it. He looked sad. I presumed he felt sorry for me, because of the unkind things Danny had said, so I told him not to worry about it, for I really didn't mind. That seemed to be the Christian thing to say. He just looked at me and shook his head. He said it wasn't that, but something else which made him sad. I suppose pastors have a lot to worry about—there are probably other people just as bad as Danny.

Danny's reference to that childish game which I taught him was most unfortunate. Even though I knew that it was only the ramblings of a drunk, I still keep thinking about it. He had no right to say it. But Danny was drunk and I shouldn't take it seriously. It's absurd to attach any importance to either Danny or the game. The game was just for fun, and Danny had no right to continue with that sort of thing.

Well, I'm not going to worry about it. I can't afford to because I have to get busy and study for next Sunday night. You see, I'm a speaker on the program for that evening. My subject is, "Am I My Brother's Keeper?" It's a **timely** subject. I'm trying to find some good illustrations to spice it, because I want to make it really practical.

Testing for Understanding

1. When Danny first met his old friend Bob, Danny believed that he
   a. had come out of genuine concern.
   b. would expect something out of him.
   c. was not sincere in coming to visit.
   d. lived as badly as Danny did.

2. Danny offered his old friend a drink
   a. as a sick gesture in friendship.
   b. because he couldn't control his own craving.
   c. as a bold sneer.
   d. to remind him of their past.

3. Bob had played the penny game with Danny when they were
   a. too young to know better.
   b. in their first years of elementary school.
   c. young teenagers.
   d. agreed on what was right and wrong.

4. Danny would not have been where he was if he had
   a. allowed no "segments" in his earlier life.
   b. drawn the line at the right places between the "segments" which his friend helped him to form.
   c. kept each of the "segments" in his life under control.
   d. known about how far each part of life extended.

5. Danny could not figure out where to draw the line in the penny game because he had
   a. an insensitive conscience.
   b. a sensitive conscience but a bad influence.
   c. less ability to see through things.
   d. an oversensitive conscience regarding details.

6. Standing between Danny and the change he needed was
   a. pride.
   b. pleasure in his present life.
   c. jealousy toward his friend.
   d. unwillingness to accept responsibility for his own mistakes.

7. Danny's attitude toward his situation was
   a. bitter and cynical.　　　b. happy-go-lucky.　　　c. desperate.　　　d. remorseful.

8. Bob's part in Danny's life was symbolized by the
   a. cracked mirror.　　　　　　　　　　c. naked light bulb.
   b. stairs.　　　　　　　　　　　　　　d. cards.

9. The pastor looked sad when he heard how the visit went because he
   a. had expected it to help Danny.
   b. felt that the young man had done his best during the visit.
   c. realized some truth in Danny's words.
   d. was reminded of the many wretched people who needed his help.

10. The Scripture that best expresses the theme of this story is
    a. "He that hateth his brother is in darkness and walketh in darkness."
    b. "It is good neither to eat flesh, nor to drink wine, nor any thing whereby thy brother stumbleth, or is offended, or is made weak."
    c. "If ye forgive not men their trespasses, neither will your Father forgive your trespasses."
    d. "The fear of man bringeth a snare."

Reading for Understanding

1. *My own philosophy was to let Danny alone. When a fellow sinks into the muck and persists in wallowing in it, I get disgusted. I believe in letting sleeping dogs lie.*
   Bob thought if he visited Danny, his drunkard friend might
   a. ignore him.　　　　　　　　　　　　c. make him even more disgusted.
   b. get angry.　　　　　　　　　　　　　d. take him seriously.

2. *I climbed gingerly up the twenty or thirty dirt-laden steps to the second floor of the cheap lodgings. Room 21 was at the end of the hall on my right. I brushed off my neat pin-striped suit, and tapped on the door.*
   The narrator wanted to do all of these except
   a. symbolize a perfect life to repel Danny.
   b. make a striking contrast between himself and Danny.
   c. keep his clothes spotless.
   d. place a distinction between himself and Danny.

3. *"Sure, sure, come in; the mansion is yours," and Danny stepped back with an air of mock grace.*
   Danny's words reveal that he
   a. didn't mind living in disgraceful quarters.
   b. wanted the writer to share his misery for awhile.
   c. was determined to make his visitor feel welcome.
   d. felt the hurt already of his visitor's attitude toward his situation.

4. *"You squeamish, Bob? You are slumming, aren't you?"*
    When Danny said this, he gave the most emphasis to the word

    a. *you.*   b. *squeamish.*   c. *are.*   d. *slumming.*

5. *He set the empty glass down carefully, too carefully for a sober man, and gathered the cards in his hands.*
    Danny likely set the glass down the way he did because he

    a. was not used to being sober.
    b. became ridiculously particular when he drank.
    c. could control himself only with conscious effort.
    d. could not tell it was empty.

Meditating for Meaning

1. Danny may have been drunk, but he quickly sensed the attitude of his visitor.
    a. What attitude did the visitor have when he went to see Danny?
    b. What contrast was evident between the visitor and Danny when they first met?
    c. What attitude did the visitor have in relation to this contrast?
    d. How did Danny feel when he first recognized his visitor?
    e. Danny switched to a tone of bitter irony in his second response. There was a difference between what he said and what he actually meant. What responses of his old friend caused him to make this switch?

2. This tone of irony carries through much of the story and helps give it much of its meaning.
    a. What ironic offer did Danny make to his visitor and why?
    b. What was Danny trying to tell his old friend when he said, "Whiskey is my friend—one of the few that I have left"?
    c. What ironic phrase of Danny's reply (p. 69) testified to his Christian background? Explain.

3. Though he did not realize it, the visitor's next response, "Danny, I'd like to help you," was ironic. He wasn't really interested in helping Danny. He told us in the beginning that he was only there because of duty.
    a. How does this tone make you as a reader feel toward the events and characters of the story?
    b. What is ironic about the visitor's reaction to Danny's "joke"?
    c. Where does this tone of irony reach its bitterest impact?

4. The visitor posed before Danny as a flawless Christian. The story proves him otherwise.
    a. What does Jesus call such persons who profess goodness they do not have?
    b. Considering the definition of irony, why is it such an effective tone to portray such a person?

5. Danny felt that he was where he was because of his friend's influence.
    a. If both boys played the penny game, why do you think Danny fell to this state while his friend remained in the church?
    b. Was Danny's accusation of his friend as the cause of his present condition valid? Explain.
    c. How might Danny's old friend have helped him now?

6. The title "The Mote and the Beam," refers to Matthew 7:3-5. Who does the author feel had the mote and who had the beam? Explain. Make sure you understand Jesus' illustration.

Looking for Literary Technique

Robert Baker writes with a fresh, lively style. Much of this effect depends upon his use of crisp, connotative words that call up clear pictures to your mind.

1. Analyze the method by which the author showed the contrast between Danny and his visitor in the first paragraphs of this story.
    a. What connotative words and phrases did he use to describe the visitor?
    b. What tone do you feel in this description?
    c. What connotative words and phrases did he use to describe Danny?
    d. What tone do you feel in this description?
    e. What connotative words and phrases did he use to describe the apartment?
    f. What tone do you feel in this description?
2. The author chose his words carefully throughout the story.
    a. For each of the following italicized nouns and verbs, tell what connotation the author achieved by them.

    Danny *caressed* the cards. . .   He got a silly *smirk* on his face . . .

    They *rippled* through his hands,   The cards *fluttered* about wildly,

    Gracefully he *flipped* them out on the table,

    b. Now for each example give a common noun or verb which a boring writer might have used.

Writing for Skill

1. Think of a time when you were sure you were right but discovered later that you were wrong. Use vivid, connotative words to show that you felt you were right, but prove by the use of an ironic tone that you were actually wrong. Try, as Baker did, to show the reader that you were wrong without actually saying so.
2. Each of the following scenes or situations suggest a definite tone. Choose one and state the tone it would have. Then write a 200-300 word description with connotative words and phrases that convey the appropriate tone to the reader.

library reading room	airport	family picnic
rush-hour traffic	cow barn	forage harvester cutting corn
school playground	funeral parlor	cabinet shop
thunderstorm	doctor's office	song service

Where Love Is, There Is God Also

by Leo Tolstoy

Sooner or later most of us will face the pain of losing people we love. Can the empty place in our lives ever be filled? Must our experience be narrowed by such a deep loss? If a man's wife and all his children die, how could his life ever take on its complete dimensions again? Or does such a loss enlarge one's life in some ironic way? Martin found some surprising answers to all these questions.

Defining for Comprehension

Choose the word or phrase below which best defines each word at the left as it is used in the story.

1. cobbler	a. poor peasant	b. shoemaker	c. widower
2. loath	a. unwilling	b. powerless	c. too absorbed
3. dotard	a. feeble-minded old person	b. one persuaded by feelings	c. strong-willed thinker
4. awl	a. cobbler's knife	b. stitching needle	c. leather punch
5. worsted	a. badly worn	b. made from yarn	c. home-woven
6. pawned	a. exchanged for money	b. lost	c. worn to shreds

| 7. **entreating** | a. rebuking | b. teaching | c. begging |
| 8. **morocco** | a. African cloth | b. prairie weed | c. goatskin leather |

Where Love Is, There Is God Also

In a certain town there lived a **cobbler,** Martin Avdeich. He had a tiny room in a basement, the one window of which looked out into the street. Through it one could see only the feet of those who passed by, but Martin recognized the people by their boots. He had lived long in the place and had many acquaintances. There was hardly a pair of boots in the neighborhood that had not been once or twice through his hands, so he often saw his own handiwork through the window. Some he had resoled, some patched, some stitched up, and to some he had even put fresh uppers. He had plenty to do, for he worked well, used good material, did not charge too much, and could be relied on; so he was well known and never short of work.

Martin had always been a good man, but in his old age he began to think more about his soul and to draw nearer to God. While he still worked for a master, before he set upon his own account, his wife had died, leaving him with a three-year-old son. None of his elder children had lived; they had all died in infancy. At first Martin thought of sending his little son to his sister's in the country, but then he felt sorry to part with the boy, thinking: *It would be hard for my little Kapiton to have to grow up in a strange family; I will keep him with me.*

Martin left his master and went into lodgings with his little son. But no sooner had the boy reached an age when he could help his father and be a support as well as a joy to him, than he fell ill and, after being laid up for a week with a burning fever, died. Martin buried his son, and gave way to despair so great and overwhelming that he murmured against God. In his sorrow he prayed again and again that he too might die, reproaching God for having taken the son he loved, his only son, while he, old as he was, remained alive. After that Martin left off going to church.

One day an old man from Martin's native village came in to see him. Martin opened his heart to him and told him of his sorrow.

"I no longer even wish to live," he said. "All I ask of God is that I soon may die. I am now quite without hope in the world."

The old man replied, "You have no right to say such things, Martin. We cannot judge God's ways. Not our reasoning, but God's will, decides. If God willed that your son should die and you should live, it must be best so. As to your despair—that comes because you wish to live for your own happiness."

"What else should one live for?" asked Martin.

"For God, Martin," said the old man. "He gives you life, and you must live for Him."

Martin was silent awhile, and then asked, "But how is one to live for God?"

The old man answered, "How one may live for God has been shown us by Christ. Can you read? Then buy the Gospels and read them; there you will see how God would have you live. You have it all there."

These words sank deep into Martin's heart, and that same day he went and bought himself a Testament in large print, and began to read.

At first he meant only to read on holidays, but having once begun he found it made his heart so light that he read every day. Sometimes he was so absorbed in his reading that the oil in his lamp burnt out before he could tear himself away from the book. As he continued to read every night, his heart grew lighter and lighter. Before, when he went to bed, he used to lie with a heavy heart, moaning as he thought of his little Kapiton, but now he only repeated again and again; "Glory to Thee, glory to Thee, O Lord! Thy will be done!"

From that time Martin's whole life changed. It became peaceful and joyful. He sat down to his work in the morning, and when he had finished his day's work he took the lamp down from the wall, stood it on the table, fetched his book from the shelf, opened it, and sat down to read. The more he read the better he understood and the clearer and happier he felt in his mind.

It happened once that Martin sat up late, absorbed in his book. He was reading Luke's Gospel; and in the sixth chapter he came upon the verses:

"Unto him that smiteth thee on the one cheek offer also the other; and him that taketh away thy cloak, forbid not to take thy coat also. Give to every man that asketh of thee; and of him that taketh away thy goods ask them not again. And as ye would that men should do to you, do ye also to them likewise."

He also read the verses where our Lord says:

"And why call ye me, Lord, Lord, and do not the things which I say? Whosoever cometh to me, and heareth my sayings, and doeth them, I will show you to whom he is like: He is like a man which built an house and digged deep, and laid the foundation on a rock: and when the flood arose, the stream beat vehemently upon that house, and could not shake it: for it was founded upon a rock. But he that heareth and doeth not, is like a man that without a foundation built a house upon the earth, against which the stream did beat vehemently

and immediately it fell; and the ruin of that house was great."

When Martin read these words his soul was glad within him. He took off his spectacles and laid them on the book, and leaning his elbows on the table pondered over what he had read. He tried his own life by the standard of those words, asking himself:

Is my house built on the rock, or on sand? If it stands on the rock, it is well. It seems easy enough while one sits here alone, and one thinks one has done all that God commands; but as soon as I cease to be on my guard, I sin again. Still I will persevere. Help me, O Lord.

He thought all this, and was about to go to bed, but was **loath** to leave his book. So he went on reading the seventh chapter and came to the part where a rich Pharisee invited the Lord to his house; and he read how the woman who was a sinner anointed His feet and washed them with her tears, and how the Lord justified her. Coming to the forty-fourth verse, he read:

"And turning to the woman, he said unto Simon, Seest thou this woman? I entered into thine house, thou gavest me no water for my feet: but she hath wetted my feet with her tears, and wiped them with her hair. Thou gavest me no kiss; but she, since the time I came in, hath not ceased to kiss my feet. My head with oil thou didst not anoint; but she hath anointed my feet with ointment."

Martin took off his spectacles once more, laid them on his book, and pondered.

He must have been like me, that Pharisee. He too thought only of himself—how to get a cup of tea, how to keep warm and comfortable; never a thought of his guest. He took care of himself, but for his guest he cared nothing at all. Yet who was the guest? The Lord Himself! If He had come to me, would I have behaved like that?

Then Martin laid his head upon both his arms and, before he was aware of it, he fell asleep.

"Martin!" he suddenly heard a voice, as if someone had breathed the word above his ear.

He started from his sleep. "Who's there?" he asked.

He turned round and looked at the door. No one was there. He called again. Then he heard quite distinctly: "Martin, Martin! Look out into the street tomorrow, for I shall come."

Martin roused himself, rose from his chair and rubbed his eyes, but did not know whether he had heard these words in a dream or awake. He put out the lamp and lay down to sleep.

Next morning he rose before daylight, and after saying his prayers he lit the fire and prepared his cabbage soup and buckwheat porridge. Then he lit the samovar, put on his apron, and sat down by the window to his work. As he sat working Martin thought over what had happened the night before. At times it seemed to him like a dream, and at times he thought that he had really heard the voice.

So he sat by the window, looking out into the street more than he worked, and whenever anyone passed in unfamiliar boots he would stoop and look up, so as to see not the feet only but the face of the passerby as well. A house porter passed in new felt boots, then a water carrier. Presently an old soldier came near the window, spade in hand. Martin knew him by his boots, which were shabby old felt ones, galoshes with leather. The old man was called Stepanich; a neighboring tradesman kept him in his house for charity, and his duty was to help the house porter. He began to clear away the snow before Martin's window. Martin glanced at him, and then went on with his work.

I must be growing crazy with age, said Martin, laughing at his fancy. *Stepanich comes to clear away the snow, and I must needs imagine it's Christ coming to visit me. Old **dotard** that I am!*

Yet after he had made a dozen stitches he felt drawn to look out of the window again. He saw that Stepanich had leaned his spade against the wall and was either resting himself or trying to get warm. The man was old and broken down, and had evidently not enough strength to clear away the snow.

What if I called him in and gave him some tea? thought Martin. *The samovar is just on the boil.*

He stuck his **awl** in its place, and rose; and putting the samovar on the table, made tea. Then he tapped the window with his fingers. Stepanich turned and came to the window. Martin beckoned to him to come in and went

himself to open the door.

"Come in," he said, "and warm yourself a bit. I'm sure you must be cold."

"May God bless you!" Stepanich answered. "My bones do ache to be sure." He came in, first shaking off the snow, and lest he should leave marks on the floor he began wiping his feet, but as he did so he tottered and nearly fell.

"Don't trouble to wipe your feet," said Martin; "I'll wipe up the floor—it's all in the day's work. Come, friend, sit down and have some tea."

Filling two tumblers, he passed one to his visitor, and pouring his own out into the saucer, began to blow on it.

Stepanich emptied his glass, and turning it upside down, put the remains of his piece of sugar on the top. He began to express his thanks, but it was plain that he would be glad of some more.

"Have another glass," said Martin, refilling the visitor's tumbler and his own. But while he drank his tea Martin kept looking out into the street.

"Are you expecting anyone?" asked the visitor.

"Am I expecting anyone? Well now, I'm ashamed to tell you," said Martin. "It isn't that I really expect anyone; but I heard something last night which I can't get out of my mind." And Martin began to tell Stepanich what he had read in the Gospels, and how he had dreamt that Christ would visit him that day.

Stepanich shook his head in silence, finished his tumbler and laid it on its side; but Martin stood it up again and refilled it for him.

"Here, drink another glass," he said. "And I was thinking, too, how our Lord walked on earth and despised no one, but went mostly among common folk. He went with plain people, and chose His disciples from among the likes of us, sinners that we are. 'He who raises himself,' He said, 'shall be humbled; and he who humbles himself shall be raised. He who would be first,' He said, 'let him be the servant of all': because He said, 'blessed are the poor, the humble, the meek, and the merciful.'"

Stepanich forgot his tea. He was an old man, easily moved to tears, and as he sat and listened the tears ran down his cheeks.

"Come, drink some more," said Martin. But Stepanich thanked him, moved away his tumbler, and rose.

"Thank you, Martin Avdeich," he said, "you have given me food and comfort for both soul and body."

"You're very welcome. Come again another time. I am glad to have a guest," said Martin.

Stepanich went away; and Martin poured out the last of the tea and drank it up. Then he put away the tea things and sat down to his work, stitching the back seam of a boot. And as he stitched he kept looking out of the window, wondering what his dream had meant and thinking about Christ and His doings. And his head was full of Christ's sayings.

Two soldiers went by: one in government boots, the other in boots of his own; then the master of a neighboring house, in shining galoshes; then a baker carrying a basket. All these passed on. Then a woman came up in **worsted** stockings and peasant-made shoes. Martin glanced up at her through the window and saw that she was a stranger, poorly dressed, with a baby in her arms. She stopped by the wall with her back to the wind, trying to wrap the baby up though she had hardly anything to wrap it in. Through the window Martin heard the baby crying, and the woman trying to soothe it but unable to do so. Martin rose, and going out of the door and up the steps, he called to her.

"My dear, I say, my dear!"

The woman heard and turned round.

"Why do you stand out there with the baby in the cold? Come inside. You can wrap him up better in a warm place. Come this way!"

The woman was surprised to see an old man in an apron, with spectacles on his nose, calling to her, but she followed him in.

They went down the steps and entered the little room.

"There, sit down, my dear, near the stove. Warm yourself and the baby."

Martin saw that the woman was thin and starved-looking. He brought out a basin and some bread. Then he opened the oven door and poured some cabbage soup into the basin. He spread a cloth on the table and served the soup and bread.

"Sit down and eat, my dear, and I'll mind the baby. I've had children of my own; I know how to manage them."

The woman sat down at the table and began to eat, while Martin put the baby on the bed and sat down by it. He chucked and chucked, but having no teeth he could not do it well and the baby continued to cry. Then Martin tried poking at him with his finger; he drove his finger straight at the baby's mouth, then quickly drew it back, and did this again and again. He did not let the baby take his finger in its mouth, because it was all black with cobbler's wax. But the baby first grew quiet watching the finger, and then began to laugh. Martin felt quite pleased.

The woman sat eating and talking, and told him who she was, and where she had been.

"I'm a soldier's wife," said she. "They sent my husband somewhere, far away, eight months ago, and I have heard nothing of him since. I had a place as cook till my baby was born, but then they would not keep me with the child. For three months now I have been struggling, unable to find a place, and I've had to sell all I had for food. Now I have just been to see a tradesman's wife (a woman from our village is in service with her), and she has promised to take me. I thought it was all settled at last, but she tells me not to come till next week. It is far to her place, and I am fagged out, and baby is quite starved, poor mite. Fortunately our landlady has pity on us, and lets us lodge free, else I don't know what we should do."

Martin sighed. "Haven't you any warmer clothing?" he asked.

"How could I get warm clothing?" said she, "Why, I **pawned** my last shawl yesterday."

Then the woman came and took the child, and Martin got up. He went to look among some things that were hanging on the wall, and brought back an old cloak.

"Here," he said, "though it's a worn-out old thing, it will do to wrap him up in."

The woman looked at the cloak, then at the old man, and taking it, burst into tears. Martin turned away, and groping under the bed brought out a small trunk. He fumbled about in it, and again sat down opposite the woman. And the woman said:

"The Lord bless you, friend. Surely Christ must have sent me to your window, else the child would have frozen. It was mild when I started, but now see how cold it has turned. Surely it must have been Christ who made you look out of your window and take pity on me, poor wretch!"

Martin smiled and said, "It is quite true; it was He made me do it. It was no mere chance made me look out."

And he told the woman his dream, and how he had heard the Lord's voice promising to visit him that day.

"Who knows? All things are possible," said the woman. And she got up and threw the cloak over her shoulders, wrapping it around herself and round the baby. Then she bowed, and thanked Martin once more.

"Take this for Christ's sake," said Martin, and gave her a coin to get her shawl out of pawn. The woman thanked him again and then Martin saw her out.

After the woman had gone, Martin ate some cabbage soup, cleared the things away, and sat down to work again. He sat and worked, but did not forget the window. Every time a shadow fell on it he looked up at once to see who was passing. People he knew and strangers passed by, but no one remarkable.

After a while Martin saw an apple-woman stop just in front of his window. She had a large basket, but there did not seem to be many apples left in it; she had evidently sold most of her stock. On her back she had a sack full of wood chips, which she was taking home. The sack evidently hurt her and she wanted to shift it from one shoulder to the other, so she put it down on the footpath and, placing her basket on a post, began to shake down the chips in the sack. While she was doing this a boy in a tattered cap ran up, snatched an apple out of the basket and tried to slip away; but the old woman noticed it and, turning, caught the boy by his sleeve. He began to struggle, trying to free himself, but the old woman held on with both hands, knocked his cap off his head, and

seized hold of his hair. The boy screamed and the old woman scolded.

Martin dropped his awl, not waiting to stick it in its place, and rushed out of the door. Stumbling up the steps, and dropping his spectacles in his hurry, he ran out into the street. The old woman was pulling the boy's hair and threatening to take him to the police. The lad was struggling and protesting, saying, "I did not take it. What are you beating me for? Let me go!"

Martin separated them. He took the boy by the hand and said, "Let him go, Granny. Forgive him."

"I'll pay him out, so that he won't forget it for a year! I'll take the rascal to the police!"

Martin began **entreating** the old woman.

"Let him go, Granny. Let him go. Forgive him for Christ's sake."

The old woman let go, and the boy wished to run away, but Martin stopped him.

"Ask the Granny's forgiveness!" said he. "And don't do it another time. I saw you take the apple."

The boy began to cry and to beg pardon.

"That's right. And now here's an apple for you." Martin took an apple from the basket and gave it to the boy, saying, "I will pay you, Granny."

"You will spoil them that way, the young rascals," said the old woman. "He ought to be whipped so that he should remember it for a week."

"Oh, Granny, Granny," said Martin, "if he should be whipped for stealing an apple, what should be done to us for our sins?"

The old woman was silent.

And Martin told her the parable of the lord who forgave his servant a large debt, and how the servant went out and seized his debtor by the throat. The old woman listened to it all, and the boy, too, stood by and listened.

"God bids us forgive," said Martin, "or else we shall not be forgiven. Forgive every one, and a thoughtless youngster most of all."

The old woman wagged her head and sighed.

"It's true enough," said she, "but they are getting terribly spoilt."

"Then we old ones must show them better ways," Martin replied.

"That's just what I say," said the old woman. "I have had seven of them myself, and only one daughter is left." And the old woman began to tell how and where she was living with her daughter, and how many grandchildren she had. "There now," she said, "I have but little strength left, yet I work hard for the sake of my grandchildren; and nice children they are, too. No one comes out to meet me but the children. Little Annie, now, won't leave me for anyone. It's 'grandmother, dear grandmother, darling grandmother.'" And the old woman completely softened at the thought.

"Of course it was only his childishness," said she, referring to the boy.

As the old woman was about to hoist the sack on her back, the lad sprang forward to her, saying, "Let me carry it for you, Granny. I'm going that way."

The old woman nodded her head and put the sack on the boy's back, and they went down the street together, the old woman quite forgetting to ask Martin to pay for the apple. Martin stood and watched them as they went along talking to each other.

When they were out of sight Martin went back to the house. Having found his spectacles unbroken on the steps, he picked up his awl and sat down again to work. He worked a little, but could soon not see to pass the bristle through the holes in the leather; and presently he noticed the lamplighter passing on his way to light the street lamps.

Seems it's time to light up, thought he. So he trimmed his lamp, hung it up, and sat down again to work. He finished off one boot and, turning it about, examined it. It was all right. Then he gathered his tools together, swept up the cuttings, put away the bristles, the thread and the awls, and, taking down the lamp, placed it on the table. Then he took the Gospels from the shelf. He meant to open them at the place he had marked the day before with a bit of **morocco** but the book opened at another place. As Martin opened it, his yesterday's dream came back to his mind. No sooner had he thought of it than he seemed to hear footsteps, as though someone were moving behind him. Martin turned round, and it seemed to him as if people were standing in the dark corner, but he could not make out who they were. And a voice whispered in his ear; "Martin, Martin, don't you know me?"

"Who is it?" muttered Martin.

"It is I," said the voice. And out of the dark corner stepped Stepanich, who smiled, and vanishing like a cloud was seen no more.

"It is I," said a voice again. And out of the darkness stepped the woman with the baby in her arms; the woman smiled and the baby laughed, and they too vanished.

"It is I," said the voice once more. And the old woman and the boy with the apple stepped out and both smiled. Then they too vanished.

And Martin's soul grew glad. He put on his spectacles and began reading the Gospel just where it had opened, and at the top of the page he read:

"I was an hungered, and ye gave me meat: I was thirsty, and ye gave me drink: I was a stranger, and ye took me in."

And at the bottom of the page he read:

"Inasmuch as ye have done it unto one of the least of these my brethren, ye have done it unto me" (Matthew 25).

And Martin understood that his dream had come true; and that the Saviour had really come to him that day, and he had welcomed Him.

Testing for Understanding

1. Martin set up his own business of shoemaking
   a. to earn enough for his family and himself.
   b. so he could be alone with his grief.
   c. for privacy to raise his son.
   d. when he finished his responsibilities as an apprentice.

2. An old man told Martin that all despair comes from
   a. the pursuit of money.   c. selfishness.
   b. reasoning.   d. misunderstanding God's will.

3. The story tells us that Martin's meditation on the New Testament added all these to his life except
   a. happiness.   b. pride.   c. understanding.   d. a standard.

4. Martin's vision about Christ coming to visit him was a result of his thinking about
   a. Luke 6.
   b. the woman who touched the hem of Jesus' garment.
   c. the house built on the rock.
   d. Simon, the Pharisee.

5. Martin first imagined that Christ was present when he
   a. saw Stepanich.
   b. fed the poorly-dressed woman and clothed her baby.
   c. helped Granny and the young thief.
   d. had finished helping everyone.

6. Martin's most important ministry to Stepanich was
   a. tea for his empty stomach.   c. a place to rest his bones.
   b. warmth.   d. spiritual encouragement.

7. When Martin ministered to the woman with the child, the greatest need was
   a. food.   c. a job.
   b. clothing for the baby.   d. spiritual encouragement.

8. Martin helped Granny most by
   a. insisting that she forgive.
   b. showing her the corrective power of love.
   c. getting the thief to make his wrong right.
   d. inspiring the boy to carry her heavy load for her.

9. The shoemaker lamented for all of these reasons except that God had
   a. cut off all future generations of his family.
   b. made him live a meaningless life.
   c. not put an end to his misery.
   d. left him to live a life of poverty.

10. The Scripture which best restates the title of this story is
    a. "Love is the fulfilling of the law."
    b. "This is love that we walk after his commandments."
    c. "He that dwelleth in love dwelleth in God."
    d. "Greater love hath no man than this, that a man lay down his life for his friends."

Reading for Understanding

1. *"We cannot judge God's ways. Not our reasoning, but God's will, decides. If God willed that your son should die, and you should live, it must be best so."*

   The old man believed that God willed the death of Martin's son
   a. because it would promote the best interests of all involved.
   b. since that was best for the son, even if Martin had to suffer.
   c. to benefit Martin at the expense of some others.
   d. primarily to please Himself, even if Martin's life had to be marred.

2. *It seems easy enough while one sits here alone, and one thinks one has done all that God commands; but as soon as I cease to be on my guard, I sin again. Still I will persevere. Help me, O Lord!*

   According to these words of Martin, the Christian struggles with a tendency to
   a. justify his wrongdoing.   c. judge himself by an easy standard.
   b. drop his guard.   d. set his ideals too high.

3. *"Don't trouble to wipe your feet," said Martin; "I'll wipe up the floor—it's all in a day's work."*

   Martin meant that cleaning up the floor would
   a. not be a difficult job.   c. be nothing more than he usually did.
   b. make his day of work full.   d. give him a special satisfaction.

4. *"Now I have just been to see a tradesman's wife, and she has promised to take me. I thought it was all settled at last, but she tells me not to come till next week. It is far to her place, and I am fagged out, and the baby is quite starved, poor mite."*

   The woman with the baby was
   a. on her way to begin her new job.   c. coming home from work.
   b. on her way to inquire about a new job. d. returning from a job interview.

5. *"Oh, Granny, Granny," said Martin, "if he should be whipped for stealing an apple, what should be done to us for our sins?"*

   Martin believed his and the old woman's sins were
   a. as bad as the boy's misbehavior.
   b. so bad that the boy was justified for his wrong.
   c. worse than the boy's theft.
   d. too bad for correction.

Meditating for Meaning

1. Martin's past had prepared him for his experiences in this story.
   a. What were several important happenings in Martin's life to which he had responded wrongly?
   b. Why did Martin murmur against God and wish to die?

c. Study James 1:2-4. What irony would Martin have seen in the truth of these verses about his experiences, especially the truth in verse 4b?

d. How did this truth, nevertheless, come to pass in Martin's life?

e. Why was Martin able to sense the special needs of people in misfortune?

2. Martin took a delight in reading the Bible that many Christians must admit they do not have. Search for his secret.

a. What would most people think of the commands Martin read in Luke 6?

b. Yet what does Jesus say in the first sentence of the next verses Martin read?

c. What does Jesus go on to say will happen to His true followers in the realistic blasts of life?

d. How did Martin react to Jesus' teachings about building on the rock, and why could he react in this way?

e. What attitude did Martin have toward Simon the Pharisee?

f. How would such an attitude have led to a delight in Bible reading?

3. Many boots passed Martin's window, but he did not look up to see faces of most of their wearers.

a. What boots caught his special attention?

b. According to Proverbs 19:17, why was Martin wise for paying special attention to such boots?

4. Study Martin's ministry to Stepanich.

a. In ministering to Stepanich, what Biblical principle concerning whom we should be willing to serve did Martin obey?

b. How did Martin give Stepanich food and comfort for his soul?

5. Study Martin's ministry to the woman with the child.

a. What Biblical principle did Martin obey in ministering to them? It is not directly stated. (See Luke 3:8, 11 and 1 John 3:17.)

b. Study the woman's last words to Martin. What were they, and why do you think she said them?

6. Study Martin's ministry to Granny and the young thief.

a. What Biblical principle did Martin teach Granny?

b. What Biblical principle did Martin teach the boy?

c. Martin objected to Granny's motive for insisting the boy be whipped. What was her motive?

d. Why did Martin object to this motive?

e. To Martin, the purpose of discipline should be _____ , not _____ .

f. How do we know that Martin's method of discipline was realistic and did not spoil the boy as Granny predicted?

7. What meaning does this story give to its title?

Looking for Literary Technique

Before a writer begins his story, he must decide who is going to tell it. If he decides to narrate it himself, it will read like the following paragraphs from the story "The Mote and the Beam."

> It took Danny but a moment to recognize me. Then he knew, and for a second his bloodshot eyes came to life as he stuck out his hand and said, "Well, well, what brings you slumming, old pal?"
>
> I touched the proffered hand lightly and gave him a businesslike smile. "I wanted to see you, Danny, to talk with you if I may."

"Sure, sure, come in; the mansion is yours," and Danny stepped back with an air of mock grace.

In this **first-person** point of view, we see everything through the eyes of the main character, in this case, Bob. The clue to the first-person point of view is the pronoun *I*. By using this *I* it seems as though the author is relating a personal experience; this may not always be true.

With this point of view, the writer could tell only what Bob was thinking and feeling. At no point in the story could the writer get inside Danny's mind and tell you what was going on there. He could suggest what Danny was thinking by telling you that "Danny stepped back with an air of mock grace" and said, "Sure, sure, come in; the mansion is yours." But he could not describe Danny's inner life directly like he did his own when he said earlier in the story'

When a fellow sinks into the muck and persists in wallowing in it, I get disgusted. I believe in letting sleeping dogs lie."

When a writer gives direct explanations of a character's mind and heart, he is presenting that character in a *subjective manner*. On the other hand, he is giving *objective* treatment to a character when he shows you only the outside facts and lets you make your own interpretation of what is going on inside the character.

With the first-person point of view, only the first person narrator can be treated subjectively. All the other characters must be given objective treatment.

If a writer wants to be subjective with all his characters, he must use the **all-knowing** point of view such as you see in "The Horse." There the storyteller is not a character taking part in the story action at all. He has perched himself somewhere outside the action and skips from character to character explaining directly what they are thinking and feeling.

We first see Martha talking to Mr. Edwards about entrance into the Sageville School. Throughout the story we see deeper into her life through her thoughts as she assesses the "different" students of Sageville, as her heart sings over the literary society's invitation, and finally as the brutality of her classmates' jeers sears her sensitive soul.

At other places in the story we see behind the scenes things Martha does not know. We know the cruel plot of the students because the all-knowing point of view allows us to listen to their thoughts and conversations.

This subjective, all-knowing point of view can be difficult to handle. The writer must have a deep understanding of people in order to create believable characters that think and feel like real human beings do.

Many writers find it easier and more effective to be objective in using the all-knowing point of view. Here the storyteller still remains outside the story, but he also stays outside the minds of the story characters as well.

Observe the contrast in a story where the inventor of a primitive airplane is to be put to death. First, see a subjective treatment of the flier's response:

The flier fell to his knees, his being flooded with frantic grief, and his mind grasping wildly for splinters of thought for his defense.
"Surely I have done nothing worse than the Emperor," he said over and over to himself.

Now compare this response from an objective view:

"But, oh, Emperor!" pleaded the flier, on his knees, the tears pouring down his face. "I have done a similar thing . . ."

This objective version does not explain how the flier felt and thought. It shows you only what he did. It lets you relate personal experiences and feelings to the character's actions rather than specifying the mental details for you. For this reason the objective all-knowing point of view can have a greater impact on the reader than the subjective approach. The all-knowing, objective point of view does not focus on a particular character. Instead, the story is told by treating all the characters with approximately equal emphasis.

One other way to tell a story appears in the story you have just read. This **third-person** point of view shows the story through the eyes of a person in the story much the same as the first-person point of view. You see all the events in this story through Martin's eyes. But, because Martin does not pose as the writer of his own story, the pronouns *he* and *him* replaced the distinctive *I* and *me* of the first-person.

The third-person point of view can be subjective. But as in the first-person story, it can only explain the inner experience of the main character. In "Where Love Is, There Is God Also" you can observe Martin's thoughts and feelings, but the minds of all the other characters are closed to you unless they speak or unless Martin guesses what they are thinking. You can not move from Martin's mind to theirs as you can in the all-knowing subjective point of view.

A third-person story can also be objective. Then even the thoughts and feelings of the third-person, main character will not be revealed. All of the characters will be described only by their speech and actions. This third-person objective point of view is very difficult for a writer to use successfully. As a beginning writer, you would be wise to use the other points of view you have studied.

Further analyze the point of view in the story which you have just read.

    1. Is the point of view subjective or objective?

    2. Prove your answer to *1* from the story.

 *Writing for Skill*

1. The story "Shago" is from the first-person point of view, but the storyteller is a person other than Shago. Choose an incident from "Shago" and write it from the first-person point of view again, using Shago as the storyteller. Remember, Shago's mind can be opened to the reader now, but not the minds of any other characters.

2. The point of view can drastically affect the tone of a story. Choose an incident from "The Mote and the Beam" and write it in the first-person point of view again through the eyes of the Danny. This will give the story an altogether different tone.

3. Most Bible stories are written from the all-knowing point of view. Choose a Bible story and write it from the third-person subjective point of view. Choose one of the characters to be the third person main character. Then, using third person pronouns, describe the actions of all the other characters through the eyes of this person.

4. Write a story of your own from the all-knowing point of view.

Whom Shall I Fear?

by Joseph Stoll

Fear sustains life. Refuse to fear gravity, and you will fall to your death. Take a raging infection lightly, and life will ebb away.

On the other hand, use fire with fear and it will protect you. Respect the white line on the highway and live. Above all, reverence the Word of the all-knowing Creator. "He that feareth God shall come forth of them all" (Ecclesiastes 7:18).

But what should you do when this fear clashes with the fear of man? That's what the Mulier family will show you.

Defining for Comprehension

Choose the word or phrase below which best defines each word at the left as it is used in the story.

1. dean	a. king	b. sergeant	c. high official
2. mused	a. meditated	b. whispered	c. grieved
3. iconoclasm	a. rebellion	b. destruction of images	c. bloody uprising
4. bailiffs	a. lawyers	b. minor officers	c. church leaders
5. menacingly	a. threateningly	b. disdainfully	c. bitterly
6. rustic	a. tumbledown	b. country-style	c. discolored
7. abandon	a. reject	b. let down	c. forsake
8. recanted	a. renounced	b. proved false	c. told the untruth

Whom Shall I Fear?

"Welcome to Meenen," called the tall man as he got out of his cart. "My name is Nicholas Zager. I saw you working in the garden, so I thought I would stop in and get acquainted."

Piersom Mulier rested on his hoe and shook hands with the friendly visitor. "I'm glad you stopped," he spoke in a quiet voice. "We haven't met very many of the villagers yet."

"Oh, you will soon. And you'll like it in Meenen, I'm sure. It's a friendly little town."

"But you're the first man to talk to us."

"I am? That's strange, indeed. But then . . ." Mr. Zager paused, and lowered his voice, "I think I know why. You're Anabaptists, aren't you?"

Piersom was startled and dropped his hoe. "I . . . we," he stuttered.

"Don't worry," the visitor hastened to add. "The villagers wish you no harm. You'll be as safe here as anywhere in Flanders."

"But how did you know?"

"The report came straight from your hometown of Bruges. You had to flee the city, didn't you?"

"Yes," admitted Piersom, "but I don't see how you knew who we were."

"Never mind that. We want to be friends, and though I'm not an Anabaptist I have a great respect for those I've met." Mr. Zager glanced behind him. He did not want just anyone to hear him say these words.

Piersom sighed with relief. "I'm glad to hear that, though I will say you really shocked me at first. But come, you must meet my wife and children." He led the way toward the house.

"I have just a minute, but—"

"Do come in. We have a new baby, just a few weeks old, and the trip from Bruges was hard on both my wife and the baby. Claudine will want to meet you."

"You have a nice home here," commented the visitor, as he followed Piersom into the house. The room was neatly furnished, and in one corner were boxes that had not yet been unpacked.

"Yes, we are more than content with our earthly home," answered Piersom, and then he added, "that is, if we could just live in it in peace, without the constant fear of arrest."

"Well, I assure you," said the visitor, "I . . . oh, is this your wife?"

"Yes," and Piersom turned to her, "Claudine, this is Nicholas Zager, and he knows all about us."

"He does!" Claudine was holding the baby in one arm, but her free hand flew to her mouth.

"It's true," said Mr. Zager, "and as I was about to say, I'm sure you'll be as safe here as anywhere, even if we know more than we should." He smiled reassuringly. "I'm on the town council, and you'll excuse me if I say I do have influence. The villagers were shy to talk to you, having heard what they did, but now that I've been here you'll soon have friends. And as long as the **Dean** of Ronse does not hear about you, no one will trouble you."

"But might someone not tell the Dean?" asked Piersom anxiously.

"There is the possibility, yes. But the Dean is not very popular hereabouts."

Weeks passed, and Piersom Mulier and his family were indeed well accepted in Meenen. The people shrugged their shoulders and said to each other, "They're nice people, and after all, we don't *know* that they're Anabaptists. There was a rumor that came over from Bruges, but who can trust a rumor?"

But not everyone in Meenen was friendly to the Muliers. Piersom told his wife one day, "I'm happy we are so well settled in this town, but I'm worried about one man."

"Who? Our neighbor?"

"Yes, Franz Ledersnyder. He never smiles to me, and when I wave from the street, he ignores me."

"He is not nearsighted or blind, is he? Perhaps he doesn't see you."

"He sees well enough," said Piersom flatly. "He is angry about something. I wonder if he wanted to buy this property? His shop is pretty small for his leather business and perhaps he wanted to expand. Whatever it is, he doesn't like us."

"Can't we win him for a friend somehow, Piersom?"

"We must watch our opportunity to return good for evil, as the Bible says," her husband replied.

"If he knew you are an Anabaptist minister," **mused** Claudine, "what do you suppose he would do?"

"Well, I don't know, but if it is possible we must win him for a friend. There's one thing we can't afford in this town and that is an enemy. Paul writes that if it is possible we should live peaceably with all men, so there must be times when it isn't."

Piersom sat down to his books to study. He picked up the Bible and paged through it. "Claudine," he called at length. "Can you help me?"

"What is it?" she asked.

"We were talking of returning good for evil. Paul writes in Romans 12, 'If thine enemy hunger, feed him; if he thirst, give him drink: for in so doing thou shalt heap coals of fire on his head.' Wasn't Paul quoting from the Old Testament?"

"Yes, I think so, Piersom."

"I thought it was written in Psalms, but I can't find it."

"No, it is in Proverbs, and if I'm not mistaken, it is Chapter 25."

"Yes, here it is, almost quoted word for word as Paul quoted it. I wish I could remember verses and references as well as you do, Claudine."

"But you do very well."

"Indeed, I should, for I am a minister. And it is a great help to have a wife who knows her Bible so well."

"The Bible is worth knowing well," remarked his wife. "The Word of God is what brought us to the faith."

"Yes, but it was the preaching of Leonard Bouwens that brought us to the Word of God, don't forget that," added Piersom.

"Quite true. God can do wonders through His Word, but He also uses His servants to win souls."

"I am praying that He may use us, as His humble servants, to build up a church in His name here in Meenen," Piersom concluded fervently.

And his wife added, "Let's not forget Franz Ledersnyder. His soul is worth as much in God's sight as yours or mine."

* * * * * * *

The summer of 1567 was a restless one in the Netherlands. In August of the previous year, the **Iconoclasm,** a wave of anti-Catholic violence had broken out, beginning in Flanders and spreading northward as far as Friesland. There had been riots and public demonstrations, but in these the Anabaptists took no part. Quietly they watched as the Calvinists rebelled against the church of Rome.

But now summer had come again, and there were rumors that King Philip was sending the Duke of Alba to the Netherlands to punish his unwilling subjects. A few months before Alba arrived, Piersom and Claudine Mulier were studying the Bible together in the peace of a June morning when the door suddenly burst open. It was Nicholas Zager, the friendly councillor.

"Friends," he cried out anxiously, "Flee for your lives at once! A message has come from Ypres that the Dean of Ronse is on his way here with **bailiffs** and soldiers. But tell no one who warned you."

Claudine turned toward her husband, her face becoming pale. "It is you they are after," she cried. "Go hide at once in the woods!"

"But you must come, too, Claudine."

"I will as soon as I can. The children are fast asleep. You go, and I will follow."

Piersom hurried out the door, and struck out for the nearby woods, being careful to conceal himself behind the hedge as much as possible.

Claudine woke her oldest child and said, "Margriete, listen to me. The Dean of Ronse is coming to capture Father, but he has run to the woods. I am going, too, with the baby, but you stay here till we come back. Take good care of Pieter and Nicholas when they wake up. Goodbye."

Little Margriete's eyes opened wide, but she did not say anything.

Just then the sound of horses' hoofs were heard on the street. Claudine grabbed Baby Jan and wrapping a blanket about him, she hurried out the back way.

The Dean of Ronse followed the bailiffs into the house. The soldiers surrounded the home so no one could escape. Neighbors came running to watch.

The Dean and the bailiffs quickly searched the house. It was empty except for three young children.

"Where are your father and mother?" a bailiff asked Margriete.

"Yes, tell us and be quick," added the Dean. Then he turned around and saw neighbors gathering in the yard outside.

"Does anyone know where the occupants of this house have fled?" he barked, looking **menacingly** at the people.

No one spoke. Some of the neighbors must have known but they were not about to tell.

Just then a baldish little man came puffing up. He was wearing a leather apron and no hat. He waved the scissors in his hand. "Mr. Bailiff," he cried.

"And who are you? Please identify yourself," said the Dean haughtily.

"I am Franz Ledersnyder," puffed the excited man. He pointed his scissors toward the woods. "There she goes," he shouted.

All eyes turned toward the woods. Claudine was hurrying across the field with the babe in her arms.

"After her, men," commanded the Dean.

Piersom watched from behind a bush in the thick woods. His heart sank as he saw the men on horseback start across the field, and rapidly gain on his struggling wife. Claudine had no chance.

"Oh, why didn't I insist that she come with me at once?" moaned Piersom, as the soldiers caught Claudine, and placed chains on her hands. "But I thought she was coming right after me. There was no time to spare."

There were frowns on the faces of the village folk as Claudine was brought back to the house. A few bold fellows dared to cast angry glances at Franz Ledersnyder, the traitor. Just wait till the soldiers were gone, and they would show him a thing or two!

Claudine was led down the road to Ypres, still holding the baby in her arms. Meenen was an unwalled city, and the bailiffs feared that friends of the prisoners would break in and free them. This had happened in a neighboring village, where four hundred prisoners had been enclosed. On a certain day the peasants came in great numbers and broke open the prison, freeing them all. But in Ypres Claudine would be safe.

Piersom remained hidden in the woods for several days. Meanwhile, the priest of Meenen ordered the children brought to him. Friends did so, and little Margriete, Pieter, and Nicholas were baptized.

Nicholas Zager came to the empty house the next day and gathered up Piersom's books and some of their household belongings. "Piersom is my friend," he said to himself. "I will hide these things for him until he can use them again. The bailiff will have enough if he takes the house."

One night not long after Claudine had been captured, a mob of rough-looking men swarmed up the street past the empty house where Piersom's family had lived. They turned in at neighbor Franz Ledersnyder's house, and roused him out of bed.

A drunken fellow grabbed the poor man by the throat and shook him. "Traitor!" he hissed. "Meenen has no need for the likes of you."

At the same time the other men tore apart the leathermaking shop, and smashed the tools. Then they carried Franz out to the road and set him free. "Get out of here, you traitor!" they cried. "And don't come back!"

Franz Ledersnyder set off down the road toward Ypres, going a hard trot in his bare feet. Echoes of "Judas! Judas! Traitor!" followed him into the darkness.

Piersom Mulier was anxious to hear news of his wife in prison, so he went to Ypres. In this large city it was easy to hide, and he looked for a place to stay. Past the great Cloth Hall he walked and as near to the prison as he dared. Then he turned around and retraced his steps, back to the city gates.

The road from Meenen came winding over the Flemish hills, and just as it entered Ypres it dipped into a beautiful valley. Here, just under the walls of the city, stood a **rustic** old mill.

Piersom spoke to the miller, who lounged in the doorway brushing the flour from his huge hands. "Would you know of a place where a man could find work, and a place to sleep?" he asked.

The miller raised his shaggy eyebrows, white with flour dust. "Can you heave a bag of flour, sir?"

"I think so," and Piersom straightened his shoulders.

"I need a man just now, for I have a bin of wheat that needs gristing before the new crop ripens. And if our bed and board is good enough for you, you are welcome to stay at our house," said the miller.

"Thank you. That is an offer too good to turn down, for I need employment for a month or two."

"My name is Herman," explained the miller. "Herman, the miller, I am called. The work is done for today, and as soon as I've cleaned up, I'll take you to the house—that stone one just over there," and the miller pointed up the hill.

In the little stone cottage Piersom met the miller's wife. She was a round little woman with a ready tongue, but friendly and kind of heart. "My name is Catherine," she announced. "Herman has been grumbling that he's behind in his work. He is glad for the help, and I don't mind cooking for an extra stomach."

Piersom sat down to the simple meal and bowed his head in thanks. He could feel the miller and his wife eyeing him curiously.

The miller's wife was soon chattering. "You know, Herman," she said to her husband, "that Anabaptist woman I was telling you about, the one from Meenen that is in prison? She has her child with her, though I'm sure I don't know how the baby lives with the food its mother gets. They tell me the woman won't listen to the priests, but talks right back to them as if she knew the Scriptures as well as they. Can you imagine that? I wonder where her husband got to. They tell me he hid in a woods and escaped."

Piersom listened, but said not a word.

The miller's wife went up to the city quite often, and she never came home without news. There was always something to report.

Months passed, and one evening when Piersom came home from working at the mill, he found the mistress of the house quite excited. "Last night the prisoners broke out of the city hall. The burgomaster is in a rage, and is breathing death upon whoever helped them out."

Piersom's heart beat faster. "Did they all get out?" he ventured to ask timidly.

"As far as I know," answered Catherine. "Isn't that something!"

But two days later the miller's wife knew more. "The woman from Meenen, the Anabaptist—Claudine, they call her—she didn't leave."

"She didn't? I wonder why not?" asked Herman, the miller.

"She didn't want to **abandon** her child, someone told me. The little fellow was asleep in another room, and she couldn't go without him. And another prisoner, an old feeble man, stayed there too."

Piersom's heart sank again.

"That Claudine woman must not be in her right mind," stated Catherine breezily. "If I were in prison and had a chance to escape, you wouldn't see me hesitating!"

Winter came, but still Claudine was held in prison. Piersom often wondered how the older children were faring in Meenen. One day he decided to brave the danger, and investigate. He walked to Meenen and sought out Nicholas Zager.

"How are my children?" he asked.

Mr. Zager looked away and did not answer at once. At last he said, "Piersom, I regret to say little Pieter died."

This came as a shock to Piersom. Sadly he retraced his steps to Ypres. He had suffered much in the past year, especially since Claudine had been captured and the older children had been put into Catholic homes. He had hoped his wife might be released and the family reunited, but that hope had dimmed. The future on earth looked dark, but Piersom believed with all his heart that a blessed future in heaven awaited the faithful. And he was comforted.

And then the letters from Claudine began to arrive. Through friends and brethren in the city, her letters were brought to Piersom and his letters in answer were delivered safely to the lonely prisoner and her child behind the thick walls.

Claudine wrote that she was of good cheer, though one thing saddened her. Some brethren and sisters who had been brought in did not remain faithful. Under threat of death they **recanted** and promised to attend mass and confession regularly. Some were thereupon released, though a few were kept in prison for further questioning.

The miller and his wife never suspected Piersom's identity. They did not even know he was an Anabaptist.

One evening Catherine had news to report. "I heard today in the streets that the child has been taken away from the Anabaptist woman. The bailiffs think this may make her recant faster than anything else can. I don't know what they did with the child, but likely they gave it to a nurse to be cared for."

Piersom breathed a quick prayer for Claudine.

Her letter came the next day.

She wrote,

My dear husband,

My heart is full of sorrow. This is almost more than I can bear, for they have taken the babe Jan from me, and God only knows where they have taken him. He was such a comfort and pastime to me these long hours in prison. Oh, what shall I do? I pray every day to be delivered from this imprisonment, and I trust that God will answer according to His will.

Oh, Piersom, it is too much! I could bear it to be parted from you and the older children only because I still had the baby with me. But now he is taken, too. Pray for me, that I may submit to His will.

Your loving wife,

Claudine.

Each evening Piersom hurried home from work, anxious to know if the miller's wife had heard any news of Claudine.

One evening she announced, "The Duke of Alba has sent word throughout Flanders to empty the prisons. That means we shall see some executions this summer, or I miss my guess. It seems the duke wants to save some money, and thinks some of the prisoners have been fed long enough. Or maybe he wants the prisons emptied so he can fill them again. He has had thousands executed already."

"I wouldn't want all that blood on my hands," said the miller piously.

"Neither would I," continued Catherine, as Piersom listened, "but Herman, what would you do with a woman such as Claudine the Anabaptist? If you were the bailiff, would you set her free?"

"I think I would," said Herman stoutly.

"But she is not in her right mind," objected his wife. "She was rebaptized, and I'd allow her that if she has such a fancy to it, but to carry on the way she has, just because of this matter of baptism. Tut, tut, I tell you, the woman's mad. She has been tortured, and I do believe she's ready to die rather than to give up to the priests. Such stubbornness is not natural; it is more than human."

"It is the grace of God," said Piersom softly, and tears flowed down his cheeks. He got up and left the room.

"Did you hear that?" whispered Catherine to her husband. "How strangely this news of the prisoner affects Piersom."

"It is strange," agreed Herman.

* * * * * * *

"Will you go with me to the city today?" the miller's wife asked Piersom.

"No, I would rather not."

"But today is a special day. I wouldn't miss it. Don't you want to see the Anabaptist woman Claudine executed? She is to be buried alive."

"I prefer to stay at home. You can tell me about it when you return."

"Just as you say, Piersom. You look so troubled lately. I thought a holiday might do you good."

"I will be satisfied if you give me a detailed account of it afterwards."

And so the miller's wife hurried to the prison to see what she could see. And Piersom went to an empty room of the old mill and spent the day on his knees, praying for his wife.

With anxious face Piersom met Catherine as she returned home. "Tell me about the execution," he implored.

"Oh!" she began, swelling with the news, "you should have gone along! That woman Claudine was a queen, even if she was mad. I was one of the first ones there, and we stood in front of the prison waiting for them to bring her out. Of a sudden we heard singing, a wonderful voice she had, and when the door opened she stood there, and I tell you she looked more like a queen than a prisoner going to her death. She was beautiful, though a bit pale, of course. I could see the crowd was impressed, and so was I. Then she began to sing, a sweet sad smile on her face—"

"What did she sing?" asked the miller.

"Oh, I remember the words so well, though I can't sing the way she did. Some say it is the twenty-seventh Psalm."

Hereupon the miller's wife tried to sing the song Claudine had sung,

"The LORD is my light and my salvation;
Whom shall I fear?
The LORD is the strength of my life;
Of whom shall I be afraid."

The excited woman resumed her story before the last echo of her song had died. "Do you know what she did next? She began to praise God, and she would have kept it up as long as she had any breath left if the executioner had not gagged her. Cruel fellow! But I suppose he was afraid her madness would spread. Even after she was gagged, you could see on her face that her spirit was not conquered."

Herman the miller said mildly, "Well, my good wife, it appears to me you have a better opinion of the woman than you had this morning."

"Yes, I do, but . . . " she hesitated.

"But what?"

"But what was the Spirit that made her die like that? Surely it was madness."

Piersom could no longer contain himself. Great waves of emotion swept over him, and he struggled for control of his voice. "My dear friends," he began. "It was not madness that

About the Author

Joseph Stoll, (b. 1935) born in Indiana and now living in Ontario, serves as an Old Order Amish minister. He has written several books based on the stories of Anabaptists including *The Drummer's Wife* in which this selection appears.

made my . . . that caused the woman to die as she did. It was the Spirit of God dwelling in her. She died gloriously for her faith in Jesus Christ just as the early Christians at Jerusalem did. They, too, suffered persecution, but they did it gladly and boldly, just as the woman you saw today."

The miller and his wife listened with open mouths. Never had Piersom made such a long speech in their presence. He had been satisfied with listening.

"In our day," continued Piersom Mulier, "the Anabaptists are everywhere persecuted and despised. It is not easy to be a true Christian, to take up the cross of Christ and follow Him. But it is the only way to get to heaven."

The miller's wife at last found her tongue. "I'm surprised at you, Piersom. And if I had not seen what I did today, I would say you are mad. But now . . . "

She was interrupted by Piersom's earnest words, "For a year I have lived with you, and have kept from you a secret. Tonight I feel compelled to tell you." He paused, then continued solemnly, "I am an Anabaptist minister. And the woman you saw executed today was my own dear wife, Claudine."

Herman and Catherine were stunned beyond words.

Piersom eagerly explained the faith of the Anabaptists, and his listeners heard his words respectfully. Claudine had not died in vain, for it is doubtful that the miller and his wife would have listened otherwise.

As the old chronicle concludes, "This so deeply affected the miller and his wife, that they also resolved to amend their life. They were baptized upon their faith, and shortly after sealed the truth with their blood."

Testing for Understanding

1. This story took place in
    a. one of Switzerland's Calvinist territories.
    b. a severely persecuted area of Austria.
    c. the Netherlands (lowlands of north-western Europe).
    d. a Protestant town in northern Germany.

2. The main character in this story is
    a. Piersom.
    b. Claudine.
    c. the miller's wife.
    d. the Dean of Ronse.

3. Nicholas Zager made acquaintance with Piersom Mulier's family
    a. the day they moved to Meenen.
    b. no sooner than he had to.
    c. to warn them.
    d. some days after they arrived.

4. Mr. Zager may have been reluctant to meet Piersom's wife and children because he was
    a. suspicious of them.
    b. only doing his duty.
    c. afraid of others seeing him in close contact with this strange family.
    d. spiritually uneasy in Piersom's presence.

5. Piersom's family was well accepted in Meenen because the people there
    a. didn't know anything about the Anabaptists.
    b. were favorably impressed with the Mulier family.
    c. were suspicious because of rumors that they had heard.
    d. disliked the Dean of Ronse.

6. Before the arrest the greatest challenge to the Muliers' Anabaptist beliefs came from
    a. Franz Ledersnyder.
    b. the Dean of Ronse.
    c. Nicholas Zager.
    d. the miller's wife.

7. Piersom took the job in the flour mill
    a. because it was safer there than at Meenen.
    b. to be close to the prison.
    c. for the living he now needed desperately.
    d. to keep his mind off his family tragedy.

8. The miller's wife thought Claudine was insane because she
    a. insisted on keeping her children.
    b. had so many children.
    c. had an unnatural knowledge of the Scriptures.
    d. did not escape with the other prisoners.

9. The thing that discouraged Claudine the most was
    a. brethren who gave up their faith under threat of death.
    b. separation from her family.
    c. the loss of her baby.
    d. Pieter's death.

10. Claudine greatly impressed the miller's wife by
    a. her singing.
    b. her spirit.
    c. her looks.
    d. all of these.

Reading for Understanding

1. *"I am praying that He may use us, as His humble servants, to build up a church in His name here in Meenen,"* Piersom concluded fervently.
   The town of Meenen had
   a. a weak Anabaptist fellowship that needed leadership.
   b. people who did not attend any church at all.
   c. no Anabaptist congregation.
   d. driven all true believers away by persecution.

2. *There had been riots and public demonstrations, but in these the Anabaptists took no part. Quietly, they watched as the Calvinists rebelled against the church of Rome. But now summer had come again, and there were rumors that King Philip was sending the Duke of Alba to the Netherlands to punish his unwilling subjects.*
   Piersom and Claudine had to flee at this time because
   a. apparently the authorities made no difference between Anabaptists and Calvinists.
   b. they were unwilling subjects of King Philip.
   c. there was danger that an unfriendly neighbor would report them.
   d. of their refusal to take part in the rebellion.

3. *Claudine was led down the road to Ypres, still holding her baby in her arms. Meenen was an unwalled city, and the bailiffs feared that friends of the prisoners would break in and free them.*
   The city of Ypres was a/an
   a. unwalled city with a stronger prison.   c. city with walls.
   b. long way from Meenen.   d. place where the Anabaptists had no friends.

4. *Piersom sat down to the simple meal and bowed his head in thanks. He could feel the miller and his wife eyeing him curiously.*
   Apparently, the miller and his wife
   a. thanked God for their food in a different way.   c. did not pray before eating.
   b. thought Piersom was doing wrong.   d. admired Piersom for his courage.

5. *"Tut, tut, I tell you, the woman's mad. She has been tortured, and I do believe she's ready to die rather than to give up to the priests. Such stubbornness is not natural; it is more than human."*
   The miller's wife possibly believed that Claudine had
   a. God's supernatural assistance.   c. the cooperation of the devil.
   b. no way to help herself.   d. the nature of an animal.

Meditating for Meaning

1. The title of this story asks an important question.
   a. As the story opens, how do Nicholas, Piersom, and Claudine each show fear?
   b. All these characters seem to fear _____ .

c. If you follow the actions of Piersom and Claudine through the whole story, you will see that they have a fear different from Nicholas's. They showed by their actions that they feared _____ more than _____ .

d. Give examples from the story that show this.

e. What warning does Proverbs 29:25 give to those who fear men?

2. Those who fear the wrong thing will also misplace their trust.

a. What were the Muliers tempted to trust in at Meenen?

b. How does the story prove that such a trust would have been a cruel delusion?

3. The experience of the Muliers with Franz Ledersnyder shows how the right kind of fear affects the decisions people make.

a. Why did Piersom and his wife have reasons in the natural realm to fear Franz?

b. As Piersom saw it, what did the Bible say could happen when they tried to make friends with Franz?

c. If they had shown love to Franz only because they feared him, what might have happened later in the story?

d. How can you tell that the Muliers' love for Franz was not rooted in their fear of him?

4. A proper fear makes a person bold. But such character is not gained automatically.

a. What was Claudine's most outstanding characteristic before the summer of 1567?

b. How did this make her bold under persecution?

5. What fear do you suppose made Claudine refuse to abandon her child and escape from the prison?

6. The forces at work in the Christian are so radically different from the motives of the unbeliever that his actions appear unreasonable to the carnal mind.

a. Why did Claudine seem mad to the miller's wife?

b. How was Claudine actually living a more sane life than the people around her?

c. What did the executioners do that proved they realized that something more powerful than madness controlled Claudine?

d. How did Piersom explain Claudine's "madness"?

 *Looking for Literary Technique*

Unlike the other stories so far, this one is not fiction in the strictest sense. It tells the facts about people who actually lived in Flanders over four centuries ago. You will find the history of Piersom and Claudine on pages 737, 738 of the *Martyrs Mirror*. The storywriter stayed very close to the facts given there.

The short story, however, differs from the *Martyrs Mirror* account in several important ways. Of course, the storywriter has rearranged some facts, devised imaginary conversation, and named some of the minor characters. But this alone would not change nonfiction into a good short story. We must look deeper to see the important differences.

The *Martyrs Mirror* sticks to the facts about Piersom and Claudine, except for one place where it goes beyond a listing of facts and explains the beliefs which condemned the Anabaptists. But the short story illustrates the truth of the Anabaptist beliefs in a way that a listing of facts could not.

One of these truths is the theme on which the story is built. The title introduces the theme taken from Claudine's song at the end of her life. All of the story happenings are arranged to emphasize this theme—"Whom shall I fear?"

As the story opens, the main characters are struggling with their natural fear of man. The story goes on to show how they resolve their fear of Franz Ledersnyder in obedience to God. After Claudine's capture, we see her victory over the fear of man as she refuses to escape from prison, stands her ground with Scripture, and endures the loss of her baby. The theme climaxes in her brilliant witness on the day of her death as she sings, "The LORD is my light and my salvation; Whom shall I fear?" The story then quickly ends with the effect of such a godly fear on Piersom. He now has the courage to reveal himself to the awed miller and his wife, who came to fear God also.

As the theme develops, some meaningful contrasts emerge that we also do not see in the *Martyrs Mirror* account. The fears of the main characters at the beginning of the story contrast with their boldness at the end. The first impressions of the miller's wife about Claudine contrast ironically with her final impression. Claudine's response at her death surprises the expectations of the onlookers. And death proves to be Claudine's greatest triumph.

As you can see, the story version does far more than "spice up" the facts. It unifies all the facts around an idea that gives them fresh meaning. The account tells you what happened. The story moves you to a new understanding about life in Christ Jesus.

1. Read the account of Piersom and Claudine in the *Martyrs Mirror,* pages 737, 738. Don't miss the "Further Account of the Aforesaid Claudine" on page 738.
   a. Besides the imaginary conversation, what details did the storywriter add to the facts in the history? You will be surprised how few there are.
   b. What details did the storywriter omit and what was the possible reason each was dropped?
2. Decide who is the teller of this story.
   a. What is the point of view?
   b. Is it subjective or objective?
3. What tone does the talk of the miller's wife have?

Writing for Skill

Use the following account taken from pages 449, 450 of the *Martyrs Mirror* as an outline to write a short story. Use any point of view you choose. Be sure to carry a single theme throughout the story. A possible theme would be "The providence of God." Stick to the *Martyrs Mirror* account as closely as possible, but you will need to add details to make it interesting.

JOHN STYAERTS, AND PETER. A.D. 1538

About this year, there were, in Flanders, two cousins, one named Styaerts, the other Peter. These two blooming and God-seeking youths resided with their parents in a village called Mereedor, in Flanders. And as they were very zealous for God, and searched the holy Scriptures, they soon perceived, that the believing and regenerated—according to the doctrine of Christ, as a sign of having buried the former sins, and risen with Christ, and walking in newness of life—had to receive Christian baptism, in the water; and since they were desirous of this, they journeyed to Germany, to seek others of their fellow believers. But as they could not find such as suited their wishes, they soon returned to their parents in Flanders, where they earnestly sought the Lord their God, so that they had a good report, doing much good to the poor, and saying with Zacchaeus, that if they had defrauded any one, they would restore it fourfold (Luke 19:8). When the blinded papists, who most bitterly hated the light of truth, perceived this, they took these two young lambs out of the houses of their parents, at Mereedor, and brought them beyond Ghent, into a village called Vinderhout, where they most severely imprisoned them in a dungeon (Jer. 38:6). Once when their sister came to bring them some fine shirts, they told her that they could not keep them from the worms, which were in their food, eating it, and in their clothes and shirts on their bodies. They further said: "Here is a Bible, the contents of which, as well as the cause of our bonds, will yet come to light after our death." The aforesaid John Styaerts was once released from prison, on account of sickness, and, as is thought, could easily have obtained his liberty; but he voluntarily returned to prison, desiring gladly to die with his dear brother for the name of Jesus. Thus after a certain time they were led to the slaughter. Peter, who came forth first to die, casting his eyes up to heaven, boldly called out to John Styaerts: "Fight valiantly, my dear brother; for I see the heavens open above us" (Acts 7:56). They were together put to death with the sword at Vinderhout. Thus these young branches in the court of the Lord (Jer. 17:8; Ps. 1:3), were also devoured by the awful beast which rose up out of the sea (Rev. 13:1), but they had no power over their immortal souls, which escaped from them unto God, where they shall forever live in unspeakable joy. When their parents came from Mereedor to Vinderhout, and inquired for their children, the villagers told them that they had already been executed with the sword. And thus they were deprived of their children by these tyrants.

UNITY

Jesus carried Himself through life with perfect poise. His enemies could never trip Him in word, nor catch Him off guard in action. Rude interruptions, trick questions, and impossible tasks always found Him in calm control.

Once, 5,000 of His followers needed food on a moment's notice. The problem baffled Philip, but not Jesus, "for he himself knew what he would do" (John 6:6). With Jesus, it was never otherwise. He always met life with foresight and quiet power.

What secret did Jesus possess?

Certainly, as God, He had unusual authority. But much of His power lay in the perfect wholeness of His humanity. He allowed no conflicts in His being.

Jesus let God's Spirit master and unify all parts of His soul (mind, will, feelings) and body. These worked together in perfect agreement. With such unity of being, Jesus could always be "filled with the Spirit" (Ephesians 5:18). Nothing could hinder its supernatural flow.

The poise in Jesus' life can be seen in His stories. They tell their truth with power because they have unity. Of course, a story cannot be Spirit-filled in the same way as a person can. But it can have all its parts tied together with truth.

The thread of truth in a story is its theme. If a story is to have unity, every part of it must help in some way to develop this one main truth.

Take the account of "The Good Samaritan" in Luke 10. The characters, actions, and setting all emphasize its theme: "Your neighbor is anyone who needs your help." Jesus did not allow one unnecessary character or action in His story to lead you away from the theme and spoil its unity. Every character and action serves a purpose.

The thieves violently upset life and give the account its opening problems. In the robbery, we see their belief: "What's yours is mine, and I'll take it." Nothing could differ more sharply from the attitude of a true neighbor, so the theme is introduced by contrast. Religion now comes walking down the road in the form of a priest. When he sees the man, he must decide whether or not to show mercy to a fellowman. A tone of irony creeps in as religion walks by without even stopping to investigate and proves itself only a hair above the robbers.

A Levite now comes by and so another religious man gets a chance to recognize a neighbor. He stops for a close-up look, then turns a callous eye from the misery he has clearly seen. He and the priest show their belief that "What's mine is mine, and I'll keep it." Again we sense a tone of irony as these "servants of God" miss the point of their religion. The story theme has been emphasized once again by contrast.

The irony climaxes in the last scene when a religious heretic, the Samaritan, stops to do the godly act of mercy. He obviously believed "What's mine is yours and I'll gladly give it to the full extent of your need." With this, the story ends squarely on the theme which every character and action helped to develop.

Let's see how the setting ties into the theme. It shows a man going down a road that drops over 3,000 feet from Jerusalem to Jericho.

Some readers see the steep descent of that road as symbolizing the victim's fall into tragic need. Going down the same road, the priest also fell frightfully, but in a different way. Such symbolism can add to the unity of the story.

Now suppose the account had told us what the thieves did with their stolen money. Or what if it had gone on to show us the character of the innkeeper? These details have nothing to do with the theme of this particular story. They would have broken its unity and weakened its force. The account, as Jesus told it, has power because He harmonized all its parts around one truth. He made every word serve His theme.

The Spirit of Christ uses truth to produce unity and power. As you read the following stories, observe how lives become forceful as the Spirit unifies them. See how truth can unify a story and sharpen its impact. Above all, let the truth in these stories work out a harmony and power in your own life.

Checking for Understanding

1. Give two reasons why Jesus could exercise great power.
2. Study the characteristics that give stories a powerful impact.
   a. Every part of such a story is _____ around its _____ .
   b. What characteristic will you find in a weak story?

The Great Stone Face

by Nathaniel Hawthorne

"What we love, we shall grow to resemble," said Bernard of Clairvaux, a medieval church leader. If a man really believes that, he will select only the grandest and noblest things to love. In a hymn Bernard wrote, "Jesus the very thought of Thee with sweetness fills my breast." But many people choose to focus on lesser things. In truth, they probably don't make a conscious choice at all. They ignorantly let their "eye" get centered on some superficial person with a striking face and a dashing figure. But the unyielding natural tendency to imitate others leads them to grow unconsciously shallow. Then there are those who don't focus on people at all. They love cars, trucks, money, or fine furniture. And slowly but surely they become insensitive, impersonal, and cold like the object they love. You can choose your focus, but you cannot choose its control over you. See how this subtle law works with the people in this story.*

Defining for Comprehension

Choose the word or phrase below which best defines each word at the left as it is used in the story.

1. **phenomenon**   a. unusual object   b. lofty truth   c. wisdom lover

2. **perpendicular**   a. beside   b. jagged   c. vertical

3. **ponderous**   a. easily angered   b. thoughtful   c. heavy; weighty

4. **infusing**   a. misleading   b. igniting   c. instilling

5. **purport**   a. claim   b. foundation   c. launching pad

6. **ardor**   a. trellis   b. zeal   c. strength

7. **pensive**
   a. deep in thought
   b. punishing
   c. dividing

8. **unobtrusive**
   a. quiet; unnoticed
   b. simple
   c. unlikely

9. **veneration**
   a. air circulation
   b. honor; respect
   c. exposure

10. **inscrutable**
    a. impossible
    b. mysterious
    c. contrary

11. **effulgence**
    a. radiance
    b. extravagance
    c. foolishness

12. **inured**
    a. accustomed
    b. persuaded
    c. completed

13. **harbingers**
    a. dancers
    b. heralds
    c. swords

14. **beneficence**
    a. charity
    b. closing prayer
    c. convenience

15. **benignant**
    a. cancerous
    b. kind; gracious
    c. angry

16. **physiognomy**
    a. mental illness
    b. exercise
    c. facial features

17. **sordid**
    a. miserable
    b. partial
    c. frank

18. **conceded**
    a. ended
    b. withdrew
    c. admitted

19. **ignoble**
    a. disgraceful
    b. desperate
    c. kingly

20. **consigned**
    a. entrusted
    b. poised
    c. surety

21. **infirm**
    a. feeble
    b. incorrect
    c. dishonest

22. **sylvan**
    a. fancy
    b. of the city
    c. of the woods

23. **vista**
    a. small town
    b. porch
    c. view

24. **verdant**
    a. enthusiastic
    b. lush; thriving
    c. poisonous

25. **profusely**
    a. mistakenly
    b. abundantly
    c. swiftly

26. **toasts**
    a. honors
    b. groceries
    c. coverlets

27. **ruthlessly**
    a. cruelly
    b. carelessly
    c. dishonestly

28. **reverberating**
    a. scolding
    b. echoing
    c. renewing

29. **imbibed**
    a. developed
    b. encouraged
    c. assimilated

30. **auditors**
    a. listeners
    b. moneylenders
    c. entertainers

31. **inevitably**
    a. securely
    b. unavoidably
    c. undesirably

32. **truculent**
    a. juicy
    b. fierce
    c. laughing

33. **eminent**
    a. threatening
    b. famous
    c. urgent

34. **buoyantly**
    a. enthusiastically
    b. gentlemanly
    c. elegantly

35. **emulation**
    a. waviness
    b. imitation
    c. sacrifice

36. **sublimity**
    a. loftiness
    b. obedience
    c. peace

37. **etherealized**
    a. reasoned
    b. recognized
    c. made heavenly

38. **vociferous**
    a. noisy; boisterous
    b. cone-bearing
    c. ferocious

39. sage	a. anger	b. wise man	c. old person
40. imbued	a. quieted	b. filled	c. followed
41. spontaneously	a. defiantly	b. irregularly	c. naturally
42. obliquely	a. dully	b. carefully	c. slantedly

The Great Stone Face

One afternoon, when the sun was going down, a mother and her little boy sat at the door of their cottage, talking about the Great Stone Face. They had but to lift their eyes, and there it was plainly to be seen, though miles away, with the sunshine brightening all its features.

And what was the Great Stone Face?

Embosomed amongst a family of lofty mountains, there was a valley so spacious that it contained many thousand inhabitants. Some of these good people dwelt in log huts, with the black forest all around them, on the steep and difficult hillsides. Others had their homes in comfortable farm houses, and cultivated the rich soil on the gentle slopes or level surfaces of the valley. Others, again, were congregated into populous villages, where some wild, highland rivulet, tumbling down from its birthplace in the upper mountain region had been caught and tamed by human cunning, and compelled to turn the machinery of cotton factories. The inhabitants of this valley, in short, were numerous, and of many modes of life. But all of them, grown people and children, had a kind of familiarity with the Great Stone Face, although some possessed the gift of distinguishing this grand natural **phenomenon** more perfectly than many of their neighbors.

The Great Stone Face, then, was a work of nature in its "mood" of majestic playfulness, formed on the **perpendicular** side of a mountain by some immense rocks, which had been thrown together in such a position as, when viewed at a proper distance, precisely to resemble the features of the human countenance. It seemed as if an enormous giant, or a *Titan*[1], had sculptured his own likeness on the precipice. There was the broad arch of the forehead, a hundred feet in height; the nose, with its long bridge; and the vast lips, which, if they could have spoken, would have rolled their thunder accents from one end of the valley to the other. True it is, that if the spectator approached too near, he lost the outline of the gigantic visage, and could discern only a heap of **ponderous** and gigantic rocks, piled in chaotic ruin one upon another. Retracing his steps, however, the wondrous features would again be seen; and the farther he withdrew from them, the more like a human face, with all its original divinity intact, did they appear; until, as it grew dim in the distance, with the clouds and glorified vapor of the mountains clustering about it, the Great Stone Face seemed positively to be alive.

It was a happy lot for children to grow up to manhood or womanhood with the Great Stone Face before their eyes, for all the features were

---

1. Titan: A person gigantic in size or power.

noble, and the expression was at once grand and sweet, as if it were the glow of a vast, warm heart, that embraced all mankind in its affections, and had room for more. It was an education only to look at it. According to the belief of many people, the valley owed much of its fertility to this benign aspect that was continually beaming over it, illuminating the clouds, and **infusing** its tenderness into the sunshine.

As we began with saying, a mother and her little boy sat at their cottage door, gazing at the Great Stone Face, and talking about it. The child's name was Ernest.

"Mother," said he, while the Titanic visage smiled on him, "I wish that it could speak, for it looks so very kindly that its voice must needs be pleasant. If I were to see a man with such a face, I should love him dearly."

"If an old prophecy should come to pass," answered his mother, "we may see a man, some time or other, with exactly such a face as that."

"What prophecy do you mean, dear mother?" eagerly inquired Ernest. "Pray tell me all about it!"

So his mother told him a story that her own mother had told to her, when she herself was younger than little Ernest; a story, not of things that were past but of what was yet to come; a story, nevertheless, so very old, that even the Indians, who formerly inhabited this valley, had heard it from their forefathers, to whom, as they affirmed, it had been murmured by the mountain streams, and whispered by the wind among the tree-tops. The **purport** was, that, at some future day, a child should be born hereabouts, who was destined to become the greatest and noblest personage of his time, and whose countenance, in manhood, should bear an exact resemblance to the Great Stone Face. Not a few old-fashioned people, and young ones likewise, in the **ardor** of their hopes, still cherished an enduring faith in this old prophecy. But others, who had seen more of the world, had watched and waited till they were weary, and had beheld no man with such a face, nor any man that proved to be much greater or nobler than his neighbors, concluded it to be nothing but an idle tale. At all events, the great man of the prophecy had not yet appeared.

"O mother, dear mother!" cried Ernest, clapping his hands above his head, "I do hope that I shall live to see him!"

His mother was an affectionate and thoughtful woman, and felt that it was wisest not to discourage the generous hopes of her little boy. So she only said to him, "Perhaps you may."

And Ernest never forgot the story that his mother told him. It was always in his mind, whenever he looked upon the Great Stone Face. He spent his childhood in the log cottage where he was born, and was dutiful to his mother, and helpful to her in many things, assisting her much with his little hands, and more with his loving heart. In this manner, from a happy yet often **pensive** child, he grew up to be a mild, quiet, **unobtrusive** boy, and sun-browned with labor in the fields, but with more intelligence brightening his aspect than is seen in many lads who have been taught at famous schools. Yet Ernest had had no teacher, save only that the Great Stone Face became one to him. When the toil of the day was over, he would gaze at it for hours, until he began to imagine that those vast features recognized him, and gave him a smile of kindness and encouragement, responsive to his own look of **veneration**. We must not take upon us to affirm that this was a mistake, although the Face may have looked no more kindly at Ernest than at all the world besides. But the secret was that the boy's tender and confiding simplicity discerned what other people could not see; and thus the love, which was meant for all, became his peculiar portion.

About this time there went a rumor throughout the valley, that the great man, foretold from ages long ago, who was to bear a resemblance to the Great Stone Face, had appeared at last. It seems that, many years before, a young man had migrated from the valley and settled at a distant seaport, where, after getting together a little money, he had set up as a shopkeeper. His name—but I could never learn whether it was his real one, or a nickname that had grown out of his habits and success in life—was Gathergold. Being shrewd and active, and endowed by Providence with that **inscrutable** faculty which develops itself in what the world calls luck, he became an exceedingly rich merchant, and owner of a whole fleet of bulky-bottomed ships. All the countries of the globe appeared to join hands for the mere purpose of adding heap after heap to the mountainous accumulation of this one man's wealth. The cold regions of the north, almost within the gloom and shadow of the Arctic Circle, sent him their tribute in the shape of furs; hot Africa sifted for him the golden sands of her rivers, and gathered up the ivory tusks of her great elephants out of the forests; the East came bringing him the rich shawls, and spices, and teas, and the **effulgence** of diamonds, and the gleaming purity of great pearls. The ocean, not to be behindhand with the earth, yielded up her mighty whales, that Mr. Gathergold might sell their oil, and make a profit on it. Be the original commodity what it might, it was gold within his grasp. It might be said of him, as of Midas in the fable, that whatever he touched with his finger immediately glistened, and grew yellow, and was changed at once into sterling metal, or, which suited him still better, into piles of coin. And, when Mr. Gathergold had become so rich that it would have taken him a hundred years only to count his wealth, he bethought himself of his native valley, and resolved to go back thither, and end his days where he was born. With this purpose in view, he sent a skillful architect to build him such a palace as should be fit for a man of his vast wealth to live in.

As I have said above, it had already been rumored in the valley that Mr. Gathergold had turned out to be the prophetic personage so long and vainly looked for, and that his visage was a perfect and undeniable similitude of the Great Stone Face. People were the more ready to believe that this must needs be the fact, when they beheld the splendid edifice that rose, as if by enchantment, on the site of his father's old weather-beaten farm house. The exterior was of marble, so dazzlingly white that it seemed as though the whole structure might melt away in the sunshine, like those humbler ones which Mr. Gathergold, in his play days, before his fingers were gifted with the touch of *transmuta-*

tion[2], had been accustomed to build of snow. It had a richly ornamented *portico,*[3] supported by tall pillars, beneath which was a lofty door, studded with silver knobs, and made of a kind of variegated wood that had been brought from beyond the sea. The windows, from the floor to the ceiling of each stately apartment, were composed, respectively, of but one enormous pane of glass, so transparently pure that it was said to be a finer medium than even the vacant atmosphere. Hardly anybody had been permitted to see the interior of this palace; but it was reported, and with good semblance of truth, to be far more gorgeous than the outside, insomuch that whatever was iron or brass in other houses was silver or gold in this; and Mr. Gathergold's bedchamber, especially made such a glittering appearance that no ordinary man would have been able to close his eyes there. But, on the other hand, Mr. Gathergold was now so **inured** to wealth, that perhaps he could not have closed his eyes unless where the gleam of it was certain to find its way beneath his eyelids.

In due time, the mansion was finished; next came the upholsterers, with magnificent furniture; then, a whole troop of black and white servants, the **harbingers** of Mr. Gathergold, who, in his own majestic person, was expected to arrive at sunset. Our friend Ernest, meanwhile, had been deeply stirred by the idea that the great man, the noble man, the man of prophecy, after so many ages of delay, was at length to be made manifest to his native valley. He knew, boy as he was, that there were a thousand ways in which Mr. Gathergold, with his vast wealth, might transform himself into an angel of **beneficence,** and assume a control over human affairs as wide and **benignant** as the smile of the Great Stone Face. Full of faith and hope, Ernest doubted not that what the people said was true, and that now he was to behold the living likeness of those wondrous features on the mountainside. While the boy was still gazing up the valley, and fancying, as he always did, that the Great Stone Face

---

2. transmutation: Supposed act of changing base metals to gold or silver.
3. portico: Entranceway with roof supported by columns.

returned his gaze and looked kindly at him, the rumbling of wheels was heard, approaching swiftly along the winding road.

"Here he comes!" cried a group of people who were assembled to witness the arrival. "Here comes the great Mr. Gathergold!"

A carriage, drawn by four horses, dashed round the turn of the road. Within, thrust partly out of the window, appeared the **physiognomy** of the old man, with a skin as yellow as if his own Midas-hand had transmuted it. He had a low forehead, small, sharp eyes, puckered about with innumerable wrinkles, and very thin lips, which he made still thinner by pressing them forcibly together.

"The very image of the Great Stone Face!" shouted the people. "Sure enough, the old prophecy is true; and here we have the great man come, at last!"

And, what greatly perplexed Ernest, they seemed actually to believe that here was the likeness which they spoke of. By the roadside there chanced to be an old beggar-woman and two little beggar-children, stragglers from some far-off region, who, as the carriage rolled onward, held out their hands and lifted up their doleful voices, most piteously beseeching charity. A yellow claw—the very same that had clawed together so much wealth—poked itself out of the coach-window, and dropped some copper coins upon the ground; so that, though the great man's name seems to have been Gathergold, he might just as suitably have been nicknamed Scattercopper. Still, nevertheless, with an earnest shout, and evidently with as much good faith as ever, the people bellowed:

"He is the very image of the Great Stone Face!"

But Ernest turned sadly from the wrinkled shrewdness of that **sordid** visage, and gazed up the valley, where, amid a gathering mist, gilded by the last sunbeams, he could still distinguish those glorious features which had impressed themselves into his soul. Their aspect cheered him. What did the benign lip seem to say?

"He will come! Fear not, Ernest; the man will come!"

The years went on, and Ernest ceased to be a boy. He had grown to be a young man now. He attracted little notice from the other inhabitants of the valley; for they saw nothing remarkable in his way of life, save that, when the labor of the day was over, he still loved to go apart and gaze and meditate upon the Great Stone Face. According to their idea of the matter, it was a folly, indeed, but pardonable, inasmuch as Ernest was industrious, kind, and neighborly, and neglected no duty for the sake of indulging this idle habit. They knew not that the Great Stone Face had become a teacher to him, and that the sentiment which was expressed in it would enlarge the young man's heart, and fill it with wider and deeper sympathies than other hearts. They knew not that thence would come a better wisdom than could be learned from books, and a better life than could be molded on the defaced example of other human lives. Neither did Ernest know that the thoughts and affections which came to him so naturally, in the fields and at the fireside, and wherever he communed with himself, were of a higher tone than those which all men shared with him. A simple soul—simple as when his mother first taught him the old prophecy—he beheld the marvelous features beaming down the valley, and still wondered that their human counterpart was so long in making his appearance.

By this time poor Mr. Gathergold was dead and buried; and the oddest part of the matter was that his wealth, which was the body and spirit of his existence, had disappeared before his death, leaving nothing of him but a living skeleton, covered over with a wrinkled, yellow skin. Since the melting away of his gold, it had been very generally **conceded** that there was no striking resemblance, after all, betwixt the **ignoble** features of the ruined merchant and that majestic face upon the mountainside. So the people ceased to honor him during his lifetime, and quietly **consigned** him to forgetfulness after his decease. Once in a while, it is true, his memory was brought up in connection with the magnificent palace which he had built, and which had long ago been turned into a hotel for the accommodation of strangers, multitudes of whom came, every summer, to visit that famous natural curiosity, the Great Stone Face. Thus, Mr. Gathergold, being discredited and thrown into the shade, the man of prophecy was yet to come.

It so happened that a native-born son of the valley, many years before, had enlisted as a soldier, and, after a great deal of hard fighting, had now become an illustrious commander. Whatever he may be called in history, he was known in camps and on the battlefield under the nickname of Old Blood-and-Thunder. This war-worn veteran, being now **infirm** with age and wounds, and weary of the turmoil of a military life, and of the roll of the drum and the clangor of the trumpet, that had so long been ringing in his ears, had lately signified a purpose of returning to his native valley, hoping to find repose where he remembered to have left it. The inhabitants, his old neighbors and their grown-up children, were resolved to welcome the renowned warrior with a salute of cannon and a public dinner; and all the more enthusiastically, it being affirmed that now, at last, the likeness of the Great Stone Face had actually appeared. An aide-de-camp of Old Blood-and-Thunder, traveling through the valley, was said to have been struck with the resemblance. Moreover the schoolmates and early acquaintances of the general were ready to testify, on oath, that, to the best of their recollection, the aforesaid general had been exceedingly like the majestic image, even when a boy, only that the idea had never occurred to them at that period. Great, therefore, was the excitement throughout the valley; and many people, who had never once thought of glancing at the Great Stone Face for years before, now spent their time in gazing at it, for the sake of knowing exactly how General Blood-and-Thunder looked.

On the day of the great festival, Ernest, with all the other people of the valley, left their work and proceeded to the spot where the **sylvan** banquet was prepared. As he approached, the loud voice of the Rev. Dr. Battleblast was heard, beseeching a blessing on the good things set before them, and on the distinguished friend of peace in whose honor they were assembled. The tables were arranged in a cleared space of the woods, shut in by the surrounding trees, except where a **vista** opened eastward, and afforded a distant view of the Great Stone Face. Over the general's chair, which was a relic from the home of Washington, there was an arch of **verdant** boughs, with the laurel **profusely** intermixed, and surmounted by his country's banner, beneath which he had won his victories. Our friend Ernest raised himself on his tiptoes, in hopes to get a glimpse of the celebrated guest; but there was a mighty crowd about the tables anxious to hear the **toasts** and speeches, and to catch any word that might fall from the general in reply; and a volunteer company, doing duty as a guard, pricked **ruthlessly** with their *bayonets*[4] at any particularly quiet person among the throng. So Ernest, being of an unobtrusive character, was thrust quite into the background, where he could see no more of Old Blood-and-Thunder's physiognomy than if it had been still blazing on the battlefield. To console himself, he turned towards the Great Stone Face, which, like a faithful and long-remembered friend, looked back and smiled upon him through the vista of the forest. Meantime, however, he could overhear the remarks of various individuals, who were comparing the features of the hero with the face on the distant mountainside.

" 'Tis the same face, to a hair!" cried one man, cutting a caper for joy.

"Wonderfully like, that's a fact!" responded another.

"Like! why, I call it Old Blood-and-Thunder himself, in a monstrous looking glass!" cried a third. "And why not? He's the greatest man of this or any other age, beyond a doubt."

And then all three of the speakers gave a great shout, which communicated electricity to the crowd, and called forth a roar from a thousand voices, that went **reverberating** for miles among the mountains, until you might have supposed that the Great Stone Face had poured its thunder-breath into the cry. All these comments, and this vast enthusiasm, served the more to interest our friend; nor did he think of questioning that now, at length, the mountain-visage had found its human counterpart. It is

---

4. bayonet: Short knife attached near the end of a gun barrel for hand-to-hand combat.

true, Ernest had imagined that this long-looked-for personage would appear in the character of a man of peace, uttering wisdom, and doing good, and making people happy. But, taking an habitual breadth of view, with all his simplicity, he contended that Providence should choose its own method of blessing mankind, and could conceive that this great end might be effected even by a warrior and a bloody sword, should inscrutable wisdom see fit to order matters so.

"The general! the general!" was now the cry. "Hush! Silence! Old Blood-and-Thunder's going to make a speech."

Even so, for the cloth being removed, the general's *health had been drunk*,[5] amid shouts of applause, and he now stood upon his feet to thank the company. Ernest saw him. There he was, over the shoulders of the crowd, from the two glittering *epaulets*[6] and embroidered collar upward, beneath the arch of green boughs with intertwined laurel, and the banner drooping as if to shade his brow! And there, too, visible in the same glance, through the vista of the forest, appeared the Great Stone Face! And was there, indeed, such a resemblance as the crowd had testified? Alas, Ernest could not recognize it! He beheld a war-worn and weather-beaten countenance, full of energy, and expressive of an iron will; but the gentle wisdom, the deep, broad, tender sympathies, were altogether wanting in Old Blood-and-Thunder's visage; and even if the Great Stone Face had assumed his look of stern command, the milder traits would still have tempered it.

"This is not the man of prophecy," sighed Ernest to himself, as he made his way out of the throng. "And must the world wait longer yet?"

The mists had congregated about the distant mountainside, and there were seen the grand and awful features of the Great Stone Face, awful but benignant, as if a mighty angel were sitting among the hills, and enrobing himself in a cloud-vesture of gold and purple. As he looked, Ernest could hardly believe but that a smile beamed over the whole visage, with a radiance still brightening, although without motion of the lips. It was probably the effect of the western sunshine, melting through the thinly diffused vapors that had swept between him and the object that he gazed at. But—as it always did—the aspect of his marvelous friend made Ernest as hopeful as if he had never hoped in vain.

"Fear not, Ernest," said his heart, even as if the Great Face were whispering to him—"fear not, Ernest; he will come."

More years sped swiftly and tranquilly away. Ernest still dwelt in his native valley, and was now a man of middle age. By imperceptible degrees, he had become known among the people. Now, as heretofore, he labored for his bread, and was the same simplehearted man that he had always been. But he had thought and felt so much, he had given so many of the best hours of his life to unworldly hopes for some great good to mankind, that it seemed as though he had been talking with the angels, and had **imbibed** a portion of their wisdom unawares. It was visible in the calm and well-considered beneficence of his daily life, the quiet stream of which had made a wide green margin all along its course. Not a day passed by that the world was not the better because this man, humble as he was, had lived. He never stepped aside from his own path, yet would always reach a blessing to his neighbor. Almost involuntarily, too, he had become a preacher. The pure and high simplicity of his thought, which, as one of its manifestations, took shape in the good deeds that dropped silently from his hand, flowed also forth in speech. He uttered truths that wrought upon and molded lives of those who heard him. His **auditors**, it may be, never suspected that Ernest, their own neighbor and familiar friend, was more than an ordinary man; least of all did Ernest himself suspect it; but, **inevitably** as the murmur of a rivulet, came thoughts out of his mouth that no other human lips had spoken.

When the people's minds had had a little time to cool, they were ready enough to

---

5. health had been drunk: The crowds had served drink in honor of the general.
6. epaulets (e pə lets'): Shoulder ornaments on military uniform.

acknowledge their mistake in imagining a similarity between General Blood-and-Thunder's **truculent** physiognomy and the benign visage on the mountainside.

But now, again, there were reports and many paragraphs in the newspapers, affirming that the likeness of the Great Stone Face had appeared upon the broad shoulders of a certain **eminent** statesman. He, like Mr. Gathergold and Old Blood-and-Thunder, was a native of the valley, but had left it in his early days, and taken up the trades of law and politics. Instead of the rich man's wealth and the warrior's sword, he had but a tongue, and it was mightier than both together. So wonderfully eloquent was he, that whatever he might choose to say, his auditors had no choice but to believe him; wrong looked like right, and right like wrong; for when it pleased him, he could make a kind of illuminated fog with his mere breath, and obscure the natural daylight with it. His tongue, indeed, was a magic instrument: sometimes it rumbled like the thunder; sometimes it warbled like the sweetest music. It was the blast of war—the song of peace; and it seemed to have a heart in it, when there was no such matter. In good truth, he was a wondrous man; and when his tongue had acquired him all other imaginable success; when it had been heard in halls of state, and in the courts of princes and potentates; after it had made him known all over the world, even as a voice crying from shore to shore; it finally persuaded his countrymen to select him for the Presidency. Before this time—indeed, as soon as he began to grow celebrated—his admirers had found out the resemblance between him and the Great Stone Face; and so much were they struck by it, that throughout the country this distinguished gentleman was known by the name of Old Stony Phiz. The phrase was considered as giving a highly favorable aspect to his political prospects; for, as is likewise the case with the Popedom, nobody ever becomes President without taking a name other than his own.

While his friends were doing their best to make him President, Old Stony Phiz set out on a visit to the valley where he was born. Of course, he had no other object than to shake hands with his fellow citizens, and neither thought nor cared about any effect which his progress through the country might have upon the election. Magnificent preparations were made to receive the illustrious statesman; a cavalcade of horsemen set forth to meet him at the boundary line of the state, and all the people left their business and gathered along the wayside to see him pass. Among these was Ernest. Though more than once disappointed, as we have seen, he had such a hopeful and confiding nature, that he was always ready to believe in whatever seemed beautiful and good. He kept his heart continually open, and thus was sure to catch the blessing from on high when it should come. So now again, as **buoyantly** as ever, he went forth to behold the likeness of the Great Stone Face.

The cavalcade came prancing along the road, with a great clattering of hoofs and a mighty cloud of dust, which rose so dense and high that the visage of the mountainside was completely hidden from Ernest's eyes. All the great men of the neighborhood were there on horseback; militia officers in uniform; the member of Congress; the sheriff of the county; the editors of newspapers; and many a farmer, too, had mounted his patient steed, with his Sunday coat upon his back. It really was a very brilliant spectacle, especially as there were numerous banners flaunting over the cavalcade, on some of which were gorgeous portraits of the illustrious statesman and the Great Stone Face, smiling familiarly at one another, like two brothers. If the pictures were to be trusted, the mutual resemblance, it must be confessed, was marvelous. We must not forget to mention that there was a band of music, which made the echoes of the mountains ring and reverberate with the loud triumph of its strains; so that airy and soul-thrilling melodies broke out among all the heights and hollows, as if every nook of his native valley had found a voice, to welcome the distinguished guest. But the grandest effect was when the far-off mountain precipice flung back the music; for then the Great Stone Face itself seemed to be swelling the triumphant chorus, in acknowledgement that, at length, the man of prophecy was come.

All this while the people were throwing up their hats and shouting, with enthusiasm so contagious that the heart of Ernest kindled up, and he likewise threw up his hat, and shouted, as loudly as the loudest. "*Huzza*[7] for the great man! Huzza for Old Stony Phiz!" But as yet he had not seen him.

"Here he is, now!" cried those who stood near Ernest. "There! There! Look at Old Stony Phiz and then at the Old Man of the Mountain, and see if they are not alike as twin brothers!"

In the midst of all this gallant array came an open *barouche*,[8] drawn by four white horses; and in the barouche, with his massive head uncovered, sat the illustrious statesman, Old Stony Phiz himself.

"Confess it," said one of Ernest's neighbors to him, "the Great Stone Face has met its match at last!"

Now, it must be owned that, at his first glimpse of the countenance which was bowing and smiling from the barouche, Ernest did fancy that there was a resemblance between it and the old familiar face upon the mountainside. The brow, with its massive depth and loftiness, and all the other features, indeed, were boldly and strongly hewn, as if in **emulation** of a more than heroic, of a Titanic model. But the **sublimity** and stateliness, the grand expression of a divine sympathy, that illuminated the mountain visage and **etherealized** its ponderous granite substance into spirit, might here be sought in vain. Something had been originally left out, or had departed. And therefore the marvelously gifted statesman had always a weary gloom in the deep caverns of his eyes, as of a child that has outgrown its playthings, of a man of mighty faculties and little aims, whose life, with all its high performances, was vague and empty, because no high purpose had endowed it with reality.

Still, Ernest's neighbor was thrusting his elbow into his side, and pressing him for an answer.

"Confess! confess! Is not he the very picture of your Old Man of the Mountain?"

"No!" said Ernest, bluntly, "I see little or no likeness."

"Then so much the worse for the Great Stone Face!" answered his neighbor; and again he set up a shout for Old Stony Phiz.

But Ernest turned away, melancholy, and almost despondent; for this was the saddest of his disappointments, to behold a man who might have fulfilled the prophecy, and had not willed to do so. Meantime, the cavalcade, the banners, the music, and the barouches swept past him, with the **vociferous** crowd in the rear, leaving the dust to settle down, and the Great Stone Face to be revealed again, with the grandeur that it had worn for untold centuries.

"Lo, here I am, Ernest!" the benign lips seemed to say. "I have waited longer than thou, and am not yet weary. Fear not; the man will come."

The years hurried onward, treading in their haste on one another's heels. And now they began to bring white hairs, and scatter them over the head of Ernest; they made reverend wrinkles across his forehead, and furrows in his cheeks. He was an aged man. But not in vain had he grown old; more than the white hairs on his head were the sage thoughts in his mind; his wrinkles and furrows were inscriptions that Time had graved, and in which he had written legends of wisdom that had been tested by the tenor of a life. And Ernest had ceased to be obscure. Unsought for, undesired, had come the fame which so many seek, and made him known in the great world, beyond the limits of the valley in which he had dwelt so quietly. College professors, and even the active men of cities, came from far to see and converse with Ernest; for the report had gone abroad that this simple husbandman had ideas unlike those of other men, not gained from books, but of a higher tone—a tranquil and familiar majesty, as if he had been talking with the angels as his daily friends. Whether it were **sage**, statesman, or *philanthropist*,[9] Ernest received these visitors

---

7. Huzza: An exclamation of joy, encouragement, or triumph.

8. barouche (bə rüsh'): A four-wheeled carriage with collapsible top and two double seats facing each other.

9. philanthropist: One dedicated to the good of mankind.

with the gentle sincerity that had characterized him from boyhood, and spoke freely with them of whatever came uppermost, or lay deepest in his heart or their own. While they talked together, his face would kindle, unawares, and shine upon them, as with a mild evening light. Pensive with the fullness of such discourse, his guests took leave and went their way; and passing up the valley, paused to look at the Great Stone Face, imagining that they had seen its likeness in a human countenance, but could not remember where.

While Ernest had been growing up and growing old, a bountiful Providence had granted a new poet to this earth. He, likewise, was a native of the valley, but had spent the greater part of his life at a distance from that romantic region, pouring out his sweet music amid the bustle and din of cities. Often, however, did the mountains which had been familiar to him in his childhood lift their snowy peaks into the clear atmosphere of his poetry. Neither was the Great Stone Face forgotten, for the poet had celebrated it in an *ode*,[10] which was grand enough to have been muttered by its own majestic lips. This man of genius, we may say, had come down from heaven with wonderful endowments. If he sang of a mountain, the eyes of all mankind beheld a mightier grandeur reposing on its breast, or soaring to its summit, than had before been seen there. If his theme were a lovely lake, a celestial smile had now been thrown over it, to gleam forever on its surface. If it were the vast old sea, even the deep immensity of its dread bosom seemed to swell the higher, as if moved by the emotions of the song. Thus the world assumed another and a better aspect from the hour that the poet blessed it with his happy eyes. The Creator had bestowed him, as the last best touch to his own handiwork. Creation was not finished till the poet came to interpret, and so complete it.

The effect was no less high and beautiful, when his human brethren were the subject of his verse. The man or woman, sordid with the common dust of life, who crossed his daily path, and the little child who played in it, were glorified if he beheld them in his mood of

poetic faith. He showed the golden links of the great chain that intertwined them with an angelic kindred; he brought out the hidden traits of a celestial birth that made them worthy of such kin. Some, indeed, there were, who thought to show the soundness of their judgment by affirming that all the beauty and dignity of the natural world existed only in the poet's fancy. Let such men speak for themselves, who undoubtedly appear to have been spawned forth by Nature with a contemptuous bitterness; she having plastered them up out of her refuse stuff, after all the swine were made. As respects all things else, the poet's ideal was the truest truth.

The songs of this poet found their way to Ernest. He read them after his customary toil, seated on the bench before his cottage door, where for such a length of time he had filled his repose with thought, by gazing at the Great Stone Face. And now as he read stanzas that caused the soul to thrill within him, he lifted his eyes to the vast countenance beaming on him so benignantly.

"O majestic friend," he murmured, addressing the Great Stone Face, "is not this man worthy to resemble thee?"

The Face seemed to smile, but answered not a word.

Now it happened that the poet, though he dwelt so far away, had not only heard of Ernest, but had meditated much upon his character, until he deemed nothing so desirable as to meet this man, whose untaught wisdom walked hand in hand with the noble simplicity of his life. One summer morning, therefore, he took passage by the railroad, and, in the decline of the afternoon, alighted from the cars at no great distance from Ernest's cottage. The great hotel, which had formerly been the palace of Mr. Gathergold, was close at hand, but the poet, with his carpetbag on his arm, inquired at once where Ernest dwelt and was resolved to be accepted as his guest.

Approaching the door, he there found the good old man, holding a volume in his hand, which alternately he read, and then, with a finger between the leaves looked lovingly at the

---

10. ode. A lyric poem of praise.

Great Stone Face.

"Good evening," said the poet. "Can you give a traveller a night's lodging?"

"Willingly," answered Ernest; and then he added smiling, "Methinks I never saw the Great Stone Face look so hospitably at a stranger."

The poet sat down on the bench beside him, and he and Ernest talked together. Often had the poet held intercourse with the wittiest and the wisest, but never before with a man like Ernest, whose thoughts and feelings gushed up with such a natural freedom, and who made great truths so familiar by his simple utterance of them. Angels, as had been so often said, seemed to have wrought with him at his labor in the fields; angels seemed to have sat with him by the fireside; and, dwelling with angels as friend and friends, he had imbibed the sublimity of their ideas, and **imbued** it with the sweet and lowly charm of household words. So thought the poet. And Ernest, on the other hand, was moved and agitated by the living images which the poet flung out of his mind, and which peopled all the air about the cottage door with shapes of beauty, both grave and pensive. The sympathies of these two men instructed them with a profounder sense than either could have attained alone. Their minds accorded into one strain, and made delightful music which neither of them could have claimed as all his own, nor distinguished his own share from the other's. They led one another, as it were, into a high pavilion of their thoughts, so remote, and hitherto so dim, that they had never entered it before, and so beautiful that they desired to be there always.

As Ernest listened to the poet, he imagined

Photo: Kevin & Bethany Shank

that the Great Stone Face was bending forward to listen too. He gazed earnestly into the poet's glowing eyes.

"Who are you, my strangely gifted guest?" he said.

The poet laid his finger on the volume that Ernest had been reading.

"You have read these poems," said he. "You know me, then—for I wrote them."

Again, and still more earnestly than before, Ernest examined the poet's features; then turned towards the Great Stone Face; then back, with an uncertain aspect, to his guest. But his countenance fell; he shook his head, and sighed.

"Wherefore are you sad?" inquired the poet.

"Because," replied Ernest, "all through life I have awaited the fulfillment of a prophecy; and, when I read these poems, I hoped that it might be fulfilled in you."

"You hoped," answered the poet, faintly smiling, "to find in me the likeness of the Great Stone Face. And you are disappointed, as formerly with Mr. Gathergold, and Old Blood-and-Thunder, and Old Stony Phiz. Yes, Ernest, it is my doom. You must add my name to the illustrious three, and record another failure of your hopes. For—in shame and sadness do I speak it, Ernest—I am not worthy to be typified by yonder benign and majestic image."

"And why?" asked Ernest. He pointed to the volume. "Are not those thoughts divine?"

"They have a strain of the Divinity," replied the poet. "You can hear in them the far-off echo of a heavenly song. But my life, dear Ernest, has not corresponded with my thought. I have had grand dreams, but they have been only dreams, because I have lived—and that, too, by my own choice—among poor and mean realities. Sometimes even—shall I dare to say it?—I lack faith in the grandeur, the beauty and the goodness, which my own works are said to have made more evident in nature and in human life. Why, then, pure seeker of the good and true, shouldst thou hope to find me, in yonder image of the divine?"

The poet spoke sadly, and his eyes were dim with tears. So, likewise, were those of Ernest.

At the hour of sunset, as had long been his frequent custom, Ernest was to discourse to an assemblage of the neighboring inhabitants in the open air. He and the poet, arm in arm, still talking together as they went along, proceeded to the spot. It was a small nook among the hills, with a gray precipice behind, the stern front of which was relieved by the pleasant foliage of many creeping plants that made a tapestry for the naked rock, by handing their festoons from all its rugged angles. At a small elevation above the ground, set in a rich framework of verdure, there appeared a niche, spacious enough to admit a human figure, with freedom for such gestures as **spontaneously** accompany earnest thought and genuine emotion. Into this natural pulpit Ernest ascended, and threw a look of

About the Author

Nathaniel Hawthorne (1804-1864) born in Salem, Massachusetts, of Puritan ancestry, graduated from Bowdoin College. With his wife, Sophie Peabody, Hawthorne lived in the now famous Old Manse of Concord. A close friend of Franklin Pierce, he served as a U.S. consul to England. His novels portray his insight into the darker aspects of human nature. Most famous of these are *The Scarlet Letter* and *The House of the Seven Gables*.

familiar kindness around upon his audience. They stood, or sat, or reclined upon the grass, as seemed good to each, with the departing sunshine falling **obliquely** over them, and mingling its subdued cheerfulness with the solemnity of a grove of ancient trees, beneath and amid the boughs of which the golden rays were constrained to pass. In another direction was seen the Great Stone Face, with the same cheer, combined with the same solemnity, in its benignant aspect.

Ernest began to speak, giving to the people of what was in his heart and mind. His words had power, because they accorded with his thoughts; and his thoughts had reality and depth because they harmonized with the life which he had always lived. It was not mere breath that this preacher uttered; they were the words of life, because a life of good deeds and holy love was melted into them. Pearls, pure and rich, had been dissolved into this precious draught. The poet, as he listened, felt that the being and character of Ernest were a nobler strain of poetry than he had ever written. His eyes glistening with tears, he gazed reverentially at the venerable man, and said within himself that never was there an aspect so worthy of a prophet and a sage as that mild, sweet, thoughtful countenance, with the glory of white hair diffused about it. At a distance, but distinctly to be seen, high up in the golden light of the setting sun, appeared the Great Stone Face, with hoary mists around it, like the white hairs around the brow of Ernest. Its look of grand beneficence seemed to embrace the world.

At that moment, in sympathy with a thought which he was about to utter, the face of Ernest assumed a grandeur of expression, so imbued with benevolence, that the poet, by an irresistible impulse, threw his arms aloft, and shouted— "Behold! Behold! Ernest is himself the likeness of the Great Stone Face!"

Then all the people looked, and saw that what the deep-sighted poet said was true. The prophecy was fulfilled. But Ernest, having finished what he had to say, took the poet's arm, and walked slowly homeward, still hoping that some wiser and better man than himself would by and by appear, bearing a resemblance to the GREAT STONE FACE.

 *Testing for Understanding*

1. The Great Stone Face seemed to take on life especially when the viewer
   a. stood close enough to see each facial feature clearly.
   b. glanced at it casually without straining to study it deliberately.
   c. had avoided the opportunity to get an education at a famous school.
   d. was so far away that he could see only dimly.

2. The legend about the Great Stone Face said that
   a. some person who had left the valley would return bearing a likeness to the face.
   b. some individual from the valley would resemble the face from his childhood.
   c. the person who resembled the face from birth would become a great man.
   d. some noble member of the valley would acquire a likeness to the face when he became a man.

3. It was said that the prophecy of the Great Stone Face was spoken first by
   a. the first inhabitants of the valley.   c. the forefathers of the Indians.
   b. nature.   d. the Indians.

4. The person who resembled the Great Stone Face the most, but flawed his opportunity, was
   a. Old Stony Phiz.   c. Gathergold.
   b. Old Blood-and-Thunder.   d. Scattercopper.

5. The author symbolized the ironic end of Mr. Gathergold's fortune by
   a. Mr. Gathergold's name.   c. the fable of Midas.
   b. Mr. Gathergold's copper pennies.   d. the outcome of Mr. Gathergold's palace.

6. The basic characteristic reflected in the Great Stone Face could be described as
   a. all-knowing wisdom.   c. generous love.
   b. enduring faith.   d. strict justice.

7. Ernest's life proves that
   a. the growth of character is largely unfelt by the person himself.
   b. character cannot be achieved by conscious effort.
   c. notable characters do not achieve their greatness far away and then return home.
   d. winsome speech is the mark of great character.

8. The man least like the Great Stone Face both in appearance and character was
   a. Mr. Gathergold.   c. Old Stony Phiz.
   b. Old Blood-and-Thunder.   d. the poet genius.

9. The difference between Ernest and the poet genius was mostly a matter of
   a. aspiration.   b. thought.   c. practice.   d. speech.

10. The statement which best expresses the theme of the story is
    a. "Wisdom comes to those who carefully meditate on their surroundings."
    b. "Imperfect men can never recognize true greatness."
    c. "What we love, we shall grow to resemble."
    d. "If you believe something firmly, it will come true at last."

Reading for Understanding

1. *But the secret was that the boy's tender and confiding simplicity discerned what other people could not see; and thus the love, which was meant for all, became his peculiar portion.*
   Most people were untouched by the Great Stone Face's influence because
   a. their approach to life was not as simple and trustful.
   b. they would not confide in the Great Stone Face.
   c. they were not naturally gifted with the discernment that Ernest had.
   d. they were no longer in their young and tender years.

2. *He knew, boy as he was, that there were a thousand ways in which Mr. Gathergold, with his vast wealth, might transform himself into an angel of beneficence, and assume a control over human affairs as wide and benignant as the smile of the Great Stone Face.*
   Ernest believed that Mr. Gathergold
   a. had the power to fake a resemblance to the Great Stone Face.
   b. had enough money to change himself into a world dictator.
   c. could use his wealth to carry out the goodness in the Great Stone Face.
   d. couldn't bring himself to do what he would have had the resources to do.

3. *While his friends were doing their best to make him President, Old Stony Phiz, as he was called, set out on a visit to the valley where he was born. Of course, he had no other object than to shake hands with his fellow-citizens, and neither thought nor cared about any effect which his progress through the country might have upon the election.*
   Old Stony Phiz visited his boyhood community to
   a. win votes for his election.
   b. renew friendships rather than win votes.
   c. rest while his friends worked to get him elected.
   d. ignore his friend's idea of making him President.

4. *This man of genius, we may say, had come down from heaven with wonderful endowments. If he sang of a mountain, the eyes of all mankind beheld a mightier grandeur reposing on its breast, or soaring to its summit, than had before been seen there.*
   The poet described here had the ability to
   a. make nature seem better than it really was.
   b. add imaginary beauties to natural features.

c. give people deeper insight into nature's beauty.

d. get everyone to take an interest in the study of nature.

5. *Often had the poet held intercourse with the wittiest and the wisest, but never before with a man like Ernest, whose thoughts and feelings gushed up with such a natural freedom, and who made great truths so familiar by his simple utterance of them.*

Ernest had the rare ability to

a. express complex ideas in everyday terms.

b. discover truth with little effort on his part.

c. take a simple truth and make it lofty and profound.

d. make a trivial fact seem like a great truth just by saying it.

Meditating for Meaning

1. It was an education simply to look at the Great Stone Face.
   a. What made this true?
   b. What effect did many people think the face had on the valley?
   c. In what sense might this have been true?

2. Some people lost faith in the prophecy about the face.
   a. What caused them to lose faith?
   b. What then must a person avoid in order to keep a lofty vision?

3. The Great Stone Face became a teacher to Ernest as he grew to manhood. What did it teach him?

4. The four men associated with the face during Ernest's life represent the four basic paths to fame.
   a. Name these four paths.
   b. By observing these four men, what do you conclude is the difference between fame and greatness?

5. The first resemblance to the Great Stone Face was credited to Mr. Gathergold.
   a. According to Hawthorne, where had he gotten his extraordinary ability to acquire more wealth than others?
   b. Check *wealth* in a Bible concordance or topical Bible to find a verse that proves this as the source of wealth.
   c. What characteristic did Mr. Gathergold lack which was a dominant trait of the Great Stone Face?
   d. How did Mr. Gathergold's life prove this lack?

6. Ernest attracted little notice from his neighbors.
   a. What was Ernest's one oddity which his neighbors noticed?
   b. Why were they willing to overlook this "folly"?
   c. What is ironic about the fact that they pardoned his "folly" on the basis of his good characteristics?
   d. How might this same thing take place in the Christian's life today?

7. The next prospective resemblance to the face was Old Blood-and-Thunder.
   a. What "recollection" did his old schoolmates have about him?
   b. What was somewhat amusing and strange about their recollection?
   c. By this, what is Hawthorne saying about the "impressive" associations many people make to "prove" their points?

8. Even before Ernest saw him, he considered Old Blood-and-Thunder an unlikely candidate to resemble the face.
   a. Why did Ernest feel this way?
   b. On what basis then did he trust that this was the long-looked-for personage?
   c. To his dismay, what contrast did Ernest see between the two faces?

9. Meanwhile Ernest continued to acquire wisdom.
   a. By what means did he acquire this wisdom?
   b. In what way was he a preacher?

10. Next appeared Old Stony Phiz.
    a. What great ability did he have?
    b. How had he perverted his ability?
    c. Note that this man changed his name to become a politician. What could such a change symbolize about him?
    d. What does the sound of the last part of his name suggest about him?
    e. What sad observations, in accord with the idea suggested by his name, did Ernest make of Old Stony Phiz in spite of the vague similarity to the Great Stone Face?

11. Ernest had to admit to his neighbor that he saw little or no likeness between Old Stony Phiz and the Great Stone Face.
    a. What did his neighbor respond to this?
    b. According to this example, what will a fool do when truth does not fit his wishes?

12. Ernest became an old man. "But," the story says, "not in vain had he grown old."
    a. Why was this said of him?
    b. What significance do you see in his name?

13. Compare Ernest's anticipation of each of the long-looked-for personages with that of his neighbors'.
    a. How did their reasons for wanting to see this personage differ? Hint: Whom did each give the most glory, the personage or the face?
    b. How did their responses upon first seeing the people with the supposed likeness differ?
    c. How do you account for these contrasting responses?
    d. At what point in each instance did Ernest's neighbors come to the same conclusions as Ernest about the likeness of each man to the Stone Face?
    e. It seems Ernest's neighbors finally gave up waiting for a person who would resemble the Great Stone Face. Why did Ernest never give up?

14. The poet genius came on the scene last.
    a. What unusual ability did he have?
    b. Why were his words only an echo and not powerfully moving like Ernest's?

15. Not Ernest's neighbors, but the poet was the first to recognize Ernest's resemblance to the Great Stone Face.
    a. Why do you think Ernest's neighbors failed to see this resemblance?
    b. How did Ernest respond to the poet's identification?
    c. Why would you expect him to respond in this way?

16. Compare the truth of this story to 2 Corinthians 3:18.
    a. The picture in this Scripture portrays the Christian looking into a mirror. What is opposite about the way this mirror works from the way ordinary mirrors work?
    b. What do we see as we look into this mirror?
    c. What happens as we look into this mirror?
    d. There are two aspects involved in this process. What besides looking must we do in order for this to take place? (See James 1:22-25.)
    e. According to 2 Corinthians 3:18, what else is essential for this to take place?
    f. What was the mirror which Ernest was looking into?
    g. What besides looking did Ernest do in order for this mirror to be effective in his life?

Looking for Literary Technique

Have you ever listened to someone tell a story that was like a puzzle from which several of the key pieces are lost? When they were finished you looked at someone else, frowned, and shook your head. The story just didn't add up. There were missing links.

A good short story, however, has no missing links, no lost puzzle pieces. Every part of the story fits neatly into the final picture, nothing extra, nothing missing. This unity most often occurs in a complication plot type story. Notice how Hawthorne, by repeating key ideas throughout the mounting crises, created unity.

1. Outline or diagram the complication plot of "The Great Stone Face." The crises will be the various appearances of supposed likenesses of the Stone Face.

2. Look for unifying details of the plot you just outlined.
   a. At what time of the day does the story beginning, most of the crises, and ending take place?
   b. What convinced the people each time that the expected visitor was the long-awaited likeness?
   c. How did Ernest's neighbors anticipate each appearance?
   d. How did Ernest anticipate each appearance?
   e. What did Ernest's neighbors conclude upon first witnessing each supposed likeness?
   f. What did Ernest conclude upon first witnessing each supposed likeness?
   g. How did Ernest's neighbors respond as the popularity of each person waned?
   h. How did Ernest respond?

3. To arrive at an effective climax and conclusion, there must be differences between the crises to accent the unity.
   a. What differences in the mounting crises add impact to them?
   b. How does the author convince you that the likeness to the Stone Face was at last found and that the people will not need to conclude, as always before, that they were mistaken?

Writing for Skill

Develop the following situation into a story with carefully planned characterization and plot. Try to develop carefully unified crises which build to a climax.

A boy gets permission from his parents to have his clean-cut friend, the son of a drunkard, move in with him when the friend's family breaks up. Later, some money is lost, and the evidence points to the drunkard's son, who at the same time purchases some articles worth the amount that is missing. The money, which was mislaid, is finally found, and the family learns that the innocent boy earned the money he spent.

The Doctor of Afternoon Arm

by Norman Duncan

The day had been a hard one, a cold one, and a long one. Doctor Rolfe was an old man and tonight retirement sounded sweet. But when it was a question of Dolly West's eyesight or his own comfort, Doctor Rolfe knew what he must do. Read with bated breath the narrow escapes of a Newfoundland doctor who placed his life on the line for the good of a patient.

Defining for Comprehension

Choose the word or phrase below which best defines each word at the left as it is used in the story.

1. **hilarious**	a. sophisticated	b. uproarious	c. assorted
2. **appalling**	a. dismaying	b. hesitating	c. attractive
3. **detonation**	a. voice inflection	b. explosion	c. demand
4. **plainted**	a. lisped	b. established	c. wailed
5. **tedious**	a. cruel	b. winding	c. wearisome
6. **chagrined**	a. annoyed	b. amused	c. wearied
7. **indubitably**	a. undoubtedly	b. permanently	c. reluctantly
8. **ominous**	a. threatening	b. momentary	c. hungry

9. petulant	a. careful	b. impulsive	c. irritable
10. dispatch	a. disconnect	b. send	c. remedy
11. impenetrable	a. unconvinced	b. dense	c. contrary
12. contemplated	a. considered	b. argued	c. circled
13. catastrophe	a. decay	b. tragedy	c. tomb
14. conjecture	a. divide	b. speculate	c. insert
15. unromantic	a. realistic; harsh	b. arrogant	c. heathen
16. callow	a. insensitive	b. pale	c. careless
17. inert	a. heedless	b. motionless	c. unharmed
18. stanched	a. posed	b. stopped	c. whitened
19. succinct	a. brief; concise	b. surrounding	c. completed
20. mincing	a. careful; small	b. cringing	c. arguing
21. marooned	a. embarrassed	b. isolated	c. dangerously tilted
22. contorted	a. abused	b. twisted	c. replied angrily
23. incumbrance	a. memory	b. trespass	c. hindrance
24. agitated	a. disturbed	b. exercised	c. removed
25. impending	a. hanging in midair	b. imminent	c. forcing upon
26. contingencies	a. uncertainties	b. requirements	c. hints
27. laved	a. bathed	b. stitched	c. allowed
28. pecuniary	a. ridiculous	b. insignificant	c. paying

The Doctor of Afternoon Arm

It was March weather. There was sunshine and thaw. Anxious *Bight*[1] was caught over with rotten ice from Ragged Run Harbor to the *heads of Afternoon Arm.*[2] A rumor of seals on the Arctic drift ice off shore had come in from the Spotted Horses. It inspired instant haste in all the cottages of Ragged Run—an eager, stumbling haste. In Bad-Weather Tom West's kitchen, somewhat after ten o'clock in the morning, in the midst of this **hilarious** scramble to be off to

---

1. Bight: A wide bay formed by a curve in a shoreline.
2. heads of Afternoon Arm: Outer ends of a projection of land.

the floe, there was a flash and spit of fire, and the clap of an explosion, and the clatter of a sealing gun on the bare floor; and in the breathless, dead, little interval between the **appalling detonation** and a man's groan of dismay followed by a woman's choke and scream of terror, Dolly West, Bad-Weather Tom's small maid, stood swaying, wreathed in gray smoke, her little hands pressed tight to her eyes.

She was—or rather had been—a pretty little creature. There had been yellow curls—in the Newfoundland way—and rosy cheeks and grave blue eyes; but now of all this shy, fair loveliness—

"You've killed her!"

"No—no!"

Dolly dropped her hands. She reached out, then, for something to grasp. And she **plainted**, "I ithn't dead, Mother. I juth—I juth can't thee." She extended her hands. They were discolored, and there was a slow, red drip. "They're all wet!" she complained.

By this time the mother had the little girl gathered close in her arms. She moaned, "The doctor!"

Terry West caught up his cap and mittens and sprang to the door.

"Not by the Bight!" Bad-Weather shouted.

"No, sir."

Dolly West whimpered, "It thmart-th, Mother!"

"By Mad Harry an' Thank-the-Lord!"

"Ay, sir."

Dolly screamed—now, "It hurt-th! Oh, oh, it hurt-th!"

"An' haste, lad!"

"Ay, sir."

There was no doctor in Ragged Run Harbor; there was a doctor at Afternoon Arm, however—across Anxious Bight. Terry West avoided the rotten ice of the Bight and took the longshore trail by way of Mad Harry and Thank-the-Lord. At noon he was past Mad Harry, his little legs wearing well and his breath coming easily through his expanded nostrils. He had not paused; and at four o'clock—still on a dogtrot—he had hauled down the chimney smoke of Thank-the-Lord and was bearing up for Afternoon Arm.

Early dusk caught him short-cutting the doubtful ice of Thank-the-Lord Cove; and half an hour later, midway of the passage to Afternoon Arm, with two miles left to accomplish—dusk falling thick and cold, then, a frosty wind blowing—Creep Head of the Arm looming black and solid—he dropped through the ice and vanished.

Returning from a professional call at Tumble Tickle in clean, sunlit weather, with nothing more **tedious** than eighteen miles of wilderness trail and rough floe ice behind him, Doctor Rolfe was **chagrined** to discover himself fagged out. He had come heartily down the trail from Tumble Tickle, but on the ice in the *shank of the day*[3] there had been eleven miles of the floe—he had lagged and complained under what was **indubitably** the weight of his sixty-three years. He was slightly perturbed. He had been fagged out before, to be sure. A man cannot practice medicine out of a Newfoundland outport harbor for thirty-seven years and not know what it means to stomach a physical exhaustion. It was not that. What perturbed Doctor Rolfe was the singular coincidence of a touch of melancholy with the **ominous** complaint of his lean old legs. And presently there was a more disquieting revelation. In the drear, frosty dusk, when he rounded Creep Head, *opened the lights*[4] of Afternoon Arm, and caught the warm, yellow gleam of the lamp in the surgery window, his expectation ran all at once to his supper and his bed. He was hungry—that was true. Sleepy? No; he was not sleepy. Yet he wanted to go to bed. Why? He wanted to go to bed in the way that old men want to go to bed—less to sleep than just to sigh and stretch out and rest. And this anxious wish for bed—just to stretch out and rest—held its definite implication. It was more than symptomatic—it was shocking.

"That's age!"

It was.

---

3. shank of the day: Latter part of the day.

4. opened the lights: Sighted the lights ahead.

"Hereafter, as an old man should," Doctor Rolfe resolved, "I go with caution and I take my ease."

And it was in this determination that Doctor Rolfe opened the surgery door and came gratefully into the warmth and light and familiar odors of the little room. Caution was the wisdom and the privilege of age, wasn't it? He reflected after supper in the glow of the surgery fire. There was no shame in it, was there? Did duty require of a man that he should practice medicine out of Afternoon Arm for thirty-seven years—in all sorts of weather and along a hundred and thirty miles of the worst coast in the world—and go recklessly into a future of increasing inadequacy? It did not! He had stood his watch. What did he owe life? Nothing—nothing! He had paid in full. Well, then, what did life owe him? It owed him something, didn't it? Didn't life owe him at least an old age of reasonable ease and self-respecting independence? It did!

By this time the more he reflected, warming his lean, aching shanks the while, the more he dwelt upon the bitter incidents of that one hundred and thirty miles of harsh coast, through the thirty-seven years he had managed to survive the winds and seas and frosts of it; and the more he dwelt upon his straitened circumstances and increasing age, the more **petulant** he grew.

It was in such moods as this that Doctor Rolfe was accustomed to recall the professional services he had rendered and to **dispatch** bills therefor; and now he fumbled through the litter of his old desk for pen and ink, drew a dusty, yellowing heap of statements of accounts from a dusty pigeonhole, and set himself to work, fuming and grumbling all the while. "I'll *tilt the fee!*[5]" he determined. This was to be the new policy—to "tilt the fee," to demand payment, to go with caution; in this way to provide for an old age of reasonable ease and self-respecting independence. And Doctor Rolfe began to make out statements of accounts due for services rendered.

From this labor and petulant reflection Doctor Rolfe was withdrawn by a tap on the surgery

door. He called "Come in!" with no heart for the event. It was no night to be abroad on the ice. Yet the tap could mean but one thing—somebody was in trouble; and as he called "Come in!" and looked up from the statement of account, and while he waited for the door to open, his pen poised and his face in a pucker of trouble, he considered the night and wondered what strength was left in his lean old legs.

A youngster—he had been dripping wet and was now sparkling all over with frost and ice—intruded.

"Thank-the-Lord Cove?"

"No, sir."

"Mad Harry?"

"Ragged Run, sir."

"Bad-Weather West's lad?"

"Yes, sir."

"Been in the water?"

The boy grinned. He was ashamed of himself. "Yes, sir. I falled through the ice, sir."

"Come across the Bight?"

The boy stared. "No, sir. A cat couldn't cross the Bight the night, sir. 'Tis all rotten. I come alongshore by Mad Harry an' Thank-the-Lord. I dropped through all of a sudden, sir, in Thank-the-Lord Cove."

"Who's sick?"

"Pop's gun went off, sir."

Doctor Rolfe rose. "'Pop's gun went off!' Who was in the way?"

"Dolly, sir."

"And Dolly in the way! And Dolly—"

"She've gone blind, sir. An' her cheek, sir—an' one ear, sir—"

"What's the night?"

"Blowin' up, sir. There's a scud. An' the moon—"

"You didn't cross the Bight? Why not?"

"'Tis rotten from shore t' shore. I'd not try the Bight, sir, this night."

"No?"

"No, sir." The boy was very grave.

"Mm-m."

All this while Doctor Rolfe had been moving about the surgery in sure haste—packing a waterproof case with little instruments and vials and whatnot. And now he got quickly into

---

5. tilt the fee: Raise his profesional fees.

his boots and jacket, pulled down his coonskin cap, pulled up his sealskin gloves, handed Bad-Weather West's boy over to his housekeeper for supper and bed (he was a bachelor man), and closed the surgery door upon himself.

Doctor Rolfe took to the harbor ice and drove head down into the gale. There were ten miles to go. It was to be a night's work. He settled himself doggedly. It was heroic. In the circumstances, however, this aspect of the night's work was not stimulating to a tired old man. It was a mile and a half to Creep Head, where Afternoon Tickle led a narrow way from the Shelter of Afternoon Arm to Anxious Bight and the open sea; and from the lee of Creep Head—a straightaway across Anxious Bight—it was nine miles to Blow-me-Down Dick of Ragged Run Harbor. And Doctor Rolfe had rested but three hours. And he was old.

Impatient to revive the accustomed comfort and glow of strength, he began to run. When he came to Creep Head and there paused to survey Anxious Bight in a flash of the moon, he was tingling and warm and limber and eager. Yet he was dismayed by the prospect. No man could cross from Creep Head to Blow-me-Down Dick of Ragged Run Harbor in the dark. Doctor Rolfe considered the light. Communicating masses of ragged cloud were driving low across Anxious Bight. Offshore there was a sluggish bank of black cloud. The moon was risen and full. It was obscured. The intervals of light were less than the intervals of shadow. Sometimes a wide, **impenetrable** cloud, its edges alight, darkened the moon altogether. Still, there was light enough. All that was definitely ominous was the bank of black cloud lying sluggishly offshore. The longer Doctor Rolfe **contemplated** its potentiality for **catastrophe** the more he feared it. "If I were to be overtaken by snow!"

It was blowing high. There was the bite and shiver of frost in the wind. Half a gale ran in from the open sea. Midway of Anxious Bight it would be a saucy, hampering, stinging head wind. And beyond Creep Head the ice was in doubtful condition. A man might **conjecture**;

that was all. It was mid-spring. Freezing weather had of late alternated with periods of thaw and rain. There had been windy days. Anxious Bight had even once been clear of ice. A westerly wind had broken the ice and swept it out beyond the heads. In a gale from the northeast, however, these fragments had returned with accumulations of Arctic *pans and hummocks*[6] from the Labrador current; and a frosty night had caught them together and sealed them to the cliffs of the coast. It was a most delicate attachment—one pan to the other and the whole to the rocks. It had yielded somewhat—it must have gone rotten—in the weather of that day. What the frost had accomplished since dusk could be determined only upon trial.

"Soft as cheese!" Doctor Rolfe concluded. "Rubber ice and air holes!"

There was another way to Ragged Run—the way by which Terry West had come. It skirted the shore of Anxious Bight—Mad Harry and Thank-the-Lord and Little Harbor Deep—and something more than multiplied the distance by one and a half. Doctor Rolfe was completely aware of the difficulties of Anxious Bight—the way from Afternoon Arm to Ragged Run; the treacherous reaches of young ice, bending under the weight of a man; the veiled black water; the labor, the crevices, the snow crust of the Arctic pans and hummocks; and the broken field and wash of the sea beyond the lesser island of the Spotted Horses. And he knew, too, the issue of the disappearance of the moon, the desperate plight into which the sluggish bank of black cloud might plunge a man. As a matter of **unromantic** fact he desired greatly to decline a passage of Anxious Bight that night.

Instead, he moved out and shaped a course for the black bulk of the Spotted Horses. This was in the direction of Blow-me-Down Dick of Ragged Run, and the open sea.

He sighed. "If I had a son—" he reflected.

Well, now, Doctor Rolfe was a Newfoundlander. He was used to traveling all sorts of ice in all sorts of weather. The returning fragments of the ice of Anxious Bight had been close

---

6. pans and hummocks: Pieces of drift ice broken from larger floes.

packed for two miles beyond the narrows of Afternoon Arm by the northeast gale which had driven them back from the open. This was rough ice. In the press of the wind, the drifting floe had buckled. It had been a big gale. Under the whip of it the ice had come down with a rush. And when it encountered the coast the first great pans had been thrust out of the sea by the weight of the floe behind. A slow pressure had even driven them up the cliffs of Creep Head and heaped them in a tumble below. It was thus a folded, crumpled floe, a vast field of broken bergs and pans at angles.

No Newfoundlander would adventure on the ice without a gaff. A gaff is a lithe, ironshod pole, eight or ten feet in length. Doctor Rolfe was as cunning and sure with a gaff as any old hand of the sealing fleet. He employed it now to advantage. It was a vaulting pole. He walked less than he leaped. This was no work for the half light of an obscured moon. Sometimes he halted for light; but delay annoyed him. A pause of ten minutes—he squatted for rest meantime—threw him into a state of incautious irritability. At this rate it would be past dawn before he made the cottages of Ragged Run Harbor.

Impatient of precaution, he presently chanced a leap. It was error. As the meager light disclosed the path, a chasm of fifteen feet intervened between the edge of the upturned pan upon which he stood and a flat-topped hummock of Arctic ice to which he was bound. There was footing for the tip of his gaff midway below. He felt for this footing to entertain himself while the moon delayed. It was there. He was tempted. The chasm was critically deep for the length of the gaff. Worse than that, the hummock was higher than the pan. Doctor Rolfe peered across. It was not *much* higher. It would merely be necessary to lift stoutly at the climax of the leap. And there was need of haste—a little maid in hard case at Ragged Run and a rising cloud threatening black weather.

A slow cloud covered the moon. It was aggravating. There would be no light for a long time. A man must take a chance—And all at once the old man gave way to impatience; he gripped his gaff with angry determination and projected himself toward the hummock of Arctic ice. A flash later he had regretted the hazard. He perceived that he had misjudged the height of the hummock. Had the gaff been a foot longer he would have cleared the chasm. It occurred to him that he would break his back and merit the fate of his **callow** mistake. Then his toes caught the edge of the flat-topped hummock. His boots were of soft seal leather. He gripped the ice. And now he hung suspended and **inert**. The slender gaff bent under the prolonged strain of his weight and shook in response to a shiver of his arms. Courage failed a little. Doctor Rolfe was an old man. And he was tired. And he felt unequal—

Dolly West's mother—with Dolly in her arms, resting against her bosom—sat by the kitchen fire. It was long after dark. The wind was up; the cottage shook in the squalls. She had long ago washed Dolly's eyes and temporarily **stanched** the terrifying flow of blood; and now she waited, rocking gently and sometimes crooning a plaintive song of the coast to the restless child.

Tom West came in.

"Hush!"

"Is she sleepin' still?"

"Off an' on. She's in a deal o' pain. She cries out, poor lamb!" Dolly stirred and whimpered. "Any sign of un, Tom?"

" 'Tis not time."

"He might—"

" 'Twill be hours afore he comes. I'm jus' wonderin'—"

"Hush!" Dolly moaned. "Ay, Tom?"

"Terry's but a wee feller. I'm wonderin' if he—"

The woman was confident. "He'll make it," she whispered.

"Ay; but if he's delayed—"

"He was there afore dusk. An' the doctor got underway across the Bight—"

"He'll not come by the Bight!"

"He'll come by the Bight. I knows that man. He'll come by the Bight—an' he'll—"

"If he comes by the Bight he'll never get here at all. The Bight's breaking up. There's rotten ice beyond the Spotted Horses. An' Tickle-my-Ribs is—"

"He'll come."

Bad-Weather Tom West went out again—to plod once more down the narrows to the base of Blow-Me-Down Dick and search the vague light of the coast for the first sight of Doctor Rolfe. It was not time; he knew that. There would be hours of waiting. It would be dawn before a man could come by Thank-the-Lord and Mad Harry, if he left Afternoon Arm even so early as dusk. And as for crossing the Bight—no man could cross the Bight. It was blowing up, too—clouds rising and a threat of snow abroad. Bad-Weather Tom glanced apprehensively toward the northeast. It would snow before dawn. The moon was doomed. A dark night would fall. And the Bight—Doctor Rolfe would never attempt to cross the Bight—

Hanging between the hummock and the pan, the gaff shivering under his weight, Doctor Rolfe slowly subsided toward the hummock. A toe slipped. He paused. It was a grim business. The other foot held. The leg, too, was equal to the strain. He wriggled his toe back to its grip on the edge of the ice. It was an improved foothold. He turned then and began to lift and thrust himself backward. A last thrust on the gaff set him on his haunches on the Arctic hummock, and he thanked Providence and went on. And on—and on! There was a deal of slippery crawling to do, of slow, ticklish climbing. Doctor Rolfe rounded bergs, scaled perilous inclines, leaped crevices.

It was cold as death now. Was it ten below? The gale bit like twenty below.

When the big northwest wind drove the ice back into Anxious Bight and heaped it inshore, the pressure had decreased as the mass of the floe diminished in the direction of the sea. The outermost areas had not felt the impact. They had not folded—had not "raftered." When the wind failed they had subsided toward the open. As they say on the coast, the ice had "gone abroad." It was distributed. And after that the sea had fallen flat; and a vicious frost had caught the floe—widespread now—and frozen it fast. It was six miles from the edge of the raftered ice to the first island of the Spotted Horses. The flat pans were solid enough, safe and easy going; but this new, connecting ice—the lanes and reaches of it—

Doctor Rolfe's **succinct** characterization of the condition of Anxious Bight was also keen: "Soft as cheese!"

All that day the sun had fallen hot on the young ice in which the scattered pans of the floe were frozen. Some of the wider patches of green ice had been weakened to the breaking point. Here and there they must have been eaten clear through. Doctor Rolfe contemplated an advance with distaste. And by and by the first brief barrier of new ice confronted him. He must cross it. A black film—the color of water in that light—bridged the way from one pan to another. He would not touch it. He leaped it easily. A few fathoms forward a second space halted him. Must he put foot on it? With a running start he could—Well, he chose not to touch the second space, but to leap it.

Soon a third interval stopped him. No man could leap it. He cast about for another way. There was none. He must run across. He scowled. Disinclination increased. He snarled, "Green ice!" He crossed then like a cat—on tiptoe and swiftly; and he came to the other side with his heart in a flutter. "Whew!"

The ice had yielded without breaking. It had creaked, perhaps, nothing worse. It was what is called "rubber ice." There was more of it; there were miles of it. The nearer the open sea the more widespread was the floe. Beyond—hauling down the Spotted Horses, which lay in the open—the proportion of new ice would be vastly greater. At a trot for the time over the pans, which were flat, and in delicate, **mincing** little spurts across the bending ice, Doctor Rolfe proceeded. In a confidence that was somewhat *flushed*[7]—he had rested—he went forward.

And presently, midway of a lane of green ice, he heard a gurgle as the ice bent under his weight. Water washed his boots. He had been on the lookout for holes. This hole he heard—the spurt and gurgle of it. He had not seen it. Safe across, Doctor Rolfe grinned. It was a reaction of relief. "Whew! *Whew!*" he whistled.

---

7. flushed: Excited by a feeling of accomplishment.

By and by he caught ear of the sea breaking under the wind beyond the Little Spotted Horse. He was nearing the limits of the ice. In full moonlight the whitecaps flashed news of a tumultuous open. A rumble and splash of breakers came down with the gale from the point of the island. It indicated that the sea was working in the passage between the Spotted Horses and Blow-me-Down Dick of the Ragged Run coast. The waves would run under the ice, would lift it and break it. In this way the sea would eat its way through the passage. It would destroy the young ice. It would break the pans to pieces and rub them to slush.

Doctor Rolfe must make the Little Spotted Horse and cross the passage between the island and the Ragged Run coast. Whatever the issue of the haste, he must carry on and make the best of a bad job. Otherwise he would come to Tickle-my-Ribs, between the Little Spotted Horse and Blow-me-Down Dick of Ragged Run, and be **marooned** from the main shore. And there was another reason: it was immediate and desperately urgent. As the sea was biting off the ice in Tickle-my-Ribs, so, too, it was encroaching upon the body of the ice in Anxious Bight. Anxious Bight was breaking up. Acres of ice were wrenched from the field at a time and then broken up by the sea. What was the direction of this swift melting? It might take any direction. And a survey of the sky troubled Doctor Rolfe. All this while the light had diminished. It was failing still. It was failing faster. There was less of the moon. By and by it would be wholly obscure. A man would surely lose his life on the ice in thick weather—on one or other of the reaches of new ice. And thereabouts the areas of young ice were wider. To tiptoe across the yielding film of these dimly visible stretches was instantly and dreadfully dangerous. It was horrifying. A man took his life in his hand every time he left a pan. Doctor Rolfe was not insensitive. He began to sweat—not with labor but with fear. When the ice bent under him, he gasped and held his breath; and he came each time to the solid refuge of a pan with his teeth set, his face **contorted**, his hands clenched—a shiver in the small of his back.

To achieve safety once, however, was not to win a final relief; it was merely to confront, in the same circumstances, a precisely similar peril. Doctor Rolfe was not physically exhausted; every muscle that he had was warm and alert. Yet he was weak; a repetition of suspense had unnerved him. A full hour of this, and sometimes he chattered and shook in a nervous chill. In the meantime he had approached the rocks of the Little Spotted Horse.

In the lee of the Little Spotted Horse the ice had gathered as in a back current. It was close packed alongshore to the point of the island. Between this solidly frozen press of pans and the dissolving field in Anxious Bight there had been a lane of ruffled open water before the frost fell. It measured perhaps fifty yards. It was now black and still, sheeted with new ice which had been delayed in forming by the ripple of that exposed situation. Doctor Rolfe had encountered nothing as doubtful. He paused on the brink. A long, thin line of solid pan ice, ghostly white in the dusk beyond, was attached to the rocks of the Little Spotted Horse. It led all the way to Tickle-my-Ribs. Doctor Rolfe must make that line of solid ice. He must cross the wide lane of black, delicately frozen new ice that lay between and barred his way.

He waited for the moon. When the light broke—a thin, transient gleam—he started. A few fathoms forth the ice began to yield. A moment later he stopped short and recoiled. There was a hole—gaping wide and almost under his feet. He stopped. The water overflowed and the ice cracked. He must not stand still. To avoid a second hole he twisted violently to the right and almost plunged into a third opening. It seemed the ice was rotten from shore to shore. And it was a long way across. Doctor Rolfe danced a zigzag toward the pan ice under the cliffs, spurting forward and retreating and swerving. He did not pause; had he paused he would have dropped through. When he was within two fathoms of the pan ice, a foot broke through and tripped him flat on his face. With his weight thus distributed he was momentarily held up. Water squirted and gurgled out of the break—an inch of water, forming a pool. Doctor Rolfe lay still and expectant in this pool.

Dolly West's mother still sat by the kitchen fire. It was long past midnight now.

Once more Bad-Weather Tom tiptoed in from the frosty night. "Is she sleepin' still?" he whispered.

"Hush! She've jus' toppled off again. She's having a deal o' pain, Tom. An' she've been bleedin' again."

"Put her down on the bed, dear."

The woman shook her head. "I'm afeared 'twould start the wounds, Tom. Any sign of un yet, Tom?"

"Not yet."

"He'll come soon."

"No; 'tis not near time. 'Twill be dawn afore he—"

"Soon, Tom."

"He'll be delayed by snow. The moon's near gone. 'Twill be black dark in half an hour. I felt a flake o' snow as I come in. An' he'll maybe wait at Mad Harry—"

"He's comin' by the Bight, Tom."

Dolly stirred, cried out, awakened with a start, and lifted her bandaged head a little. She did not open her eyes. "Is that you, doctor, sir?"

"Hush!" the mother whispered. " 'Tis not the doctor yet."

"When—"

"He's comin'."

"I'll take a look," said Tom. He went out again and stumbled down the path to Blow-me-Down Dick by Tickle-my-Ribs.

Doctor Rolfe lay still and expectant in the pool of water near the pan ice and rocks of the Little Spotted Horse. He waited. Nothing happened. Presently he ventured delicately to take off a mitten, to extend his hand to sink his fingernails in the ice and try to draw himself forward. It was a failure. His fingernails were too short. He could merely scratch the ice. He reflected that if he did not concentrate his weight—that if he kept it distributed—he would not break through. And once more he tried to make use of his fingernails. It turned out that the nails of the other hand were longer. Doctor Rolfe managed to gain half an inch before they slipped. They slipped again—and again and again. It was hopeless. Doctor Rolfe

lay still, pondering.

Presently he shot his gaff toward the pan ice, to be rid of the **incumbrance** of it, and lifted himself on his palms and toes. By this the distribution of his weight was not greatly disturbed. It was not concentrated upon one point. It was divided by four and laid upon four points. And there were no fearsome consequences. It was a hopeful experiment.

Doctor Rolfe stepped by inches on his hands toward the pan ice—dragging his toes. In this way he came to the line of solid ice under the cliffs of the Little Spotted Horse and had a clear path forward. Whereupon he picked up his gaff, and set out for the point of the Little Spotted Horse and the passage of Tickle-my-Ribs. He was heartened.

Tickle-my-Ribs was heaving. The sea had by this time eaten its way clear through the passage from the open to the first reaches of Anxious Bight and far and wide beyond. The channel was half a mile long; in width a quarter of a mile at the narrowest. Doctor Rolfe's path was determined. It must lead from the point of the island to the base of Blow-me-Down Dick and the adjoining fixed and solid ice of the narrows to Ragged Run Harbor. Ice choked the channel. It was continuously running in from the open. It was a thin sheet of fragments. There was only an occasional considerable pan. A high sea ran outside. Waves from the open slipped under this field of little pieces and lifted in running swells. No single block of ice was at rest.

Precisely as a country doctor might petulantly regard a stretch of hub-deep crossroad, Doctor Rolfe, the outport physician, complained of the passage of Tickle-my-Ribs. Not many of the little pans would bear his weight. They would sustain it momentarily. Then they would tip or sink. There would be foothold through the instant required to choose another foothold and leap toward it. Always the leap would have to be taken from sinking ground. When he came, by good chance, to a pan that would bear him up for a moment, Doctor Rolfe would have instantly to discover another heavy block to which to shape his **agitated** course. There would be no rest, no certainty beyond the impending moment. But, leaping thus, alert and agile and daring, a man might—

Might? Mm-m, a man might! And he might not! There were **contingencies**: A man might leap short and find black water where he had depended upon a footing of ice; a man might land on the edge of a pan and fall slowly back for sheer lack of power to obtain a balance; a man might misjudge the strength of a pan to bear him up; a man might find no ice near enough for the next immediately imperative leap; a man might be unable either to go forward or retreat. And there was the light to consider. A man might be caught in the dark. He would be in hopeless case if caught in the dark.

Light was imperative. Doctor Rolfe glanced aloft. "Whew!" he whistled.

The moon and the ominous bank of black cloud were very close. There was snow in the air. A thickening flurry ran past.

Bad-Weather Tom West was not on the look-out when Doctor Rolfe opened the kitchen door at Ragged Run Harbor and strode in with the air of a man who had survived difficulties and was proud of it. Bad-Weather Tom West was sitting by the fire, his face in his hands; and the mother of Dolly West—with Dolly still restless asleep in her arms—was rocking, rocking, as before.

And Doctor Rolfe set to work—in a way so gentle, with a voice so persuasive, with a hand so tender and sure, with a skill and wisdom so keen, that little Dolly West, who was brave enough in any case, as you know, yielded the additional patience and courage which the simple means at hand for her relief required;

About the Author

Norman Duncan (1871-1916) a Canadian journalist, educator, and author, was born in Brantford, Ontario. He taught in various colleges: Washington College, Jefferson College, and the University of Kansas. His best books portray his love of Labrador and Newfoundland where he spent much of his life.

and Doctor Rolfe **laved** Dolly West's blue eyes until she could see again, and sewed up her wounds that night so that no scar remained; and in the broad light of the next day picked out grains of powder until not a single grain was left to disfigure the child.

Three months after that it again occurred to Doctor Rolfe, of Afternoon Arm, that the practice of medicine was amply provided with hardship and shockingly empty of **pecuniary** reward. Since the night of the passage of Anxious Bight he had not found time to send out any statements of accounts. It occurred to him that he had then determined, after a reasonable and sufficient consideration of the whole matter, to "tilt the fee." Very well; he would "tilt the fee." He would provide for himself an old age of reasonable ease and self-respecting independence.

Thereupon Doctor Rolfe prepared a statement of account for Bad-Weather West, of Ragged Run Harbor, and after he had written the amount of the bill—"$4"—he thoughtfully crossed it out and wrote "$1.75."

Testing for Understanding

1. From Ragged Run Harbor to Afternoon Arm, Terry West chose a route
   a. entirely across land.
   b. entirely across frozen sea.
   c. across the firmer sections of ice.
   d. of combined land and ice.

2. All of the following influenced the route Terry chose except
   a. the need for haste.
   b. the danger of soft ice.
   c. his unfamiliarity with other routes.
   d. his father's instruction.

3. The main cause of Dr. Rolfe's fatigue as he returned from Tumble Tickle was
   a. he was overweight.   c. the wilderness trail.
   b. hunger.   d. age.

4. Dr. Rolfe began preparing to go out to help in spite of his weariness
   a. when he heard the tapping at the door.
   b. when he saw Terry sparkling with frost and ice.
   c. when he heard that Pop's gun had gone off.
   d. when he heard that Dolly was hurt.

5. Tom West's response to his wife's optimistic confidence in Dr. Rolfe's coming could best be described as
   a. optimistic.   b. contrary.   c. realistic.   d. despairing.

6. Of the following, the danger which caused Dr. Rolfe the least trouble was
   a. wind and waves.   b. snow.   c. sunshine earlier that day.   d. darkness.

7. Dr. Rolfe's greatest asset in crossing the Bight was
   a. perseverance and skill taught by years of practice.
   b. continual light.
   c. the freezing weather.
   d. untiring energy.

8. The basic strategy involved in crossing thin ice was
   a. to use a gaff.
   b. to use one's fingernails.
   c. never to place too much weight at one place for too long.
   d. to act slowly but deliberately.

9. The story covers a time span of about
   a. 1 night.   b. 12 hours.   c. 24 hours.   d. 2 days.

10. The greatest obstacle between Dr. Rolfe and "an old age of reasonable ease and self-respecting independence" was
    a. his patients' inability to pay.
    b. his lack of a son.
    c. the fact that he was a bachelor.
    d. his soft heart.

Reading for Understanding

1. *Did duty require of a man that he should practice medicine out of Afternoon Arm for thirty years—in all sorts of weather and along a hundred and thirty miles of the worst coast in world—and go recklessly into a future of increasing inadequacy? It did not!*

   Dr. Rolfe was thinking that

   a. it had not been his sense of duty which had made him endure the hardships of his profession.

   b. he was justified in taking life more easily from here on.

   c. he resented the rigors which his profession had imposed upon him throughout his life.

   d. he planned to move to an easier country to complete his practice.

2. *"You didn't cross the Bight? Why not?"*

   " 'Tis rotten from shore t' shore. I'd not try the Bight, sir, the night."

   "No?"

   "No, sir." The boy was very grave.

   "Mm-m."

   From this conversation and the events that followed we know that Dr. Rolfe

   a. is joking about the obvious impossibility of crossing the Bight.

   b. thinks Terry is exaggerating the condition of the Bight.

   c. is considering the Bight route anyway.

   d. has been convinced of the foolhardiness of crossing the Bight.

3. *As a matter of unromantic fact he desired greatly to decline a passage of Anxious Bight that night. Instead, he moved out and shaped a course for the black bulk of the Spotted Horses.*

   Dr. Rolfe

   a. allowed necessity to overrule inclination.

   b. allowed impulse to rule rather than judgment.

   c. obeyed desire rather than obligation.

   d. obeyed caution rather than impulse.

4. *"If I had a son—" he reflected.*

   The rest of Dr. Rolfe's thoughts may have been

   a. I wouldn't have sent him out in a night like this.

   b. he could go along with me on such treks.

   c. I wouldn't need to go on rigorous treks like this. My son could go.

   d. he could carry on my profession after my death.

5. *But, leaping thus, alert and agile and daring, a man might—*

   Might? Mm-m, a man might! And he might not! There were contingencies. . . .

   Dr. Rolfe was

   a. moving from considering the possibilities of success to weighing the possibilities of failure.

   b. considering that he had been unwise to take this route.

   c. moving from despair at the impossible odds to remote hope of survival.

   d. considering that a younger man might stand a greater possibility of success.

Meditating for Meaning

1. By close observation find the following details of this story's setting.
   a. What time of day did this story begin and what time of year was it?
   b. Although the story does not precisely say, what approximate year did it likely take place? Give story details to prove your answer.
   c. In what present-day province and country did this story take place?

2. In times of emergency, most people are willing to sacrifice. Tell what sacrifices or heroism are evident in each of the following characters:
   a. Tom West
   b. Dolly West's mother
   c. Terry West
   d. Dolly West
   e. Dr. Rolfe

3. Dr. Rolfe was a man of unusual character.
   a. Judging by his present age and the number of years he had practiced in this region, how old was he when he began his practice here?
   b. Why was he slightly perturbed as he headed home from Tumble Tickle?
   c. Explain how this perturbation grew into the petulance which led him to dispatch bills for his professional services.
   d. How can you tell from this scene that this petulance and his conclusion that life owed him something were not characteristic?
   e. What importance does this scene have to the rest of the story?

4. Dr. Rolfe determined to establish a new policy.
   a. State in your own words the three terms of the new policy.
   b. How is his determination to establish a new policy ironic in light of the rest of the story?
   c. What was the purpose of this new policy?
   d. What caused him for a time to forget his new policy?
   e. At what time did he again remember his determination to adopt a new policy?
   f. In the meantime he had been so busy _____ that he had no time to _____ .

5. Dr. Rolfe never succeeded in adopting the new policy.
   a. Give the final proof of this.
   b. Why did he never successfully adopt this new policy?
   c. How was the intention behind this new policy better realized by failing to adopt it than if Dr. Rolfe had enforced it? Give a Bible verse to support your answer.

Looking for Literary Technique

A unified story, as you have learned, has no extra details. However, it includes all the details necessary to portray the setting.

1.   Suggest several unnecessary details which a poor writer might have included in this story.
2.   Find a place in the story where the author supplies more detail and explain how these details fill an important place in the story.

This story is further unified by repeating word-for-word several of Dr. Rolfe's thoughts two or three times in the story. The author carefully chose these thoughts as ones to repeat to emphasize the theme of the story in an ironic way.

3.   Find and copy these thoughts.
4.   Explain how these thoughts emphasize the theme of the story ironically.

Writing for Skill

At the beginning of this story, Dr. Rolfe felt certainly that he should provide for retirement. By the end of the story he seems to have abandoned these plans.

Write about a time, real or imaginary, in which you or some other person discovered, through a remarkable experience, the error of a certain pet idea. Unify your story with appropriate details and repetition of the main character's faulty idea. Prove by the story the faultiness of the idea.

Too Dark

by Ruth Kurtz Hobbs

*The fair-weather Christian is so named because he loves Christ only if the sun shines in the experiences of his life. The moment the storm winds of the Christian struggle begin to blow, he cowers and gives up. He has no heart for cloudy weather. Such a "Christian" can no more claim the title **Christian** than the bridge that collapses under rush hour traffic can claim the title of bridge. Our truest character is revealed when we are under test. Notice how Jeanie's true character shows forth when tested in this story.*

Defining for Comprehension

Choose the word or phrase below which best defines each word at the left as it is used in the story.

1. **slicker**	a. boots	b. raincoat	c. hat
2. **canter**	a. long hook	b. fast trot	c. tall jar
3. **navigate**	a. surround	b. travel through	c. become dizzy
4. **nickered**	a. laughed	b. crawled	c. neighed softly
5. **vague**	a. feverish	b. indistinct	c. difficult
6. **petrified**	a. fear-stricken	b. angered	c. exhausted
7. **idiotic**	a. disorganized	b. foolish	c. amusing
8. **mediocre**	a. light yellow	b. average or below average	c. poverty-stricken

9. **blithely**	a. cheerfully	b. recklessly	c. bending easily
10. **moonshiner**	a. night prowler	b. stargazer	c. illegal whiskey maker
11. **coxcomb**	a. red flower	b. rooster	c. roof peak
12. **bantering**	a. sinking	b. flying	c. joking; teasing
13. **futile**	a. causing death	b. pointless	c. productive
14. **illuminated**	a. lighted	b. improved	c. surprised
15. **vexation**	a. irritation	b. exchange	c. falsehood
16. **rejoined**	a. met again	b. responded	c. scolded
17. **condescension**	a. climbing down	b. poor condition	c. haughty stooping

Too Dark

A heaving lid of clouds had closed down on the rim of the mountains. As Sinbad and I topped the ridge, the sky settled even lower and the wind began to whine fretfully. Sinbad quickened his walk unconsciously as the first drops began to spit down.

Suddenly the wind shrieked as if just discovering that it was caged between the mountains and the low-driving clouds. Off to my right, lightning ripped the heaven open from top to bottom, and a moment later, thunder mumbled ominously.

It was a night made for a man and a horse. I loved being out on Sinbad in a storm. From my saddlebag I pulled my **slicker**, and standing up in the stirrups wriggled into it. Then I urged Sinbad into a **canter**, for I was already late.

After that first thunder, there followed a curious quiet. The wind held its breath and so did I. Even the trees were hushed. Then came the sound from behind me. It couldn't be! Yet it was—the distant sound of a car. Who in the world would be foolish enough to attempt bringing a car over this abandoned old logging road?

This trail was a shortcut to the church across the mountain from my home. Around by the road was twenty-three miles; across the mountain, just six. Tonight there was a young people's meeting at the church. We had invited the youth of another congregation to spend the evening with us. They were giving us a program and we were furnishing refreshments.

Late though I was, the sound of that car did arouse my curiosity. Whoever it was would make the first several miles okay. But he would never **navigate** the wash-out that lay between him and the top of the ridge. It was at least ten feet deep. Even Sinbad and I had detoured around it.

I reined up and listened. From the sound, the car was going slower and slower. Then the motor stopped.

Five long minutes of silence. Sinbad **nickered** restlessly. The wind whinnied lonesomely. Another five minutes. Rain started to patter down gently, then harder. A **vague** uneasiness gripped me. From the sound, the car had stopped at, or nearly at, that deep washout.

I lifted my face in the rain. "What should I do, Lord?"

A moment later, with the answer certain in my heart, I wheeled Sinbad and headed back. It was as dark as only a mountain can be on a stormy night. At the edge of the washout I dismounted. The only light I had was a feeble orange ray from a finger light on my key chain. In its dull brown circle of light I saw the indistinct bulk of a car headfirst down the opposite bank. It was literally standing on its front bumper.

Then, as if too exhausted to meet the challenge, the light wavered a moment and went black.

Then I heard a cautious rolling down of a car window. A girl's voice quavered out, "Who are you?"

Talk about a scared voice! This one was absolutely **petrified**!

"I'm Bert Gardiner, at your service. Six feet, three-quarters of an inch in my socks. Black hair and eyes. One hundred sixty-eight pounds without my shoes. Also at your service is Sinbad, a Palomino, three years and seven months old with five gaits and a black saddle."

Something very like a giggle came from the car.

"I'm on my way to a young people's social at my church over the mountain and . . ."

"You are! Well, thank the Lord! Did you hear that, Amy?"

"Yes, I heard it," rejoiced another voice in immense relief. "And it's the best sound I've heard since a good while before you made the **idiotic** suggestion to drive over this mountain!"

"We are on our way to that social too," continued the first voice, ignoring the unveiled slander in the other's remark.

"Are you—?" I ventured with dawning conviction.

"Yes, we are part of that young people's group from Butler's church that is going to give you a program tonight."

"You mean that *was* going to give you a program," corrected the Amy voice. "Just try to recall your present situation long enough, my dear Jeanie, to realize that there won't be any mixed quartet; nor will there be a certain **mediocre** reading; nor will there be any ladies' chorus songs with the fair director standing on her nose in a mudhole at five minutes before the program is to start."

The Jeanie voice laughed without regret. "That quartet wasn't too good anyway," she confided. "And the chorus can sing better when I don't direct them. But I am sorry they will miss your reading."

"I'm not. I wouldn't have missed this for anything. I've gotten into a lot of crazy situations with you, Jeanie, but this tops them all," observed Amy dryly.

"You thought it was a good idea yourself," defended Jeanie. "Look where we'd be if we had driven all the way around the mountain— about fifteen miles away from the church and the program starting right now."

Amy groaned at that illogical "logic." "Where we'd *be!*" she repeated. "Just look where we *are!* Please list the overwhelming advantages of being *here!*"

"Well, for one thing," Jeanie began **blithely**. "We are not far from the church. Secondly, we have been found by a Christian gentleman instead of a drunken **moonshiner** as I was expecting. Thirdly, my car has only two smashed headlights and a crumpled grill. And fourthly . . ."

"All right, all right," interrupted Amy hastily. "I realize now that this is the most ideal spot to be in at the present. I just hate to think of leaving."

During this exchange of friendly verbal blows, I was trying to decide what to do. There was no chance of their walking out the ends of the washout, because one end was nearly straight up and the other a drop of almost thirty feet to the river.

The girls were not dismayed when I informed them of these things and warned them not to get out of the car on the river side.

"All right then, we'll crawl up to the road, worm fashion," Jeanie assured me promptly. "Come on, Amy, let's give it a try."

Never have I felt so helpless. Those sides

were as slippery as soapy glass. I listened to the girls' voices as they inched nearer to the top. There they halted, groping for a fingerhold.

I blundered off into the bushes hoping to find a stick or branch which I could hold down to them. Did you ever hunt for a **coxcomb** seed in a barrel of soot on the dark of the moon with your eyes shut? Well, you know what chance I had of finding a stick.

The girls were still **bantering** back and forth when I returned; but their joking had a forced note in it. Muddy, soaked to the bone, and weary with trying, they clung to the side of that steep bank.

"I'll see if I can dig out a step with my pocket knife," I decided. "Then I can come down at least that far and may be able to reach you from there."

Lying on my stomach at the edge of the hole, I reached down and began stabbing my knife into the bank. Under that slimy top, the clay was almost as hard as concrete. I couldn't see a thing. All I could do was jab around a while, then feel what I had done. Jab and feel; jab and feel.

Finally I wormed back from the edge and snapped my knife shut. "Well, here goes! Watch out down there! If I slip—"

"Lord, please help me now," I prayed as I eased one foot over the edge. A little exploring and I found the step and tested my weight on it. It seemed secure enough. I leaned down.

"Now here's my hand. Grab hold."

Amy was light as girls go, but it took all I had to straighten up from that awkward position and haul her to the top.

Jeanie moved to the spot where Amy had been. Guided by her voice, I again reached down in the blackness. After a few **futile** swings her cold wet hand went into mine.

"I'll never forget what you've done for us tonight," she chattered, partly from cold; partly in the intensity of her relief at being on the way out of that hole.

At that moment right above us, the sky opened and bright blue-white lightning flickered for several seconds. The washout, the car, and Jeanie's face were for an instant clearly **illuminated**. Thunder clapped above us. Then darkness closed in, blacker than before. But it had been enough.

"Oh-h-h." The cry she gave was half revulsion, half fear. She jerked her hand from mine as if she were stung. "I'd rather try some other way," she stammered agitatedly.

Bitterness rose in a slow scalding wave within me. The intensity of it almost choked me. Then the Lord laid a cool hand of peace and love upon my heart, and as I straightened up, the resentment drained from me like the raindrops that were running off my nose.

"What's wrong?" shivered Amy from behind me. "Can't you get her up?"

"Not that way," I answered briefly.

Regaining the top of the bank, I stripped off my slicker and leaning over, dangled it down. "Here's my slicker. Grab hold if you can."

Jeanie's hand finally contacted the swinging raincoat and after a desperate but brief struggle, we three stood together under the weeping trees.

The storm was grumbling its way over the mountain, but it continued to rain. The girls' teeth were chattering like jackhammers.

"We have four miles to the church and the minister's home where you will be able to get warm and dry. If you'd like me to, I can stop at a garage and have them send a wrecker after your car."

"Dad will look after it, thank you," Jeanie stated as stiffly as her quivering jaw would allow.

I smiled serenely to myself. For one moment back there, my own feelings had almost gotten the upper hand, but my Lord was back at the controls and nothing could touch me.

I handed my slicker to Amy. "Here, put this on. It isn't very warm, but will keep you from getting wetter.

"And you take this." I skinned out of my jacket and handed it to Jeanie.

"N-n-no, th-th-th-thank you. I-I-I'm not very c-c-c-cold."

"Put it on and don't be so s-s-s-silly," I mocked her with a dry laugh, leaving it in her hands. She put it on.

In another moment, after Jeanie had almost cried with **vexation** because she had to let me help her into the saddle, we were off, both girls on Sinbad and I walking at his head. Sinbad could see, and I relied on him to get us off that mountain.

Amy talked. Jeanie didn't.

"What is the matter with you?" Amy burst out at last. "You've acted so standoffish ever since you got out of that hole. You'd think Bert threw you in instead of pulling you out. You haven't said a word this whole time!"

"One doesn't have to talk all the time," Jeanie **rejoined** curtly.

"I know, but this is the first time I can remember that you acted as if you believed it. What do you think's the matter with her, Bert? Could she be getting sick?"

"Could be." I knew well enough what was wrong with her, but naturally I wouldn't say.

After a long while, lights gleamed through the darkness below us and Amy spoke again. "Bert, what you've done for us tonight reminds me of what Christ did for all of us. You know that verse about taking us out of the pit and the miry clay and setting our feet upon a rock and establishing our going? Tonight has been a beautiful illustration of that. 'Thank you' is such an inadequate thing to say to someone who has been as wonderful as you have been tonight."

"I did no more than anyone else would have done. Don't you think Christians should always remind others of Christ? If He really lives in us it's natural that others will see Him, isn't it?"

"Yes, but so often we say we have Christ living in us, and yet in trying situations we act just the opposite of the way He would. We fog things up so much with our own unsanctified feelings that the life of the Lord Jesus can't shine through, don't you think?"

"I guess you are right," I admitted as gently as I could because of Jeanie.

It had stopped raining by the time we got off

About the Author

Ruth Kurtz Hobbs (b. 1924) was born and raised in Harrisonburg, Virginia. After studying elementary education at Eastern Mennonite College, she taught for seven years in public and parochial schools of Virginia, Pennsylvania, and Kentucky. Miss Kurtz then married and moved to North Carolina as Mrs. Hobbs. During her early married life and after her family of six children were grown, she again taught elementary school for several years. Mrs. Hobbs has now returned to Harrisonburg. She has written short stories as well as *The Christian Short Story* and *The Master Teacher.*

the mountain. At the minister's driveway, the girls insisted on dismounting.

"You don't need to go to the house with us," said Amy. "If you'll just run over to the church and let the rest of the group know where we are. Then please come over and warm up good before you start home—or are you going to stay for the rest of the social?"

I heard Jeanie catch and hold her breath until I answered. "No, I am not fit to be seen. I'll borrow a flashlight from one of the fellows. Sinbad and I will take our usual detour around that hole and be home in an hour."

Ten minutes later Sinbad and I were headed back up the mountain. I laughed without bitterness as I recalled Jeanie's aloof little statement of thanks as she returned my jacket. "She could hardly keep the **condescension** out of her voice," I remarked to the Lord, who was shoving back the clouds and sprinkling stars over the sky. "But that Amy—she seemed different. I wonder how she'd have acted if she had known I'm black."

Testing for Understanding

1. The first two paragraphs make the storm sound as though it were
   a. a freight train.
   b. a person.
   c. an animal.
   d. a tornado.

2. It was foolish to travel across the mountain in a car because
   a. it was dark.
   b. the road was not kept up.
   c. it was raining.
   d. there may have been robbers hiding out.

3. From the time that Bert first heard the car to the time that he turned back to investigate,
   a. about ten minutes had elapsed.
   b. about an hour had elapsed.
   c. it had stopped raining.
   d. Bert could hear the car constantly.

4. The girls' parts in the program were to be
   a. refreshment servers.
   b. Jeanie, choir director and Amy, reader.
   c. Amy, choir director and Jeanie, reader.
   d. registrars.

5. In the exchange between the two girls, Jeanie might best be described as
   a. silly.
   b. optimistic.
   c. contrary.
   d. having poor judgment.

6. In this exchange, Amy's response might best be described as
   a. encouragement.
   b. poor logic.
   c. humor tinged with sarcasm.
   d. inconsideration.

7. Bert insisted that Jeanie put on his jacket because
   a. he was determined to show her that her fears were ungrounded.
   b. he was concerned for her physical welfare in spite of her aversion.
   c. he felt spite in his heart.
   d. he didn't want Amy to become suspicious, too.

8. Bert only rather weakly agreed with Amy's discourse about the love of Christ shining through us because
   a. it was difficult to agree after having been mistreated by Jeanie.
   b. he knew she was being insincere.
   c. he didn't want Jeanie to be embarrassed or to interpret his agreement as a return of spite.
   d. these were new concepts to him.

9. Bert did not go to the social because
   a. he could not face the people after such an insult.
   b. he felt he was too dirty.
   c. it was too late.
   d. he wanted to spare the girls any further embarrassment.

10. The happenings of this story are most like those of
    a. the story of the Good Samaritan.
    b. Naaman and Gehazi.
    c. the Ethiopian eunuch and Philip.
    d. the parable of the unmerciful servant (Matthew 18:23-35).

Reading for Understanding

1. *It was a night made for a man and a horse. I loved being out on Sinbad in a storm.*
   From this we gather that
   a. Bert had a questionable character which made him prefer darkness.
   b. Bert had a clear conscience which allowed him to be fearless of the dark and storm.
   c. Bert was a daring fellow who took unnecessary risks.
   d. Bert had chosen the mountain route when he saw the likelihood of a storm.

2. *I lifted my face in the rain. "What should I do, Lord?" A moment later with the answer certain in my heart, I wheeled Sinbad, and headed back.*
   Bert prayed to God for help because
   a. he feared that those in the car might be evil men.
   b. he was reluctant to be late to the meeting.
   c. he felt such foolhardy actions didn't deserve help.
   d. he wondered if it was the Lord's will for him to help.

3. *Then I heard a cautious rolling down of a car window. A girl's voice quavered out, "Who are you?"*
   Talk about a scared voice! This one was absolutely petrified.
   The girl was scared because
   a. the accident had frightened her.
   b. she had been afraid no one would find them.
   c. she feared that the voice may have belonged to an evil person.
   d. she was embarrassed.

4. *Thunder clapped above us. Then darkness closed in blacker than before. But it had been enough.*
   The phrase *it had been enough* means that
   a. there had been enough light for Jeanie to see Bert's skin color.
   b. the thunder was sufficient to frighten Jeanie.
   c. there had been enough light for Jeanie to see the slipperiness of the slope.
   d. Bert was glad the storm was no worse.

5. *I heard Jeanie catch and hold her breath until I answered, "No, I am not fit to be seen."*
   Jeanie caught and held her breath because
   a. she was still chattering from cold.
   b. she was afraid the young people would discover that a black man had helped her.
   c. She was embarrassed to have the young people see how muddy Bert had gotten on their account.
   d. she was embarrassed to have done such a foolish thing.

Meditating for Meaning

1. This story shows the correct course to take when facing indecision.
   a. What did Bert do in the story when he was uncertain as to whether he should stop for the stranded vehicle?
   b. Explain why this was a wise action.
   c. What must accompany such an action to guarantee its full value to a person?
2. Amy and Jeanie bantered back and forth in "fun," as friends often do.
   a. Find proof from the story that Jeanie did not consider the bantering totally "fun."
   b. Why is such bantering dangerous in spite of the fact that it is between friends?
3. Explain how each of the following aspects of the weather figure symbolically in the story.
   a. the storm at the beginning
   b. the lightning that lit up Bert's face and the thunder following
   c. the darkness that closed in after the lightning, "blacker than before"
   d. the clouds shoving back, being replaced by stars at the end of the story
4. Explain how the title fits this story symbolically.
5. The flimsiness of prejudice, particularly of racial prejudice, exposes itself when we consider the little things it hinges on.
   a. What made both girls at first (and Amy throughout the story) think that Bert was so wonderful?
   b. At what point did Jeanie's feeling change?
   c. Which standard of judgment was most valid?
   d. What does this show about the reasons for and wrongness of racial prejudice?
   e. What Biblical principle do people forget when they harbor racial prejudice?
6. Amy aptly explained the analogy between Christ's provision of salvation to man and Bert's help to the girls.
   a. Explain the irony of Amy's words about how we "fog things up with our own unsanctified feelings."
   b. How was Jeanie's refusal of Bert's help like men's refusal to accept Christ's help?
   c. How was Bert's response to Jeanie's refusal Christlike?
   d. How does Christ's response to men's refusal differ from Bert's?
7. How do you think Amy would have acted if she had known Bert was black?

Looking for Literary Technique

You have already seen how mention of weather throughout the story contributed to its unity. The storm rages and subsides to correspond to the rise and fall of conflict. A good author carefully plans these details of setting to unify his story.

A well-unified story should not include too many characters and should have a reason for each one.

   1. List the three characters in this story and explain the importance of each to the story.

In a well-unified story the characters should also remain consistent throughout.

   2. Explain how Bert maintains a consistent character throughout the story.

Writing for Skill

Write a story with a well-organized plot including three characters. Keep your characters consistent throughout. Also try to unify your story by matching a varying aspect of setting to the rise and fall of the plot. Mention this aspect at the beginning of the story and again at the end, symbolizing a resolution of conflict by the change in setting. Following are several possible settings for your story:

a family gathering

the school playground

a school bus ride

a family trip

a crew on a roofing job

Getting the Point

Match the following statements with the short stories in which they were major themes. Select the statement that best matches each story.

____ 1. If we fear God, our souls may be free though our bodies suffer imprisonment and death.

____ 2. One small act of ill will if not curbed, can grow to uncontrollable and devastating proportions.

____ 3. Peace with God is far more important than success in temporal things.

____ 4. Children who appear to be impossible to manage often simply lack parental love and attention.

____ 5. There is far more fulfillment in meeting the needs of others than in selfishly looking out for our own needs.

____ 6. The object of our heart's affection and focus has a slow but steady shaping effect upon our character.

____ 7. More important than physical perfection is perfection of character that enables us to accept disappointments calmly.

____ 8. Thoughtless cruelty often irreparably bruises the life of its victim.

____ 9. Those who sacrifice for the cause of right and the good of their fellowman frequently reap rewards that outweigh the sacrifice.

____ 10. Our true character is revealed by how we respond under test.

____ 11. He who serves the least of God's people serves Christ.

____ 12. Before we can influence a sinner's life we must first remove hypocrisy from our own.

a. "Mama and the Garfield Boys" (Grizzard)

b. "The Horse" (McNeely)

c. "Second Chance" (Baker)

d. "Shago" (Pooler)

e. "A Spark Neglected" (Tolstoy)

f. "Cache of Honor" (Hayes)

g. "The Mote and the Beam" (Baker)

h. "Where Love Is, There Is God Also" (Tolstoy)

i. "Whom Shall I Fear?" (Stoll)

j. "The Great Stone Face" (Hawthorne)

k. "The Doctor of Afternoon Arm" (Duncan)

l. "Too Dark" (Hobbs)

Taking Stock of Techniques

Place the letter of the correct answer on the blank beside the number.

____ 1. The plainest statement of a story theme usually appears
     a. in the title.   c. near the beginning of the story.
     b. in the last paragraph.   d. near the end of the story.

____ 2. The action in a short story
     a. is more important than the character.   c. determines the setting.
     b. reveals and forms character.   d. is handled indirectly.

____ 3. The conflict in a story
     a. is most often one of man versus man.
     b. is more often man versus his surroundings than man versus himself.
     c. rarely involves more than one type of conflict.
     d. may include all three types of conflict.

____ 4. The difference between a complication plot and a loose plot is
     a. a complication plot story is longer than a loose plot story.
     b. a complication plot is harder to understand than a loose plot.
     c. a complication plot is more real to life than a loose plot.
     d. a complication plot involves a succession of crises mounting to a climax, while a loose plot is merely a succession of incidents.

____ 5. Flashback is the method by which an author
     a. starts a story at an interesting or exciting point and fills in previous details later.
     b. hints what will happen later in the story.
     c. says one thing and means another.
     d. uses an object to stand for a concept.

____ 6. The author uses the setting of a story to affect the reader in all of the following ways except to
     a. reinforce feelings and ideas in the story experience.
     b. sharpen the reader's awareness of his own surroundings.
     c. highlight or influence character by contrast or similarity.
     d. provide symbols for the story.

____ 7. A figure of speech which compares two unlike things using *like* or *as* is
     a. a simile.   b. a metaphor.   c. personification.   d. onomatopoeia.

____ 8. A figure of speech which gives human qualities to a nonliving thing is
     a. a simile.   b. a metaphor.   c. personification.   d. irony.

____ 9. A figure of speech which implies a comparison between two unlike things is
     a. a simile.   b. a metaphor.   c. personification.   d. onomatopoeia.

____ 10. Connotation is
     a. a word which sounds like its meaning.
     b. the real meaning of a word.
     c. the acquired meaning of a word through association.
     d. an outcome of a situation different from what is expected.

____ 11. The feelings produced in a reader by words and expression used to describe the setting are the story's
     a. connotation.   b. point of view.   c. symbolism.   d. tone.

_____ 12. The eyes through which an author tells a story is the
  a. connotation. b. point of view. c. symbolism. d. tone.

_____ 13. An author has the most free rein in describing his characters with the
  a. first person point of view.
  b. third person point of view.
  c. all-knowing point of view.
  d. objective point of view.

_____ 14. The two points of view which are most nearly alike are
  a. first person subjective and third person subjective.
  b. first person objective and third person subjective.
  c. third person objective and all-knowing objective.
  d. first person subjective and all-knowing objective.

_____ 15. Unity is achieved by all the following methods except
  a. story details emphasizing one theme.
  b. characters remaining consistent.
  c. similarities between the different crises of a plot.
  d. careful avoidance of any repetition.

UNIT 2

Poetry

for the Joyful Life

Life pulses with energy and emotion and so does poetry. For those who love life and find it meaningful and rewarding, poetry provides an ideal expression of their exuberance. "Is any merry? let him sing psalms" (James 5:13).

In one of Robert Browning's long poems, a lowly factory girl, Pippa, enjoying her one yearly holiday, bursts forth in this song:

Pippa's Song

˘ – / ˘ ˘ –
The year's at the spring   a

˘ – / ˘ ˘ –
And day's at the morn;   b

– ˘ ˘ / – ˘
Morning's at seven;   ©

˘ – / ˘ ˘ –
The hillside's dew-pearled;   d

˘ – / ˘ ˘ –
The lark's on the wing;   a

˘ – / ˘ ˘ –
The snail's on the thorn: b

– ˘ ˘ / – ˘
God's in his heaven—   ©

˘ – / ˘ ˘ –
All's right with the world!   d

Photo: Kevin & Bethany Shank

This poem expresses feelings of joy, contentment, peace, trust, delight in nature, and delight in life. God intends that our lives be joyful. He has created us with the capacity to use poetry in communicating that joy to others.

What gives Pippa's song its joyous mood? For one

thing, it contains beautiful word pictures: a bright spring morning with the freshness of dew lingering on the hill, a songbird in the sky, and a lowly snail on a thorn bush.

But her song, like all lovely poetry, owes its feeling of delight to more than beautiful words and ideas. You could describe Pippa's surroundings with beautiful words:

> *It is a sparkling spring morning. Dew glitters on the hillside like pearls. Already the lark wings across the sky and a snail clings to a silvery thorn.*

But, while the ideas may be poetically expressed, no one would mistake these sentences for a poem. What is missing that readily alerts the ear to a poem? There is no rhythm, nor is there any rhyme. Although, as you will later study, poems sometimes exist without rhyme and sometimes even without rhythm. But much of the charm of poetry centers around these two poetic devices.

RHYTHM—The Flight of a Poem

What is rhythm? Rhythm is rocking in a rocking chair—back and forth, back and forth. Rhythm is sawing a two-by-four in half—in and out, in and out. Rhythm is jumping rope—up and down, over and under. Rhythm is pattern, and pattern is the repeated and regular alternations of two or more objects or motions.

In poetry, rhythm is the alternation of accented and unaccented syllables. When we speak, our voices fall more heavily on some words or parts of words. These are the accented syllables which poets mark with a **macron** (⁻) when they **scan** or mark off the rhythm of a line of poetry. Unaccented syllables, they mark with a **breve** (˘).

Try it with your name if your name is longer than one syllable. Listen to the rhythm of a name such as Āl ĕx ăn dĕr or of one such as Ĕ līz ă bĕth. Notice also that while *Alexander* starts with an accented syllable, *Elizabeth* begins with an unaccented syllable. This provides for variety in poetic patterns. One unit of accented and unaccented syllables in a poetic pattern is called a **foot**. Four basic patterns or four different types of feet make up most poetry.

The name *Elizabeth* illustrates perhaps the most common one, the **iambus**, in which the unaccented syllable comes before the accented. **Iambic** rhythm sounds naturally more sober and meditative. Notice that many hymns use this rhythm. For instance:

‿ –/‿ – /‿ – / ‿ –
When I sur-vey the wondrous cross

‿ – / ‿ – / ‿ –/‿ –
On which the Prince of glo-ry died,

‿ – /‿ –/‿ – / ‿ –
My rich-est gain I count but loss,

‿ – / ‿ – / ‿ –/‿ –
And pour con-tempt on all my pride.

Alexander, on the other hand, illustrates a more hopeful and exuberant type of poetry, **trochaic** verse. The **trochee** or one foot of trochaic poetry is the exact reverse of the iambus. The unaccented syllable follows rather than precedes the accented syllable, producing such joyful carols as

– ‿ /– ‿ /– ‿ / –
Hark the her-ald angels sing,

– ‿/– ‿/ – ‿ / –
"Glo-ry to the new-born King;

By just inserting another unaccented syllable in these first two **meters** of poetic rhythms, we form the other two types of feet. Add the unaccented syllable before the accented syllable of the iambic rhythm, and you have the **anapest** or **anapestic** rhythm:

‿ –/‿ ‿ – / ‿ ‿ – / ‿ ‿ –
My Je-sus, I love Thee, I know thou art mine;

You will notice that the first foot of this line lacks one unaccented syllable. This is common for anapestic rhythm.

Perhaps you have already guessed the fourth foot. Add another unaccented syllable *after* the accented syllable of trochaic rhythm, and you have the **dactyl** or **dactylic** rhythm:

– ‿ ‿ / – ‿ ‿ / – ‿ ‿/– ‿
Hail the blest morn when the great Me-di-a-tor

– ‿ ‿/ – ‿ ‿ /– ‿ ‿ / –
Down from the re-gions of glo-ry de-scends.

Both anapestic and dactylic rhythms produce a more lighthearted, freely flowing poem.

Now we have our four patterns of poetry, but there is one more aspect to meter. Just as some names are longer than others, so some lines of poetry contain more feet than others. Just scan a line of poetry, count the number of macrons or accented syllables, and you know how many feet long that line of poetry is. A one-foot line is **monometer** (mə näm′ ət ər); a two-foot line, **dimeter** (dim′ ət ər); a three-foot line, **trimeter** (trim′ ət ər); a four-foot line, **tetrameter** (te tram′ ət ər); and a five-foot line, **pentameter** (pen tam′ ət ər). Few pieces of poetry exceed five feet in length. You may understand why if you have ever sung a song with twelve syllables or six feet per line.

Look at "Pippa's Song" again noting the **scansion** or marks designating the rhythm. Now you should be able to see what gives her song some of its lighthearted joy. Browning wisely chose the tripping lilt of anapestic rhythm to convey Pippa's thrill in living. Perhaps you also noticed that lines 3 and 7 begin with accented syllables, switching the rhythm to dactylic. Skillful poets intentionally insert such variations to emphasize climaxes of thought. Line 3 forms a pinnacle of delight in the time setting of this poem while line 7 points out the reason Pippa can draw her conclusion, "All's right with the world."

RHYME—The Trill of a Poem

But we have not yet accounted for the full beauty of this bit of musical poetry. Browning might have expressed the same idea by saying, "The day's at the dawn," but look what a bond of beauty he would have robbed from lines 2 and 6. The rhyme would be gone. Rhyme, like rhythm, is repetition, but rhyme repeats sounds rather than accents. What precisely does it take to make a rhyme? Let's have a look at the delightful rhyme of lines 4 and 8, *dew-pearled* and *world*. There are four distinct observations to gather from these two words.

Notice first that the macron is above the second syllable of *dew-pearled* and above *world*:

1. Rhyming syllables must be accented.

Unlike the unaccented sounds of the ending syllable in *emerald,* the sounds of *pearled* and *world* ring clearly and distinctly because they are accented. But *emerald* could not rhyme with *pearled* and *world* for another reason:

2. The ending consonant sounds of rhyming syllables must be alike.

The /r/, /l/, and /d/ sounds occur in both *pearled* and *world*. Even though an *e* separates the *l* and *d* in *pearled*, the words still rhyme because the *e* is silent. It is the sound that counts in rhyme. If we add an *s* onto the end of *world—worlds*—we break the rhyme because now *worlds* ends in a /z/ sound unlike *dew-pearled*.

There is another identity of sound between these two words—the vowel sounds:

3. The vowel sounds of rhyming syllables must be alike.

Although they are not spelled alike, yet a dictionary pronunciation would show the same /ə/ for both. Again, it is the sound that counts. *Gnarled* does not rhyme with *world* because it has an /ä/ sound.

There the identity of sounds stops and must stop if there is to be rhyme:

4. The beginning consonant sounds of rhyming syllables must be different.

Homonyms do not rhyme. *Purled* does not rhyme with *pearled* nor does *mourn* rhyme with *morn*. The beauty of rhyme arises from this slight difference at the beginning of the syllables.

It does not matter that *dew-pearled* has another syllable, since only the accented syllable counts. One-syllable rhymes like these and like most rhymes are called *masculine* rhymes. Any rhyme containing two or more syllables is called *feminine*. If we glance at lines 3 and 7, we discover that the ending syllables are not accented in *seven* and *heaven*. Here we move backward in these words until we find accented syllables which follow all the rules for masculine rhymes. It does not matter how many syllables follow these accented syllables as long as they meet one more requirement for rhyme:

5. The unaccented syllables of feminine rhymes must sound exactly alike.

Sometimes poets, even very skilled ones, use imperfect rhymes that do not follow all these rules. If the rest of the poem is well constructed, no great harm results. Likely you never noticed the imperfect rhyme in "Joy to the World":

> Joy to the world! the Lord is *come*!
> Let earth receive her King;
> Let every heart prepare Him *room*,
> And heav'n and nature sing.

Rhyme is beautiful, but if two words only partly rhyme, then they are only partly beautiful.

Rhyme gathers delight according to how the poet fits it into the poem. Browning used an interesting rhyme scheme in "Pippa's Song," which the letters at the right of the poem highlight. Notice that the first rhyme is marked with an *a*, the second with a *b*, and so forth. Then any other lines ending in a word rhyming with *spring* would also be marked *a*. The circle around the *c* shows that it is a feminine rhyme. Any line that does not rhyme with any others would be marked with an *x*.

In your study of the next three poems, you will notice how other poets crafted poems of joy and delight with rhythm and rhyme. But primarily you will see in these three poems, three aspects of life—the joy of life in the first, the meaning of life in the second, and the steadfastness of a Christian's life in the third.

Sheer Joy

Joy is not a worked-up emotional state in which, for a few moments, everything seems to be going our way. True joy comes from confidence that God is for us and nothing can be against us (Romans 8:31). We then realize that everything He allows in our lives and every service we are called to perform is for our good and His glory. Consider the author's basis for joy as you study this poem.

Oh the **sheer** joy of it!
  Living with Thee,
God of the universe,
  Lord of a tree,
Maker of mountains,   5
  Lover of me!

Oh the sheer joy of it!
  Breathing Thy air,
Morning is dawning,
  Gone every care,   10
All the world's singing,
  "God's everywhere."

Oh the sheer joy of it!
  Walking with Thee,
Out on the hilltop,   15
  Down by the sea,
Life is so wonderful,
  Life is so free.

Oh the sheer joy of it!
  Working with God,   20
Running His errands,
  Waiting His nod,
Building His heaven,
  On common sod.

Oh the sheer joy of it!   25
  Ever to be
Living in glory,
  Living with Thee,
Lord of tomorrow,
  Lover of me!   30

Ralph Spaulding Cushman

The Poet's Language

sheer (shir) adj.: absolute

About the Author

Ralph Spaulding Cushman (1879-1960) was born and educated in Vermont. As a Methodist minister and later as a bishop, he pastored churches in Massachusetts, Connecticut, and New York. After successfully inspiring his Geneva, New York, parishioners to pay a large church debt with tithes, Cushman became a secretary on the Methodist Board of Stewardship and Tithing. Cushman wrote several books on stewardship and other devotional prose and poetry.

Checking for Understanding

1. Using the macron (‾) for accented syllables and the breve (˘) for unaccented syllables, scan the first stanza of "Sheer Joy." The scansion of the first line would be (‾˘˘‾˘˘).

2. What kind of rhythm does the poem have, iambic (˘‾), trochaic (‾˘), anapestic (˘˘‾), or dactylic (‾˘˘)? Sometimes the unaccented syllables are omitted in the last foot of a line.

3. How is the rhythm of this poem suited to its subject?

4. Count the number of feet in each line. What kind of meter do we call lines written with this number of feet?

5. Use small letters to indicate the rhyme scheme of one stanza of this poem. Use an x to indicate any lines that do not end with a rhyme.

Meditating for Meaning

1. What kind of joy is **sheer** joy?

2. Poets will sometimes mention a specific thing that is to represent an entire set of things. For example, in line 4 the word *tree* could represent the set of all living things. To what set could each of the following lines refer? Line 5? 8? 15? 16? 24?

3. Lines 9, 14, 21, 22, and 23 describe living with God in terms of natural, everyday experiences. Explain the figurative meaning of each of these lines as it applies to life in God's service.

4. Each stanza of a well-constructed poem should have a distinct theme and yet be related to the theme of the entire poem. State in one sentence the theme of each stanza of "Sheer Joy."

5. From your study of this poem, what would you say is the basic source of the author's joy?

6. In Philippians 4:4 we are strongly urged to rejoice. What thought in verses 5-7 of Philippians 4 corresponds with Cushman's reason for joy?

A Psalm of Life

What the Heart of the Young Man Said to the Psalmist

Sometimes we need to give ourselves a good talking to. Our minds may be in a turmoil and our emotions upset. Yet our hearts know that such a state of despondency is wrong and unreasonable. Then it is good for us to back away from our imaginations and feelings and face reality. That is just what Longfellow is doing in this poem. The psalmist is himself; the heart of the young man is his own. He wrote it when he was 31. His own testimony was, "I kept it some time in manuscript, unwilling to show it to anyone, it being a voice from my inmost heart at a time when I was rallying from depression."

The Poet's Language

destined (des′ tənd) adj.: planned beforehand

bivouac (biv′ ə wak) n.: temporary encampment

sublime (sə blīm′) adj.: noble; majestic

main (mān) n.: great ocean

About the Author

Henry Wadsworth Longfellow (1807-1882) born in Portland, Maine, published his first poem at thirteen. After graduating from Bowdoin College, he taught at Harvard. Sorrow struck him twice when his first wife died

Tell me not, in mournful numbers,
    Life is but an empty dream!—
For the soul is dead that slumbers,
    And things are not what they seem.

Life is real! Life is earnest!   5
    And the grave is not its goal;
Dust thou art, to dust returnest,
    Was not spoken of the soul.

Not enjoyment, and not sorrow,
    Is our **destined** end or way;   10
But to act, that each to-morrow
    Find us farther than to-day.

Art is long, and Time is fleeting,
    And our hearts, though stout and brave,
Still, like muffled drums, are beating   15
    Funeral marches to the grave.

In the world's broad field of battle,
    In the **bivouac** of Life,
Be not like dumb, driven cattle!
    Be a hero in the strife!   20

during a trip to Europe and his second in a fire. Some of his best poetry grew out of this sorrow. Two of his most famous pieces are the epic poems *Evangeline* and *The Song of Hiawatha*. Longfellow is the only American buried in the Poet's Corner of Westminster Abbey, England.

Trust no Future, howe'er pleasant!
    Let the dead Past bury its dead!
Act,—act in the living Present!
    Heart within, and God o'erhead!

Lives of great men all remind us   25
    We can make our lives **sublime**,
And, departing, leave behind us
    Footprints on the sands of time;

Footprints, that perhaps another,
    Sailing o'er life's solemn **main**,   30
A forlorn and shipwrecked brother,
    Seeing, shall take heart again.

Let us, then, be up and doing,
    With a heart for any fate;
Still achieving, still pursuing,   35
    Learn to labor and to wait.

Henry Wadsworth Longfellow

 *Checking for Understanding*

1. Scan one stanza of this poem and determine its meter. Give in two words what kind of foot is used and how many feet there are per line.

2. Poets sometimes use irregular rhythm for special effect or for emphasis.
   a. Scan line 23.
   b. How does irregularity contribute to the thought of line 23?
   c. Find one more example of irregular rhythm in this poem and suggest how it helps to emphasize the meaning.

3. Consider the rhymes used in this poem.
   a. Analyze the rhyme scheme of one stanza.
   b. Choose one example of feminine rhyme from the poem.

4. Poets use sounds in more ways.
   a. **Alliteration** is the repetition of an initial consonant sound in nearby words. For example, *find* and *farther* in line 12 both begin with the /f/ sound. Sometimes this repetition also occurs within words. Find at least one more example of alliteration in this poem.
   b. **Assonance** is the repetition of the same or similar vowel sounds in nearby words. For example,

the vowels in *spoken* and *soul* are similar (line 8); the vowels in *act* and *that* are the same (line 11). Find at least one more example of assonance in this poem.

c. **Onomatopoeia** is using the sound of a word to suggest its meaning. For example, the pronunciation of *bang* echoes its actual meaning and the sound of *jump* suggests the act of jumping. Find at least one example of onomatopoeia in this poem.

 *Meditating for Meaning*

1. In line 1, Longfellow is not likely referring to numbers such as 1, 2, and 3. Check a college dictionary to see what other meaning of *numbers* he probably intended.

2. Twice in his poem the poet refers to Scriptural quotations.
   a. To what Scripture or Scriptures does Longfellow refer in lines 7 and 8?
   b. Find another reference to Scripture in this poem and tell what Scripture is in focus.

3. This poem bristles with figures of speech. Find at least one of each of the following figures of speech.
   a. simile: a comparison that is introduced with "like" or "as"
   b. metaphor: an implied comparison
   c. personification: referring to something that is not a person as though it had human qualities and abilities

4. This poem has been rated as poor poetry because of its use of mixed and illogical metaphors.
   a. A mixed metaphor is the use of two or more comparisons together that do not belong together in actual life. For example: To reach the harbor on the highway of life, we must fight the good fight of faith. Highways do not lead to harbors nor are they the site of battle. Explain what is mixed about the metaphor in lines 17 through 20.
   b. An illogical metaphor is one that is unrealistic in actual life. For example: We need daily showers of blessings from the cloudless sky of God's grace. What is illogical about the metaphor used in lines 27 to 32? Try to think of two ways this is illogical.

5. This poem describes life with several vivid expressions. Interpret each of the following descriptions of life. Try to reword these expressions to bring out their meaning.
   a. "Art is long, and Time is fleeting" (*Art* here refers to any acquired skill, either a fine art or practical art.)
   b. "The bivouac of Life"
   c. "life's solemn main"

6. This poem has a number of weaknesses that have caused it to be severely criticized. Analyze one of these weaknesses in the following questions.
   a. What does the author say is the duty of man?
   b. In what way is he correct?
   c. In what way is the poem weak as direction for life?

7. Consider these additional weaknesses in the ideas of this poem.
   a. From a Biblical perspective, what idea in line 34 is not according to Scripture?
   b. As basic encouragement for life, what very significant concept is missing? (See 2 Corinthians 2:14; 4:7-10; 12:9.)

8. Despite these weaknesses, why do you think this poem remains among the most quoted and the best liked poems of the English language?

9. What are some "footprints" we can leave behind that could be encouragement to others?

The Pilgrim

Who are the true heroes? The world looks up to the soldier, the statesman, the explorer, and the inventor. Monuments are erected to the memory of gallant men of past wars. In the following poem, John Bunyan is calling us to consider a very different kind of hero. Here is one who will stand firm against evil in every form. His life is so different from society about him that he clearly identifies himself as a pilgrim on the way to a better country (Hebrews 11:14-16).

*This poem is from the second part of **The Pilgrim's Progress**. The first part is included in the allegory unit of this text. A study of **The Pilgrim's Progress** will help you see what it meant to Bunyan "to be a pilgrim."*

Who would true **valor** see,
    Let him come hither;
One here will **constant** be,
    Come wind, come weather;
There's no discouragement   5
Shall make him once **relent**
His first **avowed** intent
    To be a pilgrim.

Who so beset him round
    With dismal stories,   10
Do but themselves **confound**;
    His strength the more is.
No lion can him fright,
He'll with a giant fight,
But he will have a right   15
    To be a pilgrim.

Hobgoblin nor foul **fiend**
    Can **daunt** his spirit;
He knows he at the end
    Shall life inherit.   20
Then, **fancies**, fly away,
He'll fear not what men say;
He'll labour night and day
    To be a **pilgrim**.

John Bunyan

The Poet's Language

valor (val′ ər) n.: bravery

constant (kän′ stənt) adj.: steadfast

relent (ri lent′) v.: give in

avowed (ə vaủd′) adj.: declared

confound (kən faủnd′) v.: perplex; bewilder; bring to ruin

hobgoblin (häb′ gäb′ lən) n.: ghost; frightening spirit

fiend (fēnd) n.: demon

daunt (dȯnt) v.: discourage

fancies (fan′ sēz) n.: vain imaginations

pilgrim (pil′ grəm) n.: person on journey with a holy destination

About the Author

John Bunyan (1628-1688) was a tinker and traveling preacher of Bedford, England. He did not take religious life seriously until after marriage. Several times he served prison sentences for preaching without a license and dissenting from the Church of England. During his second imprisonment he wrote the allegory *The Pilgrim's Progress*, which you will study in Unit 5. Though he had little formal education, a fanciful imagination is evidenced in his writings.

Checking for Understanding

1. The rhythm of this poem is (iambic, trochaic, anapestic, dactylic).
2. What is the rhyme scheme of this poem? Circle the letters of the feminine rhyme.
3. "The Pilgrim" has four imperfect rhymes. Find them and tell which rule from page 148 each imperfect rhyme violates.
4. Find at least one example of both alliteration and assonance.

Meditating for Meaning

1. To whom is this poem addressed?
2. Explain the metaphor "Come wind, come weather."
3. Notice what happens to both Pilgrim and those who oppose him.
   a. What effect do dismal stories have on Pilgrim?
   b. What happens to those who try to discourage Pilgrim with dismal stories?
4. Pilgrim has many adversaries.
   a. Explain in what way Pilgrim may be called to face both a literal and a figurative lion. See 1 Corinthians 15:32; 2 Timothy 4:16, 17; and 1 Peter 5:8.
   b. What adversaries does Bunyan refer to in line 17?
5. Use a concordance to find the two places in the Bible where Christians and godly men are referred to as pilgrims. List each reference and tell what tests pilgrims need to endure as given in each of these Scriptures.
6. According to this poem, what character trait marks a true pilgrim?

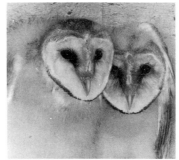

Photos: Kevin & Bethany Shank

POEMS OF A FEATHER

Kinds of Poetry

Although no two poems are alike, they can be grouped according to certain similarities. For example, depending on the type of verse that is used, a poem can be classified as blank verse, rhymed and bound verse, or free verse poetry. A poem may be any one of dozens of different poetic forms from the Abercrombie to the Zanze.[1] If a poem tells a story, it is a narrative poem. If it could be acted out in a play, it is dramatic poetry. If its basic purpose is to teach, then it is a didactic poem. The many song-like poems are called lyrics.

You will become familiar with different kinds of poetry as you study some representative examples.

The Genus of a Poem

Each of the next three poems is different in a very noticeable way. Each has a different type of line or verse. They illustrate blank verse, bound and rhymed verse, and free verse respectively.

While each poem uses a different type of verse, they are similar in theme. In each poem the author is lamenting a situation that he believes should be changed. A lament is always charged with emotion and is therefore a good subject to express in poetry.

---

1. The Abercrombie is a poetic form named for Lascelles Abercrombie, the poet who first used it. The four-line stanzas of the Abercrombie appear in sets of two, having an interlocking rhyme scheme (a b a c d b d c) and varying line lengths (pentameter, tetrameter, pentameter, trimeter).

The Zanze is a poetic form first used by Walden Greenwill. It is a four-stanza, sixteen-line poem with the following rhyme scheme: a b a b c d c d e f e f g a g a. The first line of each stanza repeats the very first line only dropping two syllables from the end each time. Stanza 1 is tetrameter. Stanza 2 is trimeter, and stanza 3 is dimeter. Stanza 4 begins with a line of monometer, followed by dimeter, trimeter, and finally a line of tetrameter which repeats the first line.

BLANK VERSE

Any poem that is written with line after line of unrhymed iambic pentameter is called blank verse. The following lines are written in blank verse:

ᵕ — ᵕ — ᵕ — ᵕ — ᵕ —
Ten syllables in five iambic feet

ᵕ — ᵕ — ᵕ — ᵕ — ᵕ —
Make up a rhythm called pentameter;

ᵕ — ᵕ — ᵕ — ᵕ — ᵕ —
And if these lines are yet without a rhyme,

ᵕ — ᵕ — ᵕ — ᵕ — ᵕ —
This kind of script is said to be blank verse.

Many of the serious well-written poems of the English language are written in blank verse. There is good reason why such a specific meter has become so prominent that a special name is given to it. First of all, the natural accent of the English language lends itself best to the iambic meter. Second, for highly developed expressions of thought, the ten-syllable pentameter is well-suited. Shorter lines of only three or four feet have the familiar song-like rhythm of many of the songs in our hymnbooks.

The meter of hymns is usually not measured in feet of accented and unaccented syllables such as trimeter, tetrameter, and pentameter. Rather, each individual syllable is counted. Thus a line of trochaic tetrameter in a hymn has eight syllables. This provides the three most frequent rhythm patterns of four-line hymns, using numbers to represent the number of syllables per line:

short meter (S.M.)—6.6.8.6
common meter (C.M.)—8.6.8.6.
long meter (L.M.)—8.8.8.8

These meters are all based on the three- and four-foot lines. At times these meters are too short to easily accommodate weighty discussions. On the other hand, if a line of poetry is more than five feet long, it tends to break up into shorter phrases.

While rhyme adds to the beauty of poetry, the restriction of rhyme pattern does hinder freedom of expression. If you have written poetry yourself, you well know the difficulty of finding pairs of words that not only rhyme but form a natural part of the phrasing. Do not think that blank verse is less than good poetry. Some of the most profound and moving poems have been written in blank verse. Your study of "The Man With the Hoe" will show you the strength of feeling and thought that can be communicated with this type of verse.

The Man With the Hoe

This poem of lament was inspired by a painting. In 1884 Edwin Markham saw a print of the painting by Jean Francois Millet called **The Man With a Hoe.** *Markham's own dismay at the plight of common laborers, combined with the fresh reminder of the abused man in the painting, moved him to write the first draft of the poem. About ten years later Markham had the opportunity to see Millet's original painting. Only then did Markham bring his poem to its final form and have it published. The poem so stirred the American public that Markham became a famous poet almost overnight.*

What about the painting aroused Markham to write this poem? The painting is one of a number of paintings by the French artist, depicting the life of the peasant with great realism. You may have seen two of these paintings called **The Angelus** *and* **The Gleaners.** **The Man With a Hoe** *presents a dejected, exhausted laborer who seems to have lost all hope of ever having a better lot in life. The heavy adz-like hoe he is leaning upon and the coarseness of the ground he has just hoed suggest exhausting labor with no pleasure or reward.*

Markham makes it clear that powerful landowners have suppressed the man to this slave position and that they will be responsible to God for their mistreatment of one of their fellow men. The Bible verse at the head of the poem is generally associated with it in anthologies and textbooks, so it must have been part of Markham's original communication of this lament.

Notice how the ponderous blank verse lends dignity to this lofty subject. The piling up of repeated phrases and pointed questions tells us that Markham felt strongly about his subject and that he believed the abuse must stop or society would suffer the tragic consequences.

The Man with a Hoe, by Jean-Francois Millet (1814-1875).

The Man With the Hoe

God made man in his own image; in the image of God made he him.
                                                    –Genesis 1:27

Bowed by the weight of centuries he leans
Upon his hoe and gazes on the ground,
The emptiness of ages in his face,
And on his back the burden of the world.
Who made him dead to rapture and despair,   5
A thing that grieves not and that never hopes,
Stolid and stunned, a brother to the ox?
Who loosened and let down this **brutal** jaw?
Whose was the hand that slanted back this brow?
Whose breath blew out the light within this brain? 10

Is this the Thing the Lord God made and gave
To have dominion over sea and land;
To trace the stars and search the heavens for power;
To feel the passion of Eternity?

The Poet's Language

stolid (stäl′ əd) adj.: showing no emotion

brutal (brüt′ l) adj.: beastly

tongued (təngd) adj.: filled with words

censure (sen′ chər) n.: criticism; condemnation

portents (pȯr′ tentz) n.: prophecies; warnings

fraught (frȯt) adj.: filled

menace (men′ əs) n.: threat of evil

plundered (plən′ dərd) adj.: spoiled; laid waste

profaned (prō fānd′) v.: debased

immemorial (im′ ə mȯr′ ē əl) adj.: reaching beyond memory

infamies (in′ fa mēz) n.: shameful evils

perfidious (pər fi′ dē əs) adj.: disloyal; treacherous

immedicable (im med′ i kə bəl) adj.: unable to be cured

About the Author

Edwin Markham (1852-1940) was born in Oregon, but grew up in California. After graduating from Santa Anna Christian College, he taught and superintended in various schools of California. Around 1900 he moved to New York City where he became a poet and lecturer. One of his most famous collections of poetry is *Lincoln and Other Poems*.

Is this the dream He dreamed Who shaped the suns 15
And marked their ways upon the ancient deep?
Down all the stretch of Hell to its last gulf
There is no shape more terrible than this—
More **tongued** with **censure** of the world's blind greed—
More filled with signs and **portents** for the soul— 20
More **fraught** with **menace** to the universe.

What gulfs between him and the seraphim!
Slave of the wheel of labour, what to him
Are Plato and the swing of Pleiades?
What the long reaches of the peaks of song, 25
The rift of dawn, the reddening of the rose?
Thru this dread shape the suffering ages look;
Time's tragedy is in that aching stoop.
Thru this dread shape humanity betrayed,
Plundered, **profaned**, and disinherited, 30
Cries protest to the Powers that made the world,
A protest that is also prophecy.

O masters, lords, and rulers in all lands,
Is this the handiwork you give to God,
This monstrous thing distorted and soul-quencht? 35
How will you ever straighten up this shape;
Touch it again with immortality;
Give back the upward looking and the light;
Rebuild in it the music and the dream;
Make right the **immemorial infamies**, 40
Perfidious wrongs, **immedicable** woes?

O masters, lords, and rulers in all lands,
How will the future reckon with this Man?
How answer his brute question in that hour
When whirlwinds of rebellion shake all shores? 45
How will it be with kingdoms and with kings—
With those who shaped him to the thing he is—
When this dumb Terror shall appeal to God,
After the silence of the centuries?

Edwin Markham

Meditating for Meaning

1. Sometimes a poet will invert a foot in the meter of a line. This is usually done at the beginning of a line and often follows a pause. Find the five such inversions from iambic to trochaic feet at the beginning of a line.

2. This poem can be outlined as follows. Find the lines where each section begins and ends.
   a. A description of the man in the painting
   b. A question as to who made this man what he is
   c. A question of whether this is the man as God created him
   d. A statement of horror at the extent of this man's degradation
   e. A condemnation of those who have wronged this man
   f. A warning of the coming judgment on those who abused this man

3. What nouns and pronouns does Markham use repeatedly in referring to the man which show that the poet believes the man is now less than a man?

4. Compare this poem with Psalm 8. What contrast do you find between man as God made him and the man with the hoe in the following sets of lines and verses?
   a. lines 13 and 24 with verse 3
   b. line 22 with verse 5
   c. line 7 with verses 6 and 7

5. The man with the hoe is missing many things that Markham believes man was created to enjoy. What general joys does each of the following specifics refer to?
   a. Plato
   b. Pleiades
   c. peaks of song
   d. the rift of dawn, the reddening of the rose

6. In good writing, the simple, expressive word is often preferred above the polysyllabic word. Many long words close together make the reading level harder and can make sentences difficult to comprehend. Lines 40 and 41 have several such words.
   a. Translate lines 40 and 41 into easy words.
   b. Why is Markham's choice of words justified and very effective at this place in his poem?

7. The man with the hoe is a poor peasant tilling the ground of a wealthy landowner. This poem has a universal message and applies to many more situations of man than the specific one portrayed.
   a. What universal problem does the man with the hoe represent?
   b. What does the poet say is the motivation behind such abuse?
   c. Line 32 speaks of a prophecy which the last stanza explains more fully. According to line 45 what does such abuse often lead to?
   d. How does the tone of this poem compare with the discussion of the same problem in James 5:1-6?

RHYMED AND BOUND VERSE

To most people, poetry must have a regular meter and at least some of the lines must be rhymed. That is because most of the poems we read *do* follow formal rhyme and rhythm patterns. Verse that follows some metrical pattern is called bound verse to distinguish it from free verse that you will study later. Verse that has rhymed lines is called rhymed verse to distinguish it from blank verse. The following poem of lament is an example of rhymed and bound verse.

The Jericho Road

Modern man is inclined to think his lifestyle is better than that of past ages. Some may be inclined to think that we are more civilized because of the benefits of science, education, and law. High-speed transportation and communication are credited with linking the world together and putting men in touch with each other. But the author of "The Jericho Road" does not agree. In this poem he is lamenting what modern technology has done to man. Be sure you do not miss the actual reason for lament as you study this poem.

I know the road to Jericho,
   It's in a part of town
That's full of factories and filth.
   I've seen the folk go down,

Small folk with roses in their cheeks   5
   And starlight in their eyes,
And seen them fall among the thieves,
   And heard their helpless cries

When toiling took their roses red
   And robbed them of their stars   10
And left them pale and almost dead.
   The while, in motor-cars

The priests and Levites speeding by
   Read of the latest crimes
In headlines spread in black or red   15
   Across the "Evening Times."

How hard for those in **limousines**
   To heal the hurt of man!
It was a slow-paced ass that bore
   The Good Samaritan.   20

Edwin McNeill Poteat

The Poet's Language

limousines (lim′ ə zēnz′) n.: large luxury automobiles

Meditating for Meaning

1. This poem is an example of rhymed and bound verse.
   a. Identify the meter of each line of the first stanza.
   b. Scan a long meter (L.M.), common meter (C.M.), and short meter (S.M.) song in a hymnbook. Which kind of meter is each stanza of "The Jericho Road"? (One value of bound, rhymed verse is that it can be easily fitted to music).
   c. What is the rhyme scheme of the first stanza? Use an *x* to indicate unrhymed lines.
   d. Which stanza has a different rhyme scheme than the rest?
   e. What is there about that stanza that makes it the pivotal stanza of the poem?

2. The author says he knows "the road to Jericho."
   a. To what Scriptural account does "the road to Jericho" refer?
   b. What in general does the road to Jericho represent?
   c. What is both the literal and figurative meaning of "go down" in line 4. (For the literal meaning, think of relative elevation of Biblical areas.)

3. This poem mentions four groups of people, giving them figurative names.
   a. Who are the "small folk" of line 5?
   b. Who are the "thieves"?
   c. Who are represented by the "priests and Levites"?
   d. Who would be a "Good Samaritan" in our day?
   e. Which two of the above groups could be the same?
   f. How may the situation today be even worse than it was in the time of Christ?

4. The author lays the blame for this sorry situation on modern conditions.
   a. What three "advances" in technology does the author cite?
   b. What ideals are these advances to be working toward?
   c. In actual practice, what have these things done to man that make it hard for him "to heal the hurt of man"?
   d. What is really the motivation behind the development of most modern technology?

5. There is a suggestion of a cure in this poem.
   a. Give several reasons why it is hard for those in limousines to heal the hurt of man.
   b. In the last two lines what does the poet suggest is needed to be of help to others?

FREE VERSE

Free verse is just that—verse that is free of any requirement to follow a rhythm pattern or rhyme scheme. In one respect, free verse is not much different from prose except that its lines are arranged according to the phrasing of speech.

> In fact, I could arrange
> These words that I am writing
> In free verse form.
> With no restrictions,
> I can make the word order
> However I wish.
> But,
> You do not need to be an expert
> In poetic analysis
> To realize that this
> Is not poetry.

To be poetry, free verse must contain poetic language. The free verse poet uses figures of speech and words that suggest deep emotion. Often the words suggest a great deal more than they say. The lines often end with strong words that would be emphasized in reading and are followed by a pause to help bring out the meaning. Stanzas are constructed to make up paragraphs of thought.

Most of what the Apostle Paul wrote is prose. But at a few places his writing can be considered poetry if put in free verse form. For example, consider Romans 11:33-36:

> O the depth of the riches
> Both of the wisdom and knowledge of God!
> How unsearchable are his judgments,
> And his ways past finding out!
> For who hath known the mind of the Lord?
> Or who hath been his counsellor?
> Or who hath first given to him,
> And it shall be recompensed unto him again?
> For of him,
> And through him,
> And to him, are all things:
> To whom be glory for ever. Amen.

There is, however, reason to give some caution about the overuse of free verse. The growth in popularity of free verse in our century coincided with a desire for the lack of restraints in many areas: government, economics, and morals. This led to the movement that promoted immorality and drug abuse in the late 1960s. The undisciplined youth of that era were often called hippies. Their clothing, behavior, music, and poetry gave evidence of an unrestrained life.

This does not mean that all free verse should be condemned. Certainly the message of the following free verse poem is proper, and its free verse form does not make it unworthy of our study.

Another reason to discourage the overuse of free verse is its lack of adaptability to music. The marriage of poetry to music has been and should continue to be a blessing to the Christian church. Hence, there is a continuing need for the writing of rhymed and bound verse.

Lament

Jesus said that on the judgment day many will plead for acceptance on the basis of doing many wonderful works in His name but will not be accepted (Matthew 7:21-23). Once, when commenting on those who would be denied access to the kingdom, Jesus said there would be weeping and gnashing of teeth. At the time, He was talking to the self-righteous Jews who thought they were doing great things for God. It is possible that some today who are busy in church work are actually deceived and are hurting those whom they think they are helping. It is for those the poet is lamenting in this poem.

Weep, weep for those
Who do the work of the Lord
With a high look
And a proud heart.
Their voice is lifted up   5
In the streets and their cry is heard.
The bruised reed they break
By their great strength, and the smoking flax
They trample.

Weep not for the quenched   10
(For their God will hear their cry
And the Lord will come to save them)
But weep, weep for the quenchers.

For when the Day of the Lord
Is come, and the vales sing   15
And hills clap their hands
And the light shines,
Then their eyes shall be opened
On a waste place,
Smouldering,   20
The smoke of the flax bitter
In their nostrils,
Their feet pierced
By broken reed-stems . . .
Wood, hay, and stubble,   25
And no grass springing
And all the birds flown.

Weep, weep for those
Who have made a desert
In the name of the Lord.   30

Evangeline Paterson

Meditating for Meaning

1. Write the scansion for the first stanza of "Lament." Notice the great variety of rhythms and an almost total lack of pattern from one line to the next.

2. An allusion is a casual and indirect reference to a person, event, or writing of another. To be effective, the thing alluded to must be familiar to the reader. If this is the case, allusions are more effective than direct reference because it engages the mind of the reader in making the implied connection. An allusion also brings with it the broad context of meaning associated with the thing alluded to. This makes writing more compact and interesting.

   This poem contains a number of allusions to Scripture. How many of them are familiar to you? Without using a Bible, write down as many of the phrases as you think are borrowed from Scripture.

3. Now look at Isaiah 42:1-3. This prophecy is mentioned as being fulfilled in Christ in Matthew 12:19, 20. Notice that the workers for the Lord in the poem do everything exactly opposite from the way Christ did His work.
   a. In what way do modern religious workers lift up their voices in the streets?
   b. In what way might a religious worker break a bruised reed? (Bruised by what?)
   c. In what way might a religious worker quench a smoking flax? (The tangled, short fibers of flax were used as wicks for oil lamps. What does the smoking flax symbolize here?)

4. The context of the allusion in Proverbs 21:4 suggests that even right pursuits from a _____ motive are _____ .

5. Another allusion to Scripture is "the Day of the Lord."
   a. Find a New Testament verse with this expression.
   b. What does it mean?

6. At that time, these pseudo-Christian workers will see what they have done (lines 18–20).
   a. How have their works now come back to torment them?
   b. What basically have they produced?
   c. According to 1 Corinthians 3:12, 13 what will happen to the works alluded to in line 25.
   d. What could be symbolized by "no grass springing"?
   e. What could be symbolized by "all the birds flown"?

7. Why is it more lamentable for these pseudo-religious workers than for those who suffer because of their labors? (Consider Matthew 23 for this question.)

Checking for Understanding

Types of Poetic Verses

Match each of the numbered characteristics with one of the three types of verse:
   a. blank verse

b. rhymed and bound verse

c. free verse

(Some descriptions apply to more than one type of verse.)

1. a b a b c c
2. well-suited to the rhythm of the English language
3. best-suited for setting to music
4. follows a definite rhythm pattern
5. lines are arranged according to the phrasing of speech
6. ⏑ — ⏑ — ⏑ — ⏑ — ⏑ —
7. depends on imagery and connotation of words to be poetic
8. "The Jericho Road"
9. unrhymed
10. well-suited for weighty discussions
11. "Lament"
12. uses a variety of rhythm patterns
13. "A Psalm of Life"
14. Gained popularity in the 1900s
15. "The Man With the Hoe"
16. ⏑ — ⏑⏑ — — ⏑ — — ⏑⏑ — ⏑ —
17. unrhymed iambic pentameter
18. no definite rhythm pattern
19. suitable for expressing concern about a social problem
20. C.M., L.M., and S.M.

 *Writing for Skill*

Select some subject worthy of poetic expression. Write three poems of four or more lines using each of the three types of verse (blank verse, rhymed and bound verse, and free verse). You may write all three on the same subject or on different subjects.

Here are some suggested topics:

Praise for the opportunity to learn

Joy in the beauty of nature

Concern for the plight of the (poor, refugees, handicapped)

Love for (friends, enemies)

The value of (honesty, cheerfulness, faith, etc.)

Desire to make right decisions

Abhorrence for (laziness, carnal pleasures, worldly fashions, etc.)

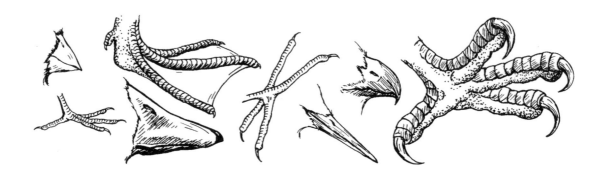

THE ANATOMY OF A POEM

Four Poetic Forms

THE ACROSTIC

There are literally dozens of poetic forms. The book *Pathways for the Poet* (Mott Media 1977, compiled by the author of the following poem) contains over 200 poetic forms explained and illustrated. Some are ancient and some are modern. They originated in many different lands. Once someone invents an interesting pattern for writing a poem, others will copy the pattern and a poetic form is born.

To help you appreciate the structure and value of poetic forms, you will study four different forms. The acrostic is as old as the Old Testament era. Both the psalmist in Psalm 119 and Jeremiah in the Book of Lamentations used the acrostic form. Their acrostics started lines or verses with successive letters of the Hebrew alphabet. Modern acrostics often use the first letter of each line to spell a word. "Infinity" is an example of a modern acrostic poem.

Infinity

I nto the future time stretches its arms,
N ewborn each moment by **omniscient** schemes,
F resh as the dew over meadows and farms,
I **nfused** are the fires of passions and dreams.
N ight follows day in the pattern of time,
I nfinite hours wait over the ridge,
T aking their turn in eternity's climb.
Y esterday's gone, and today is the bridge.

Viola Jacobson Berg

THE TRIOLET

The triolet is an eight-line poem with one of the lines used twice (lines 2 and 8) and another used three times (lines 1, 4, and 7). The rhyme scheme follows a very precise pattern using only two rhymes. Using capital letters to represent repeated lines, the rhyme scheme of a triolet is A B a A a b A B. You will notice that "The Triolet" is written in iambic trimeter with one feminine rhyme. This is not characteristic of all triolets. They may have any line length and be with or without feminine rhyme.

The triolet originated in France. Its lighthearted rhyme, clever repetition, and brevity have made it a favorite with students. Once its form is clearly understood, the triolet is not difficult to write. Examine the following triolet about triolets.

The Triolet

The triolet is **comely**;	A	
You almost hear it sing.	B	
So do not say it glumly;	a	
The triolet is comely—	A	
Nor form its lines so dumbly	a	5
It cannot joyous ring.	b	
A triolet is comely;	A	
You almost hear it sing.	B	

Lester E. Showalter

About the Author

Lester Showalter (b. 1942) born near Hagerstown, Maryland, attended Greencastle High School and Hagerstown Junior College. Raised on a farm near Greencastle, Pennsylvania, he enjoyed tinkering at an early age, and developed broad interests in science and literature. He serves as principal and teacher at Paradise Mennonite School and has written a high school science series as well as much of the *Perspectives of Literature* series. On his family farm where he and his wife Esther raised their four sons and one daughter, he now operates a small orchard as a sideline.

The Bible

The following triolet is iambic dimeter with only masculine rhymes.

> Within God's book
> The truth we read.
> And so we look
> Within God's book
> In quiet nook   5
> With souls to feed.
> Within God's book
> The truth we read.

Lester E. Showalter

A Key to Happiness

Here is a triolet with iambic pentameter.

> Happy the men who always goodness find,
> And do not search the land for bad report;
> But share with others only what is kind.
> Happy the men who always goodness find;
> For evil tends to make a sickly mind.   5
> So with this wholesome truth let us exhort:
> Happy the men who always goodness find,
> And do not search the land for bad report.

Lester E. Showalter

The Poet's Language

warily (war′ ə lē) adv.: cautiously

About the Author

Faustina Martin Garber (b. 1963) grew up on a mountain farm near Cumberland, Maryland. She wrote this triolet for a high school English assignment. Lester Showalter was her teacher at the time. Faustina taught several years in a local church school and later married Glen Garber of Martinsburg, Pennsylvania.

Winter's Coming

The following triolet written by a tenth-grade student uses trochaic meter with a feminine rhyme.

> Winter whistles **warily**;
> Winter's coming soon.
> Autumn now sings airily;
> Winter whistles warily.
> Clouds go floating merrily   5
> Round the silver moon.
> Winter whistles warily;
> Winter's coming soon.

Faustina Martin Garber

Spring

> Sweet spring speaks gentle words
> Warm breezes whisper past.
> With choirs of lowing herds,
> Sweet spring speaks gentle words.
> With **symphonies** of birds,   5
> Life's voices ring at last.
> Sweet spring speaks gentle words;
> Warm breezes whisper past.

Lester E. Showalter

The Poet's Language

symphonies (sim′ fən nēz) n.: musical compositions

Checking for Understanding

Answer the following questions about "Spring":

1. Which line is repeated three times?
2. What alliteration does it contain?
3. What line is repeated twice?
4. How is the alliteration in this line onomatopoeia?
5. What meter does this poem have?
6. What is the rhyme scheme of this poem?
7. This poem emphasizes the sounds of spring. Every line contains words about sound. List all the words of this poem that are "sound" words.
8. What mood does this triolet have?
9. List all the words that contribute to that mood.

Writing for Skill

While the subject matter of a triolet can be serious, this form does not lend itself to a profound treatment of a subject. There are no really famous triolets. The main value of the triolet is to communicate a pleasant emotion about a narrow subject and to give experience to young poets in writing in a specific verse form.

Now is the time for you to write a triolet. First, write a good lead line on some subject you feel pleasant about. Write that line on a first, fourth, and seventh line of your paper. Next, write a companion line to it and fill in the second and eighth lines on your paper. Now all that is left to do is to write the transition lines with the proper rhyme pattern for the triolet. It will be helpful for you to put the rhyme scheme of the triolet down the side of your paper to correspond with the lines on which you will construct your poem.

Don't give up on the first try. Several fresh starts may be necessary before you land on an idea that works itself into a satisfactory triolet.

THE SONNET

The sonnet provides a sharp contrast with the triolet. The triolet is short and easy to write; the sonnet is long and difficult to construct. The triolet is lighthearted in tone and does little more than express pleasant emotions about a limited subject; the sonnet is serious in tone and well-suited to discussion of a weighty subject. The triolet has much flexibility in rhythm; the sonnet sticks rigidly to iambic pentameter.

The sonnet is an old and established form, and although it is difficult to write a good sonnet, many excellent sonnets on a variety of subjects are to be found.

All true sonnets have 14 lines of iambic pentameter. These 14 lines are often grouped into thoughts like paragraphs. There are three main sonnet forms: Italian, Shakespearean, and Miltonic.

Italian Sonnet

In the Italian sonnet, the first eight lines (called the *octave)* present a situation, problem, or premise. The last six lines (called the *sestet)* give a comment, solution, or conclusion. The Italian sonnet can have a variety of rhyme schemes.

octave	sestet	Selections in *Perspectives of Truth in Literature*
a b b a a b b a	c d e c e d	"Pretty Words," *by Elmer Wylie,* p. 254.
a b a b a c d c	e d e f e f	"Ozymandias," *by Percy Bysshe Shelley,* p. 313.

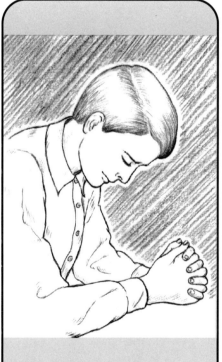

The Poet's Language

lower (laŭ′ r) v.: appear black and threatening

overborne (ō′ vər bórn′) adj.: burdened beyond capacity

Lord, What a Change

Lord, what a change within us one short hour
Spent in Thy presence will prevail to make!
What heavy burdens from our bosom take!
What parched grounds refresh as with a shower!
We kneel—and all around us seems to **lower**;   5
We rise—and all, the distant and the near,
Stands forth in sunny outline brave and clear.
We kneel—how weak! we rise—how full of power!

Why, therefore, should we do ourselves this wrong
Or others—that we are not always strong,   10
That we are ever **overborne** with care,
That we should ever weak or heartless be,
Anxious or troubled when with us is prayer,
And joy and strength and courage are with Thee!

Richard Chenevix Trench

Meditating for Meaning

1. What is the rhyme scheme of this sonnet?
2. Summarize the statement of the octave of this sonnet.
3. What comment does the poet make in the sestet?
4. Twice the poet contrasts *kneel* and *rise*.
   a. What literal pictures does he draw as results of each of these actions? Lines 5 and 6? Line 8?
   b. Explain the figurative connection between the actions and the results in each of these instances.
5. Lines 6 and 7 present the tremendous value of prayer in giving us perspective.
   a. What is "the distant"?
   b. What is "the near"?
   c. What perspective does prayer give on the distant and the near?

Shakespearean Sonnet

The Shakespearean sonnet, made famous by William Shakespeare, has three four-line stanzas called quatrains. Each quatrain gives a separate situation, problem, or premise. These particulars are then summarized or brought to some conclusion in the last two rhyming lines called a couplet. Generally, the Shakespearean sonnet rhymes within each quatrain as follows:

three quatrains	couplet
a b a b c d c d e f e f	g g

O God, I Love Thee

O God, I love Thee in the stars at night
Under the still eternity of sky;
Teach me to love Thee in the passer-by,
For Thou hast said that this is living right.

I hear Thee in the stars whose silence sings,   5
And in the shout of dawn Thy voice I know;
Teach me to hear Thee in the joy and woe
Of men who speak of **trivial** earthly things.

I see Thee when the world is full of sleep
Walking upon the moon-path of the sea;   10
Teach me by all the tears of Calvary
To know Thee in the eyes of all that weep.

There are so many things that I would say,
God-soul of beauty, teach me how to pray!

Nadejda de Braganca, (d. 1946)

The Poet's Language

trivial (triv′ ē əl) adj.: petty; unimportant

Meditating for Meaning

1. What is the rhyme scheme of this sonnet?
2. The likenesses and differences of the quatrains have been very skillfully handled.
   a. What are the first two lines of each quatrain talking about?
   b. How do the last two lines of each quatrain contrast to the first two?
   c. What is the distinct theme in each of the three quatrains? (Look for repetition of key words.)
   d. What is the prayer struggle of the poet?

3. There are three situations described in the poem where it is characteristically easy to miss God's will and Word.
   a. Stanza 1: the _____ , who is easily ignored
   b. Stanza 2: the _____ , that crowds out spiritual thoughts
   c. Stanza 3: the _____ , that causes many to question God's love.
4. How is the closing couplet related to the burden of the poem?

Miltonic Sonnet

Yet another sonnet, called the Miltonic Sonnet, was invented by John Milton. Later you will be studying a sonnet written by Milton himself (page 236), The Miltonic sonnet is not divided into sections like the Italian or Shakespearean sonnet. It is rather constructed as a unit with the thought building up and coming to a climax in the last lines.

The Poet's Language

foul (faùl) adj.: offensive; vulgar

Forgiveness

My heart was heavy, for its trust had been
Abused, its kindness answered with **foul** wrong;
So, turning gloomily from my fellow-men,
One summer Sabbath day I strolled among
The green mounds of the village burial place;   5
Where, pondering how all human love and hate
Find one sad level; and how, soon or late,
Wronged and wrongdoer, each with meekened face,
And cold hands folded over a still heart,
Pass the green threshold of our common grave,   10
Whither all footsteps tend, whence none depart,
Awed for myself, and pitying my race,
One common sorrow, like a mighty wave,
Swept all my pride away, and trembling I forgave!

John Greenleaf Whittier

About the Author

John Greenleaf Whittier (1807-1892) was a Quaker abolitionist born in Massachusetts. He received little formal education. Though critics find his poetry too didactic, many have enjoyed his poems in praise of rural New England life. His stand against slavery asserts itself in his volume *Voices of Freedom*. In 1835 Whittier served a term on the Massachusetts legislature.

Meditating for Meaning

1. What is the rhyme scheme of this sonnet?

2. Why would it not be appropriate to divide this sonnet into sections as was done in the Italian and Shakespearean sonnet?

3. Explain the meaning of each of the following phrases:
   a. "find one sad level" (line 7)
   b. "each with meekened face" (line 8)
   c. "pass the green threshold" (line 10)
   d. "whence none depart" (line 11)

4. Which line is the climax of this poem?

5. This poem gives the solution to a very difficult problem.
   a. What was the problem of the poet?
   b. What does he say stands in the way of solving this problem?
   c. What brought him to the solution?
   d. In light of Scripture, what should move the Christian to forgive?

HEBREW POETRY

Four of the 66 books of the Bible are entirely or almost entirely written in poetic form and more than 30 other books contain some poetry.

Unfortunately (from a literary viewpoint), the typeset of many Bibles does not indicate the separate lines of poetry. But even when Biblical poetry is not set up with its individual lines, it is not difficult to observe a marked difference between this poetry and our traditional form of poetry. Rhyme is entirely missing. The rhythm, if indeed it can be called rhythm, is free and irregular. And yet there is something special about the form of such passages as the Twenty-third Psalm. "The Shepherd Psalm" is not ordinary prose. It is poetry of a high order.

Parallelism gives Hebrew poetry its distinctive form. Two sentences or phrases are said to be parallel when a relationship of thought appears between them. As will be observed in the examples that follow, parallelism makes a rhythm of thought that is indeed poetical. Any patterning of language can result in poetry, not just patterns of sound such as rhyme and rhythm. In Hebrew poetry the pattern is parallelism of thought. You will observe four different kinds of parallelism in Hebrew poetry.

Synonymous Parallelism: agreement of thought.
Synonymous means "having the same meaning."

Examples of synonymous parallelism:

> The heavens declare the glory of God;
> And the firmament sheweth his handywork.   Psalm 19:1

The king shall joy in thy strength, O Lord;
And in thy salvation how greatly shall he rejoice!
Thou hast given him his heart's desire,
And hast not withholden the request of his lips.   Psalm 21:1, 2

Surely there is a vein for the silver,
And a place for gold where they fine it.   Job 28:1

Notice that in each pair of lines, the second line echoes the idea or thought of the first line in different words. The second line is not necessarily more emphatic than the first line. Really, in many cases you can reverse the order of the lines without disturbing the thought. Even though the two lines may be talking about different specifics, (as in the example from Job), the concept they are communicating is the same. Consider the following lines:

Who shall ascend into the hill of the Lord?
Or who shall stand in his holy place?   Psalm 24:3

These two questions are really expressing one basic question: What kind of person is fit to enter into the presence of God? Whether it be ascending into the Lord's hill or standing in his holy place, it is a serious matter to present oneself before God. The variety used in this repeated question adds to its beauty and forcefulness and makes it poetry.

Antithetic Parallelism: contrast of thought.
Antithetic means "being in opposition."

Examples of antithetic parallelism:

Cursed be every one that curseth thee,
And blessed be he that blesseth thee.   Genesis 27:29

A man shall eat good by the fruit of his mouth:
But the soul of the transgressors shall eat violence.   Proverbs 13:2

A soft answer turneth away wrath:
But grievous words stir up anger.   Proverbs 15:1

He hath filled the hungry with good things;
And the rich he hath sent empty away.   Luke 1:53

Note that the conjunction *but* can be a clue to antithetic parallelism.

When two colors are placed side by side, their difference tends to be emphasized. So it is with ideas. When a single idea is presented alone, we may agree that it is true enough but not be impressed with the importance of the truth until it has a contrasting idea presented beside it. For example:

Righteousness keepeth him that is upright in the way:
But wickedness overthroweth the sinner.   Proverbs 13:6

The first line is very true and would make a good verse for a motto. But such a motto may only seem like a nice platitude until the blessing of the righteousness is contrasted with the overthrow of the wicked. By putting two contrasting ideas in parallel, the writer can emphasize and clarify the truths of each. Antithetic parallelism is a forceful literary technique.

Synthetic Parallelism: completion of thought.
Synthetic means "placed together."

Examples of synthetic parallelism:

> Blessed is he that considereth the poor:
> The LORD will deliver him in time of trouble.   Psalm 41:1
>> (A reward for the first line is given in the second.)

> It is better to trust in the LORD
> Than to put confidence in man.   Psalm 118:8
>> (The comparison begun in the first line is concluded in the second.)

> Wherewithal shall a young man cleanse his way?
> By taking heed thereto according to thy word.   Psalm 119:9
>> (The question asked in the first line is answered in the second.)

> Have mercy upon us, O Lord, have mercy upon us:
> For we are exceedingly filled with contempt.   Psalm 123:3
>> (In the second line a reason is given for the prayer in the first line.)

The two lines of these couplets are definitely related. But it is not a matter of the second line repeating the thought of the first line as in synonymous parallelism. Neither do the lines provide a contrast as in antithetic parallelism. In synthetic parallelism the second line adds a thought to the idea of the first line.

Many of our ideas involve two parts. To present them we use synthetic parallelism.

This type of parallelism

states a fact	then	gives a reason
asks a question	then	gives an answer
gives a truth	then	compares it with another
states a cause	then	gives the effect

Climactic Parallelism: building up of thought.
Climactic means "building up to a climax."

Examples of climactic parallelism:

> Give unto the LORD, O ye kindreds of the people,
> Give unto the LORD glory and strength.
> Give unto the LORD the glory due unto his name.   Psalm 96:7, 8

> Till thy people pass over, O LORD,
> Till the people pass over, which thou hast purchased.   Exodus 15:16

Climactic parallelism is distinguished by the building up of thought with the repetition of certain words or phrases. Such repetition tends to emphasize a certain idea and to sustain that idea until it reaches a climax. Imagine the buildup of feeling that a multitude of worshippers could express as they chanted the following psalm together.

> Praise ye the LORD.
> Praise God in his sanctuary:
> Praise him in the firmament of his power.
> Praise him for his mighty acts:

Praise him according to his excellent greatness.

Praise him with the sound of the trumpet:
Praise him with the psaltery and harp.
Praise him with the timbrel and dance:
Praise him with stringed instruments and organs.
Praise him upon the loud cymbals:
Praise him upon the high sounding cymbals.
Let everything that hath breath praise the LORD.
Praise ye the LORD.   Psalm 150

Sometimes the climactic parallelism uses the repetition of a word to build up a theme. Notice the theme of preservation in the following lines:

The LORD shall preserve thee from all evil:
He shall preserve thy soul.
The LORD shall preserve thy going out and thy coming in
    from this time forth, and even for evermore.   Psalm 121:7, 8

The first two verses of Psalm 123 make masterful poetic use of the repetition of the word *eyes*.

Unto thee lift I up mine eyes,
O thou that dwellest in the heavens.
Behold, as the eyes of servants look unto the hand of their masters,
And as the eyes of a maiden unto the hand of her mistress;
So our eyes wait upon the LORD our God,
    until that he have mercy upon us.   Psalm 123:1, 2

Not all the lines of Biblical poetry fall neatly into these four categories of parallelism. This is because the Hebrew poets did not restrict their expressions to rigid rules of poetry. But to say that the Biblical poets used no patterns is to ignore the overwhelming number of sets of lines that do show similarity of pattern. In ordinary speech and writing, people do not express themselves in well-ordered pairs of lines like we find over and over in the Psalms. Such literary form has a special quality; it is poetry.

The unique parallelism of Hebrew poetry provides a marked advantage for accurate translation. You may have seen rhyme-and-rhythm poems that were translated from one language to another. Madame Guyon's poem on pages 239, 240 was translated from French into English. In such a case, the translator needed to take some liberty in translating the thoughts in order to retain the rhyme and rhythm pattern. In other words, some accuracy of thought needed to be sacrificed for the sake of the poetic structure.

But since most of the poetic structure in the Bible is parallelism of thought, the more accurate the translation of thought, the more faithfully the poetic structure is maintained. No accuracy of thought needed to be sacrificed to maintain the poetic form. So when you read the Psalms in the King James Version, you can benefit from the same poetic beauty that the children of Israel had in their original Hebrew. We can hardly appreciate this fact as we ought. Only the omniscient God could have planned so wisely for our benefit and for the benefit of all people of whatever tongue.

Testing for Understanding

1. Classify each of the following sets of lines according to their type of parallelism. If the parallelism is synonymous, give the basic idea that is repeated. If antithetic, give what is being contrasted. If synthetic, explain how the second line completes the thought begun in the first line. If the parallelism is climactic, give the word or phrase that is repeated in the building up of thought.

   a. "A wise son heareth his father's instruction:
      But a scorner heareth not rebuke."　　　　　　　　　　Proverbs 13:1

   b. "Awake, awake, Deborah:
      Awake, awake, utter a song."　　　　　　　　　　　　Judges 5:12

   c. "My soul doth magnify the Lord,
      And my spirit hath rejoiced in God my Saviour."　　　Luke 1:46, 47

   d. "Better is a dinner of herbs where love is,
      Than a stalled ox and hatred therewith."　　　　　　Proverbs 15:17

   e. "He that keepeth his mouth keepeth his life:
      But he that openeth wide his lips shall have destruction."　　Proverbs 13:3

   f. "Iron is taken out of the earth,
      And brass is molten out of the stone."　　　　　　　Job 28:2

   g. "Boast not thyself of tomorrow;
      For thou knowest not what a day may bring forth."　　Proverbs 27:1

   h. "He will bless us;
      He will bless the house of Israel;
      He will bless the house of Aaron.
      He will bless them that fear the LORD, both small and great."　　Psalm 115:12, 13

   i. "Who is this King of glory?
      The LORD of hosts, he is the King of glory."　　　　　Psalm 24:10

   j. "As a bird that wandereth from her nest,
      So is a man that wandereth from his place."　　　　Proverbs 27:8

2. Match the following kinds of parallelism with their meaning and the description of the parallelism.

   a. antithetic:　　　　same meaning　　　　　contrast of thought
   b. climactic:　　　　 in opposition　　　　　 agreement of thought
   c. synthetic:　　　　 ascending to climax　　 completion of thought
   d. synonymous:　　　 place together　　　　　building up of thought

3. How does the uniqueness of Hebrew poetry benefit us today?

Psalm 1

A Psalm of Moral Instruction

Blessed is the man that walketh not in the counsel
   of the ungodly,
Nor standeth in the way of sinners,
Nor sitteth in the seat of the scornful.

But his delight is in the law of the LORD;
And in his law doth he meditate day and night.   5

And he shall be like a tree planted by the rivers
   of water,
That bringeth forth his fruit in his season;
His leaf also shall not wither;
And whatsoever he doeth shall prosper.

The ungodly are not so: 10
But are like the chaff which the wind driveth away.

Therefore the ungodly shall not stand in the judgment,
Nor sinners in the congregation of the righteous.

For the LORD knoweth the way of the righteous:
But the way of the ungodly shall perish.   15

Meditating for Meaning

1.   Each of the four kinds of parallelism are found in this short Psalm.
     a. Explain what is climactic about the parallelism in the first three lines.
     b. Give the line numbers for three examples of synonymous parallelism.
     c. Give the line numbers for two examples of synthetic parallelism.
     d. Give the line numbers for one example of antithetic parallelism.

2. Note the figures of speech used in this Psalm.
   a. What two figures of speech are there?
   b. Are they similes or metaphors?

3. Interpret the meaning intended by the poetic language by completing the following statements with a phrase.
   a. The first three lines tell us that a godly man does not _____ .
   b. The fourth and fifth lines tell us that a godly man does _____ .
   c. The sixth to ninth lines tell us that a godly man is _____ .
   d. The tenth line tells us that an ungodly man is not _____ .
   e. The eleventh line tells us that an ungodly man is _____ .
   f. The last four lines warn us of _____ .

4. Each line is expressed in either the positive or negative. This shifting from positive to negative makes for a strong contrast and is a powerful literary scheme.
   a. Identify each line as either positive or negative.
   b. Note how this literary scheme is well-suited to the theme of the Psalm. Moral instructions are usually a list of _____ and _____ .

Psalm 43

A Psalm of Lament

Judge me, O God, and plead my cause against an
    ungodly nation:
O deliver me from the deceitful and unjust man.
For thou art the God of my strength:
Why dost thou cast me off?
Why go I mourning because of the oppression
    of the enemy?   5

O send out thy light and thy truth:
Let them lead me;
Let them bring me unto thy holy hill,
And to thy tabernacles.
Then will I go unto the altar of God,   10
Unto God my exceeding joy:
Yea, upon the harp will I praise thee,
O God my God.

Why art thou cast down, O my soul?
And why art thou disquieted within me?   15
Hope in God: for I shall yet praise him,
Who is the health of my countenance, and my God.

Meditating for Meaning

1. The psalmist is coming to God for the solution to a problem.
   a. According to lines 1, 2, and 5, what is the cause of his problem?
   b. According to lines 4, 14, and 15, what is it about the situation the psalmist is lamenting?
   c. What does the Psalmist ask to be done to solve this problem? (Lines 6-9)
2. Give one example from Psalm 43 of each kind of parallelism you can find.
3. Repetition can contribute much to the impact of literature.
   a. What lines are repeated as a refrain in Psalms 42 and 43?
   b. Find lines repeated as a refrain in Psalm 80.
   c. Find lines repeated as a refrain in Psalm 107.
   d. What line is repeated over and over in Psalm 136?
   e. What is the value of such repetition?
4. What two evidences do we have that the last four lines are no longer addressed to God?

Psalm 66

A Psalm of Praise

Make a joyful noise unto God, all ye lands:
Sing forth the honor of his name:
Make his praise glorious.
Say unto God, How terrible art thou in thy works!
Through the greatness of thy power shall thine
    enemies submit themselves unto thee.   5
All the earth shall worship thee,
And shall sing unto thee;
They shall sing to thy name. Selah.

Come and see the works of God:
He is terrible in his doing toward the children
    of men.   10
He turned the sea into dry land:
They went through the flood on foot:
There did we rejoice in him.
He ruleth by his power for ever;
His eyes behold the nations: 15
Let not the rebellious exalt themselves. Selah.

O bless our God, ye people,
And make the voice of his praise to be heard:
Which holdeth our soul in life,
And suffereth not our feet to be moved.   20
For thou, O God, hast proved us:
Thou hast tried us, as silver is tried.
Thou broughtest us into the net;
Thou laidst affliction upon our loins.
Thou hast caused men to ride over our heads;   25
We went through fire and through water:
But thou broughtest us out into a wealthy place.

I will go into thy house with burnt offerings:
I will pay thee my vows,
Which my lips have uttered,   30
And my mouth hath spoken,
When I was in trouble.
I will offer unto thee burnt sacrifices of fatlings,
With the incense of rams:
I will offer bullocks with goats. Selah.   35

Come and hear, all ye that fear God,
And I will declare what he hath done for my soul.
I cried unto him with my mouth,
And he was extolled with my tongue.
If I regard iniquity in my heart,   40
The Lord will not hear me:
But verily God hath heard me;
He hath attended to the voice of my prayer.

Blessed be God,
Which hath not turned away my prayer,   45
Nor his mercy from me.

 *Meditating for Meaning*

1. From the introductory section (lines 1-8), copy the line that states the psalmist's reason for praising God in this Psalm.
2. This Psalm divides into sections (lines 1-27 and 28-46). Each section has three parts: a call to praise, a reason to praise, and a blessing to God.

a. Who is being called to praise in the first part of Section 1?

b. The second part of the first section (line 9) begins "Come and *see*." The second part of the second section (line 36) begins "Come and *hear*." From the content of each section explain why the one invites you to see and the other to hear.

3. Some of the parts of Psalm 66 end with the word *Selah*. This word is used 71 times in the Psalms and three times in Habakkuk. Check a collegiate or Bible dictionary and write a summary of its meaning.

4. What earlier happening in the experience of God's people is alluded to in lines 11 to 13?

5. The psalmist uses various literary devices in lines 21-26—metaphors, similes, and a device we have not yet discussed, the *hyperbole*.

a. For what is the psalmist praising God in these lines?

b. Line 25 contains an example of a hyperbole—"Thou hast caused men to ride over our heads." A hyperbole is an exaggeration not to be taken literally. Though at some times Israel's enemies did overrun them, it is probably an exaggeration to say that the enemy actually rode over their heads. What effect does this hyperbole achieve?

Psalm 119:9-16 (Beth)

A Psalm About the Word of God

Wherewithal shall a young man cleanse his way?
By taking heed thereto according to thy word.

With my whole heart have I sought thee:
O let me not wander from thy commandments.

Thy word have I hid in mine heart,   5
That I might not sin against thee.

Blessed art thou, O LORD:
Teach me thy statutes.

With my lips have I declared
All the judgments of thy mouth.   10

I have rejoiced in the way of thy testimonies,
As much as in all riches.

I will meditate in thy precepts,
And have respect unto thy ways.

I will delight myself in thy statutes: 15
I will not forget thy word.

Meditating for Meaning

1. This section from Psalm 119 is typical of the Psalm as a whole. God's Word is referred to in all but about five verses of this long Psalm. Find seven words in this section that refer to God's Word.

2. The psalmist says a young man can cleanse his way by taking heed to God's Word. From lines 5-16 list several things which are involved in taking heed to God's Word.

3. Psalm 119 is a giant acrostic poem based on the Hebrew alphabet.
    a. What is an acrostic (page 168)?
    b. Count the number of eight-verse sections in Psalm 119. Compare this number with the number of verses in Psalm 25 and 34, and in Chapters 1–4 of Lamentations that are also in acrostic form. Considering that these acrostics are based on the Hebrew alphabet, what do you conclude is the significance of this number?
    c. The translators could not retain the acrostic form in our English Bibles and yet translate the Hebrew accurately. If they had, each verse of the "Beth" section would have started with the letter *b*. For example, the first two verses could read:

    > Being a young man, how shall I cleanse my way?
    > By taking heed thereto according to thy word.

    > Bringing my whole heart to the search, I seek thee:
    > O let me not wander from thy commandments.

    The twelfth verse already begins with *b*. Try to recast the remaining five verses so they will conform to the original acrostic form.
    d. What value is there in the acrostic form of poetry?

9 בַּמֶּה יְזַכֶּה־נַּעַר אֶת־אָרְחוֹ לִשְׁמֹר כִּדְבָרֶֽךָ׃ (ב)

10 בְּכָל־לִבִּי דְרַשְׁתִּיךָ אַל־תַּשְׁגֵּנִי מִמִּצְוֹתֶֽיךָ׃

11 בְּלִבִּי צָפַנְתִּי אִמְרָתֶךָ לְמַעַן לֹא אֶחֱטָא־לָֽךְ׃

12 בָּרוּךְ אַתָּה יְהוָה לַמְּדֵנִי חֻקֶּֽיךָ׃

13 בִּשְׂפָתַי סִפַּרְתִּי כֹּל מִשְׁפְּטֵי־פִֽיךָ׃

14 בְּדֶרֶךְ עֵדְוֹתֶיךָ שַׂשְׂתִּי כְּעַל כָּל־הֽוֹן׃

15 בְּפִקֻּדֶיךָ אָשִׂיחָה וְאַבִּיטָה אֹרְחֹתֶֽיךָ׃

16 בְּחֻקֹּתֶיךָ אֶשְׁתַּעֲשָׁע לֹא אֶשְׁכַּח דְּבָרֶֽךָ׃

Hebrew for Psalm 119:9-16.
(Hebrew is read from right to left. Note that each line in this section begins with the Hebrew letter beth ב).

From the BIBLIA HEBRAICA STUTTGARTENSIA, ©1967/77 by the German Bible Society, Stuttgart.

Psalm 126

A Song of Degrees

When the LORD turned again the captivity of Zion,
We were like them that dream.
Then was our mouth filled with laughter,
And our tongue with singing:
Then said they among the heathen,   5
The LORD hath done great things for them.
The LORD hath done great things for us;
Whereof we are glad.

Turn again our captivity, O LORD,
As the streams in the south.   10
They that sow in tears
Shall reap in joy.
He that goeth forth and weepeth, bearing precious seed,
Shall doubtless come again with rejoicing,
Bringing his sheaves with him.   15

Meditating for Meaning

1. The 15 "Songs of Degrees" (Psalms 120-134) are short poems which express simple confidence and joy in the Lord by a people who know the reality of affliction. These psalms may have been sung as "pilgrim psalms" by travelers on their way to worship at Jerusalem. Some scholars think that they were composed by Hezekiah when 15 years were added to his life and God gave him a sign of "degrees" (Isaiah 38:8). Judging from Isaiah 38:9-20, Hezekiah did have literary ability.
   a. Which of the "Songs of Degrees" would indicate that these were sung on the way to Jerusalem?

b. Find at least one "Song of Degrees" on each of the following topics that would have been close to the heart of the Jew:

> Safety from enemies
> Blessings of family life
> Blessings of brotherhood
> The sanctuary of the Lord

2. Several of these Psalms are linked with specific historical events.
   a. What event in the history of Judah may be referred to in Psalm 126?
   b. If this was written by Hezekiah, what event in his life might this refer to?
   c. How was this event like a dream? (line 2)
   d. Contrast line 4 with Psalm 137:4. What made the difference?

3. This Psalm contains an interesting repetition. Line 6 is repeated almost exactly in line 7, but not by the same people.
   a. Who said line 6? To discover who it was you must know who "they" are in line 5.
   b. Who is speaking in line 7 and what is meant by the repetition?

4. This Psalm is one of the nine Psalms that the early Anabaptists put into verse form. It is the only one of the nine that is still sung by the Amish. What interpretation of *captivity* in line 9 would make this Psalm applicable to the Christian?

THE HABITAT OF A POEM

Four Purposes for a Poem

So far you have studied how poems can be grouped according to the type of verse form: blank, bound and rhymed, and free. You then looked at a few of the many poetic forms: the triolet, the sonnet, and Hebrew poetry.

Now we will group poems in yet another way. Poems can also be classified according to their purpose. If a poem's purpose is to tell a story, then it is narrative poetry. Long poems that are written to be acted out are called dramatic poems. Lyric poems may be written to be sung. The purpose of some poems is to teach; such poems are didactic poetry. You will be studying examples of each of these kinds of poetry.

NARRATIVE POETRY

A poem that tells a story is called a narrative poem. Either the poem recounts the story of some hero or event that has made a strong impression on the poet, or it tells a made-up story to communicate a lesson or an attitude.

This first narrative you will study is about a real man and his stand for the Christian faith. This poem is hymn number 11 in the *Ausbund*, the 16th century Anabaptist hymnbook. It was written to sing the praises of the faith of a Christian hero and to inspire future generations to be as steadfast in the faith as George Wagner. Such a folk-song narrative is called a folk ballad.

The ballad is an important literary form for times and places where printed literature is scarce and much of the communication of history and truth depends on memory—aided by poems and songs.

In the original German, this ballad about an early Anabaptist martyr contains twenty-seven stanzas. Only eighteen are given here in an English translation. Interestingly, this same ballad appears in Hutterian literature with some variation. Instead of twenty-seven stanzas, the Hutterian ballad has twenty-nine. The rhymes of the stanzas are the same, but the wording in the lines is often different. The meaning of the lines is the same. Such variation would be expected of a folk ballad that is handed down by word of mouth.

George Wagner

1. Who Christ will follow now, new-born,
   Dare not be moved by this world's scorn,
   The cross must bear sincerely;
   No other way to heaven leads,
   From childhood we're taught clearly.   5

2. This did George Wagner, too, aspire,
   He went to heav'n 'mid smoke and fire,
   The cross his test and proving,
   As gold is in the furnace tried,
   His heart's desire approving.   10

3. The **falcon tower** became his **lease**,
   It brought about his soul's release,
   No human sorrowing swerved him,
   Nor was he moved by his small child,
   Nor had his wife unnerved him.   15

4. They no more his could be to aid,
   Though he gladly with them had stayed,
   His love and sorrow **welling**;
   No labor spared he on his part,
   As righteous partners dwelling.   20

5. Although he from them must depart,
   No **meanly** sacrifice of heart,
   That he from them be parting,
   No prince with all his princely gain
   Could him from this be **thwarting**.   25

6. Two barefoot monks in grey array,
   George Wagner's sorrows would **allay**,
   They would him be converting;
   He waved them to their **cloister** home,
   Their speech he'd be **averting**.   30

7. The hangman him with rope **interned**
   In the town hall four counts he learned,
   Upon which hinged his living;
   Before he one truth would deny,
   His life would he be giving.   35

8. The article which first would weigh,
   With the confession it did lay,
   No priest could be forgiving.
   For against God would he have sinned,
   Who'd only be grace giving.   40

The Poet's Language

falcon tower (fal′ kən taŭr) n.:
tower from which small cannons
were fired; probably the location of his prison cell

lease (lēs) n.: temporary dwelling

welling (wel′ ing) v.: issuing forth

meanly (mēn′ lē) adj.: meager;
insignificant (Here the poet
uses an adverb as an adjective.)

thwarting (thwȯr′ ting) v.: preventing; hindering

allay (a lā′) v.: diminish; ease

cloister (kloi′ stər) n.: place of religious seclusion

averting (ə vər′ ting) v.: hindering;
avoiding

interned (in tərnd′) v.: confined

9. Baptism is right as Christ has taught,
    When this ord'nance is not distraught,
    Portends his bitter dying,
    In symbol washes us from sins,
    And grace us signifying.   45

10. Of our Lord Christ's own sacrament,
    George Wagner testified intent,
    A symbol, it esteem I,
    Of Christ's own body offered free;
    No flattery spake he hereby.   50

11. Fourthly, he would not **fain** believe
    That God should such **constraint** receive
    And come to earth in brightness,
    Until His judgment He should hold,
    The wicked with the righteous.   55

12. Did several Christian brothers near
    Speak then into George Wagner's ear
    While still he was yet living,
    (He died in fire, a Christian true),
    Wilt us a sign be giving.   60

13. He said: This will I gladly do,
    Christ, truly God's own Son, as due,
    By mouth I'll be confessing;
    As long as privilege shall be,
    Jesus him be addressing.   65

14. Two hangmen stood now at his side.
    The ring about him they made wide.
    George Wagner spake his faith strong,
    Around him a great company,
    Men, women, an attent throng.   70

15. George Wagner's gaze did nothing **quail**,
    His lips did never once grow pale,
    He spake that many wondered.
    'Twas in the twenty-seventh year,
    One thousand and five hundred.   75

16. In February the same year,
    The eighth day, openly and clear,
    Men on a stake then hung him,
    A bag of powder, rather small,
    There took his soul quite from him.   80

17. Men fastened him to ladder firm
    The wood and straw was made to burn,
    Now was the laughter **dire**;
    "Jesus! Jesus!" Did he four times
    Call loudly from the fire.   85

The Poet's Language

portends (pór tendz´) v.: foretells

fain (fān) adj.: eagerly desirous

constraint (kən strānt´) n.: control by force

quail (kwāl) v.: shrink back in fear

dire (dīr) adj.: desperate; distressing

The Poet's Language

lighten (līt′ n) v.: come to rest

18. Elias speaks the truth entire
    That he in chariot of fire
    In paradise did **lighten**;
    So pray we then, the Holy Ghost,
    That He may us enlighten.   90

Translated by John J. Overholt

Meditating for Meaning

1. The story of George Wagner in prose is given below from page 416 of *Martyrs Mirror*, a 1,141 page book about Christian martyrs from the time of Christ to 1660. Write the stanza number from the poem which each lettered detail refers to.

2. What is the significance of the first stanza of the ballad?

3. Why was this ballad more valuable to the sixteenth century Anabaptist Christians than a prose account of the same incident?

George Wagner, A. D. 1527

George Wagner, of Emmerich, was apprehended at Munich, in Bavaria, on account of four articles of the faith (a). First, that the priest cannot forgive sins (b). Secondly, that he does not believe that a man can bring down God from heaven (c). Thirdly, that he does not believe that God or Christ is bodily in the bread which the priest has upon the altar, but that it is the bread of the Lord (d). Fourthly, that he did not hold to the belief that water baptism possessed any saving power (e). As he would not renounce these articles, he was most severely tormented, so that the prince felt great compassion for him, and personally came to him in the prison, and earnestly admonished him thereto, promising that he would call him his friend all his life time (f). Thus also the tutor of the prince earnestly admonished him to recant, and likewise made him many promises. Ultimately, his wife and child were brought before him in prison in order, on this wise to move him to recant (g). But neither was he to be moved in this way; for he said that though his wife and child were so dear to him that the prince could not buy them with all his dominion, yet he would not forsake his God and Lord on their

account (h). Many priests and others also came to him, to persuade him; but he was steadfast and immovable in that which God had given him to know (i). Hence he was finally sentenced to the fire and death.

Having been delivered into the hands of the executioner, and led into the middle of the city, he said: "Today I will confess my God before all the world" (j). He had such joy in Christ Jesus, that his face did not pale, nor his eyes show fear (k); but he went smiling to the fire, where the executioner bound him on the ladder, and tied a little bag of powder to his neck (l), at which he said: "Be it done in the name of the Father, the Son, and the Holy Ghost"; and having smilingly bid farewell to a Christian who was there, he was thrust into the fire by the executioner (m), and happily offered up his spirit, on the eighth day of February (n), A.D. 1527 (o). The sheriff, however, surnamed Eisenreich von Landsberg, while returning home from the place of execution, traveling on horseback; purposing to apprehend others of the brethren, died suddenly in the night, and was found dead in his bed in the morning, having thus been removed through the wrath of God.

The Fool's Prayer

This narrative poem is an example of a literary ballad. Unlike the folk ballad, the literary ballad is the deliberate attempt by a poet to produce a narrative poem of high literary quality. The folk ballad is very sincere and born out of much feeling and conviction, but it is often somewhat crude as a piece of literature. Usually we do not know who wrote the folk ballad. It may have been the work of various people. We commonly know who wrote a literary ballad.

Although "The Fool's Prayer" is a relatively modern literary ballad, its setting is in the Middle Ages. This was the day before movies, comics, radio, and television; but human nature still sought carnal entertainment. Kings often had in their courts a jester who had a talent to act as a fool. Some jesters were mentally deficient or physically deformed, but, nevertheless, some had keen minds. The "fool" in this story was really very wise; wiser even than the king who hired him.

The royal feast was done; the King
    Sought some new sport to **banish** care,
And to his jester cried: "Sir Fool,
    Kneel now, and make for us a prayer!"

The jester **doffed** his cap and bells,   5
    And stood the mocking court before;
They could not see the bitter smile
    Behind the painted grin he wore.

He bowed his head, and bent his knee
    Upon the Monarch's silken stool;   10
His pleading voice arose: "O Lord,
    Be merciful to me, a fool!

"No pity, Lord, could change the heart
    From red with wrong to white as wool;
Thy rod must heal the sin: but Lord,   15
    Be merciful to me, a fool!

"'Tis not by guilt the onward sweep
    Of truth and right, O Lord, we **stay**;
'Tis by our follies that so long
    We hold the earth from heaven away.   20

"These clumsy feet, still in the mire,
    Go crushing blossoms without end;
These hard, well-meaning hands we thrust
    Among the heart-strings of a friend.

"The ill-timed truth we might have kept—   25
    Who knows how sharp it pierced and stung?
The word we had not sense to say—
    Who knows how grandly it had rung!

The Poet's Language

banish (ban′ ish) v.: dismiss from
   one's thoughts

doffed (dȯft) v.: removed

stay (stā) v.: stop

balsam (bȯl′ səm) n.: comfort;
   healing agent

knave (nāv) n.: scoundrel

"Our faults no tenderness should ask,
   The chastening stripes must cleanse them all; 30
But for our blunders—oh, in shame
   Before the eyes of heaven we fall.

"Earth bears no **balsam** for mistakes;
   Men crown the **knave**, and scourge the tool
That did his will; but Thou, O Lord,   35
   Be merciful to me, a fool!"

The room was hushed; in silence rose
   The King, and sought his gardens cool,
And walked apart, and murmured low,
   "Be merciful to me, a fool!"   40

Edward Rowland Sill

About the Author

Edward Rowland Sill (1841-1887) born in Connecticut, graduated from Yale University. Seeking a better climate for his frail health, he traveled west and taught in the University of California. His poetry reflects the conflict which developed between the influences of his New England Puritan background and experiences in the more progressive West.

Meditating for Meaning

1. What similarity do you see between the immediate circumstances of the king of this poem and the kings of Esther 1:10 and Daniel 5:2?

2. The bitter smile behind the painted grin which the jester wore reveals the jester's feelings about his situation.
   a. Explain the reasons both for the bitter smile behind and the painted grin in front.
   b. Why couldn't the court see the bitter smile?

3. Notice carefully what it is for which the jester feels the need of God's mercy.
   a. Summarize the thought expressed in lines 13, 14, 17, 18, 29, and 30. For what does he say we should not expect God's mercy?
   b. What does he say must be the dealings to correct these issues?
   c. In contrast, for what general type of wrong does he beseech God's mercy in line 19, stanzas 6 and 7, and lines 31 and 32?
   d. What wrong concepts does he have of mercy and sin?

4. Consider the two metaphors in the sixth stanza.
   a. The first metaphor is a picture of a man with muddy feet tramping through a _____ .
   b. In the second he compares men's hearts to _____ into whose strings are thrust work-roughened hands.
   c. In both cases what is being spoiled? Interpret the metaphors.
   d. Interpret the metaphor "still in the mire."
   e. What then must we conclude about ourselves if we hurt others even unintentionally?
5. The final stanza of the jester's prayer is the most revealing of all.
   a. Who was the knave that was crowned?
   b. Who was the obedient tool that was being punished?
   c. What is the jester saying indirectly?
   d. What then is the meaning of line 33?
   e. What does the jester see as his only hope for relief?
6. Why was the room hushed after the fool had finished his prayer?

The Battle of Blenheim

This poem is a satirical narrative. While the poet is telling a story, he is ridiculing what some consider very noble. The story of the grandfather and his grandchildren was made up to suit the author's purpose, but the Battle of Blenheim was real. In that battle, the English and Austrians defeated the French and Bavarians on August 13, 1704, at Blenheim, Bavaria, which is now part of Germany. Do not miss the author's disgust at the glamor some people give to war.

The Poet's Language

green (grēn) n.: grassy lawn

rivulet (riv′ yə lət) n.: small stream

It was a summer evening,
  Old Kaspar's work was done,
And he before his cottage door
  Was sitting in the sun;
And by him sported on the **green**   5
His little grandchild Wilhelmine.

She saw her brother Peterkin
  Roll something large and round
Which he beside the **rivulet**
  In playing there had found;   10
He came to ask what he had found
That was so large and smooth and round.

Old Kasper took it from the boy
  Who stood expectant by;
And then the old man shook his head,   15
  And with a natural sigh
"'Tis some poor fellow's skull," said he,
"Who fell in the great victory.

The Poet's Language

rout (raȯt) n.: wild flight after military defeat

quoth (kwōth) v.: said

hard by (härd bī) prep.: close beside

"I find them in the garden,
  For there's many here about;   20
And often when I go to plow
  The plowshare turns them out.
For many thousand men," said he,
"Were slain in that great victory."

"Now tell us what 'twas all about,"   25
  Young Peterkin he cries;
And little Wilhelmine looks up
  With wonder-waiting eyes;
"Now tell us all about the war,
And what they fought each other for."   30

"It was the English," Kaspar cried,
  "Who put the French to **rout**;
But what they fought each other for
  I could not well make out.
But everybody said," **quoth** he   35
"That 'twas a famous victory.

"My father lived at Blenheim then,
  Yon little stream **hard by**;
They burnt his dwelling to the ground,
  And he was forced to fly;   40
So with his wife and child he fled,
Nor had he where to rest his head.

"With fire and sword the country round
  Was wasted far and wide.
And many a childing mother then   45
  And newborn baby died;
But things like that, you know, must be
At every famous victory.

"They say it was a shocking sight
  After the field was won;   50
For many thousand bodies here
  Lay rotting in the sun;
But things like that, you know, must be
After a famous victory.

"Great praise the Duke of Marlbro' won   55
  And our good Prince Eugene";
"Why, 'twas a very wicked thing!"
  Said little Wilhelmine.
"Nay—nay—my little girl," quoth he,
"It was a famous victory.   60

"And everybody praised the Duke
    Who this great fight did win."
"But what good came of it at last?"
    Quoth little Peterkin.
"Why that I cannot tell," said he,   65
"But 'twas a famous victory."

Robert Southey

About the Author

Robert Southey (1774-1843) orphaned at a young age, lived with his aunt in Bristol, England. While a student in school, he was expelled for writing a satire on flogging. This same bent developed later into radical views about the government. In 1813 he became poet laureate of England, famous for his ballad style of poetry. Literature classes him with the famous Lake Poets of the lake region of England. He also wrote a biography of John Bunyan.

 *Meditating for Meaning*

1. What brought about the discussion of the battle?
2. In discussing the battle, Kaspar admits to the tragic results that are the result of every war. Generalize these results as given in the following lines:
    a. line 39
    b. lines 40-42
    c. lines 45, 46
    d. lines 23, 24, 51, 52
3. To Kaspar the victory was glamorous. Notice the ironic buildup by the repetition of "great victory," and "famous victory."
    a. What two admissions did Kaspar make that show how futile the victory was?
    b. How is that victory different from the victory the Christian experiences over sin?
4. The poet tells us his opinion of the war through a child.
    a. What does the poet think of war as revealed by the child?
    b. Why is the use of a child to make the judgment on war so effective?

198   POETRY

A Fable

A short story with a moral is called a fable. Sometimes fables are put into verse form to make a short narrative poem.

The mountain and the squirrel
Had a quarrel,
And the former called the latter "Little Prig."
Bun replied,
"You are doubtless very big;   5
But all sorts of things and weather
Must be taken in together,
To make up a year
And a sphere.
And I think it no disgrace   10
To occupy my place.
If I'm not so large as you,
You are not so small as I,
And not half so spry.
I'll not deny you make   15
A very pretty squirrel track;
Talents differ; all is well and wisely put;
If I cannot carry forests on my back,
Neither can you crack a nut."

Ralph Waldo Emerson

About the Author

Ralph Waldo Emerson (1803-1882), son of a Unitarian minister, was born in Boston, Massachusetts. While Emerson was still young, his father died leaving five sons, one being mentally retarded. Emerson himself suffered from a lung disease and occasions of temporary blindness. Graduating from Harvard University, he served three years as a Unitarian pastor. As an essayist, critic, poet, and orator, Emerson stressed optimism and individualism. His somewhat novel views laid a foundation of beliefs for many literary figures who followed him.

Meditating for Meaning

1. What did the mountain mean by calling the squirrel "Little Prig"?
2. What did the squirrel mean in his reply in lines 6 to 9?
3. What advantage did the squirrel see in being small?
4. This is a fable with a figurative meaning. What is symbolized by the following words or phrases from the story?
   a. mountain
   b. squirrel
   c. carry forests on my back
   d. crack a nut
5. A fable is a story with a moral. What is the moral of this story?

Prayer Answered By Crosses

Some of our hymns are in narrative form. In such hymns, each stanza tells one part of the story. Every stanza must be present and in order to complete the thought of the story. Some narrative hymns recount a Bible story. "While Shepherds Watched Their Flocks by Night" tells the story of the shepherds at Jesus' birth. Some hymns are written as a supposed conversation. The following narrative poem, from an 1872 Brethren hymnbook, contains a conversation between the poet and God.

Prayer Answered by Crosses

I asked the Lord that I might grow
    In faith, and love, and every grace;
Might more of His salvation know,
    And seek more earnestly His face.

I hoped that in some favored hour   5
    At once He'd answer my request;
And by His love's constraining power,
    Subdue my sins, and give me rest.

Instead of this, He made me feel
    The hidden evils of my heart,   10
And let the angry powers of hell
    Assault my soul in every part.

Yea more, with His own hand He seemed
    Intent to aggravate my woe;
Crossed all the fair designs I schemed,   15
    Blasted my hopes, and laid me low.

"Lord, why is this," I trembling cried—
    "Wilt Thou pursue Thy worm to death!"
"Tis in this way," the Lord replied,
    "I answer prayer for grace and faith."   20

"These inward trials I employ,
    From self, and pride, to set thee free;
And break thy schemes of earthly joy,
    That thou may'st seek thy all in Me."

The Poet's Language

assault (ə sȯlt′) v.: attack

Meditating for Meaning

1.   God answers prayer, but not always in the manner we had hoped.
    a. What was the poet asking God to do for him?
    b. How did he want God to answer his prayer?
    c. In what ironical way did God answer the poet's prayer?

2. God's answer is better than our wish.
   a. How did the poet first interpret the answer he got?
   b. What graces did the trial bring to his life?
   c. What do the last two lines suggest may have happened if God had answered the poet's prayer the way he had hoped?
3. This poem can be sung if an appropriate tune is found.
   a. Count the syllables (not the feet) in each line of a stanza to find if it is common meter (8.6.8.6.), long meter (8.8.8.8.) or short meter (6.6.8.6.).
   b. Find a suitable tune for this poem in a hymnbook. Besides looking for the right meter, consider if the tune is appropriate to the thoughts of the poem.
   c. Find the two imperfect rhymes in this poem.

DRAMATIC POETRY

Strictly speaking, dramatic poetry provides lines to be spoken by actors on a stage. Several hundred years ago it was common for playwrights (persons who write the script for plays) to put the words of their actors into verse form. They became very skilled at writing hundreds of lines of blank verse.

Acting Violates Scriptual Principles. On the printed page, drama exists as dialogue. Two examples of this are *The Pilgrim's Progress* and many places in the *Martyrs Mirror.* Though *The Pilgrim's Progress* and the *Martyrs Mirror* are not intended to be acted out theatrically, they are examples of this type of dramatic dialogue in which the speaker's name appears separately before his speech. Well-written drama contains powerful interchanges of ideas, often in poetic language that is quotable. Thoughtful Christians can *read* drama with profit. But when drama is acted out on the stage, it takes on some very sinful aspects.

One serious problem in acted drama involves the imitation of evil. A good story involves conflict between two opposing forces, the one struggling for the right, and the other fighting against it. In the story of Moses, there must always be a Pharaoh. Joseph was opposed by his scheming brothers; Daniel by evil men in Babylon; and Jesus by the unbelieving Jews. What Christian could consent to act out the evil side of the conflict in a play? In fact, what Christian could act out the life of a "good" character? Moses once disobeyed God and struck the rock. Abraham lied about his relationship to his wife, and Peter denied his Lord. The only perfect character is Christ, but pretending to be deity would be nothing short of blasphemy. In the end, the Christian cannot really pretend to be any character in a play without getting involved with the appearance of evil (1 Thess. 5:22) or pretending to be God.

The Christian, furthermore, finds himself sensitive to the hypocrisy of acting out a part. In his pursuit of godlikeness, he values sincerity, the quality of always being his genuine self (2 Cor. 1:12). In God there is "no variableness, neither *shadow* of turning." God never gives the slightest appearance of being someone other than Himself. To be godly, then, is to be absolutely genuine at all times (Eph. 6:24). It is no accident that the word for *actor* in Greek was *hupokrites*, the term most used by Christ to denounce the worst enemies of truth. The actor actually uses a lie to promote truth. How revolting to the Christlike mind!

The Bible lays down God's methods for expressing truth, and acting is not among them. This does not mean that acting was unknown in Bible times. To the contrary, acting was used extensively among the ancient Greeks. Corinth had at least three theaters in the time of Paul. One might have expected Paul to use or refer to plays of the Corinthians to win them. But Paul ignored the theater and told the Corinthians that "it pleased God by the foolishness of *preaching* to save them that believe." We can conclude that Paul was aware of acting and rejected it.

Acting has always flourished in heathen cultures. The early church forbade its use. Acting came into the church during the Dark Ages while the church was in a lamentable state of decline, but it did nothing to bring the church out of its tragic apostasy. In fact, no widespread revival of true Christianity has ever resulted from its use. Never do you find acting listed among the gifts of the Holy Spirit in the Bible. It lacks the convicting power that preaching has to move sinners to repentance. The fearless preaching of the reformers broke through the apostasy of the Middle Ages and brought in a new age of faith. Interestingly, "Christians" are taking up acting again in a time of rapid spiritual decline.

The use of drama as written dialogue should not lead to acting in any form. Neither should we attend a play or endorse a method that deeply grieves the Holy Spirit by its very nature. Only by *reading* drama can a Christian be *truthfully* impressed by its truth.

While concerned Christians reject the use of drama itself, they can accept that dramatic poetry as literature is basically a story told in conversational form. Some writers of dramatic poetry had many insights into the problems of life and were skilled in expressing wise thoughts in striking literary form. Of the many such poets in the past, William Shakespeare is the most prominent. He wrote over thirty dramatic poems and many sonnets. Many lines from his plays have become proverbs. How many of the following lines from Shakespeare have you heard?

Better three hours too soon than a minute too late.

Cowards die many times before their deaths;
The valiant never taste of death but once.

Uneasy lies the head that wears a crown.

I'll not budge an inch.

Brevity is the soul of wit.

That's neither here nor there.

It was Greek to me.

You will be studying selections from three of Shakespeare's most important dramas. In these selections you will find more lines that have been often quoted to express universal truths.

 *Checking for Understanding*

1. Drama violates Christian character.
   a. What kind of character would a Christian least want to act out?
   b. Why would a Christian not want to act the part of Christ?
   c. What Christian virtue must a person sacrifice when acting?

2. Drama is not a Spirit-approved method of communication.
   a. What public method of promoting truth should the Christian use instead of drama?
   b. In the history of the church, the rise of drama occurred at times when _____ .

3. What is the only way a Christian can properly profit from dramatic poetry or any other form of written dialogue?

4. Scan several lines from the following selections from Shakespeare. From your observation, what kind of verses did he use to write his plays?

The Merchant of Venice

A certain merchant named Antonio borrowed a sum of money from a scheming money lender named Shylock. Since Antonio had good reason to believe that he could pay back the money in three months, he foolishly bargained that Shylock could have a pound of his flesh if the money was not paid back in time. Unforeseen tragedy fell, and Antonio was faced with the need to lose one pound of his flesh. A sympathetic woman posed as a lawyer to plead his case in court. The following selection is her appeal that Shylock would have mercy.

PORTIA:	Then must the Jew be merciful.	
SHYLOCK:	On what compulsion must I? tell me that.	
PORTIA:	The quality of mercy is not strain'd;	
	It droppeth as the gentle rain from heaven	
	Upon the place beneath: It is twice bless'd;	5
	It blesseth him that gives and him that takes.	
	'Tis mightiest in the mightiest, it becomes	
	The throned monarch better than his crown,	
	His sceptre shows the force of temporal power,	
	The **attribute** to awe and majesty,	10
	Wherein doth sit the dread and fear of kings:	
	But mercy is above this scepter'd sway,—	
	It is enthroned in the heart of kings,	
	It is an attribute to God himself;	
	And earthly power doth then show likest God's	15
	When mercy seasons justice. Therefore, Jew,	
	Though justice be thy plea consider this—	
	That in the course of justice none of us	
	Should see salvation: we do pray for mercy;	
	And that same prayer doth teach us all to render	20
	The deeds of mercy. I have spoke thus much	
	To **mitigate** the justice of thy plea;	
	Which if thou follow, this strict court of Venice	
	Must needs give sentence 'gainst the merchant there.	

The Poet's Language

attribute (aʹ trə byüt) n.: identifying quality   **mitigate** (miʹ tə gāt) v.: to make less severe

Shylock insisted on carrying out the letter of the law with respect to Antonio's bargain. Portia then told Shylock that the letter of his bargain made no provision to have any blood with the flesh. Furthermore, the law of Venice provided a stiff penalty for anyone who threatened a citizen's life. Since Shylock was indeed threatening to take Antonio's life, Shylock was guilty. This gave Antonio the opportunity to show Shylock the mercy that he would not give. By this the true "quality of mercy" was shown.

About the Author

William Shakespeare (1564-1616) was born in Stratford-upon-Avon, a market town northeast of London. He was largely self-taught because his father's financial failure terminated his formal education early. After marrying Anne Hathaway, Shakespeare took up acting in London and became perhaps the most famous playwright of all time. His sonnets and plays, which cover the range of tragedy, comedy, and history, have contributed many new words and expressions to the English language.

Meditating for Meaning

1. In light of line 2, what is the meaning of lines 3-6?
2. It would have taken a hard heart not to respond to this appeal for mercy.
   a. What double blessing does mercy bring?
   b. Explain " 'Tis mightiest in the mightiest."
   c. What will mercy do for a king that a sceptre will never do?
   d. Who above the rank of king shows mercy?
   e. Why does justice need to be seasoned with mercy?
   f. What is the very strongest reason why we should show mercy?
3. What is mercy?

Macbeth

Macbeth, an ambitious nobleman of Scotland, was tempted to aspire to the throne. His even more ambitious wife urged him to kill the existing king in order to become king himself. That murder led to more murders. Life became a complex of guilt and fear for Macbeth and his wife. Finally Lady Macbeth became insane and was tormented with nightmares. Her doctor witnessed one of these nightmares in which she implied that she was guilty of several murders. In the following conversation between Macbeth and the doctor, the doctor emphasizes that the only cure for some sicknesses lies with the patient and is beyond the help of medicine.

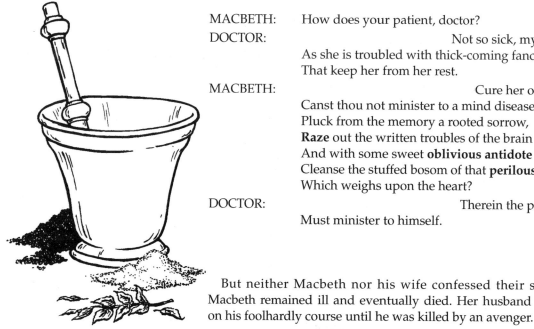

MACBETH: How does your patient, doctor?
DOCTOR: Not so sick, my lord,
As she is troubled with thick-coming fancies,
That keep her from her rest.
MACBETH: Cure her of that.
Canst thou not minister to a mind diseased,
Pluck from the memory a rooted sorrow,   5
Raze out the written troubles of the brain
And with some sweet **oblivious antidote**
Cleanse the stuffed bosom of that **perilous** stuff
Which weighs upon the heart?
DOCTOR: Therein the patient
Must minister to himself.   10

But neither Macbeth nor his wife confessed their sins. Lady Macbeth remained ill and eventually died. Her husband continued on his foolhardly course until he was killed by an avenger.

The Poet's Language

raze (rāz) v.: erase; remove completely

oblivious (ə bliv′ ē əs) adj.: unaware

antidote (ant′ i dōt) n.: cure; remedy

perilous (per′ ə ləs) adj.: dangerous

 *Meditating for Meaning*

1. What was Lady Macbeth's illness?
2. What did Macbeth want "some sweet oblivious antidote" to do?
3. What is the only effective medicine for a condition such as this?

Julius Caesar

The general plot of this story is based on historical fact. Shakespeare added many details and constructed the conversations. Julius Caesar rose to the position of dictator of the Roman empire in 49 B.C., and without doubt, was ambitious for this power. Some Romans feared what Caesar might do with his power. Others were jealous of Caesar and wanted him removed. Brutus was one of those who had honest misgivings about Caesar. The following selection is Brutus's expression of the fault of ambition.

BRUTUS: 'Tis a common proof,
That lowliness is young ambition's ladder,
Whereto the climber upward turns his face;
But when he once attains the upmost round,
He then unto the ladder turns his back,   5
Looks in the clouds, scorning the base degrees
By which he did ascend.

Brutus allowed himself to be influenced by base men into heading up an insurrection that climaxed in the murder of Caesar. The conspirators then had trouble getting along among themselves. Some loyal to Caesar raised an army to overthrow Brutus and his men. These conspirators then faced a question: Should they take the offensive and go forward to meet the loyal avengers, or should they wait until the enemy reached them? Brutus was in favor of taking the offensive. The following selection is his eloquent way of saying that opportunity should be taken when it comes.

There is a tide in the affairs of men,
Which, taken at the flood, leads on to fortune:
Omitted, all the voyage of their life
Is bound in shallows and in miseries.
On such a full sea are we now afloat;   5
And we must take the current when it serves,
Or lose our ventures.

But no amount of opportunity could save the cause of the conspirators and they were defeated by Caesar's avengers among whom was Octavian, the Roman Emperor at the time of Jesus' birth.

Meditating for Meaning

1. According to the selection about ambition, what is to be feared from those who reach great heights as a result of ambition?
2. In relation to the tides, when is the best time to launch a boat along an ocean shore?
3. What does Shakespeare use this metaphor to represent?
4. According to Shakespeare, what happens to people who do not make good use of opportunities?

LYRIC POETRY

Poetry by nature lends itself to singing. Singing here is not restricted to poems set to music, but includes all emotional expressions of joy and praise. A person could sing out in ordinary prose: "June is my favorite month. I like its delightfully warm days. It is the time of the year when flowers are prettiest and birds are happiest. I like June best."

But the emotional quality of poetry is even better than prose for singing. Poetry with highly musical wording is called lyric poetry. Our hymnbooks are full of lyric poetry. The Psalms are lyrics. Like all lyrics, our hymns and the Psalms have strong emotion and a deeply personal quality. Any poem that has praise as its main feature can be called a lyric. Lyrics may have any rhyme or rhythm pattern, but usually they are short. Most lyrics are simply songs, but some more lofty lyrics have been classified according to their particular style. You will be studying an example of three of these kinds of lyrics: the *ode*, the *apostrophe*, and the *elegy*.

What Is So Rare as a Day in June?

This lyric is the prelude to a very long narrative poem called **The Vision of Sir Launfal.** *In that poem, spring symbolizes youth. To set the mood of vigorous life and bright prospects, James Lowell introduces his poem with this lyric about June.*

What Is So Rare as a Day in June?

And what is so rare as a day in June?
    Then, if ever, come perfect days;
Then heaven tries earth if it be in tune,
    And over it softly her warm ear lays;
Whether we look, or whether we listen,   5
    We hear life murmur, or see it glisten;
Every clod feels a stir of might,
    An instinct within it that reaches and towers,
And, groping blindly above it for light,
    Climbs to a soul in grass and flowers.   10

James Russell Lowell

About the Author

James Russell Lowell (1819-1891) was born in Cambridge, Massachusetts. His father had been a member of the Second Continental Congress. After graduating from Harvard he taught at the college. During the Mexican War and again during the Civil War, he published the *Biglow Papers,* a political satire on these wars. Later he served as foreign minister to Spain and England. Perhaps his most famous literary work is the long epic poem, "The Vision of Sir Launfal," which tells how a legendary knight of King Arthur's court searched for the Holy Grail.

The Ode

The ode is a lofty lyric on a profound or philosophical theme. It can be contrasted to some ordinary songs that do not have much depth of emotion and whose poetic expressions are somewhat lacking in art.

The following ode has the theme of the existence of God as proclaimed in the starry heavens. Its poetic expressions transcend most of the ordinary lyrics in our hymnbooks. This rousing ode by Joseph Addison is often included in hymn collections with equally stirring music by Joseph Haydn.

The Spacious Firmament

The Poet's Language

ethereal (i thir′ ē əl) adj.: heavenly

terrestrial (tə res′ trē əl) adj.:
  earthly

orbs (ȯrbz) n.: spheres

The spacious firmament on high,
With all the blue **ethereal** sky,
And spangled heavens, a shining frame,
Their great Original proclaim.
The unwearied sun, from day to day,   5
Does his Creator's power display,
And publishes to every land
The work of an Almighty hand.

Soon as the evening shades prevail,
The moon takes up the wondrous tale,   10
And nightly to the listening earth
Repeats the story of her birth;
Whilst all the stars that round her burn
And all the planets in their turn,
Confirm the tidings as they roll,   15
And spread the truth from pole to pole.

What though in solemn silence all
Move round the dark **terrestrial** ball;
What though no real voice or sound
Amidst their radiant **orbs** be found: 20
In reason's ear they all rejoice,
And utter forth a glorious voice,
Forever singing as they shine,
"The hand that made us is divine."

Joseph Addison

About the Author

Joseph Addison (1672-1719) was born in Wiltshire, England, and graduated from Oxford University. With his friend Richard Steele he developed the periodical essay and published a literary magazine, *The Spectator*. Charmed by Addison's wit, many readers accepted his criticism of the social flaws of their day. Addison held several government positions, including a seat in Parliament and the office of Secretary of State. One of Addison's essays "The Works of Creation," appears in the CLP textbook *Perspectives of Truth in Literature*.

Photo: NASA

1. Good poets make excellent word choices. Find the six expressive verbs that Addison uses which mean "to tell."

2. Much of the richness of this poem will be lost to you if you do not understand the well-chosen adjectives. Find the adjective in the poem that matches each item below.
   a. cannot be made tired
   b. heavenly
   c. awe-inspiring
   d. magnificent
   e. vast
   f. decorated with small bright ornaments
   g. actual
   h. of the earth
   i. having unlimited power
   j. serious

3. This poem echoes many of the thoughts of Psalm 19:1-6. Match as many lines of poetry with verses as you can.

4. Addison tells us that the heavens are making a statement.
   a. What statement do the sun, moon, planets, and stars make?
   b. How does the poet say the heavenly bodies make that statement without saying anything?

The Apostrophe

An apostrophe is an address to someone who is absent or to something that is not alive as though it were alive. A poem that is written as such an address is also called an apostrophe. The apostrophe is similar to personification, the difference being that in personification some object is acting like a person whereas in apostrophe the object is being spoken to as if it were a person. This kind of lyric usually has an exclamatory tone as will be seen in the opening lines of "Apostrophe to the Ocean."

As you read this poem, be aware that the poet is only using the apostrophe as a figure of speech with which to say some very profound things about man and about nature. Be sure to observe punctuation carefully. Do not pause at the end of a line unless the punctuation tells you to.

Apostrophe to the Ocean

Roll on, thou deep and dark blue ocean, roll!
Ten thousand fleets sweep over thee in vain;
Man marks the earth with ruin—his control
Stops with the shore; upon the watery plain
The wrecks are all thy deed, nor doth remain   5
A shadow of man's **ravage**, save his own,
When, for a moment, like a drop of rain,
He sinks into thy depths with bubbling groan,
Without a grave, **unknelled, uncoffined** and unknown.

His steps are not upon thy paths—thy fields   10
Are not a spoil for him—thou dost arise
And shake him from thee; the vile strength he wields
For earth's destruction, thou dost all despise,
Spurning him from thy bosom to the skies,
And send'st him shivering in thy playful spray   15
And howling, to his gods, where **haply** lies
His **petty** hope in some near port or bay,
And dashest him to earth again—there let him lay.

The **armaments** which thunderstrike the walls
Of rock-built cities, bidding nations quake,   20
And monarchs tremble in their capitals,
The oak **leviathans** whose huge ribs make
Their clay creator the vain title take
Of lord of thee and **arbiter** of war;
These are thy toys, and, as the snowy flake,   25
They melt into thy **yeast** of waves, which mar
Alike the Armada's pride, or spoils of Trafalgar.

Thy shores are empires, changed in all save thee—
Assyria, Greece, Rome, Carthage, what are they?
Thy waters wasted them while they were free;   30
And many a tyrant since; their shores obey
The stranger, slave or savage; their decay
Has dried up realms to deserts—not so thou
Unchangeable, save to thy wild waves' play.
Time writes no wrinkle on thine azure brow;   35
Such as creation's dawn beheld, thou rollest now.

George Gordon Byron

Photo: Jessie M. Harris

The Poet's Language

ravage (rav′ ij) n.: raid; destruction

unknelled (ən neld′) adj.: unannounced by bells at death

uncoffined (ən kô′ fənd) adj.: unburied

spurning (spərn′ ing) v.: rejecting scornfully

haply (hap′ lē) adv.: perhaps

petty (pet′ ē) adj.: insignificant

armaments (är′ mə məntz) n.: military forces

leviathans (li vī′ ə thənz) n.: large sea monsters

arbiter (är′ bət ər) n.: dictatorial judge

yeast (yēst) n.: white foam caps of ocean waves

About the Author

George Gordon Byron (1788-1824) grew up in London, England, with his widowed mother. Throughout his childhood his mother's fits of passion and his own clubfootedness haunted him. An uncle died when Byron was ten, leaving him with the title of Lord. After graduating from Trinity College, Byron toured Europe and lived extravagantly, falling into debt and an unhappy marriage. These tours, however, sparked perhaps his greatest literary work, *Childe Harold's Pilgrimage*. From this work comes the lyric, "Apostrophe to the Ocean." Another lyric of his, "The Destruction of Sennacherib," appears in *Perspectives of Truth*. Byron died of a fever while serving as officer in a Greek army.

 *Meditating for Meaning*

1. This is a carefully constructed poem.
   a. With letters analyze the intricate rhyme scheme of one stanza of this poem.
   b. How does the rhythm of the last line of each stanza differ from the remainder of the stanza?
   c. What examples of assonance in the first two lines help to increase their beauty?
2. The poet is addressing the ocean, but his subject is man.
   a. What simile in the first stanza emphasizes the smallness of man?
   b. According to line 3, what is the result of man's control?
   c. Where does this control end? (See lines 3 and 4.)
   d. What do lines 10 and 11 imply man would do with the ocean if he could?
   e. Name at least one way in which twentieth-century man has extended his dominion to the control and ruin of the ocean's fields.

3. A reason is suggested for man's behavior.
   a. What word in the second stanza tells us that Byron feels that man is evil?
   b. For what purpose do many men use their religion? See line 16.
   c. The ocean brings such selfish men to shore. How?
   d. Considering the experience of Jonah, of what can the ocean be considered a symbol in this poem?
4. The third stanza climaxes Byron's condemnation of man.
   a. What destructive activity of man does the ocean judge in this stanza?
   b. What are the oak leviathans?
   c. Who is their clay creator?
   d. Copy the metaphor and the simile which the poet uses to show the puniness of man's efforts in relation to the sea.
   e. What vain pride does this stanza condemn?
5. The fourth stanza condemns yet another activity of man.
   a. What evil do the empires represent? See line 31.
   b. As long as the great empires were free, what did the ocean bring to them?
   c. What is the antecedent for the pronoun "their" in line 32?
   d. What became of the mighty empires?
6. What characteristic of the ocean does Byron particularly admire in stanza 4?
7. Poets are permitted a degree of poetic license.
   a. Use a college dictionary to find the definition of *poetic license*.
   b. What poetic license did Byron take in line 18?

The Elegy

The elegy as a lyric is a pensive poem about a sad subject. That subject is often death. The mood of an elegy is serious, sober, and melancholy. The poet is not overcome by grief, but is rather using sadness to reflect seriously about the sober realities of life.

The style of an elegy is polished and restful. It is the product of turning truth over and over in the mind until it can be expressed with great exactness and correctness.

Thomas Gray's "Elegy Written in a Country Churchyard" is an excellent example of an elegy. The setting of this poem is an actual graveyard near Stoke Poges, England. The church still stands and Gray himself is now buried in the graveyard.

It will be helpful for you to know that according to English custom, the prominent people of a community were buried within the church itself. The common people were buried in the churchyard. In his elegy, Gray is meditating on the significance of the common people of the land.

Mr. Gray was a perfectionist. He allowed only 12 of his poems to be published in his lifetime. He started the elegy in 1742 following the burial of an uncle. He continued work on it in 1749 after an aunt died. He finished it in 1750. That kind of effort produced what is considered by some the most perfect poem in the English language.

Elegy Written in a Country Churchyard

Darkness descends on a country churchyard and a meditating poet. The workday is over.

1. The curfew[1] tolls the knell[2] of parting[3] day,
   The lowing herd wind slowly o'er the lea,[4]
   The plowman homeward plods his weary way,
   And leaves the world to darkness and to me.

1. the ringing of a bell marking the time to cover fires and retire
2. bell rung at a funeral; hence in the poem, marking the death of the day
3. departing
4. pasture or clearing

The darkening natural world drifts into the quiet and drowsy sounds of night.

2. Now fades the glimmering landscape on
   the sight,   5
   And all the air a solemn stillness holds,
   Save where the beetle wheels his droning
   flight,
   And drowsy tinklings[5] lull[6] the distant folds;

5. tinklings of cowbells
6. put to sleep

The first three stanzas set a mood suitable for quiet, unhurried reflection on the dead.

3. Save that from yonder ivy-mantled tower[7]
   The moping owl does to the moon
   complain   10
   Of such as, wandering near her secret bower,
   Molest her ancient solitary reign.

7. the bell tower of the church

The past common men of the village lie buried in the shady church graveyard.

4. Beneath those rugged elms, that yew[8] tree's
   shade,
   Where heaves the turf[9] in many a
   mouldering heap,
   Each in his narrow cell[10] forever laid,   15
   The rude[11] forefathers of the hamlet[12] sleep.

8. a long-living ever-green; symbolizes immortality
9. sod
10. coffin
11. uncultured and uneducated; lacking refinement
12. a small country village

Never again will they be awakened by the sounds of morning.

5. The breezy call of incense-breathing morn,
   The swallow twittering from the straw-
   built[13] shed,
   The cock's shrill clarion,[14] or the echoing
   horn,[15]
   No more shall rouse them from their lowly
   bed.[16]   20

13. having a thatched roof
14. a sound similar to a clear, shrill trumpet
15. a hunter's horn
16. not the grave, but the humble bed they slept on while alive

They will never again have an honored place as head of a family.

6. For them no more the blazing hearth shall
   burn,
   Or busy housewife ply[17] her evening care:
   No children run to lisp their sire's return,
   Or climb his knee the envied kiss to share.

17. keep working at; maybe at knitting

But previously they energetically tilled the soil and cleared the land.

7. Oft did the harvest to their sickle yield, 25
   Their furrow oft the stubborn glebe[18] has broke;
   How jocund[19] did they drive their team[20] afield!
   How bowed the woods beneath their sturdy stroke![21]

It is not proper for those of high position and prestige to make fun of the poor . . .

8. Let not ambition mock[22] their useful toil,
   Their homely joys, and destiny obscure; 30
   Nor grandeur hear[23] with a disdainful smile,
   The short and simple annals[24] of the poor.

. . . since even the high-born, rulers, and those with outstanding beauty or wealth must some day die.

9. The boast of heraldry,[25] the pomp of power,
   And all that beauty, all that wealth e'er gave,
   Awaits[26] alike th' inevitable hour:—[27] 35
   The paths of glory lead but to the grave.

And the proud should not blame the survivors of the deceased for not burying in a cathedral and placing above the tomb an ornament of remembrance.

10. Nor you, ye proud, impute to these the fault,
    If memory o'er their tomb no trophies raise,
    Where through the long-drawn aisle and fretted vault[28]
    The pealing anthem swells the note of praise. 40

For the honor and flattery of a memorial vase or statue will have no effect on the dead.

11. Can storied urn[29] or animated bust[30]
    Back to its mansion[31] call the fleeting breath?
    Can honour's voice provoke[32] the silent dust,
    Or flattery soothe the dull cold ear of Death?

There may be buried in this graveyard some who had special gifts of heavenly zeal, ability to rule others, or ability to write poetry.

12. Perhaps in this neglected spot is laid 45
    Some heart once pregnant with celestial fire;[33]
    Hands, that the rod of empire might have swayed,[34]
    Or waked to ecstasy the living lyre.[35]

But a lack of education and poverty kept them from ever realizing their full potential.

13. But knowledge to their eyes her ample page[36]
    Rich with the spoils of time[37] did ne'er unroll;[38] 50
    Chill penury[39] repressed their noble rage,[40]
    And froze the genial[41] current of the soul.

Just so, nature has many examples of a seeming waste of great potential for beauty and value.

14. Full many a gem of purest ray serene
    The dark unfathomed caves of ocean bear;
    Full many a flower is born to blush unseen, 55
    And waste its sweetness on the desert air.

18. ground or soil
19. cheerful and happy
20. of horses or oxen
21. stroke of the axe

22. Ambition is here personified. It is ambitious persons who are not to mock.
23. Grandeur is also personified. Let not men of pomp make fun of the lives of the poor.
24. record or history

25. refers to the coat of arms used to signify prestigious family lines; here used to mean the pride of noted ancestry
26. The verb is singular because the subject is *hour*. The "inevitable hour" lies in wait for the boast of heraldry, the pomp of power, "and all that beauty, all that wealth e'er gave."
27. death

28. a description of the interior of a cathedral; famous men were often buried in a cathedral with monuments over them in their honor.

29. a burial vase on which is written or pictured the deeds of the deceased
30. a lifelike statue of the upper portion of the deceased
31. the dead body; the place where the breath lived
32. stir to life

33. filled and fruitful with heavenly ideas or zeal
34. The subject of *swayed* is *hands.*
35. a reference to poetry
36. the many books of learning
37. the accumulation of information through the ages
38. as a scroll; here symbolizing an education
39. poverty
40. zeal or enthusiasm for academic pursuits
41. potential for genius

These graves may contain men who could have made a mark in history or literature if they had had opportunity.

They could not seek the praise of governments with fair speeches, or seek the gratitude of the populace by heroic deeds for their benefit . . .

. . . because their station in life would not allow them. But their lot did not only limit the extent they could exercise their virtues, but it also spared them of committing many crimes. They were spared the temptation to ruthlessly strive for high government position and even commit murder in the process.

They did not try to hide what they knew was true or try to hide their guilt. Neither did they cater to the aristocrats for selfish advantage.

These sober-minded people were far removed from the evil struggles of the majority. They quietly went about their pleasant life in obscurity.

So that no one would molest the bones of the dead, a crude grave marker had been erected bearing some common poetry and unartistic sculpturing. It did serve as a sobering reminder of the dead.

15. Some village Hampden,[42] that with dauntless breast
    The little tyrant of his fields withstood.
  Some mute inglorious Milton[43] here may rest
    Some Cromwell[44] guiltless of his country's blood.   60

16. Th' applause of listening senates to command,
    The threats of pain and ruin to despise,
  To scatter plenty o'er a smiling land,
    And read their history in a nation's eyes,[45]

17. Their lot forbade: nor circumscribed alone   65
    Their growing virtues, but their crimes confined;
  Forbade to wade through slaughter to a throne,
    And shut the gates of mercy on mankind;

18. The struggling pangs of conscious truth to hide,
    To quench the blushes of ingenuous[46] shame,   70
  Or heap the shrine of Luxury and Pride
    With incense kindled at the Muse's[47] flame.

19. Far from the madding[48] crowd's ignoble[49] strife,
    Their sober wishes never learned to stray;
  Along the cool sequestered[50] vale of life   75
    They kept the noiseless tenor[51] of their way.

20. Yet ev'n these bones from insult to protect,
    Some frail memorial still erected nigh,
  With uncouth[52] rhymes and shapeless sculpture decked,
    Implores the passing tribute of a sigh.   80

42. refers to John Hampden who in 1636 resisted a tax imposed by King Charles I

43. refers to John Milton who is one of the most famous English poets

44. refers to Oliver Cromwell, a former ruler of England who was once thought to have caused the death of King Charles I because of his own ambition. See line 67. History has shown that Cromwell was not actually guilty of that crime.

45. This entire stanza is the object of the verb "forbade" in the next stanza.

46. frank, open, without guile

47. poet's; lines 71 and 72 refer to the vain practice of poets to write poems of flattery or dedicate their books to nobles in order to receive favors from them

48. acting in a wild or insane way

49. not noble; mean; dishonorable

50. secluded, apart from others

51. steady and continuous course

52. coarse, unrefined, lacking culture

The engraved name and age of the deceased, though misspelled, took the place of statements of flattery. Some Bible verses served as good reminders to the country folks that they should prepare to die.

21. Their name, their years, spelt by the unlettered Muse,[53]
    The place of fame and elegy supply;
    And many a holy text[54] around she strews,
    That teach the rustic[55] moralist to die.

53. Some uneducated poet or writer had included misspellings in the texts of the gravestones

54. Scripture verses

55. country; rural

Doesn't everyone have a tendency to look back on his life with fondness when he comes to die?

22. For who to dumb forgetfulness[56] a prey,   85
    This pleasing anxious being e'er resigned,
    Left the warm precincts[57] of the cheerful day,
    Nor cast one longing, lingering look behind.

56. death

57. a confined area; in this case a lifetime

Everyone wants to know that he was loved and appreciated when he dies.

23. On some fond breast the parting soul relies,
    Some pious drops[58] the closing eye
        requires;   90
    Ev'n from the tomb the voice of Nature cries,
    Ev'n in our ashes live their wonted[59] fires.

58. tears of a devoted friend

59. usual, customary

Photo: Kevin & Bethany Shank

Gray hopes that if someone interested in the dead should inquire about him after he is gone . . .

24. For thee,[60] who mindful of th' unhonored dead,
    Dost in these lines[61] their artless tale relate;
    If chance, by lonely contemplation led,   95
    Some kindred spirit[62] shall inquire thy fate,—

60. Gray is here talking to himself
61. this particular poem
62. someone who like Gray himself thinks about the departed and wonders how they met their end

. . . some old country-men will remember him and be able to say, "I often saw him out walking   bright and early.

25. Haply some hoary-headed swain[63] may say,
    "Oft have we seen him at the peep of dawn
    Brushing with hasty steps the dews away,
    To meet the sun upon the upland lawn;   100

63. gray-haired peasant or shepherd

"At noon he would rest under that old beech tree and gaze at the stream that runs by.

26. "There at the foot of yonder nodding beech
    That wreathes its old fantastic roots so high,
    His listless length at noontide would he
        stretch,
    And pore[64] upon the brook that babbles by.

64. Gaze intently, perhaps with deep meditation

"I have seen him talking to himself as he walked by the woods. His shoulders would be sagging as if he had a life of trouble or as if he had not been able to marry the one he loved.

27. "Hard by yon wood, now smiling as in
        scorn,   105
    Muttering his wayward fancies he would rove,
    Now drooping, woeful wan,[65] like one forlorn,
    Or crazed with care, or crossed in hopeless
        love.[66]

65. sickly, pale
66. Gray was never married.

"One day I did not see him at his usual places.

28. "One morn I missed him on the customed hill,
    Along the heath and near his favorite tree;   110
    Another came; nor yet beside the rill,[67]
    Nor up the lawn, not at the wood was he;

67. a little stream

"The next day we saw him taken to the church graveyard." Here, read this poem upon his tombstone."

29. The next, with dirges[68] due in sad array
    Slow through the church-way path we saw
        him borne.[69]
    Approach and read (for thou canst read)[70] the
        lay,[71]   115
    Graved on the stone beneath yon aged
        thorn."

68. mournful hymns suitable for use at a funeral
69. carried
70. Many country people in Gray's day were illiterate. The old man speaking cannot read himself and is inviting his listener to read for himself what is written on the tombstone.
71. poem

Here is buried one who knew only a little of wealth and nothing of fame. He had a good education despite his lowly birth. He was a man much given to sad thoughts and moods.

The Epitaph[72]

30. Here rests his head upon the lap of earth
    A youth to fortune and to fame unknown.
    Fair science frowned not on his humble birth,[73]
    And melancholy marked him for her own.
                                              120

72. This epitaph is Gray's description of himself.

73. Although he was of humble birth, he was still well-educated.

He was very generous and sincere. He lived in sorrow but was satisfied with a close friend God gave him.

31. Large was his bounty,[74] and his soul sincere,
    Heaven did a recompense as largely send;
    He gave to misery all he had, a tear;
    He gained from Heaven ('twas all he wished)
    a friend.[75]

Do not try to discover his further merits or weaknesses. He has committed them to his God and Father.

32. No farther seek his merits to disclose,   125
    Or draw his frailties from their dread abode,
    (There they alike in trembling hope repose)
    The bosom of his Father and his God.

74. generosity
75. probably referring to Horace Walpole who was a close friend of Gray.

Thomas Gray

About the Author

Thomas Gray (1716-1771) was a gentle and quiet poet of London, England. His jealous father made his early life unhappy, but Gray's mother encouraged him to attend Cambridge University where he graduated and later became a professor. Gray expressed his simple views in "Elegy Written in a Country Churchyard" and in his famous saying, "Where ignorance is bliss, 'tis folly to be wise." He is buried outside the church at Stoke Poges, England, setting of "Elegy Written in a Country Churchyard."

Meditating for Meaning

1. Gray establishes the mood of his elegy in the first three stanzas.
    a. What is the setting for this poem?
    b. What is the mood established by this setting?
    c. Give various things that are happening that contribute to this mood.

2. Consider the poetic characteristics of this poem.
    a. What meter has the poet selected that is particularly suitable for his weighty subject?
    b. What is the rhyme scheme?
    c. There are at least six imperfect rhymes in this poem. Find four of them.
    d. What assonance in the first stanza contributes to a slow, drowsy effect?
    e. Find at least two examples of alliteration in the first two stanzas.
    f. Find at least two examples of onomatopoeia in the first two stanzas.

3. Identify the stanzas included in each point of the following outline of the poem.
   a. The setting for the elegy
   b. The subject for the elegy
   c. The life of those buried in the churchyard
   d. The reason it is not fitting for aristocrats to scorn the common man
   e. The difference caused by lack of opportunity
   f. The evil from which the common man is spared
   g. The memorial left to the common man by those who loved him
   h. The common thoughts and desires of departing souls
   i. The prospect of someone inquiring about the poet after he dies
   j. The memory of an old man
   k. The epitaph on the tomb of the poet

4. Identify the lines from Stanzas 1-15 that tell each of the following:
   a. A bell signals the close of the day.
   b. Sheep are going to sleep.
   c. An owl is the only inhabitant of the church tower.
   d. The graves can be discerned by the unevenness of the ground.
   e. Those in the grave will never again be aroused by the crowing of a rooster.
   f. At the end of a workday, the children announced their father's coming.
   g. One pleasure of the farmer was to go to work with his horses.
   h. The strength of the farmer is seen in the amount of timber he cut.
   i. There is not much to record about the life of the common folk.
   j. Like the poor, the aristocrats cannot avoid the time of their death.
   k. The poor are not to be blamed for their lack of an honored burial.
   l. Having an elaborate tomb cannot give back life to the body.
   m. Given the opportunity, the poor man might have become a king.
   n. The reason the poor do not have the opportunity is because of their poverty.
   o. Nature abounds with examples of potential value going undiscovered.
   p. Someone with outstanding potential for writing poetry may be buried in the churchyard.

5. Identify the lines from Stanzas 16-32 that tell each of the following:
   a. Some may have had great oratory potential.
   b. The attainment of high government office often makes the heart unfeeling to the distress of others.
   c. Those in high positions in society are apt to cover up their wrongdoing.
   d. The poor live away from the ruthless struggles of a selfish society.
   e. Even the most lowly gravemarker stirs a sober reminder of the dead.
   f. Inscriptions on the tombstones of the poor may provide worthy meditation.
   g. It gives us all concern to give up our life that has brought us so much pleasure.
   h. When we come to die, we depend on the help of a close friend.
   i. The poet has written a poem about the common men who have died.
   j. The poet wants to be remembered as one who had a zest for life.
   k. The poet wants to be remembered for his contentment with the simple beauties of nature.
   l. The poet had a melancholy disposition.
   m. The poet wants to be active to within two days of his funeral.
   n. The poet wants to be remembered by a poem.
   o. The poet had opportunities that others of his class did not have.
   p. The poet was not ambitious.
   q. The poet does not wish to have a biography written about himself.

6. While this elegy has its setting in a graveyard and is a meditation about the dead, it is what it says about the living that makes it valuable.
   a. According to Stanzas 6 and 7, what good was accomplished by the peasant people? Compare these accomplishments with God's objectives for man in Genesis 1:28.
   b. What benefit is it to be denied the opportunity to climb in society? (See Stanzas 17-19.)
   c. What does Gray consider valuable to have when he dies? (Stanzas 23 and 31)
   d. As good as Gray's desires are, what better objective(s) can one have?
7. Good poetry will have lines worthy of being quoted. These are lines that express timeless truths in a particularly striking way. Select six such quotable lines from this poem. Then check to see how many of those you selected are in *Bartlett's Familiar Quotations* (if it is available to you).

DIDACTIC POETRY

Narrative poetry tells us a story. Dramatic poetry gives us dialogue. Lyric poetry helps us sing. But the main purpose of some poetry is to teach us something. Such poetry is called didactic poetry. To a certain extent, all poetry teaches us. Many of our hymns instruct us in the doctrines of the Bible as they provide expressions of praise to God.

But as you will see in the next few poems, the poet sometimes uses his poems *primarily* to teach. Literary critics tend to be very hard on didactic poetry. They feel that when rhyme and rhythm are simply added to moralistic teaching, the result is no longer poetry but simply verse. For example,

> "Early to bed and early to rise,
>   Makes a man healthy, wealthy, and wise"

is not regarded as poetry no matter how well the lines rhyme. Sometimes teachers will use verses to help the students remember a lesson. The simple verse

> "*I* before *e*
>   Except after *c*"

has helped many spell certain words right. But such verse does not have the emotional quality and imagery of true poetry. The verse form only helps us remember the truth better.

However, we should not belittle didactic verse since it does perform a valuable service. Neither should we scorn didactic poetry simply because it is openly trying to teach us a lesson. We want to be teachable, and if a poem helps us see truth better, or puts truth in a form that will make it easier for us to accept and remember, then we appreciate didactic poetry. Ministers often use a didactic poem to highlight a teaching in their messages.

The three examples of didactic poetry you will study vary greatly in their poetic quality. Try to decide which is the most poetic and which is hardly more than verse. All of them are teaching something. Be sure you do not miss their messages.

Bad Times

Why slander we the times?
    What crimes
  Have days and years, that we
Thus charge them with iniquity?
    If we would rightly scan,   5
It's not the times are bad, but man.
    If thy desire it be
        To see
    The times prove good, be thou
But such thyself, and surely know   10
    That all thy days to thee
Shall, spite of mischief, happy be.

Joseph Beaumont

About the Author

Joseph Beaumont (1616-1699) was born to a family of Leicestershire, England. At the age of 16, he entered Cambridge University. He later served as tutor, college master, and finally as Professor of Divinity. His once famous poem, "Love's Mystery," tells of the communion between Christ and the soul.

 *Meditating for Meaning*

1. Look up the word *slander* in a dictionary; then explain what is meant by slandering the times.
2. What does the poet teach us is the key to seeing good days?
3. How does the poet's advice compare with 1 Peter 3:10, 11?
4. What is the implied reason why people slander the times?
5. "Bad Times" is almost entirely void of imagery and emotion.
   a. There is some use of personification. What is it?
   b. Line 6 has a slight display of emotion. What is it?
   c. How would you rate this didactic poem as poetry?

Building

I watched them tearing a building down—
A gang of men in a busy town—
With a yo-heave-ho and a **lusty** yell,
They swung a beam and the side wall fell.
I asked the foreman: "Are these men skilled—   5
The kind you would hire if you wanted to build?"
He laughed and said: "Why, no indeed,
Just common labour is all I need:
They can easily wreck in a day or two
What builders have taken years to do."   10

I asked myself, as I went my way,
Which of these roles have I tried today?
Am I a builder, who works with care,
Measuring life by the rule and square,
Shaping my deeds by the well-made plan,   15
Patiently doing the best I can?
Or am I a wrecker who walks the town,
Content with the labour of tearing down?

Author unknown

The Poet's Language

lusty (ləs′ tē) adj.: vigorous; energetic

Meditating for Meaning

1. The job of building has often been used as an analogy.
   a. What word is used in Romans 14:19 that means to build?
   b. By what actions do we "build" with our lives?
   c. When do we become a "wrecker"?

Photo: David Hartzler

2. What difference between wrecking and building does the poet show?

3. What is the "rule and square" in our lives?

4. What would you say is the lesson of this didactic verse?

5. True poetry should have both emotional quality and imagery. Which does this verse lack that keeps it from ranking very high as poetry?

The Poet

Thou who wouldst wear the name
 Of poet 'mid thy brethren of mankind,
And clothe in words of flame
 Thoughts that shall live within the general mind;
Deem not the framing of a deathless **lay**   5
The pastime of a drowsy summer day.

But gather all thy powers,
 And **wreak** them on the verse that thou dost weave,
And in thy lonely hours,
 At silent morning or at wakeful eve,   10
While the warm current tingles through thy veins
Set forth the burning words in **fluent** strains.

No smooth array of phrase,
 Artfully sought and ordered though it be,
Which the cold rhymer lays   15
 Upon his page with **languid** industry,
Can wake the listless pulse to livelier speed,
Or fill with sudden tears the eyes that read.

The secret wouldst thou know
 To touch the heart or fire the blood at will?   20
Let thine own eyes o'erflow;
 Let thy lips quiver with the **passionate** thrill;
Seize the great thought, ere yet its power be past,
And bind, in words, the fleet emotion fast.

Then should thy verse appear   25
 Halting and harsh, and all unaptly wrought,
Touch the crude line with fear,
 Save in the moment of **impassioned** thought;
Then summon back the original glow, and mend
The strain with rapture that with fire was penned.   30

The Poet's Language

deem (dēm) v.: consider; regard

lay (lā) n.: poem, hymn

wreak (rēk) v.: unleash; inflict

fluent (flü′ ənt) adj.: smoothly spoken

languid (lan′ gwəd) adj.: lifeless; feeble

passionate (pash′ ə nət) adj.: with strong feeling

impassioned (im pash′ ənd) adj.: zealous; intense

limn (lim) v.: describe

rampart (ram′ pärt′) n.: fortified protection

Yet let no empty gust
    Of passion find an utterance in thy lay,
A blast that whirls the dust
    Along the howling street and dies away;
But feelings of calm power and mighty sweep,   35
Like currents journeying through the windless deep.

Seek'st thou, in living lays,
    To **limn** the beauty of the earth and sky?
Before thine inner gaze
    Let all that beauty in clear vision lie;   40
Look on it with exceeding love, and write
The words inspired by wonder and delight.

Of tempests wouldst thou sing,
    Or tell of battles—make thyself a part
Of the great tumult; cling   45
    To the tossed wreck with terror in thy heart;
Scale, with the assaulting host, the **rampart's** height,
And strike and struggle in the thickest fight.

So shalt thou frame a lay
    That haply may endure from age to age,   50
And they who read shall say:
    "What power hangs upon this poet's page!
What art is his the written spells to find
That sway from mood to mood the willing mind!"

William Cullen Bryant
(altered)

About the Author

William Cullen Bryant (1794-1878) ranks as America's first noteworthy poet. Unlike earlier writers who parroted English poets, Bryant wrote about America, particularly his native Massachusetts hills. Probably his greatest poem is "Thanatopsis," a poem about death, which he wrote in his teens and revised, history claims, 99 times. "To a Waterfowl" appears in *Perspectives of Truth*. Unable to attend Yale, Bryant studied law at Williams college of Massachusetts and became a lawyer. Much of his life he spent in New York where he edited the *New York Evening Post*.

Meditating for Meaning

1. The word *lay* is used two ways in this poem.
   a. What is the meaning of the word "lays" in line 15?
   b. What does Bryant mean by "a deathless lay" (line 5) and "living lays" (line 37)?
2. Bryant is very clear that a good poem must stir emotion.
   a. In what two general directions does he say a poem can stir the emotions? (See lines 17, 18, and 20.)
   b. What does he say is the secret to writing poetry that has feeling?
   c. By his own advice, what was necessary for Bryant to be qualified to write this poem?
   d. What is necessary to write a good nature poem? (See Stanza 7.)
   e. What is necessary to write a stirring poem about danger? (See Stanza 8.)
3. Now look at the literary qualities of this poem.
   a. What is the rhyme scheme and meter of this poem?
   b. Find three good examples of alliteration in this poem.
   c. Interpret the imagery of the sixth stanza.
   d. Find three lines that you think are good expressions of emotion and tell what emotion each expresses.
4. How would you rate this didactic verse as poetry? Does it stir in you the emotions of a true poet?

Writing With Skill

Probably there is some experience in your life in which you were deeply moved emotionally. Were you awestruck by something spectacular in nature? Were you touched with sympathy in the face of suffering or death? Did the joy of friendship ever make you feel like singing? What spiritual experience was very meaningful to you? Which things thrill your soul?

Relive that experience in your mind. Allow your heart to be quickened again. Then "bind, in words, the fleet emotion fast." Write a poem that communicates your feelings about the subject. It likely will not be a "deathless lay," but such efforts, if repeated often enough, can lead you to the skill of writing poetry that touches the hearts of people and edifies them for many years.

A FLOCK OF POEMS

Poems to Ponder

Some poems can be read easily and understood the first time they are read. They require little study because their meaning is not very deep. Such poems may not rate very highly as literature. On the other hand, a good poem has such profound meaning and intriguing turns of phrase that you can come to it again and again and find new truths and inspiration.

At first you may not like a poem that has been highly acclaimed. Its wording seems so obtuse and the meaning so obscure that you despair of reading it. Those are the poems that repay your effort to dig out their truth. The beauty of their lines will grow on you until the phrasing is like an old friend—you respond with recognition every time you hear them read or see them in print.

Sometimes a poem is deceptively simple. At first you think you understand everything it says. But there is a deeper meaning—a phrase with a double meaning, a figure of speech to unravel, a truth that is not as simple as it seems. Such is a poem to ponder.

Victory in Defeat

Defeat may serve as well as victory
To shake the soul and let the glory out.
When the great oak is straining in the wind,
The boughs drink in new beauty, and the trunk
Sends down a deeper root on the **windward** side.   5
Only the soul that knows the mighty grief
Can know the mighty rapture. Sorrows come
To stretch our spaces in the heart for joy.

Edwin Markham

The Poet's Language

windward (wind′ wərd) adj.: the
  side from which the wind blows

 *Meditating for Meaning*

1. What in our lives is symbolized by the wind in this poem?
2. Markham presents defeat as a benefit.
    a. What will happen to an oak tree that never experiences a storm?
    b. What will be missing in the character development of a person who always has things go his way?
    c. What purpose do grief and sorrow serve in our experience?
    d. How do you think grief and sorrow accomplish this?
3. Explain the title.
4. According to its mechanics, what kind of verse is this?

Conscience and Remorse

The Poet's Language

aye (ā) adv.: always; ever

"Good-bye," I said to my conscience—
  "Good-bye for **aye** and aye,"
And I put her hands off harshly,
  And turned my face away;
And conscience smitten sorely   5
  Returned not from that day.

But a time came when my spirit
  Grew weary of its pace;
And I cried: "Come back, my conscience;
  I long to see thy face."   10
But conscience cried: "I cannot;
  Remorse sits in my place."

Paul Laurence Dunbar

About the Author

Paul Laurence Dunbar (1872-1906) son of escaped slaves, was born in Dayton, Ohio. There he attended the Steele High School as the only Negro student and edited the student magazine. Though he wrote both short stories and poetry, readers love his verse best. In it he expresses with humor the sentiments of the Negro. Many of his poems appear in the collection *Lyrics of the Lowly.* Dunbar died of tuberculosis at the age of 34.

Meditating for Meaning

1. Conscience is here personified.
   a. What do the "hands" of conscience try to do?
   b. How does one "put her hands off harshly"?

c. How does the Bible describe the condition of the conscience spoken of in lines 5 and 6? (1 Timothy 4:2; Ephesians 4:19; Heb. 3:13)

2. What pace is it that Dunbar speaks of in line 8?

3. Why does he now desire the return of his conscience?

4. Conscience has been displaced.
   a. What is remorse?
   b. How does remorse take the place of conscience?

5. The conclusion leaves the impression of hopelessness about sins that are past. Explain how this idea is inconsistent with 1 John 1:9 and Psalm 103.

6. In spite of the error implied in the concluding line, this poem has a valuable warning. State this warning in your own words.

The Poet's Language

fray (frā) n.: fight; conflict

perjured (pər′ jərd) n.: corrupted by falsehood

No Enemies

You have no enemies, you say?
Alas! my friend, the boast is poor—
He who has mingled in the **fray**
Of duty, that the brave endure,
Must have made foes! If you have none,   5
Small is the work that you have done;
You've hit no traitor on the hip;
You've dashed no cup from **perjured** lip;
You've never turned the wrong to right—
You've been a coward in the fight!   10

Charles Mackay

About the Author

Charles Mackay (1814-1889) born in Perth, Scotland, was raised by a nurse because his mother died during his infancy. He received his early schooling in Brussels, moving later to London where he became editor of the *Illustrated London News*. During the Civil War in America he lived in New York, working for the *London Times*. After the death of his first wife, he married a widow. The many songs which he wrote brought him his greatest popularity.

Meditating for Meaning

1. By nature man is inclined to take the easy way. He may even consider it a virtue to avoid hardship.
   a. What boast of virtue might the natural man make that would prompt such a poem?
   b. What are two ways of acquiring enemies? (One is not mentioned in the poem.)
   c. Which way is spoken of in 1 Peter 4:15?
   d. Which way is spoken of in 2 Timothy 4:2, 3?

2. If a man has no enemies, what is he to be blamed for?

3. If a man says he has enemies, is this reason to praise him? Explain.

4. Notice accusation piled on accusation in parallel form. This is an effective literary technique.
   a. Who is a traitor?
   b. What does hitting him on the hip symbolize?
   c. What kind of lip would be a perjured lip?
   d. What does dashing a cup from perjured lips signify?

5. We surely do not want to set the making of enemies as a goal in life. What then is the call of this poem?

Betrayal

Still as of old
Men by themselves are priced—
For thirty pieces Judas sold
Himself, not Christ.

Hester H. Cholmondeley

About the Author

Hester H. Cholmondeley lived in Shropshire, England, during the latter half of the nineteenth century. She was the invalid daughter of Reverend Richard Hugh Cholmondeley. During her 22 years she wrote a lot of miscellaneous poetry. Her sister Mary Cholmondeley authored several novels.

Meditating for Meaning

1. Consider the following irony.
   a. What do we often say one person is worth (Matt. 16:26)?
   b. According to this poem, how do many people who say this, prove that they really do not believe it?

2. Psalm 105:17 speaks of Joseph being sold to be a servant.
   a. According to this poem, who was really sold?
   b. How much did they consider themselves worth? (See Genesis 37:28.)

3. Other Bible characters sold themselves. Who are the ones in the following references and by what did they value themselves?
   a. Genesis 3:6
   b. 1 Samuel 15:14, 15
   c. Acts 5:2-9

4. In a spiritual sense, who won a victory from the purchasing in each of these cases? _____

5. Then, in general, we sell ourselves anytime we agree to _____ in return for _____ _____ .

6. The poet says that this selling is still going on today. Give several examples of the prices men are putting on themselves today.

The Poet's Language

resolved (ri zälvd′) adj.: determined

Fanny Crosby in later life

Blind But Happy

O what a happy soul am I!
    Although I cannot see,
I am **resolved** that in this world
    Contented I will be;
How many blessings I enjoy   5
    That other people don't!
To weep and sigh because I'm blind,
    I cannot, and I won't.

Fanny Crosby

About the Author

Fanny Crosby (1820-1915) known as the "Queen of Gospel Hymnody,"
wrote eight or nine thousand hymn poems during her life. At the age of
six, Fanny was blinded by improper medical treatment. She attended an
institution for the blind in her native state of New York. While teaching in
this same school, Fanny met and married a blind musician, Alexander
van Alstyne. Although blind, Fanny memorized large portions of Scripture
including the five books of Moses, Ruth, many Psalms and Proverbs, The
Song of Solomon, and the four Gospels. From this Bible knowledge came
many well-loved hymn poems which she contributed to composers and
evangelists, as well as church hymnals of today.

Meditating for Meaning

1. This poem is a simple statement of the formula for happiness, written when the author was eight years old.

   a. What does the poet say is the key to her happiness despite her handicap?

   b. What is the basis for contentment as explained in lines 5 and 6?

   c. What then is contentment? (See Philippians 4:11; 1 Timothy 6:8; and Hebrews 13:5.)

2. Crosby does not consider her handicap to be without its compensations. For example, a blind person develops a very keen memory. It is said Fanny Crosby could quote Genesis to Deuteronomy and Matthew to John at a young age.

   a. What other faculties would a blind person tend to develop and enjoy more than a person with sight?

   b. In her hymns, Crosby makes many references to things she could see or hoped to see. For example: "Gushing from the rock before me, Lo! A spring of joy I see," "Visions of rapture now burst on my sight," "He hideth my soul in the cleft of the rock, where rivers of pleasure I see." What is the poet professing to be able to see?

   c. How could being blind actually contribute to this kind of vision? (See 2 Corinthians 4:4; Matthew 5:29; and 1 John 2:16.)

   d. How could being blind have contributed in a physical way to Crosby writing over 6,000 hymns in her lifetime?

3. Happiness and contentment have a prominent place in Crosby's hymns. Use a hymnbook with an index of hymn authors to locate hymns she wrote. From these hymns find at least four expressions of happiness or contentment.

On His Blindness

When I consider how my light is spent
Ere half my days, in this dark world and wide,
And that one talent which is death to hide
Lodged with me useless, though my soul more bent
To serve therewith my Maker, and present   5
My true account, lest He returning **chide**;
"Doth God **exact** day labor, light denied?"
I fondly ask. But Patience, to prevent
That murmur, soon replies, "God doth not need
Either man's work or his own gifts. Who best   10
Bear his mild yoke, they serve him best. His state
Is kingly: thousands at his bidding speed,
And **post** o'er land and ocean without rest;
They also serve who only stand and wait."

John Milton

The Poet's Language

chide (chīd) v.: scold

exact (ig zakt′) v.: demand; require

post (pōst) v.: to travel quickly

About the Author

John Milton (1608-1674) was born in Cambridge, England, and graduated from Cambridge University. The first two of his three marriages were short and marred by sorrow. Extensive study left his weak eyes sightless at the age of 44. He dictated to his daughters three book-length poems: *Paradise Lost, Paradise Regained,* and *Samson Agonistes.* These treat, respectively, the fall of Satan and man, Christ overcoming Satan, and the life of Samson.

Meditating for Meaning

1. This poem is a special poetic form.
   a. What is the rhythm and line length?
   b. What is the rhyme scheme?
   c. How many lines does it have?
   d. What special poetic form do your answers suggest?

2. This poem was written three years after Milton's light was spent.
   a. Consult an encyclopedia to find out how old he was when he went blind.
   b. Did he become blind "ere half my days"?
   c. What did he accomplish after he was blind?

3. Some of the basis for this poem is Matthew 25:14-30.
   a. To what did Milton allude when he said, "that one talent which is death to hide"?
   b. What was Milton's "one talent"?
   c. What did he desire to do with his talent?
   d. What did he fear if he did not use his talent?

4. The word "fondly" in line 8 means foolishly.
   a. In his foolishness, what was Milton inclined to think was not fair?
   b. Study lines 9 and 10. What was Milton tempted to misunderstand about God?
   c. Who pleases God best?

5. The "thousands" of line 12 are angels.
   a. How do lines 12 and 13 explain the reasonableness of the last line?
   b. How do those who are called to stand and wait serve God?

6. This poem is the best of the poems you have studied thus far in this section, "A Flock of Poems." Consider its following characteristics that make it high-quality literature.
   a. A sonnet is a clearly recognizable _____ that is well-suited to the nature of the subject.
   b. It deals with a problem that is _____ in all cultures.
   c. It contains allusion to _____ (lines 3, 6).
   d. It considers its subject in light of _____ realities.
   e. It is the sincere expression of one who has _____ .
   f. It comes to a _____ conclusion.
   g. It contains original and striking expressions. Select three expressions that impress you.

Sympathy

The author of this poem was black. His father had been a slave in Kentucky. Although the blacks were free after the Civil War, their problems were far from solved. Prejudice against the blacks kept them restricted and abused. This poem laments this situation in a unique and telling way.

The Poet's Language

opes (ōps) v.: opens

chalice (chal′ əs) n.: cup

I know what the caged bird feels, alas!
   When the sun is bright on the upland slopes;
When the wind stirs soft through the springing grass,
And the river flows like a stream of glass;
   When the first bird sings and the first bud **opes**,   5
And the faint perfume from its **chalice** steals—
I know what the caged bird feels!

I know why the caged bird beats his wing
   Till its blood is red on the cruel bars;
For he must fly back to his perch and cling   10
When he fain would be on the bough a-swing;
   And a pain still throbs in the old, old scars
And they pulse again with a keener sting—
I know why he beats his wing!

I know why the caged bird sings, ah me,   15
   When his wing is bruised and his bosom sore,
When he beats his bars and would be free;
It is not a carol of joy or glee,
   But a prayer that he sends from his heart's deep core,
But a plea, that upward to Heaven he flings—   20
I know why the caged bird sings!

Paul Laurence Dunbar

Meditating for Meaning

1. The entire poem is a skillful use of metaphor.
   a. What image does Dunbar use metaphorically?
   b. What does this image represent in his own experience?

2. The first stanza is unified around the feelings of a caged bird.
   a. What do the circumstances in lines 2 to 6 make the bird feel like doing?
   b. How then must the bird feel to be confined to a cage?
   c. What cage was Dunbar in?
   d. This poem has not one word to say about those who "caged" the author. What judgment can the white man take from this poem?

3. The second stanza centers around the *action* of the caged bird.
   a. Why does a bird beat his wings even if it is caged?
   b. What could this be a symbol of in the life of the author?

4. The last stanza gives this poem its highest dimension.
   a. What does the author imagine a caged bird is doing when it is singing?
   b. Many of the Negro spirituals express very well the longing Dunbar says is in the song. Find several phrases from Negro spirituals that express the longings of a caged man.
   c. What is noble about this response to the abuse of others?

A Little Bird I Am

A little bird I am,
   Shut in from fields of air,
And in my cage I sit and sing,
   To Him who placed me there;
Well pleased a prisoner to be,   5
Because, my God, it pleases thee!

Naught have I else to do,
   I sing the whole day long;
And He whom I most love to please
   Doth listen to my song;   10
He caught and bound my wandering wing,
And still he bends to hear me sing.

The Poet's Language

rude (rüd) adj.: crude; unrefined

Thou hast an ear to hear,
    A heart to love and bless;
And though my notes were e'er so **rude**,   15
    Thou wouldst not hear the less;
Because Thou knowest as they fall,
That love, sweet love, inspires them all.

My cage confines me round,
    Abroad I cannot fly;   20
But though my wing is closely bound,
    My heart's at liberty;
My prison walls cannot control
The flight, the freedom of the soul.

Oh, it is good to soar,   25
    These bolts and bars above,
To Him whose purpose I adore;
    Whose providence I love;
And in Thy mighty will to find
The joy, the freedom of the mind.   30

Madame Guyon

About the Author

Madame Marie De La Moth Guyon (1648-1717) was born near Paris, France, in an aristocratic, Roman Catholic family. Raised by nuns, Marie learned to read the Bible at a young age, but became beautiful and proud. When she was 16, her father arranged her marriage to Jaques Guyon, a wealthy merchant of 38 years. Calamity fell swiftly during her unhappy marriage—deaths, an abusive mother-in-law, financial failure, and finally smallpox. Robbed of her beauty, Madam Guyon was helped by a monk to a deep spiritual life. Because of her efforts to help others to this same life of death to self, Madam Guyon suffered numerous prison experiences, including four years in the dungeon of Paris's Bastille Prison. During her imprisonment and later banishment to Blois, France, Madam Guyon wrote much, including the familiar hymn, "I Would Love Thee."

Meditating for Meaning

1. Like Dunbar, author of the preceding poem, Guyon was in a cage. But Guyon's was a literal cage. She was imprisoned in the Bastille for her Christian faith. What reason for being in this cage does Guyon give in her poem?

2. The poet likens herself to a bird in a cage.
   a. Like a bird, what does the cage keep her from doing?
   b. What does she mean by line 11?
   c. Like a bird, what does the cage experience give her time to do?
   d. According to the third stanza, what quality does God look for in the songs we sing?

3. Explain what kind of freedom Guyon says she has in spite of the prison walls?

4. Both Guyon and Fanny Crosby had discovered the same secret to joy and happiness. What was it?

JOY ON THE HEIGHTS WITH CHRIST

The Poet's Language

inference (in′ fə rəns) n.: conclusion based on evidence

amiss (ə mis′) adj.: wrong; astray

Paragon (par′ ə gän) n.: model of perfection

crystal (kris′ təl) n.: a clear colorless glass of superior quality

The Crystal Christ

But Thee, but Thee, O sovereign Seer of Time,
But Thee, O poet's Poet, Wisdom's Tongue,
But Thee, O man's best Man, O love's best Love,
O perfect life in perfect labor writ,
O all men's Comrade, Servant, King, or Priest—   5
What *if* and *yet*, what mole, what flaw, what lapse,
What least defect or shadow of defect,
What rumor, tattled by an enemy,
Of **inference** loose, what lack of grace
Even in torture's grasp, or sleep's, or death's—   10
Oh, what **amiss** may I forgive in Thee,
Jesus, good **Paragon**, thou **Crystal** Christ?

Sidney Lanier

Meditating for Meaning

1. This poem is a celebration of the superlative Christ.
   a. In what ways is Christ like a crystal?
   b. Words such as *Paragon* can be called superlatives because they express excellence of the highest degree. Find three other superlative words in this poem.
   c. Find eight words that Lanier uses to contrast with the superlative. These words denote a coming short of some standard.

2. Explain the following descriptions of Christ:
   a. sovereign Seer of Time
   b. poet's Poet
   c. Wisdom's Tongue
   d. man's best Man
   e. love's best Love

3. Lanier wonders what he can forgive in Christ.
   a. When we need to ask a brother for forgiveness, what knowledge about him helps us feel less humiliated in his eyes?
   b. When we are asked to forgive another for hurting us, what helps us to be able to do this? (See Matthew 6:12.)
   c. But, when we go to Christ for forgiveness, we cannot console ourselves with any knowledge that _____ , nor does Christ have any feeling of duty to forgive us from a sense of _____ .
   d. What then does His perfection do to us when we need to ask for His forgiveness?
   e. What response does His perfection evoke in us when He does forgive us?

4. Look closely at the first part of line 6.
   a. We use the word *if* to introduce something that is desired but does not exist in reality. (This would be a beautiful dish if it were not chipped). How is the poet applying this to Christ?
   b. We use the word *yet* to introduce an exception or contrast to an observation. (It was a lovely house, yet it had a weak foundation.) How is the poet applying this word to Christ?

5. What amazing aspect of Christ's perfection is brought out in lines 9 and 10?

6. What is the answer to the question in the poem?

The Poet's Language

freighted (frā təd) v.: loaded

helm (helm) n.: steering gear of a
   ship

About the Author

George MacDonald (1824-1905)
was a Scottish novelist and poet.
Born in West Aberdeenshire, he
attended Aberdeen University
and eventually became a
Congregationalist pastor at
Arundel. Rejected by his audi-
ences as lacking dogmatic fervor,
he soon gave up his pastorship
and turned to writing, producing
some 50 volumes. The climate of
Italy, where he lived for a while
with his six sons and five daughters, favored his frail health.

The Boat

I owned a little boat a while ago,
And sailed the morning sea without a fear,
And whither any breeze might fairly blow
I steered my little craft afar or near.
    Mine was the boat   5
    And mine the air,
    And mine the sea,
    Nor mine a care.

My boat became my place of mighty toil,
I sailed at evening to the fishing ground,   10
At morn my boat was **freighted** with the spoil
Which my all-conquering work had found.
    Mine was the boat
    And mine the net,
    And mine the skill   15
    And power to get.

One day there came along that silent shore,
While I my net was casting in the sea,
A Man who spoke as never man before.
I followed Him; new life began in me.   20
    Mine was the boat,
    But His the voice,
    And His the call,
    Yet mine the choice.

Ah! 'twas a fearful night out on the lake,   25
And all my skill availed not, at the **helm**,
Till Him asleep I waked, crying, "Take
Thou the helm—lest water overwhelm!"
    And His the boat,
    And His the sea,   30
    And His the peace
    O'er all and me.

Once from the boat He taught the curious throng
Then bade me cast my net into the sea;
I murmured but obeyed, nor was it long   35
Before the catch amazed and humbled me.
    His was the boat,
    And His the skill.
    And His the catch,
    And His my will.   40

George Macdonald

1. This poem, like many poems, is written as though someone were speaking.
   a. Who is the Bible character speaking in this poem?
   b. Who is the Man in line 19?
   c. List all the things the speaker eventually turned over to the Man's ownership.
2. From the testimony of the first two stanzas, describe the person who owned the boat.
3. In the third stanza the fisherman still holds ownership of the boat. What happened to cause him to transfer that ownership?
4. What two events caused him to give over the ownership of his skill?
5. The poem follows the Biblical account closely.
   a. What do you think the poet is trying to say to you with this poem?
   b. What do you think makes this poem an effective statement of that lesson?

Calvary

Friendless and faint, with martyred steps and slow,
Faint for the flesh, but for the spirit free
Stung by the mob that came to see the show,
The Master toiled along to Calvary;
We **jibed** Him, as He went, with **houndish** glee,   5
Till His dimmed eyes for us did overflow;
We cursed His **vengeless** hands thrice wretchedly,—
And this was nineteen hundred years ago.

But after nineteen hundred years the shame
Still clings, and we have not made good the loss   10
That outraged faith has entered in His name.
Ah, when shall come love's courage to be strong!
Tell me, O Lord—tell me, O Lord, how long
Are we to keep Christ writhing on the cross!

Edwin Arlington Robinson

The Poet's Language

jibed (jībd) v.: mocked

houndish (haŭn′ dish) adj.: like a
dog after prey

vengeless (veng′ ləs) adj.: not
seeking revenge

About the Author

Edwin Arlington Robinson (1869-1935) was born at Headtide, Maine. Because of
family misfortune, he was able to complete only two years at Harvard University.
During his lifetime he won three Pulitzer Prizes for poetry. He developed particular
skill at depicting society with witty or thought-provoking character sketches. One of
these, "Richard Cory," appears in *Perspectives of Truth*.

 *Meditating for Meaning*

1. By this time you should immediately recognize the poetic form of this poem.
   a. What is the special form of this poem?
   b. Which of the three kinds of that form is this?
   c. Identify the basic theme of the octet and sestet to show how they are related.

2. The octet paints a very dark picture.
   a. What mood is established in this section?
   b. What reaction does the poet want you as a reader to make?

3. The sestet turns the accusing finger on us. But this time it is people of faith who get the blame.
   a. Line 11 is a shocking, although difficult line to interpret. Consider that there are various qualities of faith. There is weak faith, dead faith, saving faith, and great faith. Even the devils have faith (James 2:19). What then is "outraged faith"? (The poet may have used poetic license in using "outraged" instead of "outrageous." Be sure you check the meaning of these words.)
   b. In what way could a modern-day Christian have an outraged faith?
   c. What does Robinson say such a faith does ("entered") to the cause of Christ?
   d. According to line 12, what is lacking in those who have an outraged faith?
   e. What does Hebrews 6:6 say will "keep Christ writhing on the cross"?

4. Read Matthew 23:29-35. How are the people to whom Christ was speaking similar to the ones whom this poem criticizes?

Good Friday

Am I a stone, and not a sheep,
    That I can stand, O Christ, beneath Thy cross,
    To number drop by drop Thy Blood's slow loss,
And yet not weep?

Not so those women loved
    Who with exceeding grief lamented Thee;
    Not so fallen Peter weeping bitterly;
Not so the thief was moved;

Not so the Sun and Moon
    Which hid their faces in a starless sky.
    A horror of great darkness at broad noon—
I, only I.

Yet give not o'er
    But seek Thy sheep, true Shepherd of the flock;
    Greater than Moses, turn and look once more
And smite a rock.

Christina Rossetti

About the Author

Christina Rossetti (1830-1894) born in London, received her education at home. Her piety and love of nature show forth in her short lyrics. She was a sister of the painter and poet, Dante Gabriel Rossetti.

Meditating for Meaning

1. In the poem "Calvary" (page 244) Robinson condemned Christianity as a whole. This poem by Rossetti is the censor of one's self.
   a. What quality does Rossetti think a Christian should have when meditating on the sufferings of Christ?
   b. What quality does she too much find in herself?

2. She contrasts herself to the response of others.
   a. What three people or groups of peoples does she give as making a proper response to Christ's suffering?
   b. What natural objects does she give as making an appropriate response?
   c. What does the poet mean by "I, only I"?

3. The last stanza contains some interesting allusions to Scripture.
   a. Where in the Bible did Rossetti get her idea for Christ as a shepherd?
   b. When was Moses ever a shepherd? Give both the literal and figurative sense in which Moses was a shepherd.
   c. What experience in the life of Moses is alluded to in the last line?
   d. What would the smiting be in the poet's experience?
   e. How was the result of Moses smiting the rock similar to what Rossetti wants to have happen to her?

4. What is the mood of this poem?

5. Note the unity between the first and last stanzas.
   a. In the first stanza the poet laments that she is an unfeeling stone. What in the last stanza connects with this idea?
   b. In the first stanza she wishes she were a tender sheep. What kind of sheep does she admit that she is in the last stanza?

Bigot

Though you be scholarly, beware
The bigotry of doubt.
Some people take a strange delight
In blowing candles out.

Eleanor Slater

The Poet's Language

bigot (big′ ət) n.: person who will not tolerate others' opinions

About the Author

Eleanor Slater (b. 1903), was a Catholic nun and educator, often referred to as Sister Mary Eleanor.

Meditating for Meaning

1. "Scholarly" applies to more people than those who are attending school (and not everyone who goes to school is scholarly).
   a. Who is a scholarly person?
   b. In contrast to the bigot, a scholarly person would profess to _____ .
   c. But what narrow (bigoted) view does this poem warn scholars not to develop?
   d. What is bigoted about doubt?
   e. Why would a scholar be more inclined to develop the bigotry of doubt than other people? (See Colossians 2:8.) This reveals a danger in higher education.

2. Candles are used as a symbol in this poem.
   a. What does a candle symbolize? (See Matthew 5:15.)
   b. What are some candles that scholars may take a delight in blowing out?
   c. What might a scholarly person do to blow such candles out?
   d. Why does he take a "strange delight" in such activity?

Conventionality

Men wrap themselves in **smug** cocoons
Of **dogmas** they believe are wise,
And look **askance** at one who sees
In worms potential butterflies.

Eloise Hackett

The Poet's Language

conventionality (kən ven′ chə nal′ ət ē)
n.: tradition

dogmas (dog′ məs) n.: opinionated beliefs

smug (sməg) adj.: superior; self-satisfied

askance (ə skans′) adv.: sideways; scornfully

Meditating for Meaning

1. Not only education (as in "Bigot") but religion has often been used to alienate others; wrong beliefs as well as doubt can be un-Christian.
   a. What bad connotation does the word *dogma* have? Consider the connotation of the word *dogmatic*.
   b. What two other words in this poem have the idea of looking down on others?
2. What is symbolized by "in worms potential butterflies"? Consider man's contrasting attitudes towards worms and butterflies.
3. The title may seem strange, but it is very meaningful for this poem.
   a. Considering the definition of *conventionality*, explain how it fits as a title for this poem.
   b. What conventionality did Jesus condemn in Mark 7:11-13?
   c. What did Christ say was the danger of conventionality? (See Mark 7:7-9.)
   d. What conventionality should be challenged in light of the clear teaching of Luke 14:12-14?
   e. Not all tradition is dangerous conventionality. When is tradition good?
4. What does this poem suggest is the reason false conventionalities are so difficult to correct?
5. Note the unity of this poem.
   a. In relation to line 4, what is inconsistent about where men place themselves in line 1?
   b. What does the metaphor of worms and butterflies suggest should be the attitude toward the conventionalities of others?

Mending Wall

About the Author

Robert Frost (1874-1963) was born in San Francisco, California. After his father's early death, Robert and his family moved to New England. There Frost attended Dartmouth and Harvard. As a farmer, editor, and teacher, Frost composed many short, pithy poems about New England life and country, receiving four Pulitzer Prizes for poetry. Perhaps his most famous poem is "Stopping by Woods on a Snowy Evening." Frost read one of his poems at President Kennedy's inauguration and "Mending Wall" to Premier Khruschev during a visit to U.S.S.R.

Something there is that doesn't love a wall,
That sends the frozen ground-swell under it,
And spills the upper **boulders** in the sun;
And makes gaps even two can pass abreast.
The work of hunters is another thing: 5
I have come after them and made repair
Where they have left not one stone on a stone,
But they would have the rabbit out of hiding,
To please the yelping dogs. The gaps I mean,
No one has seen them made or heard them made,   10
But at spring mending-time we find them there.
I let my neighbor know beyond the hill;
And on a day we meet to walk the line
And set the wall between us once again.
We keep the wall between us as we go.   15
To each the boulders that have fallen to each.
And some are loaves and some so nearly balls
We have to use a spell to make them balance:
"Stay where you are until our backs are turned!"
We wear our fingers rough with handling them.   20
Oh, just another kind of outdoor game,
One on a side. It comes to little more;
There where it is we do not need the wall—
He is all pine and I am apple orchard.
My apples trees will never get across   25
And eat the cones under his pines, I tell him.
He only says, "Good fences make good neighbors."
Spring is the mischief in me, and I wonder
If I could put a notion in his head:
"Why do they make good neighbors? Isn't it   30
Where there are cows? But here there are no cows.
Before I built a wall I'd ask to know
What I was walling in or walling out,
And to whom I was like to give offense.
Something there is that doesn't love a wall,   35
That wants it down." I could say "Elves" to him,
But it's not elves exactly, and I'd rather
He said it for himself. I see him there
Bringing a stone grasped firmly by the top
In each hand, like an old stone savage, armed.   40
He moves in darkness as it seems to me,
Not of woods only and the shade of trees.
He will not go behind his father's saying,
And he likes having thought of it so well
He says again, "Good fences made good neighbors."   45

Robert Frost

Meditating for Meaning

1. In this poem we are faced with a conventionality.
   a. What is the tradition that Frost is challenging in this poem?
   b. What statement twice repeated opposes this tradition?
   c. What statement twice repeated is given in defense of the tradition?
   d. Note that the poet is not totally against fences. What two lines clearly indicate that he willingly cooperates in mending the wall.
   e. What then is Frost objecting to? (See lines 29-34.)

2. Now look closely at what it is that does not love a wall.
   a. What in lines 2-4 work against walls? Generalize your answer.
   b. What in lines 5-9 is destructive to walls?
   c. What is this symbolic of?
   d. From line 20, what may have been a reason Frost (who had been a farmer) did not like walls?
   e. Although this poem presents a simple situation, Frost was also speaking philosophically. What is there in all of us that does not like walls?

3. On the surface, walls seem illogical.
   a. When did Frost think a wall was needed?
   b. What absurdity does he present us as an objection to the wall?
   c. This concept sees a wall only for the purpose of _____ .

4. Frost never said that good fences did not make good neighbors. He was sorry his neighbor did not know the reason for the maxim.
   a. What was the basic command in Deuteronomy 19:14; 27:17; Proverbs 22:28; and 23:10?
   b. In the Old Testament the markers served to indicate _____ .
   c. What problems would likely have arisen between farmers who did not keep up fences they had erected along their boundaries?
   d. So in reality, keeping walls and fences shows _____ for the _____ of others.

5. This poem contrasts two kinds of persons. Both helped to mend the wall and so both benefited from its aid in making good neighbors. But both had an unsatisfactory attitude toward their work.
   a. How was the poet's attitude unsatisfactory?
   b. What was unsatisfactory about the neighbor's attitude?
   c. What is likely to happen in the future generations of both types of men?
   d. Which do you think it will happen to soonest?

6. What lesson(s) do you see in this poem
   a. about traditions?
   b. about neighborliness?

7. What type of verse did Frost use in writing this poem?

Thy Brother

When thy heart, with joy o'erflowing
   Sings a thankful prayer,
In thy joy, O let thy brother
   With thee share.

When the harvest-sheaves ingathered   5
   Fill thy barns with store,
To thy God and to thy brother
   Give thee more.

If thy soul, with power uplifted,   10
   Yearn for glorious deed,
Give thy strength to serve thy brother
   In his need.

Hast thou borne a secret sorrow   15
   In thy lonely breast?
Take to thee thy sorrowing brother
   For a guest,

Share with him thy bread of blessing,   20
   Sorrow's burden share;
When thy heart enfolds a brother
   God is there.

Theodore Chickering Williams

About the Author

Theodore Chickering Williams (1855-1915) born in Brookline, Massachusetts, was a Unitarian minister in Massachusetts and New York. He studied at Harvard University and served as headmaster in several schools. Williams wrote poetry and hymns as well as translating European literature. He traveled in Europe on several occasions.

Meditating for Meaning

1. What do each of the first four stanzas call for us to share with others?
2. In contrast to the advice of this poem, what is man so inclined to do when:
   a. the harvest fills the barns with store?
   b. the soul is lifted up with power to do a glorious deed?
   c. one is experiencing a secret sorrow?
3. Christ told a parable in answer to the question, "Who is my neighbor?" This poem can answer the question, "Who is my brother?" What is the poem's answer to that question?
4. How important is it that we heed the message of this didactic poem? (See 1 John 3:17.)

Getting the Point

Part I

Match the following statements with the poems they summarize. (pp. 145 to 189)

_____ 1. Hope of eternal life renders the Christian undaunted by fear and discouragement.

_____ 2. The condition of false religious workers is more pitiable than that of those whom they have harmed.

_____ 3. Recognizing the impartiality of death helps us to forget our grudges.

_____ 4. Life with God is supreme joy.

_____ 5. With the great power of prayer available, we need never be weak or discouraged.

_____ 6. Praise to God for His great power, deliverance, and gracious dealings with man.

_____ 7. Man will need to give account for brutal oppression of laborers.

_____ 8. The Lord will turn the sorrow of the penitent captive to freedom and joy.

_____ 9. Modern technology robs men spiritually and offers no restoration.

_____ 10. We need God's help to recognize Him in the less beautiful parts of life as well as in nature's beauty.

_____ 11. Youth can be pure by studying and following God's Word.

_____ 12. God can defend me from evil and lead me aright. Why should I be discouraged?

_____ 13. Life is intended for action and accomplishment of good, not for indulgence in pleasure or gloom.

_____ 14. The righteous man will know happiness and spiritual prosperity; the ungodly shall be destroyed.

a. "Sheer Joy"   h. "O God, I Love Thee"

b. "A Psalm of Life"   i. "Forgiveness"

c. "The Pilgrim"   j. Psalm 1

d. "The Man With the Hoe" k. Psalm 43

e. "The Jericho Road"   l. Psalm 66

f. "Lament"   m. Psalm 119

g. "Lord, What a Change" n. Psalm 126

Part II

Match the following statements with the poems they summarize. (pp. 190 to 227)

____ 1. The glamour men bestow on war appears absurd in view of the horrible realities.

____ 2. There is no cure for guilt besides confession and repentance.

____ 3. Opportunity should be taken when it first knocks.

____ 4. The common man may live and die unnoticed, but in many respects his is a better life than a prince's.

____ 5. Man may spread his control over the earth, but the sea mocks his labors.

____ 6. The apparently weaker and less important people likely possess some skill which is lacking in those who disdain them.

____ 7. God sends us trials to perfect us.

____ 8. It is worth losing our physical life to gain eternal life.

____ 9. An era is only good or bad depending on your response to it.

____ 10. Truly good poems are those which grow from the poet's own experience.

____ 11. Men may be heartless with our mistakes and thoughtless actions, but with God there is mercy.

____ 12. We either build or destroy lives around us by how we live.

____ 13. The heavens declare the glory of God.

____ 14. If we expect mercy, we must show mercy.

____ 15. After the lowly have risen to power, they often turn against those who helped them to rise.

a. "George Wagner"   i. *Julius Caesar* (Excerpt 2)

b. "The Fool's Prayer"   j. "The Spacious Firmament"

c. "The Battle of Blenheim"   k. "Apostrophe to the Ocean"

d. "A Fable"   l. "Elegy Written in a Country Churchyard"

e. "Prayer Answered by Crosses" m. "Bad Times"

f. *Merchant of Venice*   n. "Building"

g. *Macbeth*   o. "The Poet"

h. *Julius Caesar* (Excerpt 1)

Part III

Match the following statements with the poems they summarize. (pp. 228 to 252)

_____ 1. It is not the size, kind, or amount of our talents which counts, but whether we faithfully serve God with what we have.

_____ 2. If we ignore our conscience, to our sorrow it will cease to function.

_____ 3. Circumstances may seem to imprison us, but we can be free in spirit through joyful submission.

_____ 4. Jesus is perfect; there is no flaw in Him.

_____ 5. Sorrow and disappointment enlarge our capacity for joy.

_____ 6. If we give everything to Christ, He will do more with us and for us than we could ever do alone.

_____ 7. The sophisticated and educated too often scorn and destroy the faith of the simple.

_____ 8. God dwells in the heart that shares both sorrows and joys with its brother.

_____ 9. Men crucified Christ through unbelief; today men are still crucifying Christ, but through a false and warped faith.

_____ 10. Men sneer at others' traditions while holding to ones which are no less legalistic.

_____ 11. He who lives for the right cannot avoid opposition.

_____ 12. Men show what value they place on their souls by the cheapness of the things to which they sell themselves.

_____ 13. Those experiencing abuse can better understand others' sufferings and responses to their sufferings.

_____ 14. If we are contented in our handicap, we are often happier than those who have no handicap.

_____ 15. Traditions are good only if we know the reason behind them and if the reason is valid.

_____ 16. Bring from me, O Christ, the same sorrow that man and nature felt at Thy death.

a. "Victory in Defeat"   i. "The Crystal Christ"

b. "Conscience and Remorse"   j. "The Boat"

c. "No Enemies"   k. "Calvary"

d. "Betrayal"   l. "Good Friday"

e. "Blind But Happy"   m. "Bigot"

f. "On His Blindness"   n. "Conventionality"

g. "Sympathy"   o. "Mending Wall"

h. "A Little Bird I Am"   p. "Thy Brother"

UNIT 3

Biography

for the Exemplary Life

If you are like most teenagers, you already have an appreciation for biography. In the upper-elementary grades young people look up to outstanding adults as heroes. Their parents, teachers, neighbors, or church leaders may be models for their growing idealism. About this age they often begin to discover the adventure of biography. From the biographies they read, they add more individuals to the list of those they admire. If those biographies are wholesome, they can help develop strong convictions, high ideals, and worthy aspirations.

A biography is simply the story of someone's life. Like the short story, it has the interest-arousing features of setting, characters, and events. Things happen in a biography. But unlike the short story, biographies often lack a carefully worked-out plot. Actual life has many detours, interruptions, and seemingly irrelevant incidents that keep it from moving steadily forward with the mounting tension of a good short story. Of course God has a plan for every life, but it is often difficult for us to see how each part of the life fits into that plan.

But biography has something that fiction can never have. The story in a biography actually happened. The characters were real people. Often the house they lived in is still standing. The problems they faced, the battles they fought, the joys they experienced are not just typical of human experience; someone really did experience them.

Biography is history, and like all history, it has many lessons for life. Observing how God worked all things together for good in someone else's life can give us confidence to face our own problems. Seeing how the laws of God worked in another's life can serve to direct our own lives. Noting the outcome of various life choices in someone else can help us make decisions. You need not live 50 years to see how a certain course of action will work out. You can profit from seeing 50 years of cause and effect in another's experience.

The Bible has the truth that will make you wise, but we often have difficulty working that truth out in actual life. So it is not surprising that the Bible contains many biographies which illustrate the truth. They give truth flesh-and-bone reality.

But remember that no man's life is so perfect that his conduct in every situation should be copied and accepted as right. A biography presents what truly happened in a person's life. But while a person's life can challenge by illustrating truth, not everything he does is worthy of emulation. People have faults. People misjudge. People make wrong decisions. The Bible is the standard by which we measure the accomplishments of people.

In reality, truth is at work even when men do wrong. Sometimes a biographer will deliberately record a person's error to give us insight into where that error leads. Much of the Old Testament was written so that we would not repeat the mistakes of others. But, at other times a biographer does not point out the law of sowing and reaping at work in the actions and attitudes of his character. The reader must judge according to truth and follow only those qualities of a person's life that are in line with the teachings of the Bible.

At best, a biography is only a collection of selected facts about one person's life. If everything would be written about a person that could be written, the result would be bulky and boring. What kind of reading would it make to report on every thought and move you make in just one hour? The Apostle John said that if everything Jesus did would be written, he supposed "that even the world itself could not contain the books that should be written" (John 21:25). So even the facts of Jesus' life which were recorded were carefully selected.

Two things determine what is included in a biography: the availability of the facts and the purpose for writing the biography.

A good biographer will do much research into the life of the person he is writing about. Information will be carefully collected from letters, diaries, courthouse records, and if possible, interviews with those who knew the person. Even then, important links in the chain of his life may be missing. Where did he work while he was living in a certain city? Why did he decide against taking an attractive job offer? At what age did he make a certain significant notation in his Bible? These are the kinds of questions that can baffle a biographer and send him running here and there for bits and pieces to the puzzle.

Likely the biographer will collect much more information than he can use. In writing the biography, he must be selective. He will include only those facts that will help to accomplish his purpose for writing the biography. He must decide what he wants this biography to prove or demonstrate.

The Apostle John says he wrote his biography of Jesus that we "might believe that Jesus is the Christ, the Son of God; and that believing [we] might have life through his name" (John 20:31). The Holy Spirit helped him select a few choice facts and incidents for this purpose.

Maybe the biography is being written to show what life was like in colonial America. Perhaps the character was chosen to demonstrate a particular quality such as courage, conviction, or honesty. The biographer may have wanted to show how a particular character trait was developed, what events contributed to refining that character, and what responses made it grow. A biography may be written to trace the hand of God as it leads one to fulfill His purposes. It will reveal those many little but significant things in a person's life that equip the person for a special capacity.

Whatever his purpose, the biographer selects facts and arranges them in a way that will have the effect he desires. In reading a biography, try to discover the writer's purpose early in your reading, so that you can follow the unfolding of that purpose through the rest of the biography.

While purposes for biographies may vary greatly, the tone of all biographies is much the same. The writer is generally sympathetic to the person he is writing about and will, therefore, attempt to present the facts with a serious, understanding tone. This warmhearted approach gives biographies a friendly, almost intimate touch. After reading a well-written biography, you may feel almost like you have met the person. He seems so alive and real that you think of him as someone you know personally. He may even become somewhat of a hero to you and you may want to read more about the same person.

One of the biographical selections in this text is a special kind of biography called the autobiography. *Auto* means "self." An autobiography is a biography a person writes about himself. Of course, when a person writes about his own life, he can use the first person point of view. He can reveal his thoughts and feelings about the events of his life. He should be able to make you feel like you are right there, because he was there.

To be appreciated, an autobiography needs to be written with modesty. In writing the story of his own life, the good autobiographer must show his weaknesses as honestly as his strengths. He should be careful to credit others for helping him succeed and to refrain from blaming others for his failures.

If the biographer or autobiographer tells his story well, carefully selecting his material to illustrate truth, the reading of it should not only be interesting, but profitable.

Checking for Understanding

1. This is not your first encounter with biographies.
   a. From memory, list five biographies you have read.
   b. In what school grade did you begin reading biographies with real interest?

2. Biographies can be compared to short stories.
   a. What characteristics do biographies and short stories have in common?
   b. What do biographies often lack that is a prominent feature of most short stories?
   c. In what other way are biographies different from many short stories?

3. Much can be gained from reading biographies.
   a. What is a chief value in reading biographies?
   b. How are biographies a helpful supplement to the truth of the Bible?

4. Even a record of failures can be helpful.
   a. What could be the value of reading about the mistakes and failures of others?
   b. What is the danger of having such faults included in a biography?
   c. How can you avoid this danger?

5. A biographer must sort the material he collects on his subject.
   a. Why will a biographer select only certain parts of these materials?
   b. What two things determine what the biographer will include in his biography?

6. What work must precede the writing of a biography?

7. Imagine you are planning to write a biography of the Apostle Peter. Considering Peter's character strengths and weaknesses, what might you choose as your guiding purpose for the selection of material to include in the biography?

8. Watch for the tone of biographies.
   a. What tone will a biography usually have?
   b. Why will it have this tone?

9. Suppose a friend told you that he read an autobiography of Abraham Miller by Daniel Jones. How do you know this could not be true?

10. What special temptations would a person have in writing an autobiography?

Menno Simons
1496-1561

by John C. Wenger

It is only natural for a group of people to be interested in their past. The record of the past is mostly a story of people who stand out for the special contributions they have made. Therefore, in the history books of the Mennonites, we are not surprised to find various biographies of Menno Simons. Menno was not the founder of the church group bearing his name. In fact, before Menno became their noted leader, the Anabaptists in the Netherlands were called Obbenites after Obbe Philips, an early leader.

As you will see in this biography, Menno was not ambitious to become a famous leader nor to have a religious group named for himself. His desire was to be faithful to truth; God used that faithfulness and made Menno a leader in the church. God did not allow the memory of Menno's life and work to pass into oblivion. We can still be challenged by Menno's determination to do what he believed he should do, by his loyalty to truth once he had embraced it, and by his selfless sacrifice for the cause of Christ.

What did it take for a self-indulging Catholic priest to become a self-denying minister of the Gospel? Trace carefully the grace of God working through inner turmoil and outward incidents to change this moral weakling into a spiritual giant. The strength of his conviction, and the value he placed on the Bible can be seen in his own words in Unit 1 of **Perspectives of Truth in Literature.**

Defining for Comprehension	Choose the word or phrase below which most nearly defines each word at the left as it is used in the biography.
1. infallibly	a. definitely b. unerringly c. skillfully
2. transubstantiation	a. changing of Communion emblems to Christ's body and blood b. infant baptism c. literal reign of Christ on earth

Menno Simons, 1496-1561; a portrait made in 1683

3.	**confessional**	a. closing hymn	b. acknowledgment of sins to a priest
		c. payment to compensate for sins	

4.	**ultimate**	a. final; supreme	b. manifold	c. divinely appointed
5.	**abominable**	a. narrow-minded	b. false	c. loathsome; horrible
6.	**fanatical**	a. imaginary	b. radical	c. personal
7.	**deluded**	a. stripped bare	b. unsociable	c. deceived
8.	**evangelical**	a. according to the Gospel	b. heavenly	c. of angels
9.	**renounced**	a. forsook	b. criticized	c. publicized
10.	**heretic**	a. study of family relationships	b. rebel to traditional belief	c. criminal
11.	**deputation**	a. conversation	b. group of representatives	c. argument
12.	**edict**	a. prophecy	b. banishment	c. proclamation
13.	**diverse**	a. inconvenient	b. various	c. illegal
14.	**seduce**	a. lure; entice	b. choose	c. withdraw
15.	**erroneous**	a. absurd	b. false	c. forbidden
16.	**jurisdiction**	a. sentence	b. area of rule	c. judgment
17.	**apprehend**	a. understand	b. arrest	c. execute
18.	**placard**	a. regulation	b. game piece	c. public notice
19.	**disputation**	a. debate	b. assembly	c. separation
20.	**incarnation**	a. resurrection	b. crucifixion	c. taking on of flesh
21.	**dissension**	a. transgression	b. disagreement	c. conference

Menno Simons

In 1496 a Dutch couple of Witmarsum in Friesland named their infant son Menno. Since the name of Menno's father was Simon, the custom of the day in Holland made the child's name Menno Simonszoon—called Simons for short. As a youth Menno received training for the Catholic priesthood, perhaps in the Franciscan Monastery at Bolsward, near Witmarsum. In the monastery Menno received training in reading and writing Latin and in a study of the church fathers, but he never read the Bible. In 1524 he was consecrated as a priest, and for seven years he served in the Pinjum parish near Witmarsum. In 1531 he was transferred to his hometown where he served for five more years. His work as priest consisted in the celebration of the mass, in offering prayers for the living and the dead, in baptizing infants, in hearing confessions of sin and, unfortunately, in playing cards and drinking. Until this time Menno had feared to read the Bible, for only the Catholic Church, Menno had been taught, could **infallibly** interpret the Scriptures.

The story of Menno's conversion is interesting. One day in 1525, during the first year of priesthood, while he was celebrating the mass, a doubt crept into his mind as to whether the bread and wine actually became divine. This doubt of the truth of **transubstantiation** was to lead to Menno's first soul-struggle. Menno first thought this was a suggestion from the devil, and he tried by using the **confessional** to get it out of his system. After much worry Menno finally decided upon a course of action. He resolved to study the New Testament. This was a most important decision, for in the end it was

bound to lead him from the Catholic Church. He finally had to choose between following the Word of God and following the church. For Menno this was a very hard decision. It was Martin Luther who helped Menno Simons solve his problem. For Luther (through his writings) taught Menno one great truth: A violation of human commands cannot lead to eternal death. And yet Menno did not become a Lutheran; he developed his own doctrine of the Lord's Supper. But it was Martin Luther who convinced Menno that the **ultimate** authority in all matters of faith was the Word of God and nothing else. Menno was convinced of this about 1528, but strangely enough he went right on celebrating the mass.

In 1531 Menno Simons heard of an incident which became the occasion for his second soul-struggle. Jan Trijpmaker, a Melchiorite, had baptized a Dutchman named Sicke Freerks in 1530. Freerks was executed for his faith in

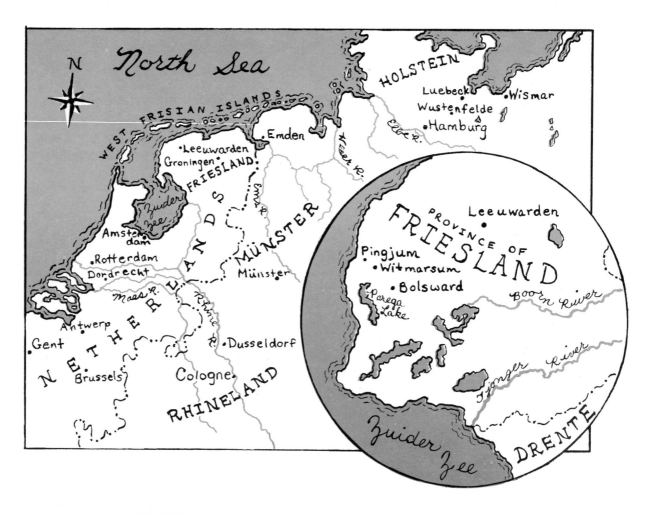

Leeuwarden on March 20, 1531. Menno Simons was exceedingly astonished; the idea of a second baptism was for him completely new. To the horrified Menno now came the question: Is the Catholic Church also unbiblical as to baptism? Again Menno turned to the writings of the leading reformers. Luther said that infant baptism was justifiable because babies have "hidden faith," just as a believing adult is also a Christian even while he is asleep. Martin Butzer said that infant baptism was a pledge that the parents would give the child a godly training. Henry Bullinger, Zwingli's successor in Zurich, said that just as the Old Testament sign of the Covenant (circumcision) was performed on infants, so also the New Testament sign of the Covenant (baptism) shall be performed on infants. To Menno these arguments seemed logical enough, but he was not so much interested in logic as in the Word of God. And he could find nothing of infant baptism in the New Testament.

Through all this strain and stress Menno remained a Catholic priest. He continued baptizing infants and saying mass. In fact he even accepted promotion to become head-pastor at Witmarsum. Menno was thus living a double life. He was believing one thing and practicing another. What would it take to make Menno Simons follow the Lord in loving obedience? The answer came in 1534-35 when the Münsterites came to Holland teaching their **abominable** and **fanatical** views. Even Menno's own brother was swept along with the **deluded** folks, and lost his life in a little battle with the authorities on April 7, 1535.

Menno of course took up the literary fight with the Münsterites. And yet he was not a happy man. For in fighting Münsterism was he not defending Catholicism? And were not those 300 misguided souls, who perished when his own brother lost his life, more honorable than he? They gave their lives for their error; was he not willing to give anything for the truth?

About April 1535, Menno surrendered to God, crying for pardon and peace. What a decision this was for the Obbenites and for the future Mennonite Church! Strangely enough Menno apparently remained in the Catholic Church for yet another nine months, preaching **evangelical** doctrines from a Catholic pulpit. But this could not go on indefinitely, and in January 1536 Menno Simons **renounced** the Catholic Church and thus took the step which he had known for a long time was God's will for him. As was already mentioned, he was probably baptized by Obbe Philips. Before we criticize Menno for his timidity, we should remember what this step meant for him. It meant that in the eyes both of the world and of the civil authorities he was a **heretic** of the worst sort, even more dangerous than an ordinary criminal. While Luther and Zwingli timed and modified their programs to secure political protection, the Anabaptists went bravely ahead and organized a church which they felt was true to the teachings of the New Testament. For this step they were willing to part with possessions, friends, family, and even life itself.

Obbe Philips and the Obbenites would not allow Menno to live a private life for any length of time. It is true that for several months he evidently devoted himself to quiet meditation and study. During this time he probably preached on occasion but had no pastoral oversight. But a number of Obbenite brethren felt that Menno Simons ought to assume the duties of an elder. Consequently a **deputation** of brethren called on Menno and pleaded with him to accept the leadership of the brotherhood. Menno hesitated. The brethren came a second time. This time Menno accepted the call. It was probably early in 1537, when Menno was ordained as elder (bishop). The ordination was assuredly performed by Obbe Philips, the Leeuwarden surgeon and founder of Dutch Anabaptism. Incidentally Obbe himself later lost heart, laid down his ministry, and withdrew from the church; because of this Menno called him a "Demas." Menno now took the lead in building up the brotherhood and saving it from the radical movements of the day.

From 1536, until 1543, Menno worked in Holland. Soon after becoming an Obbenite he married a woman named Gertrude; her last name is uncertain; it may have been Hoyer. Menno's family did not take first place in his life, although he no doubt did all he could for them. His great work was the proclamation of the Gospel of Christ. About 1539, he called himself a "homeless man." Menno's work was richly blessed of God; many souls were won and strengthened through his ministry. One tribute to the effectiveness of his work was the opposition he received. On December 7, 1542, Emperor Charles V, ruler of Europe from the Netherlands to Austria, issued the following **edict** against him:

BY THE EMPEROR

To our worthy, beloved Mayors, Boards, and Counselors, etc., of our city of Leeuwarden, Greeting:

Whereas, it has come to our knowledge... that a man [named] Menno Symonss,... being polluted with Anabaptism and other false teachings, now sojourning, endeavoring at night and other unseasonable times and in **diverse** places to **seduce** by his false teachings and sermons the simple people, our subjects, and to lead them away from the faith and unity of the Holy Church; and that he also has undertaken to make a few books treating on his aforesaid **erroneous** teachings, and to circulate and scatter the same among our aforesaid subjects, which he has no right to do.... Therefore, to take appropriate steps in this matter, we ordain and command herewith, that ye everywhere in your **jurisdiction** do publish, cry out, and proclaim... that every one in our aforesaid land... should be on his guard not to receive the same man Minne Symonss into his house or on his property, or to give him shelter or food or drink, or to accord him any favor or help, or to speak or converse with him in whatever manner or place it may be, or to accept or keep in possession any of the aforesaid books published by the same man Minne, or any other books that he may publish at any future time—all on penalty of punishment on life and property, as heretics,... and further,... they may **apprehend** the same man Minne wherever they may be able to find him, no place or jurisdiction excepted, and send him captive to our court in Friesland; for which they, in case they accomplish this, shall receive for a recompense besides the expense they have incurred in this matter, the sum of one hundred golden Karolus gulden, which shall be paid them by our General Treasurer of Friesland without any hesitancy....

Given, in our city of Leeuwarden under our secret seal, published as a **placard**, on

About the Author

John C. Wenger (1910-1995), son of Aaron and Martha Wenger, attended Goshen College and the University of Zurich. He taught in the Goshen College Biblical Seminary for many years and served as a deacon, minister, and bishop of the Indiana-Michigan Mennonite Church Conference. His studies of Anabaptism and church history led him to write numerous books including *Glimpses of Mennonite History and Doctrine* from which this biography of Menno Simons is taken. He also edited *The Complete Writings of Menno Simons.*

the seventh day of December, of the year 1542.

By the Emperor to his Majesty's Stadtholder, President and Counsellors in Friesland.

(Signed) Boeymer

During the years 1541-43, Menno labored in and about Amsterdam. In these years he also found time to do some writing. He published seven books and booklets from 1536 to 1543.

Menno spent a few months in east Friesland in 1543, then labored in northwest Germany for several years (until 1546). He engaged in a **disputation** with the noted Polish reformer, John a Lasco, 1499-1560, on January 28-31, 1544, at Emden. The two men agreed on original sin and sanctification, but disagreed on the **incarnation** of Christ, baptism, and the calling of the ministry. Without securing Menno's permission a Lasco published a statement of Menno's views. Menno then removed to the Rhineland and worked in the bishopric of Cologne for two years, 1544-46.

With his sick wife and children, Menno fled to Holstein in northern Germany, along the Baltic, in 1546. First he lived at Wismar, later at a place called Wuestenfelde. The latter was located between Hamburg and Leubeck. In 1550, Menno wrote his *Confession of the Triune God* against Adam Pastor, a Mennonite minister who had become unsound in his view of Christ. The last years of Menno's life were spent in writing. He revised a number of his earlier productions and translated them into the dialect of the region where he was then living.

The closing years of Menno's life were also darkened by **dissension** within the church. The great problem was, How strictly shall the "ban" be observed? Some of the Dutch leaders were unreasonably harsh in their views, so much so that at the great Strasburg Conference of 1557, over 50 bishops dissented from the strict views of their Dutch brethren. The next year Menno wrote to Reyn Edes, his brother-in-law, "O Brother Reyn! If only I could be with you even a half day and tell you something of my sorrow, my grief and heartache, and of the heavy burden which I carry for the future of the church.... There is nothing on earth that I love so much as the church; yet just in respect to her must I suffer this great sorrow."

Menno Simons had no easy life. He was always poor in this world's goods, being forced to appeal to his brethren for financial help. Yet the Lord stood by him and preserved him from all his enemies. He died on his sickbed January 31, 1561, twenty-five years after his renunciation of Catholicism.

Menno Simons is undoubtedly the greatest figure in the history of the church which now bears his name. He had a sane and balanced program of promoting both an evangelical faith and holiness. He was a fearless leader who aimed at complete loyalty to the Word of God.

Meditating for Meaning

1. As a youth, Menno did not drink from the fountainhead of truth.
   a. What was surprisingly lacking in young Menno's education for the priesthood?
   b. Why did he fear to read the Bible even after he had religious responsibility?

2. A turning point came in Menno's experience.
   a. What was the issue that finally led Menno to read the Bible?
   b. What great conflict entered Menno's life when he did read the Bible?
   c. What attitude toward human commandments did Menno gain from the writings of Martin Luther that helped to resolve this conflict to some extent?
   d. What great conviction about the Bible did Menno gain from Martin Luther?
   e. How do you know the conflict was not yet entirely resolved?

3. God wasn't finished with Menno yet.
   a. What did God use to plant the second seed of conflict in Menno's mind?
   b. Why did the answers to this issue from reformers such as Butzer and Bullinger seem to be right?
   c. Why didn't Menno accept these answers?
   d. Was Menno a better person after experiencing this second conflict? Why or why not?

4. Menno needed to decide whether he would be obedient or not.
   a. Explain how the death of a man who believed error made Menno willing to come clear for the truth.
   b. What probably held Menno back from immediately parting with the Catholic Church although he knew the church was wrong?
   c. Was this delay justified? Explain.

5. Before long, Menno was asked to take a leadership role.
   a. Choose as many of the following adjectives as you think describe Menno's acceptance of leadership responsibility: (reluctant, eager, submissive, confident, willing)
   b. Why did Menno later call the one who ordained him a Demas?

6. Faithfulness as a church leader cost Menno dearly.
   a. What indirect, legal evidence do we have that Menno made an outstanding contribution to the advancement of truth?
   b. For what probable reason was Menno a "homeless man" around 1539?
   c. For what additional reason was he "homeless" after 1542?

7. Besides the regular care of the church, in what other activities did Menno engage that greatly increased his sphere of influence?

8. Toward the end of his life, what gave Menno special concern for the church?

9. Menno had a hard life as a leader of the Dutch Anabaptists. What makes you think he would have made the same decision to join them if he could have lived his life over again?

Looking for Literary Technique

Billions of people freckle the face of the earth and billions more have lived and died in the centuries past. But every one of those billions has left his imprint for good or evil. It is by this imprint that men are known. Peter knew Jesus as one "who went about doing good" (Acts 10:38). But not everyone had this same view of Jesus. Peter's testimony of Jesus stunningly opposes the Jews' complaint to Pilate, "We found this fellow perverting the nation" (Luke 23:2). Obviously both could not be true; one of these testimonies was false. But why? Both were eyewitnesses of Jesus' life. The difference lies in point of view. Jealousy, hatred, and guilt corroded the Jews' point of view. Love, devotion, and full-hearted commitment haloed Peter's.

Similarly, two biographers can tell the story of the same man's life and seem to portray two totally different men. J.C. Wenger's portrait of Menno Simons frames him in all the hallowed beauty of a sincere, dedicated Christian. Why? Because J. C. Wenger loved the same God whom Menno loved, devoted himself to the same church for which Menno risked his life, and embraced the same doctrines to which Menno clung.

But were you to read John a Lasco's statement of Menno's views, likely you would form an entirely different image of Menno Simons. Again, why? Because a Lasco and Menno disagreed. A Lasco did not embrace all of the beliefs Menno did.

This is the task of the biographer—not only to hand you a pack of facts, but to interpret that pack of facts in such a way that you feel about his subject as he does. Wenger takes care to protect Menno from criticism for what, in another biographer's hands, could have appeared as cowardly reluctance to leave the Roman Catholic church. "Before we criticize Menno for his timidity," he writes, "we should remember what this step meant for him." Furthermore, Wenger does not berate Menno for improvidence because his family did not take first place in his life. He quickly explains that Menno ". . . no doubt did all he could for them. His great work was the proclamation of the Gospel of Christ."

Although a good biographer will not condone character flaws on this basis, he can lead you to love and appreciate a Christlike character such as Menno because he himself brims with love and appreciation for his subject.

1. Find another example in this biography where the author reflects his point of view by the way he handles information.

2. From what other point of view might another biographer have presented this same information?

Choose the life of a godly person who has influenced your life for good—one whom you love, admire, and appreciate. By the time you reach the end of this unit, you will have written a biography on this person's life. This person should be one in whom you are intensely interested because your job as a biographer will be to intensely interest someone else. Your subject may be deceased or living, a grandparent, a church leader, a Sunday school teacher, a Christian day school teacher, an uncle, an aunt, or any other faithful Christian who made this world a better place.

Decide on a focus for your biography, jotting down what could be its title. What was your subject's most outstanding character trait? Was he persevering, patient under trial, generous? What did he contribute to the church? To you? Notice the titles of the three other biographies from this unit. John Bunyan in the next selection calls himself the chief of sinners, borrowing from the Apostle Paul's view of himself. William Carey was the father of modern missions, and Clayton Kratz was true till death. Also, consult the biography section of your school library for ideas.

For other foundation can no man lay than that is laid, which is Jesus Christ.

Grace Abounding to the Chief of Sinners

by John Bunyan

Christian experience varies from one person to another. Some have shipwreck experiences like Paul. Some have martyr experiences like Stephen. Some have Isle of Patmos experiences like John. Some are left on an Isle of Crete like Titus to remain faithful in leadership responsibility. But all Christians must deny themselves, take up the cross, and follow Jesus. That way is a narrow way. That way will bring struggles with the flesh and opposition from Satan. Often the hardest battles of the Christian life are those fought in the heart and mind. Only the warrior himself can describe these conflicts. Only an autobiography can give the true picture of this side of a man's life.

In the spiritual autobiography you are about to read, you are shown the inner life of John Bunyan, who knew what it was like to fight Apollyon in the Valley of the Shadow of Death, to fall into the Slough of Despond, and to come under the influence of Giant Despair in Doubting Castle—characters and places in Bunyan's later book The Pilgrim's Progress. *A study of the following excerpts from Bunyan's autobiography will benefit you in two ways. First, it ought to help you understand your own soul struggles better. Second, it will provide a good background for interpreting the allegory* The Pilgrim's Progress *in Unit 5.*

Defining for Comprehension

Choose the word or phrase below which most nearly defines each word at the left as it is used in the biography.

	a.	b.	c.
1. **profanity**	a. abundance	b. cursing	c. folly
2. **hankered**	a. squatted	b. desired	c. corroded
3. **rebound**	a. bounce back	b. thrive	c. become famous
4. **consumption**	a. extravagance	b. final decision	c. illness similar to tuberculosis

5. **inertia**	a. resistance to motion	b. energy	c. extreme fright
6. **malicious**	a. spiteful	b. inexperienced	c. tasty
7. **indicted**	a. prosecuted	b. charged with guilt	c. pardoned
8. **venture**	a. expose to hazard	b. send	c. adventure
9. **flinch**	a. to settle	b. to cringe	c. to steal

Grace Abounding to the Chief of Sinners

Part 1 – Preconversion Experiences

One day it happened that, among the various sermons our parson preached, his subject was "The Sabbath Day," and the evil of breaking it either with work or sports or in any other way. Then my conscience began to prick me and I thought that he had preached this sermon on purpose to show me my evil ways. That was the first time I can remember that I felt guilty and very burdened, for the moment at least, and I went home when the sermon was ended with a great depression of spirit.

For a little while this made me bitter against my former pleasures, but it didn't last very long. Before I had had a good dinner, the trouble began to go off my mind and my heart returned to its old course. Oh, how glad I was that the fire was put out so that I might sin again without worrying about it! And so, after my dinner, I shook the sermon out of my mind and returned with great delight to my usual custom of sports that afternoon.

But the same day, as I was in the middle of a game of *cat*,[1] and had just struck one blow, and was about to strike the second time, a voice darted from heaven into my soul and said,

"Will you leave your sins and go to heaven, or keep your sins and go to hell?"

I was immeasurably surprised, and leaving my "cat" upon the ground I looked up to Heaven. I felt as though I could almost see the Lord Jesus looking down upon me with hot displeasure, as though He were severely threatening me with some terrible punishment for this and other ungodly practices.

This thought had no sooner come into my mind, when suddenly this conclusion fastened on my spirit (for my sins were suddenly very much before me again) that I had been such a great sinner that now it was too late for me to think about heaven; for Christ would not forgive me nor pardon my transgressions. Then, while I was thinking about this and fearing that it might be so, I felt my heart sink in despair, concluding it was too late; and so I decided that I might as well go on in sin. I decided that I would be miserable if I left my sins and miserable if I followed them; and, if I were going to be damned anyway, I might as well be damned for many sins as be damned for a few.

So there I stood in the middle of my play, in

---

1. cat: A rural English game of batting a small, pointed stick of wood with a larger stick.

front of all the others, but I told them nothing. Having decided this, I returned desperately to my sports again; and I well remember that presently such a despair took hold of my soul that I was persuaded that I could never again be happy except for whatever happiness I could get out of my sin. Heaven was already gone—I must not think any more about that—so I found an increasing desire to take my fill of sin and to taste the sweetness of it. I made as much haste as I could to fill my belly with its delicacies, lest I should die before I had my desires, for that was the thing that I most greatly feared. I am not making this up. These were really my desires and I wanted them with all my heart. May the good Lord whose mercy is unsearchable forgive my transgressions. I am confident that this temptation of the devil is more common among the poor creatures around us than many are aware of. They have concluded that there is no hope for them because they have loved sin; therefore, after sin they will go (Jeremiah 2:25; 18:12).

And so I went on in sin, but was disturbed because it never seemed to satisfy me. This went on for about a month or more. Then one day as I was standing at a neighbor's shop window, cursing and swearing in my usual way, the neighbor's wife was sitting inside and heard me. Although she was a very loose and ungodly wretch, she protested because I swore and cursed so much. She said she trembled to hear me. She told me that I was the ungodliest fellow for swearing that she ever heard in all her life, and that by doing this I was going to spoil all the young people in the whole town if they got into my company.

At this reproof I was silenced and put to secret shame. I stood there with my head hanging down and wishing that I might be a little child again and that my father might teach me to speak without this wicked swearing. I thought, "I'm so accustomed to it now it is useless to think of reforming, for I could never do it." But—how it happened I do not know—from this time forward I stopped my swearing to such an extent that it was a great wonder to me to see it happen. Whereas formerly I put one oath before what I said and another behind

it, to make my words have authority, now, without swearing, I could speak better and more pleasantly than ever before. But all this time I knew not Jesus Christ, nor did I leave my sports and play.

Soon after this I fell into company with a poor man who called himself a Christian. He talked very pleasantly about the Scriptures, and about religion. Liking what he said, I found the Bible and began to take quite a bit of pleasure in reading it, especially the historical parts. As for Paul's letters, and other parts of Scripture like that, I couldn't understand them at all. I was still ignorant of my own nature and of the desire and ability of Jesus Christ to save us.

So I began some outward reformation, both in my speech and life, and decided to try to keep the Ten Commandments as a way of getting to heaven. I tried hard and thought I did pretty well sometimes in keeping them, and at such times I was quite pleased with myself. But now and then I would break one and it worried my conscience so that I could hardly sleep. Then I would repent and say that I was sorry for it and promise God to do better next time, and I would begin to feel hopeful again— for I thought that at such times I was pleasing God as well as any man in England.

I continued this way for about a year and all this time our neighbors took me to be very godly and marveled greatly to see so much change in my life and actions. Indeed, there was a great change, though I knew not Christ nor His grace nor faith nor hope; but, as I have since learned, if I had died then, my situation would have been most fearful.

As I say, my neighbors were amazed at this great conversion from rebel **profanity** to something like a moral life and a sober man. So now they began to praise me and to speak well of me both to my face and behind my back. Now I was, as they said, a godly man. Now I had become honest. And how pleased I was when I heard them say these things about me for, although I was still nothing but a poor painted hypocrite, I loved to be talked about as one who was truly godly. I was proud of my godliness and indeed I did everything I could to be well-spoken of. And so I continued for a year or more.

Now I must tell you that before this time I used to have a great delight in *ringing*[2] but my conscience now began to be so tender and I thought that this was something I ought not to do. I forced myself to quit; yet, my mind still **hankered** for this, and so I would go to the steeple-house and look on, though I dared not ring myself. I decided this was not right either, but still I forced myself to stay and look on. But then I began to think, "What if one of the bells should fall?" So I stood under a main beam that lay across the steeple under the bells, thinking that I would be safe there. But then I thought: "What if the bell fell with a swing? It might hit the wall first and then **rebound** upon me and kill me anyway." This made me stand in the steeple door, and now I thought I was surely safe enough. If the bell should fall, I could slip out behind the thick walls and so be preserved.

After this, I still would go to see them ring, but would not go any farther than the steeple door. Then it came into my head: "What if the steeple itself should fall?" This thought so shook my mind that I dared no longer stand even in the steeple door, but was forced to flee for fear the steeple would fall upon my head.

Another thing was my dancing. It was a full year before I could finally leave that. But all this time, when I thought that I was keeping this or that commandment, or when I did something good, I had a fine feeling and thought that now God will surely be pleased with me; I thought no one in England could please God better than I.

But, poor wretch that I was, all this time I was ignorant of Jesus Christ and was trying to establish my own righteousness, and would have perished thereby if God had not been merciful to me.

Then on a certain day, in the good provi-

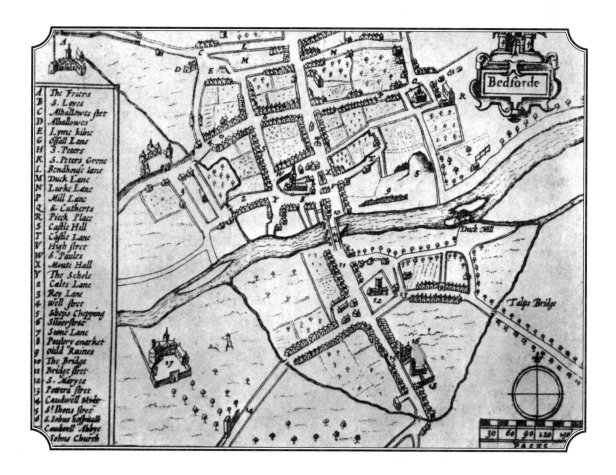

2. ringing: Striking bells in a specific order for musical effect.

dence of God, I had to make a trip to Bedford for my work; and in one of the streets of that town I came to a place where there were three or four poor women sitting in a door in the sun talking about the things of God. Since I was now willing to listen to such discussion, I came close to hear what they were saying—I was not myself a brisk talker in matters of religion—but they were far above my reach. Their talk was about a new birth, a work of God in their hearts, and how they were sure that they had been born as helpless sinners. They talked about the way that God had visited their souls with His love in the Lord Jesus, and spoke of the particular words and promises that had helped and comforted and supported them against the temptations of the devil. What's more, they talked about particular temptations they had from Satan, and told each other how God had helped them.

They also talked about their evil hearts and their unbelief and their goodness. It seemed to me that they spoke with such pleasure of the Bible, and they had so much grace in all that they said, that they had found a new sort of world; they were people that could not be compared with anyone else (Numbers 23:9).

Now my heart began to shake for I saw that all my thought about religion and salvation had never once considered the question of the new birth. I began to realize that I knew nothing about the comfort and the promise that this might give, nor about the deceitfulness and treachery of my own wicked heart. As for my secret evil thoughts, I had never taken any notice of them; I did not even recognize Satan's temptations and certainly did not know how they could be resisted.

After I had listened awhile and thought about what they said, I left them and went my way. My heart was still with them, for I was greatly affected by their words because I was convinced by them that I did not have what would make me a truly godly man, and I was convinced that those who were truly godly were really happy and blessed.

So I made it my business to go there often and be in the company of these poor people, for I could not stay away; and the more I was there,

the more I realized the seriousness of my condition. I still remember quite clearly how two things were happening to me that surprised me very much, especially considering how blind, ignorant and ungodly I had been just before. The first of these two things was a very great tenderness which caused me to be deeply convicted that whatever they told me from the Bible was true; the other was that my mind kept turning back to the things they had told me and to all good things that I had ever heard or read about.

The Bible was precious to me in those days and I began to look at it with new eyes. The letters of the apostle Paul were especially sweet to me. It seemed as though I was never out of the Bible, but was always either reading it or thinking about it. While I was reading, I came upon this passage: "To one is given by the Spirit the word of wisdom; to another the word of knowledge by the same Spirit; to another faith" (1 Corinthians 12:8, 9). I know now, of course, that this is talking about an extraordinary kind of faith, but at that time I thought that it meant ordinary faith that other Christians had. I thought about this a long time and could not tell what to do. Sometimes I questioned whether I had any faith at all, but I did not want to decide that I had none, for if I did that, I thought that I would then forever be a castaway from God.

I had not talked to anyone about this but had only thought about it myself. While I was trying to think how to begin, the tempter came in with his lies to tell me that there was no way for me to know whether I had faith until I had tried to work some miracles, and he brought to my mind Scriptures that seemed to make this idea logical. One day, as I was going along between the towns of Elstow and Bedford, the temptation was hot upon me to try to do a miracle to see if I had faith. The miracle was that I would say to the puddles to dry up and to the dry spots in the road that they should be puddles. But just as I was about to speak, the thought came into my mind that I had better go over under a hedge nearby and pray first that God would make me able. But when I had decided to pray, the terrible thought came that if I prayed and then tried and nothing happened, it would be very clear that I had no faith and would forever be lost. So I decided that I would not force the issue but would wait awhile before trying.

Now I was at a great loss to know what to think, for if only those who could do such miracles had faith, I was certainly never likely to have it, and so I was caught between the devil's temptation and my own ignorance, and I was so perplexed that I simply didn't know what to do.

It was about this time that I had sort of a vision of the wonderful state of happiness that these poor people at Bedford were in. I saw them as if they were on the sunny side of a high mountain and were there refreshing themselves in the pleasant sun, while I was shivering and shrinking in the cold with frost, snow, and dark clouds all about me. It seemed that there was between me and them a high wall that went all around the mountain. How I wanted to get through that wall so that I could enjoy myself there in the heat of the sun as they were doing!

Again and again I tried to find a way to get through the wall, but for a long time I could find no entrance, until finally I saw a tiny doorway. I tried to go through, but it was so narrow that all my efforts were in vain. At last, after a great struggle, I did get my head through, and after that, by squeezing myself along, my shoulders followed, and finally my whole body. Then I was very glad and went and sat down in the midst of them and was comforted with the light and the heat of their sun.

The mountain was the church of the living God. The sun that shone upon it was the shining from God's merciful face. The wall was the Bible that separated between the Christians and the world. The door was Jesus Christ who is the way to God the Father (John 14:6; Matt. 7:14). The fact that this door was so narrow that I could hardly get in showed me that no one could enter into this life but those who were in real earnest and left the wicked world behind them. For there is room here only for body and soul and not for a body, soul, and a load of sin.

Meditating for Meaning

1. Conviction must come first.
   a. Bunyan was first convicted on the matter of (Choose one: stealing, swearing, Sabbath Day observance, honesty).
   b. What brought this first conviction of sin?
   c. This conviction lasted about (1 hour, 1 day, 1 week, 1 month).
   d. What shows that his conscience was not entirely dead?

2. Bunyan sank deeper into sin.
   a. What wrong concept about his relation to grace made him despair of his situation?
   b. In the title of his autobiography, Bunyan calls himself the chief of sinners, borrowing an expression Paul made about himself (1 Timothy 1:15). In his despair how did Bunyan attempt to fulfill his desires?

3. Conviction brings reform.
    a. Whom did God use to bring the next round of conviction?
    b. About what was Bunyan convicted this time?
    c. In what way was this conviction of sin effective?
    d. In what way were the results deceptive?

4. Bunyan wrote, "Then I would repent and say that I was sorry for it [a sin] and promise God to do better next time, and I would begin to feel hopeful again." But this was a false hope.
    a. What was wrong with Bunyan's religion at this point?
    b. What did the neighbors think of Bunyan's religion?
    c. How does Bunyan evaluate himself now that he looks back to that time in his life?

5. When Bunyan's conscience became tender, he thought he ought not to ring bells. Some people would say that Bunyan's conscience was overly sensitive and that there is nothing wrong with ringing bells. But surely with the keen mind Bunyan had, there was some reason why he thought bell ringing was wrong.
    a. What do you think may have been his reasons?
    b. What evidence do we have that Bunyan had become almost addicted to bell ringing?
    c. Why was Bunyan suddenly so concerned about the danger of the bells falling?
    d. What was another carnal pleasure about which Bunyan became convicted?

6. After all of this reform, why did Bunyan still call himself wretched?

7. God's mercy gave Bunyan yet another eye-opener through the conversation of several women in Bedford.
    a. Explain what Bunyan meant when he said that they were far above his reach.
    b. In what way was it true that these women could not be compared to anyone else in Bunyan's experience then?
    c. What did Bunyan learn about himself through this experience?

8. A true turning to God will lead one to the Bible.
    a. What conviction about the Bible did Bunyan receive during this time?
    b. For what reason may the letters of the Apostle Paul have been especially sweet to Bunyan?

9. The abridgement of *Grace Abounding* you are studying leaves out many of the specific struggles with doubt that Bunyan had. However, some detail of one of his struggles is given.
    a. He was afraid that he had no _____ .
    b. He decided that the true test of faith is whether one could _____ .
    c. What two forces did Bunyan say were at work in producing this very perplexing situation?
    d. What false concept about faith and its purpose did Bunyan have?

10. Bunyan next reveals that he had "sort of a vision." He is very modest in claiming to have had a vision. Perhaps it was a daydream he had. At least we know from his allegorical books (such as *The Pilgrim's Progress*) that Bunyan had a very fertile mind for symbolical thinking.

    Interpret the "vision" by telling what each of the following represent. Some of the things Bunyan interpreted for you, but others are left for you to interpret.
    a. mountain   e. frost, snow, and dark clouds
    b. sun   f. repeated fruitless efforts to get through the wall
    c. wall   g. a great struggle
    d. door

11. What important concept of the Christian life did this "vision" give Bunyan?

Part 2 – Postconversion Experiences

And now I want to tell you of a few of the Lord's other dealings with me at various times, and of some of the other temptations I met. I will begin with what happened to me when I first joined in fellowship with the people of God in Bedford. I was admitted by them into the fellowship of the Lord's Supper, and that Scripture, "This do in remembrance of me" (Luke 22:19), was made very precious to me. By it, the Lord came down upon my conscience with the discovery of His death for my sins. But it was not long before it happened, when I was partaking of the ordinance, that there came fierce temptations to blaspheme the ordinance and to wish some deadly thing to those that were eating of it. To keep myself from consenting to these wicked and fearful thoughts, I had, as it were, to lean myself mightily against them, crying out to God to keep me from such blasphemies, and to bless the cup and bread to those who were drinking from it. I have since thought that the reason for this temptation was because I did not come with sufficient reverence to the table to partake thereof.

This kept on for nine months and would neither rest nor ease, but at last the Lord came in upon my soul with that same Scripture He had used before. After that, I was usually able to partake of the blessed ordinance with great comfort and, I trust, discerned therein the Lord's body broken for my sin and His precious blood shed for my transgressions.

Another time I seemed to be getting **consumption** and along during the springtime I was suddenly and violently seized with so much weakness that I thought I would not live. Once again I gave myself up to a serious examination of my state and my prospects for the future. For, blessed be the name of God, I have been enabled at all times to keep my interest in the life to come clearly before my eyes, especially in the day of affliction.

But I had no sooner begun to recall to mind my experiences of the goodness of God, than there came flocking into my mind also the remembrance of an innumerable number of sins, especially my coldness of heart, my weariness in doing good and my lack of love for God, His ways, and His people. And along with them, came this question: Are these then the fruits of Christianity? Are these the signs of a man who has been blessed of God?

Now my sickness was doubled, for now I was sick in my inward man, my soul clogged with guilt, and my experiences of God's goodness were quite taken out of mind as though they had never existed. Now my soul was tossed between these two conclusions: live I must not; die I dare not. And so I gave up all for lost. But just then as I was walking up and down in the house, in the most dreadful state of mind, this word of God took hold upon my heart: Ye are "justified freely by his grace through the redemption that is in Christ Jesus" (Romans 3:24). Oh, what a turn this made upon me! Oh, what a sudden change it made!

Then also, this Scripture came upon my spirit

with great power: "Not by works of righteousness which we have done, but according to his mercy he saved us" (Titus 3:5; 2 Timothy 1:9). Now I was walking on air, for I saw myself within the arms of grace and mercy and, whereas before I was afraid to die, now I cried out, "Let me die." Now death was lovely and beautiful in my sight, for I saw that we will never really live until we have come to the other world. This life, I saw, was but a slumber in comparison with that above. It was at this time also, that I saw more in these three words than I shall ever be able to express: "Heirs of God" (Romans 8:17). God Himself is the portion of the saints. This I saw and wondered at, but I cannot explain what it meant to me.

Another time I was very weak and ill, and again the tempter was there. I find he is most present to assault the soul when it begins to approach the grave. That was his opportunity and he worked hard to hide from me my experiences of God's goodness and set before me the terrors of death and judgment of God, and through my fear that I would be lost if I died, I was as one dead before death came. It was as if I were already descending into the pit. But then, just as I was in the midst of these fears, the words of the angel carrying Lazarus into Abraham's bosom darted in upon me, and I felt that it would be even so with me when I left this world. This thought wonderfully revived my spirits and helped me to have hope again in God. And after I had thought about this for a while, the words fell with great weight upon my mind: "O death, where is thy sting? O grave, where is thy victory?" (1 Corinthians 15:55). At once I became well both in body and in mind; my sickness vanished, and I walked comfortably in my work for God again. Another time, when I had been getting along well in spiritual things, suddenly there fell upon me a great cloud of darkness which so hid from me the things of God in Christ that it seemed as though I had never known about them in all my life. My soul was seized with **inertia**, so that I could not stir after grace and the life that is in Christ. It was as if my hands and feet were bound with chains.

I had remained in this condition for three or four days, when, as I was sitting by the fire, this word suddenly struck into my heart: I must go to Jesus. At that moment the darkness and atheism fled away and the blessed things of Heaven came into my view. I cried out to my wife, "Is there such a Scripture as this: 'I must go to Jesus'?" She said she did not know, so I sat there trying to think if I could remember such a place. I had been sitting there two or three minutes when there came bolting in upon me, "and to an innumerable company of angels" and all the twelfth chapter of Hebrews about Mount Sion especially the phrase from verse 22, along with these words in verse 24, "And to Jesus."

That night was one that I shall long remember. Christ was so precious to my soul that I could scarcely lie in my bed for joy and peace and triumph through Christ. The glory of it did not continue, but Hebrews 12:22-24 was a blessed Scripture to me for many days after that. The words are these, "Ye are come unto mount Sion, and unto the city of the living God, the heavenly Jerusalem, and to an innumerable company of angels, to the general assembly and church of the firstborn, which are written in heaven, and to God the Judge of all, and to the spirits of just men made perfect, and to Jesus the mediator of the new covenant, and to the blood of sprinkling, that speaketh better things than that of Abel." Through this sentence the Lord led me over and over first to this word and then to that and showed me wonderful glory in every one of them. These words have often refreshed my spirit. Blessed be God for having mercy on me.

Meditating for Meaning

1. What truth was particularly impressed on Bunyan through observance of the Lord's Supper?

2. Even in this observance, Satan tried to defeat him.
   a. What strong temptation came to Bunyan in relation to this ordinance?
   b. What did Bunyan think was the cause for this temptation?

3. Times of testing are sure to come to the Christian.
   a. What condition moved Bunyan to closely examine his life?
   b. Besides the goodness of God, what tended to dominate his thinking and made his condition worse?
   c. When do you think such self-examination becomes self-destructive?

4. Bunyan found triumph after testing.
   a. What finally brought victory to Bunyan?
   b. Copy the other two portions of Scripture that helped Bunyan at this time.
   c. From your study of Bunyan's life so far, what in general do you conclude brought him victory when he was downcast?
   d. What did Bunyan need to do throughout his life to have this source of victory available?
   e. What two figures of speech does Bunyan use to describe his feeling after this victory?

5. Satan brings doubt at times of weakness.
   a. What fear did a second illness bring?
   b. From this experience what could you conclude is the relationship between the health of the mind and the health of the body?

6. Explain this statement: "My soul was seized with inertia."

7. By saying "at that moment the darkness and atheism fled away," we learn that Bunyan had been actually tempted to doubt that _____ .

8. How do we know that Bunyan's experience of joy was more than just transient emotions? Clue: What did he think about?

Part 3 – Preaching Experiences

In my preaching, I have actually been in real pain travailing to bring forth children to God, and I have never been satisfied until there has been some fruit. If not, it made no difference who complimented me, but if I were fruitful I did not care who might condemn me. I have often thought of that verse: "Lo, children are an heritage of the Lord: and the fruit of the womb is his reward. As arrows are in the hand of a mighty man; so are children of the youth. Happy is the man that hath his quiver full of them: they shall not be ashamed, but they shall speak with the enemies in the gate" (Psalm 127:3-5).

It never pleased me to see people merely drinking in opinions if they were ignorant of Christ and the value of His salvation. When I saw sound conviction for sin, especially the sin of unbelief, and saw hearts set on fire to be saved by Christ, those were the souls I counted blessed.

But in this work, as in any other, I had my different temptations. Sometimes I would suffer from discouragement, fearing that I would not be of any help to anyone and that I would not even be able to speak sense to the people. At such times, I have had a strange faintness seize me. At other times, when I have been preaching, I have been violently assaulted with thoughts of blasphemy before the congregation. At times, I have been speaking with clearness and great liberty, when suddenly everything would go blank and I would not know what to say or how to finish.

Again, there have been times when I have been about to preach on some searching portion of the Word, and I have found the tempter suggesting, "What! Will you preach this? This condemns you. Your own soul is guilty of this; you must not preach on it. If you do, you must leave a door open for you to escape from the guilt of what you will say. If you preach like this you will lay that guilt upon your own soul and you will never be able to get out from under it."

I have been kept from consenting to these horrid suggestions, and instead I thought, it is far better to bring oneself under condemnation by plain preaching to others, than to save yourself by imprisoning the truth in unrighteousness. Blessed be God for His help also in this.

I have often found in this blessed work of Christ that I have been tempted to pride; but the Lord in His precious mercy has, for the most part, kept me from giving way to such a thing. Every day I have been able to see the evil of my own heart and my head has hung down with shame, despite the gifts and the attainments that He has given to me. So I feel that this thorn in the flesh is the very mercy of God to me (2 Corinthians 12:7-9).

I have also had the Word come to me with some sharp, piercing sentence concerning the perishing of the soul notwithstanding the gifts God has given. For instance: "Though I speak with the tongues of men and of angels, and have not charity, I am become as sounding brass, or a tinkling cymbal" (1 Corinthians 13:1).

A tinkling cymbal is a musical instrument with which a skillful player can make heart-inflaming melody, so that all who hear him play can scarcely keep from dancing. Yet the cymbal does not contain life, and the music does not come out of it except by the ability of the one who plays upon it. The instrument can be crushed and thrown away, even though in the past wonderfully sweet music has been played upon it.

So are all those who have gifts but do not have saving grace. They are in the hands of Christ as the cymbal was in the hand of David. As David could use the cymbal in the service of God to lift up the hearts of the worshipers, so Christ can use gifted men to affect the souls of the people in His church, yet when He has finished using them, He can hang them up with life, even though they are sounding cymbals.

Such considerations were a sledge hammer upon the head of pride and the desire of vainglory. What! thought I, shall I be proud since I am a sounding brass? Is it such a great thing to be a fiddle? Does not the person who has the least of the life of God in him have more than these instruments? Besides, I remembered that these instruments would vanish away, though love would never die. So I concluded that a little grace, a little love, a little of the true fear of God are better than all the gifts. I am convinced that it is possible for an ignorant soul who can scarcely give a right answer to have a thousand times more grace, and to be more in the love and favor of the Lord, than some who have marvelous gifts and can deliver themselves like angels.

I saw that he who has these gifts needs to be led into an understanding of the nature of them—that they do not prove that he is in a saved condition—lest he rely on them and so fall short of God.

He needs to learn to walk humbly with God, to be little in his own eyes, and to remember that his gifts are not his own—they belong to the church. By them he is made a servant of the church; he must give at the last an account of his stewardship unto the Lord Jesus; and it will be a wonderful thing if he can give a good account.

When Satan saw that this temptation would not do what he had hoped—overthrow my ministry, making it ineffectual—he tried another way. He stirred up the minds of the ignorant and **malicious** to load me with slanders and reproaches. All that the devil could devise and invent was whirled up and down the country against me, the devil thinking that in this way he could make me abandon the ministry.

It began to be rumored that I was a witch, a Jesuit, a highwayman, and so on.

To all this I only say that God knows I am innocent. As for my accusers, let them prepare to meet me before the judgment seat of the Son of God. There they shall answer for all these things they have said against me and for all the rest of their iniquities, unless—as I pray with all my heart—God gives them repentance.

Meditating for Meaning

1. In studying this section you should be aware that Bunyan was actually a very effective preacher. But God knows how to keep men humble. You may look at a prominent church leader and think that he has an easy Christian life; everything seems to go so smoothly for him. But you do not know the tremendous inner struggles he may have.
   a. Under what circumstances did Bunyan not care if he was condemned by others?
   b. What did he consider good fruit of preaching?

2. Various temptations and trials concerning his ministry brought seasons of discouragement.
   a. At times he feared that his ministry would not be _____ .
   b. He worried that what he would say would not _____ .
   c. Sometimes as he was preaching he would have thoughts of _____ .
   d. He even experienced times when his mind would _____ .

3. Bunyan was sometimes tempted not to preach the truth.
   a. Why would a minister hesitate to preach a truth he himself is not practicing?
   b. What attitude did Bunyan take about preaching such truths?

4. If Satan cannot cause a Christian to fall by casting him down, he will try by lifting him up.
   a. What special temptation does an eloquent preacher have?
   b. What did Paul say was God's purpose for his "thorn in the flesh"? (2 Corinthians 12:7).
   c. What does Bunyan say was his "thorn in the flesh"?

5. After one particularly eloquent sermon, someone commended Bunyan. He replied, "Ay, you have no need to tell me that, for the devil whispered it to me before I was well out of the pulpit."
   a. What further consideration about a tinkling cymbal helped Bunyan keep himself humble?
   b. What did he conclude was better than the gift of effective speech?
   c. Which one of the following verses best summarizes Bunyan's feeling about his ministry?
      1 Corinthians 9: (14, 16, 19)
   d. To Bunyan, gifts were not evidence that _____ .

6. Satan tries to defeat a Christian by opposition.
    a. Since Satan was not successful in causing Bunyan to fall by working in his mind, what outside opposition did he stir up?
    b. In what wrong ways is a leader tempted to respond when faced with such opposition?
    c. How did Bunyan respond?

Part 4 – Prison Experience

After I had been a Christian for a long time, and had been preaching for about five years, I was arrested at a meeting of good people in the country, among whom, if they had let me alone, I would have preached that day. They took me away from among them and before a justice. I offered security to appear at the next session, but he threw me into jail because those who were ready to make up the bond for me would not agree to be bound that I would preach no more to the people.

At the next session, I was **indicted** as one who had encouraged unlawful assemblies and for not conforming to the national worship of the Church of England. The judges thought that my plain dealing with them was proof enough, and sentenced me to life imprisonment because I refused to conform. So I was again given to the jailer and sent to prison, where I have now lain for these 12 years, waiting to see what God would let these men do with me.

In this condition I have found much contentment through grace, so there have been many turnings and goings upon my heart, from the Lord, from Satan, and from my own corruption. After all these things—glory be to Jesus Christ—I have also received much instruction and understanding. I will not speak at length of these things, but will give you at least a hint or two that may stir up the godly to bless God and to pray for me, and to take encouragement, should they find themselves in need of it, not to fear what man can do unto them.

I have never in all my life had so much of the Word of God opened up so plainly to me before. Those Scriptures that I saw nothing particular in before have been made, in this place, to shine upon me. Also, Jesus Christ was never more real to me than now; here I have seen and felt Him indeed. That "we have not followed cunningly devised fables" (2 Peter 1:16) and that God raised Christ "from the dead, and gave him glory; that your faith and hope might be in God" (1 Peter 1:21) have been blessed portions to me in this my imprisonment.

I never knew before what it really was for God to stand beside me at all times. As soon as fears have presented themselves, so have supports and encouragements. Sometimes when I have been startled by my shadow, being so full of fear, God has been very tender to me and has not suffered me to be molested by Satan, but has given me one Scripture after another to strengthen me against it all.

Before I came to prison I saw what was coming, and two things were particularly heavy upon my heart.

The first was how I would be able to encounter death if that should be my portion. Colossians 1:11 helped me greatly at this point to pray to God to be "strengthened with all might, according to his glorious power, unto all patience and longsuffering with joyfulness." For at least a year before I was in prison, I could scarcely go to prayer without this sentence thrusting itself into my mind and persuading me that if I would ever have to go through long suffering, I would need much patience especially if I were to endure it joyfully.

The second thing that bothered me was what would happen to my wife and family. Concerning this, this Scripture helped me: "But we had the sentence of death in ourselves, that we should not trust in ourselves, but in God which raiseth the dead" (2 Corinthians 1:9). By this Scripture I was made to see that if ever I must suffer properly, I must first pass the sentence of death upon everything that can be in this life; even to reckon myself, my wife, my children, my health, my enjoyments, and all, as dead to me; and myself as dead to them.

I saw, moreover, as Paul said, that the way not to faint is to "look not at the things which are seen, but at the things which are not seen: for the things which are seen are temporal; but the things which are not seen are eternal" (2 Corinthians 4:18). I reasoned: if I provide only for a prison, then I am whipped, and if I provide myself for these, then I am not fit for banishment. If I decide that I could stand banishment, then if I am killed, I would be surprised. So I saw that the best way to go through sufferings is to trust in God through Christ concerning the world to come and to expect the worst down here, to count the grave as my house, to make my bed in darkness.

This helped, but I am a man with many weaknesses. Parting with my wife and poor children has often been to me like pulling the flesh from my bones, not only because of all that they mean to me, but also because I have thought so much of many hardships, miseries and wants that they were likely to meet, were I taken from them; especially my poor blind child, who was nearer my heart than all of the others. Oh, the thoughts that went through my mind of the hardship I thought my poor blind one might undergo which would break my heart!

Poor child, I thought, what sorrows you are likely to have as your portion in this world. You will probably be beaten and have to beg and suffer hunger, cold, nakedness and a thousand calamities, though I cannot endure the thought of even the wind blowing against you.

The old bridge and prison at Bedford

But I must **venture** you all with God, though it cuts to the heart to leave you. I saw that I was as a man who was pulling down his house upon the head of his wife and children, yet I thought, I must do it, I must do it.

Let me tell you about an interesting thing that happened: I was once in a particularly sad condition for many weeks. I was only a young prisoner at the time and not acquainted with the laws, and I thought that it was probable that my imprisonment would end at the gallows. All this time, Satan was beating upon me and saying, If you are going to die, what will happen to you if you are not enjoying the things of God and have no evidence from your feelings that you are going to heaven?" Indeed, at this time all the things of God seemed to be hidden from my soul.

At this time I was so obsessed with the thought of death that I often felt myself standing on the ladder with a rope about my neck. Only this was of some encouragement to me, that I might have a last opportunity to speak to a large multitude which I thought would come to see me die. And I thought: If this must be, and God will convert even one soul by my last words, I will not count my life as thrown away.

And still the tempter kept following me around, saying, "Where are you going when you die? What will become of you? What evidence have you for heaven and glory and an inheritance among those who are sanctified?" So it was that I was tossed about for many weeks, and knew not what to do. But at last this consideration fell with great weight upon me, that it was for the Word and way of God that I was in this condition; wherefore, I was engaged not to **flinch** a hair's breadth from it.

I decided also that God might choose whether He would give me comfort now or at the hour of death, but I had no choice as to whether to hold to my profession or not. I was bound, but He was free. It was my duty to stand up for His Word, whether He would ever look upon me with mercy to save me at the last or not. I will go on, I said to myself, and venture my eternal state with Christ, whether I feel it here or not. If God does not give me joy, thought I, then I will leap off the ladder blindfolded into eternity, sink or swim, come heaven, come hell. Lord Jesus, if You will catch me, do; if not, I will venture for Your name anyway.

I had no sooner resolved this than I thought of the word: "Doth Job fear God for naught?" It was as if the accuser had said, "Lord, Job is not an upright man, he is serving You for what he can get out of it. You have given him everything he wants, but if You put forth Your hand against him and take away all that he has, then he will curse You to Your face." Well, I thought, then it must be the sign of an upright soul that is on its way to heaven to desire to serve God when all is taken from him. The truly godly man will serve God for nothing rather than giving up. Blessed be God! Then I began to hope that I did indeed have an upright heart, for I was resolved, God giving me strength, never to deny my Lord though I got nothing at all for my pains: and as I was thinking about this God put into my mind Psalm 44:12-26.

Now my heart became full of comfort, and I would not have missed this trial for a great deal. I am still comforted every time I think of it and I will bless God forever for what He has taught me out of this experience. There are of course, many more of God's dealings with me, but of the spoils won in battle these have I dedicated to maintain the house of God (1 Chronicles 26:27).

Meditating for Meaning

Bunyan wrote *Grace Abounding* during his first imprisonment of 12 years. He was freed for about three years before he was imprisoned again in 1675. It was during this second imprisonment that he started to write *The Pilgrim's Progress*.

1. Satan used legal measures to stop Bunyan's preaching.
   a. What were the charges against Bunyan?
   b. What do you think Bunyan meant by "plain dealing."

2. Prison gives much time for thought.
   a. What does Bunyan mean by "many turnings and goings upon my heart"?
   b. From what three sources does Bunyan say these "turnings and goings" come?
   c. How was Bunyan benefited by his prison experiences?

3. From what Bunyan says about the blessings he received, how was he apparently using much of his time in prison?

4. In what two ways did God help Bunyan when he was struggling with fear?

5. What two concerns did Bunyan have before he was put into prison?

6. Bunyan faced the problem of suffering and gave good advice.
   a. What did Bunyan say will happen if you make preparation for a particular kind of suffering?
   b. What did Bunyan suggest is the best preparation for suffering?

7. What was Bunyan's chief trial in leaving his family?

8. How did Satan work through Bunyan's ignorance and imagination?

9. God was leading in Bunyan's life to refine him. One of the hardest tests of faith is to obey and be faithful to God even if there is no prospect of reward. Abraham passed that test when he offered up Isaac. Job passed that test when he said, "Though he slay me, yet will I trust in him" (Job 13:15). Notice how Bunyan passed this test.
   a. What spiritual comfort did Bunyan lack?
   b. What did Bunyan decide he would do in spite of his lack of this comfort?
   c. Bunyan had learned the lesson that the truly godly will _____ God even if he gets _____ .
   d. How did God reward this kind of unconditional surrender of Bunyan?

Looking for Literary Technique

The writer of fiction is much like a paleontologist, piecing together the bones of some skeleton. When a piece is missing, he can fabricate it with plaster of Paris. The fiction author creates most of his characters' life experiences from an educated imagination. But not the biographer. The biographer is duty-bound to facts.

John Bunyan had a benefit as he wrote. *He* was his subject. He himself had lived the experiences he described and had felt those feelings. This, as you have learned, is an autobiography. But most biographers must become real archaeologists, excavating through cobwebbed, moth-eaten documents in broiling attics or courthouses; sifting through libraries; interviewing relatives, neighbors, friends, or, if possible, the subject himself.

1. What part of J. C. Wenger's biography on Menno Simons is the type of information you would find today by visiting a courthouse?

2. It is unlikely that J. C. Wenger visited any courthouses to do research for his biography. Neither would he have been able to consult primary sources such as journals and eyewitness accounts. Where did he likely get his information? You can find some clues if you have access to *Glimpses of Mennonite History and Doctrine* where this biography appears.

Writing for Skill

Now it is time for you to begin excavating for facts on your biography. You must submerge, yes, even bury yourself in your subject. Learn all there is to know. Don't worry if you find too much information. You can always sift out the rubble. But keep in mind your purpose. If you want to show how Joseph Funk contributed to the growth of four-part church music, don't spend time discovering whether or not he was an avid gardener.

Now where should you begin your excavation? If your subject is alive, willing, and able to answer questions, begin there. Before arranging an interview, make a list of questions you would like to have answered about his life. Ask for diaries, photographs, letters, journals, and even business records. As you visit, tune your ear for interesting events from his life. Take care to preserve some of his information as direct quotations because these automatically disarm the skeptical reader. Remember, however, not to demand but to ask courteously and to respond gratefully. If your subject is not living, relatives may be able to provide you with these documents.

Depending upon how widely known your subject is, there may already be books written about his life. Visit a library for books, newspapers, or magazines which may acquaint you more fully with your subject. By the time you investigate all these possibilities, he should seem like your friend. Don't only look for books on your subject but delve into the times in which he lived. Did he live during the Great Depression, during the Revolutionary War, during the presidency of Abraham Lincoln? These are the factors which shape lives. Possibly he even wrote a book himself. Keep a preying eye for original writings because these provide an acutely accurate view of your subject.

If possible, visit the places where your subject lived, attended school, and worked. You can learn volumes from such visits.

But you can't expect your memory to absorb and hold all this information. Develop the art of note-taking. Preferably, you should have a pack of 3 x 5 cards. Write only on one side and include on each card information on only one aspect of your subject's life. If that aspect is his education, jot this as a heading at the top of the note card. At the foot of the card, note the source of this information in case you should want to return to that source. Now is the time *not* to write in complete sentences. Abbreviate as much as you choose, as long as you will later remember what you meant. By all means, if you are taking notes from a book, don't copy word for word, unless you intend to quote the source and give credit to the author. Copying without crediting is plagiarism, and plagiarism is a crime because you are claiming credit for some other author's hard work. Put it in your own words.

Imagine now that you were going to take notes from the first paragraph of the biography on Menno Simons.

In 1496, a Dutch couple of Witmarsum in Friesland named their infant son Menno. Since the name of Menno's father was Simon, the custom of the day in Holland made the child's name Menno Simonszoon—called Simons for short. As a youth Menno received training for the Catholic priesthood, perhaps in the Franciscan Monastery at Bolsward, near Witmarsum. In the monastery Menno received training in reading and writing Latin and in a study of the church fathers, but he never read the Bible. In 1524, he was consecrated as a priest, and for seven years he served in the Pinjum parish near Witmarsum. In 1531, he was transferred to his home town where he . . .

Observe below how your note card might look:

```
EARLY LIFE
       born 1496, Friesland
       father, Simon
       trained to be Catholic priest, maybe in Franciscan
         Monastery near Witmarsum
       learned Latin; never read Bible
       1524, became priest of Pinjum parish for 7 years


                       —Glimpses of Mennonite History
                                       and Doctrine
```

Notice that not all the information has been included in the notes, only important facts, expressed in skeletal verb phrases.

Twenty to thirty note cards, well-filled should provide ample data for a 500-word biography. Enjoy your research.

True . . . Till Death

The Story of Clayton Kratz

by Clarence Y. Fretz

Decisions, discipline, and dedication: these are the fabric of life—the right decision, strict self-discipline, and dedication to the kingdom of God.

But what if a right decision leads to a shortened life? Can we use the length of a person's life as the criteria for determining his success? No. A short life in the will of God is not to be compared to 80 years of selfishness.

Clayton Kratz was young when he made a decision that was to cost him his life. Of course, he did not know this consequence, but to him the needs of others and the call of the church preceded personal plans and comfort.

After a quick glance at Kratz's short life, one might conclude that he never achieved his goal. Yet he did. His dauntless zeal broke a path which the Mennonite Central Committee and other relief programs afterwards pursued, providing aid for southern Russia and other war-torn areas. In terms of dedication to serve others, Clayton's life is a worthy model.

His example provided a positive challenge for Clarence Fretz, the author of this biography. When Fretz was asked to help with relief work in civil war-torn Spain in 1938, one acquaintance tried to discourage him by calling attention to what happened to Kratz. But far from being discouraged, Fretz believed Kratz's example was worthy of emulation and followed Kratz's steps with confidence in the providence of God. No doubt, having grown up in the same congregation added to Fretz's esteem for Kratz.

Years later while teaching in a Christian school, Fretz did the extensive research needed to write this biography. Now young people of a new generation can be challenged by the decisions, discipline, and dedication of Clayton Kratz . . . who was "true . . . till death."

Part 1 – From Childhood to Manhood

The telegram of August 18 was urgent:

NEED ANOTHER MAN SERIOUSLY
IN GROUP SAILING SEPT 1ST CAN
YOU GET READY IF YOU REPORT
AT SCOTTDALE THUR OR FRI THIS
WEEK CAN WE DEPEND ON YOU
WIRE TODAY

What! Leave home, go overseas to help feed the hungry, postpone marriage and **career** *plans? And report to Mennonite headquarters at Scottdale, Pennsylvania, yet this week?*

It took a levelheaded man to answer these questions and many others that kept asking for answers. At the time, 23-year-old Clayton Kratz was working at the Studebaker factory at Fort Wayne, Indiana, to raise funds to finish his schooling during the 1923-24 school term. His mother, sisters, and brothers were at home in eastern Pennsylvania, 600 miles away. There was no way he could get their advice for this sudden call to service. His pastor, too, was too remote; his trusted schoolmates were not within calling distance. He would have to make the decision on his own, all alone.

World War I had just ended, leaving a world in turmoil and distress. In eastern Europe, a fierce revolution had left famine and terror in its wake. Hard-pressed Mennonites there were calling for help. A hastily-organized Mennonite relief organization had just been formed and was planning to send three men as relief workers. Two had already been found; a third man was yet needed. More than a dozen young men had already been contacted to fill the post—none felt free to go. Would Clayton accept the call?

Why was there so little time to decide? Why hadn't there been a **preliminary intimation** of this need before Clayton became elected as president of the school's leading Christian organization, and vice-president of the senior class? And before he had become engaged to his girl friend and made plans for settling down in life?

But only on July 27 had the American Mennonite Relief Committee been organized. By August 15 Clayton received the first appeal from Orie Miller, who was to be the leader of the three-man relief unit scheduled to sail for Constantinople on September 1. Help was needed in Russia at once.

Actually Clayton had been in preparation to give attention to such a call ever since he was born. His godly parents had given him a good start. His elderly father was a quiet man, who believed in discipline and in keeping his children from running after the things of the world. His mother was also a quiet person, a soft-spoken, motherly soul, who had a pleasing way of teaching and maintaining order in the home. Together they held dear the faith of their fathers. Bible reading and prayer were familiar practices in their well-ordered home. On Sundays they regularly attended Sunday school and preaching services at the Blooming Glen Mennonite Church, four miles away.

When Clayton was six (1904), he began attending a nearby one-room school. His teacher still remembered him in 1943, when she wrote of him: "He was a very studious and obedient boy. He was thoughtful and helpful and a favorite among his playmates.... He took pride in handing in neat papers. He was a good sport and a jolly little fellow on the playground.... He was always willing to assist me and seemed to find pleasure in helping to carry water and to bring coal."

Clayton had made significant choices before the call came to go to Russia. When Clayton was eight years old, his father, then over 65, decided to retire from farming and move to the village of Blooming Glen. Here there were other boys to play with. But Clayton never became involved in the cheaper aspects of town life. A high school chum remembers that Clayton "was different from other town boys, who would hang around and talk about girls in a vulgar way." He was interested in the finer things of life—books, nature, kind deeds, and working in the out-of-doors on his uncle's farm. He found the local newspaper unsatisfactory. "It has nothing in it but visiting," he once said. "If I want to read, I want to read something more worthwhile."

In church he would often sit with older boys or with grown-up men, rather than with the boys of his own age. When his sister asked him about this, he said, "The other boys talk and 'make fun' too much and I don't like that. It isn't right." But Clayton was no religious hermit. He is remembered as having been quite an all-around person. His grammar-school (grades 5-8) teacher in later life shared his memory of Clayton: "A good student...able to do his work as required...took a great interest in different games, baseball one of the leading... a pleasant disposition...when his mind was set to do a thing, he would do it...obedient...full of life...would do most anything asked of him by other students...."

His schoolmates remembered him as a quiet, studious person, yet diligent and active, who did well in his studies, liked to play ball, was a well-behaved fellow and a good pal. One classmate thought of him as of only average ability in school, but his high school records reveal him to have stood at the head of the class, with an average grade of over 90.

In 1912, Clayton's father died. In 1914, Clayton became a Christian and on April 26 was baptized with 11 others into the church at Blooming Glen. In June he graduated from high school. During the summer he attended West Chester State Normal School to prepare for teaching. Here he came under the influence of Professor Green, a talented lecturer and inspiring teacher who imparted noble ideals.

In the fall of 1914, Kratz began teaching in a one-room school several miles from his home. He applied himself earnestly to his work. According to his high school records, he also "reviewed all the common branches after school hours" during 1914-15. In December of that winter, a Young People's Meeting was organized at the nearby Perkasie Church. Clayton began attending and occasionally was asked to serve as a speaker.

Kratz took quite an interest in speaking and literary activity. A fellow teacher recalls that on the eight-mile horse-and-buggy trips to and from county teacher's institutes, Kratz would like to get the others to join him in recalling and reciting literary gems—in which he usually excelled.

The next year, 1915-16, Kratz obtained a

teaching position nearer home, at Blue School only a mile from Blooming Glen. Here he taught for two years. One of his pupils, Harold Clymer, retained quite distinct memories of Kratz's excellence as a teacher:

> Older people spoke of him as a good teacher, but strict, and when I heard he was going to be our teacher, I was somewhat scared. However, he proved to be a very good teacher and an outstanding, clean-cut young man. He was a strict disciplinarian, but punished only if necessary as a last resort, after dealing with pupils in a kind way and giving them several warnings.
>
> Kratz was good at explaining. I had no other teacher who could read a dry article and make it live as he did. He would help you to form a picture in your mind. He made history and geography very interesting. I wasn't so good at arithmetic. He tried to make me ashamed and we didn't hit it so good in this, but if I would have a chance to talk to him today, I would thank him for it. He read Scriptures in a very sincere tone. Whenever he saw me in after years, he was sure to talk to me. He has stayed in my mind as the type of man I'd like to be.

Despite his success as a teacher, Kratz did not want to remain a teacher. His old love for the farm called him in a different direction. In high school he had especially enjoyed the course in agriculture and had made some of the best grades in it. Now he wanted to become a farmer and to study so that he could become a *scientific* farmer.

Consequently, he gave up his teaching, and in the fall of 1917, went off to a church school in Indiana instead of a state school, even though it was farther away from home. He enrolled in several courses in agriculture, besides general subjects such as English and algebra. In later years, the head of the school wrote of Kratz as a "modest, quiet, unassuming and devoted Christian gentleman," who "always attended to his own business, and went about his work

Kratz with his students

faithfully and with purpose."

As spring and summer approached, Kratz's thoughts began to turn to the home farm where he had often worked. He wrote to his sister:

> Farming appeals to me more and more as I study about it, and find out how the different plants grow and how to improve their growth. And sometimes I think that I can hardly wait until I am through school and settled down on a farm in good old Pennsylvania, however much I do like school life.
>
> This summer I think I will work on the farms in the Middle West somewhere. A fellow learns a whole lot about farming by seeing how they do it in different communities.

CONSCIENTIOUS OBJECTOR

Kratz was also thinking about the war question. The nation by this time was deeply involved in the European war, and many were being called to engage in the bloody conflict. What should a young man do and think? Kratz's own brother had just been called, and had decided to take up military training and service. Kratz went on in his letter to his sister to comment on this action of his brother Jacob and to reveal something of his own thinking on the subject:

> I got a letter from Jacob a short time ago, but I don't quite understand his stand.
> I think this is no time to worry, but a time when we all should examine our

lives, put our trust and prayers in that higher power, which is, after all, guiding and directing our conditions at present and giving us our conscientious scruples against the evils of the day.

It soon began to look as if Kratz would be drafted, and he decided that if he would be called, he would go as a conscientious objector, and take whatever hardships might befall him as such. However, his mother felt so sorry that her older son had gone into the army that she now pleaded with her younger son Clayton that he would not go away at all (even if he did not intend to take up carnal warfare), but that instead he would take up farm work, which would defer him. While Clayton did not want to do anything which would look like shirking his duty, he decided to yield to his mother's wishes, and go to his brother-in-law's farm. After all, he did like farm work, and it was considered even by the government to be more vital and necessary than soldiery.

So it was that when the fall term of college began in September 1918, Kratz was not back in school with the rest of his class. However, in November the **armistice** was signed, and on January 12, Kratz was able to go back to school and resume his studies.

RESUMING SCHOOL

Soon he was hard at work, applying himself diligently to his studies, and to such opportunities for service as came his way. For instance, a week after he was back in school he went along to help in the Gospel services held by the students in the county jail.

One of Kratz's favorite subjects was **botany**. He enjoyed going out on jaunts through the countryside gathering specimens for the botany teacher. It is not surprising then that he should have been asked to assist in this department during the summer of 1919. This helped him finance his own summer study, and so catch up with the work he had missed. A similar opportunity was granted him in the fall when he was given an assistantship in agriculture.

The 1919-1920 school term proved to be Kratz's last year in school. How he entered so fully into so many of the worthwhile phases of school life is almost a marvel. His class, the

About the Author

Clarence Y. Fretz (1911– 1996) was born in Bucks County, Pennsylvania, and grew up in the Blooming Glen congregation of which Clayton Kratz was a member. After graduating from the Millersville Teacher's College, he taught school for several years in the Lancaster, Pennsylvania, area and then volunteered on a relief program to war-torn Spain. Later he attended Eastern Mennonite College, Goshen College, and Eastern Baptist Seminary. In 1940 Fretz was ordained minister at Norris Square in Philadelphia where he served for 11 years before going to Luxembourg as a missionary with his wife, Lela. Fretz was a principal and teacher at Paradise Mennonite School of Hagerstown, Maryland, from 1959-1972.

junior class, elected him as president, and he was chosen business manager of the school annual. He served on various committees, helping to arrange for lectures, provide books for the school library, etc. He found time for active physical exercise on the baseball diamond and tennis court. As an enthusiastic orator, he spent many hours of time in preparation and practice.

Kratz seems to have been well qualified to help develop the social life of his fellow students. A cheerful, thoughtful person, he took a friendly interest in others, and was always willing to help where he could. He went out of his way to make non-Mennonites feel at home in the school.

Quiet, yet sociable, he disarmed timidity in others with a friendly broad grin as he looked their way or talked to them. Even little boys who roamed across the campus found that Kratz was their friend and would take time to romp with them.

Preeminent in all of Kratz's life and activity, however, was his interest in Christian work and life. A schoolmate says of him, "Kratz was a man of high Christian ideals. When he believed in such ideals, he disciplined himself to live them. He had a schedule for all his studies, and held himself to it. He was opposed to **dissipation** in any form, and faithfully observed appointed hours of rest. No doubt it was this self-discipline that enabled him to be such an all-around man and successfully carry through such a variety of activities."

The most outstanding example of Kratz's self-discipline was with regard to his personal devotional life. Every morning he arose at a certain time so that he would have time to observe the morning watch. One of his devotional books contains many notes, significant underscorings, and other signs of careful thought and deep meditation.

Kratz's convictions were especially strong regarding Christian service. In January 1920 he attended a convention at Des Moines, Iowa, where speakers "sounded the call of a needy world, and drove home the glorious opportunity of service." Often on Saturdays he and a friend would work together at Loomis's Creamery, **candling** eggs and testing cream, and would talk over the deeper things of life. On one such occasion, Kratz said, "Although we don't always see tangible results, yet I feel very strongly that the person who gives himself in service is the one that really lives."

In the spring of 1920, the student body recognized Kratz's spiritual leadership by electing him president of the leading Christian organization on the campus. No doubt, he took this appointment quite seriously and faithfully applied himself to the carrying out of his duties.

As the school year drew to a close, Kratz wrote to his mother of his yearning to come home, but said that it might be for only a month, as he had several good offers for the summer. Life was becoming more serious, full of significant opportunities.

Testing for Understanding

1. The August 18 telegram did not give Kratz much time for decision because
   a. the relief committee was slow in recruiting help.
   b. Kratz had been putting off making a decision.
   c. the call for relief was urgent.
   d. the new school term was about to begin.

2. Young Clayton's character as shown by his relation to town life, church life, and the local newspaper could best be described as
   a. serious-minded.
   b. pleasure-minded.
   c. high-minded.
   d. education-minded.

3. The fact that a classmate remembered Clayton as an average student would seem to prove that
   a. Clayton was not as intelligent as his schoolteachers thought.
   b. Clayton's fellow students did not appreciate him.
   c. Clayton was meek and unassuming with his successes.
   d. testimonies from personal acquaintances are frequently not reliable.

4. Clayton Kratz sat with older men and boys rather than with those his age because
   a. the younger boys made fun of him.
   b. the discussion of the younger boys violated his convictions.
   c. he was a quiet, timid boy.
   d. he preferred to appear more mature than the younger boys.

5. By approximately a year after graduating from high school, all of the following probably helped Kratz to mature except
   a. a challenging friend.
   b. self-motivated study.
   c. a model teacher.
   d. a teaching position.

6. As a teacher, Kratz excelled in all of the following except
   a. maintaining good order in the classroom.
   b. motivating students in school subjects.
   c. helping his students with learning problems to accept their limitations.
   d. inspiring respect and appreciation for himself as a teacher.

7. Kratz's life ambition was to become
   a. a college teacher in agriculture.
   b. a public speaker.
   c. an educated farmer.
   d. a church official.

8. After attending college for only one year, Kratz returned to his home community to work for his brother-in-law because
   a. he was homesick for the farm.
   b. his mother was old and he wanted to be near her in her later years.
   c. he needed more money to continue his education
   d. his mother urged him to pursue work that would exempt him from military service.

9. We gain insight into how the college faculty rated Kratz as a student by his
   a. being given an assistantship in agriculture.
   b. being asked to give a talk at the county jail.
   c. being elected the junior class president.
   d. being chosen manager of the school annual.

10. The most significant factor in Kratz's general success as a student was his
    a. socializing.
    b. disarming way with others.
    c. wise use of time.
    d. superior intellect.

11. "Although we don't always see tangible results, yet I feel very strongly that the person who gives himself in service is the one that really lives." By this statement Kratz revealed that he felt that
    a. submission is more important than popularity.
    b. quality is more important than quantity.
    c. self-sacrifice is more important than material success.
    d. humility is more important than accomplishment of great things.

Part 2 – Kratz Answers the Call

Defining for Comprehension

Choose the word or phrase below which most nearly defines each word at the left as it is used in the biography.

1. essay	a. attempt	b. speech	c. opinion
2. visas	a. views	b. luggage	c. passports
3. offensive	a. attack	b. assurance	c. retreat
4. initial	a. official	b. military	c. first
5. cordially	a. drunkenly	b. in friendly manner	c. divided
6. confirm	a. swear	b. verify	c. adapt
7. palatial	a. dull	b. lateral	c. magnificent
8. conjunction	a. combination	b. intersection	c. separation
9. misgivings	a. doubts	b. stingy actions	c. wrong assumptions
10. ardor	a. shady place	b. strong smell	c. enthusiasm
11. impending	a. dangling	b. approaching	c. imprisoning

At the close of the school term Kratz took up work for the summer at the Studebaker plant in South Bend, Indiana, in order to raise money to continue his school career.

It was while he was working at South Bend, that the Mennonite people of North America became much concerned about their brethren in southern Russia, who were suffering greatly from political revolution. Finally, on July 27, a relief effort was organized at Elkhart, Indiana, with plans to send relief before winter. Orie Miller of Pennsylvania and Arthur Slagel of Illinois were chosen for the relief unit. However, the sending committee still needed a third worker in this unit.

It was no easy task to find someone to fill this place. Finally, someone suggested Clayton Kratz. Orie Miller, director of the relief unit, wrote to Kratz at South Bend, explaining this call to service abroad.

MAKING AN IMPORTANT DECISION

It was no easy task to which the church was calling Kratz. A bitter civil war raged in Russia between various White (noncommunist) armies and the Red (communist) forces. Only a few years before, the Reds had taken over the central government by bloody revolution.

A food shortage worsened the situation, and cries for help rose from Mennonites suffering in the crossfire of southern Russia. But the same conditions which made life so bitter for them made it difficult and dangerous for American relief workers to enter Russia and distribute relief provisions among them.

To accept this call would mean interrupting Kratz's plans of finishing his schooling, marrying, and settling down to a life vocation. But Kratz did not feel he could say No, so on the same day he received Orie Miller's letter, he wired MCC's secretary, Levi Mumaw:

> RECEIVED LETTER FROM O MILLER THIS PM   I MADE DEFINITE PLANS TO BE IN SCHOOL THIS FALL   IF YOU NEED MY HELP SERIOUSLY I WOULD BE WILLING TO GIVE MY SERVICE
> C H KRATZ

A snarl of confusion delayed Mumaw's return telegram, and when his insistent appeal finally reached Kratz, September 1 was only 14 days away. There were no friends nearby to ask for counsel nor was there time to contact friends at a distance. A decision had to be made at once. The same day, August 18, Kratz wired Mumaw from South Bend:

> WILL REPORT AT SCOTTDALE ON FRI
> KRATZ

That evening he wrote to his mother: "I suppose you got the telegram which I sent tonight. All this has gone so suddenly that I was hardly able to catch my breath. I cannot conscientiously refuse, so I am going."

By Friday, Kratz was in Scottdale where he passed his doctrinal and physical examinations satisfactorily. On his application for relief work, he gave as his motive for going in this service, "I feel it my duty and privilege to help the suffering because this great world catastrophe has not caused me any inconvenience." He was now ready to suffer personal inconvenience in order to serve others. In reply to the question whether his temperament and experience were such that he could easily adapt himself to the difficult and unpleasant conditions of life in a foreign land, his modest, but significant reply was: "I think so."

Kratz reached home on Saturday. What a reunion with loved ones it must have been! How mixed must have been his mother's feelings! Kratz had only a short time left before sailing. As word spread of his plan to join the relief work in war-torn Russia, many people expressed negative opinions. But Kratz's resolve was clear.

In a farewell message, he told his home Sunday school at Blooming Glen that although many of his friends had advised him not to go, he felt it was a calling from God and it was his duty to go. To those who reminded him of the dangers, he said, "I feel that the Lord can take care of me, and deliver me out of evil. And if it is the Lord's will that I shall lose my life, it is all right with me." In a talk at the Doylestown Young People's Meeting, he said he did not know just what his work would be or what the Lord had mapped out for him to do, but as he was called to this relief work he was willing to go and do what the Lord would have him do.

At a final farewell gathering with loved ones, Kratz told his brother-in-law, "Take good care of Mother—you will be rewarded." Then he left for New York and a few days of final preparations.

THE JOURNEY TO RUSSIA

Kratz embarked September 1, 1920, on the steamer *Providence* with Arthur Slagel and Orie Miller. The 13-day ocean voyage from New York to Naples, Italy, gave Kratz the opportunity to relax after the strain of the past busy weeks. Did he begin to regret his quickly made decision and wish that he were back at school instead? Not according to a September 12 letter to the school newspaper:

"I feel convinced that the work to which I have been called is of greater importance than the completion of my schooling," Kratz wrote.

The voyage was not spent in idleness by Kratz and his companions. On the evening of the first day aboard, they "began using the after-supper hour in devotional study, using the Book of James, chapter by chapter." On the second day they added a daily hour on Russian language study and an hour a day at shuffleboard for exercise. On the third day they added a half hour devoted to oral reading of German stories by turn, with the two listeners making all comments and corrections in German. Miller concludes his diary report on this by saying: "If we continue the present reading schedule, it leaves us for general reading only the forenoon until eleven o'clock and the evening after nine." Among the books read were some on Russian life and thought, so even their general reading was of value in preparation for the work ahead.

On September 26, as they were nearing the end of their journey, Miller, Kratz, and Slagel met for an hour in the study of Matthew 4, "The Temptation of Jesus." The days of preparation for work ahead were coming to a close, but were certain to prove of value. Miller summarizes this aspect of their journey by saying, "We spent the days in discussing general principles which might guide relief work, and studying Russia. We prayed that we might be prepared for the experiences ahead, made willing for hard things, and given wisdom to deal with the situations as they might develop." In the next six weeks they were to discover what hard things they would encounter.

On September 27 the unit landed at Constantinople. They attempted to learn as quickly as possible what conditions were like in southern Russia. The American Embassy assured them that they could enter southern Russia and encouraged them to do so. The American Red Cross had been doing some relief work in southern Russia and told them about further needs and possibilities. The Near East Relief, who had supply warehouses in Constantinople, assured them of their cooperation. Miller made final plans for the first **essay** into Russia, while Kratz went to market to buy some small supplies needed for the journey. After waiting in line more than once to obtain needed **visas** to enter Russia, they were ready to go. The American Embassy had promised them transit to Russia on an American destroyer leaving at the end of the week.

On Saturday Miller withdrew 4,000 dollars to take along to start relief work in Russia, obtained a letter of introduction from the American Embassy, and together with Kratz, boarded the American destroyer which was to take them to Sevastopol, a Black Sea port in southern Russia. Slagel remained at Constantinople, gathering supplies for the relief work.

ENCOUNTERING PRESSING NEED

Miller and Kratz landed in Russia on October 6. Sevastopol, the seaport, was greatly overcrowded, and only after some inquiry did they finally find a place for the night in the home of a Mennonite, Kornelius Hiebert. Sevastopol was the headquarters of General Wrangel, the White Army leader who had at this time obtained control of all Crimea and of the territory in the Ukraine north of Crimea, containing the two largest Mennonite colonies in Russia. To these Mennonite colonies, the Molotschna and Chortitza, the American relief workers now determined to go. Wrangel had been making steady progress against the Reds all summer and with recent assurance of help from the French, it was felt that he could continue his **offensive**. The American Consul in Sevastopol encouraged Miller and Kratz in their mission and promised any assistance his office could give. The Wrangel government was quite cooperative, granting free transportation to the relief workers and any supplies they would send in, as well as providing an interpreter-guide for their **initial** trip to the interior.

The train for Melitopol left Sevastopol on October 8. Miller and Kratz had reserved a compartment in a third-class coach for themselves and their interpreter, Dr. Monastery, a lady doctor in government service. The train was crowded with refugees returning to districts which had been recently liberated by the Wrangel army. Very poorly dressed, most of them with shoes made out of cloth or even strings, and many without stockings, they jammed the aisles, covered the roofs of the train and hung on to the sides of the cars, where they got the full force of the cold wind, with the temperature at 40 degrees Fahrenheit.

Kratz wrote of this train ride as "a memorable one." He said,

"They put us into a car which had all the windows replaced with boards. The car was dark even in the daytime so that we had to burn candles. . . . About nine p.m. we decided to arrange ourselves for a little nap. I unwrapped my blanket roll, took out my blankets and went to bed. My bed consisted of a narrow piece of board about 12 inches wide fixed close to the ceiling in the form of a shelf."

Russian refugees

In spite of interruptions from a drunken Russian soldier's movements and "dreadful snoring" on the adjacent shelf, Kratz slept fairly well, even though the air at his high perch was so thick in the unventilated, crowded coach that "you could almost cut chunks out of it."

The train arrived at Melitopol on October 9. Here, Kratz says, they got their first impression of the real poverty of Russia. Miller, who had seen famine conditions in his relief work in the Near East, commented that he had never seen a poorer looking town. Most of the people seemed to be in rags. The streets were poorly paved, windows in buildings broken, horses skinny and few, and children mostly barefoot. Kratz was especially impressed with "the young, poorly clad and tough-looking Bolsheviki prisoners" they saw in town.

At the home of Jacob Neufeld, a former wealthy Mennonite miller, they learned more of local conditions. His only son, a doctor, had been recently killed together with his wife. Kratz wrote later that this was typical of reports they heard "all day long." Melitopol had been in the hands of the Bolshevists 18 times during the last three years. A number of the Mennonites had been wealthy, but were now poor, even though they owned the best wheat land in southern Russia.

Both in Neufeld's home on Saturday evening and after the sermon in the Mennonite church on Sunday morning, Miller was given the opportunity to explain what the Mennonite Committee in America was doing and planning to do. Kratz wrote, "They treated us very **cordially** and they are thankful that aid from the outside has finally come."

Before leaving Melitopol, Miller and Kratz called on the local Red Cross headquarters to learn what the Red Cross was doing and found that their supplies were mostly medical which the Red Cross distributed to existing hospitals and orphanages. Miller wrote,

> "They do or attempt very little in the way of relief for the civilian population outside of . . . hospitals. They distribute a few clothes. They **confirm** us in the thought that there is tremendous need for what we plan to do here."

On Monday, they traveled by carriage to Ohrloff, arriving at the home of preacher Jensen by one o'clock. Here they met a few of the Mennonite leaders of the colony and visited local institutions to discover relief needs. Neither the Deaf and Dumb School nor the Mennonite hospital were able to operate at more than half their capacity because they did not have enough bedclothes to provide for more.

From Ohrloff, Miller, Kratz, and Dr. Monastery pressed on to Halbstadt, the principle town in the large Mennonite colony on the Molotschna. Here again they met some of the local Mennonite leaders and made an initial explanation of their mission.

It was during these calls that they made their first acquaintance with Johann Peters, a man who was going to play an important role in Kratz's life in the next few weeks. Before the war, Brother Peters had been a very wealthy landowner. Even yet, the inside of his home appeared to the American visitors **palatial** in arrangement and furnishings. Only a week previous to their visit he had been chosen as president of a newly formed local relief committee to try to get help from the Mennonites of Holland and America. And now here were the Americans.

When the local committee met with the American relief unit, they indicated that the greatest need was in the Chortitza colonies which had only recently been liberated from the Reds by the White army and had suffered much more—not so much from the Reds as from the Machnow bandit gangs. The Halbstadt brethren felt that the first help should be given to these more needy Chortitza brethren. Later, two thirds of the relief should go to Chortitza and one third to the Halbstadt area. They advised that only one tenth of the budget should be spent locally and the rest should be spent for supplies to be sent in from outside Russia. They recommended the purchase of one auto, and felt that with Wrangel's area of occupation as it was at the time, it would be advisable to have at least six Americans on the field to look after the work. They were ready to make up a list of supplies which $10,000 could buy.

On October 12, Miller and Kratz visited local institutions to discover local needs. Here again they found the hospital in need of bedclothes. A unique need was discovered at the local printery. The local printer reported an unusual demand for Russian New Testaments. Many Russian peasants were coming with wheat and other materials and offering it for a Testament. Miller and Kratz were eager to have the American Mennonites help the printer overcome his chief problem—the shortage of paper.

Halbstadt was, at the time, the headquarters of the Mennozentrum, the Central Executive Committee representing all the Mennonites of Russia and Siberia. This committee had sent a *Studien Kommission* to America to appeal for help and also to investigate the possibilities of migration to North America. The American relief workers had brought a report from this Studien Kommission.

Plans were made for Kratz to remain at Halbstadt and proceed with investigation and organization, while Miller was to return to Constantinople for supplies and send them in as soon as possible for Kratz to distribute. It may seem surprising that the local Halbstadt brethren in both committees, who lived so close to the military front lines, should have approved Kratz's staying with them in a place of such great danger. Kratz and Miller had come from a place where orderly and controlled conditions existed and could not be expected to have as keen a sense of the gravity of the danger as these South Russian Mennonites who had lived through so much. But it must be remembered that these Russian Mennonite brethren saw need and hunger approaching by forced marches, and were fearing that soon what little they had left would be gone. Not only had they sent out appeals for help from America, but they had poured out fervent prayers to the Almighty for help. "And now," one of the Halbstadt brethren wrote, "the American brethren hastened to the rescue. That was more than we had hoped for. We saw in this the answer to our prayers, and the fulfillment of our hopes in a very unusual manner. The two brethren, Miller and Kratz, came to Halbstadt. We were permitted to see them, to speak to them. That raised wonderfully the spirits of the committee, and of the whole community. In **conjunction** with the American brethren, extensive plans for relief work were at once made." For the moment they thought more of relief than of danger.

Local **misgivings** about the safety of the new relief program were no doubt also influenced by the **ardor** and courage of the young Americans. "The American brethren," continues the Halbstadt brother, "young men, eager to undertake, full of Christian conviction and love for their fellows, the spirit of sacrifice and the will to work, seemed to have only one thing in mind—to help where help was needed. Everything else that in one form or another threatened us, which was not directly connected with hunger, but with which we had to reckon very definitely, seemed not to exist for them." And for the moment, it appears the Halbstadt brethren also forgot somewhat their continued sense of **impending** danger. At least they did not oppose the plan to leave Kratz in their midst.

Testing for Understanding

1. When Kratz took a job at the Studebaker plant, he knew it would only be temporary because
   a. he was planning to go back to school in the fall.
   b. Studebaker only needed his help for the summer.
   c. he would be leaving for Russia on September 1.
   d. factory work did not appeal to him.

2. The relief work in Russia was dangerous because
   a. the country was in the midst of World War I.
   b. the country was an enemy of the United States.
   c. there was civil war in the country.
   d. the lack of government left the country to be ruled by the bandits.

3. All of the following made the decision difficult for Kratz except
   a. he had vocational plans that would need to be changed.
   b. he was fearful of the dangers he might face.
   c. he had planned to finish his schooling.
   d. he was planning to be married soon.

4. Kratz's first response to a request to help with relief work was
   a. an absolute "yes."   b. a mild rejection.   c. an absolute "no."   d. a reserved "yes."

5. The letter to his mother revealed that he was motivated to accept the call
   a. as an opportunity to gain valuable experience.
   b. as a result of persuasion by church officials.
   c. from a sense of duty.
   d. as an answer to his desire to help the suffering Mennonites in Russia.

6. In explaining his motive to the relief board at Scottdale, he revealed
   a. a desire to be excused from serving if possible.
   b. some doubt that he was qualified for the work.
   c. some compunction for having not been inconvenienced by World War I.
   d. a delight at being chosen to help with such a worthy cause.

7. In response to reminders of the dangers he might face, Kratz expressed confidence in
   a. the grace of God.   b. the justice of God.   c. the love of God.   d. the providence of God.

8. The time spent in ocean travel was important to the three men's future work in all of the following ways except
   a. laying out a plan of action in doing the relief work.
   b. acquainting themselves with the language of the people they would work among.
   c. building up their spiritual lives for hardship.
   d. reading about the customs and attitudes of the Russian people.

9. The inquiries made at Constantinople led the relief party to believe
   a. it would be very difficult to take needed help into Russia.
   b. they were too late to do much good.
   c. the way was open and help would be available.
   d. the Russian government barred their entry.

10. The train Kratz and Miller boarded at Sevastopol carried
    a. refugees, fleeing for safety.

b. wounded soldiers headed for army hospitals.

c. civilians, returning to their homes from which they had earlier fled.

d. medical aid to war-torn areas.

11. The plight of the Mennonites at Melitopol stood in sharp contrast to
    a. the living conditions of the local Bolsheviks.
    b. the prosperity of their non-Mennonite neighbors.
    c. the former prosperity of the Mennonites.
    d. the Bolsheviki prisoners at Melitopol.

12. To the visiting Americans, Johann Peters' house "even yet . . . appeared palatial in arrangement and furnishings." From this we have a clue that before the war some of the Russian Mennonites lived in
    a. luxury.   c. poverty.
    b. simplicity and self-denial.   d. nonconformity to the world of their day.

13. In making recommendations for relief work, the Halbstadt Mennonites were
    a. wise in their warnings to be cautious.
    b. looking out for themselves.
    c. considerate of the limited resources of the relief party.
    d. unselfish.

14. The Mennonites at Halbstadt did not object to Kratz's staying with them because
    a. they were ignorant of the impending danger.
    b. their desire to meet the need was for the moment overriding their caution.
    c. they did not want to discourage the Americans by implying that it was unsafe to stay in their town.
    d. the relief work would be delayed unless Kratz remained to continue language study.

Part 3 – Calm in the Face of Terror

Defining for Comprehension

Choose the word or phrase below which most nearly defines each word at the left as it is used in the biography.

1. **quarter**	a. provide housing	b. demand	c. oppose
2. **atrocities**	a. horrible acts	b. slums	c. suburbs
3. **ruthless**	a. dishonest	b. vicious; cruel	c. fearless
4. **pessimistic**	a. annoying	b. foggy; hazy	c. gloomy-spirited
5. **evacuated**	a. vacated	b. graduated	c. destroyed
6. **amiable**	a. tillable	b. likely	c. friendly
7. **bravado**	a. boastful daring	b. noisy raid	c. horseman
8. **discreetly**	a. privately	b. carefully; wisely	c. rudely

What were Kratz's own thoughts at this time? Had he become aware of the great dangers and sufferings on every hand? Did he know how close the war front was? How did he feel about himself and the assignment he was to have? In his last letter to his mother, written at this very time, he at least indirectly answers these questions:

This is right in the district where the people have suffered untold cruelties. Since the time we have arrived in Russia, they have told us so many horrid tales of theft, cruelty, and murder, that it almost sickens a person. The front line of battle between the Reds and the Whites has passed over these people 18 times at some places, and at present it is only 25 miles away. Whenever the line of battle passes over a place, the people must **quarter** and feed the soldiers, but most of them leave

Kratz viewing one of the horses between Halbstadt and Alexandrovsk

their homes, because there is great danger of being shot.

But much worse than the Bolsheviks are bands of robbers that committed the worst **atrocities**.... At some places entire villages were destroyed....

I had started this letter yesterday, but about every five minutes I am interrupted by someone who wants information. The people want to get out of Russia and they come from villages 15 to 20 miles away to see what we know about their chances of getting out....

I am well and glad that I am here. If any clothing is collected in our church, will you get my two overcoats from my trunk and send them also....

The Halbstadt local relief committee had advised that the larger part of American relief should be given in the larger and more needy Chortitza Mennonite colony. Before Miller returned to Constantinople, he and Kratz wanted to investigate needs there and in nearby Alexandrovsk, where American Mennonite relief might be given to the very needy native Russian population. The local committee appointed their chairman, Johann Peters, as the one to find the team and take them to Alexandrovsk, which was about 50 miles northwest of Halbstadt.

On October 14, Miller and Kratz wanted to leave early in the morning, but Peters could not find a team of horses that could make the trip in one day. No one wanted to loan a team at that particular time for fear of having it taken by the military which was at the moment quite active in the Alexandrovsk area. Of Peters' own horses all but two had been taken during military operations, and the only reason he had these two was that he had driven them down to the Crimea in the time of greatest danger. Now he naturally hesitated to take them near the front lines, but on finding no others, he finally offered them, and at two o'clock on Thursday afternoon, they started off at last.

The road from Halbstadt to Alexandrovsk lay parallel to the battlefront, only 20 miles away. Miller and Kratz were passing over territory where severe fighting had taken place only four weeks previously. The atmosphere of war was all about them. Miller writes:

The whole trip was the continuation of the same sad story which we have been hearing all the way from Sevastopol, only it seemed ever so much more sad and cruel as we saw the multiplied evidences of the **ruthless** struggle. They say that 12,000 horses were killed on the plains between these two places. We saw hundreds of these lying along the roadside practically consumed by the dogs of which the country has entirely too many. Others were still lying much as they fell. Hundreds and hundreds of little mounds of earth about six feet long, with not even a cross to mark the spot, were mute evidences all along the way of the soldiers that fell there.

By nightfall the travelers had reached a Russian village about 20 miles from Alexandrovsk, and determined to put up there for the night. Here Miller and Kratz experienced even more realistically what it meant to be so near a war zone. Miller says:

This was a village of about 100 people. The chief of the village hunted a room for us. There seemed to be only one available in the village which still had windows that were not mere holes. This man had boarded up his windows, and then covered the boards with plaster on the outside. This made the room entirely dark and stuffy, but kept the cold out somewhat.... In the evening the villagers gathered in and through Brother Peters and the doctor we heard the usual sad story—how all the homes had been repeatedly robbed (of food and clothing) by occupying armies. The people have only the clothing left that they carry on themselves and cannot buy others, have not soap to wash either their clothes or themselves, have no horses left with which to put out crops, and hardly enough food ahead for the winter. Moreover, they are not at all sure that the worst is over. Eleven times during the past two years has the front passed over their village... and each time they have been robbed. The front is now only 25 miles away, and they have no assurance that the White Army will not have to retreat again. They are all extremely sad and **pessimistic** and feel utterly helpless in their misery.

The next morning the travelers were on their way. As they were entering the city of Alexandrovsk, situated on the bank of the Dnieper, Johann Peters, their driver, pointed out six of the ten large mills belonging to one Mennonite, and the immense farm implement factories, now idle, belonging to another Mennonite by the name of Koop. Peters drove to the home of a Brother Lepp, chairman of the local relief committee and owner of another large implement factory, employing 700 persons before the war, but now used as a prison for captured Bolshevik soldiers. Since Lepp's home was found to be occupied by Wrangel soldiers, Peters drove on to a younger Brother Lepp, who had remained here during the Soviet occupation and only brought in his family about a week previously, after the Soviets were driven out. Koop, too, had just returned and was trying to find out what he could still call his own.

After lunch, Miller, Kratz, and Peters walked to the headquarters of the commanding general, Passenov, to ask him about extending their tour of investigation to the Chortitza Mennonite colony just across the Dnieper. The general informed them that they were three days too late, and that the whole section on the other side of the Dnieper would be **evacuated** within a few days. He was very kind to them, however, and gave Kratz and Peters a special paper which guaranteed their safety back to Halbstadt and gave Miller and his interpreter seats in his private coach to go south as far as Melitopol.

On October 16 Kratz and Miller were awakened early by the continuous noise of wagons and horses passing on the street just outside their window. "While dressing," Miller writes, "we could see this continuous stream of wagons passing loaded with all kinds of provisions, some with horse feed, others with cooking apparatus, other wagons filled with soldiers, and then...a number of big guns loaded on wagons, followed by ammunition wagons."

Something was really going on. The big guns could be heard all morning, but a soldier in the yard said they were being fired by the Whites, so it didn't seem too serious.

The Lepp family, their hosts, were very much frightened. They had just returned within the previous week from Sevastopol where they had been fugitives for nearly a year. Besides, they had suffered so terribly at the hands of the Bolsheviks, they dreaded seeing them occupy the city again.

Miller, Dr. Monastery, and Kratz walked down to the station to see about outgoing trains. The station commandant seemed concerned that Miller and his interpreter had not already gone. He told them that a hospital train would leave for the south in an hour and a half with wounded soldiers, and that they could have a place on it. They hurried back to the Lepp home, bade them farewell, packed the baggage, and then Kratz came with them to the station.

Miller and Kratz were about to part and go their separate ways. As they walked to the station, the shots fired seemed louder and closer. In this hour of generally felt danger, Kratz would have seemed justified to have decided to go with Miller. Yet there is no evidence that either Miller or Kratz thought or spoke of it, nor that the Lepps or Koops suggested it. Peters, on his part, would have been even less inclined to do so, since the return of Kratz with Peters would more likely guarantee safe conduct for him and his team. Moreover, Miller says, "That there would be a general rout and defeat of the White Army was still not felt. The program decided upon in Halbstadt was still in mind."

Even in this apparently tense moment Kratz still retained his quiet, steady, warm, cheerful spirit.

The station commandant assigned a place to Orie Miller and Dr. Monastery on the train, and they bade Clayton Kratz good-bye. Kratz and Peters were going to start in one-half hour.

Miller soon perceived that the continued

shots came still closer and that it was his very train that was the target. The nurses of the train had been in the Kuban campaign. They knew all too well what might await them and they were terribly frightened. Soon six shells burst very close at hand, one about 200 feet from their car, wounding a man with its flying fragments. Finally, an engine hooked on to their train, but it was then discovered that one of the shells had torn up the track ahead. Shells kept on whistling by. Eventually, "after a half hour, which seemed like hours," another track was cleared and the train started to move. Miller's life had been spared. Six hours later he wrote, "I still feel tingling nerves from the experience."

Kratz and Peters left Alexandrovsk soon afterwards. With them was industrialist Koop, who was using this means of getting out of the path of the oncoming Bolsheviks.

Kratz wrote Miller about their experiences en route:

> On our way from the city we met the army coming back again. They told us that a telegram was sent from headquarters telling that the army should not withdraw from the city. We passed out from the city quietly, but all of us felt a little better

A native family of South Russia.

when we got out of gun range from the Reds. We drove all afternoon and spent the night at the same place we had spent the day before. The next morning we started out early and gathered considerable information on the way concerning the action of the Reds. We learned that about 3,000 of the Red Cavalry broke through the lines to the east of Halbstadt robbing several villages and throwing the whole region into panic. The people of Halbstadt had scarcely quieted down by the time that we arrived here. Apparently the army about Alexandrovsk was called over to the region east of Halbstadt, but after the airplanes drove the Reds back, the army was again ordered back to Alexandrovsk.

In spite of these disquieting experiences, Kratz's letter breathes a calm, relaxed tone.

Miller found his way back to Constantinople and zealously gathered together a boatload of 10,000 dollars worth of relief supplies. Kratz, on his part, set at his work with his characteristic earnestness. The people of Halbstadt could sense that he took life seriously, and that he had high ideals. One observer wrote: "The work which he had undertaken, he performed as though it were a God-given task. He esteemed it as the things of the kingdom of God. With youthful zeal he stood at his post."

His **amiable** disposition soon won him friends. The family of Johann Peters, with whom he lived, became warmly appreciative of their quiet, earnest, friendly guest. Together with other beloved brethren in Halbstadt, they sought to make his stay there as pleasant as possible.

Kratz spent almost two weeks in Halbstadt in this preliminary relief activity. During these two weeks the position of the Wrangel army forces became constantly more uncertain. Even the Wrangel officers themselves began to discuss withdrawal to the Crimea very freely and openly. The nearing approach of the Soviet army brought up the question for Kratz, "Should he flee in view of possible danger or stay at his work?" His Halbstadt friends strongly urged Kratz to withdraw to the Crimea and await the outcome there. But he considered such a move an unworthy one. It would be deserting his colors—cowardice. His hostess, Mother Kate Peters, wrote afterward: "I often told him to go away, but he answered in a calm way, 'I am not doing anything bad; nobody will harm me.'"

G. A. Peters wondered afterward: "Was it the ardor of youth—**bravado**—or did he not understand the situation—perhaps a little of both—that he answered thus? But bravado had not been characteristic of Kratz before this. He was the kind of person who thought through carefully, planned **discreetly**, and then disciplined himself to carry out his plans with steadfastness of purpose. This gave his life a clear sense of direction and kept him from much foolhardy rashness. It is rather in that clear sense of the direction defined by his life ideals that we need to look for the springs of his action in this crucial situation.

Testing for Understanding

1. The suffering of the Mennonites was caused by all of the following except
   a. providing housing for soldiers.
   b. being in the crossfire of opposing armies.
   c. becoming victims of bandits who took advantage of a bad situation.
   d. being tortured for refusing to join the military.

2. Kratz's request to send his two overcoats was most likely prompted by his
   a. concern that he may never return to need them.
   b. personal needs in light of the approaching winter.
   c. desire to make personal sacrifice to meet the need about him.
   d. decision to stay with the work indefinitely if necessary.

3. The delay in leaving for Alexandrovsk was caused by
   a. neglect.   c. altered plans.
   b. fear.   d. waiting for one member of the party.

4. Kratz and Miller's first experience with actual battlefield atmosphere was
   a. seeing bodies of dead horses.
   b. seeing lines of soldiers retreating through the streets.
   c. hearing repeated shooting in the distance.
   d. soldiers living in the house of a Mennonite.

5. We know that the Mennonite community of Alexandrovsk had been well-to-do by evidences of
   a. large and elaborate homes.   c. extensive land holdings.
   b. prosperous industries.   d. large bank accounts.

6. The relief party did not visit the Chortitza Mennonite colony because
   a. the fighting had already reached that community.
   b. they could not find a safe way to cross the Dnieper River.
   c. the people of that community would soon move out.
   d. time was running out when they needed to be back in Alexandrovsk.

7. Some of the Russian Mennonites such as the Lepp family sought refuge from the war by
   a. fleeing to the North.   c. hiding in underground shelters.
   b. hiding their identity as Mennonites.   d. moving temporarily to the South.

8. The situation at Alexandrovsk became more serious when
   a. the Red Army approached the city.
   b. the White Army retreated to Sevastopol.
   c. the city was overrun by the White Army.
   d. the Red Army retreated through the city streets.

9. In light of the dangerous situation at Alexandrovsk, it would have seemed wise
   a. for Lepp to make contact with the commanding general of the White Army.
   b. for Kratz to leave Alexandrovsk with Miller.
   c. for Peters to accompany Miller and Kratz.
   d. For Miller to go back to Halbstadt with Peters.

10. All of the following are true except
    a. Kratz was willing to be separated from Miller.
    b. Peters helped a native of Alexandrovsk leave the city.
    c. Kratz's departure from Alexandrovsk was less frightening than Miller's.
    d. Miller rode north on a train with wounded soldiers.

11. When Kratz arrived back in Halbstadt he found the people
    a. encouraged by the progress of the White Army.
    b. worried about what had become of the relief party.
    c. excited over some recent raids by the Red Army.
    d. disinclined to pursue future relief plans.

12. Kratz was especially appreciated by the Johann Peters family for his
    a. energetic helpfulness.   c. unflinching courage.
    b. likable personality.   d. keen intellect.

13. The biographer feels that Kratz's decision to stay at Halbstadt in the face of danger was not
    a. an informed choice.
    b. a carefully considered act.
    c. a desire to be faithful to the work he was called to.
    d. a forced effort to appear courageous.

Part 4 – To Serve and to Suffer

Defining for Comprehension

Choose the word or phrase below which most nearly defines each word at the left as it is used in the biography.

1. **consummate**
   a. destroyed
   b. complete; supreme
   c. handy

2. **civilian**
   a. politeness
   b. scoundrel
   c. nonmilitary citizen

3. **hostages**
   a. prisoners
   b. guests
   c. enemies

4. **negotiations**
   a. bargainings
   b. lodgings
   c. disagreements

5. **resignation**
   a. resentment
   b. submissiveness
   c. second attempt

6. **commissary**
   a. sympathy
   b. suffering
   c. government official

7. **tribunal**
   a. honor
   b. tax
   c. court of justice

8. **ascertained**
   a. implied
   b. fastened
   c. figured out

9. **martial**
   a. military
   b. brisk
   c. definite

10. **bourgeois**
    a. unusual occurrence
    b. capitalists
    c. town

11. **vice**
    a. reverse
    b. evil
    c. virtue

12. **itinerary**
    a. travel plan
    b. short life
    c. opposition

13. **composure**
    a. body position
    b. self-control
    c. assurance

14. **insanitary**
    a. mentally ill
    b. unhealthy; filthy
    c. illegal

15. **vermin-infested** filled with–
    a. small animals
    b. fear
    c. dirt

16. **convention**
    a. assembly
    b. new method
    c. belief

17. **vexation**
    a. increase
    b. irritation
    c. excitement

18. **exemplified**
    a. denied
    b. showed by example
    c. enlarged

Kratz was now ready to suffer personal inconvenience to keep on serving others in suffering. He did not want to shirk his duty. In his devotional book he had underlined the words, "In this consuming devotion which identifies an individual with a cause, and makes him ready to give up everything selfish for the people whom he loves, lies the **consummate** perfection of character.... Be used up for the sake of some cause, unnoticed. Not what you can do, but what you can endure."

Another factor in Kratz's quiet, calm steadfastness was his trust in God. More than once had he and Miller and Slagel read together Psalm 91 en route to Russia, and even now he still believed God to be an adequate refuge and fortress. And he would feel safest in staying at the place he believed God wanted him to stay and serve.

Actually, to find one's self in Soviet territory

was not at that time universally regarded as fatal. In several communities Mennonites had told Kratz and Miller that the Bolsheviks had not been as cruel as the Machnow bandits; in fact, they had at some times and places treated the **civilian** population rather decently. On November 9, Orie Miller wrote Levi Mumaw from Constantinople: "If Wrangel be entirely defeated, then I think we should try to arrange with the Soviet government for the carrying on of our work. Many here, whom I have talked to, think this could be satisfactorily arranged." (It actually was, but not immediately after the Wrangel defeat.) From a Russian representative in America, Mumaw received the opinion that there was "no cause whatever for alarm as the Bolsheviks would not knowingly or willing do him (Kratz) any harm, and therefore there need be no fear for his personal safety." (At least two American relief workers were later safely evacuated from a territory after it had been occupied by Soviets.)

When Orie Miller finally learned that the Reds had conquered the territory where Kratz was, Miller was in Sevastopol and immediately made inquiries about Kratz's safety. "No one that I have asked (American consul, etc.) anticipates that he met with any personal danger," he wrote Mumaw. "They say that he was probably hiding during the first few days, while the Bolshevik army was coming in; but that after the first 48 hours or after some local government was formed, he, as a civilian American, would be entirely safe." On November 18 the American High Commissioner at Constantinople wired the Secretary of State at Washington, D.C., saying, "Regarding Kratz there is no further information, but he was amongst friends who probably knew how to protect him and if not made prisoner, may probably escape altogether."

However, the friends of Kratz did not place him in hiding when the Soviet Army approached Halbstadt. Their plan was rather to take him away to safety before the Soviets arrived. The evening before the Whites withdrew they finally persuaded Kratz to start very early the next morning by the safest way. Everything for the trip was well thought through and carefully prepared. Johann Peters planned to use his valuable team of fine running horses to take Kratz to the Crimea, together with his own 17-year-old son.

The next morning, very early, as Peters and Kratz went out to look over the situation and to speak with their traveling companions, they were both arrested by the advance guard of the Reds. Overnight there had been a change in the government—the Whites were gone and so was the possibility of escape. When the soldiers handled Kratz and Peters roughly, Peters stepped up at once to defend Kratz. In this he succeeded. The Reds seemed to fear the American but took out their revenge on Peters. Emptying the pockets of both men, they ordered Peters to lead them to his home. When he refused, the soldiers grew angry and once more placed the men under arrest.

In the meantime the Reds had completed their occupation of Halbstadt and the surrounding territory. The prisoners were now taken to the officer in charge, who appeared to be a man with whom one could reason. He agreed to free Kratz and Peters, if the Mennonite group would furnish **hostages** to be held in their stead. G. A. Peters, Kratz's warm friend and local relief secretary, was also sent for. "After some **negotiations**," he says, "we were permitted to go home with Peters and Kratz, but only after we had made ourselves answerable for them." Before they left, Kratz was given his papers and most of his money again, but his pocketknife, flashlight, and some money had disappeared in the handling.

G. A. Peters continues, "We were glad that it had gone as well as it had, and we comforted ourselves somewhat. But everything possible was done to safeguard Brother Kratz from attacks, and at first we were successful. Kratz went about as he always had. But we had to give up all our plans and wait. Brother Kratz was of the opinion that since we had for so long suffered so much, he could also suffer with us for a while. Then he would learn to appreciate our situation better."

Mother Kate Peters says that after Kratz's first arrest he lived with them for 12 days longer. "In these 12 days we were very well befriended, had many anxious moments together." Kratz spent much time in reading the Testament he had carried with him. He took lessons in Russian and German from the daughter in the home. His quiet, calm **resignation** deeply impressed the Peters family. Mother Peters says, "I often told him, 'Yes, Brother Kratz, we are sorry you must suffer so for us.' He then said calmly, 'I am no better than you.'" He spoke of his mother, his family, and his dearest friends. It almost seemed as if he knew that he was about to make the supreme sacrifice.

A few days after the Reds had come in, a new official came to take charge. He was known to local people in former days as a less desirable character, and they expected nothing good from him now, either for the group or for individuals. Very soon after he assumed command, G. A. Peters went to him to talk over Kratz's affairs with him. (Since G. A. Peters was unmarried, he did more of this work, because there would be no tragic implications for a wife and children if he met with serious disfavor.) The new official seemed to be reasonable. "But if ever words had a false ring to them," comments Peters, "they were the words of a Soviet **commissary** in Russia."

The stroke fell about a week later. On November 10, 1920, five days after Kratz's 24th birthday, there came a sudden summons to appear before the authorities. He went, accompanied by his host, Johann Peters. Both were treated gruffly. They were struck brutally. Kratz was put under arrest and taken away by the military **tribunal**. Peters got his team and followed the arresting party at a discreet distance until descending twilight made it necessary that he return. But he had **ascertained** the direction they had taken.

Once again the Mennonites looked to G. A. Peters to intercede for Kratz.

G. A. Peters gave a vivid account of his earnest efforts:

> One day [apparently the same day, November 10] about sundown, a messenger burst into my room and announced breathlessly that Kratz had again been arrested, and was to be taken away. That was bad news. I hurried over to help get

Kratz free again. But I failed to find him anywhere in Halbstadt. At headquarters, where I presented myself, they said, "He has been taken to the 22nd Division." This group was one of the worst ones, and was stationed in the Mennonite villages between Ohrloff and Landskrone, about 20 or 30 miles from Halbstadt. As we were under **martial** law, and on that account had to be inside after sundown, we could attempt no more that day. This much was decided: I was to follow after Brother Kratz as far as possible, and attempt to bring him back to Halbstadt. I consented to do so, but to be frank, with anxiety and fear in my heart, also on my own account. That same evening I secured all the necessary passes. The next morning my driver and I started on our way. We could not appear as **bourgeois** so we put on our poorest clothing. Our appearance reminded one of a beggar's outfit of former days, when beggars still came among us. After going hither and thither, we had the good fortune to find traces of Kratz. Between hope and fear we went on until my way was barred with threats of death. I had to retreat.

> Here I want to relate briefly my last conversation with the head officer of the Checka (the Soviet secret police—the dread of the land) concerning Brother Kratz. I entered the room of the Checka. Behind a table sat a young Jew, hardly 20 years old, fumbling numerous arrest and death warrants—for what he saw was terror and what he wrote was blood. Beside the officer sat a woman, on whose face was written **vice** and cruelty. By the stove sat two armed Red soldiers. The officer asked me harshly about my business. I stated it briefly. At once he ordered the door to be guarded, asked me to come nearer, and began a severe cross-examination. Among other things he asked me, "What have you in common with this American, whom we know to be a spy of a bourgeois government?"

> "He is no spy. I doubt if you really think that he can be one. What I have with him in common is that we are working together at a task pleasing to God—relieving the need of suffering humanity."

> "You lie! We know your whole business. We shall look into this matter thoroughly. And you also shall not escape us."

> "I! We are in your hands, that I know well. But if it were not as I say, I would

never have come to you."

"What we shall do with the American doesn't concern you. We do what we must. Do you understand?"

"But I should like very much to know where you have taken him."

"That is also none of your business. Cease making any further inquiries about him, or it may go badly for you. Now get out!"

So it went on for some time. At last I asked him, "Is your mother still living?"

After he had sworn an awful oath, he said, "What has my mother to do with this?"

I replied, "The American has a mother, too, who loves him, and who with a heavy heart saw him drawn into this work; who prays for him, that the Lord may shield him from the many dangers with which he is surrounded. As soon as Russia has dealings with America and you certainly believe that the time will come—then the old mother will demand an accounting for her son, from those who stood nearest to him—also from me—do you understand something of this?"

And now he seemed quieter and more gentle. His last words were, "Yes, do not worry. I can tell you this much about it. We shall not kill the American. That might be too severe, in spite of the fact that we do not fear America. We can also not free him. Frankly, I do not believe he is a spy. The situation in which we find ourselves makes it necessary for us to act as we do. We shall send the prisoner to the chief of staff in Bachmut, from whence he will probably be sent by way of Kharkov to Moscow, and from there perhaps to Finland. Then he is free."

Then his face darkened as he proceeded. "But there is nothing better for you to do than to go home." Then to the soldier, "Conduct him out."

G. A. Peters was forced to return without being able to contact Kratz.

Kratz was last seen, on the day of his arrest, in Fürstenwerder, together with other political prisoners. He was quite decently treated, because he was an American, and given a place on a large ladder-wagon full of straw, somewhat separate from the rest, who were filled with lice. The weather was cold—an intensely cold spell had already set in two weeks earlier, during which the thermometer had gone down to 20 degrees below zero Fahrenheit. Providentially, a friend, who still had two overcoats, had given him one of them.

It is not known how much truth there was to the Cheka officer's announced **itinerary** for Kratz, but the next day he was seen in Wernersdorf, which could have been on the way to Bachmut. A Mennonite in Wernersdorf reported that he had exchanged a few words with Kratz, and that Kratz "was entirely quiet and composed in spirit." He was apparently going to his death, for he was never heard of again, but he was going to it with the same quiet **composure** that had marked his dedication to God-given tasks all through his short, but full life. And we can be sure that he maintained that quiet steadfastness in the cold, crowded, **insanitary**, damp, **vermin-infested** and disease-ridden Soviet prisons where he finally lost his life, more probably in some prison epidemic than before a firing squad.

His fate was unknown to his friends, but not to the God whom he had served so faithfully. Though his service for others cost him much, he paid the price willingly. "Greater love hath no man than this, than a man lay down his life for his friends." Clayton Kratz was "true...till death." Almost 300 years earlier his forefathers in the Mennonite faith had met in solemn **convention** and declared that "according to the example, life, and doctrine of Christ, we are not to do wrong, or cause offence or **vexation** to any one; but to seek the welfare of all men, . . . to do good in all respects, 'commending ourselves to every man's conscience in the sight of God.'" Kratz **exemplified** these ideas throughout his life, and he let it cost him something to carry them out heroically in a time of great need and danger. His life and death are an outstanding example of the Christian idealism expressed in the last stanza of his favorite hymn:

> Faith of our fathers! we will love
> Both friend and foe in all our strife;
> And preach thee, too, as love knows how,
> By kindly words and virtuous life:
> Faith of our fathers! Holy faith!
> We will be true to thee till death!

Testing for Understanding

1. The biographer is careful to show that
    a. Kratz's decisions in his last days of freedom were consistent with his philosophy of life.
    b. Kratz was unknowingly acting in a foolhardy manner.
    c. the Russian Mennonites acted wisely in providing for Kratz's safety.
    d. Miller was not to blame for what happened to Kratz.

2. The escape plan did not work because
    a. a delay in their plans made it too late to leave.
    b. the plans were hastily made and were not practical.
    c. the Red Army took over the city before the plans were carried out.
    d. horses could not be secured in time.

3. Before the authorities would release Kratz and Peters
    a. G. A. Peters needed to promise to be responsible for any problem they caused.
    b. G. A. Peters needed to go to jail in their place.
    c. they needed to turn over everything they had in their pockets.
    d. Johann Peters needed to take the soldiers to his house.

4. Responsibility to deal with government officials often fell on G. A. Peters' shoulders because
    a. he had more experience and ability in dealing with officials.
    b. he was one of the few who volunteered for such dangerous work.
    c. he had no wife and children.
    d. he had developed a warm relationship with Kratz.

5. Between the two times he was arrested, Kratz expressed the attitude that
    a. he was not worthy to suffer less than the Russians.
    b. he had done nothing wrong and therefore needed to fear no harm.
    c. one must face life's uncertainties bravely.
    d. the worst was past and soon the relief work could continue.

6. The Red Government was particularly opposed to
    a. Americans.   c. relief agencies.
    b. the Mennonites.   d. bourgeois.

7. G. A. Peters introduced the subject of the head officer's mother in an effort to
    a. divert attention from Kratz.
    b. show the officer that his own life could be brought into account.
    c. try to get on the good side of the officer by flattery.
    d. appeal to some goodness that may have yet remained in the officer's heart.

8. Kratz's benefiting from a friend's extra overcoat is best illustrated by the Scripture (remember Kratz's request to his mother)
    a. "Cast thy bread upon the waters: for thou shalt find it after many days" (Ecclesiastes 11:1).
    b. "He which soweth bountifully shall reap also bountifully" (2 Corinthians 9:6).
    c. "If any man will sue thee at the law, and take away thy coat, let him have thy cloke also" (Matthew 5:40).
    d. "Provide neither gold, nor silver, nor brass in your purses, nor scrip for your journey, neither two coats . . . for the workman is worthy of his meat" (Matthew 10:9, 10).

9. The general impression we gain from G. A. Peters' last contact with the Checka is that the Red Government
    a. was not fairly represented by the man Peters talked to.
    b. felt a need to demonstrate their authority concerning Kratz.
    c. probably intended to harm Kratz.
    d. had detailed information about Kratz's activities.

10. The final impressions we have of Kratz reveal an experience of
    a. emotional strain.
    b. joyful confidence.
    c. patient resignation.
    d. physical abuse.

11. Which of the following phrases from the Bible would make the best heading to this last section of Kratz's biography?
    a. "No good thing will he withhold from them that walk uprightly" (Psalm 84:11).
    b. "The LORD is my light and my salvation; whom shall I fear?" (Psalm 27:1).
    c. "The LORD shall preserve thee from all evil: he shall preserve thy soul" (Psalm 121:7).
    d. "Behold, the righteous shall be recompensed in the earth: much more the wicked and the sinner" (Proverbs 11:31).

12. The biographer's choice of title for his biography is based on
    a. a key phrase within the biography itself.
    b. a comment made by a Russian Mennonite about Kratz.
    c. words from Kratz's favorite hymn.
    d. a verse in the Book of Revelation.

SOURCES:

– Interviews and correspondence with Kratz's close relatives, friends, teachers, classmates, and with one of his pupils.

– Kratz's personal letters to his mother, sister, and others.

– Goshen College Record, 1917-20.

– Orie O. Miller diary, September through December, 1920.

– Files of Mennonite Central Committee relating to Kratz.

– P. C. Hiebert and Orie O. Miller, *Feeding the Hungry, Russia Famine*, 1919-25, pp. 92-99, 165-170, 343-353.

– H. E. Fosdick, *The Meaning of Prayer*. This is the devotional book owned by Kratz in which he had marked significant passages, quoted in this biography. It is one of Fosdick's earlier books.

Looking for Literary Technique

"A job well-begun is a job half done." When was that ever more true than when wielding a pen? Beginning is often the greatest hurdle in writing, but it is also one of the most important parts. "First impressions are lasting," to employ another saying. If the first few pages of a book do not hold your attention, you might reject the entire book. So how should a good biography begin? The most logical, but perhaps the most mistaken place to begin is with the details of the person's birth. Some biographies begin this way. "Clayton Kratz was born November 5, 1896, in Dublin, Pennsylvania, to William and Elizabeth Kratz." True, this sentence would begin the biography, but how excited would readers become? Everyone is born sometime, somewhere, to someone. Readers want to know what is extraordinary about this person's life. Why should they read this biography?

The biography you just read did not begin with the sentence suggested above. Instead the biographer reached right into the middle of Kratz's life and pulled out an incident fairly bursting with life— the telegram which summoned Clayton Kratz to service in Russia. The first sentence satisfies the basic requirement for the successful beginning to any good piece of literature—it arouses curiosity: "The telegram of August 18 was urgent." Immediately a dozen questions throng into your mind. Who sent the telegram? What did it say? Why was it urgent? Who received the telegram? What did he respond? The only way to answer these questions is to read on. The biographer has accomplished his purpose. He has convinced you that you should read this biography.

1. Of the other two biographies which you have read in this unit, those about Menno Simons and John Bunyan, which one seemed to you to have the most curiosity-arousing beginning? Why?

2. Why is the beginning of the other biography less ideal?

Writing for Skill

Now that you have a pack of note cards crammed with facts about your subject, it's time to begin. Thumb through your notes until you find a dramatic moment from his life, perhaps the moment which shaped the rest of his life, as in the case of Clayton Kratz; perhaps the moment of his death. Don't tell it in detail. Briefly but vividly sketch enough of the account to hold your reader. Later you can add the details in full color.

There could be other ways of beginning your biography. Perhaps if your subject contributed something of significance to the world, you could begin by describing a world handicapped by the absence of his contribution. Imagine, for instance, that you are writing about Joseph Funk whom Mennonites thank for promoting shaped notes in their hymnbooks. Your biography might begin something like this:

> The room was hot and stuffy. Several dozen heads bent over one-fourth as many curled and clammy sheets of music, which none but the leader had ever seen before. A jumble of fat, round notes sprawled up and down the scale, dragging fainthearted voices after them, voices wearied from scrambling after rising and falling notes, plunging in the approximate direction, but never arriving at the same guess in unison. Guesswork—that's what learning a new tune was for many before Joseph Funk published and promoted shaped notes in his hymnbooks.

A paragraph or two will suffice to open your biography, but make sure they are dynamic. Here again, a visit to the biography section of your school library may reward you with more ideas.

William Carey

How does God shake the lethargy of a church and move her in the direction of obedience to one of His neglected commandments? Sometimes He uses persecution; sometimes hardship. But often He raises up a prophet within the church to challenge the disobedience and lead the way to greater faithfulness. William Carey was such a man. In his day extreme Calvinistic teachings on election and grace had led many in England to feel that it was unnecessary to preach the Gospel to the heathen. They thought that if God wanted to save the heathen He could do it without the help of men and if God did not want the heathen saved, it would be utterly fruitless to preach to them. But God was working in Carey's personal life to build conviction for missions. Then, step by very slow step his vision was impressed on the hearts of his brethren. The following account of this process is excerpted from a full-length biography of Carey's life, **William Carey: Father of Modern Missions.**

Part 1: Moulton and the Missionary Call

(1785-1789, age 24-28)

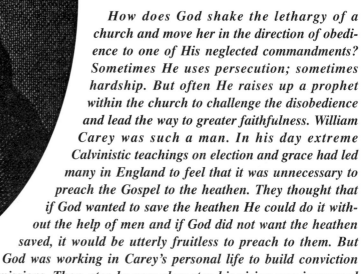

Defining for Comprehension

Choose the word or phrase below which most nearly defines each word at the left as it is used in the biography.

1. **memorable**   a. gloomy   b. unrelenting   c. unforgettable

2. **secluded**   a. prevented   b. involved   c. isolated

3. **psychology**   a. mental processes   b. mental illness   c. conviction

4. **remote**   a. distant   b. divided   c. mischievous

5. **requisite**   a. complicated   b. necessary   c. delightful

6. **inducement**   a. motivation   b. temptation   c. bonding medium

7. **romantic**   a. Latin   b. prowling   c. serenely beautiful and exciting

8. **accessible**   a. extra   b. obtainable   c. believable

9. **cannibal**   a. merrymaking   b. man-eating   c. meat-eating

10. **ransacked**   a. stowed   b. searched thoroughly   c. destroyed

11. **medieval**   a. prehistoric   b. corrupt   c. of the Middle Ages

12. **unique**   a. one of a kind   b. neat; precise   c. miniature

13. **resolutely**   a. rebelliously   b. determinedly   c. eventually

14. **mused**   a. pondered   b. deafened   c. applied

15. **casement**   a. manuscript   b. trunk   c. window

16. **reflex**   a. superfluous   b. turned backward   c. curved

17. **probationer**   a. bailiff   b. novice   c. disputer

18. **fraternal**   a. unending   b. argumentative   c. brotherly

19. **obligatory**   a. opaque   b. binding   c. exempt

20. **denounced**   a. condemned   b. broadcast   c. gave up

21. **proposition**   a. advantage   b. suggestion   c. situation

22. **colleagues**   a. graduates   b. co-workers   c. schools

23. **marshaled**   a. set in array   b. arrested   c. swamped

24. **subsistence**   a. support   b. presence   c. argument

25. **substantial**   a. steady   b. uncertain   c. considerable

The four years at Moulton[1] were **memorable** for something of far-reaching importance. It was while laboring in that **secluded** village and living in that thatched cottage that William Carey heard the missionary call. We know the actual manner in which that call came to him.

"My attention to missions was first awakened after I was at Moulton, by reading the *Last Voyage of Captain Cook*," he tells us. Surely this sentence gives us the key to the **psychology** of the call and enables us to understand the working of his mind.

---

1. In Northamptonshire, England: 1785-1789, age 24-28.

Cook's *Journal* is anything but a missionary textbook, and the idea of its being so used was certainly **remote** from the great explorer's mind. Cook was a sailor and an explorer; his object was to probe into great geographic problems, to unveil the hidden lands of the Pacific. He was not particularly interested in religion, and probably had no thought that anyone would deem it worthwhile to Christianize the savages of the islands he found. Indeed, he himself wrote concerning one of them: "No one would ever venture to introduce Christianity into Erromanga, because neither fame nor profit would offer the **requisite inducement**." Yet in spite of this, Cook's *Journal* became, in Carey's hands, a call to missionary effort. What Carey read in those **romantic** pages we know quite well, for happily they are **accessible** to us—a record of voyages, of latitudes and longitudes, of new islands and of strange peoples; narratives of canoes loaded with dusky savages swarming round the *Resolution* and the *Discovery*, and of hazardous landings on coral beaches among peoples sometimes friendly and sometimes hostile; stories of tattooed natives addicted to tribal conflicts and **cannibal** feasts. That *Journal* was probably more read and talked about than any other book published in England about that time, for Cook's tragic death had made him the hero of the hour.

To most people Cook's *Journal* was a thrilling story of adventure: To William Carey it was a revelation of human need. To him those tattooed savages were *men and women*—God's creatures, needing to know about God's love. And in his heart there arose the thought: "These South Sea islands need the gospel!"

The idea took possession of him, and he set to work to pursue that line of thought. He devoured every book he could lay his hands upon that had any bearing on the subject. He read of India and China, of Africa and America, and of the many countries of Europe; and, as he pursued his studies, the idea grew yet clearer in his soul: "The peoples of the world need Christ." The *Mercury* was advertising Guthrie's *Geographical Grammar*, and he **ransacked** it for general information, and probably the writings of the fathers and the existing church histories for information concerning the missionary efforts of the early church and of **medieval** times. It is certain that he read Jonathan Edward's *Life and Diary of David Brainerd*, and possibly a little book that had been published in 1709 by the Danish missionaries, Henry Plütschaw and Bartholomew Zeigenbalgh.

With that thoroughness that always characterized him, Carey made careful notes from the books he read. His large, homemade map of the world, which hung upon the wall of his schoolroom,[2] now began to serve a new purpose. On this map, his friend Fuller tells us, "he had drawn with a pen a place for every nation in the known world, and entered into it whatever he met with in reading, relative to its population, religion, etc."

A **unique** map truly—and the revelation of a unique man. How it reminds us of words his brother wrote concerning him: "He was always **resolutely** determined never to give up any point or particle of anything on which his mind was set till he had arrived at a clear knowledge of his subject."

Day by day, new facts were added to that first missionary map of the world. Day by day, as Carey acquired new information about world conditions, he mused over world problems, and "while he **mused**, the fire burned" in his soul. Can we doubt that wonderful map of human need became also his prayer chart? Often in the silence of night, when the day's toil was over and the **casement**-cloths were drawn across the little window of his cottage, by the dim *rushlight*[3] he would scan that map, and then kneeling before it pour out his soul to God.

Along with this ever-increasing vision of human need, there grew in Carey's soul an ever-deepening sense of his own riches in Christ. It came to him, no doubt, largely through his reading of the Scriptures and his experience of the Christian life, and also as a **reflex** influence of his preaching to his congregations.

---

2. Carey was both a schoolteacher and a cobbler.
3. rushlight: A candle that consists of the pith of a rush dipped in grease.

To William Carey the call came not in an enthusiastic missionary meeting—he never had the opportunity of attending one—but in the quiet of his own workshop. The call came to him as it came to Amos—as he worked at a humble profession. In Cook's *Journal* and other books he saw the needs of men, and in those deep needs he heard the voice of God. Changing the words (but not the meaning) of Amos, Carey might have said with truth: "I was no prophet, neither was I the son of a pro- phet...but the Lord took me as I made the shoes, and the Lord said unto me, 'Go, prophesy unto My people Israel.'"

And, in truth, his first message was "to Israel"—to the people of God slumbering in the churches of England. He had to arouse them first.

On August 10, 1786, the Olney Church meeting defi- nitely appointed Carey "to the work of the ministry, and sent him out...to preach the gospel *wherever God in His providence might call him.*" Carey probably read into those last words a deeper meaning than existed in the mind of the secretary who wrote them in the church minute book.

A few weeks later, as a young **probationer**, Carey was present at a ministers' meeting at Northampton. Toward the close of the evening, when the public services were over, some of the ministers were sitting together in **fraternal** conversation, when old Dr. Ryland entered the room and invited one of the younger men to propose a subject for general discussion. After a pause, Carey rose, and with some hesitation suggested that they should consider:

"Whether the command given to the Apostles to teach all nations was not **obligatory** on all succeeding minis- ters to the end of the world, seeing that the accompa- nying promise was of equal extent."

The question fell on the meeting like a thunderbolt. Dr. Ryland, who was addicted to forcible expressions, instantly **denounced** the **proposi- tion**, which seemed to him absurd. "Young man," he exclaimed, "sit down: when God pleases to convert the heathen, He will do it without your aid or mine!"[4]

Carey sat down—disappointed but not discouraged, for he was sure of his ground. He had read books Dr. Ryland had not read; and he realized what his senior **colleagues** did not—the depth of human need. He was

---

4. As reported by John C. Marshman. Morris of Clipstone, who was present at the meeting, represents Ryland as saying: "You are a miserable enthusiast for asking such a question. Certainly nothing can be done before another Pentecost, when an effusion of miraculous gifts, including the gift of tongues, will give effect to the Commission of Christ as at first. What, Sir! Can you preach in Arabic, in Persic, in Hindustani, in Bengali, that you think it your duty to send the Gospel to the heathens?" This was afterwards stoutly denied by Dr. Ryland's son (Carey's friend John Ryland), and as stoutly maintained by Morris in reply. Eustace Carey relates that he asked his uncle about it, and says, "I do not remember his repeating that precise expression (i.e. 'miserable enthusiast') . . . but I distinctly recollect that some strong epithet was said to have been used."

silenced for the moment, but only for the moment. He saw that his first task must be to pass on to others the information that had stirred his own heart, he must transmit to them his vision. Assured that God had called him, he embarked upon what today would be called an educational campaign. He began to talk about it to all with whom he came in contact; he preached about it to his little flock at Moulton; it echoed in his prayers.

In order to reach a wider public than would ever hear his voice, he resolved to write a book—his famous *Enquiry*.[5] And now his map became as a weapon in the hand of a mighty man; the facts he had laboriously collected and written upon it were barbed arrows in his quiver. Slowly he **marshaled** his information, developed his arguments, set forth his conclusions, and with heart aflame wrote his amazing appeal. Every sentence was an arrow winged with conviction based on knowledge.

About the time the *Enquiry* was finished, Carey happened to be in Birmingham collecting funds for the little chapel he had built at Moulton. In visiting a certain Mr. Potts, there occurred a conversation that happily, has been preserved for us by a gentleman who was present.

Mr. Potts: "Pray, friend Carey, what is it you have got into your head about missions? I understand you introduce the subject on all occasions."

Carey: "Why, I think, sir, it is highly important that something should be done for the heathen."

Mr. Potts: "But how can it be done, and who will do it?"

Carey: "Why, if you ask who, I have made up my mind, if a few friends can be found who will send me out, and support me for 12 months after my arrival, I will engage to go wherever Providence shall open a door."

Mr. Potts: "But where would you go? Have you thought of that, friend Carey?"

Carey: "Yes, I certainly have. Were I to follow my inclination, and had the means at command, the islands of the South Seas would be the scene of my labors, and I would commence at Otaheite. If any society will send me out, and land me there, allow me the means of **subsistence** for one year, I am ready and willing to go."

Mr. Potts: "Why, friend Carey, the thought is new, and the religious public are not prepared for such undertakings."

Carey: "No; I am aware of that; but I have written a piece on the state of the heathen world, which, if it were published, might probably awaken an interest on the subject."

Mr. Potts: "Why don't you publish it?"

Carey: "For the best of all reasons. I have not the means."

Mr. Potts: "We will have it published by all means. I had rather bear the expense of printing it myself, than the public should be deprived of the opportunity of considering so important a subject."

This conversation is valuable as showing the precision and clearness of Carey's mind, and it so impressed Mr. Potts that he then and there promised to contribute the sum of £10 towards the publication of the pamphlet—a **substantial** sum for those days. Here at last was encouragement.

---

5. *An Enquiry into the Obligations of Christians to use Means for the Conversion of the Heathens.*

Meditating for Meaning

1. God can use the work of secular men to accomplish His purposes.
   a. What provided the original spark for Carey's missionary zeal?
   b. This method of God calling Carey to mission work would provide some justification for your study of which school subjects?
   c. What motives did Cook think it would take to move men to the mission field?
   d. From Carey's reaction to Cook's *Journal,* what can you conclude should be the true motive for missions?

2. God does not call all men into His service in the same manner by which He called Carey. Each must recognize God's call to him and be certain that it is of the Spirit.
   a. What method did God use to call Moses (Exodus 3)?
   b. How did Jesus provide for the need of evangelism (Luke 10)?
   c. How did God call Paul to preach the Gospel in Europe (Acts 16:9)?
   d. Through what institution does God call men into the harvest of souls today?

3. Convictions are rarely born in their full potential; they grow.
   a. What unique project did Carey undertake to keep his interest in missions alive?
   b. What does this project reveal about Carey?
   c. What use did he likely make of this map? Try to think of uses not mentioned in the biography.

4. Biographers try to present an accurate picture of their subject.
   a. What is the most convincing way the author demonstrates that this account of Carey's life is based on fact?
   b. Give two examples where the author went beyond known facts.
   c. How did the biographer handle these additions so that you know they are conjecture and you do not lose confidence in the overall accuracy of the biography?
   d. What problem in writing biographies does footnote 4 reveal?

5. In describing Carey's call to be a missionary, the author quotes the words of the Prophet Amos.
   a. How has the author changed Amos's words to adapt them to Carey's life?
   b. Explain why the author made this change.
   c. Explain what the author means when he says that Carey's "first message truly was to Israel."
   d. To what Scripture or Scriptures does this idea allude? (Check *missions* in a topical Bible.)

6. Carey saw that he must first enlighten his own church people.
   a. What is meant by saying, "The question fell on the meeting like a thunderbolt"?
   b. What false assumption does Dr. Ryland's answer to Carey reveal which made Carey's question seem absurd to him? (See the introduction at the beginning of this biography.)
   c. How did Carey account for Dr. Ryland's response, so that instead of being discouraged he could gain further insight into what needed to be done?
   d. List three of the four approaches Carey took in his educational campaign.

7. Besides being instructive, this biography is a good example of effective writing.
   a. Find and write the sentence about Carey's *Enquiry* that summarizes the quality of all effective writing.
   b. What extended figure of speech does the author use to picture Carey's effort to write his book?
   c. Why is this such an appropriate figure?

8. What does the conversation with Mr. Potts reveal about each of the following?
   a. the strength of Carey's conviction for the need for missions
   b. the precision of Carey's forethought
   c. Carey's financial standing
   d. Carey's ability to influence others

Part 2: The Formation of the Baptist Missionary Society

(1792, age 31)

Within a few years, at the age of 31, Carey was able to see the pamphlet published. Its long title read: **An ENQUIRY into the OBLIGATIONS OF CHRISTIANS to use means for the CONVERSION of the HEATHENS, in which the religious state of the different nations of the world, the success of former undertakings, and the practicability of further undertakings are considered, by William Carey.** *But Carey did not think his work complete with the publication of this booklet. The writing was for one end, to stimulate action; and Carey was not satisfied until he had seen some fruits of his labors.*

Defining for Comprehension

Choose the word or phrase below which most nearly defines each word at the left as it is used in the biography.

1. **garret**	a. pantry	b. attic	c. garage
2. **epoch-making**	a. beginning a new era	b. disruptive	c. defacing
3. **last**	a. leather	b. a workbench	c. a form
4. **epigrammatized**	a. expressed in a witty saying	b. spoke boldly	c. showed emotion
5. **annals**	a. historical records	b. yearbooks	c. one-season flowers
6. **sluices**	a. slow creatures	b. water channels	c. tropical fruits
7. **criminality**	a. shame; wrongfulness	b. unjust blame	c. province
8. **supineness**	a. ill temper	b. remorse	c. lack of energy
9. **propagating**	a. reproducing	b. spreading rumor	c. suggesting
10. **hither**	a. here	b. there	c. beyond
11. **layman**	a. mason	b. printer	c. ordinary church member
12. **inopportune**	a. unsuitable	b. insistent	c. unlikely
13. **subsequent**	a. below	b. oppressed	c. following
14. **in lieu of**	a. in view of	b. instead of	c. for the purpose of
15. **launched**	a. jerked	b. began	c. reclined

In the spring of 1792 the Baptist Ministers' Association was to meet at Nottingham, and Carey had been previously chosen to be the preacher. There was no need to ask what his subject would be—they must have known that when they appointed him. It is easy to imagine the prayerful diligence with which he chose his text and prepared the address that he trusted would be used by God to accomplish his great purpose. He would shut himself away in his top **garret** and pray for a message that would move the hearts of his brethren.

The appointed day was May 30, and the place—the Baptist chapel beside the old almshouses in Park Street (Nottingham). In that simple sanctuary, Carey preached a sermon that was nothing short of **epoch-making**. It is probable that the young preacher made a rather strange figure as he stood in the pulpit: somewhat short of stature, rather thin, and with a decided stoop—the result of constant bending over his shoemaker's **last**. But there could be no mistaking the resolution manifest in every line of his face, the fire in his keen eye, or the earnestness of his voice. He was a man with a message—called by God and sure of his call.

His text is not one we should have expected. Few men would have chosen it for a missionary sermon. It may have been suggested to him by the words Cowper had recently penned in his study at Olney:

> Lord at Thy commanding Word
> We stretch the curtain and the cord.

Be that as it may, Carey announced as his theme:

"Enlarge the place of thy tent, and let them stretch forth the curtains of thine habitations: spare not, lengthen thy cords, and strengthen thy stakes; for thou shalt break forth on the right hand and on the left" (Isa. 54:2, 3).

After a brief and rather weak introduction he took up what he regarded as the spirit of the passage and **epigrammatized** it in two memorable exhortations:

EXPECT GREAT THINGS FROM GOD
ATTEMPT GREAT THINGS FOR GOD

These magnificent words must be forever written large on the first page of the **annals** of British missionary enterprise.

The earnestness with which Carey presented his case and the skill with which he marshaled his arguments moved his hearers profoundly. "It was as if the **sluices** of his soul were thrown fully open and the flood that had been accumulating for years rushed forth in full volume and irresistible power," said Dr. Ryland. "If all the people had lifted up their voices and wept.... I should not have wondered at the effect, it would have only seemed proportionate to the cause; so clearly did he prove the **criminality** of our **supineness** in the cause of God." Copies of the *Enquiry* appear to have been on sale at this service. We wonder how many members of the congregation bought a copy when the meeting broke up.

The following morning the ministers met alone for their usual conference, and Carey's proposal to form a missionary society came up for discussion. But the enthusiasm kindled by the previous day's sermon had passed and the cold logic of practical difficulties seemed overpowering. That little band of comparatively insignificant preachers felt the task to be beyond their strength. They came to the conclusion that Carey's proposal was, for the time being impossible; they turned it down, and the gathering prepared to break up. In distress, Carey seized Fuller by the arms and asked whether they were once more to separate without doing something definite. Then a change came over the company, and after further discussion, and passionate exhortation from Carey, it was decided to place on their minutes a resolution that: "A plan be prepared against the next ministers' meeting for forming a Baptist Society for **propagating** the Gospel among the heathen."

On October 2, 1792, the autumn meeting of the association was held in Andrew Fuller's chapel in the town of Kettering, Northamptonshire, and **hither** Carey journeyed.

The missionary scheme does not appear to have been discussed in the full public meeting that day. In the evening a small group of 12 ministers, a student, and a **layman** met in the spacious dwelling of Widow Wallis—a fine old Georgian house so noted for hospitality to preachers that it was commonly known among them as "the Gospel Inn." That memorable October evening they gathered in a little back parlor. It can safely be described as a "crowded" meeting, for those 14 grave men were squeezed into a room measuring about eighteen feet by nine!

Again the brethren wavered. Let us not blame them too severely. They one and all had come to share Carey's desire to make Christ known to the world. We may perhaps assume that they had all read the *Enquiry*. But most of them still felt that the time was **inopportune**. Once again the great project was on the point of being turned down. But when hesitation and fear were about to triumph Carey made one more appeal. Pulling from his pocket a little volume entitled, *Periodical Account of Moravian Missions*, he cried, "If you had only read this and knew how these men overcame all obstacles for Christ's sake, you would go forward in faith!" There are moments when the faith of one man is contagious, and the strength of one becomes the strength of many. It was so in that little back parlor. Their resolution once taken, those 14 men threw themselves heartily into the great enterprise, and ere they separated the following minute was passed:[1]

> Desirous of making an effort for the propagation of the Gospel among the heathen, agreeable to what is recommended in brother Carey's late publication on that subject, we, whose names appear to the **subsequent** subscription, do solemnly agree to act in society together for that purpose.

No money was taken at the memorable meeting just described, but the men wrote their promises on slips of paper.

---

1. What follows is only one section of a seven-point minute.

2. This amount was equivalent to approximately eight months' wages for the common laborer of those times.

SUBSCRIPTION LIST

John Ryland	£2	2	0
Reynold Hogg	2	2	0
John Sutcliff	1	1	0
Andrew Fuller	1	1	0
Abraham Greenwood	1	1	0
Edward Sharman	1	1	0
Samuel Pearce	1	1	0
Joseph Timms	1	1	0
William Highton	0	10	6
William Staughton	0	10	6
Joshua Burton	0	10	6
Thomas Blundel	0	10	6
John Eayre	0	10	6
	£13	2	6

Glancing over that subscription list we immediately notice that one name is missing from it—that of William Carey. The man whose unquenchable zeal and "plod" had brought the new society into existence was so poor that he could not promise a definite subscription to its funds! But **in lieu of** a subscription, Carey had previously promised that, should there be any profit on his book he would give it to the society.

Thus, with a promised annual income of thirteen pounds, two shillings, and sixpence,[2] the Baptist Missionary Society was **launched**!

House at Kettering in which the Baptist Missionary Society was formed.

Meditating for Meaning

1. What about the Baptist Ministers' Association's appointing of Carey to speak at the minister's meeting shows that the general attitude toward missions was changing?

2. The content and text of thousands of sermons have been forgotten. But an occasional sermon is such a crossroads in the life of the church that it becomes part of her written history.
    a. Why do you think Carey chose Isaiah 54:2, 3 for his text rather than the familiar great commission verses of Matthew 28:19, 20?
    b. Look at the context of Carey's text and suggest a phrase from the surrounding Scripture that Carey may have used to support the theme of his message.
    c. What was Carey's text actually saying that related to mission work?

3. One part of Carey's sermon is called an epigram.
    a. What is the characteristic of all epigrams?
    b. In your own words express the great truth contained in Carey's epigram.
    c. Aside from the great truth it expresses, find at least two literary techniques that contribute to making these words memorable.

4. The response to the sermon immediately after and the next morning differed greatly.
    a. "If all the people had lifted up their voices and wept . . . I should not have wondered at the effect." This testimony shows that much of the immediate effect of the sermon was mainly
    _____ .
    b. The next day "the cold logic of practical difficulties seemed overpowering." What then was the enemy of the good effect of the sermon?
    c. What did these men lack that changed their attitude so quickly?
    d. Consider your above answers along with Hebrews 4:2 and tell what place each of the elements in a, b, and c must take in order for a sermon to do us good.

5. What helped to strengthen the ministers' faith at the autumn meeting where the proposal for a missionary society was considered?

6. How does Carey's absence from the subscription list put special meaning in his appeal to "Expect great things from God; attempt great things for God"?

Looking for Literary Technique

A job well begun may be half done, but it's only that—half done. The other half or perhaps two-thirds remains. Be the beginning ever so catchy, the biographer can lose his reader if the beginning is only a facade for a collection of boring facts. In the *Meditating for Meaning* questions, you have already noticed some of the excellent literary quality of the biography you are reading. Walker doesn't hand over to you the bare bones which he unearthed in his research. Instead, he interprets them, ties them together with the living sinews of his point of view so that William Carey lives again as you read the account of his life. How does the biographer achieve this? By several methods.

Let's examine the very first paragraph of the biography. The "bones" for this paragraph are Carey's quotation, "My attention to missions was first awakened after I was at Moulton, by reading the *Last Voyage of Captain Cook*." Also Walker had discovered that Carey spent four years at Moulton. Walker might have simply told us: "Carey decided to be a missionary after reading the *Last Voyage of Captain Cook* during his four years at Moulton." Rather, he begins by saying, "The four years at Moulton were memorable for something of far-reaching importance." The rather insignificant four-year part, he tosses in as an unobtrusive fact which you catch out of the corner of your eye while absorbed by the curiosity-arousing idea that something important happened at Moulton (what it was, you must wait to discover).

In the next sentence, "It was while laboring in that secluded village and living in that thatched cottage that William Carey heard the missionary call," Walker gives you another side glimpse, this time at Carey's environment—a thatched cottage in a secluded village.

In the last sentence, "Surely this sentence gives us the key to the psychology of the call and enables us to understand the working of his mind," the biographer comments on Carey's words in the sentence before and prepares to expound them in the paragraph to come. His comments reveal that, as a researcher, he saw more than the surface of the facts he gathered. He saw into them, understood what parts they played in his subject's life, and clearly explained them to us.

Another temptation to biographers besides handing across "bare bones" is to begin every sentence alike with the subject first and to chop each one to the same length. This produces monotony. Notice how the third paragraph of this biography might have appeared beneath the stroke of a less-skilled pen:

> Cook's *Journal* was a thrilling story of adventure to most people. It revealed human need to William Carey. Those tattooed savages were *men and women* to him. They were God's creatures, needing to know about God's love. The thought arose in his heart: "These South Sea islanders need the gospel!"

Although sentences usually begin with the subject, it adds variety to begin with some other type of phrase. Walker begins with the preposition *to*. These prepositional phrases, "To most people," "to William Carey," and "To him," not only add variety, but they accent the contrast between what most people gained from Cook's *Journal* and what Carey gained. Also, they provide coherence in the buildup of thought.

1. Find another paragraph from this biography in which the biographer deviated from the usual subject-first order. Rewrite the paragraph, placing the subject first in each sentence, to see how monotonous and less emphatic it becomes.

2. Find and copy an example from the biography in which the author repeats a key phrase or idea to achieve contrast, coherence, or buildup of thought.

Writing for Skill

With your pack of archaeological findings in hand, you are now ready to assemble the main part of your paper. First, sort all your note cards so that all cards containing information on one topic or similar topics are together. Then place the topics in logical order as they would come in your subject's life.

Beginning with the first topic, begin putting "muscle" and "flesh" on the "bones." Try to interpret your notes for your reader. Judging by the way in which your subject approached life's activities, what were his work habits? What was his life philosophy? Be sure you don't guess or jump to conclusions. Have a basis for your generalizations, but don't leave your reader wondering. Remember, he doesn't know your subject as well as you do. Again, keep in mind your point of view. If some fact just doesn't seem to fit into your biography, discard it.

Try to vary your sentences. Use repetitions and contrasts to achieve coherence. Later you may choose to rearrange your paragraphs and sharpen them. Do what it takes to make your subject come to life for your reader.

Part 3: Converts, Trials, and Progress

(1800-1813, Age 39-42)

Obviously, William Carey was not just a sounding brass or a tinkling cymbal. He put his convictions into action. In less than two years after the founding of the missionary society, Carey landed in India. Once he left England to do missionary work, he never planned to return. But the vineyard of Carey's planting bore slow fruit.

Defining for Comprehension

Choose the word or phrase below which most nearly defines each word at the left as it is used in the biography.

1. wane	a. increase	b. decrease	c. curse
2. disposed	a. inclined	b. reclined	c. opened
3. broached	a. opened	b. rebuked	c. ignored
4. vernacular	a. upright	b. external	c. native language
5. perpetuated	a. lengthened existence	b. pierced	c. encouraged
6. arbitrary	a. unreasonable	b. surrounding	c. docile
7. imposes	a. opens	b. forces upon	c. hints
8. coercion	a. weariness	b. force	c. joint effort

Carey labored in India under great difficulties. For two years, he heard nothing from his friends in England. Then they wrote to tell him he was crazy. No one sent him any money. Even his own wife did not share his missionary zeal and had only reluctantly consented to go with him to India in the first place. After the loss of a child in India, she became insane and needed to be restrained. This mental affliction lasted for 12 years until her death in 1807.

The climate in the part of India where Carey served was so oppressive that four of the first seven missionaries died within a few years of reaching the field.

More reverses hit Carey in swift succession. Fire burned his print shop and years of his translating work went up in flames. A bank failure wiped out his hard-earned finances. The government of India made laws against his work. The riverbank gave way, and the enraged heathen blamed him for the disastrous flood. But William Carey stuck to his motto and the call of God. He expected great things from God and attempted great things for God.

By the end of his fruitful life in 1834, he had supervised the translation of the Bible or parts of it into 40 Asiatic languages and dialects, a labor that marked Carey's missionary efforts as "modern." Most earlier missionaries had not recognized the need for people to read Bibles in their native language. Carey became such a recognized language expert that he was asked to teach native languages in a government school in Calcutta.

This undaunted missionary was instrumental in starting the first organized publishing operation in India which even involved a paper mill.

He helped set up several schools in India, including a college, and assisted in establishing about 30 mission outposts.

As a result of his protests, Carey rejoiced to see two heathen customs abolished—the sacrifice of children by throwing them into the river and the burning of a widow with her dead husband.

The last days of 1800 witnessed the baptism of the first Indian convert of the mission. It was an event long looked for and prayed for, both by Carey and his colleagues, and by their supporters in England. For seven years Carey had labored without the joy of leading a single Indian to Christ. This was a source of great distress to him, for all his labors were but means to the one end of winning Indian peoples to definite allegiance to Christ. Moreover, he often feared that his inability to report conversions might discourage the friends at home and cause their interest to **wane**. To what purpose the translations, the

press, the schools, the evangelistic preaching, if the main object were not achieved?

It often happened that some man was attracted by the gospel message, and for a time seemed **disposed** to respond to the call of Jesus. But for Hindus and Mohammedans to respond to His "Follow me" meant the loss of all that men hold dear, and when the hour of decision came they drew back. This happened so often that whenever a new "enquirer" showed promise, the missionaries "rejoiced with fear" lest they should experience a new disappointment.

It was given to Dr. John Thomas, Carey's companion missionary, to win the first real convert.

In October 1800, Thomas visited his missionary brethren at Serampore, bringing with him a Mohammedan sugar-boiler named Fukeer whom he had led to the point of decision. Great was the joy of all the brotherhood when they heard the man's story and listened to his simple confession of faith in Jesus. They all rose to their feet and with full hearts sang "Praise God from whom all blessings flow." The question of Fukeer's early baptism was raised, and Fukeer suggested that he should first go home and take leave of his family before separating from them, perhaps forever. He went home—and the missionaries never saw him again. Another disappointment!

But on the very day the brethren sang that doxology over Fukeer, a poor Serampore carpenter, a Hindu named Krishna Pal, met with an accident in which he dislocated his shoulder. Hearing of this, the kindhearted Dr. Thomas immediately went off to his assistance. Surgical treatment was somewhat rough in those days. They tied the poor man to a tree, and while Carey and Marshman held out the arm, Thomas jerked the bone back into its socket. In his pain, the man cried, "I am a great sinner! A great sinner am I! Save me, Sahib! Save me!" Thomas was not the man to treat any patient without also speaking to him of the Lord Jesus, and he made the most of the opportunity in this case. Ten times over he repeated the words, "He that covereth his sins shall not prosper, but whoso confesseth and forsaketh

Dr. Carey and his pundit

them shall find mercy," and he tried to get Krishna Pal to repeat them after him. Even "line upon line, line upon line" did not seem to make the meaning clear to the poor fellow, and so to help him Thomas called it the true *gayatri*[1] which if a man could truly pronounce and act upon, he would be saved—

> *He that confesseth his sins,*
> *And forsakes them,*
> *Obtaining the righteousness of Jesus,*
> *Is free.*

On his recovery Krishna, together with a friend named Goluk, often visited the mission house for further instruction, and one day, meeting Thomas in the street, he said to him: "Oh, Sahib, I am a very great sinner, but I have confessed my sin . . . *and I am free!*" He came daily for Christian instruction, and his wife and daughter determined to join him in following Christ. The subject of baptism was **broached**— and of breaking caste—and to the missionaries' joy the converts did not shrink. Three days before Christmas Krishna and Goluk openly renounced caste by joining the missionaries at a meal, and the same evening they, with Krishna's wife and daughter, came before the church to confess their faith. When this breaking of caste became known, a riot followed. Two thousand people gathered before the houses of the converts and dragged Krishna and Goluk to a magistrate—who promptly ordered the mob to dissolve. To prevent violence, the Governor placed a soldier before their dwellings.

The baptism was fixed for Sunday, December 28, and it was resolved to baptize them in the Hooghly, at the landing steps near to the mission house. This was decided upon after very careful discussion, for the Hooghly is really one mouth of the sacred Ganges, and there was some fear that the Hindus might regard it as a recognition of the sanctity of the river. There was, however, once more a measure of disappointment—on the Saturday Goluk and the women held back. But Krishna himself stood firm, and it was resolved to baptize him along with Felix Carey, who had fully decided thus to pledge his allegiance to Christ.

It was indeed a great day for Carey. That Sunday morning the missionaries assembled in their chapel and then walked through a dense crowd of Hindus, Moslems and Europeans to the landing place. Governor Bie was present, and with him a company of Danish and Portuguese Christians. Carey, as pastor of the little church, was to officiate and he walked down to the water with his son Felix and Krishna Pal, one on either hand. Addressing the multitude, Carey explained the meaning of the ceremony and what it means to become a disciple of Jesus; and then, amid intense silence, the Hindu carpenter and the young Englishman were baptized together. In baptizing his son,

---

1. gayatri: A sacred invocation solemnly repeated every day by caste Hindus.

Carey repeated the sentences in English; in baptizing Krishna Pal he spoke in Bengali.

Two things followed: that Sunday evening the Holy Communion was administered for the first time in the Bengali language. Next day, the **vernacular** school was left without a scholar! All had been withdrawn lest they too should become Christians.

That first baptism was speedily followed by others. Early in the New Year (1801) Krishna's sister-in-law was baptized—the first Hindu woman—and also Mr. Fernandez, whom Carey had so helped at Dinajpur. A month later Krishna's wife and another woman received baptism. In the following August, Goluk took up his cross and followed Jesus, and in November his wife also confessed Christ in baptism. On the first Sunday in 1802, the first convert of the Kayust or writer caste was baptized—a man nearly 60 years of age and of high intelligence.

At the beginning of 1803, the first Brahmin was baptized; he had become acquainted with the Gospel through reading one of the mission tracts. His baptism produced a profound impression on the Hindus. By this time there were 13 baptized Bengalis and eight enquirers.

The coming of Bengali converts into the church created several questions that called for solution. One was as to the advisability of giving Christian names in place of their old Hindu or Mohammedan names to those who received baptism. Some urged that it would be a useful way of proclaiming the fact that they were Christians; but Carey opposed it, and after discussion it was resolved not to do it.

A vastly more important matter was that of the attitude to be adopted toward caste among the converts. The missionaries well knew that their Danish predecessors in South India had allowed converts to retain their caste, and caste distinctions were thus **perpetuated** within the church of Christ. After looking at the question very carefully, Carey and his colleagues felt that such a state of things could not be tolerated and that from the very beginning the Bengali Christians must not be divided by such **arbitrary** social distinctions as the Hindu caste system **imposes**; they must be "one in Christ Jesus," and it was resolved to allow no compromise. Not that they contemplated **coercion**; but they hoped to lead all their converts to see that the caste system is contrary to the Spirit of Christ. A little over two years after the baptism of Krishna Pal, the first Bengali Christian wedding was celebrated—Krishna's daughter was married to the Brahmin convert, a glorious triumph over caste.

Six months later they had the first funeral of a Bengali Christian—Goluk, who had been led to Christ with Krishna Pal. Carey was in Calcutta and Ward at Dinajpur; the arrangements, therefore, were in the hands of Marshman. Instead of employing low-class Portuguese as bearers—men who as likely as not would come to their duty drunk—Marshman decided to give a concrete illustration of the meaning of Christian brotherhood. So, to the amazement of the onlookers, he and Felix Carey, Bhyrub, a converted Brahmin, and Piru, a converted Mohammedan, themselves lifted the coffin and placed it upon their shoulders. Singing a Bengali hymn, "Salvation Through the Name of Christ," those four men slowly carried the body of their low-caste brother through the streets of Serampore. Thus was proclaimed the unity of all Christians at Holy Communion, at the marriage altar, and at the graveside.

The missionaries had their joys and sorrows strangely interwoven, but those men had "signed on for life."

The pioneering of this famous missionary has earned for him the title of Father of Modern Missions. The work progressed slowly at first and Carey faced many discouragements. Yet, 18 years after he had baptized the first Indian convert, the Baptist Church in India numbered well over a thousand souls.

Carey recognized the value of education in meeting the Indians' spiritual needs, and with the support of the British government he established approximately 50 schools and a college as well. Earlier, as the professor of a college in Calcutta, Carey encountered a lack of books in the native language of his students. The solution was to write his own grammar and literature books with the help of Indian scholars.

Later, with the help of these same Indian scholars, Carey and his fellow missionaries translated parts of the Bible into 40 different Indian languages. Among Carey's greatest triumphs was his role in influencing the British government to ban human sacrifice of infants and widows in India.

In spite of all these accomplishments, Carey was very modest. The only special trait that he would acknowledge was plodding. Close to the end of his life, when praised by a visitor, he responded, "You have been speaking of Dr. Carey, Dr. Carey. When I am gone, say nothing about Dr. Carey—speak about Dr. Carey's Saviour."

Carey's rigorous life as a missionary took its toll at last. Weakened by repeated attacks of fever, he died two months before his 73rd birthday. In the land where he had labored and struggled, Carey was buried beside several of his converts. The only inscription he would allow on his tombstone was:

WILLIAM CAREY, BORN AUGUST 17, 1761
DIED JUNE 9, 1834
A WRETCHED, POOR, AND HELPLESS
WORM
ON THY KIND ARMS I FALL

His epitaph is accurate. Carey died a poor man. Even his books were sold to meet a need of his son. However, this does not mean that he did not earn much money in his lifetime. He with two other families, who put their earnings in a common fund, contributed £90,000 ($153,000) to the mission work in India.

Few missionaries have labored under more adverse circumstances than Carey, but his life was dedicated to a cause that he believed was God's commission to the church.

Dr. Carey's tomb at Serampore

Meditating for Meaning

1. In commenting on the cost of discipleship, Christ said, "So likewise, whosoever he be of you that forsaketh not all that he hath, he cannot be my disciple" (Luke 14:33).
   a. What evidence do we have that it was especially hard for the Indians to become disciples?
   b. What un-Christian system existed in India that made it hard to be a Christian?
   c. Using an encyclopedia, report briefly on how this system operated.

2. A crisis provided the turning point in the missionary effort.
   a. What brought Krishna Pal to confess that he was a sinner?
   b. What prevented Krishna Pal from finding immediate freedom from his sin?
   c. What eventually helped him to gain that freedom?
   d. What two tests to his faith did he endure before his baptism?

3. Another crisis immediately followed the baptism of Krishna Pal. Why was the vernacular school left without a scholar the next day?

4. Church expansion soon followed the baptism of Krishna Pal.
   a. List all the converts to Christianity who were baptized within one year of Krishna Pal's baptism.
   b. Why do you think there was a sudden influx of natives into the church after seven years with no converts?
   c. What does this aspect of Carey's experience in India teach us about witnessing?

5. Find at least one Scripture that supports the decision of the missionaries not to allow the caste system in the church.

Looking for Literary Technique

According to Solomon, the end of an endeavor is more important than the beginning, or at least better than the beginning (Ecclesiastes 7:8). While nothing can end that never begins, yet a poor ending can destroy the effect of a good beginning.

Contrary to the way a news article ends, shutting off after announcing the last bit of information, a good story must not bring you to a crash landing or leave you dangling without ever landing. A good biography, like any good story, should leave you with the satisfied feeling that it was worth reading, with the firm understanding of how and why the subject affected the world as he did, and with the firm resolve that you will or will not follow in his footsteps.

To stop where the person's life stopped, at his death, leaves the reader dissatisfied. Actually no life stops there. Influence lives for years after a person's physical death. The biographer's task is to track down that influence and point out to his reader the reason for the success or failure of the person's life. In the biography which you have just read, the author does this quite well. The various experiences which he earlier recounted in vivid detail, he now crystallizes in two words—joys and sorrows.

Then he shows us the key to Carey's effective influence—he refused to give up.

Often biographers will harmonize their entire biography by ending with an idea similar to the one with which they began.

1. Consider the biography of Clayton Kratz, "True...Till Death." How does the idea of the last paragraph connect with the opening paragraph?
2. Not all the biographies in this unit end in this way.
    a. Besides the biographies of Clayton Kratz and William Carey, which other biography in this unit ends satisfactorily because it summarizes the subject's life?
    b. Why do you think the other biography does not end in a similar way?

Writing for Skill

Your biography is almost complete. Now write a paragraph or two in conclusion, tying together the facts of your subject's life and reflecting his influence on the world. Try to connect your conclusion with your beginning. Let your reader lay down your biography with a satisfied smile.

"Go ye therefore,
and teach all nations,
baptizing them in the name of the Father,
and of the Son, and of the Holy Ghost:
teaching them to observe all things
whatsoever I have commanded you:
and, lo, I am with you alway,
even unto the end of the world.
Amen."

—Matthew 28:19, 20

UNIT 4

Reflections
for the Victorious Life

A schoolteacher once faced the difficulty of friction among her students of various races. As an object lesson one morning, she brought to the classroom two bouquets of dahlias. One bouquet was totally one color. The other bouquet included the whole spectrum of dahlia hues. "Which bouquet is prettier?" she asked the children. The children didn't disappoint her. With one voice, they chose the multicolored bouquet. She agreed and explained that that was why she preferred her "multicolored" classroom. Variety with harmony is an asset to any setting.

This unit is somewhat like the multicolored bouquet. While the other units in this book concentrate on one form of literature—the short story, poetry, biography, or allegory—this unit includes a wider scope of literature.

While the "single-colored" unit has its benefit in being a concentrated look at the structure and form of one type of literature, the "multicolored" unit yields other benefits. In this unit we focus more on the central theme which harmonizes it—the victorious life.

You will see in this unit not only the perfecting power of discipline, but also the destructive power of misaimed ambition; not only the far-reaching good of well-ordered steps of men of God throughout all ages, but also the widespread sadness that wrong choices can bring.

Life itself is "multicolored" with variegated experiences, but the path to happiness and eternal life is the same for all. Happiness and eternal life are God's eternal purposes for all men. To these purposes He sent Jesus to earth, but it is our choice whether we will fulfill these purposes and reap His promised joys. Our choices will turn life either to a millstone about our necks or a diadem on our brow.

If we wish life to be a diadem, we must have a settled and all-pervading focus on the principle of right. The influence and example of others is invaluable in living by this principle of right, but we must look first and last to God to aid us in this great task of life. Don't wait for the lash of guilt to scourge you into the path of God and heaven. Learn from the wisdom and experiences of others. Be one of the prudent, who foresee the evil and hide themselves from it; not of the simple, who pass on and are punished (Proverbs 22:3). Be wise in time, that you may be happy in eternity.

These are the warnings and admonitions which you will find in the unit ahead. Read the selections, compare them with truth, and apply the truths to your own life.

Checking for Understanding

1. How does this unit differ from other units in this book?
2. What is the benefit of each type of focus?
3. Though all lives are different, how are they all alike?
4. What is the highest happiness which God wants us to enjoy?
5. How can we find this happiness?

Reflections on
Discipline

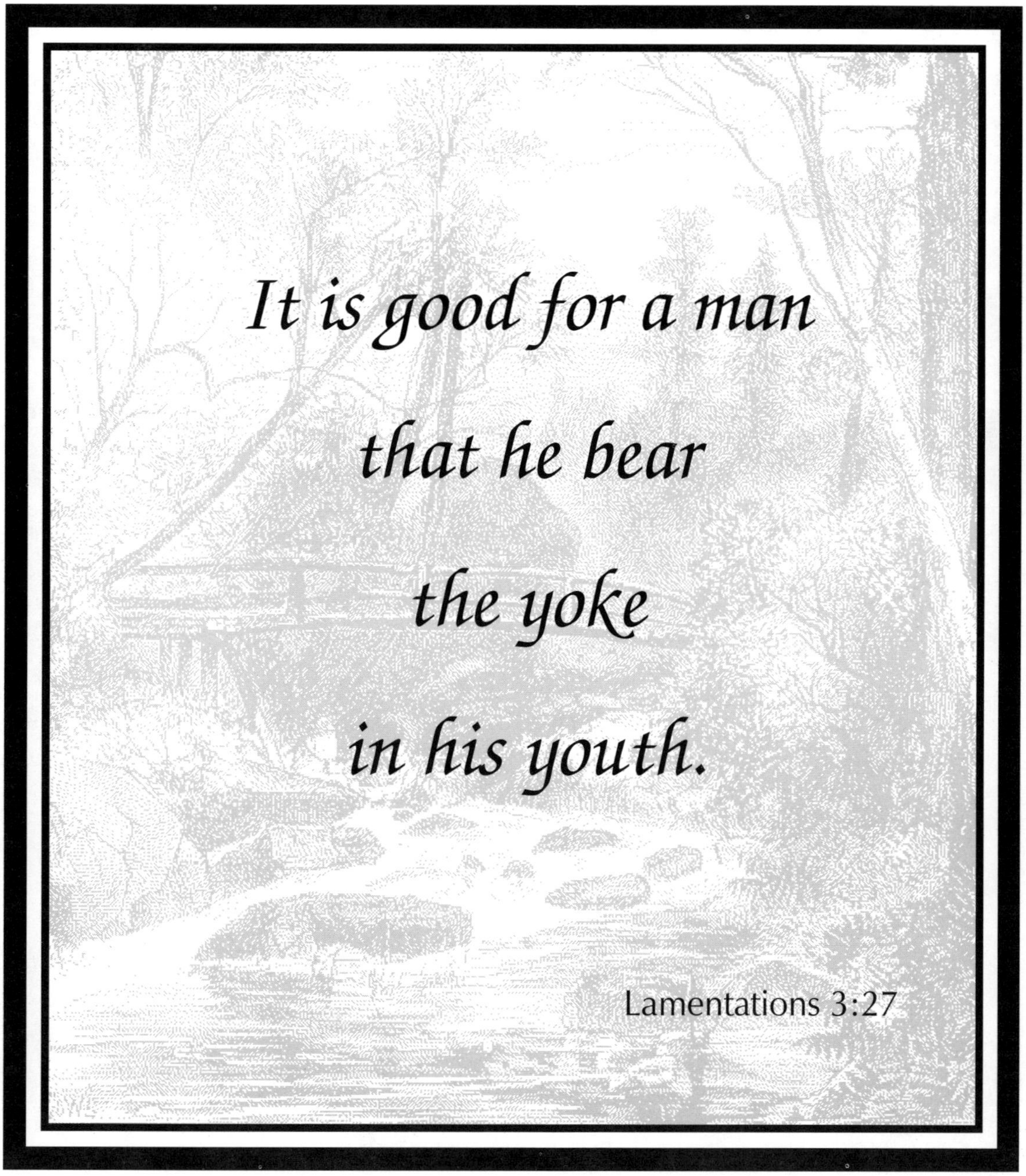

It is good for a man

that he bear

the yoke

in his youth.

Lamentations 3:27

Discipline

by William MacDonald

What do all people have in common?—the inborn tendency toward laziness. What do all successful students, all prosperous business-men, and all victorious Christians have in common?—the cultivated trait of diligence. And what does it take to acquire this diligence?—discipline—making yourself do what you know is for your best interest, even though you would rather not do it. Read the following selection and see what discipline demanded of those who succeeded in the past.

Defining for Comprehension

Choose the word or phrase below which most nearly defines each word at the left as it is used in this selection.

1. **rigorous**	a. energetic; strong	b. inventive	c. demanding; harsh
2. **catering**	a. frolicking	b. satisfying	c. supporting
3. **insipid**	a. empty; tasteless	b. lazy	c. ridiculous
4. **surfeited**	a. glutted	b. floated	c. successful
5. **sated**	a. filled to full	b. settled	c. angered
6. **buffet**	a. polish	b. strike	c. clown
7. **prowess**	a. trickery	b. wanderer	c. skill
8. **passion**	a. strong desire	b. sensitivity	c. shortness
9. **bayous**	a. chariots	b. weapons	c. marshy areas
10. **clamant**	a. angry; disturbed	b. thieving	c. loud; urgent

Discipline

In the Christian life, it is possible to follow the path of least resistance and to escape the **rigorous** demands of personal discipline. By **catering** to the soft and flabby desires of the flesh, we can avoid the pain of weariness, hunger and discomfort. But in striving so hard to baby the self-life, we become barren and **insipid**.

The flesh struggles unceasingly for pampering. It wants to be **surfeited** with food, satisfied with sleep, surrounded with pleasure, and **sated** with attention. Until we learn to say NO! and mean it, there can be little progress for God. We must **buffet** our body and bring it into subjection. We must crucify the flesh with its darling affections and lusts. We must make it our business to rise early, redeem the time, and refuse the pathway of self-indulgence.

By its shocking lack of discipline, Christendom has become a powerless giant. It enjoys the contempt of the world. The disciplined lives of unbelievers often put the Christian in a very bad light.

When asked the secret of his **prowess** as a pianist, Paderewski said, "Practicing scales hour after hour, day after day, till these poor fingers were nearly worn to the bone."

It is said that Milton used to rise at four every morning to write *Paradise Lost*. Noah Webster worked for 36 years before the first edition of his dictionary was finished.

Many would like to enjoy the reward of a job well done, but they don't want the toil, heartache, and loneliness that often lead to it. For Gibbon it meant 26 long years of discipline to write the *Decline and Fall of the Roman Empire*. For Bryant it meant rewriting *Thanatopsis* 99 times.

Jowett said, "Vast ambitions are not kept burning in the soul without fuel. They suck the very energies of the body into their own flame. Fine **passion** makes a heavy drain upon the nerves; the suburbs are scoured to feed the fire at the center. There is not a man or woman of holy Christian passion today who is not burning the candle at both ends."

Audubon, the great naturalist, was willing to undergo prolonged discomfort to learn more of the world of birds. Let Robert G. Lee tell it:

> He counted his physical comforts as nothing compared with success in his work. He would rise at midnight, night after night, and go out into the swamps to study the habits of certain night hawks. He would crouch motionless for hours in the dark and fog, feeling himself well rewarded, if, after weeks of waiting he secured one additional fact about a single bird. During one summer he went, day after day, to the **bayous** near New Orleans to observe a shy waterfowl. He would have to stand almost to his neck in the nearly stagnant water, scarcely breathing, while countless poisonous moccasin snakes swam past his face, and great alligators passed and repassed his silent watch.
>
> "It was not pleasant," he said, as his face glowed with enthusiasm, "but what of that? I have the picture of the bird." He would do that for the picture of a bird.

The great military commanders of history learned the lesson of discipline. Famous musicians had to bow their necks to the yoke of discipline. Leaders in every walk of life

About the Author

William MacDonald (b. 1917) born in Leominster, Massachusetts, received degrees at Tufts and Harvard Universities. Following his employment as an investment analyst at a bank in Boston, he served on the Emmaus Bible School faculty of Oak Park, Illinois, acting as President from 1959-1965. Later MacDonald joined a Bible-teaching ministry in Europe and Asia, writing numerous books, pamphlets, and Bible correspondence courses. Presently he lives in California and is a faculty member of the Discipleship Intern Training Program.

worked, practiced, suffered and endured before they reached the pinnacle.

Men are willing to endure tremendous hardship for earthly honors. Sir Ernest Shackleton, the Irish explorer of Antarctica, once placed this ad in a London paper.

> Men wanted for hazardous journey. Small wages, bitter cold, long months of complete darkness, constant danger, safe return doubtful. Honor and recognition in case of success.

All those who ventured their lives with him returned to their homes in safety, and were given honor and recognition. They did it to obtain a corruptible crown; how much more should we be willing to do for an incorruptible crown.

> *The heights by great men reached and kept*
> *Were not attained by sudden flight,*
> *But that while their companions slept*
> *Were toiling upward through the night.*

God calls every Christian to a life of discipline. There must be discipline in prayer, discipline in studying the Word, discipline in the use of time, discipline in witnessing to others, discipline in sacrificial living. By the example of the Lord Jesus, by the **clamant** needs of a perishing world and by the personal peril of being a castaway at last, let us discipline ourselves so that Christ will get the most and the best out of these passing lives of ours.

 *Meditating for Meaning*

1. The word *discipline* is closely related to the word *disciple*.
   a. Define *disciple*.
   b. Find and copy a definition of *discipline* as it is used in this article.
   c. Using a dictionary with word origins, check the meaning of the root word of *disciple* and *discipline*. Then explain how these words are associated.
2. The first sentence says, "It is possible to follow the path of least resistance."
   a. Apparently, discipline requires following a path of _____ .
   b. While it is possible to follow the path of least resistance, what does the first paragraph suggest is the result of such a course?
   c. What part of man wants to avoid discipline? Why?
   d. What does this part of man desire instead of discipline?
   e. What does the second paragraph say must be done to this part of man?
   f. What practical suggestions does this paragraph give for accomplishing this?
3. Christ called His followers disciples. It is ironic that Christians should have such a "shocking lack of discipline."
   a. Following _____ requires discipline; following _____ does not.
   b. In light of these statements, what might we conclude about someone who lacks discipline?
   c. Give a Scripture to prove your answer.
4. The article specifies seven men who exercised discipline in their lives.
   a. What characteristic do you recognize in each of these men which is the key to exercise of discipline? Note the stanza of poetry.
   b. Can we conclude that these men were Christians on the basis that they exercised discipline?

c. Explain the difference between this type of discipline and the discipline required to live a Christian life. Consider the goal of both kinds of discipline.

d. Give some examples of the type of discipline required in the Christian life. See Ephesians 4, 5, and Colossians 3.

e. Do you think the discipline of the men mentioned in this article was a wrong exercise of discipline? Explain.

5. The last paragraph says, "God calls every Christian to a life of discipline."

a. From this paragraph list five areas of the Christian life which require discipline.

b. From this same paragraph give three encouragements to discipline ourselves.

c. According to the last sentence, what will be the fruit of a disciplined life?

6. To many people the Christian life appears narrow and discipline looks like a self-hating method of avoiding anything pleasant. In your own words, summarize the purpose and fruit of discipline which proves this view of the Christian life incorrect.

 *Looking for Literary Technique*

Why do visitors to Niagara Falls come home with postcards? Why do tourists of Yellowstone National Park return with miniature plush grizzlies? Why do vacationers in Florida leave with tufts of Spanish moss? And why are souvenir shops always full? The reason is simple. People like things. They like things they can touch, see, hear, smell, taste, and finally keep. We call such items that can be discerned by the five senses *concrete*. Ideas and memories, on the other hand, are *abstract*. Though we can remember the sound of Niagara thundering through her gorge, the image of Old Faithful spouting every 65 minutes, or the feel of Spanish moss between our fingers, these are only abstract memories that soon die. Through souvenirs the memories remain alive.

Readers, just like tourists, look for souvenirs in the literature they "tour." They want something to touch, something to see, something to hear, something to smell, and something to taste. They want something to "take along home." One way authors provide readers with these "souvenirs" is to give specific examples of the ideas they are trying to express.

The author of the article you just read was expressing the abstract idea of discipline. But you as the reader would have understood and remembered much less if he had not made the article concrete by giving examples.

An author should give sufficient examples to illustrate his point, but not so many that they hide rather than highlight his point. If an author gives many examples, each one should illustrate a different aspect of his point.

1. List the seven men whom the author gave as concrete examples to illustrate the abstract idea of discipline. Then briefly tell how each exercised discipline.

2. Summarize the various fields of achievement represented by these examples of discipline.

3. What has the author included in the stories of some of these men which makes his examples especially effective?

Writing for Skill

Choose a character quality which every Christian should have. Prove its value by a short article of several paragraphs. Make your article concrete by inserting several good examples. You may wish to choose illustrations from the lives of Bible characters. Give your reader interesting, memorable "souvenirs." Following is a list of possible qualities you may choose from.

commitment   punctuality   honesty   unselfishness   courtesy   humility

The Chariots of God

by Hannah Whitall Smith

Most people, as the expression goes, want to have their cake and eat it too. Human nature wants to stand on the mountaintops, wreathed in clouds of triumph, without ever risking the rugged cliffs and precipices of the mountainside. In short, we want the victory without the struggle. But such a life is as unreal as traveling on a bicycle without pedaling. Without effort there is no transportation. Think with Hannah Smith as she explains how difficulties provide the transportation to success.

Defining for Comprehension

Choose the word or phrase below which most nearly defines each word at the left as it is used in this selection.

1. chafed	a. discarded	b. fretted	c. heated
2. tangible	a. tasty	b. touchable; real	c. unstable
3. substantial	a. solid; sound	b. below average	c. upright
4. deprivations	a. compartments	b. hardships	c. distributions
5. taunting	a. stretching	b. visiting frequently	c. mocking
6. traverse	a. oppose	b. travel	c. move backward
7. mortification	a. complete change	b. hardening process	c. humiliation

The Chariots of God

It has been well said that "earthly cares are a heavenly discipline." But they are even something better than discipline,—they are God's chariots, sent to take the soul to its high places of triumph.

They do not look like chariots. They look instead like enemies, sufferings, trials, defeats, misunderstandings, disappointments, unkindnesses. They look like *Juggernaut cars*[1] of misery and wretchedness, which are only waiting to roll over us and crush us into the earth. But could we see them as they really are, we should recognize them as chariots of triumph in which we may ride to those very heights of victory for which our souls have been longing and praying. The Juggernaut car is the visible thing; the chariot of God is the invisible. The King of Syria came up against the men of God with horses and chariots that could be seen by every eye, but God had chariots that could be seen by none save the eye of faith. The servant of the prophet could only see the outward and visible; and he cried, as so many have done since, "Alas, my master! how shall we do?" But the prophet himself sat calmly within his house without fear, because his eyes were opened to see the invisible; and all he asked for his servant was, "Lord, I pray thee open his eyes that he may see."

This is the prayer we need to pray for ourselves and for one another, "Lord, open our eyes that we may see"; for the world all around us, as well as around the prophet, is full of God's horses and chariots, waiting to carry us to places of glorious victory. And when our eyes are thus opened, we shall see in all the events of life, whether great or small, whether joyful or sad, a "chariot" for our souls.

Everything that comes to us becomes a chariot the moment we treat it as such; and on the other hand, even the smallest trials may be a Juggernaut car to crush us into misery or despair if we so consider them. It lies with each of us to choose which they shall be. It all depends, not upon what these events are, but upon how we take them. If we lie down under them and let them roll over us and crush us, they become Juggernaut cars, but if we climb up into them, as into a car of victory, and make them carry us triumphantly onward and upward, they become the chariots of God.

Whenever we mount into God's chariots the same thing happens to us spiritually that happened to Elijah. We shall have a translation. Not into the heavens above us, as Elijah did, but into the heaven within us; and this, after all, is almost a grander translation than his. We shall be carried away from the low, earthly, groveling plane of life, where everything hurts and everything is unhappy, up into the "heavenly places in Christ Jesus," where we can ride in triumph over all below.

These "heavenly places" are interior, not exterior, and the road that leads to them is interior also. But the chariot that carries the soul over this road is generally some outward loss or trial or disappointment, some chastening that does not indeed seem for the present to be joyous, but grievous, but that nevertheless afterward "yieldeth the peaceable fruits of righteousness to them that are exercised thereby."

In the *Canticles*[2] we are told of "chariots paved with love." We cannot always see the love-lining to our own particular chariot. It often looks very unlovely. It may be a cross-grained relative or friend; it may be the result of human malice or cruelty or neglect; but every chariot sent by God must necessarily be paved with love, since God is love; and God's love is the sweetest, softest, tenderest thing to rest one's self upon that was ever found by any soul anywhere. It is His love, indeed, that sends the chariot.

Look upon your chastenings then, no matter how grievous they may be for the present, as

1. Juggernaut cars: carts which carried a Hindu god under which worshippers were sometimes crushed to death.
2. Canticles: Song of Solomon.

God's chariots sent to carry your soul into the "high places" of spiritual achievement and uplifting, and you will find that they are, after all, "paved with love."

The Bible tells us that when God went forth for the salvation of His people, then He "did ride upon His horses and chariots of salvation." And it is the same now. Everything becomes a "chariot of salvation" when God rides upon it. He maketh even the "clouds his chariot," we are told, and "walketh on the wings of the wind." Therefore the clouds and storms that darken our skies and seem to shut out the shining of the sun of righteousness are really only God's chariots, into which we may mount with Him, and "ride prosperously" over all the darkness. Have you made the clouds in your life your chariots? Are you "riding prosperously" with God on top of them all?

I knew a lady who had a very slow servant. She was an excellent girl in every other respect, and very valuable in the household; but her slowness was a constant source of irritation to her mistress, who was naturally quick, and was always **chafed** at slowness. This lady would consequently get out of temper with the girl twenty times a day, and twenty times a day would repent of her anger and resolve to conquer it, but in vain. Her life was made miserable by the conflict. One day it occurred to her than she had for a long while been praying for patience, and that perhaps this slow servant was the very chariot the Lord had sent to carry her soul over into patience. She immediately accepted it as such, and from that time used the slowness of her servant as a chariot for her soul; and the result was a victory of patience that no slowness of anybody was ever after able to disturb.

I knew another lady, at a crowded convention, who was put to sleep in a room with two others on account of the crowd. She wanted to sleep, but they wanted to talk; and the first night she was greatly disturbed, and lay there fretting and fuming long after the others had hushed and she might have slept. But the next day she heard something about God's chariots, and at night she accepted these talking friends as her chariots to carry her over into sweetness

and patience, and was kept in undisturbed calm. When, however, it grew very late, and she knew they all ought to be sleeping, she ventured to say quietly, "Friends, I am lying here riding in a chariot!" The effect was instantaneous, and perfect quiet reigned! Her chariot had carried her over to victory, not only inwardly, but at last outwardly as well.

If we would ride in God's chariots instead of our own we should find this to be the case continually.

Our constant temptation is to trust in the "chariots of Egypt," or, in other words, in earthly resources. We can *see* them; they are **tangible**, and real, and look **substantial,** while God's chariots are invisible and intangible, and it is hard to believe they are there.

We try to reach high spiritual places with the "multitude of our chariots." We depend first on one thing and then on another to advance our spiritual condition, and to gain our spiritual victories. We "go down to Egypt for help." And God is obliged often to destroy all our own earthly chariots before He can bring us to the point of mounting into His.

The "chariot of God" which alone can carry us to the places where we hoped to be taken by the instrumentalities upon which we have been depending is to be found in the very **deprivations** we have so mourned over. God must burn up with the fire of His love every chariot of our own that stands in the way of our mounting into His.

We have to be brought to the place where all other refuges fail us before we can say, "He only." We say, "He *and*—something else," "He and my experiences," or "He and my relationships," or "He and my Christian work"; and all that comes after the "and" must be taken away from us, or must be proved useless, before we can come to the "He only." As long as visible chariots are at hand, the soul will not mount into the invisible ones.

Let us be thankful, then, for every trial that will help to destroy our earthly chariots, and that will compel us to take refuge in the chariot of God which stands ready and waiting beside us in every event and circumstance of life. We are told that "God rideth upon the heavens," and if we would ride with Him there we need to be brought to the end of all riding upon the earth.

When we mount into God's chariot, our goings are "established," for no obstacles can hinder His triumphal course. All losses, therefore, are gains that bring us to this. Paul understood this, and he gloried in the losses which brought him such unspeakable rewards. "But what things were gain to me, those I counted loss for Christ. Yea doubtless, and I count all things but loss for the excellency of the knowledge of Christ Jesus my Lord: for whom I have suffered the loss of all things, and do count them but dung, that I may win Christ, and be found in him."

Even the "thorn in the flesh," the messenger of Satan sent to buffet him, became a "chariot of God" to his willing soul and carried him to the heights of triumph which he could have reached in no other way. To "take pleasure" in one's trials, what is this but to turn them into the grandest of chariots?

Joseph had a revelation of his future triumphs and reigning, but the chariots that carried him there looked to the eye of sense like dreadful Juggernaut cars of failure and defeat. Slavery and imprisonment are strange chariots to take one to a kingdom, and yet by no other way could Joseph have reached high exaltation. And our exaltation to the spiritual throne that awaits us is often reached by similar chariots.

The great point, then, is to have our eyes opened to see in everything that comes to us a "chariot of God," and to learn how to mount into these chariots. We must recognize each thing that comes to us as being really God's chariot for us, and must accept it as from Him. He does not command or originate the thing, perhaps; but the moment we put it into His hands, it becomes His, and He at once turns it into a chariot for us. He makes all things, even bad things, work together for good to all those who trust Him. All He needs is to have them entirely committed to Him.

When your trial comes, then, put it right into the will of God, and climb into that will as a little child climbs into its mother's arms. The baby carried in the chariot of its mother's arms

rides triumphantly through the hardest places, and does not even know they are hard. And how much more we who are carried in the chariot of the "arms of God!"

No doubt the enemy will try to turn your chariot into a Juggernaut car by **taunting** you with the suggestion that God is not in your trouble, and that there is no help for you in Him. But you must utterly disregard all such suggestions, and must overcome them with the assertion of a confident faith. "God is [my] refuge and strength, a very present help in trouble," must be your continual declaration, no matter what the seemings may be.

Moreover, you must not be half-hearted about it. You must climb wholly into your chariot, not with one foot dragging on the ground. There must be no "ifs," or "buts," or "supposings," or questionings. You must accept God's will fully, and must hide yourself in the arms of His love, that are always underneath to receive you, in every circumstance and at every moment.

The soul that thus rides with God "on the sky" has views and sights of things that the soul which grovels on the earth can never have. The poor crushed and bleeding victim under the Juggernaut car can see only the dust and stones and the grinding wheels, but the triumphant rider in the chariot sees far fairer sights.

Do any of you ask where your chariots are to

be found? The Psalmist says, "The chariots of God are twenty thousand, even thousands of angels." There is never in any life a lack of chariots. One dear Christian said to me, "I am a poor woman, and have all my life long grieved that I could not drive in a carriage like some of my rich neighbors. But I have been looking over my life and I find that it is so full of chariots on every side that I am sure I shall never need to walk again."

If all our eyes could be opened today we should see our homes, and our places of business, and the streets we **traverse**, filled with the "chariots of God." There is no need for any one of us to walk for lack of chariots. That misunderstanding, that **mortification**, that unkindness, that disappointment, that loss, that defeat,—all these are chariots waiting to carry you to the very heights of victory you have so longed to reach.

Mount into them, then, with thankful hearts, and lose sight of all second causes in the shining of His love, who will "carry you in his arms" safely and triumphantly over it all.

 ## Testing for Understanding

1. When the author speaks of earthly cares, she means
    a. worries over material riches.
    b. pressures of life which we have control over.
    c. unpleasant experiences which we cannot change.
    d. the consequences of our wrongdoings.

2. Earthly cares are a distress to the soul because
    a. we fail to see their true worth in helping us to rise higher in our Christian experience.
    b. they bring misery and wretchedness.
    c. we bring them upon ourselves.
    d. they are a tool of Satan's rather than of God's.

3. In order to face earthly cares calmly, the author says we need
    a. others around us who are calm.
    b. faith in the invisible chariot of God moving in our lives.
    c. a full understanding of the good that this experience will work in our lives.
    d. time to leave these cares and lose ourselves in some other satisfaction.

4. Some people are more subject to self-pity and despair than others because
    a. they seek out tribulation.
    b. they encounter tribulation more often.
    c. the trials they encounter are usually more severe.
    d. they interpret trials as instruments of misery rather than of victory.

5. We can say that our chariots of life experiences are "paved with love"
    a. when we find them pleasant and easy.
    b. if we allow God to make them lovely and pleasant experiences.
    c. because they help us to show love to others.
    d. when we recognize that God, in His love, sent them.

6. According to this article, sometimes our prayers seem unanswered because
   a. we have not prayed fervently enough.
   b. we do not really have sufficient faith that God can answer them.
   c. God is really answering us in a different way from what we imagine.
   d. we have not waited long enough.

7. Men are inclined to trust in earthly things rather than in God because
   a. they have insufficient proof of God's ability to help them.
   b. God does not offer His help unless we demand it.
   c. earthly things are easily seen and felt by human sense and therefore easier to believe.
   d. trust in earthly things yields swifter results.

8. By destroying our earthly chariots God shows
   a. vengeance.
   b. severity and sternness.
   c. love and mercy.
   d. omnipotence.

9. The solution to life's problems is found in
   a. God and our own experiences.
   b. God and our relationships.
   c. God and our Christian work.
   d. God alone.

10. Disappointments and trials seem severe because
    a. their immediate earthly discomfort looms greater than the eventual heavenly joy to be gained by them.
    b. we can not understand the reason for any of them in this life.
    c. God makes them severe to us in order that we may learn the intended lesson.
    d. we forget that others have suffered trials, too.

 *Reading for Understanding*

1. *And when our eyes are thus opened, we shall see in all the events of life, whether great or small, whether joyful or sad, a "chariot" for our souls.*
   This sentence is saying that
   a. if God allows an experience to come into our lives, He can use it to make us grow spiritually.
   b. we can grow spiritually in any circumstance in the world.
   c. some of God's chariots are capable of carrying us further than others and we must choose the best ones.
   d. All of God's chariots can be seen if our spiritual eyes are open.

2. *These "heavenly places" are interior, not exterior, and the road that leads to them is interior also. But the chariot that carries the soul over this road is generally some outward loss or trial or disappointment.*
   The author is saying that
   a. both the trial and the result it works in us are states of the mind.
   b. the trial is usually physical and tangible but the result it works in us is spiritual.
   c. we will not experience the triumph from our trials until we reach heaven.
   d. others will be able to see our trial but never the result which it works in us.

3. *One day it occurred to her that she had for a long while been praying for patience, and that perhaps this slow servant was the very chariot the Lord had sent to carry her soul over into patience.*

The mistress

a. had expected the Lord to remove the slowness of the servant.

b. had been praying for patience without really expecting the Lord to give it to her.

c. had been praying for patience long before this servant began to work for her.

d. had expected the Lord to bestow upon her tolerance for her servant's slowness without any effort on her part.

4. *She ventured to say quietly, "Friends, I am lying here riding in a chariot!" The effect was instantaneous, and perfect quiet reigned!*

The response of the other ladies is evidence that

a. they had not been aware of her presence.

b. they were insulted.

c. they also had heard about "chariots" and understood that they were disturbing her.

d. they had been discussing chariots.

5. *And God is obliged often to destroy all our own earthly chariots before He can bring us to the point of mounting into His.*

From this we learn that

a. God would allow us to keep our earthly chariots if we would also ride in His.

b. the powers of evil are sometimes stronger than the powers of good.

c. God sometimes removes our earthly resources so that we realize that He alone is substantial to trust.

d. we are not truly trusting in God unless we have suffered severe material loss or disappointment.

Meditating for Meaning

1. The first sentence says that "earthly cares are a heavenly discipline."

a. Define *discipline* as it is used in this sentence.

b. How does this discipline differ from the discipline you considered in the last selection?

c. Explain how earthly cares are a heavenly discipline.

d. Chariots provide transportation. Why does seeing earthly cares as chariots make them "better than discipline"?

2. Rather than looking like chariots, these earthly cares look like Juggernaut cars. From a dictionary discover the connotation(s) accompanying a chariot which contrast(s) with the connotation of Juggernaut cars. What characteristics would an experience need to have in order to look like a chariot?

3. Both the Juggernaut car and the chariot of God are associated with deities. Contrast them after studying the footnote on page 340.

a. What contrast do you see in the part the deity plays in each?

b. What contrast do you see in what each deity does for the worshiper?

c. What contrast do you see in the visibility of each type of conveyance?

d. Summarize your answers to a, b, and c. What contrast do you see in the natures of these two deities?

4. The story of the prophet of God and his servant confronted by the army of the King of Syria shows us the source of fear (2 Kings 6:13-18).
   a. What caused the servant to cry out in fear?
   b. Why could the prophet sit calmly without fear?
   c. What then can we conclude is lacking in our experience when we begin to fear?

5. The same circumstance can be a Juggernaut car or a chariot of God to us.
   a. What two responses determine which it becomes in our experience?
   b. Who turns our experience into a chariot? Into a Juggernaut car?

6. Consider the wisdom of the paradox that God uses unpleasant experiences to bring us happiness. This is not, on God's part, a perverse delight in man's misfortune.
   a. What must God do to our earthly chariots?
   b. What would happen to man if he had only pleasant experiences? (See Deuteronomy 6:10-12.)
   c. How does removal of the pleasant experiences carry him to heights of Christian experience?
   d. List the two Bible characters mentioned in this article whose earthly cares became chariots of God and briefly explain the "chariot" experience of each.

7. The author suggests that we climb into God's will as a child climbs into its mother's arms. What quality of a child is she telling us to imitate?

Looking for Literary Technique

Difficult concepts are more easily understood when we compare them to a familiar idea. Authors do this in various ways. In this article, besides the basic symbol of a chariot, the author used several stories, both Biblical and modern. When an author or a speaker tells a short story of a person's experience to illustrate his point, we say he is giving an anecdote.

1. Find two anecdotes in this article and tell the point each illustrated.

The author also used allusions to emphasize her points. An allusion is an indirect reference to a well-known piece of literature or fact, as the mention of the Juggernaut car. Unlike an anecdote, an allusion is often little more than a hint. A reader must be familiar with the literature or fact which is the origin of the allusion if he is to understand the author's point. Allusions are like seasonings in food. They are most delightful when they are merely hints.

2. Find two Scriptural allusions in this article and briefly explain the comparison the author is making in each.

Writing for Skill

Choose a concept which may be easily illustrated by anecdotes. In an article explain how this concept affects the Christian's life. Illustrate your point with anecdotes and allusions. The anecdotes may be from your own personal experience or those of others. Although allusions may be taken from other pieces of literature or history besides the Bible, you will probably find it easier to use Biblical allusions. Choose a symbol to represent your concept. For instance, if you choose to write on *pride*, you might title your article "The Dragon of Pride."

The Discipline of Deformity

by V. Raymond Edman

If a cow doesn't produce much milk, the dairyman sells her. If a piece of oak is full of knots, the cabinetmaker tosses it aside. If a piece of fabric bears a blemish, the seamstress cuts around it. No one wants to work with inferior materials. But if a human being is physically deformed, does God cast him out because he's imperfect? In the following article you will see what perfect use God can make of "inferior materials."

Defining for Comprehension

Choose the word or phrase below which most nearly defines each word at the left as it is used in this selection.

1. **defamation**   a. hunger   b. slander   c. decay

2. **recompense**   a. payment   b. promise   c. punishment

3. **cankered**   a. corrupted   b. irritated   c. desired

4. **indelible**   a. tasteless   b. unreadable   c. permanent

5. **engenders**   a. attacks   b. supports   c. produces

6. **fain**   a. mocking   b. exhausted   c. eagerly desirous

7. **introspection**   a. self-analysis   b. criticism   c. detective work

8. **introversion**   a. indrawnness   b. complete change   c. translation

9. **exultation**   a. praise; fame   b. rejoicing   c. secrecy

10. **solicitude**	a. aloneness	b. forbiddenness	c. concern
11. **intimate**	a. close in association	b. famous	c. fearful; shy
12. **pale**	a. container	b. territory	c. fear
13. **bane**	a. blessing	b. exile	c. curse
14. **preposterous**	a. ridiculous	b. impossible	c. announced beforehand
15. **remonstrated**	a. protested	b. showed an example	c. destroyed
16. **inconspicuous**	a. argumentative	b. not obvious	c. not neat
17. **impotence**	a. rudeness	b. indistinctness	c. powerlessness
18. **rudimentary**	a. formed in layers	b. undeveloped	c. coarse

The Discipline of Deformity

There are few, if any, disciplines of the soul that sink as deeply into the human spirit as that of physical deformity. Doubt, discouragement, **defamation**, desperation, even disease does not dig so deeply into the inner heart as does bodily handicap. Frustration and fear follow it, so that life itself seems mad folly and utter futility; while the Most High, in His infinite tenderness and mercy says, "Strengthen ye the weak hands, and confirm the feeble knees. Say to them that are of a fearful heart, Be strong, fear not: behold, your God will come with vengeance, even God with a **recompence**; he will come and save you. Then the eyes of the blind shall be opened, and the ears of the deaf shall be unstopped. Then shall the lame man leap as an hart, and the tongue of the dumb sing: for in the wilderness shall waters break out, and streams in the desert" (Isaiah 35:3-6).

One remembers Lord's Byron's bitterness of soul over his physical handicap, as he said,

My poor mother was generally in a rage every day and used to render me sometimes almost frantic; particularly when, in her passion, she reproached me with my personal deformity, I have left her presence to rush into solitude, where, unseen, I could vent the rage and mortification I endured, and curse the deformity, that I now began to consider as a signal work of the injustice of Providence. Those were bitter moments; even now, the impression of them is vivid in my mind; and they **cankered** a heart that I believe was naturally affectionate, and destroyed a temper always disposed to be violent. It was my feeling at this period that suggested the idea of

"The Deformed Transformed." I often look back on the days of my childhood, and am astonished at the recollection of the intensity of my feelings at that period;—the first impressions are **indelible**. My poor mother, and after her my school-fellows by their taunts, had led me to consider my lameness as the greatest misfortune, and I have never been able to conquer this feeling. It requires great natural goodness of disposition, as well as reflection, to conquer the corroding bitterness that deformity **engenders** in the mind, and which, while preying on itself, sours one toward all the world. I have read, that where personal deformity exists, it may be always traced in the face, however handsome the face may be. I am sure that what is meant by this is, that the consciousness of it gives to the countenance an habitual expression of discontent, which I believe is the case; yet it is too bad (added Byron with bitterness) that, because one had a defective foot, one cannot have a perfect form.

One sits beside Byron in sorrow of spirit, for one would **fain** have him turn from the **introspection** and **introversion** of the "corroding bitterness . . . which while preying on itself, sours one toward all the world" to the assurance and uplift of Isaiah's promise, "The lame take the prey" (Isaiah 33:23). If he, and thousands with him, could only hearken to the testimony of one who had an unspeakably cruel "thorn" in his flesh the nature of which is nowhere revealed, from which "thorn" he prayed earnestly to be delivered, but without avail. He learned, however, and would teach Lord Byron if he could, that there is a delight higher than deliverance; for he learned from the Lord Jesus Christ, that, "My grace is sufficient for thee: for my strength is made perfect in weakness" (2 Corinthians 12:9). Therefore he could say with inner **exultation**, "Most gladly therefore will I rather glory in my infirmities, that the power of Christ may rest upon me. Therefore I take pleasure in infirmities, in reproaches, in necessities, in persecutions, in distresses for Christ's sake: for when I am weak, then am I strong" (2 Corinthians 12:9, 10).

Grace that is sufficient, strength made perfect in weakness, pleasure in infirmities, strength when I am weak, that the power of Christ may rest upon me: this is the discipline of deformity. This is the triumph over the thorn, the song over the suffering, the rejoicing over reproach, the glorying in grace, the defeat of deformity.

The lame have access to the king, and are the special object of his **solicitude**. Is there story lovelier than that of David's desire to help the son of Jonathan, because of the heart covenant he had made with the companion of his youth! (1 Samuel 20:14-16; 23:18; 2 Samuel 21:7). He found that there remained one son of Jonathan, Mephibosheth by name, "which is lame on his feet" (2 Samuel 9:3). For the lame there was love, thoughtfulness, tenderness, care and provision, even privilege to eat at the king's table. "So Mephibosheth dwelt in Jerusalem: for he did eat continually at the king's table; and was lame on both his feet" (9:13). Handicapped, but a special home in the court; infirm, but on **intimate** terms with his Majesty; lame, but loved by David; deformed, but dining with the king. And has the Lord of Glory, David's greater Son, less compassion for the crippled?

The leper has service for his king. Outside the **pale** of his people, "unclean" by highest judgment, unwanted by fellow humans, the leper seemed a burden to himself and a **bane** to others. Yet it was the leper whom God sent to show that the enemy had fled, that food had become available in abundance to the starving multitudes of Samaria, as he had promised through his servant Elisha (2 Kings 7). The promise, "Tomorrow about this time shall a measure of fine flour be sold for a shekel, . . . in the gate of Samaria" seemed so **preposterous** that a minister of state **remonstrated**, "Behold, if the LORD would make windows in heaven, might this thing be?" (vv. 1, 2).

The Almighty does have windows in heaven (Malachi 3:10), from which to pour blessings upon His needy children; but He delights in using the useless, in dispatching the deformed, to open them. The four lepers in the story led their king and country to the accomplishment of God's promise. The **inconspicuous** have their inning, the incompetent make their contribution, the unsightly serve their God and fellow men, and the handicapped help open windows in heaven!

Who can have more compassion on the weak than have the crippled, or more heart for the helpless than the handicapped?

God's "lame ones" and "lepers" can bring love and lilt of laughter to others. His blind ones can cause them to see glories hitherto hidden. Is there a Christian heart unmoved by the message of that hymn, "O, Love That Wilt Not Let Me Go," especially when it remembers that its author was blind? The late Rev. George Matheson, D.A., of Edinburgh was blind; yet he could see the wonders of God's love, and point others to them. With a heart overflowing with faith he could say to his fellow-handicapped, and to all of us:

> My soul, it was by the gate of the temple called Beautiful that the lame man was laid; in the moments of thine **impotence**, remember that. Remember that thine experience of the cross is itself the gate into the temple of sympathy. It may be that here thy lot is simply to lie low— to be prostrated on a bed of pain. That battered gate is the most beautiful of all.

About the Author

V. Raymond Edman (1900-1967) born in Chicago, Illinois, was educated in Boston University and Clark University of Massachusetts. He served as a missionary to the Quichua Indians of Ecuador and was president of Wheaton College, Wheaton, Illinois, for 25 years. Edman died of a heart attack while speaking to the Wheaton student body. He had written over a dozen devotional books, including *The Disciplines of Life*.

> It is thy training for the right service. It is thy school for learning the art of mercy. The barrier that chains thee is a **rudimentary** wing; one day thou shalt fly with it.

Seeing in the shadow of blindness, singing in the sadness of sorrow, serving in the loneliness of lameness, strengthened in the grace that is sufficient: this is the discipline of deformity, that makes sweet our spirit, and strengthens that of others.

Meditating for Meaning

1. This essay says that, "Doubt, discouragement, defamation, desperation, even disease does not dig so deeply into the inner heart as does bodily handicap."
   a. How does the nature of doubt, discouragement, defamation, and desperation differ from the nature of bodily handicap?
   b. Why do you think these would be easier to bear than bodily handicap?

2. Isaiah speaks of God showing special interest in the bodily handicapped through the entrance of Christ into the world.
   a. Find a Bible reference of a time when Christ literally performed each of the following:
      opened the eyes of the blind
      unstopped the ears of the deaf
      made the lame to walk
      made the dumb to speak
   b. Today Christ is not here to work miracles in this same way. How can the physically blind, deaf, lame, and dumb of Christ's kingdom see, hear, walk in, and speak the truths of God though they may not experience bodily healing? (Consider people like Fanny Crosby and Helen Keller.)
   c. Christ made blind men to see, deaf to hear, lame to walk, and dumb to speak who never experienced physical handicaps. Explain how this could be. (Matt. 13:15, John 3:1-21).
   d. Which of these two types of handicap is greater? Explain.

3. Physical deformity can have one of two effects on a person.
   a. How did Lord Byron allow his physical handicap to affect him, and how did he come to regard it?
   b. What two factors influenced him to react in this way?
   c. Byron reflects that "it is too bad that, because one had a defective foot one cannot have a perfect form." What was he probably referring to by a perfect form?

4. The author uses a metaphor from Isaiah and reverses it to show the mistake which Byron made in relation to his handicap.
   a. Find and explain the author's use of this metaphor.
   b. What did this mistake cause in Byron's experience?
   c. Why do you think the attitude Byron had about his deformity had this effect and why is this attitude a mistake?

5. Isaiah, though speaking of Judah overcoming Assyria, was prophesying the deliverance and victory which would come to the new Zion, Christ's church. The mention of the lame is figurative.
   a. What paradox do you see in Isaiah's metaphor?
   b. How is this true in relation to salvation and the church?
   c. How should this be an encouragement to the physically handicapped?

6. A poem written by Byron appears on page 212.
   a. Check a biographical dictionary or encyclopedia and tell briefly who Byron was.
   b. In spite of Byron's wrong response to his handicap, what do his accomplishments prove about a handicapped person?

7. Paul, too, suffered physical handicap.
   a. What did Paul, like most handicapped people, crave in relation to his handicap?
   b. What did he discover was far better than the realization of this craving?

8. God loves the handicapped.
   a. What two Bible accounts does this article mention to prove this?
   b. Do you think God allows handicaps because He enjoys seeing people suffer? Explain.

9. Handicapped people quite often do respond properly to their handicap.
   a. From the article give several ways in which a handicapped person can benefit others.
   b. From the article give several ways in which a person's handicap can be a benefit to himself.

10. What significance in relation to handicapped persons did George Matheson see in the blind man being laid at the temple gate called Beautiful?

Looking for Literary Technique

Likely no other selection of literature in this text is as outstanding in its use of alliteration as the one which you have just read. Alliteration, you will recall from earlier study, is the repetition of initial consonant sounds of consecutive or nearly consecutive words. This repetition produces a music which is pleasant to both the ear and the tongue.

Alliteration, like music, loses some of its beauty when it is too loud and raucous, when the tones stand out rather than blending in. For best effect, alliteration should enter subtly. We should enjoy its music without really being conscious of what we are enjoying. Simply put, alliteration should not be overdone. The point at which alliteration is overdone must be a personal judgment for each reader.

Some examples of alliteration in the essay are particularly pleasing.

1. From this essay, find five examples of alliteration which you consider particularly pleasing.

While some related ideas, such as doubt and discouragement, are naturally alliterated, it takes special skill to compose a wholly alliterated series like *doubt, discouragement, defamation, desperation,* even *disease*. Notice how the author achieves this. Perhaps he recognized the trend toward the repeated *d* in *doubt* and *discouragement*, but the rest of his series could have been thought of as *shame, hopelessness,* and *sickness*. To complete his pattern of alliteration, he needed simply to look for synonyms of shame, hopelessness, and sickness in a thesaurus. A mental thesaurus is sometimes more reliable because it is less likely to suggest illogical and forced synonyms.

2. Using a thesaurus (mental or mechanical), find synonyms for the following words to form a logical, alliterated series of character traits:

       endurance,   dependability,   harmony,   refinement,   carefulness

Writing for Skill

Choose a paragraph of at least 75 to 100 words from one of the first two selections of this unit. Rewrite this paragraph, inserting as much alliteration into it as you can. Try to make your alliteration sound natural rather than "loud and raucous." Also retain as nearly as possible the author's meaning. You will likely find it easier if you choose a paragraph with compound nouns, verbs, and adjectives.

Reflections on
Ambition

Follow after charity,

and desire spiritual gifts,...

forasmuch as ye are

zealous of spiritual gifts,

seek that ye may excel

to the edifying

of the church.

1 Corinthians 14:1,12

Acres of Diamonds

by Russell H. Conwell

Two girls may own identical wardrobes. Yet the one may be rich while the other is poor. Two boys may own identical pocketknives. Yet the one may be wealthy and the other poverty-stricken. How can this be when the parents have the same financial net worth? God said of the church at Smyrna, "I know thy . . . poverty, (but thou art rich)." The farmer in this story began the day a wealthy man, but ended it as a poor man. Yet he had not lost anything between morning and evening. In this story you will see clearly this paradox of riches.

When going down the Tigris and Euphrates rivers many years ago with a party of English travelers I found myself under the direction of an old Arab guide whom we hired up at Bagdad, and I have often thought how that guide resembled our barbers in certain mental characteristics. He thought that it was not only his duty to guide us down those rivers and do what he was paid for doing, but also to entertain us with stories curious and weird, ancient and modern, strange and famil-

iar. Many of them I have forgotten, and I am glad I have, but there is one I shall never forget.

The old guide was leading my camel by its halter along the banks of those ancient rivers, and he told me story after story until I grew weary of his story-telling and ceased to listen. I did not become irritated with that guide when he lost his temper as I ceased listening. But I remember that he took off his Turkish cap and swung it in a circle to get my attention. I could see it through the corner of my eye, but I determined not to look straight at him for fear he would tell another story. But I did finally look, and as soon as I did he went right into another story.

Said he, "I will tell you a story now which I reserve for my particular friends." When he emphasized the words "particular friends," I listened, and I have ever been glad I did.

The old guide told me that there once lived not far from the River Indus an ancient Persian by the name of Ali Hafed. He said that Ali Hafed owned a very large farm, that he had orchards, grain-fields, and gardens: that he had money at interest, and was a wealthy and contented man. He was contented because he was wealthy, and wealthy because he was contented. One day there visited the old Persian farmer one of those ancient Buddhist priests, the wise men of the East. He sat down by the fire and told the old farmer how this world of ours was made. He said that this world was once a mere bank of fog, and that the Almighty thrust His finger into this bank of fog, and began slowly to move His finger around, increasing the speed until at last He whirled this bank of fog into a solid ball of fire. Then it went rolling through the universe, burning its way through other banks of fog, and condensed the moisture without, until it fell in floods of rain upon its hot surface, and cooled the outward crust. Then the internal fires bursting outward through the crust threw up the mountains and hills, the valleys, the plains and the prairies of this wonderful world of ours. If this internal molten mass came bursting out and cooled very quickly it became granite: less quickly copper, less quickly silver, less quickly gold, and, after gold, diamonds were made.

Said the old priest, "A diamond is a congealed drop of sunlight." The old priest told Ali Hafed that if he had one diamond the size of his thumb, he could purchase the county, and that if he had a mine of diamonds he could place his children upon thrones through the influence of their great wealth.

Ali Hafed heard all about diamonds, how much they were worth, and went to bed that night a poor man. He had not lost anything, but he was poor because he was discontented, and discontented because he feared he was poor. He said, "I want a mine of diamonds," and he lay awake all night.

Early in the morning he sought out the priest. I know by experience that a priest is very cross when awakened early in the morning. And when he shook that old priest out of his dreams, Ali Hafed said to him:

"Will you tell me where I can find diamonds?"

"Diamonds! What do you want with diamonds?"

"Why, I wish to be immensely rich."

"Well, then, go along and find them. That is all you have to do: go and find them, and then you have them."

"But I don't know where to go."

"Well, if you will find a river that runs through white sands, between high mountains, in those white sands you will always find diamonds."

"I don't believe there is any such river."

"Oh yes, there are plenty of them. All you have to do is go and find them, and then you have them."

Said Ali Hafed, "I will go."

So he sold his farm, collected his money, left his family in charge of a neighbor, and away he went in search of diamonds. He began his search, very properly to my mind, at the Mountains of the Moon. Afterward he came around into Palestine, then wandered on into Europe, and at last when his money was all spent and he was in rags, wretchedness, and poverty, he stood on the shore of that bay at Barcelona, in Spain, where a great tidal wave came rolling in between the pillars of Hercules, and the poor, afflicted, suffering, dying man could not resist the awful temptation to cast himself into that incoming tide, and he sank beneath its foaming crest, never to rise in this life again.

When that old guide had told me that awfully sad story he stopped the camel I was riding on and went back to fix the baggage that was coming off another camel, and I had an opportunity to muse over his story while he was gone. I remember saying to myself, "Why did he reserve that story for his 'particular friends'?" There seemed to be no beginning, no middle, no end, nothing to it. That was the first story I had ever heard in my life in which the hero was killed in the first chapter. I had but one chapter of that story, and the hero was dead.

When the guide came back and took up the halter of my camel, he went right ahead with the story, into the second chapter, just as though there had been no break. The man who purchased Ali Hafed's farm one day led his camel into the garden to drink, and as that camel put its nose into the shallow water of that garden brook, Ali Hafed's successor noticed a curious flash of light from the white sands of the stream. He pulled out a black stone having an eye of light reflecting all the hues of the rainbow. He took the pebble into the house and put it on the mantel which covers the central fires, and forgot all about it.

A few days later this same old priest came in to visit Ali Hafed's successor, and the moment he opened that drawing-room door he saw that flash of light on the mantel, and he rushed up to it, and shouted: "Here is a diamond! Has Ali Hafed returned?"

"Oh no, Ali Hafed has not returned, and that is not a diamond. That is nothing but a stone we found right out here in our own garden."

"But," said the priest, "I tell you I know a diamond when I see it. I know positively that is a diamond."

Then together they rushed out into that old garden and stirred up the white sands with their fingers, and lo! there came up other more beautiful and valuable gems than the first. "Thus," said the guide to me, and, friends, it is historically true, "was discovered the diamond mine of Golcanda, the most magnificent diamond mine in all the history of mankind, excelling the Kimberly itself. The Kohinoor, and the Orlof of the crown jewels of England and Russia, the

About the Author

Russell H. Conwell (1843–1925) was born to abolitionist parents in South Worthington, Massachusetts. At the age of 15, he left his home, which was a station on the Underground Railroad, and worked his way to Europe on a cattle ship. Later he returned and studied in Yale University where he became an atheist. He served as a recruiting officer during the Civil War and later as a lawyer in Minneapolis and Boston. War injuries and finally the death of his wife turned him back to God, and he became a Baptist minister in Lexington, Massachusetts. Conwell founded Temple University in Philadelphia for working people and became an editor, author, and lecturer. He gave "Acres of Diamonds" many times as a lecture, donating the proceeds to education.

largest on earth, came from that mine."

When the old Arab guide told me the second chapter of his story, he then took off his Turkish cap and swung it around in the air again to get my attention to the moral. As he swung his hat, he said to me, "Had Ali Hafed remained at home and dug in his own cellar, or underneath his own wheat fields, or in his own garden, instead of wretchedness, starvation, and death by suicide in a strange land, he would have had 'acres of diamonds.' For every acre of that old farm, yes, every shovelful, afterward revealed gems which since have decorated the crowns of monarchs."

When he had added the moral to his story I saw why he reserved it for "his particular friends." It was his way of saying indirectly what he did not dare say directly, that "in his private opinion there was a certain young man then traveling down the Tigris River that might better be at home in America."

Testing for Understanding

1. The narrator of the *entire* story was
    a. an American.   b. an Arab.   c. an Englishman.   d. a Persian farmer.

2. The Arab guide
    a. told stories for his own entertainment.
    b. made up the stories he told.
    c. didn't like to talk to inattentive listeners.
    d. told stories, hoping his tourists would pay more.

3. Ali Hafed's basic mistake was
    a. he listened to the old priest's story.
    b. he sold his farm.
    c. he fancied that diamonds would bring him contentment.
    d. he began his search at the wrong place.

4. The fact that Ali Hafed sold his farm and left home to begin his search best demonstrates the saying
    a. The grass is always greener on the other side of the fence.
    b. Happiness is not in doing but in being.
    c. A prophet is not without honor except in his own country.
    d. Riches take wings and fly away.

5. The climax of the guide's story was when
    a. Ali sold his farm.
    b. Ali jumped into the bay at Barcelona.
    c. Ali's successor found a pebble in his garden brook.
    d. a diamond mine was discovered in Ali Hafed's old garden.

6. Ali Hafed did not recognize his farm as a diamond mine because
    a. the diamonds only came to the surface of the soil after his successor bought it.
    b. he did not know what a diamond looks like.
    c. the priest had told him he would need to travel far away to find diamonds.
    d. he believed that immense riches could not be found at home.

7. The fact that Ali Hafed's successor placed the pebble on the mantel shows
    a. his recognition of its value.
    b. his appreciation of beauty.
    c. his superstition.
    d. his inclination to hoard.

8. In his storytelling the Arab guide could best be described as
    a. amusing and entertaining.
    b. pesky and tiresome.
    c. frank and impudent.
    d. insightful and discreet.

9. The Arab's skill as a storyteller came from all the following except
    a. his insistence on first having his hearer's attention.
    b. inserting appropriate pauses.
    c. his ability to get his point across without causing offense.
    d. his insensitivity to when his listener would rather hear no more.

10. The point of the Arab's story was
    a. Life's greatest riches are found through contentment where we are.
    b. He that will be rich troubleth his own house.
    c. What doth it profit a man if he gain the whole world and lose his own soul?
    d. Don't despair; success may lie just ahead.

Reading for Understanding

1. *I have often thought how that guide resembled our barbers in certain mental characteristics. He thought that it was not only his duty to guide us down those rivers and do what he was paid for doing, but also to entertain us with stories curious and weird, ancient and modern, strange and familiar.*

   The author was commenting that barbers are known
   a. to have odd mental characteristics.
   b. to be vivid storytellers.
   c. to give their customers more than their money's worth.
   d. to be good tourist guides.

2. *Ali Hafed heard all about diamonds, how much they were worth, and went to bed that night a poor man. He had not lost anything, but he was poor because he was discontented, and discontented because he feared he was poor.*

   Ali Hafed was poor now instead of wealthy as he had been at the beginning of the day because
   a. he now realized that in comparison to diamonds he owned little.
   b. he realized this would set him on a course to poverty.
   c. he had sold his farm.
   d. his greed had been awakened, and he no longer appreciated what he had.

3. *"Well, then, go along and find them. That is all you have to do: go and find them, and then you have them."*

   The old priest meant that
   a. diamonds are easy to find.
   b. diamonds are of little value.
   c. He may not have been trying to imply anything from the statements but merely wished to be left alone.
   d. he did not want to give away the secret location of diamonds.

4. *When he had added the moral to his story I saw why he reserved it for "his particular friends."*
   The author realized that when the storyteller spoke of his particular friends
   a. he meant those who listened most politely to him.
   b. he meant those with whom he felt a special oneness.
   c. he meant those in whom he recognized a special need for the morals of his stories.
   d. he was speaking ironically and actually meant those whom he liked least.

5. *It was his way of saying indirectly what he did not dare say directly, that "in his private opinion there was a certain young man then traveling down the Tigris River that might better be at home in America."*
   The storyteller
   a. felt imposed upon to guide the main character.

b. felt it was unsafe for the main character to be traveling down the Tigris River.

c. wished he lived in America.

d. thought the main character was wasting his time and money on the curiosities of travel.

Meditating for Meaning

1. When we encounter ideas which oppose Scripture in our reading, this does not necessarily totally discount the value of the piece of literature, but should cause us to root ourselves more firmly in Bible truths. Compare the Buddhist priest's version of how the world was made with Genesis 1.

    a. What true cause of Creation did he recognize which evolutionists mainly reject?

    b. Why do you think evolutionists reject this cause?

    c. If you were confronted by an evolutionist and his false theories, what argument(s) would you use to dispute his beliefs?

    d. What is basically wrong with his description of Creation? Support your answer by Scripture.

2. There are two kinds of riches and two kinds of poverty.

    a. Identify these four states from Proverbs 13:7.

    b. Of the two kinds of riches, which is the greater? Explain.

    c. Of the two kinds of poverty, which is the worse? Explain.

    d. Only one of these four states is actually condemned in Scripture, and only one is commanded. Identify these two. (See Revelation 3:17, 18.)

3. These four states of riches and poverty occur in pairs in the experiences of mankind.

    a. List four different pair combinations in which these states could occur in a person's life.

    b. At the beginning of the story, Ali Hafed was materially rich and "spiritually" rich in the sense that he was content. Find two other combinations that occur in this story. Explain when and how they occur in the story.

    c. If Ali had discovered the acres of diamonds he sought, would he have been richer than he had been at the beginning? Explain.

4. There is an irony which often occurs in the experience of those who are greedy of gain. Often in their greedy endeavors, men defeat their own ends.

    a. Explain how this irony took place in Ali Hafed's experience.

    b. What do you think is the reason that this irony occurs?

5. Wealth alone does not condemn a man. Many men of God such as Abraham have been wealthy men.

    a. Study the following verses and describe the conditions under which wealth becomes a curse.

        (1) Psalm 62:10b

        (2) Proverbs 13:11

        (3) Ecclesiastes 5:13

        (4) Jeremiah 9:23

        (5) James 2:6

        (6) 1 Timothy 6:9

    b. Which of these verses seems to best define Ali Hafed's problem? Explain.

    c. Think of your answers to 5a. Give ways money can become a snare to us.

    d. Give examples of ways in which wealth can be a blessing rather than a curse.

Looking for Literary Technique

Stories are interesting. Everyone recognizes this fact. So naturally a story within a story could make that story doubly interesting. But the story-within-a story technique which you have just encountered is valuable from another standpoint.

Some stories can be likened unto pills in that both are intended to cure ills. But a story without a theme has no curing power.

Not all cures, however, are pleasant. Like many pills, stories are distasteful and hard to "swallow" when their themes are too pertinent, too aggressive with their curing power. So good stories, like some pills, are candy-coated to make them easier to swallow. This coaxes the reader to take the medicine.

The Arab storyteller recognized the value of this, and he gave his cure in a story. The author also recognized the value of this and gave the Arab's story in a story. Notice the several paragraphs in this story which are *not* part of the old Arab's story.

1. What details and aspects of these paragraphs make them valuable to the story?

2. How is the point of this story easier to accept as a result of the author telling that someone told it to him?

Writing for Skill

Think of a time when someone, perhaps your father, mother, grandfather or grandmother, told you a story to teach you a lesson. Tell the story of how you were told that story. Show what effect the story had on you, thus bringing the same effect on your readers. To add flavor to your story, include interesting characteristics of your storyteller as Conwell did in the story you just read.

The Man Who Planted Hope and Grew Happiness

by Jean Giono

Landfills are full to overflowing. Environmentalists say "recycle." But we may counter with "I'm only one person. What difference will it make what I do with my half-dozen plastic bottles and cardboard cartons?"

The country's finances are deplorable. Economists say "budget." But we reply "I'm only one citizen. What difference will my five dollars make?"

World morals hit new lows daily. The Bible says, "Let your light so shine." But our logic says "I'm only one Christian. What difference will my witness make in this midnight of sin?"

Elzéard Bouffier, too, faced seemingly insurmountable odds in the story you are about to read. But he proved that one person can make a difference.

Defining for Comprehension	Choose the word or phrase below which most nearly defines each word at the left as it is used in this selection.		
1. egoism	a. irritability	b. freedom	c. self-interest
2. vestiges	a. garments	b. hallways	c. traces
3. ferocity	a. speed	b. viciousness	c. association
4. meticulous	a. tiny; small	b. painstaking	c. slow-moving

5. **servile**	a. simple	b. fierce	c. acting lowly; humble
6. **irrational**	a. unreasonable	b. unusual	c. selfish
7. **indiscretion**	a. crossing place	b. lack of wisdom	c. boisterousness
8. **solitude**	a. aloneness	b. concern	c. height
9. **caprice**	a. wealth	b. whim	c. youthful activity
10. **attributed**	a. gained	b. gave credit to	c. paid taxes to
11. **predisposes**	a. discards early	b. makes susceptible	c. purchases
12. **incontestable**	a. hateful	b. unrestrained	c. undebatable
13. **dilapidated**	a. shabby	b. separated into layers	c. spread out
14. **tenacity**	a. anger	b. steadfastness	c. unspeaking
15. **benevolence**	a. criminal acts	b. unclearness	c. generosity

The Man Who Planted Hope and Grew Happiness

For a human character to reveal truly exceptional qualities, one must have the good fortune to be able to observe its performance over many years. If this performance is devoid of all **egoism**, if its guiding motive is unparalleled generosity, if it is absolutely certain that there is no thought of recompense and that, in addition, it has left its visible mark upon the earth, then there can be no mistake.

About forty years ago I was taking a long trip on foot over mountain heights quite unknown to tourists in that ancient region where the Alps thrust down into Provence. All this, at the time I embarked upon my long walk through these deserted regions, was barren and colorless land. Nothing grew there but wild lavender.

I was crossing the area at its widest point, and after three days walking found myself in the midst of unparalleled desolation. I camped near the **vestiges** of an abandoned village. I had run out of water the day before, and had to find some. These clustered houses, although in ruins, like an old wasps' nest, suggested that there must once have been a spring or well here. There was, indeed, a spring, but it was dry. The five or six houses, roofless, gnawed by wind and rain, the tiny chapel with its crumbling steeple, stood about like the houses and chapels in living villages, but all life had vanished.

It was a fine June day, brilliant with sunlight, but over this unsheltered land, high in the sky, the wind blew with unendurable **ferocity**. It growled over the carcasses of the houses like a lion disturbed at its meal. I had to move my camp.

After five hours' walking I had still not found water, and there was nothing to give me any hope of finding any. All about me was the same dryness, the same coarse grasses. I thought I glimpsed in the distance a small black silhouette, upright, and took it for a trunk of a solitary tree. In any case I started towards it. It was a shepherd. Thirty sheep were lying about him on the baking earth.

He gave me a drink from his watergourd and, a little later, took me to his cottage in a fold of the plain. He drew his water—excellent water—from a very deep natural well above which he had constructed a primitive winch.

The man spoke little. This is the way of those who live alone, but one felt that he was sure of himself, and confident in his assurance. That was unexpected in this barren country. He lived, not in a cabin, but in a real house built of stone that bore plain evidence of how his own efforts had reclaimed the ruin he had found there on his arrival. His roof was strong and sound. The wind on its tiles made the sound of the sea upon its shores.

The place was in order, the dishes washed, the floor swept, his rifle oiled; his soup was boiling over the fire. I noticed then that he was cleanly shaved, that all his buttons had been mended with the **meticulous** care that makes the mending invisible. He shared his soup with me. His dog, as silent as himself, was friendly without being **servile**.

It was understood from the first that I should spend the night there; the nearest village was still more than a day and a half away. And besides I was perfectly familiar with the nature of the rare villages in that region. There were four or five of them scattered well apart from each other on these mountain slopes, among white-oak thickets, at the extreme end of the wagon roads. They were inhabited by charcoal-burners, and the living was bad. Families, crowded together in a climate that is excessively harsh both in winter and in summer, found no escape from the unceasing conflict of personalities. **Irrational** ambition reached inordinate proportions in the continual desire for escape. The men took their wagonloads of charcoal to the town, then returned.

The soundest characters broke under the perpetual grind. The women nursed their grievances. There was rivalry in everything, over the price of charcoal as over a pew in the church. And over all there was the wind, also ceaseless to rasp upon the nerves. There were epidemics of suicide and frequent cases of insanity, usually homicidal.

The shepherd went to fetch a small sack and poured out a heap of acorns on the table. He began to inspect them, one by one, with great concentration, separating the good from the bad. I did offer to help him. He told me that it was his job. And in fact, seeing the care he devoted to the task, I did not insist. That was the whole of our conversation. When he had set aside a large enough pile of good acorns he counted them out by tens, meanwhile eliminating the small ones or those which were slightly cracked, for now he examined them more closely. When he had thus selected one hundred perfect acorns he stopped and he went to bed.

There was peace in being with this man. The next day I asked if I might rest here for a day. He found it quite natural—or, to be more exact, he gave me the impression that nothing could startle him. The rest was not absolutely necessary, but I was interested and wished to know more about him. He opened the pen and led his flocks to pasture. Before leaving, he plunged his sack of carefully selected and counted acorns into a pail of water. I noticed that he carried for a stick an iron rod as thick as my thumb and about a yard and a half long. Resting myself by walking, I followed a path parallel to his. His pasture was in a valley. He left the little flock in the charge of the dog and climbed towards where I stood. I was afraid that he was about to rebuke me for my **indiscretion**, but it was not that at all; this was the way he was going, and he invited me to go along if I had nothing better to do. He climbed to the top of the ridge about a hundred yards away.

There he began thrusting his iron rod into the earth, making a hole in which he planted an acorn; then he refilled the hole. He was planting oak trees. I asked him if the land belonged to him. He answered no. Did he know whose it was? He did not. He supposed it was community property, or perhaps belonged to people who cared nothing about it. He was not interested in finding out whose it was. He planted his hundred acorns with the greatest of care. After the midday meal he resumed his planting. I suppose I must have been fairly insistent in my questioning, for he answered me. For three years he had been planting trees in this wilderness. He had planted 100,000. Of these, 20,000 had sprouted. Of the 20,000 he still expected to lose about half to rodents or to the unpredictable designs of Providence. There remained 10,000 oak trees to grow where nothing had grown before.

That was when I began to wonder about the age of this man. He was obviously over fifty. Fifty-five he told me. His name was Elzéard Bouffier. He had once had a family in the lowlands. There he had had his life. He had lost his only son, then his wife. He had withdrawn into this **solitude**, where his pleasure was to live leisurely with his lambs and his dog. It was his opinion that this land was dying for want of trees. He added that, having no very pressing business of his own, he had resolved to remedy this state of affairs.

Since I was at that time, in spite of my youth, leading a solitary life, I understood how to deal gently with solitary spirits. But my very youth forced me to consider the future in relation to myself and to a certain quest for happiness. I told him that in thirty years his 10,000 oaks would be magnificent. He answered quite simply that if God granted him life, in thirty years he would have planted so many more that these 10,000 would be like a drop of water in the ocean.

Besides, he was now studying the reproduction of beech trees and had a nursery of seedlings grown from beechnuts near his cottage. The seedlings, which he protected from his sheep with a wire fence, were very beautiful. He was also considering birches for the valleys where, he told me, there was a certain amount of moisture a few yards below the surface of the soil.

The next day we parted.

During the following year came the war of 1914, during which I hardly had time for reflecting upon trees. To tell the truth, the thing itself had made no impression upon me; I had considered it as a hobby, a stamp collection, and forgotten it.

Six years later I again took the road to the barren lands.

The countryside had not changed. However, beyond the deserted village I glimpsed in the distance a sort of greyish mist that covered the mountaintops like a carpet. Since the day before, I had begun to think again of the shepherd tree-planter. "Ten thousand oaks," I reflected, "really take up quite a bit of space." I had seen too many men die during those five years of war not to imagine easily that Elzéard Bouffier was dead, especially since, at twenty, one regards men of fifty as old men with nothing left to do but die. He was not dead. As a matter of fact he was extremely spry. He had changed jobs. Now he had only four sheep but, instead, a hundred beehives. He had got rid of the sheep because they threatened his young trees. For, he told me (and I saw for myself), the war had disturbed him not at all. He had imperturbably continued to plant.

The oaks of 1910 were then ten years old and taller than either of us. It was an impressive spectacle. I was literally speechless and, as he did not talk, we spent the whole day walking in silence through his forest. In three sections, it measured eleven kilometers in length and three kilometers at its greatest width.

He had pursued his plan, and beech trees as high as my shoulder, spreading out as far as the eye could reach, confirmed it. He showed me handsome clumps of birch planted five years before—that is, in 1915. He had set them out in all the valleys where he had guessed—and rightly—that there was moisture almost at the surface of the ground. They were delicate and very well established.

It all seemed to come about in a sort of chain reaction. He did not worry about it; he was determinedly pursuing his task in all its simplicity; but as we went back towards the village I saw water flowing in brooks that had been dry since the memory of man. This was the most impressive result of chain reaction that I had seen. These dry streams had once, long ago, run with water. Some of the dreary villages I mentioned before had been built on the sites of ancient Roman settlements, traces of which still remained; and archaeologists, exploring there, had found fishhooks where, in the twentieth century, cisterns were needed to assure a small supply of water.

The wind, too, scattered seeds. As the water reappeared, so there reappeared willows, rushes, meadows, gardens, flowers, and a certain purpose in being alive. But the transformation took place so gradually that it became part of the pattern without causing any astonishment. Hunters, climbing into the wilderness in pursuit of hares or wild boar, had of course noticed the sudden growth of little trees, but had attributed it to some **caprice** of the earth. That is why no one meddled with Elzéard Bouffier's work. If he had been detected he would have had opposition. He was undetectable. Who in the villages or in the administration could have dreamed of such perseverance in a magnificent generosity?

I saw Elzéard Bouffier for the last time in June of 1945. He was then eighty-seven. I had started back along the route through the wastelands; but now, in spite of the disorder in which the war had left the country, there was a bus running between the Durance Valley and the mountain. I **attributed** the fact that I no longer recognized the scenes of my earlier journeys to this relatively speedy transportation. It took the name of a village to convince me that I was actually in that region that had been all ruins and desolation.

The bus put me down at Vergons. In 1913 this hamlet of ten or twelve houses had three inhabitants. They had been savage creatures, hating one another, living by trapping game. All about them nettles were feeding upon the remains of abandoned houses. Their condition had been beyond hope. For them, nothing but to await death—a situation which rarely **predisposes** to virtue.

Everything was changed. Even the air. Instead of the harsh dry winds that used to attack me, a gentle breeze was blowing, laden with scents. A sound like water came from the

About the Author

Jean Giono (1895-1970) only son of a traveling cobbler, was born in Manosque, France. He left college to help his aging father, and began writing poetry and plays. During World War I he fought at Verdun. After the war he spoke and wrote passionately opposing war, occasioning his imprisonment in 1939. Adopting views similar to Tolstoy, Giono lived simply with his wife, two daughters, and blind mother in their native village where he wrote novels about the peasants.

mountains; it was the wind in the forest; most amazing of all, I heard the actual sound of water falling into a pool. I saw that a fountain had been built, that it flowed freely and—what touched me most—that someone had planted a linden beside it, a linden that must have been four years old, already in full leaf, the **incontestable** symbol of resurrection.

Besides, Vergons bore evidence of labor at the sort of undertaking for which hope is required. Hope, then, had returned. Ruins had been cleared away, **dilapidated** walls torn down and five houses restored. Now there were twenty-eight inhabitants, four of them young married couples. There new houses, freshly plastered, were surrounded by gardens where vegetables and flowers grew in orderly confusion, cabbages and roses, leeks and snapdragons, celery and anemones. It was now a village where one would like to live.

From that point I went on foot. The war just finished had not allowed the full blooming of life, but Lazarus was out of the tomb. On the lower slopes of the mountain I saw little fields of barley and rye; deep in that narrow valley the meadows were turning green.

It has taken only the eight years since then for the whole countryside to glow with health and prosperity. On the site of the ruins I had seen in 1913, now stand neat farms, cleanly plastered, testifying to a happy and comfortable life. The old streams, fed by the rains and

THE MAN WHO PLANTED HOPE   365

snows that the forest conserves, are flowing again. Their waters have been channeled. On each farm, in groves of maples, fountain pools overflow on to carpets of fresh mint. Little by little the villages have been rebuilt. People from the plains, where land is costly, have settled here, bringing youth, motion, the spirit of adventure. Along the roads you meet hearty men and women, boys and girls who under-stand laughter and have recovered a taste for picnics.

When I compute the unfailing greatness of spirit and the **tenacity** of **benevolence** that it must have taken to cause this land of Canaan to spring from wasteland, I am taken with an immense respect for that old and unlearned peasant who was able to complete a worthy work with God's help.

 *Testing for Understanding*

1. The setting of this story is
   a. western Canada.
   b. France.
   c. southern Italy.
   d. mid-southern Asia.

2. The man found the shepherd
   a. coldly hostile.
   b. rough and indifferent.
   c. quiet and precise.
   d. eager for fellowship.

3. This story shows that to maintain sanity and healthy relations, humans need
   a. a carefully planned and executed form of government.
   b. time for undisturbed relaxation and recreation.
   c. substantial material means and modern education.
   d. to think of others and to do good.

4. By planting acorns in land whose owner he did not know, the man showed his
   a. ignorance of local villages.
   b. disinterest in human companionship.
   c. preference of long- and wide-range good over personal advancement.
   d. eccentric nature willfully void of recognition of property rights.

5. The shepherd was accustomed to a survival rate on his oak trees of
   a. one percent.   b. ten percent   c. twenty percent   d. fifty percent.

6. The region had most likely become a windswept desert because
   a. the trees which were the natural means of water retention had been destroyed.
   b. it had suffered decades of drought.
   c. unwise crop farming methods had encouraged severe wind erosion.
   d. it was an unprosperous region by nature.

7. The fact that the deserted villages had been built on the sites of ancient Roman villages where fishhooks were found shows us that
   a. this was once the site of a highly advanced civilization.
   b. war had destroyed civilization in the area.
   c. people of centuries past had succumbed to the area's discouraging odds.
   d. there once had been dependable water sources in the region.

8. The lapse of time between the young man's first two visits to the mountain region was approximately
   a. one year.   b. five years.   c. seven years.   d. ten years.

9. Elzéard Bouffier's work was largely unnoticed because
   a. he avoided society.
   b. it happened so gradually.
   c. it had little effect.
   d. no one ever ventured that far into the wilderness.

10. The author wrote this story to show
    a. the necessity of not disturbing natural ecology.
    b. the importance of solitude for some personalities.
    c. the interesting oddities of Elzéard Bouffier's personality.
    d. the far-reaching good that we can work by unselfish pursuits.

 *Reading for Understanding*

1. *For a human character to reveal truly exceptional qualities, one must have the good fortune to be able to observe its performance over many years. If this performance is devoid of all egoism, if its guiding motive is unparalleled generosity, if it is absolutely certain that there is no thought of recompense and that, in addition, it has left its visible mark upon the earth, then there can be no mistake.*
   The author is commenting that
   a. unless we watch a person's character for many years we are sure to misjudge it.
   b. character of unusual worth is recognized by its consistent and unselfish labor for mankind.
   c. any character unusual enough to affect the world permanently can have no flaws.
   d. it is a blessing to live around an outstanding character for many years and be molded by its influence.

2. *It was understood from the first that I should spend the night there; the nearest village was still more than a day and a half away.*
   When the traveler met the shepherd
   a. he asked if he could spend the night there.
   b. the shepherd insisted that he spend the night there.
   c. the shepherd had been expecting his visit and had prepared overnight lodging.
   d. both understood without much discussion of it that the traveler would spend the night there because there was no other lodging within a day's travel.

3. *But my very youth forced me to consider the future in relation to myself and to a certain quest for happiness. I told him that in thirty years his 10,000 oaks would be magnificent.*
   The young man
   a. found it difficult to understand how Elzéard Bouffier could spend so much effort on something so apparently unprofitable to himself.
   b. considered Bouffier's oaks folly because he could not see any benefit in them for himself.
   c. took no interest in the trees but wanted to make Bouffier feel good.
   d. was interested in the oaks as a future logging venture for himself.

4. *To tell the truth, the thing itself had made no impression upon me; I had considered it as a hobby, a stamp collection, and forgotten it.*
   The young man
   a. disdained hobbies.
   b. hadn't foreseen the long-range effects of the man's efforts.
   c. ridiculed the trees as a waste of time.
   d. had failed to see the beauty of the trees.

5. *Now there were twenty-eight inhabitants, four of them young married couples.*
   It is significant that one-seventh of the population were young married couples because
   a. only young people could survive the rigors of this land.
   b. it proved that the land now offered entertainment to attract the young.
   c. it showed that the inhabitants were now able to live in peace.
   d. it promised new life for the area, new hope, and population growth.

Meditating for Meaning

1. When we reflect upon the first paragraph of the story, we realize that the author had concluded that Elzéard Bouffier had truly exceptional qualities of character.
   a. Find and copy the phrase in which he said each of the following about Bouffier:
      He never expected to be paid for his efforts
      He was not striving for personal fame
      He worked for the sole purpose of giving to others
   b. The author also mentions that Bouffier left a visible mark upon the earth. Do you think this is necessary to leave a tangible mark in order to have a character with exceptional qualities? Explain.
   c. What does the author say is necessary in order to see such qualities in another person?
   d. How did his own experience with Bouffier prove the value of this?
   e. How can this help us in our experiences with others?

2. Men often create their own perils.
   a. Check a dictionary or encyclopedia and tell what a charcoal-burner is.
   b. How did these villagers probably create their own perils?
   c. How did this affect their morals and why?
   d. How might they have avoided their problem?
   e. What other similar perils can you think of which men have created for themselves?

3. The villagers were obviously unhappy.
   a. What causes does the author give for their unhappiness?
   b. Besides correcting these problems, what else would have been necessary in order to restore happiness to them?
   c. Explain how your answer to *b* could actually have corrected the problem of *a*.

4. Elzéard Bouffier shows a proper way of responding to trial.
   a. What trials did he suffer in early life?
   b. What response of his is often the mistake of those who suffer trial?
   c. Explain why this response can be wrong.
   d. In what proper way did he respond that usually helps one to overcome trial?

5. Although this story is fictitious, we can apply its truths to our own lives. Suggest how you could follow the example of Elzéard Bouffier.

Looking for Literary Technique

This story effectively uses several literary techniques which you have studied earlier.
1. Copy two similes from the first four paragraphs. Explain how the connotation is fitting.
2. Find and explain the metaphor which the author used to describe the abandoned houses.
3. Find and explain an allusion to a New Testament event used near the end of the story.

The author uses another tool called a **synecdoche** when he speaks of "men and women, boys and girls who . . . have recovered a taste for picnics." One meaning of synecdoche is a part used to symbolize the whole. The author is mentioning more than the mere fact that these people take picnics. Picnicking conveys a connotation of freedom, lightsomeness, and joy in living, perhaps even merriment. Rather than stating the larger and more abstract concept, the author more efficiently gets his point across by giving an example of the concept.

Writing for Skill

Choose five concepts (such as *joy*) and give a *synecdoche* to colorfully express each.

RMS Titanic

by Hanson Baldwin

The source of many of mankind's greatest calamities and severest catastrophes can be traced backward through quivering neurons to the deadly stimulus of pride. Satan, the Bible tells us, was lifted up in pride, and God cast him out of heaven. Rare is the age that has not known its Babel enterprise, an aircastle of man's conceit that God crumpled with one blow. But perhaps no single event of more recent times so colorfully portrays the painful fall that awaits the haughty spirit as the story of the **Titanic.** *Read and interpret the facts of this disaster as Baldwin presents them.*

Defining for Comprehension

Choose the word or phrase below which most nearly defines each word at the left as it is used in this selection.

1. **quay**
   a. bird of open meadow
   b. expression of fear
   c. pier; wharf

2. **writhed**
   a. twisted like a snake
   b. resented
   c. sought escape

3. **promenade**
   a. stroll
   b. demand action
   c. supply

4. **proximity**
   a. closeness
   b. outer edge
   c. youth

5. **ascertain**
   a. determine with certainty
   b. acquire
   c. close off

6. **quorum**
   a. question
   b. select group
   c. politeness

7. **warren**
   a. guard
   b. reminder
   c. maze

8. **corroborated**	a. folded up	b. became rough	c. supported
9. **leviathan**	a. anything very large	b. long life	c. musical instrument
10. **launched**	a. snacked	b. set out; began	c. musical instrument
11. **perfunctory**	a. out of use	b. uncommon	c. halfhearted
12. **foundered**	a. sunk	b. established	c. fabricated

RMS Titanic

The White Star liner *Titanic*, largest ship the world had ever known, sailed from Southhampton on her *maiden voyage*[1] to New York on April 10, 1912. The paint on her *strakes*[2] was fair and bright; she was fresh from Harland and Wolff's Belfast yards, strong in the strength of her forty-six thousand tons of steel, bent, hammered, shaped and riveted through the three years of her slow birth.

There was little fuss and fanfare at her sailing; her sister ship, the *Olympic*—slightly smaller than the *Titanic*—had been in service for some months and to her had gone the thunder of the cheers.

But the *Titanic* needed no whistling steamers or shouting crowds to call attention to her superlative qualities. Her bulk dwarfed the ships near her as *longshoremen*[3] *singled up*[4] her mooring lines and cast off the turns of heavy rope from the *dock bollards*[5]. She was not only the largest ship afloat, but was believed to be the safest. Carlisle, her builder, had given her double bottoms and had divided her hull into sixteen watertight compartments, which made her, men thought, unsinkable. She had been built to be and had been described as a gigantic lifeboat. Her designers' dreams of a *triple-screw*[6] giant, a luxurious, floating hotel, which could speed to New York at *twenty-three knots*,[7] had been carefully translated from blueprints and *mold-loft lines*[8] at the Belfast yards into a living reality.

The *Titanic's* sailing from Southhampton, though quiet, was not wholly uneventful. As the liner moved slowly toward the end of her dock that April day, the surge of her passing sucked away from the **quay** the steamer *New York*, moored just to seaward of the *Titanic's* berth. There were sharp cracks as the manila mooring lines of the *New York* parted under the

---

1. maiden voyage: the first voyage of a ship.
2. strakes: metal plates along the side of a ship.
3. longshoremen: dock workers who load and unload ships.
4. singled up: let run freely.
5. dock bollards: thick posts on the dock to which a ship is secured by ropes.
6. triple-screw: The ship had three propellers.
7. twenty-three knots: twenty-three nautical miles per hour; approximately 26.45 land miles per hour.
8. mold-loft lines: a pattern for ship building.

strain. The frayed ropes **writhed** and whistled through the air and snapped down among the waving crowd on the pier; the *New York* swung toward the *Titanic's* bow, was checked and dragged back to the dock barely in time to avert a collision. Seamen muttered, thought it an ominous start.

Past Spithead and the Isle of Wight the *Titanic* steamed. She called at Cherbourg at dusk and then laid her course for Queenstown. At 1:30 p.m. on Thursday, April 11, she *stood out*[9] of Queenstown harbor, screaming gulls soaring in her wake, with 2,201 persons—men, women, and children—aboard.

Occupying the Empire bedrooms and the Georgian suites of the first-class accommodations were many well-known men and women—Colonel John Jacob Astor and his young bride; Major Archibald Butt, military aide to President Taft, and his friend, Frank D. Miller, the painter; John B. Thayer, vice-president of the Pennsylvania Railroad, and Charles M. Hays, president of the Grand Trunk Railway of Canada; W. T. Stead, the English journalist; Jacques Futrelle, French novelist; H. B. Harris, theatrical manager, and Mrs. Harris; Mr. and Mrs. Isidor Straus; and J. Bruce Ismay, chairman and managing director of the White Star line.

Down in the plain wooden cabins of the *steerage*[10] class were 706 immigrants to the land of promise, and trimly stowed in the great holds was a cargo valued at $420,000: oak beams, sponges, wine, *calabashes*,[11] and an odd miscellany of the common and the rare.

The *Titanic* took her departure on Fastnet Light and, heading into the night, laid her course for New York. She was due at Quarantine the following Wednesday morning.

Sunday dawned fair and clear. The *Titanic* steamed smoothly toward the west, faint streamers of brownish smoke trailing from the funnels. The *purser*[12] held services in the saloon in the morning; on the steerage deck aft the immigrants were playing games and a

Scotsman was puffing "The Campbells Are Coming" on his bagpipes in the midst of the uproar.

At 9 a.m. a message from the steamer *Caronia* sputtered into the wireless shack:

CAPTAIN, TITANIC—WESTBOUND STEAMERS REPORT BERGS *GROWLERS*[13] AND FIELD ICE IN 42 DEGREES N. FROM 49 DEGREES TO 51 DEGREES W. 12TH APRIL.

COMPLIMENTS—

BARR.

It was cold in the afternoon; the sun was brilliant, but the *Titanic*, her screws turning over at 75 revolutions per minute, was approaching the Banks.

In the Marconi cabin Second Operator Harold Bride, earphones clamped on his head, was figuring accounts; he did not stop to answer when he heard MWL, Continental Morse for the nearby Leyland liner, *Californian*, calling the *Titanic*. The *Californian* had some message about three icebergs; he didn't bother then to take it down. About 1:42 p.m. the rasping spark of those days spoke again across the water. It was the *Baltic*, calling the *Titanic*, warning her of ice on the steamer track. Bride took the message down and sent it up to the bridge. The officer-of-the-deck glanced at it; sent it to the bearded master of the *Titanic*, Captain E. C. Smith, a veteran of the White Star service. It was lunch time then; the Captain, walking along the **promenade** deck, saw Mr. Ismay, stopped, and handed him the message without comment. Ismay read it, stuffed it in his pocket, told two ladies about the icebergs, and resumed his walk. Later, about 7:15 p.m., the Captain requested the return of the message in order to post it in the chart room for the information of officers.

Dinner that night in the Jacobean dining room was gay. It was bitter on deck, but the night was calm and fine; the sky was moonless but studded with stars twinkling coldly in the

---

9. stood out: moved; traveled.
10. steerage: cheap passenger accommodations near the rudder.
11. calabashes: large hard-shelled gourds.
12. purser: ship officer in charge of passengers' comfort and welfare.
13. growlers: small icebergs.

clear air.

After dinner some of the second-class passengers gathered in the saloon, where the Reverend Mr. Carter conducted a "hymn sing-song." It was almost ten o'clock and the stewards were waiting with biscuits and coffee as the group sang:

> O, hear us when we cry to Thee
> For those in peril on the sea.

On the bridge Second Officer Lightoller—short, stocky, efficient—was relieved at ten o'clock by First Officer Murdock. Lightoller had talked with other officers about the **proximity** of ice; at least five wireless ice warnings had reached the ship; lookouts had been cautioned to be alert; captains and officers expected to reach the field at any time after 9:30 p.m. At twenty-two knots its speed unslackened, the *Titanic* plowed on through the night.

Lightoller left the darkened bridge to his relief and turned in. Captain Smith went to his cabin. The steerage was long since quiet; in the first and second cabins lights were going out; voices were growing still, people were asleep. Murdock paced back and forth on the bridge, peering out over the dark water, glancing now and then at the compass in front of Quartermaster Hichens at the wheel.

In the crow's nest, Lookout Frederick Fleet and his partner, Leigh, gazed down at the water, still and unruffled in the dim, starlit darkness. Behind and below them the ship, a white shadow with here and there a last winking light; ahead of them a dark and silent and cold ocean.

There was a sudden clang. "Dong-dong. Dong-dong. Dong-dong. Dong!" The metal clapper of the great ship's bell struck out 11:30. Mindful of the warnings, Fleet strained his eyes, searching the darkness for the dreaded ice. But there were only the stars and the sea.

In the wireless room, where Philips, first operator, had relieved Bride, the buzz of the *Californian's* set again crackled into the earphones:

Californian: "Say, old man, we are stuck here, surrounded by ice."

Titanic: "Shut up, shut up; keep out. I am talking to Cape Race; you are jamming my signals."

Then, a few minutes later—about 11:40 . . .

Out of the dark she came, a vast, dim, white, monstrous shape directly in the *Titanic's* path. For a moment Fleet doubted his eyes. But she was a deadly reality, this ghastly thing. Frantically, Fleet struck three bells—something dead ahead. He snatched the telephone and called the bridge:

"Iceberg! Right ahead!"

The First Officer heard but did not stop to acknowledge the message.

"Hard starboard!"

Hichens strained at the wheel; the bow swung slowly to port. The monster was almost upon them now.

Murdock leaped to the engine-room telegraph. Bells clanged. Far below in the engine room those bells struck the first warning. Danger! The indicators on the dial faces swung round to "Stop!" Then "Full speed astern!" Frantically the engineers turned great valve wheels; answered the bridge bells. . . .

There was a slight shock, a brief scraping, a small list to port. Shell ice—slabs and chunks of it—fell on the foredeck. Slowly the *Titanic* stopped. Captain Smith hurried out of his cabin.

"What has the ship struck?"

Murdock answered, "An iceberg, sir. I *hard-astarboarded*[14] and reversed the engines, and I was going to *hard-aport*[15] around it, but she was too close. I could not do any more. I have closed the watertight doors."

Fourth Officer Boxhall, other officers, the carpenter, came to the bridge. The Captain sent Boxhall and the carpenter below to **ascertain** the damage.

A few lights switched on in the first and second cabins; sleepy passengers peered through porthole glass; some casually asked the stewards:

"Why have we stopped?"

---

14. hard-astarboarded: turned sharply to the right.
15. hard-aport: turn sharply to the left.

"I don't know, sir, but I don't suppose it is anything much."

In the smoking room a **quorum** of gamblers and their prey were still sitting round a poker table; the usual crowd of *kibitzers*[16] looked on. They had felt the slight jar of the collision and had seen an eighty-foot ice mountain glide by the smoking-room windows, but the night was calm and clear, the *Titanic* was "unsinkable"; they had not bothered to go on deck.

But far below, in the **warren** of passages on the starboard side forward, in the forward holds and boiler rooms, men could see that the *Titanic's* hurt was mortal. In No. 6 boiler room, where the red glow from the furnaces lighted up the naked, sweaty chests of coal-blackened firemen, water was pouring through a great gash about two feet above the floor plates. This was no slow leak; the ship was open to the sea; in ten minutes there was eight feet of water in No. 6. Long before then the stokers had raked the flaming fires out of the furnaces and had scrambled through the watertight doors into No. 5 or had climbed up the long steel ladders to safety. When Boxhall looked at the mail room in No. 3 hold, twenty-four feet above the keel, the mailbags were already floating about in the slushing water. In No. 5 boiler room a stream of water spurted into an empty bunker. All six compartments forward of No. 4 were open to the sea; in ten seconds the iceberg's jagged claw had ripped a three-hundred-foot slash in the bottom of the great *Titanic*.

Reports came to the bridge; Ismay in dressing gown ran out on deck in the cold, still, starlit night, climbed up the bridge ladder.

"What has happened?"

Captain Smith: "We have struck ice."

"Do you think she is seriously damaged?"

Captain: "I'm afraid she is."

Ismay went below and passed Chief Engineer William Bell fresh from an inspection of the damaged compartments. Bell **corroborated** the Captain's statement; hurried back down the glistening steel ladders to his duty. Man after man followed him—Thomas Andrews, one of the ship's designers, Archie Frost, the builder's chief engineer, and his twenty assistants—men who had no posts of duty in the engine room but whose traditions called them there.

On deck, in corridor and stateroom, life flowed again. Men, women, and children awoke and questioned; orders were given to uncover the lifeboats; water rose into the firemen's quarters; half-dressed stokers streamed up on deck. But the passengers—most of them—did not know that the *Titanic* was sinking. The shock of the collision had been so slight that some were not awakened by it; the *Titanic* was so huge that she must be unsinkable; the night was too calm, too beautiful, to think of death at sea.

Captain Smith ran to the door of the radio shack. Bride, partly dressed, eyes dulled with sleep, was standing behind Philips, waiting.

"Send the call for assistance."

The blue spark danced: "*CQD–CQD–CQD–CQ–*"[17]

Miles away Marconi men heard. Cape Race heard it, and the steamships *La Provence* and *Mt. Temple.*

The sea was surging into the *Titanic's* hold. At 12:20 the water burst into the seamen's quarters through a collapsed fore-and-aft wooden bulkhead. Pumps strained in the engine rooms—men and machinery making a futile fight against the sea. Steadily the water rose.

The boats were moving out—slowly; for the deckhands were late in reaching their stations, there had been no boat drill, and many of the crew did not know to what boats they were assigned. Orders were shouted; the safety valves had lifted, and steam was blowing off in a great rushing roar. In the chart house Fourth Officer Boxhall bent above a chart, working rapidly with pencil and dividers.

12:15 A.M. Boxhall's position is sent out to a fleet of vessels: "Come at once; we have struck a berg."

To the Cunarder *Carpathia* (Arthur Henry Rostron, Master, New York to Liverpool, fifty-

---

16. kibitzers: meddlesome onlookers.
17. CQD: come quick, danger—International distress signal used before days of S.O.S.

eight miles away): "It's a CQD, old man. Position *41-46 N; 50-14 W*."[18]

The blue spark dancing: "Sinking; cannot hear for noise of steam."

12:30 A.M. The word is passed: "Women and children in the boats." Stewards finish waking their passengers below; life preservers are tied on. Some men smile at the precaution. "The *Titanic* is unsinkable." The *Mt. Temple* starts for the *Titanic*: the *Carpathia*, with a double watch in her stokeholds, radios, "Coming hard." The CQD changes the course of many ships—but not of one; the operator of the *Californian*, near by, has just put down his earphones and turned in.

The CQD flashes over land and sea from Cape Race to New York; newspaper city rooms leap to life and presses whir.

On the *Titanic*, water creeps over the bulkhead between Nos. 5 and 6 firerooms. She is going down by the head; the engineers—fighting a losing battle—are forced back foot by foot by the rising water. Down the promenade deck, Happy Jock Hume, the bandsman, runs with his instrument.

12:45 A.M. Murdock, in charge on the *starboard*[19] side, eyes tragic, but calm and cool, orders boat No. 7 lowered. The women hang back; they want no boat ride on an ice-strewn sea; the *Titanic* is unsinkable. The men encourage them, explain that this is just a precautionary measure: "We'll see you again at breakfast." There is little confusion; passengers stream slowly to the boat deck. In the steerage the immigrants chatter excitedly.

A sudden sharp hiss—a streaked flare against the night; Boxhall sends a rocket towards the sky. It explodes, and a parachute of white stars lights up the icy sea. The band plays ragtime.

No. 8 is lowered, and No. 5. Ismay, still in dressing gown, calls for women and children, handles lines, stumbles in the way of an officer, is told to get back. Third Officer Pitman takes charge of No. 5; as he swings into the boat Murdock grasps his hand. "Good-by, best

wishes, old man."

No. 6 goes over the side. There are only twenty-eight people in a lifeboat with a capacity of sixty-five.

A light stabs from the bridge; Boxhall is calling in Morse flashes, again and again, to a strange ship stopped in the ice jam five to ten miles away. Another rocket drops its shower of sparks above the ice-strewn sea and the dying ship.

1:00 A.M. Slowly the water creeps higher; the fore ports of the *Titanic* are dipping into the sea. Rope squeaks through blocks; lifeboats drop jerkily seaward. Through the shouting on the decks comes the sound of the band playing ragtime.

The "Millionaires' Special" leaves the ship—boat No. 1, with a capacity of forty people, carries only Sir Cosmo and Lady Duff Gorden and ten others. Aft, the frightened immigrants mill and jostle and rush for a boat. An officer's fist flies out; three shots are fired into the air, and the panic is quelled. . . . Four men sneak unseen into a boat and hide in its bottom.

1:20 A.M. Water is coming into No. 4 boiler room. Stokers slice and shovel as water laps about their ankles—steam for the dynamos, steam for the dancing spark! As the water rises, great ash hoes rake the flaming coals from the furnaces. Safety valves pop; the stokers retreat aft, and the watertight doors clang shut behind them.

The rockets fling their splendor toward the stars. The boats are more heavily loaded now, for the passengers know the *Titanic* is sinking. Women cling and sob. The great screws aft are rising clear of the sea. Half-filled boats are ordered to come alongside the cargo ports and take on more passengers, but the boats are never filled. Others pull for the steamer's light miles away but never reach it; the light disappears. The unknown ship steams off.

The water rises and the band plays ragtime.

1:30 A.M. Lightoller is getting the *port*[20] boats

---

18. 41-46 N; 50-14 W: the point of intersection of 41 degrees 46 minutes north latitude and 50 degrees 14 minutes west longitude.
19. starboard: right side of a ship.
20. port: left side of a ship.

off; Murdock the starboard. As one boat is lowered into the sea a boat officer fires his gun along the ship's side to stop a rush from the lower decks. A woman tries to take her Great Dane into a boat with her; she is refused and steps out of the boat to die with her dog. Millet's "little smile which played on his lips all through the voyage" plays no more; his lips are grim, but he waves good-by and brings wraps for the women.

Benjamin Guggenheim, in evening clothes, smiles and says, "We've dressed up in our best and are prepared to go down like gentlemen."

1:40 A.M. Boat 14 is clear, and then 13, 16, 15, and C. The lights still shine, but the *Baltic* hears the blue spark say, "Engine room getting flooded."

The *Olympic* signals, "Am lighting up all possible boilers as fast as can."

Major Butt helps women into the last boats and waves good-by to them. Mrs. Straus puts her foot on the *gunwale*[21] of a lifeboat, then she draws back and goes to her husband: "We have been together many years; where you go I will go." Colonel John Jacob Astor puts his young wife in a lifeboat, steps back, "Good-by, dearie; I'll join you later."

1:45 A.M. The foredeck is under water, the *fo'c'sle*[22] head almost awash; the great stern is lifted high toward the bright stars; and still the band plays. Mr. and Mrs. Harris approach a lifeboat arm in arm.

Officer: "Ladies first, please."

Harris bows, smiles, steps back: "Of course, certainly; ladies first."

Boxhall fires the last rocket, then leaves in charge of boat No. 2.

2:00 A.M. She is dying now; her bow goes deeper, her stern higher. But there must be steam. Below in the *stokeholds*[23] the sweaty firemen keep steam up for the flaring lights and the dancing spark. The glowing coals slide and tumble over the slanted grate bars; the sea pounds behind that yielding bulkhead. But the spark dances on.

The *Asian* hears Philips try the new signal—SOS.

Boat No. 4 has left now; boat D leaves ten minutes later. Jacques Futrelle clasps his wife: "Go! It's your last chance; go!" Madame Futrelle is half forced into the boat. It clears the side.

There are about 660 people in the boats, and 1,500 still on the sinking *Titanic*.

On top of the officers' quarters men work frantically to get the two collapsibles stowed there over the side. Water is over the forward part of A deck now; it surges up the companionways toward the boat deck. In the radio shack, Bride has slipped a coat and lifejacket about Philips as the first operator sits hunched over his key, sending—still sending—"41-46 N.; 50-14 W. CQD—CQD—SOS—SOS—"

The Captain's tired white face appears at the radio-room door: "Men, you have done your full duty. You can do no more. Now, it's every man for himself." The Captain disappears—back to his sinking bridge, where Painter, his personal steward, stands quietly waiting for orders. The spark dances on. Bride turns his back and goes into the inner cabin. As he does so, a stoker grimed with coal, mad with fear, steals into the shack and reaches for the lifejacket on Philips' back. Bride wheels about and strikes him with a wrench.

2:10 A.M. Below decks the steam is still holding, though the pressure is falling—rapidly. In the gymnasium on the boat deck the athletic instructor watches quietly as two gentlemen ride the bicycles and another swings casually at the punching bag. Mail clerks stagger up the boat-deck stairways, dragging soaked mail sacks. The spark still dances. The band still plays—but not ragtime:

> *Nearer my God to Thee,*
> *Nearer to Thee . . .*

A few men take up the refrain; others kneel on the slanting decks to pray. Many run and scramble aft, where hundreds are clinging above the silent screws on the great uptilted

---

21. gunwale: upper edge of a boat's side.
22. fo'c'sle: forecastle; section of a ship's upper deck in the bow.
23. stokeholds: compartments surrounding the openings of a ship's furnaces and boilers.

stern. The spark still dances and the lights still flare; the engineers are on the job. The hymn comes to its close. Bandmaster Hartley, Yorkshireman violinist, taps his bow against a bulkhead, calls for "Autumn" as the water curls about his feet, and the eight musicians brace themselves against the ship's slant. People are leaping from the decks into the nearby water—the icy water. A woman cries, "Oh, save me, save me!" A man answers, "Good lady, save yourself. Only God can save you now." The band plays "Autumn":

> God of Mercy and Compassion!
> Look with pity on my pain . . .

The water creeps over the bridge where the *Titanic's* master stands; heavily he steps out to meet it.

2:17 A.M. "CQ—" The *Virginia* hears a ragged, blurred CQ, then an abrupt stop. The blue spark dances no more. The lights flicker out; the engineers have lost their battle.

2:18 A.M. Men run about blackened decks; leap into the night; are swept into the sea by the curling wave which licks up the *Titanic's* length. Lightoller does not leave the ship; the ship leaves him; there are hundreds like him, but only a few who live to tell of it. The funnels still swim above the water, but the ship is climbing to the perpendicular; the bridge is under and most of the foremast; the great stern rises like a squat **leviathan**. Men swim away from the sinking ship; others drop from the stern.

The band plays in the darkness, the water lapping upwards;

> Hold me up in mighty waters,
> Keep my eyes on things above,
> Righteousness, divine atonement,
> Peace and everlas . . .

The forward funnel snaps and crashes into the sea; its tons of steel hammer out of existence swimmers struggling in the freezing water. Streams of sparks, of smoke and steam, burst from the after funnels. The ship upends to fifty; to sixty degrees.

Down in the black abyss of the stokeholds, of the engine rooms, where the dynamos have whirred at long last to a stop, the stokers and the engineers are reeling against hot metal, the rising water clutching at their knees. The boilers, the engine cylinders, rip from their bed plates; crash through bulkheads; rumble—steel against steel.

The *Titanic* stands on end, poised briefly for the plunge. Slowly she slides to her grave—slowly at first, and then more quickly—quickly—quickly.

2:20 A.M. The greatest ship in the world has sunk. From the calm, dark waters, where the floating lifeboats move, there goes up, in the white wake of her passing, "one long continuous moan."

The boats that the *Titanic* had **launched** pulled safely away from the slight suction of the sinking ship, pulled away from the screams that came from the lips of the freezing men and women in the water. The boats were poorly manned and badly equipped, and they had been unevenly loaded. Some carried so few seamen that women bent to the oars. Mrs. Astor tugged at an oar handle; the Countess of Rothes took a tiller. Shivering stokers in sweaty, coal-blackened singlets and light trousers steered in some boats; stewards in white coats rowed in others. Ismay was in the last boat that left the ship from the starboard side; with Mr. Carter of Philadelphia and two seamen he tugged at the oars. In one of the lifeboats a man with a broken wrist—disguised in a woman's shawl and hat—huddled on the floor boards, ashamed now that fear had left him. In another rode the only baggage saved from the *Titanic*—the carry-all of Samuel L. Goldenberg, one of the rescued passengers.

There were only a few boats that were heavily loaded; most of those that were half empty made but **perfunctory** efforts to pick up the moaning swimmers, their officers and crew fearing that they would endanger the living if they pulled back into the midst of the dying. Some boats beat off the freezing victims; fear-crazed men and women struck with oars at the heads of swimmers. One woman drove her fist into the face of a half-dead man as he tried feebly to climb over the gunwale. Two other women helped him in and stanched the flow of blood from the ring cuts on his face.

One of the collapsible boats, which had floated off the top of the officers' quarters when the *Titanic* sank, was an icy haven for thirty to forty men. The boat had capsized as the boat sank; men swam to it, clung to it, climbed upon its slippery bottom, stood knee deep in water in the freezing air. Clunks of ice swirled about their legs; their soaked clothing clutched their bodies in icy folds. Colonel Archibald Gracie was cast up there. Gracie who had leaped from the stern as the *Titanic* sank; young Thayer who had seen his father die; Lightoller who had twice been sucked down with the ship and twice blown to the surface by a belch of air; Bride, the second operator, and Philips, the first. There were many stokers, half-naked; it was a shivering company. They stood there in the icy sea, under the far stars, and sang and prayed—the Lord's Prayer. After a while a lifeboat came and picked them off, but Philips was dead then or died soon afterward in the boat.

Only a few of the boats had lights; only one—No. 2—had a light that was of any use to the *Carpathia*, twisting through the ice field to the rescue. Other ships were "coming hard" too; one, the *Californian*, was still dead to opportunity.

The blue sparks still danced, but not the *Titanic's*, *La Provence* to *Celtic:* "Nobody has heard the *Titanic* for about two hours."

It was about 2:40 when the *Carpathia* first sighted the green light from No. 2 boat; it was 4:10 when she picked up the first boat and

About the Author

Baldwin Hanson (1907–1971) son of a *Baltimore Sun* editor, was born in Baltimore, Maryland. After serving three years as a naval lieutenant, he reported for *Times* magazine, winning the Pulitzer Prize in journalism. He traveled widely with the military, reporting on war events.

learned that the *Titanic* had **foundered**. The last of the moaning cries had just died away then.

Captain Rostron took the survivors aboard, boatload by boatload. He was ready for them, but only a small minority of them required much medical attention. Bride's feet were twisted and frozen; others were suffering from exposure; one died, and seven were dead when taken from the boats, and were buried at sea.

It was then that the fleet of racing ships learned they were too late; the *Parisian* heard the weak signals of MPA, the *Carpathia*, report the death of the *Titanic*. It was then—or soon afterward, when her radio operator put on his earphones—that the *Californian*, the ship that had been within sight as the *Titanic* was sinking, first learned of the disaster.

And it was then, in all its white-green majesty, that the *Titanic's* survivors saw the iceberg, tinted with the sunrise, floating idly, pack ice jammed about its base, other bergs heaving slowly nearby on the blue breast of the sea.

Testing for Understanding

1. The *Titanic* was built by the
   a. Americans.   b. British.   c. French.   d. Canadians.

2.   The efforts of the crew to avoid the iceberg at the last moment are a good illustration of
     a. closing the door after the horse is stolen.
     b. being between a rock and a hard place.
     c. leaping before you look.
     d. many hands making light work.

3.   The author depicts the night of the sinking as
     a. stern and austere, symbolic of justice about to fall.
     b. superficially peaceful, symbolic of the people's careless, unsuspecting attitude.
     c. stormy and turbulent, symbolic of the conflict between man and Providential will.
     d. ominously hilarious, foreshadowing the fall of tragedy.

4.   The ship radioing for help from ships whose warnings they had ignored reminds one of the story of
     a. Peter crying for help when he was sinking on the Sea of Galilee.
     b. Paul's shipwreck on the way to Rome.
     c. the five foolish virgins asking for oil from the five wise.
     d. Ahab calling on Jehoshaphat to help him fight Syria.

5.   In describing the "Millionaires' Special" leaving the ship, the author wants to show
     a. the luxury with which the ship was equipped.
     b. the injustice and inefficiency involved in evacuating the ship.
     c. the confidence the passengers still had in the ship.
     d. the important personages who shared the peril.

6.   The listing of the different people who rowed lifeboats shows
     a. the folly of insisting on "ladies first."
     b. the underestimated ability of women.
     c. that emergency brings all people to the same level.
     d. the value of unified effort.

7.   Most of the passengers and crew of the *Titanic* might have been spared if
     a. the other ships had made more diligent effort to come to the rescue.
     b. more rockets had been launched.
     c. the *Californian* had been aware of the *Titanic's* plight earlier.
     d. the firemen had not given up quite as soon.

8.   The total time from the collision with the iceberg to the final sinking was approximately
     a. one hour.
     b. four hours.
     c. two hours, forty minutes.
     d. six hours, twenty minutes.

9.   All of the following contributed to the tragedy of the *Titanic* except
     a. equipment malfunction.
     b. insufficient preparation.
     c. refusal to heed warnings.
     d. misplaced trust.

10. In the last paragraph the iceberg is shown as
     a. a hostile enemy.
     b. a surprisingly small creature.
     c. a being with human characteristics.
     d. awesome, serene, yet oblivious to the "minor" event of the previous night.

Reading for Understanding

1. *Murdock paced back and forth on the bridge, peering out over the dark water, glancing now and then at the compass in front of Quartermaster Hichens at the wheel.*
   Murdock's actions reveal

   a. boredom.   b. excitement.   c. uneasiness.   d. inexperience.

2. *Titanic: "Shut up, shut up; keep out. I am talking to Cape Race; you are jamming my signals."*
   The *Titanic* is here a picture of

   a. a young, ill-trained child, disrespecting his parent.

   b. a parent, taking out its frustration on an insistent child.

   c. an old person, out of step with modern realities.

   d. an independent teenager, resenting safeguards which "spoil his fun."

3. *The deckhands were late in reaching their stations, there had been no boat drill, and many of the crew did not know to what boats they were assigned.*
   The failure here was due to

   a. the lateness of the hour.

   b. the fright and confusion of the occasion.

   c. insufficient preparation because of a reckless trust.

   d. incompetence of the crew selected.

4. *Third Officer Pitman takes charge of No. 5; as he swings into the boat Murdock grasps his hand. "Good-by, best wishes, old man."*
   Murdock recognized that

   a. Officer Pitman is unaccustomed to handling a lifeboat.

   b. Officer Pitman would likely have difficulty controlling his hysterical passengers.

   c. likely the ship would be spared and the precaution of leaving in lifeboats would be proven needless.

   d. possibly the two would never see each other alive again.

5. *The band still plays—but not ragtime.*
   The author mentions the change of music to show that

   a. the situation had become too serious for lighthearted music.

   b. although the situation was perilous, people were still carousing.

   c. the band had not been notified of the danger.

   d. the oceanliner was truly luxurious.

Meditating for Meaning

1. The description and details of this account are not idle filler but carefully crafted to convey a tone and connotation. Tell what tone is achieved by each of the following:

   a. the list of passengers and cargo—well-known men and women, 706 immigrants to the land of promise, trimly stowed cargo worth $420,000

b. the Sunday activities of the passengers

c. "a dark and silent and cold ocean"

d. "naked, sweaty chests of coal-blackened firemen"

2. People reveal much about themselves by their actions and reactions. Tell what the following reveal about the ship's crew and passengers.

a. the crew's first responses to iceberg warnings

b. the first reactions of the passengers after the collision with the iceberg

c. the gentlemen riding bicycles and swinging casually at a punching bag in the gymnasium

3. What symbolism do you see in the mention of the striking of the ship's bell at 11:30 just prior to the collision?

4. After a tragedy men often ask "Why?"

a. What activities and attitudes of the builders, crew, and passengers of this ship do you think brought this catastrophe upon them?

b. What tragedies can you think of which happened in Scripture under similar circumstances? Suggest one.

5. The responses of the crew and passengers of the *Titanic* are good insights into the response of sinners when warned of judgment. Tell how each of the following responses and facts is typical of the sinner's experience.

a. The radio operator and captain ignored the *California's* warnings about icebergs.

b. The lookout and his partner "gazed down at the water, still and unruffled in the dim, starlit darkness."

c. Philips told the *Californian* to shut up because they were jamming the *Titanic's* signals.

d. Officers and engineers worked frantically after the ship struck the iceberg.

e. Gamblers felt a slight jar and saw the iceberg but continued to play because the night was calm and they thought the *Titanic* was unsinkable.

f. Many of the passengers slept through the slight shock of the collision.

g. Deckhands reached lifeboats late, unassigned, and undrilled.

h. Men smiled at precautions, refused to enter lifeboats, and talked of seeing each other again at breakfast.

i. A stoker tried to steal a lifejacket from Philips.

j. One long continuous moan went up from the scene of the sinking.

6. The band playing in the darkness stopped in the middle of a line.

a. Judging by the rhyming scheme, complete the unfinished line of the hymn.

b. What do you think is significant about the point in the wording at which they stopped?

 *Looking for Literary Technique*

A weather watcher looks at the sky, sees wisps of cirrus clouds, and says, "Precipitation within twenty-four hours." He knows what will happen because he remembers other days when cirrus clouds hung in the sky and the next day it rained. We call this a forecast or a prediction.

When you read a story you also do some forecasting. Because you know that icy roads often cause accidents in real life, you predict that when a motorist in a story is driving on icy roads, he will wreck his vehicle. Of course, not every driver on icy roads wrecks, so how do you know that this motorist will?

Foreshadowing is introduced in Unit One with the story, "Cache of Honor." Skillful authors use *foreshadowing* to hint at later happenings. The skillful reader detects these hints and makes his predictions. Foreshadowing is often very subtle, merely enough to lead the reader on, but not enough to spoil the suspense of the plot.

1. Find an incident of foreshadowing which took place during the launching of the *Titanic*.

2. Which hymn's words, sung by passengers and quoted in this account, serve as foreshadowing?

 *Writing for Skill*

Choose one of the following tragedies of history. Imagine you were writing a stirring account of this tragedy. Write one paragraph which might appear early in such an account, including some foreshadowing of the event itself. Be sure not to give the plot away. Merely hint.

—the Chicago Fire
—the Johnstown Flood
—the burning of the *Hindenburg*
—the eruption of Vesuvius at Pompeii
—the explosion of the *Challenger*

Top Man

by James Ramsey Ullman

What is it that makes men important? Who is the greatest in life? Is he the man who owns the most property, who gives the most money, whom the most people know, who tastes the most success? Jesus used a child as an illustration to answer this question for His disciples. The account you will read is an answer to this recurring question, pulled from the masses of mankind scrambling for the top. As you read, ask yourself, "Who really climbed highest?"

Defining for Comprehension

Choose the word or phrase below which most nearly defines each word at the left as it is used in this selection.

1. **taut**	a. teasing	b. stretched tightly	c. nervous
2. **bereft**	a. deprived	b. resting at anchor	c. disappeared
3. **perception**	a. understanding	b. principle	c. trickery
4. **stupendous**	a. ridiculous	b. tremendous; incredible	c. easily bent
5. **precipices**	a. steep cliffs	b. peace treaties	c. land divisions
6. **transfixed**	a. pierced	b. repaired	c. supported
7. **imminent**	a. wise; famous	b. looming	c. urgent
8. **cannonading**	a. rock climbing	b. firing cannons	c. applying for office

9. **acclimated**	a. changed from solid to gas	b. mounted	c. adjusted to climate
10. **inevitable**	a. unavoidable	b. important	c. impossible
11. **grueling**	a. crawling	b. testing	c. exhausting
12. **pre-eminently**	a. finally	b. famously	c. most importantly
13. **dissimilar**	a. in pretense	b. unlike	c. arguing
14. **audacious**	a. bold	b. roomy	c. able to be heard
15. **taciturn**	a. not talkative	b. in exchange	c. defensive
16. **capitulated**	a. overturned	b. acted as chief	c. relented; gave in
17. **arduous**	a. fervent	b. laborious	c. disagreeing
18. **reconnaissance**	a. awakening	b. inspection; exploration	c. gathering of forces
19. **caches**	a. blockades	b. hidden supplies	c. recessed areas
20. **malignant**	a. intending harm	b. pretending illness illness	c. dawdling
21. **presumably**	a. supposedly	b. swiftly	c. assuredly
22. **mettle**	a. anger	b. courageous disposition	c. interference
23. **sparred**	a. excelled	b. fought	c. parceled out
24. **pennon**	a. banner	b. punishment	c. enclosure
25. **indomitable**	a. distasteful	b. unconquerable	c. doubtless
26. **gesticulating**	a. motioning	b. figuring	c. joking
27. **abyss**	a. concern	b. beast of burden	c. bottomless hole
28. **inert**	a. complete	b. injured	c. motionless
29. **rarefied**	a. extinct	b. less dense	c. extremely frightened
30. **insuperable**	a. insurmountable	b. inferior	c. united
31. **paroxysm**	a. contrast	b. spasm	c. unconsciousness
32. **negotiated**	a. accomplished	b. distributed	c. disbelieved
33. **obliquely**	a. vaguely	b. at an angle	c. on requirement
34. **epilogue**	a. listing	b. gravestone verse	c. ending comment

Top Man

The gorge bent. The walls fell suddenly away, and we came out on the edge of a bleak, boulder-strewn valley. And there it was.

Osborn saw it first. He had been leading the column, threading his way slowly among the huge rock masses of the gorge's mouth. Then he came to the first flat, bare place and stopped. He neither pointed nor cried out, but every man behind him knew instantly what it was. The long file sprang **taut**, like a jerked rope. As swiftly as we could, but in complete silence, we came out into the open ground where Osborn stood, and raised our eyes with his.

In the records of the Indian Topographical Survey it says:

> Kalpurtha: A mountain in the Himalayas, altitude 28,000 ft. The highest peak in British India and fourth highest in the world. Also known as K 3. A formation of *sedimentary*[1] limestone. . . .

There were men among us who had spent months of their lives—in some cases, years—reading, thinking, planning about what now lay before us, but at that moment statistics and geology, knowledge, thought and plans were as remote and forgotten as the faraway western cities from which we had come. We were men **bereft** of everything but eyes, everything but the single, electric **perception**: There it was!

Before us the valley stretched away into miles of rocky desolation. To right and left it was bounded by low ridges which, as the eye followed them, slowly mounted and drew closer together until the valley was no longer a valley at all, but a narrowing, rising corridor between the cliffs. What happened then I can describe only as a single, **stupendous** crash of music. At the end of the corridor and above it—so far above it that it shut out half the sky—hung the blinding white mass of K 3.

It was like the many pictures I had seen, and at the same time utterly unlike them. The shape was there, and the familiar distinguishing features—the sweeping skirt of glaciers; the monstrous vertical **precipices** of the face and the jagged ice line of the east ridge; finally the symmetrical summit pyramid that **transfixed** the sky. But whereas in the pictures of the mountain it had always seemed unreal—a dream image of cloud, snow, and crystal—it was now no longer an image at all. It was a mass, solid, **imminent**, appalling. We were still too far away to see the windy whipping of its snow plumes or to hear the **cannonading** of its avalanches, but in that sudden silent moment every man of us was for the first time aware of it, not as a picture in his mind but as a thing, an antagonist. For all its twenty-eight thousand feet of lofty grandeur, it seemed, somehow, less to tower than to crouch—a white-hooded giant, secret and remote, but living. Living and on guard.

I turned my eyes from the dazzling glare and looked at my companions. Osborn still stood a little in front of the others. He was absolutely motionless, his young face tense and shining, his eyes devouring the mountain as a lover's might devour the face of his beloved. One could feel in the very set of his body the overwhelming desire that swelled in him to act, to come to grips, to conquer. A little behind him were ranged the other white men of the expedition: Randolph, our leader, Wittmer and Johns, Doctor Schlapp and Bixler. All were still, their eyes cast upward. Off to one side a little stood Nace, the Englishman, the only one among us who was not staring at K 3 for the first time. He had been the last to come up out of the gorge and stood now with arms folded on his chest, squinting at the great peak he had known so long and fought so tirelessly and fiercely. His lean, British face, under its mask of stubble and windburn, was expressionless. His lips were a colorless line, and his eyes seemed almost shut. Behind the *sahibs*[2] ranged the porters, bent over their staffs, their brown, seamed faces straining

---

1. sedimentary: formed by fragments of other rock deposited by water.
2. sahibs: Indian title meaning "sir" or "master" used when referring to Englishmen.

upward from beneath their loads.

For a long while no one spoke or moved. The only sounds between earth and sky were the soft hiss of our breathing and the pounding of our hearts.

Through the long afternoon, we wound slowly between the great boulders of the valley and at sundown pitched camp in the bed of a dried-up stream. The porters ate their rations in silence, wrapped themselves in their blankets, and fell asleep under the stars. The rest of us, as was our custom, sat close about the fire that blazed in the circle of tents, discussing the events of the day and the plans for the next. It was a flawlessly clear Himalayan night, and K 3 tiered up into blackness like a monstrous sentinel lighted from within. There was no wind, but a great tide of cold air crept down the valley from the ice fields above, penetrating our clothing, pressing gently against the canvas of the tents.

"Another night or two and we'll be needing the sleeping bags," commented Randolph.

Osborn nodded. "We could use them tonight, would be my guess."

Randolph turned to Nace. "What do you say, Martin?"

"Rather think it might be better to wait," he said at last.

"Wait? Why?" Osborn jerked his head up.

"Well, it gets pretty nippy high up, you know. I've seen it thirty below at twenty-five thousand on the east ridge. Longer we wait for the bags, better **acclimated** we'll get."

Osborn snorted. "A lot of good being acclimated will do if we have frozen feet."

"Easy, Paul, easy," cautioned Randolph. "It seems to me Martin's right."

Osborn bit his lip, but said nothing. The other men entered the conversation, and soon it had veered to other matters: the weather, the porters, and pack animals, routes, camps, and strategy—the **inevitable**, inexhaustible topics of the climber's world.

There were all kinds of men among the eight of us, men with a great diversity of background and interest. Sayre Randolph, whom the Alpine Club had named leader of our expedition, had for years been a well-known explorer and lecturer. Now in his middle fifties, he was no longer equal to the **grueling** physical demands of high climbing but served as planner and organizer of the enterprise. Wittmer was a Seattle lawyer, who had recently made a name for himself by a series of difficult ascents in the Coast Range of British Columbia. Johns was an Alaskan, a fantastically strong, able *sourdough*[3] who had been a ranger in the U.S. Forest Service and had accompanied many famous Alaskan expeditions. Schlapp was a practicing physician from Milwaukee; Bixler, a government meteorologist with a talent for photography. I, at the time, was an assistant professor of geology at an eastern university.

Finally, and **pre-eminently**, there were Osborn and Nace. I say "pre-eminently," because even at this time, when we had been together as a party for little more than a month, I believe all of us realized that these were the two key men of our venture. None, to my knowledge, ever expressed it in words, but the conviction was there, nevertheless, that if any of us were eventually to stand on the hitherto unconquered summit of K 3, it would be one of them, or both. They were utterly **dissimilar** men. Osborn was twenty-three and a year out of college, a compact, buoyant mass of energy and high spirits. He seemed to be wholly unaffected by either the physical or mental hazards of mountaineering and had already, by virtue of many spectacular ascents in the Alps and Rockies, won a reputation as the most skilled and **audacious** of younger American climbers. Nace was in his forties—lean, **taciturn**, introspective. An official in the Indian Civil Service, he had explored and climbed in the Himalayas for twenty years. He had been a member of all five of the unsuccessful British expeditions to K 3 and in his last attempt had attained to within five hundred feet of the summit, the highest point which any man had reached on the unconquered giant. This had been the famous tragic attempt in which his fellow climber and lifelong friend, Captain Furness,

---

3. sourdough: nickname for prospectors in Alaska and northwestern Canada.

had slipped and fallen ten thousand feet to his death. Nace rarely mentioned his name, but on the steel head of his ice ax were engraved the words: TO MARTIN FROM JOHN. If fate were to grant that the ax of any one of us should be planted upon the summit of K 3, I hoped it would be his.

Such were the men who huddled about the fire in the deep, still cold of that Himalayan night. There were many differences among us, in temperament as well as in background. In one or two cases, notably that of Osborn and Nace, there had already been a certain amount of friction, and as the venture continued and the struggles and hardships of the actual ascent began, it would, I knew, increase. But differences were unimportant. What mattered—all that mattered—was that our purpose was one—to conquer the monster of rock and ice that now loomed above us in the night; to stand for a moment where no man, no living thing, had ever stood before. To that end we had come from half a world away, across oceans and continents to the vastnesses of inner Asia. To that end we were prepared to endure cold, exhaustion, and danger, even to the very last extremity of human endurance. Why? There is no answer, and at the same time every man among us knew the answer; every man who has ever looked upon a great mountain and felt the fever in his blood to climb and conquer, knows the answer. George Leigh Mallory, greatest of mountaineers, expressed it once and for all when he was asked why he wanted to climb unconquered Everest. "I want to climb it," said Mallory, "because it's there."

Day after day we crept on and upward. The naked desolation of the valley was unrelieved by any motion, color, or sound, and as we progressed, it was like being trapped at the bottom of a deep well or in a sealed court between great sky-scrapers. Soon we were thinking of the ascent of the shining mountain not only as an end in itself but as an escape.

In our nightly discussions around the fire, our conversation narrowed more and more to the immediate problems confronting us, and during them I began to realize that the tension between Osborn and Nace went deeper than I

had at first surmised. There were rarely any outright arguments between them—they were both far too able mountain men to disagree on fundamentals—but I saw that at almost every turn they were rubbing each other the wrong way. It was a matter of personalities chiefly. Osborn was talkative, enthusiastic, optimistic, always chafing to be up and at it, always wanting to take the short, straight line to the given point. Nace, on the other hand, was matter-of-fact, cautious, slow. He was the apostle of trial-and-error and watchful waiting. Because of his far greater experience and intimate knowledge of K 3, Randolph almost invariably followed his advice, rather than Osborn's, when a difference of opinion arose. The younger man usually **capitulated** with good grace, but I could tell that he was irked.

During the days in the valley I had few occasions to talk privately with either of them, and only once did either mention the other in any but the most casual manner. Even then, the remarks they made seemed unimportant, and I remember them only in view of what happened later.

My conversation with Osborn occurred first. It was while we were on the march, and Osborn, who was directly behind me, came up suddenly to my side.

"You're a geologist, Frank," he began without preamble. "What do you think of Nace's theory about the ridge?"

"What theory?" I asked.

"He believes we should traverse under it from the glacier up. Says the ridge itself is too exposed."

"It looks pretty mean through the telescope."

"But it's been done before. He's done it himself. All right, it's tough—I'll admit that. But a decent climber could make it in half the time the traverse will take."

"Nace knows the traverse is longer," I said; "but he seems certain it will be much easier for us."

"Easier for him is what he means." Osborn paused, looking moodily at the ground. "He was a great climber in his day. It's a shame a man can't be honest enough with himself to know when he's through." He fell silent and a moment later dropped back into his place in line.

It was that same night, I think, that I awoke to find Nace sitting up in his blanket and staring at the mountain.

"How clear it is," I whispered.

The Englishman pointed. "See the ridge?"

I nodded, my eyes fixed on the great, twisting spine of ice that climbed into the sky. I could see now, more clearly than in the blinding sunlight, its huge indentations and jagged, wind-swept pitches.

"It looks impossible," I said.

"No, it can be done. Trouble is, when you've made it, you're too done in for the summit."

"Osborn seems to think its shortness would make up for its difficulty."

Nace was silent a long moment before answering. Then for the first and only time I heard him speak the name of his dead companion. "That's what Furness thought," he said quietly. Then he lay down and wrapped himself in his blanket.

For the next two weeks the uppermost point of the valley was our home and workshop. We established our base camp as close to the mountain as we could, less than half a mile from the tongue of its lowest glacier, and plunged into the **arduous** tasks of preparation for the ascent. Our food and equipment were unpacked, inspected and sorted, and finally repacked in lighter loads for transportation to more advanced camps. Hours on end were spent poring over maps and charts and studying the monstrous heights above us through telescope and binoculars. Under Nace's supervision, a thorough **reconnaissance** of the glacier was made and the route across it laid out; then began the back-breaking labor of moving up supplies and establishing the advance stations.

Camps I and II were set up on the glacier itself, in the most sheltered sites we could find. Camp III we built at its upper end, as near as possible to the point where the great rock spine of K 3 thrust itself free of ice and began its precipitous ascent. According to our plans, this would be the advance base of operations during the climb; the camps to be established higher up, on the mountain proper, would be

too small and too exposed to serve as anything more than one or two nights' shelter. The total distance between the base camp and Camp III was only fifteen miles, but the utmost daily progress of our porters was five miles, and it was essential that we should never be more than twelve hours' march from food and shelter. Hour after hour, day after day, the long file of men wound up and down among the hummocks and crevasses of the glacier, and finally the time arrived when we were ready to advance.

Leaving Doctor Schlapp in command of eight porters at the base camp, we proceeded easily and on schedule, reaching Camp I the first night, Camp II the second and the advance base the third. No men were left at Camps I and II, inasmuch as they were designed simply as **caches** for food and equipment; and, furthermore, we knew we would need all the man power available, for the establishment of the higher camps on the mountain proper.

For more than three weeks now the weather had held perfectly, but on our first night at the advance base, as if by **malignant** prearrangement of Nature, we had our first taste of the supernatural fury of a high Himalayan storm. It began with great streamers of lightning that flashed about the mountain like a halo; then heavily, through the weird glare, snow began to fall. The wind howled about the tents with hurricane frenzy, and the wild flapping of the canvas dinned in our ears like machine-gun fire.

There was no sleep for us that night or the next. For thirty-six hours the storm raged without lull, while we huddled in the icy gloom of the tents. At last, on the third morning, it was over, and we came out into a world transformed by a twelve-foot cloak of snow. No single landmark remained as it had been before, and our supplies and equipment were in the wildest confusion. Fortunately, there had not been a single serious injury, but it was another three days before we had regained our strength and put the camp in order.

Then we waited. The storm did not return, and the sky beyond the ridges gleamed flawlessly clear, but night and day we could hear the roaring thunder of avalanches on the mountain above us. To have ventured so much as one step into that savage, vertical wilderness before the newfallen snow froze tight would have been suicidal. We chafed or waited patiently, according to our individual temperaments, while the days dragged by.

It was late one afternoon that Osborn returned from a short reconnaissance up the ridge. His eyes were shiny and his voice jubilant.

"It's tight!" he cried. "Tight as a drum! We can go!" All of us stopped whatever we were doing. His excitement leaped like an electric spark from one to another. "I went about a thousand feet, and it's sound all the way. What do you say, Sayre? Tomorrow?"

Randolph hesitated a moment, then looked at Nace.

"Better give it another day or two," said the Englishman.

Osborn glared at him. "Why?" he challenged.

"It's generally safer to wait until . . ."

"Wait! Wait!" Osborn exploded. "Don't you ever think of anything but waiting? The snow's firm, I tell you!"

"It's firm down here," Nace replied quietly, "because the sun hits it only two hours a day. Up above it gets the sun twelve hours. It may not have frozen yet."

"The avalanches have stopped."

"That doesn't necessarily mean it will hold a man's weight."

"It seems to me, Martin's point . . ." Randolph began.

Osborn wheeled on him. "Sure," he snapped. "I know, Martin's right, always right. Let him have his way, and we'll be sitting here twiddling our thumbs until the mountain falls down on us." His eyes flashed to Nace. "Maybe with a little less of that cautiousness, you English wouldn't have made such a mess of Everest. Maybe your pals Mallory and Furness wouldn't be dead."

"Osborn!" commanded Randolph sharply.

The youngster stared at Nace for another moment, breathing heavily. Then, abruptly, he turned away.

The next two days were clear and windless, but we still waited, following Nace's advice. There were no further brushes between him and Osborn, but an unpleasant air of restlessness and tension hung over the camp. I found myself chafing almost as impatiently as Osborn himself for the moment when we would break out of that maddening inactivity and begin the assault.

At last the day came. With the first paling of the sky, a roped file of men, bent almost double beneath heavy loads, began slowly to climb the ice slope just beneath the jagged line of the great east ridge. In accordance with prearranged plans, we proceeded in relays, this first group consisting of Nace, Johns, myself, and eight porters. It was our job to ascend approximately two thousand feet in a day's climbing and establish Camp IV at the most level and sheltered site we could find. We would spend the night there and return to the advance base next day, while the second relay, consisting of Osborn, Wittmer, and eight more porters, went up with their loads. This process was to continue until all necessary supplies were at Camp IV, and then the whole thing would be repeated between Camps IV and V, V and VI. From VI, at an altitude of about 26,000 feet, the ablest and fittest men—**presumably** Nace and Osborn—would make the direct assault on the summit. Randolph and Bixler were to remain at the advance base throughout the operations, acting as directors and co-ordinators. We were under the strictest orders that any man, sahib or porter, who suffered illness or injury should be brought down immediately.

How shall I describe those next two weeks beneath the great ice ridge of K 3? In a sense, there was no occurrence of importance, and at the same time everything happened that could possibly happen, short of actual disaster. We established Camp IV, came down again, went up again, came down again. Then we crept laboriously higher. The wind increased, and the air grew steadily colder and more difficult to breathe. One morning two of the porters awoke with their feet frozen black; they had to be sent down. A short while later Johns developed an uncontrollable nosebleed and was forced to descend to a lower camp. Wittmer was suffering from splitting headaches, and I from a continually dry throat. But providentially, the one enemy we feared the most did not again attack us—no snow fell. And day by day, foot by foot we ascended.

It is during ordeals like this that the surface trappings of a man are shed and his secret **mettle** laid bare. There were no shirkers or quitters among us—I had known that from the beginning—but now, with each passing day, it became more manifest which were the strongest and ablest among us. Beyond all argument, these were Osborn and Nace.

Osborn was magnificent. All the boyish impatience and moodiness which he had exhibited earlier were gone, and, now that he was at last at work in his natural element, he emerged as the peerless mountaineer he was. His energy was inexhaustible, and his speed, both on rock and ice, almost twice that of any other man in the party. He was always discovering new routes and shortcuts; and there was such vigour, buoyancy, and youth in everything he did that it gave heart to all the rest of us.

In contrast, Nace was slow, methodical, unspectacular. Since he and I worked in the same relay, I was with him almost constantly, and to this day I carry in my mind the clear image of the man—his tall body bent almost double against endless, shimmering slopes of ice; his lean brown face bent in utter concentration on the problem in hand, then raised searchingly to the next; the bright prong of his ax falling, rising, falling with tireless rhythm, until the steps in the glassy incline were so wide and deep that the most clumsy of the porters could not have slipped from them had he tried. Osborn attacked the mountain, head on. Nace studied it, **sparred** with it, wore it down. His spirit did not flap from his sleeve like a **pennon**; it was deep inside him, patient, **indomitable**.

The day came soon when I learned from him what it is to be a great mountaineer. We were making the ascent from Camp IV to V, and an almost perpendicular ice wall had made it necessary for us to come out for a few yards on the exposed crest of the ridge. There were six of us in the party, roped together, with Nace lead-

ing, myself second, and four porters bringing up the rear. The ridge at this particular point was free of snow, but razor-thin, and the rocks were covered with a smooth glaze of ice. On either side, the mountain dropped away in sheer precipices of five thousand feet.

Suddenly the last porter slipped. In what seemed to be the same instant I heard the ominous scraping of boot nails and, turning, saw a wildly **gesticulating** figure plunge sideways into the **abyss**. There was a scream as the next porter followed him. I remember trying frantically to dig into the ridge with my ax, realizing at the same time it would no more hold against the weight of the falling men than a pin stuck in a wall. Then I heard Nace shout, "Jump!" As he said it, the rope went tight about my waist, and I went hurtling after him into space on the opposite side of the ridge. After me came the nearest porter.

What happened then must have happened in five yards and a fifth of a second. I heard myself cry out, and the glacier, a mile below, rushed up at me, spinning. Then both were blotted out in a violent spasm, as the rope jerked taut. I hung for a moment, an **inert** mass, feeling that my body had been cut in two; then I swung in slowly to the side of the mountain. Above me the rope lay tight and motionless across the crest of the ridge, our weight exactly counterbalancing that of the men who had fallen on the far slope.

Nace's voice came up from below. "You chaps on the other side!" he shouted. "Start climbing slowly. We're climbing too!"

In five minutes we had all regained the ridge. The porters and I crouched panting on the jagged rocks, our eyes closed, the sweat beading our faces in frozen drops. Nace carefully examined the rope that again hung loosely between us.

"All right, men," he said presently. "Let's go on to camp for a cup of tea."

Above Camp V the whole aspect of the ascent changed. The angle of the ridge eased off, and the ice, which lower down had covered the mountain like a sheath, lay only in scattered patches between the rocks. Fresh enemies, however, instantly appeared to take the place of the old. We were now laboring at an altitude of more than 25,000 feet—well above the summits of the highest surrounding peaks—and day and night, without protection or respite, we were buffeted by the savage fury of the wind. Worse than this was that the atmosphere had become so **rarefied** it could scarcely support life. Breathing itself was a major physical effort, and our progress upward consisted of two or three painful steps, followed by a long period of rest in which our hearts pounded wildly and our burning lungs gasped for air. Each of us carried a small cylinder of oxygen in his pack, but we used it only in emergencies and found that, though its immediate effect was salutary, it left us later even worse off than before.

But the great struggle was now mental rather than physical. The lack of air induced a lethargy of mind and spirit; confidence and the powers of thought and decision waned. The mountain, to all of us, was no longer a mere giant of rock and ice; it had become a living thing, an enemy, watching us, waiting for us, hostile, relentless.

On the fifteenth day after we had first left the advance base, we pitched Camp VI at an altitude of 26,000 feet. It was located near the uppermost extremity of the great east ridge, directly beneath the so-called shoulder of the mountain. On the far side of the shoulder the stupendous north face of K 3 fell sheer to the glaciers, two miles below. Above it and to the left rose the symmetrical bulk of the summit pyramid. The topmost rocks of its highest pinnacle were clearly visible from the shoulder, and the intervening fifteen hundred feet seemed to offer no **insuperable** obstacles.

Camp VI, which was in reality no camp at all but a single tent, was large enough to accommodate only three men. Osborn established it with the aid of Wittmer and one porter; then, the following morning, Wittmer and the porter descended to Camp V, and Nace and I went up. It was our plan that Osborn and Nace should launch the final assault—the next day, if the weather held—with myself in support, following their progress through binoculars and going to their aid or summoning help from below if anything went wrong. As the three of us lay in the tent that night, the summit seemed already within arm's reach, victory securely in our grasp.

And then the blow fell. It snowed.

For a day and a night the great flakes drove down upon us, swirling and swooping in the wind, blotting out the summit, the shoulder, everything beyond the tiny white-walled radius of our tent. At last, during the morning of the following day, it cleared. The sun came out in a thin blue sky, and the summit pyramid again appeared above us, now whitely robed in fresh snow. But still we waited. Until the snow either froze or was blown away by the wind, it would have been the rashest courting of destruction for us to have ascended a foot beyond the camp. Another day passed and another.

By the third nightfall our nerves were at the breaking point. For hours on end we had scarcely moved or spoken, and the only sounds in all the world were the endless moaning of the wind outside and the harsh, sucking noise of our breathing. I knew that, one way or another, the end had come. Our meager food supply was running out; even with careful rationing, there was enough left for only two more days.

Presently Nace stirred in his sleeping bag and sat up. "We'll have to go down tomorrow," he said quietly.

For a moment there was silence in the tent. Then Osborn struggled to a sitting position and faced him.

"No," he said.

"There's still too much loose snow above. We can't make it."

"But it's clear. As long as we can see . . ."

Nace shook his head. "Too dangerous. We'll go down tomorrow and lay in a fresh supply. Then we'll try again."

"Once we go down we're licked. You know it."

Nace shrugged. "Better to be licked than . . ." The strain of speech was suddenly too much for him and he fell into a violent **paroxysm** of coughing. When it had passed, there was a long silence.

Then, suddenly, Osborn spoke again. "Look,

Nace," he said, "I'm going up tomorrow."

The Englishman shook his head.

"I'm going—understand?"

For the first time since I had known him, I saw Nace's eyes flash in anger. "I'm the senior member of this group," he said. "I forbid you to go!"

With a tremendous effort, Osborn jerked himself to his feet. "You forbid me? This may be your sixth time on this mountain, and all that, but you don't own it! I know what you're up to. You haven't got it in you to make the top yourself, so you don't want anyone else to get the glory. That's it, isn't it? Isn't it?" He sat down again suddenly, gasping for breath.

Nace looked at him with level eyes. "This mountain has licked me five times," he said softly. "It killed my best friend. It means more to me to lick it than anything else in the world. Maybe I'll make it and maybe I won't. But if I do, it will be as a rational, intelligent human being, not as a fool throwing my life away . . ."

He collapsed into another fit of coughing and fell back in his sleeping bag. Osborn, too, was still. They lay there inert, panting, too exhausted for speech.

It was hours later that I awoke from dull, uneasy sleep. In the faint light I saw Nace fumbling with the flap of the tent.

"What is it?" I asked.

"Osborn. He's gone."

The words cut like a blade through my lethargy. I struggled to my feet and followed Nace from the tent.

Outside, the dawn was seeping up the eastern sky. It was very cold, but the wind had fallen and the mountain seemed to hang suspended in a vast stillness. Above us the summit pyramid climbed bleakly into space, like the last outpost of a spent and lifeless planet. Raising my binoculars, I swept them over the gray waste. At first I saw nothing but rock and ice; then, suddenly, something moved.

"I've got him," I whispered.

As I spoke, the figure of Osborn sprang into clear focus against a patch of ice. He took three or four upward steps, stopped, went on again. I handed the glasses to Nace.

The Englishman squinted through them a moment, returned them to me and re-entered the tent. When I followed, he had already laced his boots and was pulling on his outer gloves.

"He's not far," he said. "Can't have been gone more than half an hour." He seized his ice ax and started out again.

"Wait," I said. "I'm going with you."

Nace shook his head. "Better stay here."

"I'm going with you," I said.

He said nothing further but waited while I made ready. In a few moments we left the tent, roped up, and started off.

Almost immediately we were on the shoulder and confronted with the paralyzing two-mile drop of the north face, but we **negotiated** the short exposed stretch without mishap and in ten minutes were working up the base of the summit pyramid. Our progress was creepingly slow. There seemed to be literally no air at all to breathe, and after almost every step we were forced to rest.

The minutes crawled into hours, and still we climbed. Presently the sun came up. Its level rays streamed across the clouds far below and glinted from the summits of distant peaks. But, although the pinnacle of K 3 soared a full five thousand feet above anything in the surrounding world, we had scarcely any sense of height. The stupendous wilderness of mountains and glaciers that spread beneath us to the horizon was flattened and remote, an unreal, insubstantial landscape seen in a dream. We had no connection with it, or it with us. All living, all awareness, purpose, and will, was concentrated in the last step and the next—to put one foot before the other; to breathe; to ascend. We struggled on in silence.

I do not know how long it was since we had left the camp—it might have been two hours, it might have been six—when we suddenly sighted Osborn. We had not been able to find him again since our first glimpse through the binoculars, but now, unexpectedly and abruptly, as we came up over a jagged outcropping of rock, there he was. He was at a point, only a few yards above us, where the mountain steepened into an almost vertical wall. The smooth surface directly in front of him was obviously unclimbable, but two alternate routes were presented. To the left, a chimney cut **obliquely** across the wall, forbiddingly steep, but seeming to offer adequate holds. To the right was a gentle slope of snow that curved upward and out of sight behind the rocks. As we watched, Osborn ascended to the edge of the snow, stopped and tested it with his foot; then, apparently satisfied that it would bear his weight, he stepped out on the slope.

I felt Nace's body tense. "Paul!" he cried out.

His voice was too weak and hoarse to carry. Osborn continued his ascent.

Nace cupped his hands and called his name again, and this time Osborn turned. "Wait!" cried the Englishman.

Osborn stood still, watching us, as we struggled up the few yards to the edge of the snow slope. Nace's breath came in shuddering gasps, but he climbed faster than I had ever seen him climb before.

"Come back!" he called. "Come off the snow!"

"It's all right. The crust is firm!" Osborn called back.

"But it's melting! There's"—Nace paused, fighting for air— "there's nothing underneath!"

In a sudden, horrifying flash I saw what he meant. Looked at from directly below, at the point where Osborn had come to it, the slope on which he stood appeared as a harmless covering of snow over the rocks. From where we were now, however, a little to one side, it could be seen that it was in reality no covering at all, but merely a *cornice*[4] or unsupported platform clinging to the side of the mountain. Below it was not rock, but ten thousand feet of blue air.

"Come back!" I cried. "Come back!"

Osborn hesitated, then took a downward step. But he never took the next. For in that instant the snow directly in front of him disappeared. It did not seem to fall or to break away. It was just soundlessly and magically no longer there. In the spot where Osborn had been about to set his foot there was now revealed the abysmal drop of the north face of K 3. I shut my eyes, but only for a second, and when I reopened them Osborn was still, miraculously, there.

Nace was shouting, "Don't move! Don't move an inch!"

"The rope." I heard myself saying.

The Englishman shook his head. "We'd have to throw it, and the impact would be too much. Brace yourself and play it out." As he spoke his eyes were traveling over the rocks that bordered the snow bridge. Then he moved forward.

I wedged myself into a cleft in the wall and let out the rope which extended between us. A few yards away, Osborn stood in the snow, transfixed, one foot a little in front of the other. But my eyes now were on Nace. Cautiously, but with astonishing rapidity, he edged along the rocks beside the cornice. There was a moment when his only support was an inch-wide ledge beneath his feet, another where there was nothing under his feet at all and he supported himself wholly by his elbows and hands. But he advanced steadily, and at last reached a shelf wide enough for him to turn around on. At this point he was perhaps six feet away from Osborn.

"It's wide enough here to hold both of us," he said in a quiet voice. "I'm going to reach out my ax. Don't move until you're sure you have a grip on it. When I pull, jump."

He searched the wall behind him and found a hold for his left hand. Then he slowly extended his ice ax, head foremost, until it was within two feet of Osborn's shoulder.

"Grip it!" he cried suddenly. Osborn's hands shot out and seized the ax. "Jump!"

There was a flash of steel in the sunlight and a hunched figure hurtled inward from the snow to the ledge. Simultaneously another figure hurtled out. The half of the ax jerked suddenly from Nace's hand, and he lurched forward and downward. A violent, sickening spasm convulsed my body as the rope went taut. Then it was gone. Nace did not seem to hit the snow; he simply disappeared through it, soundlessly. In the same instant the snow itself was gone. The frayed, yellow end of broken rope spun lazily in space.

---

4. cornice: An overhanging mass of rock, snow, or ice.

Somehow my eyes went to Osborn. He was crouched on the ledge where Nace had been a moment before, staring dully at the ax in his hands. Beyond his head, not two hundred feet above, the white, untrodden pinnacle of K 3 stabbed the sky.

Perhaps ten minutes passed, perhaps a half hour. I closed my eyes and leaned forward motionless against the rock, my face against my arm. I neither thought nor felt: my body and mind alike were enveloped in a suffocating numbness. Through it at last came the sound of Osborn moving. Looking up, I saw he was standing beside me. "I'm going to try to make the top," he said tonelessly.

I merely stared at him.

"Will you come?"

I shook my head slowly. Osborn hesitated a moment, then turned and began slowly climbing the steep chimney above us. Halfway up he paused, struggling for breath. Then he resumed his laborious upward progress and presently disappeared beyond the crest.

I stayed where I was, and the hours passed. The sun reached its zenith above the peak and sloped away behind it. And at last I heard above me the sound of Osborn returning. As I looked up, his figure appeared at the top of the chimney and began his descent. His clothing was in tatters, and I could tell from his movements that only the thin flame of his will stood between him and collapse. In another few minutes he was standing beside me.

"Did you get there?" I asked.

He shook his head slowly. "I couldn't make it," he answered. "I didn't have what it takes."

We roped together silently and began the descent to the camp.

There is nothing more to be told of the sixth assault on K 3—at least not from the experi-

About the Author

James Ramsey Ullman (1907-1971) an American, was a newspaper reporter, playwright, short story writer, novelist, professor, and explorer. His zeal and skill in mountain climbing developed in Switzerland during a vacation from Princeton University of Switzerland. He joined the expedition on Mt. Kalpurtha, which "Top Man" describes.

ences of the men who made it. Osborn and I reached Camp V in safety, and three days later the entire expedition gathered at the advance base. It was decided, in view of the appalling tragedy that had occurred, to make no further attempt on the summit, and we began the evacuation of the mountain.

It remained for another year and other men to reveal the **epilogue**.

The summer following our attempt a combined English-Swiss expedition stormed the peak successfully. After weeks of hardship and struggle, they attained the topmost pinnacle of the giant, only to find that what should have been their greatest moment of triumph was, instead, a moment of the bitterest disappointment. For when they came out at last upon the summit, they saw that they were not the first. An ax stood there. Its shaft was embedded in rock and ice, and on its steel head were the engraved words: TO MARTIN FROM JOHN.

They were sporting men. On their return to civilization they told their story, and the name of the conqueror of K 3 was made known to the world.

Testing for Understanding

1. Osborn and Nace differed most in
   a. technique.   b. personality.   c. experience.   d. stamina.

2. Nace's ax was special because
   a. it had been a gift to him from his friend who lost his life on an earlier expedition.
   b. Nace had engraved his friend's name on it.
   c. it had been to the top of Mount Everest.
   d. Nace had taken it with him on all his previous expeditions.

3. The narrator of this story had the greatest admiration for
   a. Osborn.   b. Nace.   c. Sayre Randolph.   d. the native porters.

4. Nace preferred the longer route up the ridge for all of the following reasons except
   a. his friend had fallen to his death from the shorter route.
   b. the shorter route consumed too much energy which would be needed for the final climb to the summit.
   c. all previous attempts had been unsuccessful, and he wanted to observe all caution necessary to achieve success at last.
   d. Osborn preferred the shorter route, and the rivalry between them prevented him from agreeing with Osborn.

5. The responsibility for the friction between Osborn and Nace lay
   a. mostly on Osborn.
   b. mostly on Nace.
   c. equally on Osborn and Nace.
   d. in a rivalry between Great Britain and America.

6. The "up two steps, down one" progress from camp to camp was necessary
   a. to allow time for adjusting to the change in climate.
   b. as a defense against frequent storms.
   c. because of the periodic delay of injury and ill health.
   d. because all necessary supplies could not be carried between camps in one day in addition to the time needed to set up a camp.

7. All of the following were liabilities to the climbers except
   a. thin atmosphere.   b. extreme cold.   c. fresh snow.   d. periodic thaws.

8. The two greatest contributions Osborn and Nace made to the party respectively were
   a. unmatched skill and familiarity with the mountain.
   b. spirited energy and cautious wisdom.
   c. impulsiveness and quietness.
   d. leadership ability and determination.

9. The reason for the contrast between the grandeur of the summit in the opening paragraphs of the story and its bleakness, "like the last outpost of a spent and lifeless planet," near the end of the story was
   a. now they were closer to it and could see it more realistically.
   b. distant appreciation had been tempered by realistic struggle.
   c. recent snows had changed its appearance.
   d. friction had increased between Nace and Osborn.

10. Nace set out after Osborn because
    a. he now thought the snow was safe for travel.
    b. he didn't want Osborn to reach the top before or without him.
    c. he recognized the rashness of Osborn's venture, and knew it was unsafe for Osborn to continue alone.
    d. he knew Osborn was planning to return to the lower camp without them.

Reading for Understanding

1. *What happened then I can describe only as a single, stupendous crash of music.*
   The crash of music was
   a. the sound of an avalanche ringing through the mountains.
   b. the exultant and awed cries of the climbing party.
   c. the sound of a mountain stream tumbling down the mountainside.
   d. his way of expressing the effect of the inexpressible grandeur of the sight.

2. *For all its twenty-eight thousand feet of lofty grandeur, it seemed, somehow, less to tower than to crouch—a white-hooded giant, secret and remote, but living. Living and on guard.*
   The mountain appeared
   a. smaller to the men now that they were actually conquering it.
   b. now a fearsome force ready to conquer rather than a majestic monument ready to be conquered.
   c. less alluring to the mountain climbers than it had earlier.
   d. less majestic than earlier expeditions had reported.

3. *"Once we go down we're licked. You know it."*
   Nace shrugged. "Better to be licked than . . ."
   The men's conversation revealed that
   a. Osborn felt death would come one way or the other and they might as well try for the top.
   b. if they returned to the base they would never launch another expedition.
   c. they couldn't make another try on this expedition if they went down now, but Nace felt that would be better than trying and losing their lives.
   d. Nace would rather they reach the top and lose their lives than face defeat alive.

4. *"Did you get there?" I asked.*
   He shook his head slowly. "I couldn't make it," he answered. "I didn't have what it takes."
   Osborn answered this way because
   a. he didn't realize that he had reached the top.
   b. he was too exhausted and never reached the top.
   c. he did not have equipment adequate for the terrain.
   d. in view of Nace's sacrifice, he felt he could not rightly claim credit for reaching the top.

5. *They were sporting men. On their return to civilization they told their story, and the name of the conqueror of K 3 was made known to the world.*
   The last paragraph means that
   a. these men claimed the glory that belonged to someone else.
   b. these men were willing to tell the world that Osborn had reached the top first.
   c. Nace had actually fallen from the top.
   d. the English-Swiss expedition was actually the first to reach the top.

Meditating for Meaning

1. Although the worthiness of such an expedition could be questioned, yet many worthwhile lessons may be gained from this account.
   a. List several things essential to this expedition which are also essential to any successful venture.
   b. In spite of his best precautions, man will not always be able to complete every venture he undertakes. Explain why this is true.
   c. Explain how this occurred in this story.

2. The expedition failed on one point, a point which the author says was all that mattered—that their purpose was one.
   a. In what way was their purpose one?
   b. In what way did they fail in this oneness of purpose?
   c. When do you get the first inkling of this failure?

3. The author says, "There were all kinds of men among the eight of us, men with a great diversity of background and interest."
   a. What was an advantage of this diversity?
   b. List as many differences as you can between Nace and Osborn, perhaps the two most unlike men of the group.
   c. What difference seemed to cause the most friction between them?
   d. How could this difference, if correctly handled, have been an asset to them?
   e. Why was it right that Osborn give in to Nace?

4. In one event the author said Nace showed him what it was to be a great mountaineer.
   a. What was this event?
   b. What were qualities which Nace demonstrated during this event?

5. The proof of a great mountaineer comes at the end of the story.
   a. Why did Nace forbid Osborn to go to the top as he desired?
   b. Of what did Osborn accuse Nace as his reason for forbidding him?
   c. Nace did not answer this accusation directly. In your own words, what was he saying by his answer?

6. The title of the story is "Top Man."
   a. By human reasoning what would be required of a mountain climber in such an expedition to merit this title?
   b. On this basis who was "Top Man"?
   c. Who do you think merited the title of "Top Man"? Explain.
   d. In what way did Osborn also show some high character qualities?

7. What lesson can we learn from this story which should help us to temper our selfish passions?

Looking for Literary Technique

The beginning paragraphs of this story are quite effective. The pronoun *it* is used, telling us something is in focus, but we are not told what it is.

1. At what point are you first told definitely what the "it" is?

2. Why do you think this is an effective way of beginning a story? A similar technique is employed in the last two paragraphs of the story.

3. What makes these ending paragraphs particularly effective?

Writing for Skill

Think of an important discovery or invention and imagine that you are writing an account about it. Write three paragraphs which could be the introduction to your story, but do not tell in the first two paragraphs what the invention or discovery was. Stimulate your reader's interest by making him wonder. Then satisfy his curiosity in the third paragraph. Try to satisfy it as effectively as James Ullman did when he quoted the records of the Indian Topographical Survey.

Reflections on
Faithful Christians

Wherefore seeing we also

are compassed about with

so great a cloud of witnesses,

let us lay aside every weight,

and the sin which doth

so easily beset us, and let us

run with patience the race

that is set before us.

Hebrews 12:1

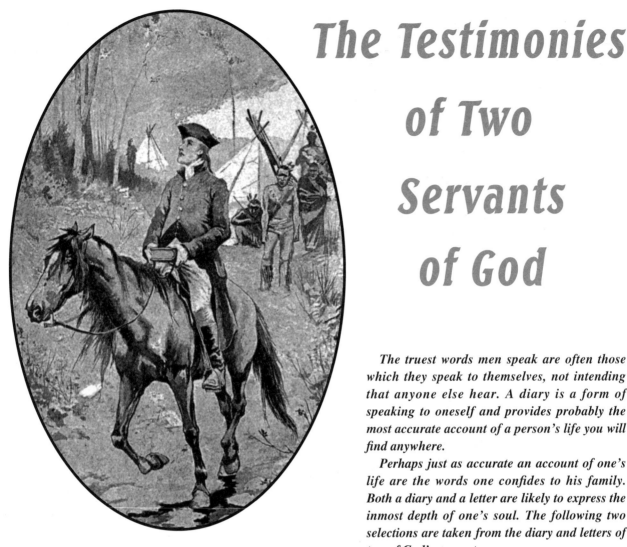

The Testimonies of Two Servants of God

The truest words men speak are often those which they speak to themselves, not intending that anyone else hear. A diary is a form of speaking to oneself and provides probably the most accurate account of a person's life you will find anywhere.

Perhaps just as accurate an account of one's life are the words one confides to his family. Both a diary and a letter are likely to express the inmost depth of one's soul. The following two selections are taken from the diary and letters of two of God's servants.

The Diary of David Brainerd

These excerpts from David Brainerd's diary, published after his death, depict the zeal and fervor that characterized his twenty-nine years.

Born in 1718, in Connecticut, Brainerd was known from his childhood for his intense interest in spiritual matters. After studying at Yale College, he accepted an appointment by a Presbyterian society as a missionary to the Kaunameek tribe of Delaware Indians.

Working through a Christian Indian interpreter, Brainerd won many Indians to Christianity with

his preaching. He spent nearly three years with the Kaunameek tribe, baptizing more than seventy.

In 1746, he began work among the Susquehanna Indians, but the rigors of his self-sacrificing, wilderness life took their toll in the form of tuberculosis. One year later at the age of twenty-nine, he died in the home of Jonathan Edwards, a Congregational minister.

Brainerd's burden and labors for the lost are a worthy example for Christians in the "wilderness" of our world today.

Choose the word or phrase below which most nearly defines each word at the left as it is used in this selection.

1. obliged	a. permitted	b. compelled	c. angled
2. mortified	a. self-denying	b. ended	c. lazy
3. dissolution	a. death	b. disappointment	c. misunderstanding
4. melancholy	a. anger	b. mental depression	c. sacredness
5. conjurers	a. judges	b. enemies	c. magicians
6. propagating	a. supporting	b. spreading	c. guessing
7. profane	a. weary	b. vulgar; godless	c. eagerly longing
8. nominal	a. chosen	b. in name only	c. distinguished
9. superscribe	a. address	b. recopy	c. complete
10. insupportable	a. awkward	b. mediocre	c. unbearable
11. eminently	a. immediately	b. closely	c. noteworthily
12. ardently	a. fervently	b. with difficulty	c. rapidly

The Diary of David Brainerd

TUESDAY, April 20. This day I am twenty-four years of age. Oh, how much mercy I have received the year past! How often has God caused His goodness to pass before me! And how poorly have I answered the vows I made this time twelve month to be wholly the Lord's, to be forever devoted to His service! The Lord help me to live more to His glory for the time to come. This has been a sweet, a happy day to me; blessed be God. I think my soul was never so drawn out in intercession for others as it has been this night. Had a most fervent wrestle with the Lord tonight for my enemies. I hardly ever so longed to live to God and to be altogether devoted to Him. I wanted to wear out my life in His service, and for His glory.

FRIDAY, April 1, 1743. I rode to Kaunameek near twenty miles from Stockbridge, where the Indians live with whom I am concerned, and there lodged on a little heap of straw. I was greatly exercised with inward trials and distresses all day. In the evening, my heart was sunk and I seemed to have no God to go to. Oh, that God would help me!

WEDNESDAY, April 20. Set apart this day for fasting and prayer, to bow my soul before God for the bestowment of divine grace; especially that all my spiritual afflictions and inward distresses might be sanctified to my soul. And endeavored also to remember the goodness of God to me the year past, this day being my birthday. Having obtained help of God, I have hitherto lived and am now arrived at the age of twenty-five years. My soul was pained to think of my barrenness and deadness; that I have lived so little to the glory of the eternal God. I spent the day in the woods alone, and there poured out my complaint to God. Oh, that God would enable me to live to His glory for the future!

SATURDAY, July 30. Just at night, moved into my own house [a little hut, which he made chiefly by his own hands, by long and hard labor], and lodged there that night;

found it much better spending time alone than in the wigwam where I was before.

MONDAY, August 15. Spent most of the day in labor to procure something to keep my horse on in the winter. Enjoyed not much sweetness in the morning; was very weak in body through the day, and thought this frail body would soon drop into the dust. Had some very realizing apprehensions of a speedy entrance into another world. And in this weak state of body I was not a little distressed for want of suitable food. I had no bread, nor could I get any. I am forced to go or send ten or fifteen miles for all the bread I eat, and sometimes it is moldy and sour before I eat it, if I get any considerable quantity.

And then again I have none for some days together for want of an opportunity to send for it, and cannot find my horse in the woods to go myself; and this was my case now. But through divine goodness I had some Indian meal, of which I made little cakes, and fried them. Yet felt contented with my circumstances and sweetly resigned to God. In prayer I enjoyed great freedom and blessed God as much for my present circumstances as if I had been a king and thought I found a disposition to be contented in any circumstances. Blessed be God.

TUESDAY, October 4. This day rode home to my own house and people. The poor Indians appeared very glad of my return. Found my house and all things in safety. I presently fell on my knees and blessed God for my safe return after a long and tedious journey, and a season of sickness in several places where I had been, and after I had been ill myself. God has renewed His kindness to me, in preserving me one journey more. I have taken many considerable journeys since this time last year, and yet God has never suffered one of my bones to be broken, or any distressing calamity to befall me, excepting the ill turn I had in my last journey. I have been often exposed to cold and hunger in the wilderness where the comforts of life were not to be had; have frequently been lost in the woods; and sometimes **obliged** to ride much of the night; and once lay out in the woods all night. Yet,

blessed be God, He has preserved me!

TUESDAY, November 29. Began to study the Indian tongue with Mr. Sergeant at Stockbridge. Was perplexed for want of more retirement. I love to live alone in my own little cottage where I can spend much time in prayer.

WEDNESDAY, January 4. Was in a resigned and **mortified** temper of mind, much of the day. Time appeared a moment, life a vapor, and all its enjoyments as empty bubbles and fleeting blasts of wind.

LORD'S DAY, July 22. When I waked my soul was burdened with what seemed to be before me. I cried to God before I could get out of my bed. As soon as I was dressed I withdrew into the woods to pour out my burdened soul to God, especially for assistance in my great work, for I could scarcely think of anything else. I enjoyed the same freedom and fervency as the last evening, and did with unspeakable freedom give up myself afresh to God, for life or death, for all hardships He should call me to among the heathen. I felt as if nothing could discourage me from this blessed work. I had a strong hope that God would "bow the heavens and come down" and do some marvelous work among the heathen. And when I was riding to the Indians, three miles, my heart was continually going up to God for His presence and assistance; and hoping, and almost expecting, that God would make this the day of His power and grace amongst the poor Indians.

When I came to them, I found them engaged in their frolic. Through divine goodness I got them to break up and attend to my preaching, yet still there appeared nothing of the special power of God among them. Preached again to them in the afternoon and observed the Indians were more sober than before, but still saw nothing special among them. From whence Satan took occasion to tempt and buffet me with these cursed suggestions: There is no God, or if there be, He is not able to convert the Indians, before they have more knowledge. I was very weak and weary, and my soul borne down with perplexity; but was mortified to all the world, and was determined still to wait upon God for the conversion of the heathen, though the devil tempted me to the contrary.

THURSDAY, November 22. Came on my way from Rockciticus to Delaware River. Was very much disordered with a cold and pain in my head. About six at night, I lost my way in the wilderness, and wandered over rocks and mountains, down hideous steeps, through swamps, and most dreadful and dangerous places. The night being dark, so that few stars could be seen, I was greatly exposed. I was much pinched with cold, and distressed with an extreme pain in my head, attended with sickness at my stomach, so that every step I took was distressing to me. I had little hope for several hours together, but that I must lie out in the woods all night, in this distressed case. But about nine o'clock, I found a house, through the abundant grace of God, and was kindly entertained. Thus I have frequently been exposed, and sometimes lain out the whole night; but God has hitherto preserved me. Blessed be His name.

Such fatigues and hardships as these serve to wean me more from the earth, and, I trust, will make heaven the sweeter. Formerly, when I was thus exposed to cold and rain, I was ready to please myself with the thoughts of enjoying a comfortable house, a warm fire, and other outward comforts. But now these have less place in my heart (through the grace of God), and my eye is more to God for comfort. In this world I expect tribulation; and it does not now, as formerly, appear strange to me. I do not in such seasons of difficulty flatter myself that it will be better hereafter, but rather think, how much worse it might be; how much greater trials others of God's children have endured; and how much greater are yet perhaps reserved for me. Blessed be God, that He makes the thoughts of my journey's end and of my **dissolution** a great comfort to me, under my sharpest trials, and scarce ever lets these thoughts be attended with terror or **melancholy**; but they are attended frequently with great joy.

FRIDAY, April 26. Conversed with a Christian friend with some warmth; felt a spirit of mortification to the world in a very great degree. Afterwards was enabled to pray fervently, and to rely on God sweetly for "all things pertaining to life and godliness." Just in the evening was visited by a dear Christian friend, with whom I spent an hour or two in conversation, on the very soul of religion. There are many with whom I can talk *about religion;* but alas! I find few with whom I can talk *religion itself.* But, blessed be the Lord, there are some that love to feed on the kernel, rather than the shell.

September 5. Discoursed to the Indians from the parable of the sower, afterwards conversed particularly with sundry persons, which occasioned them to weep, and even to cry out in an affecting manner, and seized others with surprise and concern. I doubt not but that a divine power accompanied what was then spoken. Sundry of these persons had been with me to Crossweeksung, and had there seen, and some of them, I trust, felt the power of God's Word in an effectual and saving manner.

I asked one of them, who had obtained comfort and given hopeful evidences of being truly religious, why he now cried. He replied, "When I thought how Christ was slain like a lamb, and spilt His blood for sinners, I could not help crying, when I was all alone": and thereupon burst out into tears and cried again. I then asked his wife, who had likewise been abundantly comforted, wherefore she cried. She answered, "I was grieved that the Indians here would not come to Christ, as well as those at Crossweeksung." I asked her if she found a heart to pray for them and whether Christ had seemed to be near to her of late in prayer, as in time past (which is my usual method of expressing a sense of the divine Presence). She replied, "Yes, He has been near to me; and at some times when I have been praying alone, my heart loved to pray so, that I could not bear to leave the place, but wanted to stay and pray longer."

Lord's Day, September 22. Spent the day with the Indians on the island. As soon as they were well up in the morning, I attempted to instruct them, and labored for that purpose to get them together, but quickly found they had something else to do. Near noon they gathered together all their powwows (or **conjurers**), and set about half a dozen of them to playing their juggling tricks, and acting their frantic distracted postures, in order to find out why they were then so sickly upon the island, numbers of them being at that time disordered with a fever, and bloody flux.

After they had done powwowing, I attempted to discourse with them about Christianity. But they soon scattered, and gave me no opportunity for anything of that nature, A view of these things, while I was entirely alone in the wilderness, destitute of the society of anyone that so much as "named the name of Christ," greatly sunk my spirits, gave me the most gloomy turn of mind imaginable, almost stripped me of all resolution and hope respecting further attempts for **propagating** the Gospel, and converting the pagans, and rendered this the most burdensome and disagreeable Sabbath that ever I saw.

But nothing, I can truly say, sunk and distressed me like the loss of my hope respecting their conversion. This concern appeared so great, and seemed to be so much my own that I seemed to have nothing to do on earth, if this failed. A prospect of the greatest success in the saving conversion of souls under Gospel light, would have done little or nothing towards compensating for the loss of my hope in this respect; and my spirits now were so damped and depressed that I had no heart nor power to make any further attempts among them for that purpose, and could not possibly recover my hope, resolution, and courage, by the utmost of my endeavors.

The Indians of this island can many of them understand the English language considerably well, having formerly lived in some part of Maryland among or near the white people, but are very vicious, drunken, and **profane,** although not so savage as those who have less acquaintance with the English. Their customs in divers respects differ from those of other

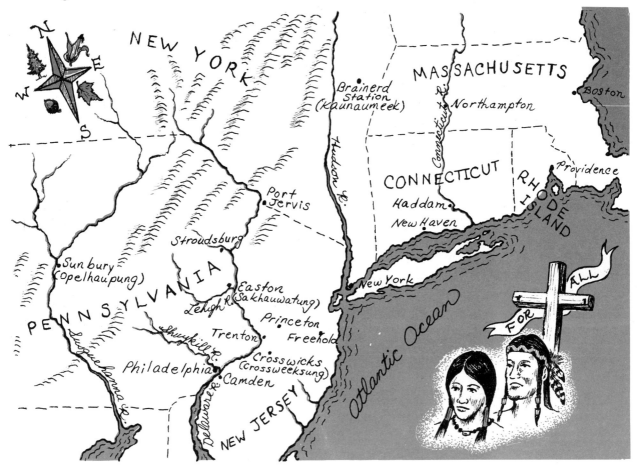

Indians upon this river. They do not bury their dead in a common form, but let their flesh consume above ground in close cribs made for that purpose; and at the end of a year, or sometimes a longer space of time, they take the bones, when the flesh is all consumed, and wash and scrape them, and afterwards bury them with some ceremony.

Their method of charming or conjuring over the sick seems somewhat different from that of other Indians, though for substance the same. The whole of it, among these and others, perhaps is an imitation of what seems, by Naaman's expression, II Kings 5:11, to have been the custom of the ancient heathens. For it seems chiefly to consist in their "striking their hands over the diseased," repeatedly stroking them, "and calling upon their gods," excepting the spurting of water like a mist, and some other frantic ceremonies, common to the other conjurations I have already mentioned.

But alas! how deplorable is the state of the Indians upon this river! The brief representation I have here given of their notions and manners is sufficient to show that they are "led captive by Satan at his will," in the most eminent manner. Methinks they might likewise be sufficient to excite the compassion, and engage the prayers of pious souls for these their fellow men, who sit in "the regions of the shadow of death."

September 23. Made some further attempts to instruct and Christianize the Indians on this island, but all to no purpose. They live so near the white people that they are always in the way of strong liquor, as well as the ill examples of **nominal** Christians; which renders it so unspeakably difficult to treat with them about Christianity.

March 24. Numbered the Indians to see how many souls God had gathered together here since my coming into these parts, and found there were now about an hundred and thirty persons together, old and young. Sundry of those that are my stated hearers, perhaps to the number of fifteen or twenty, were absent at this season. So that if all had been together, the number would now have been very considerable; especially considering how few were together at my first coming into these parts, the whole number not amounting to ten persons at that time.

SATURDAY, November 1. Took leave of friends after having spent the forenoon with them and returned home to my own house. Was much disordered in the evening and oppressed with my cough; which has now been constant for a long time with a hard pain in my breast, and fever.

After this, having perhaps taken some cold, I began to decline as to bodily health; and continued to do so, till the latter end of January, 1747. Having a violent cough, a considerable fever, an asthmatic disorder, and no appetite for any manner of food, nor any power of digestion, I was reduced to so low a state that my friends, I believe, generally despaired of my life. Some of them for some time together thought I could scarce live a day. At this time I could think of nothing with any application of mind, and seemed to be in a great measure void of all affection, and was exercised with great temptations; but yet was not, ordinarily, afraid of death.

THURSDAY, June 18, I was taken exceedingly ill, and brought to the gates of death, by the breaking of small ulcers in my lungs, as my physician supposed. In this extreme weak state I continued for several weeks, and was frequently reduced so low as to be utterly speechless, and not able so much as to whisper a word. Even after I had so far revived as to walk about the house, and to step out of doors, I was exercised every day with a faint turn, which continued usually four or five hours; at which times, though I was not so utterly speechless but that I could say Yes or No, yet I could not converse at all, nor speak one sentence, without making stops for breath. Divers times in this season, my friends gathered round my bed to see me breathe my last, which they looked for every moment as I myself also did.

THURSDAY, September 24. My strength began to fail exceedingly; which looked further as if I had done all my work; however, I had strength to fold and **superscribe** my letter. About two I went to bed, being weak and much disordered, and lay in a burning fever till night, without any proper rest. In the evening, I got up, having lain down in some of my clothes; but was in the greatest distress that ever I endured, having an uncommon kind of hiccough, which either strangled me or threw me into a straining to vomit; and at the same time was distressed with griping pains. Oh, the distress of this evening! I had little expectation of my living the night through, nor indeed had any about me, and I longed for the finishing moment! I was obliged to repair to bed by six o'clock, and through mercy enjoyed some rest. But was grievously distressed at turns with the hiccough. My soul breathed after God, "When shall I come to God, even to God, my exceeding joy?" Oh, for His blessed likeness!

(This last section was added by Jonathan Edwards.)

On Tuesday, October 6, he lay, for a considerable time as if he were dying. At which time, he was heard to utter, in broken whispers, such expressions as these: "He will come, He will not tarry. I shall soon be in glory. I shall soon glorify God with the angels." But after some time he revived.

The next day, Wednesday, October 7, his brother John arrived from New Jersey; where he had been detained much longer than he intended, by a mortal sickness prevailing among the Christian Indians, and by some other circumstances that made his stay with them necessary. Mr. Brainerd was affected and refreshed with seeing him and appeared fully satisfied with the reasons of his delay; seeing the interest in religion and of the souls of his people required it.

The next day, Thursday, October 8, he was in great distress and agonies of body; and for the greater part of the day was much disordered as to the exercise of his reason. In the evening, he was more composed and had the use of his reason well; but the pain of his body continued and increased. He told me it was impossible for any to conceive of the distress he felt in his breast. He manifested much concern lest he should dishonor God by impatience under his extreme agony; which was such that he said the thought of enduring it one minute longer was almost **insupportable.** He desired that others would be much in lifting up their hearts continually to God for him that God would support him and give him patience. He signified that he expected to die that night, but seemed to fear a longer delay; and the disposition of his mind with regard to death appeared still the same that it had been all along.

Notwithstanding his bodily agonies, the interest of Zion lay still with great weight on his mind; as appeared by some considerable discourse he had that evening with the Reverend Mr. Billing, one of the neighboring ministers (who was then present), concerning the great importance of the work of the ministry. Afterwards, when it was very late in the night, he had much very proper and profitable discourse with his brother John concerning his congregation in New Jersey and the interest of religion among the Indians.

In the latter part of the night, his bodily distress seemed to rise to a greater height than ever; and he said to those then about him that it was another thing to die than people imagined; explaining himself to mean that they were not aware what bodily pain and anguish is undergone before death. Towards day, his eyes fixed; and he continued lying immovable till about six o'clock in the morning, and then expired on Friday, October 9, 1747, when his soul, as we may well conclude, was received by his dear Lord and Master as an **eminently** faithful servant, into that state of perfection of holiness and fruition of God, which he had so often and so **ardently** longed for; and was welcomed by the glorious assembly in the upper world, as one peculiarly fitted to join them in their blessed employ and enjoyment.

Letters of Hermann Stohr

(Introduction by Julian E. Kulski)

*Dr. Hermann Stohr, born in 1888, was a professor of political science and secretary of the German Union for Conciliation; his life was dedicated, through writing, organizing, and teaching, to the ideals of social welfare and peace inspired by his **evangelical** Christian faith. His historical study was concerned chiefly with the overseas relief work of the United States. In this he saw an **exemplar** of political policy **transcending** national self-interest and full of possibilities for the future.*

*Under the Hitler **regime** he refused to render military service, and on June 21, 1940, he was executed for "undermining the **morale** of the armed forces." He died **staunchly** upholding the principles he had laid down at the founding of the Union for Conciliation in 1914: "Love, as it is made manifest in the life and death of Christ, is the only power that can conquer evil and the only enduring foundation for human society. That is why it is forbidden us Christians to wage war."*

Defining for Comprehension

Choose the word or phrase below which most nearly defines each word at the left as it is used in this selection.

	a.	b.	c.
1. evangelical	a. heavenly	b. beneficial	c. Gospel-centered
2. exemplar	a. model	b. beginner	c. accuser
3. transcending	a. exceeding	b. rising	c. crossing
4. regime	a. literary work	b. evil	c. rule
5. morale	a. mushroom	b. principle	c. spirit
6. staunchly	a. steadfastly	b. contrarily	c. joyously
7. mundane	a. grimy	b. earthly	c. humorous
8. dearth	a. scarcity	b. fondness	c. fireplace sill
9. paltry	a. hot and humid	b. stingy	c. insignificant
10. assent	a. rise; growth	b. approval	c. command
11. incomprehensible	a. not understandable	b. unending	c. unconquerable

FROM A LETTER TO HIS SISTER-IN-LAW
June 3, 1940

This is my situation: ever since March 2, 1939, I have been explaining to the military authorities that I could serve my country only with work, not with arms (Matthew 5:21-26, 38-48) nor with an oath (Matthew 5:33-37, James 5:12). And God's commandments have force for me unconditionally (Acts 5:29). For this I was sentenced to death on March 16, 1940, and the judgment was confirmed on April 13, 1940.

To be daily prepared to die is of course enjoined upon every Christian. Therefore this present state is for me a discipline. In the midst of it I rejoice in my leisure, which I use above all for Bible study.

TO HIS MOTHER
March 19, 1940

Wherever there is still any shrinking from death, something is wrong. I have been thinking much about this recently and have studied the problem with the help of the Bible and the hymnal. From a purely **mundane** point of view, being sentenced to death is indeed the worst thing that can happen to us on this earth. But from the point of view of faith we say: What harm can come to us from men? With that we know that we are securely sheltered in the hand of the Almighty. . . .

There has been no **dearth** of more or less well-meant attempts to make me change my mind. But this has resulted only in strengthening me in my awareness that God has also commanded the nations to love and to help one another. But to lie in matters relating to an awareness granted by God, only in order to save my own **paltry** life—that was impossible. It would have meant contempt of God and basing my life on a lie.

A year ago Gertrude nailed over my bed a plaque bearing the motto, "Be thou faithful unto death, and I will give thee a crown of life." At first this saying seemed to me too harsh, because it made me think immediately of situations of the sort I am in now. I have worked a great deal at spelling it out and have finally given it **assent.** After all, a great promise lies in these words. If we really have the faith symbolized by Easter, faith in a resurrection of the body, it is precisely in the face of death that we

are filled with a great joy that radiates toward us all the more brightly amidst earthly adversities. But if we let go this faith, then indeed it becomes dark around us. Therefore above everything I wish all of you and myself a never-faltering faith in the resurrection of the Lord.

TO HIS SISTER
June 20, 1940

This evening I was informed that my appeal for mercy has been rejected, and so tomorrow, that is, June 21, around six o'clock in the morning, the sentence will be carried out.

This is, then, the will of God, who loves us all, and we who in turn love Him must accept this too as for the best. It is for the best. And, in so far as it may seem at the moment **incomprehensible** to you or to anyone else, we pray to the Lord that He may soon give us revelation.

For me, as for others, it holds true that Christ has freed us from the fear of death, and that perfect love drives out fear. Perfect love—that is HE. And may He draw us all into this love. And once we stand within it, all suffering must vanish for us, and we shall partake of great joy. Whatever we have to reproach one another for, let us forgive completely with the petition of the Lord's Prayer: "Our Father . . . forgive us our trespasses, as we forgive those who trespass against us." —And let us go thus to meet the day that will unite us all in eternity.

Since we live in this grace, even this, my last journey, must not frighten us. Christ has freed us from all fears, including this one. The execu-

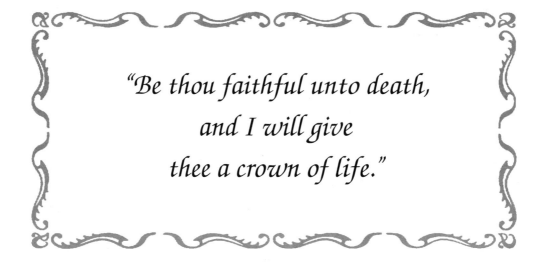

"Be thou faithful unto death, and I will give thee a crown of life."

tion of this sentence is for me the will of God— God's benevolent and merciful will. And in obedience to Him I want to make this last journey, as it were, to meet Him. Greet my relatives, and heartfelt greetings to you in the feeling that we shall all see each other again in eternity.

Do not sorrow about this my departure and my homecoming; rather, rejoice with me, as is suggested to us in 1 Peter 4:13-16. I should like to call out to everyone: Farewell until we meet again in the presence of that Lord who has summoned us to an eternal life.

 **Testing for Understanding**

1. Tuesday, April 20 was a sweet and happy day to David Brainerd because
   a. it was his birthday.
   b. he had wrought much victory among the Indians that day.
   c. it was the anniversary of his conversion.
   d. he had that day been filled with a fervent devotion to God and desire for the good of others.

2. Brainerd found his greatest relief from afflictions in
   a. the help of his fellowmen.
   b. anticipation of heaven.
   c. prayer.
   d. the pleasure of thoughts of his home.

3. Brainerd considered it a proof that one experienced divine presence when
   a. he testified of visions he had received.
   b. Christ seemed near in prayer.
   c. he was willing to discuss religion.
   d. he gave his life for the good of others.

4. Brainerd's greatest distress came from
   a. physical illness.
   b. deprivation of material comforts.
   c. loss of hope in the conversion of the Indians.
   d. a feeling that he had not fully kept his vows to God.

5. The greatest hindrance in Brainerd's work with the Indians was
   a. their ignorance of the English language.
   b. their lack of civilized ways.
   c. the influence of white men's profane practices and insincere lives.
   d. their belief in heathen gods.

6. The excerpts of Brainerd's diary likely cover the scope of
   a. six months.   b. one year.   c. five years.   d. ten years.

7. Hermann Stohr was in conflict with the governmental authorities in all of the following areas except
   a. refusal to serve in the military.
   b. influence on the military men.
   c. refusal to take an oath.
   d. efforts to convert other Germans.

8. According to his letters, Stohr found death easier to face by all the following means except
   a. meditation on a motto hanging over his bed.
   b. recognizing that God has greater power over us than men.
   c. faith in a resurrected body.
   d. the encouragement of fellow prisoners.

9. Both Brainerd and Stohr considered physical hardships and distresses valuable as a means of
   a. increasing their desire for heaven.
   b. securing the sympathies of their fellowmen.
   c. drawing other men to the Lord.
   d. bringing them to acknowledge past sins.

10. Brainerd's and Stohr's experiences differed in that
    a. the one had the support of his family while the other did not.
    b. the one sacrificed his life in his devotion to God while the other did not.
    c. the one was officially opposed while the other was not.
    d. the one was more influential than the other.

 *Reading for Understanding*

1. *There are many with whom I can talk about religion; but alas! I find few with whom I can talk religion itself. But, blessed be the Lord, there are some that love to feed on the kernel, rather than the shell.*
   Brainerd thanked God that
   a. there were some Indians who responded to the truth.
   b. there were fellow believers who could discuss the Gospel out of firsthand experience of its powerful effect in their lives.
   c. although many scorned his work, some few supported it.
   d. although some Indians responded only for material advancement, others wanted peace with God.

2. *To be daily prepared to die is of course enjoined upon every Christian. Therefore this present state is for me a discipline.*
   Stohr meant that
   a. his imprisonment was God's chastening for an earlier reluctance to face death.
   b. his right response to his imprisonment was daily making him more willing to die.
   c. he was encouraged by realizing that every Christian must sometime die.
   d. it was a sore trial to him to never know when his next day would be his last.

3. *There has been no dearth of more or less well-meant attempts to make me change my mind . . . But to lie in matters relating to an awareness granted by God, only in order to save my own paltry life—that was impossible.*
   Stohr was telling his mother that
   a. he had been encouraged by government officials to be dishonest.
   b. no one bothered to try to convince him to save his life.
   c. for him to recant just to avoid death would be lying, denying a faith that he still believed.
   d. it was too late now for him to save his life even if he recanted.

4. *This is, then, the will of God. . . . And in so far as it may seem at the moment incomprehensible to you or to anyone else, we pray to the Lord that He may soon give us revelation.*
    Stohr was telling his sister that

    a. if she was not reconciled to his death, he desired that God would help her to become reconciled.
    b. he wished that the Lord would soon reveal to him when his end would come.
    c. if she could not understand why he maintained his faith, he prayed that God would help her to see the truth.
    d. since he could not live, he wished to die as soon as possible.

5. *"Our Father . . . forgive us our trespasses, as we forgive those who trespass against us." —And let us go thus to meet the day that will unite us all in eternity.*
    Stohr was exhorting his sister to

    a. maintain a forgiving spirit until death.
    b. forgive him of any wrongs that he had done against her so that he might die in peace the following day.
    c. prepare for her death which would also come the next day.
    d. seek forgiveness for her sins so that he might die with the peace of knowing that she was saved.

Meditating for Meaning

1. It is an unfortunate assumption among many that young people need not be expected to be as deeply devoted to God as older people.
    a. How do you think this assumption would have affected Brainerd's life if he had maintained it?
    b. Why is this a wrong assumption?
    c. Give a Scriptural reference to show that God expects wholeheartedness from youth.
    d. Why do you think Brainerd had such a fervent zeal for God at the age of twenty-four?

2. What men consider essential to happiness is often not what brings us the greatest happiness.
    a. What did Brainerd say originally pleased him?
    b. What brought him to the place of finding less pleasure in these things?
    c. What word did he use to describe this process of finding less pleasure in these things?
    d. In what light does the connotation of this word place his former pleasures?
    e. What brought great joy to Brainerd?
    f. Why was that a greater joy than earthly pleasures?

3. Brainerd followed the command of Matthew 6:33.
    a. Did God fail to keep His promise in this verse in Brainerd's experience? Explain.
    b. How would it likely have affected Brainerd's work if he had reversed his priorities?

4. Both Brainerd and Stohr had time to realize that they would soon face death.
    a. What is the natural response of those who face death?
    b. How did the devil try to use this to his advantage in Stohr's experience?
    c. How did Stohr feel about this natural response to death?
    d. How did he think we can overcome this natural response?
    e. In his letter to his sister, what metaphorical description did he give of death?
    f. What will maintaining this view of death do for us?

Looking for Literary Technique

A diary or a letter is very personal and gives the impression of events happening right now. Compare the first sentences of David Brainerd's diary with the following paragraph which might appear in an article written for a more public audience:

> On Tuesday, April 20, I was twenty-four years of age. I had received so much mercy during the year that was past. How often had God caused His goodness to pass before me! And how poorly had I fulfilled the vows I had made twelve months before to be wholly the Lord's, to be forever devoted to His service! I asked the Lord to help me to live more to His glory for the time to come. It was a sweet, a happy day to me.

Instead of the present and present perfect tense verbs, you now have past and past perfect tenses.

1. What differences do you see between Stohr's letters and Brainerd's diary.

Writing for Skill

1. Keep a diary for a week. Include in it feelings and thoughts. Particularly include thoughts that you gain from your personal devotions.
2. Write a letter to a friend. Share with him not only daily happenings, but convictions and spiritual insights as well.

Though He Slay Me

by E. J. Swalm

From the beginning of the Gospel era, nonresistance has been a basic doctrine of the true Christian church. "All they that take the sword," Christ said, "shall perish with the sword." Throughout the war-clouded history of Europe, conservative Christians refused to fight and often suffered imprisonment or death as a result. In the seventeenth, eighteenth, and nineteenth centuries, persecuted Christians found refuge in the free countries of the New World. But war ravaged the New World as well. All able-bodied men were forced into service during much of the Civil War and the World Wars. In World War II, peace churches of the United States and Canada appealed to their governments for exemption from service and gained some consideration in the form of alternative service. But as the following selection describes, some conscientious objectors in World War I suffered imprisonment and mistreatment.

Defining for Comprehension

Choose the word or phrase below which most nearly defines each word at the left as it is used in this selection.

1. **brevity**
   a. simplicity   b. sobriety   c. shortness

2. **hysteria**
   a. high-pitched music   b. depression   c. rage; frenzy

3. **torturous**
   a. twisting   b. disrespectful   c. agonizing

4. **ominous**
   a. threatening   b. encouraging   c. immediate

5. **retrospect**
   a. examination   b. honor   c. looking back

6. **suave**
   a. smoothly sophisticated   b. wealthy   c. proud; arrogant

7. casualty	a. grace; ease	b. commonness	c. loss
8. abrogated	a. canceled	b. questioned	c. irritated
9. obscene	a. foul; evil	b. outdated	c. detected
10. menaced	a. threatened	b. practiced	c. trembled
11. repudiate	a. revise	b. reject	c. give off
12. denominational	a. of a church group	b. worldwide	c. patriotic
13. remanded	a. decreed	b. ordered back	c. reinspected
14. convene	a. congregate	b. interrupt	c. make pleasant
15. surveillance	a. wisdom	b. careful watch	c. seclusion
16. intimidate	a. hint	b. associate	c. frighten
17. ethical	a. just; proper	b. cautious	c. legal
18. confirmation	a. debate	b. strengthening	c. encounter
19. prerogative	a. question	b. introduction	c. right of choice

Though He Slay Me

I was fortunate in having been exposed to the Biblical teachings of nonresistance from my earliest memory. On approaching maturity I endeavoured to rethink these positions for myself. This resulted in a staunch decision that I could not participate in any form of army service.

Early in the summer of 1918, the last year of World War I, I was drafted into the Canadian Army. Orders were to report to "D" Company, 1st Depot Battalion, 2nd C. O. R., at Scott Street Barracks, Hamilton, Ontario, on May 7th. My number was D-3109171.

The sudden adjustment to such an emergency is difficult to describe. The religious, emotional and financial involvements created hours of mental anguish. The **brevity** of only one week to prepare for leaving home, and a persistent feeling that I might never return alive, all contributed to the strain of those painful days.

We read in the papers of several boys who were conscientiously opposed to serving in carnal warfare. They did not belong to any peace churches but stood firmly on personal convictions. They were maltreated by unauthorized men in the army. Some were held under a cold water pump until they died from exposure. No case was made of it as the days for the Allies were desperate and conscientious objectors were made victims of a patriotic **hysteria** that ignored law.

The last Sunday at church, teaching my Sunday school class of boys for what I thought was the last time, and receiving the tearful farewells of scores of friends, were emotional moments. However, none of them equaled the agony of saying good-bye to my family.

The awful moment of parting from my sister arrived. Memory of her pathetic cries and relentless clinging to my arms haunts me to this moment. I literally dragged her out on the lawn before she let me go.

The day was just breaking as my father and I walked toward the road. In the grey dawn we could see Pearl and my stepmother standing in front of our house, and their anguished sobs made it a most **torturous** moment.

Father and son walked solemnly the two miles to the railroad depot where we took the train to Hamilton. Our conversation was punctuated with **ominous** periods of silence. At one point Dad finally spoke.

"I feel this morning something like Abraham must have felt on his way to Mount Moriah."

Certainly, I would not be so immodest as to elevate my parent to the status of the "father of the faithful." I cannot escape, however, remembering his bravery and Christian fortitude as he faced the whole ordeal. One instance of this heroism may suffice.

While doing the morning chores shortly before my departure, he directed the following conversation. "My boy, you will soon be leaving me, and we cannot tell what the consequences will be. I want to ask you; if the worst comes to the worst, how is it with your soul?"

To this I took a rapid **retrospect** of my past and recalled the two crises in my spiritual life of which he was aware. They were my conversion at 12 years and my entire commitment to Christ at 19 years.

All I said in reply was, "It holds good this morning."

What followed was a bit dramatic. He put that bony left arm around my neck and said, "My boy, I do not know how I can get along without you here on the farm with only one arm, but I want you to stand true to God and your convictions at any price. I would rather get word that you were shot than to know you compromised your position and disobeyed the Lord."

Such rugged faith and staunch belief produced a buoyancy in my soul that I needed. I can never forget it. We then went into our granary and had a season of prayer together. What a prayer meeting that was!

The train ride to Hamilton had none of the delightsome experiences of former trips. Arriving late, we took a taxi to the camp. Being very ignorant of army routine, we made a few blundering approaches to the wrong officers and eventually arrived at our company headquarters.

Major Stanley of Company "D" was away so I was referred to Major Bennett of "A" Company. He was a **suave** trained militarist, and tried to flatter me into accepting army life. When this did not succeed, he tried to scare me with groundless threats. Although I did not know that he was so insincere at that time, I later discovered him telling a bare-faced lie. Someone has well said, "The first **casualty** in war is truth." It becomes a virtue to lie if it aids the war effort.

My father was armed with a number of official documents which clearly pointed to certain exemption privileges given to the historic peace churches when admitted to Canada. The Major emphatically told us that those treaties were all **abrogated**, declaring, "One stroke of the pen can suddenly remove any favors granted to persons or groups." I learned since that he over-simplified the process.

In a few days I was ordered to appear at the Quartermaster Stores to receive my army uniform and kit. At this point I decided to register my protest and take a positive stand regardless of cost. I refused to accept the uniform and kit. Cursed with abusive, **obscene** language such as I had never heard before, I was **menaced** with alarming threats. These did not affect me unduly for I had settled all such eventualities before leaving home.

With the corporal carrying my uniform, I was then taken to the bunk-house. Once more I was ordered to put it on. I refused. They disrobed me of my civilian clothes and put the fatigue suit of the Army Ordnance on me. I was immediately arrested and taken to the Guard House.

There I met eight other CO's. What a pleasant surprise after being told by Major Bennett there was not one other conscientious objector in the battalion! He said they had all been treated harshly enough that they had gladly fallen in line.

The next morning two other "objectors" and I were paraded before Colonel Belson for a preliminary hearing. He was very discourteous, to say the least. He accused us of being yellow, and declared he would shoot every one of us if he had authority.

One of our group belonged to the Plymouth Brethren, who **repudiate** any identification with a **denominational** label. I made a mental record of the following dialogue:

"What church do you belong to?" asked the colonel.

"The Church of Jesus Christ."

"Do you have a creed?"

"Yes, the Bible," replied my friend.

"Where do you originate?"

"At Calvary."

"But where are your headquarters?"

"Heaven."

"Don't get smart, kid," snapped the officer.

The colonel did not know that the Plymouth Brethren boy was answering sincerely in the tradition of his accepted belief. With no further words he **remanded** all three of us for a district court-martial to **convene** one month later.

We were held under **surveillance** in the "clink," as the guard house was called. Under escort of military police we were taken out on the grounds twice daily to pick up papers and keep the place looking respectable. In a few weeks our battalion moved to Niagara-on-the-Lake.

The day of the court-martial arrived. Nine of us were on trial, charged with "disobeying a lawful command given by a superior officer, in that while on active duty we refused to put on our uniform when ordered to do so by a superior officer." To this we pleaded guilty, and were all sentenced to two years hard labour.

Space will not permit repeating all the arguments, threats, and logics presented in the trial. However, one case of special interest follows. One of the older "objectors," David J. Nichols, was singled out for particular questioning.

Court: "Nichols, are you married?"

Nichols: "No."

Court: "We will suppose a case. Nichols, if you were married and your wife died unsaved (as you use the term), what would happen to her?"

Nichols: "Most decidedly she would go to hell."

Court: (pretending to be shocked) "Let us suppose you are married, your wife is not a Christian, here comes a company of the German army, and they plan to shoot her. Suppose you take a gun and shoot back holding them at bay for six months, and in the meantime your wife becomes a Christian. Then, you can hold them back no longer and they finally kill her. Would you not be doing God's will in fighting that period, seeing she would go to heaven with you?"

Without a moment's hesitation Nichols boldly replied, "In the first place this is only supposition. Second, I am not married. And third, if I ever do marry, I will marry a Christian."

Court: "No use fooling with this guy."

He was sentenced with the rest of us. Let it be reported that Nichols did marry a fine Christian girl a few years later.

In a few days the whole battalion was arranged in what they called a hollow square, one side left open. We prisoners were led into the square and one by one had our sentences read. The battalion sergeant-major removed our caps as each man's sentence was announced. All this emotion-packed ceremony was intended to **intimidate** us and warn the onlookers.

That same evening we were taken to the Lincoln County Jail at St. Catharines, Ontario. A very touching scene was evidenced as we left the camp. Nine of us prisoners sang great hymns of the church as we were paraded through the lines. The CO's remaining at the camp, and as yet unsentenced, joined us in song as long as we could hear them.

We had conducted a song service for fifteen minutes before leaving the camp, and scores of deeply-moved soldiers wept out of sympathy for us and because of the spiritual impact gospel singing creates on human hearts.

Outside the lines we boarded a crowded street car bound for St. Catharines and the prison. I was seated beside my Plymouth Brethren friend again and facing us were two noncommissioned officers, one of whom had committed the Plymouth Brethren boy for trial. He really despised conscientious objectors.

My pal held on his knees a briefcase with a Biblical motto artistically inscribed on each side. The irate officer was forced to look at the words: "But know thou that for all these things God shall bring thee into judgment."

His anger reached the point of explosion. "I don't have to sit here and look at that! You just turn that satchel around."

The Plymouth Brethren most gladly obliged, and the officer was confronted with "Except ye repent, ye shall all likewise perish." The Gospel must go forth.

All too soon our car came to a stop directly in front of the jail. We were met at the door by the prison governor, Mr. Bush. He registered us and asked the "turnkey," Garley Clinch, to search us and then take us up to the second corridor. He gave us our prison clothes and assigned us to our cells. I shared Cell 23 with another CO by the name of Allen Ironside Morrison.

Satan made a vicious attack on my spirit that beautiful June evening as I was locked in a cell with whitewashed brick all around and no furniture but a crude bed. Was I being foolish? Immediately there flashed into my mind the lines of an old hymn:

> But prisons would palaces prove
> If Jesus would dwell with me there.

I had immediate and complete victory. This prison proved to be exactly what the hymn said it would.

At 7:00 the next morning the steel door of our narrow cell was unlocked and we sat on benches in the corridor where we received our breakfast. The meals consisted of a pint of oatmeal porridge sprinkled with a dessert spoonful of sugar, but no milk, three slices of unbuttered bread and a cup to get water at the spigot. This three-times-a-day fare was occasionally replaced by a pint of beef stew at noon.

Mr. Bush was a very fine Baptist with a rare sense of humour. He extended to the conscientious objectors all the consideration possible within the legal and **ethical** boundaries of his responsiblity.

He had a large garden outside the wall and often took us out to hoe, because we had the rating of "Trusties." In the middle of a rather large corn section stood a loaded cherry tree. One of our fellows cleverly said, "Mr. Bush, do you know the Bible says: 'Thou shalt not muzzle the ox that treadeth out the corn'?"

Mr. Bush grinned. "All right, boys, fifteen minutes on the cherries."

What a treat that was! After we had resumed hoeing corn, Mr. Bush ordered; "Now boys, I want you to hoe corn until noon, and no stopping."

Early in our jail experience we were forcibly made to feel the hatred of the turnkey, Garley Clinch. Having been a former country sheriff, his career was associated with law violators most of his life. Now at seventy years of age, he was very hostile to our position. He left no stones unturned to be mean up to the limits of his authority. He stopped us from our group singing and prohibited a number of other pleasures we were enjoying. We could have gone over his head and appealed to the governor, but we felt that would not enhance our testimony. We *were* pleased that all eighteen of us were occupying a corridor by ourselves.

The second morning after our arrival, the grand jury of Lincoln County came to inspect the jail. They were escorted through our cell row by Garley. While we were sitting on the benches along the corridor, I overheard one of the jurymen say to Garley, "Who are these prisoners?"

Garley snorted in contempt. "I don't know who they are. They're a bunch of 'Unconscious Rejectors' they brought up from the camp yesterday." Poor Garley didn't know what to properly call us, but he knew positively that he resented us.

Bishop S. F. Coffman of the Mennonite Church lived nearby in Vineland, Ontario. He was a personal friend of Governor Bush and he frequently visited me. Mr. Bush allowed him to take me out beyond the wall. I can never forget the kindly interest Bishop Coffman took in me.

After I had served about ten weeks of my sentence, the War Department granted me a parole because of holding membership in a historic peace church. I had only to report every month to military headquarters. The war ended four months later and, strange to say, I was released with an honourable discharge.

Just a few days before my release, Garley had shown a great change of attitude by asking us to sing one of our hymns for him. Upon my leaving, he accompanied me to the prison lawn and with tearful face asked me to pray for him.

"You boys are getting more out of your religion than I am out of mine."

I promised to remember him in prayer, and did. A few days later Garley came to my cell mate, Allan Morrison, and asked him to pray for him. Using his Bible, a familiar book to the Plymouth Brethren, Allan led him to a saving knowledge of the truth in Christ.

Garley was very happy. He renounced his former way of life and rejoiced exceedingly in his new experience.

The Asian "Flu" was spreading its initial contagion around the world. In a few weeks Garley was a victim. Among his last words spoken to Mr. Bush, who was summoned to his bedside, were, "I am glad I ever met the conscientious objectors. They helped me to get saved."

One year later I visited Mr. Bush in the prison office and received the above story from his own lips. Mr. Bush then assured me, "So you see, you fellows were not in here for nothing."

After a ten-day delay while waiting for my papers, I was released from Camp. At noon on July 10th, I left Camp headquarters at Niagara-on-the-Lake, bound for home. After dismissal from Camp I walked to the dock, and learned that a boat would be leaving for Toronto in about an hour.

The boat arrived on schedule, and the trip across Lake Ontario to Toronto was enjoyable. I narrowly caught the night train for Collingwood, my home town 90 miles distant. The walk of five miles to my home in the country that hot, dark, summer night did not seem far. It seemed providential that I arrived at the farm gate just as my parents and Pearl were returning from the midweek prayer meeting.

As I heard the horse's hooves reveal that familiar slackening pace, I ran forward and said, "Let me open the gate."

"That's Ernie's voice!" exclaimed Pearl.

All three jumped out of the buggy and there at the very spot where weeks before we had such a sad parting, we now shared in a glorious reunion. After stabling the horse, we gathered around the family table and spent a delightful time until 3:00 a.m. We talked, laughed, cried and particularly enjoyed a period of thanksgiving to our Master.

This experience gave occasion for my further consideration of the Biblical doctrine of peace. By no means have I exhausted all the possibilities of research on this perplexing subject, but I have given it some study in depth. The result has been a deepening **confirmation** of my earlier convictions.

I can now present more clearly the teaching of God's Word regarding the sacredness of life. I am deeply convinced that we were never created to kill each other. Only God has the **prerogative** to give life or take life. A careful, unbiased approach to the Holy Scriptures reveals that war is not the will of God and this position is positively declared in the New Testament.

War never settles anything properly, but rather postpones a settlement. It would appear to be society's greatest menace. Calvary love is the only all-conquering force in our world. While I do not think war can ever be outlawed in this dispensation, yet surely Christians should abstain from participating in it. We are commanded by Christ to love our enemies and to overcome evil with good.

I am very thankful to God for having been cradled and nurtured in the Scriptural atmosphere of what is known as a Peace Church.

Testing for Understanding

1. Conscientious Objectors were abused for all the following reasons except
   a. their objection to war was interpreted as a lack of allegiance to their country.
   b. the law outlined such treatment for them.
   c. those who dealt with them were accustomed to dealing with lawbreakers.
   d. the situation of the Allies had driven many people nearly frantic.

2. The young man and his father entered the company headquarters with the hopes that
   a. they could convince the Major to allow him to return home.
   b. they could pay a fine so that he could escape service in the military.
   c. the boy would be exempted from the military on the basis of promises made to their church by the government.
   d. the boy could take up noncombatant service.

3. The boy saw all the following proofs of war's first casualty except
   a. he found himself resorting to lies to escape rough treatment.
   b. being flattered to convince him to join the military.
   c. being told that earlier treaties could be easily made void.
   d. being told that there were no other CO's in the battalion.

4. The court's reasoning with Nichols was illogical for all the following reasons except that
   a. the Christian does not value the life of one over another.
   b. Nichols did not have a wife.
   c. the Germans would not likely kill his wife.
   d. Nichols would not marry a non-Christian.

5. The early treatment of the CO's at camp was intended mostly to
   a. fulfill the terms of the law.
   b. spare the government expense.
   c. keep others from becoming CO's.
   d. frighten the CO's into recanting.

6. The incident of the Plymouth Brethren boy's Scripture-inscribed briefcase shows that
   a. whether in pretense or in truth Christ will be preached.
   b. truth will always prevail.
   c. we should not antagonize the ungodly.
   d. truth will always win those to whom it is presented.

7. The young man's victory over his temptation the first evening in prison shows the value of
    a. Bible truth learned at an early age.
    b. parental discipline.
    c. exposure to spiritual music.
    d. the beauties of surroundings.

8. Garley Clinch treated the CO's roughly until
    a. they felt he had sufficiently intimidated them.
    b. he discovered the reality of their faith.
    c. the CO's responded in a way inconsistent with their profession.
    d. higher officials ordered that he cease.

9. The part of the CO's religion that most impressed Garley Clinch was their
    a. ignoring him.
    b. living their faith before him.
    c. praying for him.
    d. attending to him when he was ill.

10. The CO's experiences were most valuable as opportunities to
    a. witness to the unsaved.
    b. help others in civilian service.
    c. help them define their own beliefs.
    d. broaden their knowledge of the world.

Reading for Understanding

1. *"I feel this morning something like Abraham must have felt on his way to Mount Moriah."*
    The father meant that
    a. he thought God would provide a way of escape for his son.
    b. he knew God was requiring too much of him.
    c. he knew his son didn't fully realize what was ahead of him.
    d. he felt as though he were having to give up his son.

2. *It becomes a virtue to lie if it aids the war effort.*
    This is an example of
    a. how men justify sin when they have wrong priorities.
    b. a time when God winks at men's ignorance.
    c. a situation when we must interpret God's laws on the basis of circumstance.
    d. the cost of living for the good of others.

3. *"But where are your headquarters?"*
    "Heaven."
    "Don't get smart, kid," snapped the officer.
    This dialogue shows that
    a. CO's suffered mistreatment because they disrespected the officials.
    b. officials often tried to corner the CO's.
    c. the boy thought that he would need to give up his life.
    d. the things of the spiritual world are not discerned by men of the flesh.

4. *Without a moment's hesitation Nichols boldly replied, "In the first place this is only supposition. Second, I am not married. And third, if I ever do marry, I will marry a Christian."*
    Nichols' reply shows that
    a. he was college educated.
    b. he had heard of this tactic before and had premeditated an answer.
    c. God will give those who trust Him the words to speak in time of need.
    d. Nichols was being arrogant.

5. *Calvary love is the only all-conquering force in our world.*
    The author feels that
    a. it is possible to completely eradicate war.
    b. if we have the love of God in our hearts, we can expect others to live at peace with us.
    c. God's love is too great to send anyone to hell.
    d. love that is willing to lay down its life for another is more effective than physical force.

 **Meditating for Meaning**

1. The doctrine of nonresistance is a Biblical doctrine.
    a. Find a Scripture that teaches this.
    b. What two things contributed to the author embracing this doctrine?
    c. Why are both of these valuable in the establishment of conviction?

2. Many people believe in what they call "situational ethics." Under certain situations, they think, it is permissible to disobey God.
    a. Give two examples from this story of situational ethics evidenced in military life.
    b. Give an example of a time when the young man and his friends might have been tempted to resort to situational ethics.
    c. What danger might this have posed to them in light of their CO position?
    d. How does their experience show the reward of standing firm in such situations?

3. The title of this selection is taken from Job 13:15.
    a. Find and copy the first sentence of this verse.
    b. In this verse the antecedent of *he* and *him* is the same. Who is it?
    c. As used for the title of this selection, who is more likely the antecedent of *he*?

4. Men generally put their trust in something they feel will not disappoint them.
    a. How can Job and the author say they will put their trust in someone at the expense of being slain?
    b. What else must be necessary, according to the last part of the verse, if we want to claim this trust?

Looking for Literary Technique

Unlike the previous two selections, this selection is written entirely in the past tense. However, like the earlier selections, the main character's name is replaced with *I*.

1. What do you call this point of view?

Some other *I* stories which you read earlier were not written about the author's actual experience. Rather he took an imaginary happening or the experience of someone else and wrote it as though it were his own. A personal experience has a sound of reality and conviction which other stories cannot have.

A personal account can include conversations which we know are actual.

2. Approximately how many conversations or direct quotations are included in this story? Count as one all conversations in which speakers change several times.

3. One conversation is recorded in an unusual way.
    a. What is different about the way this conversation is recorded?
    b. What effect does this method of recording conversation give?

Writing for Skill

Think of a time when you needed to stand on your convictions in a difficult situation. Show how you gained this conviction and what benefit it proved to be to you. Tell it with conviction as it happened to you. Include as much actual conversation as you can. Try recording some of the conversation with the speaker's name first.

Reflections on
Bible Characters

*Now all these things
happened unto them
for ensamples:
and they are written for
our admonition, upon whom
the ends of the world
are come.*

1 Corinthians 10:11

The Last Night of Sodom

by Daniel March

The story of Sodom is one of the most striking Bible stories of all Scripture. Lot, the two angels, the vile citizens, the heedless sons-in-law, fire, a disobedient wife, and the pillar of salt—we've heard it, and perhaps we think the story grows old. But those who find this story growing old ought to consider on which side of Sodom's wall their own affections lie. Read the story again as Daniel March tells it. Smell the acrid smoke stinging your nostrils. Feel the heat from the inferno of flames. Hear the wails of the once careless Sodomites. And "remember Lot's wife."

Defining for Comprehension

Choose the word or phrase below which most nearly defines each word at the left as it is used in this selection.

1. **impending**	a. soon to occur	b. dangling	c. pushing
2. **consumptive**	a. physically wasting	b. extravagant	c. uncertain
3. **deluded**	a. ignored	b. introduced	c. misguided
4. **siren**	a. enticing	b. desperate	c. senior
5. **woos**	a. entices	b. comforts	c. drips
6. **voluptuous**	a. breaking open	b. disturbing	c. pleasing the flesh
7. **indolent**	a. sympathetic	b. lazy	c. old time
8. **profusion**	a. radiation	b. lack of order	c. abundance

9. indulgence	a. carefulness	b. reckless pleasure	c. abuse
10. sensual	a. fleshly pleasing	b. logical	c. observant
11. incredulity	a. disbelief	b. inability to learn	c. disunity
12. infamy	a. dishonor; shame	b. unfriendliness	c. inconsideration
13. venerable	a. exposed	b. respectable	c. friendly
14. leering	a. mocking	b. looking evilly	c. staggering
15. rabble	a. trash	b. dispute	c. noisy mob
16. besotted	a. looked for	b. drunken	c. surrounded
17. dissolute	a. morally unrestrained	b. liquid	c. discouraged
18. teeming	a. gathering in lines	b. driving horses	c. swarming
19. reiteration	a. travel plan	b. renewal	c. repetition
20. profligate	a. morally corrupt	b. abundant	c. scornful
21. conflagration	a. extravagant praise	b. assembly	c. great fire
22. lurid	a. black and blue	b. enticing	c. fiery; horrifying
23. conceded	a. ended	b. yielded	c. withdrew
24. revenues	a. tree-lined streets	b. deserving	c. incomes
25. seductive	a. deceitfully enticing	b. reduced	c. logical
26. lethargy	a. poison	b. lack of energy	c. hatred
27. monitions	a. counsels	b. supervisors	c. payments
28. tenure	a. intended meaning	b. act of holding	c. weakness
29. transitory	a. short-lived	b. leveling device	c. necessary

The Last Night of Sodom

"Tarry all night."
"Escape for thy life."

The words of man and the words of angels. The man, a master of courtesy and hospitality; the angels, ministers of mercy and of vengeance. The man speaks of house and home and feasting and rest; the angels speak of **impending** wrath and swift destruction. The man persuades to the enjoyment of a quiet evening in a luxurious clime, and promises the return of a beautiful day; the angels would hasten an escape from the scene of enchantment and delight, at the sacrifice of all earthly possessions. The man speaks from mere feeling and a vivid impression of things as they are passing before his eyes; the angels speak of things as they are,—and behind the calm and peaceful aspect of the closing day, they see the fiery tempest of the coming morn.

Such is the contrast between feeling and fact, shadow and substance, appearance and reality. So unlike and so allied to each other are the sensual and the spiritual; the earthly and the heavenly; the aspect of peace and safety, and the near approach of danger and destruction. Such is the difference between the judgment of man, who is all involved in the cares and toils and pleasures of the passing day, and the judgment of beings who stand outside the range of our mistakes and temptations, and who see the affairs of time in the light of eternity.

The scene which arrests our attention is one of quietness and security. It is evening. A fair city lies upon the border of a plain that looks like a garden in beauty and fertility. A bright lake stretches away northward between dark frowning hills, and the steep wall of the eastern shore is reflected in perfect outline beneath the mirror-like surface of the water. Laborers are coming in from the vineyards and fields on the plain, and shepherds are folding their flocks on the distant hills. There are no signs of wrath in the sky, no voices of wailing in the air, no tremor in the "sure and firm-set earth." And yet the last night is casting its shadows upon the walls and battlements of the doomed city.

According to the custom of the land and the time, the chief men are sitting in the gate. Old and young are all abroad in the open air. The idle multitude are coming and going to gather the gossip of the day, and enjoy the cool wind that comes up from the lake outside of the walls. The sun has gone down behind the western hills, and the brief twilight lingers as if loth to go, like a purple fringe on the dusky garments of the coming night. So lingers the crimson flush of health upon the pale cheek of the **consumptive,** while the fires of fever are draining the fountains of life within. So the **deluded** youth, enticed by the **siren** voice of pleasure, hesitates at the threshold of the house of death, and then sets his feet in the way to hell with a smile.

The evening is so mild and beautiful in the cloudless clime of the East that the idle and pleasure-loving population give themselves up with childish freedom to its bewitching charm, and the streets of the city and its walks outside the gates resound with the voices of the gay, and the loud laugh of the "vacant mind." Theirs is the land of the olive and the vine. The flowers blossom through all the year. The air is loaded with perfume. The light clothes the landscape with dreamy fascination. The evening air **woos** to **voluptuous** ease. The night persuades to passion and pleasure.

The plains surrounding the city are like the garden of the Lord in fertility. The most **indolent** culture secures an abundance for the supply of every want. The distant hills are covered with flocks. The merchants of the East bring their treasures from afar. The camels and *dromedaries*[1] of the desert lay down their burdens at her gates. And the fair city in the vale of Siddim revels in the **profusion** of everything that nature and art can produce. The chief men display the luxury and the pride of princes. The common people make a holiday of the whole year. The multitude look as if they were strangers equally to want and to work. Like birds in summer, they enjoy the season as it passes, and they take no thought for the morrow. Idleness and riches stimulate the appetite for pleasure, and they go to every excess in **indulgence.** They have everything that the sensual can desire, and their only study is to find new ways of gratifying the coarsest and basest passion. According to the testimony of One who knew all history, they eat and drink, they buy and sell, they plant and build, and their whole thought and effort and desire is given to a life of the senses, denying God and debasing the soul. And they are so passionate and haughty in their devotion to earthly

---

1. dromedaries: one-humped camels.

possessions and **sensual** pleasures as to count it a mockery for one to say that there may be guilt or danger in such a life.

Such is the throng of the thoughtless and the gay around the gate of the beautiful city in the vale of Siddim, while for them the shadows of evening are deepening into night for the last time. It would only provoke a smile of **incredulity** or derision if they were told that they were sporting upon their funeral *pile*,[2] and that the breath of the divine wrath was just ready to kindle the pile into devouring flame.

Two strangers were seen approaching the city. The softened radiance of the evening light shows nothing unusual in their appearance. They seem to be only common travelers coming down from the hill-country, and turning in for shelter by night, that they may rise up early in the morning and go on their journey.

There was but one man at the gate of Sodom sufficiently attentive to notice the strangers and invite them to his own house. He did not know who they were, nor did he suspect the awful errand upon which they came. But by treating them with such courtesy as was due to the character of strangers, in which they came, he secured for himself such help as angels alone could give in the time of his greatest need.

The idle throng in the streets deride the hospitable old man for taking the two strangers home to his own house. They see nothing in them worthy of such attention. They are much more ready to treat them with rudeness and contempt, or to make them the subjects of the passion which has given their city a name of **infamy** throughout all generations. They hoot and jeer at the **venerable** patriarch when he rises up from his seat in the gate to meet the travellers, and bows himself with his face to the ground, and says with eastern courtesy, "Behold now, my lords, turn in, I pray you, into your servant's house, and tarry all night." The vilest suggestions are passed to and fro among the lewd and **leering rabble** as the old man leads his guests away. The hour of rest has not come before a crowd gathers in the streets and besets the house where the strangers have gone

to repose. They become more clamorous, with infamous outcries and rude assault, as night wears on. They are so blinded and **besotted** in their sensuality that they would do violence to God's mighty angels, who can wrap their city in flames and open the pit of destruction beneath their habitations in a moment.

The celestial messengers had come to see whether there were any, in all that city, who could be persuaded to escape from the impending doom. And the iniquity of the inhabitants was full; the last drop was added to the fiery cup of wrath to be poured upon their heads, when they received the warning as an idle tale and treated the messengers with contempt.

The men of Sodom did not think they were doing anything unusual when they beset the house of Lot and came near to break the door. They were no more riotous or **dissolute** on this last night than they had been many nights before. But there is a point beyond which the divine forbearance cannot go. And they had reached that point, when they clamoured against Lot, and would have beaten him down in the streets for protecting his angel-guests. When blindness fell upon them, and they wearied themselves to find the door, they had already passed

> "The hidden boundary between
> God's patience and His wrath."

For the sake of the righteous man, Lot, there was just one thing more to be done. The aged father is permitted to go out and urge his sons-in-law to flee from the doomed city. He makes his way to their houses through the blinded rabble in the streets, and gives the warning. But he seems to them as one that mocked. They cannot think it possible that he is in his right mind, to be coming to them at that late hour of the night with such an alarming message. They only tell him to go home and quiet his fears by dismissing the suspicious strangers and going to sleep in his own house. They cannot think of troubling themselves about the anxieties of a wakeful and weakminded old man, when nothing is wanted but a little rest to dismiss his fears. They will sleep on till morning, and

---

2. pile: a heap of combustible material for burning a corpse.

tomorrow they will laugh at the kind-hearted old father about his midnight call.

When the disappointed father comes back to his own house, the angels of rescue are waiting for him. And now the first streaks of dawn begin to appear in the east. As yet there is no apparent change in the earth or the sky. No trumpet of wrath has blown through the midnight. No earthquake has shaken the hills. No sulphurous fires have flamed up from the bed of the peaceful valley. No threatening wave has rolled upon the shore of the quiet lake. No cloud of vengeance darkens the coming day. The morning star shines with its customary brightness over the mountains of Moab. The cool air, mingled with the perfume of flowers, comes up like refreshing incense from the placid sea, and the song of birds welcomes the returning light. There is nothing to fear save that one word of the angels: "The Lord will destroy this city." The beautiful skies speak peace and safety. The **teeming** earth promises riches and abundance. The sleeping city dreams of long life and continued pleasure. The coming day looks down from the eastern hills with a smile. But the angels have said, "The Lord will destroy this city," and that is reason enough for alarm and for immediate flight.

It is hard for the old man to go and leave a part of his own family and all his worldly possessions behind to perish. But go he must, or even *he* cannot be saved. He lingers with divided heart and hesitating mind, while the door of doom is fast coming on. The angels urge him to hasten, but he lingers still. With merciful violence, they lay hold upon his hands and upon the hands of those of his family that are with him in the house, and hurry them forth out of the city. And then comes the startling and vehement charge: "Escape for thy life! Look not behind thee, neither stay thou in all the plain. Escape to the mountain, lest thou be consumed."

A few moments' delay will cost him his life. If he only turn to take one longing, lingering look of house and home, and of all that his heart holds dearest on earth—if he only wait to see what will become of the city—he will be consumed in the coming storm. The overthrow

is delayed only to give the fugitives time to escape. Their steps across the plain are counting out the last moments of the doomed city. Still the weary and distracted old man begs to be permitted to rest at a little town short of the safe mountains. It is so small that he thinks it need not be involved in the ruin of the greater and guiltier city below. The fond and fearful request is granted, but with a solemn **reiteration** of the charge to hasten, for the fiery storm cannot long be restrained from its outbreaking wrath. One of the four fugitives pauses to look back, with a vain curiosity to see what would become of the city, and so fails to escape.

The sun is already risen upon the earth, and the bright morning promises a beautiful day. The early risers in Sodom are making themselves merry about the frightened old man who has fled with his family to the mountains. The sons-in-law are on the way to his house, to laugh at him for walking in his sleep the night before. The idle and voluptuous are devising new pleasures for the day; and the **profligate** are sleeping through the fresh hours of the morning to compensate for the late revels of the night.

And just now the hour of doom strikes. The Lord rains fire and brimstone out of heaven upon the city, and upon the beautiful plain that seemed like Paradise the day before; and the smoke of the burning goes up as the smoke of a great furnace; and the glare of the mighty **conflagration** is seen far off by shepherds on the hills of Hebron and the mountains of Moab. In one moment the fair vale, which had been as the garden of the Lord in beauty and fertility, becomes a desolation—a place never to be inhabited from generation to generation—a valley of desolation and of death, where the wandering Arab shall never dare to pitch his tent, nor the shepherd to make his fold—a horrible region, doleful in reality, and clothed with additional terrors by gloomy superstition and evil imaginations. And God made this great desolation in His own beautiful and glorious work because the sin of Sodom was great and the cry of its iniquity had come up to heaven. The last night was as serene and beautiful as ever hung its starry curtain over the sleeping world. And when the golden dawn broke into day, the rising sun had not seen a fairer city than Sodom in all the "gorgeous East." In one moment her last cry went up to heaven amid tempests of fire that rained down from above, and fountains of fire that burst up from the deep. And Sodom has become a name of infamy for all generations; and its awful doom stands forth as a perpetual sign that God's patience with sin has a bound beyond which it will not go.

The Scriptures expressly declare that the fiery fate of this doomed city in ancient time is set forth as an example, to warn men in all subsequent ages against leading ungodly lives. The **lurid** flame of this great act of the divine justice sends its warning light through all the centuries of human history, to show that there is a God in heaven, before whom the cry of man's iniquity goes up day and night. The things that are told of Sodom may be said of many a city that has not shared in Sodom's doom. The prophet Ezekiel says that the sin of that city was "pride and fulness of bread and abundance of idleness." Millions would count it happiness to revel in abundance and have nothing to do. Thus far in the world's history the highest rank in human society has been **conceded** to those who have the greatest **revenues** secured to them without effort on their part, and who never touch the common burdens of humanity with one of their fingers. And we all know how naturally pride enthrones itself as the master-passion in the heart, when all fear of want and all necessity to work are taken away.

The sin of Sodom, however gross in reputation and in reality, was the offspring of wealth and leisure—the two things which the worldly heart most desires, and of which, when possessed, the worldly heart is most proud. If men could have all that they desire of both, how hard it would be for them to think or care at all for the life to come. Many are ashamed of work;—all are afraid of want. And yet it is work which makes worth in men, and the deepest sense of want is the beginning of immortal life in the soul.

This awful lesson in sacred history may be all summed up in two messages. The one is from man and the world;—the other is from heaven and God. One says to the careless and the worldly, "Tarry, be at ease, enjoy yourself while you can;"—the other says, "Escape for thy life." One says, "Wait, be not alarmed: make yourself comfortable where you are;"—the other says, "Haste, look not behind thee; flee to the mountain, lest thou be consumed." One says, "Soul, take thine ease; eat, drink, and be merry;"—the other says, "Thou fool! this night thy soul may be required of thee."

The question which every one must answer for himself is always this, Which of these two voices shall I obey? Shall I sit down in that **seductive** and false security which is all absorbed in earthly things, and fears no evil because at present there is no appearance of danger? Or shall I obey the voice from heaven, which commands me to arise and shake off the dangerous **lethargy** of the world and escape for my life? Shall I listen to the voice of earth, which cries peace and safety, or the voice of heaven, which says that destruction lies in the path of souls that are at ease without God?

To many it seems like mockery to talk of danger to the young and the gay, the healthful and the happy. But who was the mocker on the peaceful night when the cities of the plain rioted in pleasure for the last time—the righteous man, Lot, who exposed himself to the jeers of the mob and made his way through the darkened streets to warn his sons-in-law, and fled himself for his life; or the sons-in-law themselves, who laughed at the warning and perished in the flames?

All the seductions and falsehoods of temptation, and all the dangers and sorrows of perdition, are bound up in that one word—*wait*. The voice of love speaks to the careless in terms of terror and alarm. God's patience will not always last. The day of grace must have an end. And with many it is much shorter than they expect. The God who rained a fiery tempest upon the cities of the plain, and destroyed them, is the God who holds our everlasting destiny in His hands. He will not always be mocked. He will not long be trifled with.

And the loving and compassionate Jesus Himself declares that there is a greater sin than that for which Sodom and Gomorrah were overthrown. It is the sin of those who hear the Gospel call to repentance, and heed it not. It is the sin of those who see the Son of God agonizing in the garden and dying on the cross for their salvation, and who still refuse to give Him their hearts. It is the sin of those who have been many times warned and entreated, and who nevertheless spend their lives in waiting for a more convenient season to repent and turn to God. It is the sin of those who put off the first great work of life to the dying hour, and death finds them with the work all undone. It shall be more tolerable for Sodom and Gomorrah in the day of judgment than for those who spent their lives in such utter neglect of the great salvation.

The blessed and merciful Jesus gave forth that solemn warning to the neglecters and despisers in His day, that the echo of His voice might resound through all time, and that all who hear might be saved from such a doom. His most awful threatening involves and includes an invitation of equal extent. He would awaken fear that He may kindle hope. He commands effort that He may save from despair. He draws back the veil from the pit of darkness that we may be constrained to look up when He unfolds the glories of paradise.

The angels hastened Lot while he lingered and was loth to go. The voices of the divine mercy are ever repeating the cry, HASTE, ESCAPE FOR THY LIFE. Wait not for better opportunities to begin a better life. Any oppor-

About the Author

Daniel March (1816-1909) graduated from Yale College and Yale Divinity School. After serving as principal at Chester Academy in Vermont, he pastored several Congregationalist and Presbyterian churches of New England. He wrote numerous books about Bible times including *Night Scenes in the Bible*, from which "The Last Night of Sodom" is taken. Several of his books have been translated into German and Swedish.

tunity to secure infinite and eternal blessing is a good one. And a better one than the present may never come. Look not behind to see what will become of our worldly pleasures and vanities. When the soul is in peril, no earthly interest can be a sufficient reason for an hour's delay. The solemn **monitions** of conscience, the uncertain **tenure** of all earthly possessions, the embittered and **transitory** nature of all earthly joys, the admonitions of divine providence in affliction and death, the sweet and mighty constraint of the love of Christ, and all the perils and sorrows and necessities of the soul, continually say to the hesitating and the halting: Haste thee; escape for thy life; make sure thy flight to the stronghold of hope before the voice of mercy shall cease to call, and the wrath that is ready to burn, burst in an endless storm.

Testing for Understanding

1. The difference between the words of Lot and the words of the angels is the difference between all except
   a. feeling and fact.
   b. courtesy and mercy.
   c. hospitality and firmness.
   d. stubbornness and vengeance.

2. Lot's sons-in-law sealed their doom when
   a. they reveled in the beauty of this night.
   b. they ignored Lot's warnings.
   c. Lot first entered Sodom and they were not influenced by him.
   d. they spent the previous day in idleness.

3. Lot's sons-in-law did not believe him because
   a. Lot had often threatened them like this.
   b. Lot was senile.
   c. nothing this severe had ever happened to punish them before.
   d. there was not harmony between them.

4. The mercy of God is shown in all of the following except
   a. the visit of the angels.
   b. the tarrying of the angels until Lot could warn his family.
   c. the angels taking Lot's hand and leading him out.
   d. turning Lot's wife into a pillar of salt.

5. Lot's failure to grasp the complete seriousness of the situation is seen in
   a. his invitation to the angels to lodge with him that night.
   b. his failure to convince his sons-in-law to come along.
   c. the backward look of his wife.
   d. his request to be allowed to take refuge in a small nearby town.

6. Lot's wife failed to escape because
   a. God did not intend to save her in the first place.
   b. she left some of her family in Sodom.
   c. she did not hurry fast enough.
   d. she disobeyed the command of the angels of God.

7. This story shows that wealth and leisure are dangerous because they
   a. subject us to the envy of others.
   b. are the product of selfishness.
   c. lead to moral and spiritual ruin.
   d. are often gotten by ill means.

8. Those who mock the righteous should remember that
   a. they will eventually face a righteous judge.
   b. they will only be young once.
   c. they probably do things worthy of mocking themselves.
   d. they are preparing themselves for the retaliation of those who mock.

9. The greatest mistake of mankind is
   a. procrastination in the preparation of the soul.
   b. heaping up of riches.
   c. mockery of the poor.
   d. enjoyment of pleasure.

10. The strongest message of Sodom to us is
    a. Be not forgetful to entertain strangers.
    b. Do not accumulate riches.
    c. Seek God's kingdom, not pleasure and wealth.
    d. Beware of evil influence.

Reading for Understanding

1. *The things that are told of Sodom may be said of many a city that has not shared in Sodom's doom.*
    From this we know that
    a. Sodom was more wicked than any other city.
    b. just because other cities were not destroyed like Sodom does not say they were less wicked.
    c. God does not use the same methods of punishment today as He did in Sodom's day.
    d. there are different degrees of sin and punishment.

2. *The deepest sense of want is the beginning of immortal life in the soul.*
    The author means that
    a. those who are materially poor are most likely to reach heaven.
    b. we must recognize our severe need before we will seek eternal life.
    c. the most wicked sinner is likely to obtain salvation.
    d. greed for material things is similar to the desire for immortality.

3. *The voice of love speaks to the careless in terms of terror and alarm.*
    This sentence is saying that
    a. sensual love tends to dull us to reality.
    b. love frightens those who do not expect it.
    c. it is God's love to warn those who are content in their sins.
    d. those who are not spiritually alert fear expressions of God's love.

4. *He draws back the veil from the pit of darkness that we may be constrained to look up when He unfolds the glories of paradise.*
    The author is expressing the idea that
    a. there is a pathway to hell near to the very gate of heaven.
    b. those who go to hell will be tormented by the thought of others in heaven.
    c. God will be the final judge in all circumstances.
    d. God allows us to see the punishment of evil that we may fear and prepare ourselves for heaven.

5. *It shall be more tolerable for Sodom and Gomorrah in the day of judgment than for those who spend their lives in such utter neglect of the great salvation.*
    When Jesus expressed this idea He was emphasizing that
    a. many innocent were destroyed in Sodom and Gomorrah who will be spared in judgment.
    b. there are varying degrees of punishment to be experienced in hell.
    c. hell will only be for a measured length of time.
    d. in the Gospel era we have less excuse for our sin than the people of Sodom and Gomorrah who lived before the time of Christ.

Meditating for Meaning

1. The sin of Sodom was not unique. This account helps to show how people reach the point of coming under God's judgment.
   a. Find the first Biblical reference to Sodom that refers to the moral character of its men. Copy the verse.
   b. According to the selection you just read, what natural benefits did the city of Sodom have?
   c. How did they use and respond to these natural benefits?
   d. Explain how such a response to natural benefits can lead to sin.

2. Because those who enjoy natural benefits sometimes fall into sin does not mean that such benefits are wrong.
   a. Show from Scripture that this is true.
   b. What is wrong when men respond in wrong ways to natural benefits? (See Deuteronomy 8.)
   c. How does God intend for natural benefits to be used?

3. The author says, "Like birds in summer, they enjoy the season as it passes, and they take no thought for the morrow." Explain the difference between this condemnation and the command of Matthew 6:34 to "Take therefore no thought for the morrow."

4. God's mercy on sinners will come to an end as it did in the case of Sodom.
   a. Read the account of Genesis 18:16-33. Why had God decided it was time to destroy Sodom?
   b. Though we do not know exactly when the Lord will destroy the world, what does the Bible tell us about the times near the end? (See 2 Timothy 3:1-5.)
   c. What was Abraham's personal concern as he bargained with the Lord in Genesis 18:16-33?
   d. With what act of mercy did God answer this concern?
   e. Why did so few respond to this mercy?
   f. How has God shown this same mercy to the world in general?

5. Sodom and Lot served as examples to many generations.
   a. With the help of a concordance, find the number of times the New Testament makes reference to Sodom or Lot and list these references.
   b. What general warning do these references give in the mention of Lot?
   c. What encouraged Lot to move toward Sodom?
   d. What rather should he have taken into consideration in this move?
   e. Though Lot escaped, how does this experience show the danger of such a choice?

6. Unlike the story of Lot fleeing Sodom, we cannot literally leave this world. Jesus recognized this in John 17:15. How can we "flee Sodom"?

Looking for Literary Technique

This is a familiar Bible story, retold with new vividness. But in retelling this story, the author takes most of the facts from the Bible account.

1. Compare this story with Genesis 19. Give the number of the verse which corresponds with each

of the following phrases from Daniel March's story.

    a. Two strangers are seen approaching the city.

    b. One man at the gate of Sodom

    c. To notice the strangers and invite them to his own house

    d. The celestial messengers had come to see . . . who could be persuaded to escape from the impending doom.

    e. The men of Sodom . . . beset the house of Lot and came near to break the door.

    f. Blindness fell upon them

    g. The aged father is permitted to go out and urge his sons-in-law to flee from the doomed city.

    h. But he seems to them as one that mocked.

    i. He lingers with divided heart.

    j. The angels urge him to hasten.

    k. They lay hold upon his hands . . . and hurry them forth.

    l. The weary and distracted old man begs to be permitted to rest at a little town.

    m. The fond and fearful request is granted.

    n. One of the four fugitives pauses to look back . . . and so fails to escape.

    o. The sun is already risen upon the earth.

    p. And just now the hour of doom strikes.

The author also employs his imagination and adds some details. These details, however, do not violate the Bible account.

2.   Give two examples of details added by the author but not found in the Bible.

    Also the author uses colorful imagery to make this story live.

3.   Find one example each of simile and metaphor in this story.

The account includes many other historical and geographical facts about Sodom which may have come from history books, Bible dictionaries, or various Bible helps.

4.   Give one example of a fact which the author likely found in a source such as this.

 *Writing for Skill*

Choose a Bible story. Familiarize yourself with the facts of the Biblical account. Research facts of history and geography in encyclopedias and Bible dictionaries. Tell the story in a fresh, new way. Refrain from copying exact wording from the Bible. Add color by using imagery and imagination, but be sure you do not turn your story into fiction. Stick to facts. Show, as the author of this selection did, the truth to be gained from the Bible story you have chosen.

The Self-Made Fool—Saul

by Clovis G. Chappell

What picture is sadder than that of crumbling sticks where once a white-painted, pasture fence stood, of tumbling brambles where once a neatly trimmed meadow lay. Rubble and decay are ugly at best, but how much sadder, how much uglier when they lie where once stood the brightest beauty and promise. When we remember the beauty of the past and consider what beauty might be blooming even now, who can reproach our tears? And how bitter are those tears when the broken-down beauty is the character of a man! But much more is the bitterness when the tears come from the eyes of a fallen man! Such are the tears we hear in the words of Saul, "I have played the fool."

Defining for Comprehension

Choose the word or phrase below which most nearly defines each word at the left as it is used in this selection.

1. **pathos** — a. highway — b. bitterness — c. quality to arouse sympathy

2. **physique** — a. strategy — b. build of body — c. hairdo

3. **conspicuous** — a. demanding — b. obvious — c. careful

4. **arbitrarily** — a. randomly — b. with careful thought — c. in detail

5. **unction** — a. inclination — b. guilt — c. earnestness

6. **glibly** — a. boldly — b. smoothly; nonchalantly — c. swiftly

7. **palpable**   a. blameworthy   b. easily noticeable   c. likely

8. **adder**   a. poisonous serpent   b. mental disturbance   c. approval

9. **forebodings**   a. dwellings   b. forewarnings of evil   c. refusals

10. **impostor**   a. intruder   b. fake   c. offspring

11. **epitaph**   a. conclusion   b. gravestone verse   c. symbol

The Self-Made Fool—Saul

"I have played the fool" (1 Samuel 26:21). This is the confession of King Saul. He is referring especially to one act, or to one series of acts in his life. He is condemning his conduct toward a young man that he once admired and loved, named David. But this same confession might have been used as a final summing up of Saul's life. It might serve as his autobiography. And that which deepens the **pathos** of this confession is the fact that this role was self-chosen. Saul was not sent into the world to play the part of a fool. God did not plan to deck him out with *cap and bells*[1]. He was intended to play the part of a king. God planned that he should wear the garments of royalty. But he thwarted God's plan. He chose the role of fool. But he is not the type of fool that makes us laugh. He is a fool over whom we must weep if we can find any tears bitter enough.

When we first meet Saul there is much in him to admire.

He was a man of splendid **physique.** The record tells us that he was a choice young man. He stood head and shoulders above any man in Israel. He was kingly in his appearance. He was princely in his bearing.

Then Saul was a modest man. This is evident from his words to Samuel. When the prophet came to anoint him king he told him frankly that he was of the tribe of Benjamin and that Benjamin was the smallest of the tribes of Israel; that his father's house was the smallest of the families of Benjamin. Then, too, he was not too big to work honestly at a lowly task. He was in search of his father's asses, you remember, when he found his kingdom. It is often the case that in the faithful doing of the commonplace duty we find ourselves called to the higher and the more **conspicuous.**

In the third place Saul had youth. He was in the springtime of life. His best years were yet before him. He was yet brushing the dewy flowers of life's morning. He was at the age when choice can be most easily made and most easily adhered to. He was at that hour in which a right choice might bring to him and to the world the largest results. He was a young man.

Next, Saul had a great friend. When Charles Kingsley was asked for a secret of his own beautiful life, he answered: "I had a friend." This same great blessing was granted to Saul. It was his privilege to have Samuel for his friend

---

1. cap and bells: fool's cap with small attached bells, worn by court jesters.

and for his pastor. Samuel loved him with patient devotion. When Saul went wrong Samuel did all that human power could do to win him from his wrong. And to the very end of his life this faithful prophet never ceased to pray for him. He clung to him as a father might cling to a wayward son.

He was chosen for a great task. He was chosen for this task not **arbitrarily,** but because he had more fitness for it at the time than any other man in sight. He was not simply the choice of Samuel, the prophet, nor of the people. He was God's choice. Not that he was in any sense perfect. He was far from it. But he was the best that God could find in all Israel at that time. So God set His seal upon him. The word says that the Spirit of God came upon him and that God gave him another heart.

What use did Saul make of his opportunities? What returns did he render for the big investment that God had made in him?

He played the fool. If we should ask in what specific way he played the fool, the answer would be readily given by all who are acquainted with his life. Saul sinned. He rebelled against God. He turned from following after the Lord who had lifted him out of his lowly place and put a crown on his head.

But, while that answer would be in a sense correct, it is not the truest answer. Saul did sin. He sinned deeply. But there have been countless others who have sinned in a far more ugly and hideous way than he, whose lives yet ended in glory and in victory. Saul was never guilty of any sin half so detestable as the sin of his successor, who came to be a man after God's own heart. The tragedy of the life of Saul was not so much in the fact that he sinned as in the fact that he could never be brought to face his sin and to confess it and to hate it and to put it away.

For instance, God sent him one day with a command to destroy the Amalekites. He was to utterly destroy all their sheep and cattle, everything they had. Saul gathered his army in good faith and set out to the accomplishment of the task assigned. He defeated the Amalekites, but he took their king captive and saved the best of the sheep and the fattest of the cattle. And with

these he returned home seemingly in perfect confidence that he had thoroughly fulfilled the command of his Lord.

But the Lord never counts a partial obedience as a wholehearted obedience. Therefore, the word of the Lord came to Samuel saying: "Saul has turned from following after me." Not that Saul refused to do anything that the Lord commanded,—he only refused to do all. That is, he obeyed God in so far as it suited him, and beyond that he would not go. He killed the cattle that he did not want and kept the rest. He clung to the sins that appealed to him and threw the rest away. And such half-hearted obedience God counts as absolute rebellion.

When Samuel heard of Saul's failure, it broke his heart. "Saul has turned from following after me." Samuel never heard worse news than that. Every word is soaked in tears. Every syllable staggers under a weight of agony. There was no sleep for the old prophet that night. The record says that he cried unto God all night. What a privilege to have a man like that for your friend! What a privilege to have somebody, a father or mother or wife or pastor, who thinks enough of you to break his heart over your wrongdoing! "Samuel cried unto the Lord all night." But he was not content even with this. Not only did he speak to the Lord about Saul's sin, but he resolved to speak to the king himself. That was fine. That was courageous.

So after a sleepless night we see this brave old preacher setting out to try to bring the rebellious king to repentance. All the way to Saul's tent we can imagine this prophet is praying. At last he arrives. But when the two men stand eye to eye, only one face is drawn with pain. Only one face is stained with tears, and that is the face of the preacher. Saul is seemingly as happy and carefree as a little child. He greets his friend in a tone that is so pious that it fairly oozes **unction.** "Blessed be thou of the Lord," he cries. "I have performed the commands of the Lord." You see he has no disposition to acknowledge his sin. Seemingly he has no consciousness of wrongdoing whatsoever. He lies as **glibly** as if he were morally color-blind.

Then suddenly an embarrassing situation

develops. The lie is scarcely out of his mouth when some of those fat sheep begin to bleat, and some of those prize cattle begin to low. Possibly Saul had the grace to blush. Possibly he was not too hardened to show a bit of confusion. But if he did, he recovered himself quickly. He never lost his power of speech. He had an answer right on the tip of his tongue. "Oh, those cattle?" he said. "There are cattle there, it is true. They are not all dead, but that is no fault of mine."

When these cattle began to low Saul had a big chance. His sin became open and **palpable.** Had David been in his place, I feel confident that he would then and there have burst into tears and have asked the old prophet to pray for him. But not so Saul. Saul was just ready for more talk. He said, "I did not absolutely destroy all the sheep and cattle, but the reason I did not was the fault of the people. The people spared them. I am not to blame. They are to blame. A sin has been committed, but it is not mine, it is theirs."

Oh, this fatal excuse making! There is nothing that more surely shows an utter lack of repentance on the part of a man than the fact that he makes excuse for his sin. Just so long as you blame circumstances, just so long as you blame the church, just so long as you blame anybody in the world but yourself, just that long will you remain unrepentant. Just that long, too, will you remain unforgiven. For if there is an excuse for sin, then you are not guilty. If you are not guilty, then you do not need pardon. If you are not guilty, you have no part in the redemption wrought through Christ. He is come to seek and to save that which is lost.

But the people, Saul, who was their leader? Were you not their king? Could you not control them? Had you commanded them to carry out the Lord's command, would they not have done so? Certainly they would. Saul knows, as Samuel knows, that the fault is all his own; that the guilt is all his; that he has nobody to blame but himself. But when he is driven from this hiding place, he still will not come clean and confess. He tries to put a religious face on his sin: "Yes, we spared the best of the sheep and oxen, it is true, but we did it for religious reasons. We brought them along to sacrifice to the Lord, your God."

And what answer does the prophet make? "Hath the Lord as great pleasure in sacrifice as in obeying the voice of the Lord?" You see what Saul is trying to do. He is trying to buy an *indulgence.*[2] He wants to pay God for the privilege of sinning. He wants to do wrong and then get excused from it by giving to the Lord a few fat sheep and cattle. But the Lord rejected Saul's offer, as He rejects ours. There is nothing that will take the place of wholehearted obedience. Driven thus from this last refuge, Saul makes confession. He says, "I have sinned."

Saul made that confession more often than any other man in all the Bible. It was on his lips again and again. From the number of times he uttered it, you might fancy that he was the most penitent of men. How often he is saying, "I have sinned, I have sinned!" But under what circumstances does he make these confessions? He makes them only when he is in some kind of difficulty. Whenever you hear Saul confessing after this fashion, you may know he is in some kind of trouble from which he wants immediate release. Here the prophet has told him that because of his sin God is going to take the kingdom from him. He does not want to lose the kingdom. Therefore he acknowledges his guilt. But never would he make such an acknowledgement except under pressure of some impending calamity.

And, mark you, Saul is not in a class to himself. How many of us never think seriously of Christ or of His salvation until we get into some kind of trouble! A family member is near death and we want help. We ourselves are nearing the crossing and we are afraid. A cyclone is on hand and we feel the need of a refuge. But the same winds that carry the clouds away, carry away our penitence and our prayers. There are few folks so hopeless as

---

2. indulgence: Roman Catholic practice involving remission of purgatorial punishment for sins whose eternal punishment has already been remitted.

those who never want Christ except when they are threatened by some kind of disaster.

What was the outcome of Saul's foolishness?

He became a godless man. Hear that pathetic cry! "God hath departed from me and heareth me no more." We pity the man who has lost his sight or the man who has lost his hearing, or the man who has lost his health. We pity the man who has lost his loved ones. We even pity the man who has lost his money, who from a man of means has become poor. But what of the man who has lost his God? Certainly he has suffered the supreme loss. The most tragic figure on this side of the river of death, or on the other side, is the man who has no God. Saul became a man without God.

Saul became a wretched man. From this time on the light dies out of his skies. The flowers all wither in his garden. His springs all dry up. Gloom settles down upon him as deep as that woven out of the warp and woof of loneliness and despair. There is no laughter in his soul, no peace in his heart, no hope for the dawning of tomorrow. He has lost God, and, losing God, he is wretched.

He becomes fretful and feverish and suspicious. He lets himself fall into the hands of that torturing fiend called envy. One day when he returned from the battle he was greeted with a song: "Saul has slain his thousands and David has slain his ten thousands." That song put an **adder** in his bosom. That song became a fire in his soul. And henceforth he suffers the pangs of hell because he has become a prey to envy.

Last of all he becomes a plaything of his evil **forebodings**. Once he had been a brave man. But now the sight of the army of the enemy fills him with terror. Like a hunted thing he turns here and there seeking some kind of help. He must have help, but he knows not where to find it. He cannot appeal to God, for he has never repented of his sin. During the days of his rebellion he has not learned how to pray. He feels that it is too late to learn the secret now. What is he to do? Where is he to go? In sheer desperation he turns to an old witch that has hidden herself away in a cave—a cave to which he himself had banished her in his better days.

Man is incurably religious. If he has not a

About the Author

Clovis G. Chappell (1882-1972) born into a farming family in Flatwoods, Tennessee, became one of the most popular preachers in the southern United States. He attended Duke and Harvard Universities, and was ordained a minister in the Methodist Episcopal Church in 1908, serving as a pastor in various cities of the South until his retirement in 1949. Chappell wrote more than 20 books, many of them compilations of his sermons.

true religion, he will have a false. There are times when everybody must pray. There are times when the strongest of us must needs seek help. There are times when the most self-sufficient must turn somewhere or to some thing in search of assistance. Saul had flung away God. He had flung away the truth. Therefore, goaded on by the demons of wretchedness and fear, he throws himself at the feet of a woman who is a miserable **impostor**.

From this scene he goes unhelped and unencouraged to his last fight. The battle goes against him. His faithful soldiers, his courageous sons fall about him. At last the fatal day is closing in utter disaster. Everything is lost. Then it is that we see a great kingly figure standing sweat-grimed and blood-stained, among the slain. He calls upon his armor bearer to thrust him through that he may not fall into the hands of his enemies. But that individual shrinks back with fear and sorrow. Then the poor lost king falls on his own sword. What does he mutter as he bites the dust in death? This, I imagine, "I have played the fool."

And, Saul did not go to his ruin alone. If he had played the fool in a hidden stage it would not have been so tragic. When I was a boy I used to help get timber in the forests in our great hills. Here and there we would saw trees that measured from four to five feet in diameter. Now and then a friend who was passing would stop and say: "It seems a pity to cut a great tree like that." But there was something even more tragic than the falling of this great giant of the forests. It was this: As it went crashing to its ruin it flung out its arms and carried other trees with it. Here it caught a graceful young poplar, there a tall slender hickory, and yonder a beech, over there an elm. It did not go to its death alone. Neither did Saul. And neither will anyone who rejects God's plan for his life.

How differently his story might have ended! How Saul might have been a blessing to his children and a blessing to his nation; how after-generations might have been enriched by his life if he had only proven true to God! And what was his tragedy? Not so much the fact that he sinned, but the fact that he could never be brought to face and confess his sin and put it away. He refused to repent. Thus refusing, he flung away his here and he flung away his hereafter. Therefore, we can think of no better **epitaph** to be carved upon his tomb than this: "He played the fool."

Testing for Understanding

1. "I have played the fool" was said by Saul
   a. after he performed a sacrifice out of impatience.
   b. after the slaughter of the Amalekites.
   c. after David spared his life in return for Saul's ill treatment.
   d. at his death.

2. Youth is a valuable time, this article says, because then we
   a. have the sharpest mental powers.
   b. can most easily make and follow right choices.
   c. have a long life ahead of us.
   d. have not yet committed binding sins.

3. The story tells us that Saul had all the following opportunities except
   a. youth.
   b. good influence.
   c. great wealth.
   d. God's favor.

4. Saul's greatest mistake in the case of the Amalekites was failure to
   a. ask God's permission to spare the flocks.
   b. consult Samuel before sparing the flocks.
   c. control his people.
   d. fully obey God.

5. A friend's greatest worth is shown when he
   a. recognizes his friend's accomplishments.
   b. intercedes for and influences his friend for good.
   c. shields his friend from slander.
   d. overlooks the faults of his friend.

6. Saul's experience shows that worship is worthless if
   a. there is sin in one's life.
   b. it is not of the mode that others use.
   c. we do not engage in it often enough.
   d. we engage in it alone.

7. Saul used confession
    a. as a sincere expression of his penitence.
    b. to try to avoid consequences and get his own way.
    c. very rarely in his life.
    d. as a cover-up for his sin.

8. The greatest loss we can suffer is the loss of
    a. a family member.
    b. God's presence.
    c. material goods.
    d. sanity.

9. According to this author, Saul's death is made more tragic because he
    a. took his own life.
    b. was the king of God's people.
    c. knew that he was dying a lost man.
    d. took others with him to ruin.

10. The strongest lesson for us from Saul's life is
    a. Seek not to be great.
    b. Repent of your sins and start over anew.
    c. Never take your own life.
    d. Don't be proud of your station in life.

Reading for Understanding

1. *That which deepens the pathos of this confession is the fact that this role was self-chosen.*
    Saul's confession is
    a. more sincere because he came to it himself.
    b. sadder because Saul came to his pitiable state through his own choices.
    c. less acceptable because Saul chose to be king.
    d. more pathetic because Saul did not want to be forgiven.

2. *God did not plan to deck him out with cap and bells.*
    It had not been God's intention
    a. for Saul to become a fool.
    b. to dethrone Saul.
    c. for Saul to become king.
    d. for Saul to become proud and famous.

3. *And to the very end of his life this faithful prophet never ceased to pray for him. He clung to him as a father might cling to a wayward son.*
    These sentences are saying that
    a. Saul pled with Samuel not to reject him.
    b. Samuel threw his arms around Saul just as did the father of the prodigal son.
    c. Samuel was as reluctant to see Saul rejected by God as a father would be to see his wayward son be lost.
    d. Samuel was unwilling to accept that Saul had sinned.

4.   *Saul was never guilty of any sin half so detestable as the sin of his successor, who came to be a man after God's own heart.*

The difference between Saul and David was

a. a difference of intention.

b. God had a greater love for David.

c. David was a greater sinner than Saul.

d. Saul refused to repent of his sin.

5.   *Saul knows, as Samuel knows, that the fault is all his own; that the guilt is all his; that he has nobody to blame but himself. But when he is driven from this hiding place, he still will not come clean and confess.*

Saul thought that at this point

a. he could find an excuse that would satisfy Samuel.

b. he was not at fault and so refused to confess.

c. Samuel was being unreasonable.

d. he could ignore Samuel.

 *Meditating for Meaning*

1.   Perhaps the saddest part of Saul's life is the contrast between the bright promise at the start and the dark doom at the end.

a. List five things as the author lists them which were assets to Saul.

b. Which one of these five assets would you classify as least essential?

c. How might this be an asset?

d. How might it become a detriment?

e. What other asset of Saul's do all men have at one time and only one time?

f. What is necessary for this to be counted an asset?

g. Explain why each of the other three are very important.

2.   Sadly, Saul did not use these assets wisely throughout life. Choose any two of these assets and tell how Saul misused them.

3.   Saul called himself a fool, a judgment which God alone reserves the right to make. Yet Saul was right.

a. From the following references tell what kinds of people God considers foolish.

    Psalm 53:1;   Proverbs 1:22; 10:18; 13:19; 14:9; 15:5; 18:6; 20:3;

    Ecclesiastes 7:9;   Jeremiah 17:11

b. Which of these types of fools do you see in Saul? Explain. You will likely find more than one.

4.   Foolishness takes its toll on men.

a. From the story give four things that happened to Saul as a result of his foolishness. Explain them in your own words.

b. What final act of foolishness did Saul engage in before his death?

c. What made this act seem extremely foolish?

d. What drove Saul to commit this act?

5.   Perhaps the most foolish act men can commit is suicide.

a. What drove Saul to this act? (See 1 Samuel 31:4.)

b. How do we see this same pattern in some who commit suicide today?

c. Explain how this is the height of folly.

Looking for Literary Technique

Why is an orderly toolbox important? So you can find the hammer when the fence needs repairing. Why is your mother so insistent that your room be neat? So you know where your shoes are when it's time for school.

Every bit as important is an orderly story or article. Otherwise you will not be able to find what the author is trying to say. A cluttered piece of writing is not a pleasure to read.

The story which you have just read is very well organized. Every sentence fits neatly into place. In fact you could easily fit the ideas of this story into an outline. Now fit the following topics from the story into the outline below. Look first for three main topics.

This kind of outline is called a topic outline. Each point is a noun with perhaps a few modifiers or modifying phrases. Some outlines are sentence outlines in which each point is a complete sentence. Notice that the points under each Roman numeral are all parallel; that is, they have the same grammatical structure.

An outline should follow a specific layout. First comes the title. Then subpoints may follow in this order: Roman numerals, capital letters, Arabic numerals, small letters, Arabic numerals in parentheses, and then letters in parentheses. Few outlines include that many subheadings. But remember, you can not divide a topic into subheadings if it has only one point. If you list any subheadings under a point, you must list at least two.

Also notice the indentation of the subtopics.

The Self-Made Fool—Saul

I. _____

   A. _____

   B. _____

   C. _____

   D. _____

   E. _____

II. _____

   A. _____

   B. _____

   C. _____

   D. _____

III. _____

   A. _____

   B. _____

   C. _____

   D. _____

   E. _____

3a Godlessness

3 Outcome of Saul's foolishness

2d Insincere confession

3b Wretchedness

3c Envy

3e Defeat and death by suicide

3d Visit to a witch

1c Refusal to confess sin

2b Lying

1c Youth

1b Modesty

1a Splendid physique

1e A great friend

1d Appointment by God

2a Partial obedience

2 Ways in which Saul played the fool

1 Qualities to be admired in Saul

Writing for Skill

1. Choose an outstanding Bible character. Outline his life, following the rules for a topic outline.
2. Following your outline, write a story about your character, pointing out his worthy or unworthy example.

Ruth, the Moabitess

from the Bible

Rare beauty is sometimes found in the most unlikely places. A flower pokes its pretty face out of a rocky crevice. In the murky depths of the ocean, a sea plant flaunts its bright colors. The rainbow stands out against the drabness of a rainy sky.

So it is with the story of Ruth. Its recital of noble love and loyal devotion emerges like a gem from the sordid days of the judges when "every man did that which was right in his own eyes."

This story is not an ordinary romance of impatient passion. Both Ruth and Boaz sacrificed personal preferences to carry out a deep sense of responsibility to God concerning the dead.

Ruth and Boaz still stand out with winsome beauty in our day, when much courtship and marriage is but thinly disguised lust. As you read, you will see that joy comes unsought to those who sacrifice everything to the will of God.

Defining for Comprehension

Choose the word or phrase below which most nearly defines each word at the left as it is used in this selection.

1. **sojourn**   a. journey through   b. investigate   c. stay temporarily

2. **kinsman**   a. friend   b. tribal leader   c. relative

3. **hap**   a. unplanned experience   b. fortunate plan   c. delight

4. **damsel**   a. young lady   b. relation   c. helper

5. **recompense**   a. empower   b. repay   c. honor

6. **handmaid**   a. home crafted   b. small child   c. female servant

7. **morsel**   a. sorrow   b. bite of food   c. treasure

8. sufficed	a. gave	b. satisfied	c. endured pain
9. winnoweth	a. bleats sadly	b. rakes onto piles	c. removes chaff
10. virtuous	a. morally excellent	b. practical	c. requiring effort

Ruth, the Moabitess

Now it came to pass in the days when the judges ruled, that there was a famine in the land. And a certain man of Bethlehem-judah went to **sojourn** in the country of Moab, he, and his wife, and his two sons. And the name of the man was Elimelech, and the name of his wife Naomi, and the name of his two sons Mahlon and Chilion, Ephrathites of Bethlehem-judah. And they came into the country of Moab, and continued there. And Elimelech Naomi's husband died; and she was left, and her two sons. And they took them wives of the women of Moab; the name of the one was Orpah, and the name of the other Ruth: and they dwelled there about ten years. And Mahlon and Chilion died also both of them; and the woman was left of her two sons and her husband.

Then she arose with her daughters-in-law, that she might return from the country of Moab: for she had heard in the country of Moab how that the LORD had visited his people in giving them bread. Wherefore she went forth out of the place where she was, and her two daughters-in-law with her; and they went on the way to return unto the land of Judah. And Naomi said unto her two daughters-in-law, Go, return each to her mother's house: the LORD deal kindly with you, as ye have dealt with the dead, and with me. The LORD grant you that ye may find rest, each of you in the house of her husband. Then she kissed them; and they lifted up their voice, and wept. And they said unto her, Surely we will return with thee unto thy people. And Naomi said, Turn again, my daughters: why will ye go with me? Are there yet any more sons in my womb, that they may be your husbands? Turn again, my daughters, go your way; for I am too old to have an husband. If I should say, I have hope, if I should have an husband also tonight, and should also bear sons; Would ye tarry for them till they were grown? Would ye stay for them from having husbands? nay, my daughters; for it grieveth me much for your sakes that the hand of the LORD is gone out against me. And they lifted up their voice, and wept again: and Orpah kissed her mother-in-law; but Ruth clave unto her.

And she said, Behold, thy sister-in-law is gone back unto her people, and unto her gods: return thou after thy sister-in-law. And Ruth said, Entreat me not to leave thee, or to return from following after thee: for whither thou goest, I will go; and where thou lodgest, I will lodge: thy people shall be my people, and thy God my God: Where thou diest, will I die, and there will I be buried: the LORD do so to me, and more also, if ought but death part thee and me. When she saw that she was stedfastly minded to go with her, then she left speaking unto her. So they two went until they came to Bethlehem. And it came to pass, when they were come to Bethlehem, that all the city was moved about them, and they said, Is this *Naomi*?[1] And she said unto them, Call me not Naomi, call me *Mara*:[2] for the Almighty hath dealt very bitterly with me. I went out full, and the LORD hath brought me home again empty: why then call ye me Naomi, seeing the LORD hath testified against me, and the Almighty hath afflicted me? So Naomi returned, and

1. Naomi means "pleasantness."
2. Mara means "bitter."

Ruth the Moabitess, her daughter-in-law, with her, which returned out of the country of Moab: and they came to Bethlehem in the beginning of barley harvest.

And Naomi had a **kinsman** of her husband's, a mighty man of wealth, of the family of Elimelech; and his name was Boaz. And Ruth the Moabitess said unto Naomi, Let me now go to the field, and glean ears of corn after him in whose sight I shall find grace. And she said unto her, Go, my daughter. And she went, and came, and gleaned in the field after the reapers: and her **hap** was to light on a part of the field belonging unto Boaz, who was of the kindred of Elimelech. And, behold, Boaz came from Bethlehem, and said unto the reapers, The LORD be with you. And they answered him, The LORD bless thee. Then said Boaz unto his servant that was set over the reapers, Whose damsel is this? And the servant that was set over the reapers answered and said, It is the Moabitish **damsel** that came back with Naomi out of the country of Moab: And she said, I pray you, let me glean and gather after the reapers among the sheaves: so she came, and hath continued even from the morning until now, that she tarried a little in the house.

Then said Boaz unto Ruth, Hearest thou not, my daughter? Go not to glean in another field, neither go from hence, but abide here fast by my maidens: Let thine eyes be on the field that they do reap, and go thou after them: have I not charged the young men that they shall not touch thee? and when thou art athirst, go unto the vessels, and drink of that which the young men have drawn. Then she fell on her face, and bowed herself to the ground, and said unto him, Why have I found grace in thine eyes, that thou shouldest take knowledge of me, seeing I am a stranger? And Boaz answered and said unto her, It hath fully been shewed me, all that thou hast done unto thy mother-in-law since the death of thine husband: and how thou hast left thy father and thy mother, and the land of thy nativity, and art come unto a people which thou knewest not heretofore. The LORD **recompense** thy work, and a full reward be given

thee of the LORD God of Israel, under whose wings thou art come to trust. Then she said, Let me find favour in thy sight, my lord; for that thou hast comforted me, and for that thou hast spoken friendly unto thine **handmaid**, though I be not like unto one of thine handmaidens.

And Boaz said unto her, At mealtime come thou hither, and eat of the bread, and dip thy **morsel** in the vinegar. And she sat beside the reapers: and he reached her parched corn, and she did eat, and was **sufficed**, and left. And when she was risen up to glean, Boaz commanded his young men, saying, Let her glean even among the sheaves, and reproach her not: And let fall also some of the handfuls of purpose for her, and leave them, that she may glean them, and rebuke her not.

So she gleaned in the field until even, and beat out that she had gleaned: and it was about an *ephah*[3] of barley. And she took it up, and went into the city: and her mother-in-law saw what she had gleaned: and she brought forth, and gave to her that she had reserved after she was sufficed. And her mother-in-law said unto her, Where hast thou gleaned today? and where wroughtest thou? blessed be he that did take knowledge of thee. And she shewed her mother-in-law with whom she had wrought, and said, The man's name with whom I wrought today is Boaz. And Naomi said unto her daughter-in-law, Blessed be he of the LORD, who hath not left off his kindness to the living and to the dead. And Naomi said unto her, The man is near of kin unto us, one of our next kinsmen. And Ruth the Moabitess said, He said unto me also, Thou shalt keep fast by my young men, until they have ended all my harvest. And Naomi said unto Ruth her daughter-in-law, It is good, my daughter, that thou go out with his maidens, that they meet thee not in any other field. So she kept fast by the maidens of Boaz to glean unto the end of barley harvest and of wheat harvest; and dwelt with her mother-in-law.

Then Naomi her mother-in-law said unto her, My daughter, shall I not seek rest for thee, that it may be well with thee? And now is not Boaz of our kindred, with whose maidens thou

---

3. ephah: measure slightly more than a bushel.

wast? Behold, he **winnoweth** barley tonight in the threshingfloor. Wash thyself therefore, and anoint thee, and put thy raiment upon thee, and get thee down to the floor: but make not thyself known unto the man, until he shall have done eating and drinking. And it shall be, when he lieth down, that thou shalt mark the place where he shall lie, and thou shalt go in, and uncover his feet, and lay thee down; and he will tell thee what thou shalt do. And she said unto her, All that thou sayest unto me I will do.

And she went down unto the floor, and did according to all that her mother-in-law bade her. And when Boaz had eaten and drunk, and his heart was merry, he went to lie down at the end of the heap of corn: and she came softly, and uncovered his feet, and laid her down. And it came to pass at midnight, that the man was afraid, and turned himself: and, behold, a woman lay at his feet. And he said, Who art thou? And she answered, I am Ruth thine handmaid: spread therefore thy skirt over thine handmaid; for thou art a near kinsman. And he said, Blessed be thou of the LORD, my daughter: for thou hast shewed more kindness in the latter end than at the beginning, inasmuch as thou followedst not young men, whether poor or rich. And now, my daughter, fear not; I will do to thee all that thou requirest: for all the city of my people doth know that thou art a **virtuous** woman. And now it is true that I am thy near kinsman: howbeit there is a kinsman nearer than I. Tarry this night, and it shall be in the morning, that if he will perform unto thee the part of a kinsman, well; let him do the kinsman's part: but if he will not do the part of a kinsman to thee, then will I do the part of a kinsman to thee, as the LORD liveth: lie down until the morning.

And she lay at his feet until the morning: and she rose up before one could know another. And he said, Let it not be known that a woman came into the floor. Also he said, Bring the veil that thou hast upon thee, and hold it. And when she held it, he measured six measures of barley, and laid it on her: and she went into the city. And when she came to her mother-in-law, she said, Who art thou, my daughter? And she told her all that the man had done to her. And

she said, These six measures of barley gave he me; for he said to me, Go not empty unto thy mother-in-law. Then said she, Sit still, my daughter, until thou know how the matter will fall: for the man will not be in rest, until he have finished the thing this day.

Then went Boaz up to the gate, and sat him down there: and, behold, the kinsman of whom Boaz spake came by; unto whom he said, Ho, such a one! turn aside, sit down here. And he turned aside, and sat down. And he took ten men of the elders of the city, and said, Sit ye down here. And they sat down. And he said unto the kinsman, Naomi, that is come again out of the country of Moab, selleth a parcel of land, which was our brother Elimelech's: And I thought to advertise thee, saying, Buy it before the inhabitants, and before the elders of my people. If thou wilt redeem it, redeem it: but if thou wilt not redeem it, then tell me, that I may know: for there is none to redeem it beside thee; and I am after thee. And he said, I will redeem it. Then said Boaz, What day thou buyest the field of the hand of Naomi, thou must buy it also of Ruth the Moabitess, the wife of the dead, to raise up the name of the dead upon his inheritance. And the kinsman said, I cannot redeem it for myself, lest I mar mine own inheritance: redeem thou my right to thyself; for I cannot redeem it.

Now this was the manner in former time in Israel concerning redeeming and concerning changing, for to confirm all things; a man plucked off his shoe, and gave it to his neighbour: and this was a testimony in Israel. Therefore the kinsman said unto Boaz, Buy it for thee. So he drew off his shoe. And Boaz said unto the elders, and unto all the people, Ye are witnesses this day, that I have bought all that was Elimelech's, and all that was Chilion's and Mahlon's, of the hand of Naomi. Moreover Ruth the Moabitess, the wife of Mahlon, have I purchased to be my wife, to raise up the name of the dead upon his inheritance, that the name of the dead be not cut off from among his brethren, and from the gate of his place: ye are witnesses this day. And all the people that were in the gate, and the elders, said, We are witnesses. The LORD make the woman that is come into thine house like Rachel and like Leah, which two did build the house of Israel: and do thou worthily in Ephratah, and be famous in Bethlehem: And let thy house be like the house of Pharez, whom Tamar bare unto Judah, of the seed which the LORD shall give thee of this young woman.

So Boaz took Ruth, and she was his wife: and when he went in unto her, the LORD gave her conception, and she bare a son. And the women said unto Naomi, Blessed be the LORD, which hath not left thee this day without a kinsman, that his name may be famous in Israel. And he shall be unto thee a restorer of thy life, and a nourisher of thine old age: for thy daughter-in-law, which loveth thee, which is better to thee than seven sons, hath borne him. And Naomi took the child, and laid it in her bosom, and became nurse unto it. And the women her neighbours gave it a name, saying, There is a son born to Naomi; and they called his name Obed: he is the father of Jesse, the father of David. Now these are the generations of Pharez: Pharez begat Hezron, And Hezron begat Ram, and Ram begat Amminadab, And Amminadab begat Nahshon, and Nahshon begat Salmon, And Salmon begat Boaz, and Boaz begat Obed, And Obed begat Jesse, and Jesse begat David.

Testing for Understanding

1. Ruth's husband had been
    a. Elimelech.   b. a Moabite.   c. Mahlon.   d. Chilion.

2. When Naomi decided to return to Judah,
    a. her daughters-in-law meant to walk with her a short way and then bid her farewell.
    b. both daughters-in-law meant to leave Moab with her.
    c. Orpah meant to say farewell, but Ruth planned to go with her.
    d. both daughters-in-law were disappointed about the journey.

3. Naomi felt that her life was bitter, because
    a. one daughter-in-law deserted her.
    b. she had lost her property in Bethlehem.
    c. the people in her hometown did not recognize her.
    d. her posterity had been cut off.

4. The thing that impressed Boaz most about Ruth was
    a. her diligence in gleaning.   c. her relation to his maidens.
    b. her reverence for God.   d. her devotion to her mother-in-law.

5. Naomi's land was sold (see Deuteronomy 25:5, 6)
    a. as a means of keeping her family from dying out.
    b. because she was too poor to keep it.
    c. because the nearest kinsman wanted to buy it.
    d. because Ruth didn't want it.

6. The nearest kinsman refused to purchase Naomi's land because he
    a. didn't want to mar his own inheritance.   c. couldn't pay for it.
    b. didn't want to add to his own inheritance.   d. didn't want to marry Naomi.

7. The story tells us all of the following except
   a. what happened when the women came into the land of Judah.
   b. that Ruth was physically beautiful.
   c. that Ruth lived in Judah a relatively short time until she married Boaz.
   d. Naomi's home town.

8. Ruth found favor with God because she
   a. sought a husband among God's people.
   b. never went back to visit the land of Moab.
   c. gave up her own interests to serve Naomi and Naomi's God rather than her own.
   d. expressed her determination to die and be buried in the land of Judah.

9. This story places the greatest emphasis on the love between
   a. Ruth and Boaz.
   b. Ruth and Naomi.
   c. Naomi and her two daughters-in-law.
   d. Naomi and her God.

10. The account of Ruth is important to us mainly because it shows
    a. the strong devotion of the Jews to their families.
    b. how a Gentile joined the ancestry of Christ.
    c. the way Jews lived during the time of the judges.
    d. who the grandmother of Jesse was.

Reading for Understanding

1. *And Naomi said unto her two daughters-in-law, Go, return . . . The LORD grant you that ye may find rest, each of you in the house of her husband.*
   Naomi was advising her daughters-in-law to stay in Moab where they could
   a. remarry.
   b. live with their parents.
   c. depend on the care of friends.
   d. be buried with their husbands.

2. *I went out full, and the LORD hath brought me home again empty: why then call ye me Naomi, seeing the LORD hath testified against me, and the Almighty hath afflicted me?*
   Naomi is saying that
   a. God had used suffering to test her faith.
   b. God had displayed His displeasure with her.
   c. she had plenty of food when she left Judah.
   d. there was a famine in Moab when she left.

3. *And Naomi had a kinsman of her husband's, a mighty man of wealth, . . . and his name was Boaz . . . and her hap was to light on a part of the field belonging unto Boaz, who was of the kindred of Elimelech.*
   From this we can conclude that
   a. Naomi sent Ruth to Boaz's field. c. God led Ruth to the field of Boaz.
   b. gleaners customarily chose the fields of Boaz. d. Ruth chose Elimelech's field by coincidence.

4. *And he said, Who art thou? And she answered, I am Ruth thine handmaid: spread therefore thy skirt over thine handmaid; for thou art a near kinsman.*
    Ruth was asking Boaz to
    a. protect her from the cold.
    b. take her for a servant.
    c. promise her financial help.
    d. take her as his wife according to the law.

5. *And he said, Blessed be thou of the LORD, my daughter: for thou hast shewed more kindness in the latter end than at the beginning, inasmuch as thou followedst not young men, whether poor or rich.*
    These words suggest that
    a. Boaz was not a young man.
    b. Ruth had followed young men in the beginning.
    c. Boaz had a low opinion of young men.
    d. Ruth was somewhat unkind to Boaz at the first.

 *Meditating for Meaning*

1. The story of Ruth fits into the same time frame as the Book of Judges.
    a. According to Judges 2, what was likely the reason that Israel was experiencing a famine at this time?
    b. Elimelech and his sons went to Moab to make a living. What was the ironical outcome of this venture?
    c. Why do you think this happened?

2. Ruth's character shines forth in the sacrifice which she was willing to make by returning to Israel with Naomi.
    a. In Ruth 1:9a, 12, 13, what opportunity did Naomi recognize her daughters-in-law would miss by returning with her?
    b. According to Nehemiah 13:23-27, why was there little hope for this opportunity in Israel?
    c. Considering this, what does Ruth's decision to return to Israel reveal about her character?
    d. What do you think had caused the devotion Ruth expressed so beautifully in 1:16, 17?

3. Leviticus 19:9, 10 gives insight into the life of the gleaner.
    a. What was Ruth admitting by going into the fields to glean?
    b. What quality does this admission reveal in her character?

4. In 2:10 Ruth could not understand why Boaz took notice of her, a stranger. One possible reason for her question may be found in the genealogy of Matthew 1:5.
    a. According to Matthew 1:5, who was the mother of Boaz? Check the entry for this name in a concordance or other Bible help to find the familiar Old Testament spelling.
    b. What other reason did Boaz give in verse 11?

5. What does Boaz's salutation to his reapers reveal about his character?

6. Naomi's understanding of Jewish law gave her an advantage over Ruth in interpreting Boaz's actions in 2:14-16.
    a. How did Boaz treat Ruth in these two verses?
    b. Compare 2:20 with Deuteronomy 25:5, 6. What motive might Naomi have recognized behind Boaz's actions in 2:14-16?
    c. How would Boaz be showing "kindness...to the dead" by following the command of Deuteronomy 25:5, 6?

7. Boaz did not rush into marrying Ruth.
   a. From 3:10b, give one possible reason Boaz had not pursued marriage with Ruth.
   b. From 3:12, why did Boaz not marry Ruth immediately after she expressed a willingness for this?
8. Boaz reveals his quality of character in obeying the law of God by marrying Ruth.
   a. According to Deuteronomy 25:5, 6, to whose family line would the first son of Boaz and Ruth (as well as that son's inheritance) belong?
   b. What does the refusal of the kinsman in Ruth 4:5, 6 show about his character?
   c. According to Deuteronomy 25:9, 10, what was the purpose of the action described in Ruth 4:7, 8?
   d. What qualities of character did Boaz reveal by marrying Ruth and performing the kinsman's part?
9. Ruth's life is a worthy example.
   a. What rewards in this life did Ruth reap by leaving her homeland and its possibilities?
   b. According to Ruth 4:22, what longer-range rewards did she reap?
   c. What spiritual lesson does Ruth's example teach?

 *Looking for Literary Technique*

Many volumes have been compiled of famous written or spoken quotations. Close scrutiny of these quotations reveals why they became famous. Sometimes a quotation owes its fame to its meaning, other times to its literary beauty, and often to both.

1. Using *Bartlett's Familiar Quotations* find three quotations listed from the Book of Ruth. Classify each quotation according to how you think it gained its fame—meaning, literary beauty, or both.

Ruth's commitment in Ruth 1:16, 17 gains its literary beauty from *parallel construction*. Several of the phrases follow an identical grammatical pattern, retaining many of the same words, and changing key words.

2. Copy three such phrases from Ruth's commitment. Copy the phrases with identical words directly under each other. Underline the key words which have been changed.

3. Find another example of parallel construction from Scripture.

 *Writing for Skill*

Imagine that you were being advised to give up your Christian life. After considering the commitment which Ruth spoke to Naomi, write a similar commitment which you might give in response to such advice. Structure it carefully with parallel construction. Be sure, however, to use original wording.

Getting the Point

Match the following statements with the selections from this unit which they summarize.

____ 1. Physical handicap can be a blessing to a person.

____ 2. Happiness is best found by contentment in one's God-appointed sphere.

____ 3. God will bring judgment on those who engage in the sins which spring from ease and luxury.

____ 4. If one commits his life to God, He will bless him with what is best.

____ 5. Difficult experiences can carry one to heights of Christian experience.

____ 6. Pride and disregard of warnings bring man to destruction.

____ 7. The highest good in this life is to sacrifice one's life for another.

____ 8. The Christian life cannot be lived successfully by avoiding difficulty.

____ 9. That life is worthwhile which is spent for another's spiritual good.

____ 10. It is better to lose one's life than to save it by taking another's.

____ 11. To refuse to admit one's mistakes is the biggest mistake a person can make.

____ 12. It is better to be mistreated than to sacrifice one's convictions.

____ 13. Happiness is in spending one's life for the long-range good of others.

    a. "Discipline" – *MacDonald*

    b. "The Chariots of God" – *Smith*

    c. "The Discipline of Deformity" – *Edman*

    d. "Acres of Diamonds" – *Conwell*

    e. "The Man Who Planted Hope and Grew Happiness" – *Giono*

    f. "RMS *Titanic*" – *Baldwin*

    g. "Top Man" – *Ullman*

    h. "Diary of David Brainerd" – *Brainerd*

    i. "Letters of Hermann Stohr" – *Stohr*

    j. "Though He Slay Me" – *Swalm*

    k. "Last Night of Sodom" – *March*

    l. "The Self-Made Fool"—Saul – *Chappell*

    m. "Ruth—the Moabitess" – *The Bible*

UNIT 5

The Allegory
for the Fruitful Life

Ever since you learned to talk, you have been thinking with words. Words are merely symbols that represent objects or ideas. For example, the word *seed* stands for the small kernel produced by plants, a germ of life that can grow into a new plant. So when you read about God's fiat, "Let the earth bring forth grass, the herb yielding seed" (Genesis 1:11), you know what the word *seed* stands for or symbolizes. Your mind knows the meaning of thousands of such symbols. But God made the mind for more complex communication than just the use of word symbols. The object or concept a word stands for can also be a symbol. Seeds have certain characteristics that resemble other things that grow and are fruitful. Notice how the word *seed* illustrates something greater in the simile of Isaiah 55:10, 11:

> For as the rain cometh down, and the snow from heaven, and returneth not thither, but watereth the earth, and maketh it bring forth and bud, that it may give **seed** to the sower, and bread to the eater: So shall my word be that goeth forth out of my mouth: it shall not return unto me void, but it shall accomplish that which I please, and it shall prosper in the thing whereto I sent it.

Here the valuable and fruitful quality of seed is like the blessing that will surely follow God's teaching. By comparing the effect of God's Word with seed, Isaiah helps us to understand a truth that is somewhat difficult to comprehend. Consider the metaphor in Jeremiah 2:21:

> Yet I had planted thee a noble vine, wholly a right **seed**: how then art thou turned into the degenerate plant of a strange vine unto me?

The seed in this case represents the children of Israel. When we plant good seed, we expect a valuable plant. God had a right to expect that the Hebrew people would become a fruitful and God-honoring people. They came from good seed that He had carefully planted. How disappointing to see what a loathsome vine they had become by Jeremiah's day. This metaphor helps us understand how God felt about His people.

Similes and metaphors are not new to you. You have used and understood many figures of speech. But figurative language can extend even further. A whole story can be symbolic. The various parts of the story can stand for something different from the common meaning of the words. These symbolic parts go together to explain a central truth. Such stories that have a symbolic meaning are called *allegories*. If an allegory is quite short, it is called a *parable*.

For example, in the parable of the sower, the seed is the Word of God. But unlike a simple metaphor, an allegory includes many other symbols. The seed is sown by a man, who himself is a symbol. The seed falls on different kinds of soil, which are also symbolic. Birds come, weeds grow, the sun shines, and the various soils yield from zero to one hundred times what had been sown.

Each of these details has a figurative meaning.

Jesus explained this parable, but He left many others to speak for themselves. God would not have left these parables unexplained if He had not created your mind with the ability to think in terms of allegories.

Often allegories arise from real-life situations. The lost sheep, the pearl of great price, and the prodigal son are all stories that either did or could have happened. But sometimes allegories tell stories that are imaginary. In a dream God showed Pharaoh seven thin cows eating seven fat cows. Such an event is unreal, yet the dream had a very real allegorical meaning. The characters in an allegory may even be talking animals or plants. The parable of the trees in Judges 9:8-15 is an example of this kind of allegory:

The trees went forth on a time to anoint a king over them; and they said unto the olive tree, Reign thou over us. But the olive tree said unto them, Should I leave my fatness, wherewith by me they honour God and man, and go to be promoted over the trees? And the trees said to the fig tree, Come thou, and reign over us. But the fig tree said unto them, Should I forsake my sweetness, and my good fruit, and go to be promoted over the trees? Then said the trees unto the vine, Come thou, and reign over us. And the vine said unto them, Should I leave my wine, which cheereth God and man, and go to be promoted over the trees? Then said all the trees unto the bramble, Come thou, and reign over us. And the bramble said unto the trees, If in truth ye anoint me king over you, then come and put your trust in my shadow: and if not, let fire come out of the bramble, and devour the cedars of Lebanon.

This allegory raises a question: What is the value of such figurative stories?

ALLEGORIES REVEAL TRUTH

As already mentioned, the allegory, like other figures of speech, helps us understand truths that are difficult to comprehend. Often these truths are *abstract*; that is, they are ideas that we cannot touch or see. In contrast, things we **can** touch or see are said to be *concrete*.

A round, blue ball is a concrete article; the idea of Christian liberty is abstract. An allegory is not needed to communicate the idea of a round, blue ball. But Paul helped the Galatians understand the abstract truth of Christian liberty by use of an allegory about the experience of the Old Testament characters, Hagar and Sarah (Galatians 4:22, 23). Allegories help to communicate abstract truths by expressing them in concrete terms.

ALLEGORIES AROUSE INTEREST

In the case of the parable of the trees, the truth taught is not as abstract as the idea of Christian liberty. This parable deals with concrete events. Following the death of Gideon, his son Abimelech took over his father's position of leadership in a very wicked and ruthless manner, intending to kill all of his brothers. Jotham, however, escaped. It was Jotham who shouted the parable of the trees from the top of a mountain. Just imagine a lone man standing on a hill and shouting at the top of his voice to warn the people of their terrible mistake. How could Jotham convince such a foolish people to change their minds? He told a story. Inevitably, stories create interest, and this story with trees talking would have caught the attention of even the most arrogant man.

A message of truth will do no good unless it arouses interest. And when the receiver of a message resists the truth, a story may be the only way to get through to him. An example is Nathan's story of a little lamb which he told to King David (2 Sam. 12:1-6). Stories arouse interest as well as reveal truth.

ALLEGORIES CONCEAL TRUTH

Why did Christ teach with parables? On one occasion His disciples asked this question. He answered, "Because it is given unto you to know the mysteries of the kingdom of heaven, but to them it is not given" (Matthew 13:11). It does require some skill and spiritual interest to discover the hidden meaning of allegories. For those who want to learn truth, the allegories are like a window; they let in the light of truth; they make truth vivid and clear. But for scoffers who are confused already and don't want truth, the deep meaning of the allegory is withheld from their ridicule. Although they hear and may even enjoy the story, they miss its point.

ALLEGORIES MAKE TRUTH FRUITFUL

Christ told parables to reveal truth only "as [His listeners] were able to hear it." Even those who want to know the truth may find an allegory difficult to understand. But as long as a parable is within the ability of the hearers to interpret, some difficulty and complexity helps to make the truth fruitful. Man tends to be more impressed with truths and ideas he has worked to discover for himself. If a plain truth is presented, he may be inclined to reject it at first. But if he has struggled to discover the same truth when it has been concealed in an allegory, he will be more likely to accept it.

You may say, "Any rejection of truth is because of our sinful nature." And you are right. Because God knows we have this inclination and because He yearns that we accept His message of truth, He has given it a form that we will most likely accept in spite of our nature. The Bible contains many allegories. Furthermore, to the diligent reader, an allegory bears many harvests of truth. For example, Christ Himself gave the clues to interpreting the parable of the sower, but whole sermons have been preached extracting further meaning from that parable. Christ simply said that the thorns are the deceitfulness of riches. This prickly character of wealth suggests that its briars seize the lover of riches and subtly strangle his spiritual life.

This is just one example of how allegories reveal truth by the many metaphors they present.

INTERPRETING ALLEGORIES

How then can you get the point of an allegory and reap its full harvest of meaning? This comes basically through background, effort, practice, and most of all, openness to truth.

You may miss the meaning of an allegory because you do not have enough background information about the story. Consider this nursery rhyme:

> Little Jack Horner,
> Sat in the corner,
> Eating his Christmas pie;
> He stuck in his thumb,
> And pulled out a plum,
> And cried, "What a good boy am I."

To us this seems like a nonsense rhyme, and maybe it is. But the rhyme may refer to a John Horner, who while delivering some land deeds to King Henry VIII, "put in his thumb" and stole a tract of land. In which case, if we had been living in England during the early 1500s, we may have readily caught the meaning of the allegory.

To a child, *The Pilgrim's Progress* may seem like nothing more than an exciting tale. But to the struggling Christian it is a true-to-life account whose symbolism yields fresh insights into his experience.

To safeguard you against misinterpreting allegories, observe a few cautions. Do not try to make an allegory say more than it does. Just because a symbol is similar in many respects to what it symbolizes does not mean that every characteristic applies. For example, it would be incorrect to conclude that a lost person has a limited IQ because he is compared to a lost sheep. When Jesus presented the sower broadcasting the seed, He was not implying that mass evangelism is the only Scriptural method of soul winning.

Neither should you use an allegory to argue for sub-Christian practices. Just because the father of the prodigal put a ring on his son's finger does not mean that Jesus condoned the wearing of jewelry. Nor does Paul's use of metaphors from boxing and warfare promote these activities for the Christian. Decisions about such practices should be made on the basis of Scriptures that directly address these subjects. These cautions should not dull your appetite for the luscious truths of a fruitful allegory. The sampling in this unit is intended to help you to cultivate a gourmet relish for allegories.

Checking for Understanding

1. Now you should easily recognize an allegory.
   a. An allegory is a _____ in which the objects, characters, and events are _____ .
   b. A _____ is a short allegory.

2. In each of the following references sheep symbolize the person or group of persons given after it in parentheses. Match the reference with the characteristic of sheep typical of the person or group of persons being symbolized.
   a. 2 Samuel 24:17 (Jews)   —harmless
   b. Psalm 44:11 (Hebrew nation)   √—innocent
   c. Psalm 100:3 (humanity)   —dependent for food
   d. Isaiah 53:6 (humanity)   √—helpless when lost
   e. Isaiah 53:7 (Jesus)   √—source of meat
   f. Matthew 7:15 (false prophets)   √—prone to wander
   g. Matthew 18:13 (sinners)   √—silent in face of danger, meek
   h. Matthew 25:32 (saints at judgment) √—mild and agreeable nature
   i. John 21:16 (Christians)   √—owned by someone

3. An allegory often communicates an abstract idea.
   a. Explain abstract ideas by giving three examples.
   b. How do allegories help to communicate abstract ideas?

4. Occasionally an allegory may communicate a concrete idea.
   a. Under what condition may an allegory be useful in communicating concrete ideas?
   b. Why is an allegory especially helpful in this circumstance?

5. An allegory serves several purposes.
   a. In what way does an allegory conceal truth?
   b. In what two ways does an allegory make truth fruitful in our lives?

6. Give two dangers you should avoid when interpreting an allegory.

The Parable of the Ten Virgins

Matthew 25:1-13

Regret, it is said, began in the Garden of Eden when Adam, hiding among the trees, no doubt, thought bitterly, I wish I hadn't eaten that fruit. For centuries men have voiced that same basic sentiment, "If I had that to do over again . . . ," a most apt proof that "hindsight is better than foresight." But not every look of retrospect offers with it the privilege to try again. This allegory illustrates that those who neglect the foresight to provide for their eternal welfare will someday experience the tearful hindsight which finds no place for repentance.

Then shall the kingdom of heaven be likened unto ten virgins, which took their lamps, and went forth to meet the bridegroom. And five of them were wise, and five were foolish. They that were foolish took their lamps, and took no oil with them: But the wise took oil in their vessels with their lamps. While the bridegroom tarried, they all slumbered and slept.

And at midnight there was a cry made, Behold, the bridegroom cometh; go ye out to meet him.

Then all those virgins arose, and trimmed[1] their lamps. And the foolish said unto the wise, Give us of your oil; for our lamps are gone out.[2]

But the wise answered, saying, Not so; lest there be not enough for us and you: but go ye rather to them that sell, and buy for yourselves.

And while they went to buy, the bridegroom came; and they that were ready went in with him to the marriage: and the door was

---

1. trimmed: removed the charred portion from the wick and pulled the wicks up so that the lamps might burn more brightly.

2. gone out: going out.

shut. Afterward came also the other virgins, saying, Lord, Lord, open to us. But he answered and said, Verily I say unto you, I know you not. Watch therefore, for ye know neither the day nor the hour wherein the Son of man cometh.

Testing for Understanding

1. The setting of this parable is
   a. an Oriental housewarming.
   b. an Oriental marriage.
   c. a wedding feast following a marriage.
   d. the homecoming of a traveling merchant.

2. The difference between the wise and the foolish virgins was a difference in
   a. intellect.
   b. obedience.
   c. foresight.
   d. sobriety.

3. The foolish virgins
   a. carried empty lamps.
   b. were too poor to afford oil.
   c. took no extra vessels of oil.
   d. didn't expect to need their lamps.

4. While they waited for the bridegroom
   a. the virgins took turns sleeping.
   b. the foolish virgins slept while the wise virgins watched.
   c. the virgins rested without sleeping.
   d. both the wise and the foolish virgins slept.

5. When the bridegroom's arrival was announced,
   a. the foolish virgins slept a while longer.
   b. all the virgins arose to trim their lamps.
   c. the wise virgins filled their lamps with oil.
   d. only the foolish virgins needed to trim their lamps.

6. The foolish virgins apparently
   a. knew they had insufficient oil but had planned to borrow.
   b. knew they had insufficient oil but had planned to buy more before the bridegroom came.
   c. knew the possibility of running out of oil but thought they could walk by the light of the wise virgins' lamps.
   d. did not know they had insufficient oil.

7. In refusing to share their oil, the wise virgins demonstrated their
   a. wisdom.
   b. selfishness.
   c. respect for the bridegroom.
   d. stubbornness.

8. The foolish virgins could have entered only if they had
   a. hurried more swiftly to the marketplace.
   b. left several of their company behind to tell the bridegroom to wait.
   c. been content to go without lamps.
   d. been prepared when the bridegroom came.

9. The foolish virgins were not given entrance because
   a. they had not been invited.
   b. they had no oil when the bridegroom came.
   c. they were too late.
   d. the bridegroom did not want to be disturbed.

10. The primary emphasis of this allegory is
   a. the necessity of sympathy for the lost.
   b. the importance of sufficient preparation and readiness.
   c. the hazards of slothfulness.
   d. the need for divine wisdom.

Meditating for Meaning

1. Many of Christ's parables liken the kingdom of heaven to some account or element of the material realm. Matthew uses the phrase "the kingdom of heaven," over 30 times.
   a. What people are the subjects or servants of the King of heaven?
   b. Often these parables begin by comparing the kingdom of heaven to a singular element ("a certain king," Matthew 18:23; 22:2; "a man," as he relates to his servants and laborers. Matthew 20:1; 25:14). What truth concerning entrance into the kingdom of heaven may Jesus have been pointing to by making the comparison plural—"the kingdom of heaven shall be likened unto *ten* virgins"?

2. In another of Christ's parables, Matthew 22:1-14, the marriage feast seems to refer to Christ's bringing of salvation, which the Jews rejected. In this parable, however, the virgins have previously accepted Christ.
   a. What figure represents Christ in this allegory?
   b. What encounter with Christ does this marriage feast symbolize?
   c. What symbol, possessed by all the virgins, represents the fact that each of them has previously accepted salvation?

3. This parable shows various degrees of preparation for the marriage.
   a. What is particularly noted that the foolish virgins neglected to bring along?
   b. What physical relation does this substance have to a lamp?
   c. What then does the foolish virgins' lack represent, considering that they had once received salvation?

4. The sleep of the virgins does not seem to represent sin considering that the wise virgins slept as well as the foolish; perhaps it represents the daily pursuits of life.
   a. Only to the foolish virgins was slumber a mistake. What should they have been doing rather than slumbering?
   b. Based on this observation, when is "slumber" as interpreted here wrong for the professing Christian?

5. When the virgins awoke, the foolish virgins discovered that their oil was nearly gone. The oil supplies in their lamps were perhaps concealed or they would likely have noticed that they were low.
   a. What outward sign alerted them to their tragedy?
   b. What outward signs in the Christian's life alert him to the level of his inner supply of fuel?

6. The wise virgins refused to share their oil with the foolish virgins on the basis that there may not have been enough for both. There is no limit to the scope and provision of salvation.
   a. What spiritual truth does their not sharing their oil symbolize?
   b. The wise virgins were not being selfish or unfeeling when they said, "Go ye rather to them that sell, and buy for yourselves." Explain what duty of the Christian this saying represents.

7. After the bridegroom was sighted, it was too late to go to the market, buy oil, and return in time for the wedding.
   a. How will this be true in real life?
   b. What does the shutting of the door represent in real life?

8. When the foolish virgins cried, "Lord, Lord, open to us," the Lord replied, I know you not." The basic wording of the Lord's answer appears several times in Scripture.
   a. Find and copy at least one other Scripture where this general idea occurs.
   b. What is required for a person to be known of the Lord? (2 Timothy 2:19)
   c. In the final judgment, why will Christ say to some, "I know you not"?

Wheelbarrows

by Don Kraybill

This allegory and the next one are modern-day parables about current weakness in the church. Like the Pharisees of Christ's day, we may be very complacent about serious inconsistencies. When we are wrong and think we are right, we need a forceful yet acceptable awakening. An allegory will sometimes answer this purpose when other forms of communication would fail.

Defining for Comprehension

Choose the word or phrase below which most nearly defines each word at the left as it is used in this allegory.

1. **status**
   a. information
   b. inactivity
   c. rank

2. **accessories**
   a. essentials
   b. entryways
   c. optional extras

3. **elaborate**
   a. extreme
   b. painstaking
   c. fancy

4. **luxurious**
   a. costly; elegant
   b. oppressive
   c. tremendous

5. **extravagant**
   a. wandering
   b. expensive
   c. unusual

6. **hilarious**
   a. boisterously funny
   b. risky
   c. unique

7. **absurd**
   a. empty
   b. ridiculous
   c. indefinite

Wheelbarrows

Once upon a time a group of White Vantress chickens lived together on Barnyard Hill and all of them used wheelbarrows. It was considered important and necessary to have wheelbarrows in order to haul things around the barnyard. It was interesting to see the different kinds of wheelbarrows which the chickens had. Some roosters had big, expensive wheelbarrows and other ones had smaller wheelbarrows.

In a sense, a wheelbarrow was a **status** symbol because if a rooster did not have a wheelbarrow, he was out of the "in group." All the other roosters avoided him. So as a social symbol it was very important for each rooster to have a wheelbarrow. When all the roosters would gather together in a social gathering, there would be inspection parties (self-appointed) which would stand in a circle and inspect the wheelbarrows. They would check out carefully the workmanship. They would check the **accessories**, the type of wheels, the kind of steel used, and the value of the wheelbarrow. The biggest and the most **elaborate** wheelbarrows always got the nod.

Soon the chickens in Barnyard Hill knew that if they had a big wheelbarrow, they would get more attention and bigger inspection parties. So all the roosters tried to outdo each other by getting bigger and more **luxurious** wheelbarrows. They added such things as chrome-plated handlebars, rubber finger grips, gold tires, fancy spokes, gold-plated bolts and nuts, rubber linings on the steel of the wheelbarrow, lights (for fog), and horns (for fast moving cows). Some of the roosters who didn't even have much to haul got extra big wheelbarrows just to impress everyone with how important they were.

Some of the roosters who felt inferior and didn't have much social power in the community organization got **extravagant** wheelbarrows. They pushed them around in the barnyard in circles just to show off. This way they could demonstrate their power and prove to all the hens that they were important and all-powerful, too.

Some of the roosters got huge wheelbarrows just to impress the hens and they would take the hens for rides around the barnyard. The hens were even stupid enough to like some of the roosters just because of the fancy wheelbarrows they owned. It was all so **hilarious** because most of the roosters really didn't need a wheelbarrow in the first place, and the ones who did need a wheelbarrow could easily have made out with wheelbarrows that were much smaller and cost half as much. It was also kind of thought provoking because a few miles away in another barnyard, some Red Cross chickens lived together. These chickens didn't have wheelbarrows. In fact, they didn't even have corn to eat, and many of them were dying. If the White Vantress chickens in Barnyard Hill would have used smaller and more economical wheelbarrows, they could have bought corn for the Red Cross hens and roosters. It was really **absurd** because once a week all the White Vantress chickens went into a chicken coop and talked about the needs of the chicken world and how the Great Farmer loved all the chickens—but they never sold their wheelbarrows.

About the Author

Donald Kraybill (b. 1945) was born in Mt. Joy, Pennsylvania, to Mennonite parents. He attended the Millersville State College, Eastern Mennonite College, and Temple University, later teaching in the Elizabethtown College. His wife, Frances Mellinger, was a registered nurse. Kraybill has served as pastor of a Mennonite church and as director of Mennonite Voluntary Service and Mennonite Youth Service in Salunga, Pennsylvania. He has written various books for Herald Press as well as a column in *Christian Living*, "Nuts and Bolts."

Testing for Understanding

1. What reason would most roosters have given for owning a wheelbarrow?
   a. "To provide necessary transportation."
   b. "To haul feed to the Red Cross chickens."
   c. "To satisfy the demands of society."
   d. "To gain acceptance with the hens."

2. A rooster who did not have a wheelbarrow could expect to be
   a. pitied.
   b. poor.
   c. unimportant.
   d. honored.

3. The inspection parties especially valued
   a. wheelbarrows with large wheels.
   b. extravagant wheelbarrows.
   c. wheelbarrows with quality workmanship.
   d. fast wheelbarrows.

4. The White Vantress chickens were living for
   a. financial security.
   b. intellectual advancement.
   c. personal independence.
   d. social approval.

5. Some roosters felt justified in adding horns and lights because
   a. they were solving practical problems.
   b. they added to the resale value of the wheelbarrow.
   c. they improved their standard of living.
   d. they caused the wheelbarrow to attract more attention.

6. The hens were friendly to roosters with fancy wheelbarrows because
   a. such roosters were more intelligent.
   b. the hens had cultivated good tastes.
   c. fancy wheelbarrows were evidence of good character.
   d. the hens were not smart enough to make good judgments.

7. If all roosters would have been governed only by need in the purchase of wheelbarrows,
   a. all of the roosters would have bought small wheelbarrows.
   b. no rooster would have bought a wheelbarrow.
   c. a few roosters would have bought two wheelbarrows.
   d. no rooster would have bought a big, extravagant wheelbarrow.

8. That the White Vantress chickens could probably have lived without wheelbarrows altogether is shown in the allegory by the fact that
   a. they had no use for wheelbarrows.
   b. some chickens did live without wheelbarrows.
   c. wheelbarrows were of recent invention.
   d. a chicken cannot push a wheelbarrow.

9. The White Vantress chickens' attitude toward other chickens could be summarized as
   a. love.
   b. ignorance.
   c. hatred.
   d. lack of empathy.

10. One subject that apparently never came up at the chicken coop meeting was
    a. the owner of the chicken coop.
    b. wheelbarrows.
    c. corn for food.
    d. other chickens.

Meditating for Meaning

1. In this allegory the chickens represent people.
   a. What kind of people are represented by the White Vantress chickens?
   b. What possession of these people do the wheelbarrows represent?
   c. What luxurious features do the people in 1a get on their "wheelbarrows"?
   d. Besides the size and luxury features, what added area of extreme waste can be true of the possession in question 1c which is not true of wheelbarrows?

2. This allegory highlights a popular trend among people.
   a. From the parable find several factors which contribute to the trend toward extravagant automobiles.
   b. What could young men stop doing that would help reverse this trend?
   c. What could young women stop doing that would help reverse this trend?

3. The allegory mentions a second group of chickens.
   a. Whom do the Red Cross chickens represent?
   b. Do you think extravagant automobiles would be acceptable if there were no "Red Cross chickens"? Explain your answer after considering carefully what the Bible says about extravagance and waste. (Proverbs 18:9; Luke 16:19, 25; 1 Timothy 2:9)

4. Several other aspects of this parable are symbolic.
   a. What does the chicken coop symbolize?
   b. What weekly exercise among Christians corresponds to the White Vantress weekly meetings?
   c. Who is the "Great Farmer"?

5. Since the time this allegory was written, an energy crisis drove the price of fuel up, making it economically desirable to drive a smaller car that uses less gas. But this does not exempt us from the author's warning. Explain the present-day absurdity that the author is trying to show us in this allegory.

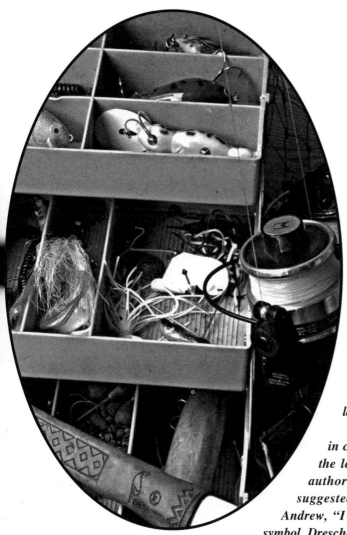

A Plea for Fishing

by John M. Drescher

Part of the skill in good allegory writing is selecting appropriate symbols. In the last parable you studied, wheelbarrows were a well-chosen symbol for automobiles. Both have wheels, both are available in a variety of sizes and styles, and both are used for transportation. These similarities develop into an effective allegory. We judge how ridiculous it was for the chickens to have luxurious wheelbarrows and know that when we laugh at them we are really seeing ourselves.

But selecting the symbols is not the only problem in composing allegories. Applications must be made to the lesson or problem the author wants us to see. The author of the following allegory had his main symbol suggested by Jesus Himself when He said to Peter and Andrew, "I will make you fishers of men." From this basic symbol, Drescher has drawn a dozen or more parallels to present-day negligence. See how many of these parallels you can discover.

Defining for Comprehension

Choose the word or phrase below which most nearly defines each word at the left as it is used in this allegory.

1. **slogans**
   a. lazy persons
   b. heavy shoes
   c. catchy mottos

2. **psychological**
   a. influenced by mind or emotion
   b. relating to mental illness
   c. reasonable

3. **doctorates**
   a. surgeons
   b. college degrees
   c. legal papers

4. **lauded**
   a. elevated
   b. praised highly
   c. filled to overflowing

5. **solely**
   a. only
   b. gloomily
   c. heartily

6. **analyzed**
   a. destroyed
   b. examined
   c. set in line

7. **waxed**
   a. decreased
   b. improved
   c. grew; became

8. **eloquent**	a. ornamented	b. forceful in speech	c. centrally located
9. **appropriate**	a. fitting	b. difficult	c. likely
10. **potential**	a. activity	b. capacity for development	c. power

A Plea for Fishing

Now it came to pass that a group existed who called themselves fishermen. And lo, there were many fish in the waters all around. In fact the whole area was surrounded by streams and lakes filled with fish. And the fish were hungry.

Week after week, month after month and year after year, these, who called themselves fishermen, met in meetings and talked about their call to fish, the abundance of fish, and how they might go fishing. Year after year they carefully defined what fishing means, defended fishing as an occupation and declared that fishing is always to be a primary task of fishermen.

Continually they searched for new and better methods of fishing and for new and better definitions of fishing. Further they said, "The fishing industry exists by fishing as fire exists by burning." They loved **slogans** such as "Fishing is the task of every fisherman," and "Every fisherman is a fisher," and "A fisherman's outpost for every fisherman's club." They sponsored special meetings called "Fisherman's Campaigns" and "The Month for Fishermen to Fish." They sponsored costly nationwide and worldwide congresses to discuss fishing and to promote fishing and hear about all the ways of fishing such as the new fishing equipment, fish calls, and whether any new bait was discovered.

These fisherman built large beautiful build-ings called "Fishing Headquarters." The plea was that everyone should be a fisherman and every fisherman should fish. One thing they didn't do however; they didn't fish.

In addition to meeting regularly they organized a board to send out fishermen to other places where there were many fish. All the fishermen seemed to agree that what is needed is a board that could challenge fishermen to be faithful in fishing. The board was formed by those who had the great vision and courage to speak about fishing, to define fishing and promote the idea of fishing in faraway streams and lakes where many other fish of different colors lived.

Also the Board hired staffs and appointed committees and held many meetings to define fishing, to defend fishing and to decide what new streams should be thought about. But the staff and committee members did not fish.

Large, elaborate, and expensive training centers were built whose original and primary purpose was to teach fishermen how to fish. Over the years courses were offered on the needs of fish, the nature of fish, where to find fish, the **psychological** reactions of fish and how to approach and feed fish. Those who taught had **doctorates** in fishology. But the teachers did not fish. They only taught fishing. Year after year, after tedious training, many were graduated and were given fishing licenses. They were sent to do full-time fishing, some to distant waters which were filled with fish.

Some spent much study and travel to learn the history of fishing and to see faraway places where the founding fathers did great fishing in the centuries past. They **lauded** the faithful fishermen of years before who handed down the idea of fishing.

Further, the fishermen built large printing houses to publish fishing guides. Presses were kept busy day and night to produce materials **solely** devoted to fishing methods, equipment, programs to arrange and to encourage meetings to talk about fishing. A speakers' bureau was also provided to schedule special speakers on the subject of fishing.

Many who felt the call to be fishermen responded. They were commissioned and sent to fish. But like the fishermen back home they never fished. Like the fishermen back home they engaged in all kinds of other occupations. They built power plants to pump water for fish, and tractors to plow new waterways. They made all kinds of equipment to travel here and there to look at fish hatcheries, fish slaughterhouses and fishing boats. Some also said that they wanted to be part of the fishing party, but they felt called to furnish fishing equipment.

Others felt their job was to relate to the fish in a good way so the fish would know the difference between good and bad fishermen. Others felt that simply letting the fish know they were nice, land-loving neighbors and how loving and kind they were was enough. A few felt what was needed was swimming lessons for the fish and better fish food so the fish would grow bigger. Some spoke of methods of purifying the water for the fish or moving fish to other waters or getting rid of the natural enemies fish have.

After one stirring meeting on "The Necessity for Fishing" one young fellow left the meeting and went fishing. The next day he reported he had caught two outstanding fish. He was honored for his excellent catch and scheduled to visit all the big meetings possible to tell about the experience to the other fishermen. He was also placed on the Fishermen's General Board as a person with considerable

About the Author

John M. Drescher (b. 1928), son of a builder, was born in Manheim, Pennsylvania. Educated at the Elizabethtown College, Eastern Mennonite College, and Goshen College, he now lives at Harrisonburg, Virginia, with his wife Betty Keener Drescher. Drescher has served as minister and bishop of the Ohio Eastern Mennonite Conference, president of the Ohio Mennonite Mission Board, and also as editor of the *Gospel Herald*. Besides his contributions to numerous magazines, he has written the book *Seven Things Children Need*.

experience.

As for the rest, it could hardly be expected that those sent out would do much fishing because those who made up the Board which sent them didn't catch fish. Those on the Board to promote fishing didn't catch a fish a year. Those who trained persons to find fish, to define fishing, to doctor fish and teach fish how to swim didn't fish themselves.

And almost no one in the meeting held weekly to talk about fishing, ever fished. So those who were sent out to fish did exactly as those who sent them did. They formed groups and special meetings to define fishing, to defend fishing and to declare how important fishing was. They talked about the great need for fishing. They prayed much that many fish might be caught. They **analyzed** the fish and discussed what is necessary in order to catch fish. They **waxed eloquent** on how others fished wrongly and bemoaned the fact that fish were not processed properly when they were caught. But one thing they did not do. They did not fish.

However, they were still called fishermen by those that sent them. The senders affirmed everywhere it was **appropriate** that they were indeed fishermen. And fish were in abundance all around. They wrote back to the board, and home fishing clubs which met each week, glowing letters about all the fishing

potential. A little criticism came sometimes that no fish were caught. But since those who criticized didn't catch fish either, the criticism was not taken so seriously.

Now it's true that many of the fishermen sacrificed and put up with all kinds of difficulties. Some lived near the water and bore the smell of dead fish every day. They received the ridicule of some who made fun of their fishermen's clubs and the fact that they claimed to be fishermen and yet never fished. They wondered about those who felt it was of little use to attend the weekly meetings to talk about fishing. After all, were they not following the Master who said, "Follow me, and I will make you fishers of men"?

Imagine how hurt some were when one day a person suggested that persons who don't catch fish were really not fishermen no matter how much they claimed to be. Yet it did sound correct. Is a person a fisherman if year after year he never catches a fish? Is one following if he isn't fishing?

 *Testing for Understanding*

1. The fishermen had all of the following incentives to fish except
    a. equipment to fish.
    b. desire to fish.
    c. fish to catch.
    d. encouragement to fish.

2. Some of the fishermen had an excuse for not fishing because
    a. they did not know how to fish.
    b. they were never told they should fish.
    c. they were busy teaching others how to fish.
    d. they lived in an area where there were no fish.

3. All of the following efforts were made to promote fishing except to
    a. appoint men to tell fishermen to fish.
    b. hold meetings to encourage fishing.
    c. have young fishers fish with experienced fishermen.
    d. educate the younger fishermen in the art of fishing.

4. Much of the effort to promote fishing was devoted to
    a. describing what fishing is.
    b. making people believe they were fishing.
    c. proving that there were not many fish to catch.
    d. organizing fishing expeditions.

5. The problem with some who were commissioned and sent to fish was
    a. they did not stay long enough to catch fish.
    b. they made friends with the fish.
    c. they allowed the fish they caught to die.
    d. they worked at making living conditions better for the fish.

6. Others justified the fact that they did not fish by
    a. pointing out that fishing is hard on the fish.
    b. assuming that it was enough to befriend the fish.
    c. proving that fishing is an inferior method of getting food.
    d. demonstrating the need for conserving fish.

7. The young man who caught two fish stopped fishing because
   a. he disliked fishing.
   b. he was not a very successful fisherman.
   c. those who didn't fish wanted him to tell about his fishing experience.
   d. those who didn't fish asked him to stop fishing.

8. From the story we gather that
   a. people were losing interest in the subject of fishing.
   b. there was a recent trend to catch more fish.
   c. the knowledge of fishing was being lost.
   d. fishing was at one time a successful occupation.

9. Someone pointed up the following inconsistency:
   a. Those who taught fishing didn't know how to fish.
   b. Much effort was put forth to promote catching fish that didn't want to be caught.
   c. People who didn't fish were being called fishermen.
   d. Much effort was put forth to promote an occupation that did not pay.

10. The last paragraph of this parable leaves you with the impression that to not catch fish is
    a. justifiable.   b. understandable.   c. inexcusable.   d. unpopular.

Meditating for Meaning

1. In this allegory winning lost souls to salvation is compared to fishing. Interpret the following symbols from the allegory.
   a. fish
   b. fisherman
   c. streams and lakes
   d. fisherman's clubs
   e. fisherman's outposts
   f. fishing headquarters
   g. fishing board
   h. fish of different colors
   i. training centers
   j. faithful fishermen of years before
   k. printing houses
   l. power plants and tractors
   m. teaching fish to swim
   n. purifying the water for fish
   o. catching two outstanding fish
   p. fishing wrongly
   q. not processing fish properly
   r. smell of dead fish
   s. weekly meetings
   t. the Master

2. Christ first used the basic metaphor of this allegory. Give at least one way in which soul winning is like fishing.

3. The problem presented in this allegory persists today.
   a. Is "fishing" required or optional for Christians? Give a Bible verse to support your answer.
   b. The allegory strongly emphasizes defining fishing and defending fishing. Why do you think people who do not fish would give such attention to defining and defending fishing?
   c. In this allegory *fish* or some form of the word is used over 130 times and in every sentence but three. In what way does this repetition contribute to the message of the allegory?

4. The excuses these fishermen gave for not fishing are very prevalent among professing Christians today.
   a. Of all the excuses given in the allegory, which do you think is the most common today?
   b. What does the last sentence of the allegory suggest about Christians who are not active in soul winning?

The Pilgrim's Progress

by John Bunyan

"Can there any good thing come out of Nazareth?" Nathanael asked Philip when Philip told him of Jesus. Perhaps a similar gasp of surprise may leap from your tongue when you discover that you are about to study an allegory written by a common mender of pans while he was imprisoned in England's Bedford Jail. Indeed, when John Bunyan first wrote **The Pilgrim's Progress,** *many did ask this question. They predicted that it would be a failure. But, it has become one of the most widely read pieces of Christian literature, translated into over 100 languages and sold in numerous editions and myriads of copies.*

Actually, John Bunyan produced this religious classic somewhat unintentionally.[1] His purpose was a personal one of avoiding the temptation of evil thoughts.[2] Although he was not educated in any of the universities of his day, he was educated many years in the school of spiritual struggles, as you learned from your study of his autobiography, **Grace Abounding to the Chief of Sinners** *(pages 268-285).*

The Pilgrim's Progress *lacks some of the literary polish that you have noticed in other pieces of literature in this textbook. However, two things more than offset any literary weakness that it might have.*

The first strength of this literary piece is its form. The allegory, as you have noticed, is a very fascinating form, and Bunyan used this form with particular genius. His mind, as he admits in his poetical introduction to the book, was a fertile seedbed for metaphorical language.

> *In more than twenty things which I set down,*
> *This done, I twenty more had in my crown;*
> *And they [metaphors] again began to multiply*
> *Like sparks that from the coals of fire do fly.*

---

1. When at the first I took my pen in hand / Thus for to write, I did not understand / That I at all should make a little book / In such a mode; nay, I had undertook / To make another; which, when almost done / Before I was aware I this begun. (From *The Author's Apology for His Book*)

2. ...I did not think/ To show to all the world my pen and ink / In such a mode; I only thought to make / I knew not what; nor did I undertake / Thereby to please my neighbour: no, not I; / I did it my own self to gratify, / Neither did I but vacant seasons spend / In this my scribble; nor did I intend / But to divert myself in doing this / From worser thoughts which make me do amiss.

Artist: J. D. Watson

As an allegory, **The Pilgrim's Progress** *is considered the greatest ever written.*

The second strength of this book is its depth of spiritual content. And no wonder! Bunyan's scholarship consisted mainly in the personal study of two books: **Foxe's Book of Martyrs** *and the Bible. As you study* **The Pilgrim's Progress**, *you will quickly notice that even the wording of the Bible is interwoven with Bunyan's own phraseology as he expounds the height and depth of profound Scriptural truth.*

This does not mean that **The Pilgrim's Progress** *is difficult to understand. By using an allegory, Bunyan was able to present in clear, easy form his keen insight into truth about the Christian life. This book has helped many Christians in their own pilgrimage.*

Bunyan's ability to clothe rich spiritual truths in an allegory was so rich and startling to the Christians of his day that he felt he needed to prefix his story with 236 lines of poetry defending his use of this literary form. In this introduction, he likens himself to a fisherman, catching certain very elusive fish by a special technique, and to a fowler, luring a particular kind of bird in an unusual way. He also argues that the Bible contains many allegories.

> *My dark and cloudy words, they do but hold*
> *The truth, as cabinets enclose the gold.*

> *The prophets used much by metaphors*
> *To set forth truth; yea, whoso considers*
> *Christ, His apostles too, shall plainly see,*
> *That truths to this day in such mantles be.*

Bunyan himself knew the true power of allegorical writing when he wrote

> *Truth's golden beams: nay, by this method may*
> *Make it cast forth its rays as light as day.*

He knew that allegories not only make truth understandable, but they help to make the truth stick in the mind.

> *Art thou forgetful? Wouldst thou remember*
> *From New-year's day to the last of December?*
> *Then read my fancies; they will stick like burrs,*
> *And may be to the helpless, comforters.*

Typical of his literary wit, Bunyan includes in his expansive apology (or reason for writing in allegory form) a homely metaphor.

> *If that* [allegories] *thou wilt not read, let it alone;*
> *Some love the meat, some love to pick the bone.*

How aptly this figure of speech describes the "cold water pourer" who, as we might say, has "a crow to pick" or "an axe to grind." Bunyan portrays peevish critics spurning the delicious, healthful meat of an allegory in order to "pick the bone." Perhaps Bunyan did lack the education of other literary masters. Perhaps men did ask, "Can there any good come out of a tinker-prisoner?" But Bunyan certainly was an artist with words. To use Philip's response to Nathanael's skeptical question—"Come and see."

Chapter 1: Christian Begins His Journey

Defining for Comprehension

Choose the word or phrase below which most nearly defines each word at the left as it is used in this allegory.

1. **plight**	a. ruin	b. difficulty	c. acreage
2. **restrained**	a. hummed	b. continued	c. withheld from expression
3. **perceive**	a. to exclude	b. grasp; understand	c. accept
4. **frenzy**	a. wildly excited	b. uncomfortable	c. unusual
5. **surly**	a. certain	b. sullenly rude	c. confused
6. **deride**	a. wreck	b. comfort	c. mock; scorn
7. **chide**	a. soothe	b. obscure	c. rebuke; scold
8. **condole**	a. lend sympathy	b. share out	c. join together
9. **solitarily**	a. moodily	b. in loneliness	c. quietly
10. **wont**	a. desirous	b. accustomed	c. absent
11. **obstinate**	a. stubborn	b. blocking from view	c. not exact
12. **pliable**	a. useful	b. fitting	c. easily bent
13. **resolved**	a. determined	b. complete	c. reasoned
14. **incorruptible**	a. pure	b. unbreakable	c. unable to decay
15. **revile**	a. draw back	b. speak abusively	c. fill again

As I walked through the wilderness of this world, I lighted on a certain place where was a den, and laid me down in that place to sleep; and as I slept, I dreamed a dream. I dreamed, and behold I saw a man clothed with rags standing in a certain place, with his face from his own house, a book in his hand, and a great burden upon his back. I looked, and saw him open the book, and read therein; and as he read, he wept and trembled; and not being able longer to contain, he brake out with a lamentable cry, saying, What shall I do?

In this **plight** therefore, he went home, and **restrained** himself as long as he could, that his wife and children should not **perceive** his distress; but he could not be silent long, because that his trouble increased. Wherefore at length he brake his mind to his wife and children; and thus he began to talk to them. O my dear wife, said he, and you the children of my bowels, I, your dear friend, am in myself *undone*[1] by reason of a burden that lieth hard upon me; moreover, I am for certain informed that this our city will be burned with fire from

---

1. undone: doomed; ruined.

heaven; in which fearful overthrow, both myself, with thee my wife, and you my sweet babes, shall miserably come to ruin, except (the which yet I see not) some way of escape can be found, whereby we may be delivered. At this his relations were sore amazed; not for that they believed that what he had said to them was true, but because they thought that some **frenzy** *distemper*[2] had got into his head; therefore, it drawing towards night, and they hoping that sleep might settle his brains, with all haste they got him to bed. But the night was as troublesome to him as the day; wherefore, instead of sleeping, he spent it in sighs and tears. So, when the morning was come, they would know how he did. He told them, Worse and worse: he also set to talking to them again; but they began to be hardened. They also thought to drive away his distemper by harsh and **surly** *carriages*[3] to him: sometimes they would **deride**, sometimes they would **chide**, and sometimes they would quite neglect him. Wherefore he began to retire himself to his chamber, to pray for and pity them, and also to **condole** his own misery; he would also walk **solitarily** in the fields, sometimes reading, and sometimes praying: and thus for some days he spent his time.

Now I saw, upon a time ,when he was walking in the fields, that he was (as he was **wont**) reading in his book, and greatly distressed in his mind; and as he read, he burst out as he had done before, crying, What shall I do to be saved?

I saw also that he looked this way, and that way, as if he would run; yet he stood still, because (as I perceived) he could not tell which way to go. I looked then, and saw a man named Evangelist coming to him, and asked, Wherefore dost thou cry?

He answered, Sir, I perceive by the book in my hand that I am condemned to die, and after that to come to judgment; and I find that I am not willing to do the first, nor able to do the second.

Then said Evangelist, Why not willing to die, since this life is attended with so many evils? The man answered, Because I fear that this burden that is upon my back will sink me lower than the grave, and I shall fall into *Tophet*.[4] And, sir, if I be not fit to go to prison, I am not fit to go to judgment, and from thence to execution; and the thoughts of these things make me cry.

Then said Evangelist, If this be thy condition, why standest thou still? He answered, Because I know not whither to go. Then he gave him a parchment roll, and there was written within, Fly from the wrath to come.

The man therefore read it, and, looking upon Evangelist very carefully, said, Whither must I fly? Then said Evangelist, pointing with his finger over a very wide field, Do you see yonder *Wicket-gate?*[5] The man said, No. Then said the other, Do you see yonder shining light? He said, I think I do. Then said Evangelist, Keep that light in your eye, and go up directly thereto, so shalt thou see the gate; at which when thou knockest, it shall be told thee what thou shalt do. So I saw in my dream that the man began to run. Now he had not run far from his own door, but his wife and children, perceiving it, began to cry after him to return; but the man put his fingers in his ears, and ran on, crying, Life! life! eternal life! So he looked not behind him, but fled towards the middle of the plain.

The neighbours also came out to see him run; and as he ran, some mocked, others threatened, and some cried after him to return; and, among those that did so, there were two that were resolved to fetch him back by force. The name of the one was **Obstinate**, and the name of the other **Pliable**. Now by this time the man was got a good distance from them; but however they were **resolved** to pursue him, which they did, and in a little time they overtook him. Then said the man, Neighbours,

---

2. distemper: mental disorder.

3. carriages: acts of behavior.

4. Tophet (tō´ fət): hell.

5. Wicket-gate: small door or gate built into or near a larger one.

wherefore are you come? They said, To persuade you to go back with us. But he said, That can by no means be: you dwell, said he, in the City of Destruction, the place also where I was born: I see it to be so; and dying there, sooner or later you will sink lower than the grave, into a place that burns with fire and brimstone: be content, good neighbours, and go along with me.

OBST. What! said Obstinate, and leave our friends and our comforts behind us?

CHR. Yes, said Christian (for that was his name), because that all which you shall forsake is not worthy to be compared with a little of that I am seeking to enjoy; and if you will go along with me, and hold it, you shall fare as I myself; for there, where I go, is enough and to spare. Come away, and prove my words.

OBST. What are the things you seek, since you leave all the world to find them?

CHR. I seek an inheritance **incorruptible**, undefiled, and that fadeth not away; and it is laid up in heaven, and safe there, to be bestowed, at the time appointed, on them that diligently seek it. Read it so, if you will, in my book.

OBST. Tush! said Obstinate, away with your book; will you go back with us or no?

CHR. No, not I, said the other, because I have laid my hand to the plough.

OBST. Come then, neighbour Pliable, let us turn again and go home without him; there is a company of these crazy-headed *coxcombs*[6], that when they take a fancy by the end, are wiser in their own eyes than seven men that can render a reason.

PLI. Then said Pliable, Don't **revile**; if what the good Christian says is true, the things he looks after are better than ours: my heart inclines to go with my neighbour.

OBST. What! more fools still! Be ruled by me, and go back; who knows whither such a brain-sick fellow will lead you? Go back, go back, and be wise.

_____

6. coxcombs: vain, conceited persons.

Artist: J. D. Watson

CHR. Come with thy neighbour, Pliable; there are such things to be had which I spoke of, and many more glories besides. If you believe not me, read here in this book; and for the truth of what is expressed therein, behold, all is confirmed by the blood of Him that made it.

PLI. Well, neighbour Obstinate, said Pliable, I begin to come to a point; I intend to go along with this good man, and to cast in my lot with him: but, my good companion, do you know the way to this desired place?

CHR. I am directed by a man, whose name is Evangelist, to speed me to a little gate that is before us, where we shall receive instructions about the way.

PLI. Come then, good neighbour, let us be going. Then they went both together.

OBST. And I will go back to my place, said Obstinate; I will be no companion of such misled, *fantastical*[7] fellows.

---

7. fantastical: queer; having wild ideas.

Meditating for Meaning

1. Bunyan uses several metaphors to explain the writing of *The Pilgrim's Progress*.
   a. From what you have learned of where Bunyan wrote this book, what does he mean by the "den"?
   b. How is a dream well suited for the form of the story?

2. The man experiencing the plight in the opening scene of Bunyan's dream is
   a. a wayward father who is returning in sorrow to do his duty to his children.
   b. a mentally incompetent man overcome by the realities of life.
   c. a sinner being awakened to his true condition.
   d. a poverty-stricken man unable to face the responsibilities of providing for a family.

3. Interpret the following figurative descriptions of a man in this state:
   a. clothed with rags (Isaiah 64:6)
   b. facing away from his house
   c. holding a book
   d. carrying a great burden upon his back (Psalm 38:4)
   e. weeping and trembling
   f. saying, "What shall I do?" (Acts 2:37; 16:30)

4. The man's family notes his distress.
   a. What does he finally tell his family is the reason for his condition?
   b. What alarms his family when he reveals this reason?

5. Men attempt to quiet conviction in many ways.
   a. What attempt does the family first make to cure him?
   b. Next they try deriding, chiding, and neglecting him. What three effects do you think they intend by these methods?
   c. Finally he himself seeks relief by _____ .
   d. What other "cures" do guilty people sometimes use to try to relieve themselves?

Note: In many respects *The Pilgrim's Progress* is a revelation of Bunyan's own spiritual pilgrimage. For example, the Evangelist was a Mr. Gifford in Bunyan's own experience who pointed out the true way to him.

6. What reason did Christian give Evangelist for his reluctance to die?

7. Evangelist gives Christian a parchment roll.
   a. What is written on the roll?
   b. Why is this message not immediately helpful?

8. The Wicket-gate is a very important part of the pilgrim's "progress," symbolizing conversion or entrance into the Christian life. In Matthew 7:13, 14 Jesus calls this gate "strait."
   a. Considering the meanings of *Wicket-gate* and *strait*, explain why you think Christian cannot see the gate.
   b. Christ's teaching about the "strait gate" is near the end of the Sermon on the Mount. Give an example of a strict, narrow Christian principle which Jesus taught in this sermon.

9. Though Christian cannot see the wicket-gate, he can see the light which will lead him there. What is likely represented by this light? (Psalm 119:105; 2 Peter 1:19)

10. Now Christian begins to run toward the shining light.
    a. What in the Christian life is symbolized by leaving his family and friends behind? (Luke 14:26, 33)
    b. What does putting his fingers into his ears symbolize?
    c. He doesn't look back, but flees, crying, "Life! life! eternal life!" What does this illustrate about how the Christian life is to begin?

11. Bunyan names his characters according to the kinds of people they are. He then has his characters act consistently with their names. True to his name, Obstinate refuses to be persuaded by Christian, blindly holding to his opinion even when shown a better way.
    a. What is worth more to Obstinate than escaping destruction to come?
    b. Find three derogatory expressions Obstinate makes about Christian that are typical of the world's attitude. Clue: Two of the expressions involve alliteration.

12. True to his name as well, Pliable yields easily to Christian's new way of life.
    a. What is Pliable's basic reason for wanting to go along with Christian?
    b. Is this a wrong motivation? (Hebrews 12:2)
    c. What motivation does Christian have that seems to be totally lacking in Pliable?

Chapter 2: Christian Falls in the Slough of Despond

Defining for Comprehension

Choose the word or phrase below which most nearly defines each word at the left as it is used in this allegory.

1. discourse	a. way of life	b. disagreement	c. discussion
2. firmament	a. heavens	b. dry land	c. affliction
3. immortality	a. everlasting life	b. sensual living	c. death
4. ravish	a. to delight	b. to spoil	c. to fill with fear
5. slough	a. ladder across fence	b. swamp; mire	c. laziness
6. wallowed	a. engulfed	b. slowed down	c. rolled in the mud
7. bedaubed	a. frightened	b. dulled	c. smeared with mud
8. apprehensions	a. doubts; fears	b. arrests	c. inclinations
9. substantial	a. difficult	b. steady; solid	c. obvious
10. hazarding	a. endangering	b. blocking	c. discarding

Now I saw in my dream, that when Obstinate was gone back, Christian and Pliable went talking over the plain; and thus they began their **discourse**.

CHR. Come, neighbour Pliable, how do you do? I am glad you are persuaded to go along with me. Had even Obstinate himself but felt what I have felt of the powers and terrors of what is yet unseen, he would not thus lightly have given us the back.

PLI. Come, neighbour Christian, since there are none but us two here, tell me now further, what the things are, and how to be enjoyed, whither we are going.

CHR. I can better conceive of them with my mind than speak of them with my tongue: but yet, since you are desirous to know, I will read of them in my book.

PLI. And do you think that the words of your book are certainly true?

CHR. Yes, verily; for it was made by Him that cannot lie.

PLI. Well said; what things are they?

CHR. There is an endless kingdom to be inhabited, and everlasting life to be given us, that we may inhabit that kingdom for ever.

PLI. Well said; and what else?

CHR. There are crowns of glory to be given us, and garments that will make us shine like the sun in the **firmament** of heaven!

PLI. This is excellent; and what else?

CHR. There shall be no more crying, nor sorrow: for He that is owner of the place will wipe all tears from our eyes.

PLI. And what company shall we have there?

CHR. There we shall be with *seraphims*[1] and *cherubims*;[2] creatures that will dazzle your eyes to look on them. There also you shall meet

---

1. seraphims: angels, possibly the highest order.
2. cherubims: angels, possibly the second highest order.

with thousands and ten thousands that have gone before us to that place; none of them are hurtful, but loving and holy; every one walking in the sight of God, and standing in His presence with acceptance for ever. In a word, there we shall see the elders with their golden crowns; there we shall see the holy virgins with their golden harps; there we shall see men, that by the world were cut in pieces, burnt in flames, eaten of beasts, drowned in the seas, for the love that they bare to the Lord of the place; all well, and clothed with **immortality** as with a garment.

PLI. The hearing of this is enough to **ravish** one's heart. But are these things to be enjoyed? How shall we get to be sharers thereof?

CHR. The Lord, the governor of the country, hath recorded that in this book; the substance of

which is, If we be truly willing to have it, He will bestow it upon us freely.

PLI. Well, my good companion, glad am I to hear of these things; come on, let us mend our pace.

CHR. I cannot go so fast as I would, by reason of this burden that is on my back.

Now I saw in my dream, that just as they had ended this talk, they drew nigh to a very miry **slough**, that was in the midst of the plain; and they, being heedless, did both fall suddenly into the bog. The name of the slough was *Despond*.[3] Here, therefore, they **wallowed** for a time, being grievously **bedaubed** with dirt; and Christian, because of the burden that was on his back, began to sink in the mire.

PLI. Then said Pliable, Ah, neighbour Christian, where are you now?

CHR. Truly, said Christian, I do not know.

PLI. At that Pliable began to be offended, and angrily said to his fellow, Is this the happiness you have told me all this while of? If we have such ill speed at our first setting out, what may we expect 'twixt this and our journey's end? May I get out again with my life, you shall possess the *brave*[4] country alone for me. And with that he gave a desperate struggle or two, and got out of the mire on that side of the slough which was next to his own house: so away he went, and Christian saw him no more.

Wherefore Christian was left to tumble in the Slough of Despond alone: but still he endeavored to struggle to that side of the slough that was further from his own house, and next to the Wicket-

---

3. despond: despondency, mental depression.
4. brave: excellent; fine.

gate; the which he did, but could not get out because of the burden that was upon his back: but I beheld in my dream, that a man came to him, whose name was Help, and asked him, What he did there?

CHR. Sir, said Christian, I was bid go this way by a man called Evangelist, who directed me also to yonder gate, that I might escape the wrath to come. And as I was going thither I fell in here.

HELP. But why did not you look for the steps?

CHR. Fear followed me so hard, that I fled the next way and fell in.

HELP. Then said he, Give me thy hand: so he gave him his hand, and he drew him out, and set him upon sound ground, and bid him go on his way.

Then I stepped to him that plucked him out, and said, Sir, wherefore, since over this place is the way from the City of Destruction to yonder gate, is it that this *plat*[5] is not mended, that poor travellers might go thither with more security? And he said unto me, This miry slough is such a place as cannot be mended: it is the descent whither the scum and filth that attends conviction for sin doth continually run, and therefore it is called the Slough of Despond; for still, as the sinner is awakened about his lost condition, there arise in his soul many fears and doubts, and discouraging **apprehensions**, which all of them got together, and settle in this place. And this is the reason of the badness of this ground.

It is not the pleasure of the King that this place should remain so bad. His labourers also have, by the directions of His Majesty's survey-ors, been for above these sixteen hundred years employed about this patch of ground, if perhaps it might have been mended: yea, and to my knowledge, said he, here have been swallowed up at least twenty thousand cart-loads, yea, millions of wholesome instructions, that have at all seasons been brought from all places of the King's dominions (and they that can tell, say, they are the best materials to make good ground of the place) if so be it might have been mended; but it is the Slough of Despond still, and so will be when they have done what they can.

True, there are, by the direction of the Lawgiver, certain good and **substantial** *steps*,[6] placed even through the very midst of this slough; but at such time as this place doth much spew out its filth, as it doth against change of weather, these steps are hardly seen; or if they be, men, through the dizziness of their heads, step besides, and then they are bemired to purpose, notwithstanding the steps be there; but the ground is good when they are once got in at the gate.

Now I saw in my dream that by this time Pliable was got home to his house. So his neigh-bours came to visit him; and some of them called him wise man for coming back, and some called him fool for **hazarding** himself with Christian: others, again, did mock at his cowardliness; saying, Surely, since you began to venture, I would not have been so base to have given out for a few difficulties: so Pliable sat sneaking among them. But at last he got more confidence, and then they all turned their tales, and began to deride poor Christian behind his back. And thus much concerning Pliable.

---

5. plat: place; plot of ground.
6. steps: the promises of forgiveness and acceptance to life by faith in Christ.

Meditating for Meaning

1. According to Christian, what realization would have kept Obstinate from turning back?

2. Why does Pliable wish to travel faster?

3. The Slough of Despond is a well-chosen metaphor.
   a. Describe the condition of despondency.
   b. How is a slough a good symbol for despond?

4. Christian and Pliable find themselves mired in the slough.
   a. Why do the two travelers fall in?
   b. Who sinks the deeper and why?
   c. Why is Pliable offended?

5. How and where does Pliable get out?

6. Christian responds differently from Pliable.
   a. What aspect of Christian's behavior in the slough shows what is necessary for successful Christian living?
   b. What kind of help does a Christian need when he is despondent? (Psalm 40:2)

7. Help comes to Christian's rescue.
   a. According to Help, what three things lead to despondency in the life of a young Christian?
   b. What efforts have been made to help correct the slough?

8. From this account of the Slough of Despond, what are two things you can do if you feel despondency threatening your life?

9. What three opinions do the neighbors have of Pliable when he returns?

Chapter 3: Christian Meets Mr. Worldly Wiseman

Defining for Comprehension

Choose the word or phrase below which most nearly defines each word at the left as it is used in this allegory.

	a.	b.	c.
1. **carnal**	a. deathly	b. festive	c. fleshly
2. **inkling**	a. slight clue	b. young bird	c. chain link
3. **distractions**	a. confusions	b. acts of removal	c. accidents
4. **morality**	a. high spirits	b. good conduct	c. encouragement
5. **legality**	a. strict keeping of the law	b. gaiety	c. laziness
6. **judicious**	a. criticizing	b. wise; shrewd	c. meddlesome
7. **perdition**	a. added part	b. second book	c. complete ruin
8. **odious**	a. smelly	b. offensive	c. strange; weird
9. **simpering**	a. boiling	b. crying quietly	c. grinning in a silly way
10. **beguile**	a. deceive	b. become evil	c. increase
11. **confirmation**	a. proof; witness	b. harmony	c. design
12. **abandoned**	a. parted	b. deserted	c. attacked
13. **God-speed**	a. swift passage	b. Christ's return	c. good success

Now as Christian was walking solitarily by himself, he espied one afar off, come crossing over the field to meet him; and their *hap*[1] was to meet just as they were crossing the way of each other. The gentleman's name that met him was Mr. Worldly Wiseman: he dwelt in the town of **Carnal** Policy, a very great town, and also hard-by from whence Christian came. This man then, meeting with Christian, and having some **inkling** of him (for Christian's setting forth from the City of Destruction was much noised abroad, not only in the town where he dwelt, but also it began to be the town talk in some other places), Mr. Worldly Wiseman, therefore, having some guess of him, by beholding his laborious going, by observing his sighs and groans, and the like, began thus to enter into some talk with Christian.

WORLD. How now, good fellow, whither away after this burdened manner?

CHR. A burdened manner, indeed, as ever I think poor creature had! And whereas you ask me, Whither away? I tell you, sir, I am going to yonder Wicket-gate before me; for there, as I am informed, I shall be put into a way to be rid of my heavy burden.

WORLD. Hast thou a wife and children?

CHR. Yes; but I am so laden with this burden, that I cannot take that pleasure in them as formerly; *methinks*[2] I am as if I had none.

---

1. hap: circumstance.
2. methinks: it seems to me.

WORLD. Wilt thou hearken to me if I give thee counsel?

CHR. If it be good, I will; for I stand in need of good counsel.

WORLD. I would advise thee then, that thou with all speed get thyself rid of thy burden; for thou wilt never be settled in thy mind till then: nor canst thou enjoy the benefits of the blessings which God hath bestowed upon thee, till then.

CHR. That is that which I seek for, even to be rid of this heavy burden: but get it off myself I cannot; nor is there any man in our country that can take it off my shoulders; therefore am I going this way, as I told you, that I may be rid of my burden.

WORLD. Who bid thee go this way to be rid of thy burden?

CHR. A man that appeared to me to be a very great and honourable person: his name, as I remember, is Evangelist.

WORLD. I *beshrew*[3] him for his counsel! There is not a more dangerous and troublesome way in the world than is that unto which he hath directed thee; and that thou shalt find, if thou wilt be ruled by his counsel. Thou hast met with something, as I perceive, already; for I see the dirt of the Slough of Despond is upon thee; but that slough is the beginning of the sorrows that do attend those that go on in that way. Hear me; I am older than thou: thou art like to meet with, in the way which thou goest, wearisomeness, painfulness, hunger, perils, nakedness, sword, lions, dragons, darkness, and, in a word, death, and what not. These things are certainly true, having been confirmed by many testimonies. And should a man so carelessly cast away himself, by giving heed to a stranger?

CHR. Why, sir, this burden upon my back is more terrible to me than are all these things which you have mentioned: nay, methinks I care not what I meet with in the way, if so be I can also meet with deliverance from my burden.

WORLD. How camest thou by thy burden at first?

CHR. By reading this book in my hand.

WORLD. I thought so; and it is happened unto thee as to other weak men, who, meddling with things too high for them, do suddenly fall into thy **distractions**; which distractions do not only *unman*[4] men, as thine I perceive have done thee, but they run them upon desperate ventures to obtain they know not what.

CHR. I know what I would obtain; it is ease for my heavy burden.

WORLD. But why wilt thou seek for ease this way, seeing so many dangers attend it? Especially since (hadst thou but patience to hear me) I could direct thee to the obtaining of what thou desirest, without the dangers that thou in this way wilt run thyself into? Yea, and the remedy is at hand. Besides, I will add, that instead of those dangers, thou shalt meet with much safety, friendship, and content.

CHR. Sir, I pray open this secret to me.

WORLD. Why, in yonder village (the village is named **Morality**) there dwells a gentleman whose name is **Legality**, a very **judicious** man, and a man of a very good name, that has skill to help men off with such burdens as thine are from their shoulders: yea, to my knowledge, he hath done a great deal of good this way;

Mr. Worldly Wiseman

---

3. beshrew: curse.

4. unman: cause to lose courage.

ay, and besides, he hath skill to cure those that are somewhat crazed in their wits with their burdens. To him, as I said, thou mayest go, and be helped presently. His house is not quite a mile from this place; and if he should not be at home himself, he hath a pretty young man to his son, whose name is *Civility*,[5] that can do it (to speak on) as well as the old gentleman himself; there, I say, thou mayest be eased of thy burden; and if thou art not minded to go back to thy former habitation, as indeed I would not wish thee, thou mayest send for thy wife and children to thee to this village, where there are houses now standing empty, one of which thou mayest have at reasonable rates; provision is there also cheap and good; and that which will make thy life the more happy is, to be sure there thou shalt live by honest neighbours, in credit and good fashion.

Now was Christian somewhat at a stand; but presently he concluded, If this be true which this gentleman hath said, my wisest course is to take his advice; and with that he thus further spoke.

CHR. Sir, which is my way to this honest man's house?

WORLD. Do you see yonder *high hill*[6]?

CHR. Yes, very well.

WORLD. By that hill you must go, and the first house you come at is his.

So Christian turned out of his way to go to Mr. Legality's house for help; but behold, when he was got now hard by the hill, it seemed so high, and also that side of it that was next the way-side did hang so much over, that Christian was afraid to venture further, lest the hill should fall on his head; wherefore there he stood still, and *wotted*[7] not what to do. Also his burden now seemed heavier to him than while he was in his way. There came also flashes of fire out of the hill, that made Christian afraid that he should be burned: here, therefore, he sweat, and did quake for fear. And now he began to be sorry that he had taken Mr. Worldly Wiseman's counsel; and with that he

saw Evangelist coming to meet him, at the sight also of whom he began to blush for shame. So Evangelist drew nearer and nearer; and coming up to him, he looked upon him with a severe and dreadful countenance, and thus began to reason with Christian.

EVAN. What dost thou here, Christian? said he: at which words Christian knew not what to answer; wherefore at present he stood speechless before him. Then said Evangelist further, Art not thou the man that I found crying without the walls of the City of Destruction?

CHR. Yes, dear sir, I am the man.

EVAN. Did not I direct thee the way to the little Wicket-gate?

CHR. Yes, dear sir, said Christian.

EVAN. How is it then that thou art so quickly turned aside? For thou art now out of the way.

CHR. I met with a gentleman so soon as I had got over the Slough of Despond, who persuaded me that I might, in the village before me, find a man that could take off my burden.

EVAN. What was he?

CHR. He looked like a gentleman, and talked much to me, and got me at last to yield: so I came hither; but when I beheld this hill, and how it hangs over the way, I suddenly made a stand; lest it should fall on my head.

EVAN. What said that gentleman to you?

CHR. Why, he asked me whither I was going; and I told him.

EVAN. And what said he then?

CHR. He asked me if I had a family: and I told him. But, said I, I am so laden with the burden that is on my back, that I cannot take pleasure in them as formerly.

EVAN. And what said he then?

CHR. He bid me with speed get rid of my burden; and I told him 'twas ease that I sought. And, said I, I am therefore going to yonder gate, to receive further direction how I may get to the place of deliverance. So he said that he would show me a better way, and short, not so attended with difficulties as the way, sir, that

5. civility: morally good but not sanctified by faith.
6. high hill: Mt. Sinai.
7. wotted: knew.

you set me; which way, said he, will direct you to a gentleman's house that hath skill to take off these burdens: so I believed him, and turned out of that way into this, if haply I might be soon eased of my burden. But when I came to this place, and beheld things as they are, I stopped, for fear (as I said) of danger: but I now know not what to do.

EVAN. Then, said Evangelist, Stand still a little, that I may show thee the words of God. So he stood trembling. Then said Evangelist, See that ye refuse not him that speaketh: for if they escaped not who refused him that spake on earth, much more shall not we escape, if we turn away from him that speaketh from heaven. He said, moreover, Now the just shall live by faith; but if any man draw back, my soul shall have no pleasure in him. He also did thus apply them; Thou art the man that art running into this misery; thou hast begun to reject the counsel of the Most High, and to draw back thy foot from the way of peace, even almost to the hazarding of thy **perdition**.

Then Christian fell down at his feet as dead, crying, Woe is me, for I am undone! At the sight of which Evangelist caught him by the right hand, saying, All manner of sin and blasphemies shall be forgiven unto men. Be not faithless, but believing. Then did Christian again a little revive, and stood up trembling, as at first, before Evangelist.

Then Evangelist proceeded, saying, Give more earnest heed to the things that I shall tell thee of. I will now show thee who it was that deluded thee, and who it was also to whom he sent thee. The man that met thee is one Worldly Wiseman and rightly is he so called; partly because he favoureth only the doctrine of this world (therefore he always goes to the town of Morality to church); and partly because he loveth that doctrine best, for it saveth him best from the cross: and because he is of this carnal temper, therefore he seeketh to pervert my ways, though right. Now there are three things in this man's counsel that thou must utterly abhor.

1. His turning thee out of the way. 2. His labouring to render the cross **odious** to thee. 3. And his setting thy feet in that way that lead-

eth unto the administration of death.

First, Thou must abhor his turning thee out of the way; yea, and thine own consenting thereto; because this is to reject the counsel of God for the sake of the counsel of a Worldly Wiseman. The Lord says, Strive to enter in at the strait gate; the gate to which I send thee; for strait is the gate that leadeth unto life, and few there be that find it. From this little Wicket-gate, and from the way thereto, hath this wicked man turned thee, to the bringing of thee almost to destruction: hate, therefore, his turning thee out of the way, and abhor thyself for hearkening to him.

Secondly, Thou must abhor his labouring to render the cross odious unto thee; for thou art to prefer it before the treasures of Egypt. Besides, the King of glory hath told thee, that he that will save his life shall lose it. And he that comes after Him, and hates not his father, and mother, and wife, and children, and brethren, and sisters, yea, and his own life also, he cannot be His disciple. I say, therefore, for man to labour to persuade thee that that shall be thy death, without which, the truth hath said, thou canst not have eternal life: this doctrine thou must abhor.

Thirdly, Thou must hate his setting of thy feet in the way that leadeth to the ministration of death. And for this thou must consider to whom he sent thee, and also how unable that person was to deliver thee from thy burden.

He to whom thou was sent for ease, being by name Legality, is the son of the bond-woman which now is, and is in bondage with her children; and is, in a mystery, this Mount Sinai, which thou has feared will fall on thy head. Now if she with her children are in bondage, how canst thou expect by them to be made free? This Legality, therefore, is not able to set thee free from thy burden. No man was as yet ever rid of his burden by him; no, nor ever is like to be: ye cannot be justified by the works of the law; for by the deeds of the law no man living can be rid of his burden. Therefore, Mr. Worldly Wiseman is an alien, and Mr. Legality is a cheat; and for his son Civility, notwithstanding his **simpering** looks, he is but a hypocrite, and cannot help thee. Believe me, there is nothing in all this noise that thou hast heard of these *sottish*[8] men, but a design to **beguile** thee of thy salvation, by turning thee from the way in which I had set thee. After this, Evangelist called aloud to the heavens for **confirmation** of what he had said; and with that there came words and fire out of the mountain under which poor Christian stood, that made the hair of his flesh stand up. The words were thus pronounced: As many as are of the works of the law are under the curse; for it is written, Cursed is every one that continueth not in all things which are written in the book of the law to do them.

Now Christian looked for nothing but death, and began to cry out lamentably; even cursing the time in which he met with Mr. Worldly Wiseman; still calling himself a thousand fools for hearkening to his counsel. He also was greatly ashamed to think that this gentleman's arguments, flowing only from the flesh, should have the *prevalency*[9] with him as to cause him to forsake the right way. This done, he applied himself again to Evangelist in words and sense as follows:

CHR. Sir, what think you? Is there any hope? May I now go back and go up to the Wicket-gate? shall I not be **abandoned** for this, and sent back from thence ashamed? I am sorry I have hearkened to this man's counsel: but may my sins be forgiven?

EVAN. Then said Evangelist to him, Thy sin is very great, for by it thou hast committed two evils; thou hast forsaken the way that is good, to tread in forbidden paths. Yet will the man at the gate receive thee, for he has goodwill for men; only, said he, take heed that thou turn not aside again, lest thou perish from the way, when His wrath is kindled but a little. Then did Christian address himself to go back; and Evangelist, after he had kissed him, gave him one smile, and bid him **God-speed**.

---

8. sottish: stupid; dull; like a drunk.

9. prevalency: control; "upper hand."

 *Meditating for Meaning*

1. Christian soon meets Mr. Worldly Wiseman of Carnal Policy. What is significant for their residents about the fact that this town is close to the City of Destruction from which Christian came?

2. Mr. Worldly Wiseman tries to convince Christian not to believe Evangelist.
    a. What does he say Christian will yet meet if he follows Evangelist's advice?
    b. According to John 16:33 and 2 Corinthians 11:24-27, is Mr. Worldly Wiseman correct?

3. Mr. Worldly Wiseman notices Christian's burden.
    a. How does Christian say he received his burden?
    b. What does Mr. Worldly Wiseman say reading the book does to men?

4. Christian's meeting with Mr. Worldly Wiseman turned out to be a snare to him. What does Mr. Worldly Wiseman say about Evangelist that should have alerted Christian to the danger of taking his advice?

5. Mr. Worldly Wiseman advises Christian to get rid of his burden an easier way.
   a. To what village does he direct Christian?
   b. To what man does he direct Christian?
   c. What skill is this man reported to have?
6. Which of the following Biblical statements would you expect to hear from persons "cured" by following Mr. Worldly Wiseman's advice? (Choose all that apply.)
   a. "God be merciful to me a sinner."
   b. "I fast twice in the week. I give tithes of all that I possess."
   c. "We are Moses' disciples." "We be Abraham's seed, and were never in bondage to any man."
   d. "I am not worthy that thou shouldest come under my roof."
   e. "All these have I kept from my youth."
7. According to a footnote which Bunyan himself added, the high hill is Mount Sinai.
   a. Considering what Moses received at Mount Sinai in the Scripture, what does Christian's detour to this mountain symbolize?
   b. What happens to his burden here?
   c. Considering the relationship between the concepts symbolized by the mount and Christian's burden, why does approaching the mount have this effect on his burden?
8. Of what is Evangelist warning Christian by his first two quotes from Scripture?
9. Why could Legality not have removed Christian's burden?

Chapter 4: Christian Passes Through the Wicket-gate

Defining for Comprehension

Choose the word or phrase below which most nearly defines each word at the left as it is used in this allegory.

1. vouchsafe	a. condescend to grant	b. guarantee protection	c. agree with
2. railing	a. limping	b. lamenting	c. speaking abusively
3. light upon	a. come upon unexpectedly	b. illuminate	c. remove weights
4. cheat	a. lack of discernment	b. deceptive person	c. slander

So he went on with haste, neither spake he to any man by the way; nor if any asked him, would he **vouchsafe** them an answer. He went like one that was all the while treading on forbidden ground, and could by no means think himself safe, till again he was got into the way which he left to follow Mr. Worldly Wiseman's counsel, so in process of time Christian got up to the gate. Now over the gate there was written, Knock, and it shall be opened unto you.

He knocked, therefore, more than once or twice, saying,

> May I now enter here? Will he within
> Open to sorry me, though I have been

An undeserving rebel? Then shall I
Not fail to sing his lasting praise on high.

At last there came a grave person to the gate, named Goodwill, who asked who was there, and whence he came, and what he would have.

CHR. Here is a poor burdened sinner. I come from the City of Destruction, but am going to Mount Zion, that I may be delivered from the wrath to come: I would, therefore, sir, since I am informed that by this gate is the way thither, know if you are willing to let me in.

GOODWILL. I am willing with all my heart, said he; and with that he opened the gate.

So when Christian was stepping in, the other gave him a pull. Then said Christian, What means that? The other told him, A little distance from this gate, there is erected a strong castle, of which Beelzebub is the captain; from thence both he and they that are with him shoot arrows at those that come up to this gate, if haply they may die before they can enter in. Then said Christian, I rejoice and tremble. So when he was got in, the man of the gate asked him who directed him thither?

CHR. Evangelist bid me come hither and knock, as I did: and he said, that you, sir, would tell me what I must do.

GOOD. An open door is set before thee, and no man can shut it.

CHR. Now I begin to reap the benefits of my hazards.

GOOD. But how is it that you came alone?

CHR. Because none of my neighbours saw their danger, as I saw mine.

GOOD. Did any of them know of your coming?

CHR. Yes, my wife and children saw me at the first, and called after me to turn again: also some of my neighbours stood crying and calling after me to return; but I put my fingers in my ears, and so came on my way.

GOOD. But did none of them follow you, to persuade you to go back?

CHR. Yes, both Obstinate and Pliable: but when they saw that they could not prevail,

Obstinate went **railing** back, but Pliable came with me a little way.

GOOD. But why did he not come through?

CHR. We indeed came both together until we came at the Slough of Despond, into the which we also suddenly fell. And then was my neighbour Pliable discouraged, and would not adventure farther. Wherefore getting out again on the side next to his own house, he told me I should possess the brave country alone for him: so he went his way, and I came mine; he after Obstinate, and I to this gate.

GOOD. Then said Goodwill, Alas, poor man! is the celestial glory of so small esteem with him, that he counteth it not worth running the hazard of a few difficulties to obtain it?

CHR. Truly, said Christian, I have said the truth of Pliable, and if I should also say all the truth of myself, it will appear there is no betterment *betwixt*[1] him and myself. 'Tis true, he went back to his own house, but I also turned

---

1. betwixt: between

aside to go in the way of death, being persuaded thereto by the carnal argument of one Mr. Worldly Wiseman.

GOOD. Oh! did he **light upon** you? What! he would have had you a sought for ease at the hands of Mr. Legality! They are both of them a very **cheat**. But did you take his counsel?

CHR. Yes, as far as I *durst*.[2] I went to find out Mr. Legality, until I thought that the mountain that stands by his house would have fallen upon my head; wherefore there I was forced to stop.

GOOD. That mountain has been the death of many, and will be the death of many more: 'tis well you escaped being by it dashed in pieces.

CHR. Why truly I do not know what had become of me there had not Evangelist happily met me again, as I was musing in the midst of my dumps; but 'twas God's mercy that he came to me again, for else I had never come hither. But now I am come, such a one as I am, more fit indeed for death by that mountain, than thus to stand talking with my Lord; but, oh! what a favour is this to me, that yet I am admitted entrance here!

GOOD. We make no objections against any, notwithstanding all that they have done before they come hither: they in no wise are cast out. And therefore, good Christian, come a little way with me, and I will teach thee about the way thou must go. Look before thee; dost thou see this narrow way? THAT is the way thou must go. It was cast up by the patriarchs, prophets, Christ and His apostles, and it is as straight as a rule can make it: this is the way thou must go.

CHR. But, said Christian, are there no turnings or windings, by which a stranger may lose his way?

GOOD. Yes, there are many ways butt down upon this; and they are crooked and wide: but thus thou mayest distinguish the right from the wrong, the right only being *strait*[3] and narrow.

Then I saw in my dream, that Christian asked him further, if he could not help him off with his burden that was upon his back. For as yet he had not got rid thereof, nor could he by any means get it off without help.

He told him, As to thy burden, be content to bear it, until thou comest to the place of deliverance; for there it will fall from thy back of itself.

---

2. durst: dared
3. strait: difficult, strict, rigorous

Meditating for Meaning

1. What attitude does Christian now have that will safeguard him from further deception until he gets to the Wicket-gate?
2. Christian arrives safely at the Wicket-gate, which symbolizes conversion.
   a. What encouragement does Christian receive when he first arrives?
   b. Why do you think we must knock to enter the Christian life?
   c. How does a person "knock" to gain entrance into the Kingdom?
   d. What good thing do we observe about Christian's knocking?

3. Goodwill opens the gate for Christian.
   a. What unusual thing does Christian observe about the way he is brought in through the gate.
   b. Why is he brought in this way?
4. Christian sees himself as no better than Pliable.
   a. On what basis does Christian make this conclusion?
   b. Why do you think Christian makes it to the Wicket-gate while Pliable does not?
5. Goodwill gives Christian two hints to help him avoid taking the wrong road again.
   a. What characteristics will identify the right road?
   b. What characteristics will identify the wrong road?

Chapter 5: Christian Visits the Interpreter's House

Defining for Comprehension	Choose the word or phrase below which most nearly defines each word at the left as it is used in this allegory.		
1. address	a. direct efforts to	b. criticize	c. chase
2. vanquished	a. disappeared	b. forgotten	c. conquered
3. lavished	a. spent liberally	b. cleansed	c. delighted
4. amity	a. friendship; harmony	b. spite	c. misfortune
5. despite	a. act of contempt	b. decay	c. discouragement
6. grapple	a. rustle noisily	b. wrestle	c. splatter
7. garner	a. red gemstone	b. granary	c. attic

Then Christian began to gird up his loins, and to **address** himself to his journey. So the other told him, that by that he was gone some distance from the gate, he would come at the house of the Interpreter, at whose door he should knock, and he would show him excellent things. Then Christian took his leave of his friend, and he again bid him God-speed.

Then he went on till he came to the house of the Interpreter, where he knocked over and over. At last one came to the door, and asked who was there.

CHR. Sir, here is a traveller, who was bid by an acquaintance of the good man of this house to call here for my profit; I would therefore speak with the master of the house. So he called for the master of the house, who, after a little time, came to Christian, and asked him what he would have.

CHR. Sir, said Christian, I am a man that am come from the City of Destruction, and am going to Mount Zion; and I was told by the man that stands at the gate at the head of this way, that if I called here you would show me excellent things, such as would be an help to me on my journey.

INTER. Then said the Interpreter, Come in; I will show thee that which will be profitable to thee. So he commanded his man to light the candle, and bid Christian follow him; so he had him into a private room, and bid his man open a door; the which when he had done, Christian saw the picture of a very grave person hang up against the wall; and this was the fashion of it: it had eyes lifted up to heaven, the best of books in its hand, the law of truth was written upon its lips, the world was behind its back; it stood as if it pleaded with men, and a crown of gold did hang over its head.

CHR. Then said Christian, What means this?

INTER. The man whose picture this is, is one of a thousand. He can beget children, travail in birth with children, and nurse them himself when they are born. And whereas thou seest him with his eyes lift up to heaven, the best of books in his hand, and the law of truth writ on his lips, it is to show thee, that his work is to know and unfold dark things to sinners; even as also thou seest him stand as if he pleaded with men. And whereas thou seest the world as cast behind him, and that a crown hangs over his head, that is to show thee that slighting and despising the things that are present, for the love that he hath to his Master's service, he is sure in the world that comes next to have glory for his reward. Now, said the Interpreter, I have showed thee this picture first because the man whose picture this is, is the only man whom the Lord of the place whither thou art going hath authorized to be thy guide, in all difficult places thou mayest meet with in the way: wherefore take good heed to what I have showed thee, and bear well in thy mind what thou hast seen, lest in thy journey thou meet with some that pretend to lead thee right, but their way goes down to death.

Then he took him by the hand and led him into a very large parlour that was full of dust because never swept; the which after he had reviewed a little while, the Interpreter called for a man to

sweep. Now when he began to sweep, the dust began so abundantly to fly about, that Christian had almost therewith been choked. Then said the Interpreter to a damsel that stood by, Bring hither the water, and sprinkle the room; the which, when she had done, it was swept and cleansed with pleasure.

CHR. Then said Christian, What means this?

INTER. The Interpreter answered, This parlour is the heart of a man that was never sanctified by the sweet grace of the Gospel. The dust is his original sin, and inward corruptions, that have defiled the whole man. He that began to sweep at first is the Law; but she that brought water, and did sprinkle it, is the Gospel. Now whereas thou sawest, that so soon as the first began to sweep, the dust did so fly about, that the room by him could not be cleansed, but that thou wast almost choked therewith; this is to show thee that the law, instead of cleansing the heart (by its working) from sin, doth revive, put strength into, and increase it in the soul, even as it doth discover and forbid it, for it doth not give power to subdue.

Again, as thou sawest the damsel sprinkle the room with water, upon which it was cleansed with pleasure; this is to show thee, that when the gospel comes in the sweet and precious influences thereof to the heart, then, I say, even as thou sawest the damsel lay the dust by sprinkling the floor with water, so is sin **vanquished** and subdued, and the soul made clean, through the faith of it,

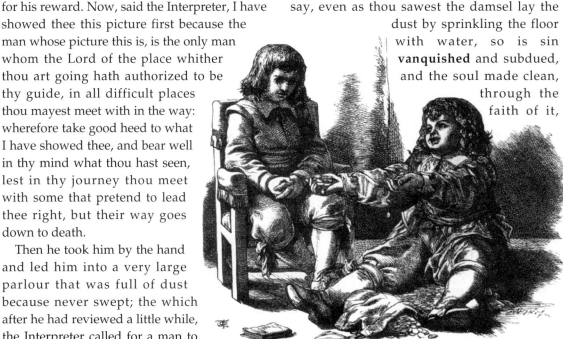

and consequently fit for the King of glory to inhabit.

I saw moreover in my dream, that the Interpreter took him by the hand and had him into a little room, where sat two little children, each one in his chair. The name of the eldest was Passion, and the name of the other Patience. Passion seemed to be much discontented, but Patience was very quiet. Then Christian asked, What is the reason of the discontent of Passion? The Interpreter answered, The governor of them would have him stay for his best things till the beginning of the next year; but he will have all now; but Patience is willing to wait.

Then I saw that one came to Passion, and brought him a bag of treasure, and poured it down at his feet: the which he took up and rejoiced therein, and withal laughed Patience to scorn. But I beheld but a while, and he had **lavished** all away, and had nothing left him but rags.

CHR. Then said Christian to the Interpreter, Expound this matter more fully to me.

III. INTER. So he said, These two lads are figures; Passion, of the men of this world, and Patience of the men of that which is to come: for as here thou seest, Passion will have all now; this year, that is to say, in this world; so are the men of this world; they must have all their good things now; they cannot stay till next year, that is, until the next world, for their portion of good. That proverb, A bird in the hand is worth two in the bush, is of more authority with them, than are all the Divine testimonies of the good of the world to come. But as thou sawest that he had quickly lavished all away, and had presently left him nothing but rags; so will it be with all such men at the end of this world.

CHR. Then said Christian, Now I see that Patience has the best wisdom, and that upon many accounts. 1. Because he stays for the best things. 2. And also because he will have the glory of his, when the other had nothing but rags.

INTER. Nay, you may add another, to wit, the glory of the next world will never wear out; but these are suddenly gone. Therefore Passion had not so much reason to laugh at Patience, because he had his good things first, as Patience will have to laugh at Passion, because he had his best things last; for first must give place to last, because last must have his time to come; but last gives place to nothing, for there is not another to succeed; he therefore that hath his portion first, must needs have a time to spend it; but he that hath his portion last, must have it lastingly; therefore it is said of Dives, In thy life-time thou receivedst thy good things, and likewise Lazarus evil things; but now he is comforted, and thou art tormented.

CHR. Then I perceive 'tis not best to covet things that are now, but to wait for things to come.

INTER. You say truth: for the things that are seen are temporal: but the things that are not seen are eternal. But though this be so, yet since things present and our fleshly appetite are such near neighbours one to another; and again, because things to come and carnal sense are such strangers one to another; therefore it is that the first of these so suddenly fall into **amity**, and that distance is so continually between the second.

Then I saw in my dream, that the Interpreter took Christian by the hand, and led him into a place where was a fire burning against a wall, and one standing by it, always casting much water upon it to quench it; yet did the fire burn higher and hotter.

Then said Christian, What means this?

IV The Interpreter answered, This fire is the work of grace that is wrought in the heart; he that casts water upon it to extinguish and put it out, is the devil: but in that thou seest the fire notwithstanding burn higher and hotter, thou shalt also see the reason of that. So he had him about to the back side of the wall, where he saw a man with a vessel of oil in his hand, of the which he did also continually cast (but secretly) into the fire.

Then said Christian, What means this?

The Interpreter answered, This is Christ, who continually, with the oil of His grace, maintains the work already begun in the heart; by the means of which, notwithstanding what the devil can do, the souls of His people prove gracious still. And in that thou sawest, that the man stood behind the wall to maintain the fire; that is to teach thee, that it is hard for the tempted to see how this work of grace is maintained in the soul.

I saw also, that the Interpreter took him again by the hand, and led him into a pleasant place, where was builded a stately palace, beautiful to behold; at the sight of which Christian was greatly delighted. He saw also upon the top thereof certain persons walking, who were clothed all in gold.

Then said Christian, May we go in thither?

V Then the Interpreter took him and led him up toward the door of the palace; and behold, at the door stood a great company of men, as desirous to go in, but durst not. There also sat a man at a little distance from the door, at a table-

side, with a book and his ink-horn before him, to take the name of him that should enter therein; he saw also that in the doorway stood many men in armour to keep it, being resolved to do to the men that would enter what hurt and mischief they could. Now was Christian somewhat in *amaze*[1]. At last, when every man started back for fear of the armed men, Christian saw a man of a very stout countenance come up to the man that sat there to write, saying, Set down my name, sir; the which when he had done, he saw the man draw his sword, and put an helmet upon his head, and rush toward the door upon the armed men, who laid upon him with deadly force; but the man, not at all discouraged, fell to cutting and hacking most fiercely. So after he had received and given many wounds to those that attempted to keep him out, he cuts his way through them all, and pressed forward into the palace; at which there was a pleasant voice heard from those that were within, even of those that walked upon the top of the palace, saying,

Come in, come in;
Eternal glory thou shalt win.

So he went in, and was clothed with such garments as they. Then Christian smiled and said, I think verily I know the meaning of this.

Now, said Christian, let me go hence. Nay, stay, said the Interpreter, till I have showed thee a little more, and after that thou shalt go on thy way. So he took him by the hand again, and led him into a very dark room, where there

VI sat man in an iron cage.

Now the man, to look on, seemed very sad; he sat with his eyes looking down to the ground, his hands folded together, and he sighed as if he would break his heart. Then said Christian, What means this? At which the Interpreter bid him talk with the man.

CHR. Then said Christian to the man, What art thou? The man answered, I am what I was not once.

CHR. What wast thou once?

MAN. The man said, I was once a fair and flourishing *professor*,[2] both in mine own eyes

---

1. amaze: bewilderment.
2. professor: one who openly declares his faith.

Artist: E. F. Brewtnall

and also in the eyes of others: I once was, as I thought, fair for the Celestial City, and had then even joy at the thoughts that I should get thither.

CHR. Well, but what art thou now?

MAN. I am now a man of despair, and am shut up in it, as in this iron cage. I cannot get out. Oh, now I cannot!

CHR. But how camest thou in this condition?

MAN. I left off to watch and be sober; I laid the reins upon the neck of my lusts; I sinned against the light of the Word, and the goodness of God; I have grieved the Spirit, and He is gone; I tempted the devil, and he is come to me; I have provoked God to anger, and He has left me: I have so hardened my heart, that I cannot repent.

Then said Christian to the Interpreter, But is there no hope for such a man as this? Ask him, said the Interpreter.

CHR. Then said Christian, Is there no hope, but you must be kept in the iron cage of despair?

MAN. No, none at all.

INTER. Why? the Son of the Blessed is very pitiful.

MAN. I have crucified Him to myself afresh. I have despised His person, I have despised His righteousness; I have counted His blood an unholy thing; I have done **despite** to the Spirit of grace. Therefore I have shut myself out of all the promises, and there now remains to me nothing but threatenings, dreadful threatenings, fearful threatenings of certain judgment and fiery indignation, which shall devour me as an adversary.

CHR. For what did you bring yourself into this condition?

MAN. For the lusts, pleasures, and profits of this world; in the enjoyments of which I did then promise myself much delight: but now every one of those things also bite me, and gnaw me, like a burning worm.

CHR. But canst thou not now repent and turn?

MAN. God hath denied me repentance. His Word gives me no encouragement to believe;

yea, Himself hath shut me up in this iron cage: nor can all the men in the world let me out. Oh, eternity! eternity! how shall I **grapple** with the misery that I must meet with in eternity?

INTER. Then said the Interpreter to Christian, Let this man's misery be remembered by thee, and be an everlasting caution to thee.

CHR. Well, said Christian, this is fearful! God help me to watch and be sober, and to pray, that I may shun the cause of this man's misery. Sir, is it not time for me to go on my way now?

INTER. Tarry till I shall show thee one thing more, and then thou shalt go on thy way.

So he took Christian by the hand again, and led him into a chamber, where there was one rising out of bed; and as he put on his raiment, he shook and trembled.

Then said Christian, Why doth this man thus tremble?

The Interpreter then bid him tell to Christian the reason of his so doing.

So he began, and said, This night, as I was in my sleep, I dreamed, and behold the heavens grew exceeding black; also it thundered and lightened in most fearful wise, that it put me into an agony. So I looked up in my dream, and saw the clouds *rack*,[3] at an unusual rate; upon which I heard a great sound of a trumpet, and saw also a man sitting upon a cloud, attended with the thousands of heaven; they were all in flaming fire; also the heavens were in a burning flame. I heard then a voice, saying, Arise, ye dead, and come to judgment.

And with that the rocks rent, the graves opened, and the dead that were therein came forth: some of them were exceeding glad, and looked upward; and some sought to hide themselves under the mountains. Then I saw the man that sat upon the cloud, open the book, and bid the world draw near. Yet there was, by reason of a fierce flame which issued out and came from before him, a convenient distance betwixt him and them, as betwixt the judge and the prisoners at the bar.

I heard it also proclaimed to them that attended on the man that sat on the cloud,

---

3. rack: to fly or be driven by a high wind.

Gather together the tares, the chaff, and stubble, and cast them into the burning lake. And with that the bottomless pit opened, just whereabout I stood; out of the mouth of which there came, in an abundant manner, smoke and coals of fire, with hideous noises. It was also said to the same persons, Gather My wheat into the **garner**. And with that I saw many catched up and carried away in the clouds; but I was left behind. I also sought to hide myself, but I could not; for the man that sat upon the cloud still kept his eye upon me: my sins also came into my mind; and my conscience did accuse me on every side. Upon this I awaked from my sleep.

CHR. But what was it that made you so afraid of this sight?

MAN. Why, I thought that the day of judgment was come, and that I was not ready for it: but this frightened me most, that the angels gathered up several, and left me behind: also the pit of hell opened her mouth just where I stood. My conscience too afflicted me; and as I thought, the Judge had always His eye upon me, showing indignation in His countenance.

Then said the Interpreter to Christian, Hast thou considered all these things?

CHR. Yes, and they put me in hope and fear.

INTER. Well, keep all things so in thy mind, that they may be as a goad in thy sides, to prick thee forward in the way thou must go. Then Christian began to gird up his loins, and to address himself to his journey. Then said the Interpreter, The Comforter be always with thee, good Christian, to guide thee in the way that leads to the city. So Christian went on his way, saying,

Here I have seen things rare and profitable;
Things pleasant, dreadful things to make
  me stable
In what I have begun to take in hand:
Then let me think on them, and understand
Wherefore they showed me were, and let
  me be
Thankful, O good Interpreter, to thee.

Meditating for Meaning

1. Of course Christian is going to need help to follow the strict path. Although Christian has been reading his Bible, it not only condemns him, but it leaves him perplexed as to what he should do about his guilt. What he needs is help to understand truth.
    a. Whose house is Christian directed to visit?
    b. How is lighting a candle symbolic of making truth clear and plain?
    c. Who is this Interpreter who illuminates truth and helps us understand? (John 14:26)

Now the Interpreter shows Christian seven scenes. Observe how each scene would help Christian understand truth.

Scene I. A True Servant of God

2. Christian has already been led astray once. He needs to know how to judge whom he should learn from and whom he should avoid. Find the seven characteristics of the man in the picture that indicate he is a reliable guide. Match them with their interpretations below.
    a. sober; serious-minded
    b. gives attention to spiritual things

c. has a working knowledge of the Bible

d. outspoken in defense and proclamation of the truth

e. separate from and despising the evils of the world

f. calling sinners to repentance

g. anticipating a reward in the next world

Scene II. The Dusty Parlour

3. Bunyan carefully interprets this allegory for you. Identify the following symbols:
   a. the dusty room
   b. the dust
   c. the first sweeper
   d. the girl who sprinkled water

4. This scene shows the Gospel's supremacy over the law.
   a. What does the law fail to do?
   b. How is the work of the water like the work of the Gospel?

Scene III. Passion and Patience

5. Bunyan wisely chooses children to represent passion and patience. On your paper copy the names of these two children. Then match each of the following traits of children to the name of the one who demonstrated it. (meek, shortsighted, teachable, forgiving, trusting, selfish)

6. The Interpreter compares Passion and Patience to the story of The Rich Man and Lazarus in Luke 16:19-31.
   a. Which man in this story corresponds to Passion? to Patience?
   b. If a Christian is to be successful, he must be willing to _____ for future pleasures and not yield to the appetites of his _____ .
   c. What basic difference will you see in the life of a Passion compared to that of a Patience?

Scene IV. The Fire Burning Against the Wall

7. Christian views yet another scene of conflict.
   a. What great conflict in the heart of a Christian does this scene illustrate?
   b. What confidence and encouragement does this scene give Christian?

Scene V. The Palace and the Book

8. Christian now sees a palace, a place of grandeur which many desire to enter.
   a. What do you think this palace symbolizes?
   b. Considering that the man at the door is recording the names of all who enter, what do you think the book symbolizes?
   c. Whom does the man of stout countenance represent?
   d. Christian thinks he knows the meaning of this scene. What do you think it means?

Scene VI. The Man in the Iron Cage

9. The man in the iron cage says, "I am what I was not once."
   a. What had this man been one day?
   b. What is his condition now?

10. The man in despair admits that he has brought this condition upon himself. What nine things does he say led to this? (Group all references to Christ into one.)

11. Since we no longer use horses as a basic means of transportation and power, you may not understand the expression "laid the reins upon the neck of my lust." When a driver was in

control of a horse, he had the reins somewhat taut. The horse knew he must submit to the driver. But when the reins were allowed to go slack (perhaps from the driver falling asleep) to the point that the horse could feel them against its neck, then it knew it could go where it wanted as fast as it wanted. A wayward horse would take advantage of such freedom and run wild. Explain what the man in the iron cage meant by using this expression.

12. What three things does Christian recognize that he must do if he is to avoid such an end as the man in the iron cage?

Scene VII. A Dream of Judgment

13. This is a dream within a dream!
    a. Why does this dream make the man tremble?
    b. What do you suppose the Interpreter wants Christian to remember from this scene?

14. According to Christian's farewell song, what was the purpose of the scenes shown by the Interpreter?

15. The Holy Spirit is our Interpreter to help us understand the truth of the Bible. Match each of the seven scenes with one of the following Bible passages or sets of passages that teach the same truth as the scene.
    a. Luke 16:19-31
    b. Hebrews 6:4-8; 10:26-29
    c. 1 Timothy 3:1-13; 2 Timothy 1:11, 13
    d. 2 Corinthians 12:9, 10
    e. Revelation 20:11-15
    f. 1 Timothy 6:12; Luke 13:24
    g. Romans 7:7-10; Ephesians 5:26

16. Match each of the seven scenes with each of the following instructions.
    a. Beware that you do not turn back from the way of salvation.
    b. Apply the Gospel of Grace for cleansing from sin.
    c. Be careful from whom you receive instruction.
    d. Enter into salvation with determined perseverance.
    e. Let the prospect of coming judgment keep you in daily readiness.
    f. Wait for eternal pleasures that last rather than seeking fleshly pleasures that are but for a short time.
    g. Depend on the grace of God to keep you spiritually alive even if Satan opposes you severely.

Chapter 6: Christian Reaches the Cross

Defining for Comprehension	Choose the word or phrase below which most nearly defines each word at the left as it is used in this allegory.

1. presumption	a. effort to establish a claim	b. rash boldness	c. complete ruin
2. proffering	a. offering	b. dividing evenly	c. stealing small things

3. **espied**	a. saw	b. robbed	c. turned traitor
4. **formalist**	a. one who follows tradition	b. murderer	c. bookkeeper
5. **hypocrisy**	a. disdain	b. insincerity	c. criticism
6. **vain-glory**	a. praise	b. extravagance	c. boasting; pride
7. **fancies**	a. theatrical acts	b. imaginations	c. mythical creatures
8. **intimate**	a. famous	b. threatening	c. closely associated

Now I saw in my dream, that the highway up which Christian was to go, was fenced on either side with a wall, and that wall was called Salvation. Up this way, therefore, did burdened Christian run, but not without great difficulty, because of the load on his back.

He ran thus till he came at a place somewhat ascending; and upon that place stood a cross, and a little below, in the bottom, a sepulchre. So I saw in my dream, that just as Christian came up with the cross, his burden loosed from off his shoulders, and fell from off his back, and began to tumble, and so continued to do till it came to the mouth of the sepulchre, where it fell in, and I saw it no more.

Then was Christian glad and *lightsome*,[1] and said with a merry heart, He hath given me rest by his sorrow, and life by his death. Then he stood still awhile to look and wonder; for it was very surprising to him that the sight of the cross should thus ease him of his burden. He looked therefore, and looked again, even till the springs that were in his head sent the waters down his cheeks. Now as he stood looking and weeping, behold, three Shining Ones came to him, and saluted him with Peace be to thee. So the first said to him, Thy sins be forgiven thee; the second stripped him of his rags, and clothed him with change of raiment; the third also set a mark in his forehead, and gave him a roll with a seal upon it, which he bid him look on as he

ran, and that he should give it in at the celestial gate: so they went their way. Then Christian gave three leaps for joy, and went on, singing,

Thus far did I come laden with my sin;
Nor could *aught*[2] ease the grief that I was in
Till I came hither: What a place is this!
Must here be the beginning of my bliss?
Must here the burden fall from off my back?
Must here the strings that bound it to me crack?
Blest cross! blest sepulchre! blest rather be
The Man that there was put to shame for me!

---

1. lightsome: joyous; lighthearted.
2. aught: anything.

I saw then in my dream, that he went on thus, even until he came at a *bottom*,[3] where he saw, a little out of the way, three men fast asleep, with fetters upon their heels. The name of the one was Simple, another Sloth, and the third **Presumption.**

Christian then seeing them lie in this case, went to them, if peradventure he might awake them, and cried, You are like them that sleep on the top of a mast, for the dead sea is under you, a gulf that hath no bottom: awake, therefore, and come away; be willing also, and I will help you off with your irons. He also told them, If he that goeth about like a roaring lion comes by, you will certainly become a prey to his teeth. With that they looked upon him, and began to reply in this sort: Simple said, I see no danger; Sloth said, Yet a little more sleep; and Presumption said, Every *fat*[4] must stand upon his own bottom. And so they lay down to sleep again, and Christian went on his way.

Yet was he troubled to think, that men in that danger should so little esteem the kindness of him that so freely offered to help them, both by awakening of them, counselling of them, and **proffering** to help them off with their irons. And as he was troubled thereabout, he **espied** two men come tumbling over the wall on the left hand of the narrow way; and they made up apace to him. The name of the one was **Formalist**, and the name of the other **Hypocrisy.** So, as I said, they drew up unto him, who thus entered with them into discourse.

CHR. Gentlemen, whence came you, and whither go you?

FORM. and HYP. We were born in the land of **Vain-glory**, and are going for praise to Mount Zion.

CHR. Why came you not in at the gate which standeth at the beginning of the way? Know you not that it is written, that he that cometh not in by the door, but climbeth up some other way, the same is a thief and a robber?

FORM. and HYP. They said, that to go to the gate for entrance was by all their countrymen counted too far about; and that therefore their usual way was to make a short cut of it, and to climb over the wall as they had done.

CHR. But will it not be counted a trespass against the Lord of the city whither we are bound, thus to violate His revealed will?

FORM. and HYP. They told him, that, as for that, he needed not to trouble his head thereabout: for what they did they had custom for, and could produce (if need were), testimony that would witness it, for more than a thousand years.

CHR. But, said Christian, will it stand a trial at law?

FORM. and HYP. They told him, that custom, it being of so long a standing as above a thousand years, would doubtless now be admitted as a thing legal by any impartial judge: and besides, said they, if we get into the way, what's matter which way we get in? If we are in, we are in: thou art but in the way, who, as we perceive, came in at the gate; and we are also in the way, that came tumbling over the wall: wherein now is thy condition better than ours?

CHR. I walk by the rule of my Master: you walk by the rude working of your **fancies**. You are counted thieves already by the Lord of the way; therefore I *doubt*[5] you will not be found true men at the end of the way. You come in by yourselves without His direction, and shall go out by yourselves without His mercy.

To this they made him but little answer; only they did bid him look to himself. Then I saw that they went on every man in his way, without much conference one with another; save that these two men told Christian, that as to laws and ordinances, they doubted not but they should as conscientiously do them as he. Therefore, said they, we see not wherein thou differest from us, but by the coat that is on thy back, which was, as we *trow*[6] given thee by some of thy neighbours, to hide the shame of thy nakedness.

---

3. bottom: low-lying land.

4. fat: tub; vat.

5. doubt: fear; suspect.

6. trow: think; suppose.

CHR. By laws and ordinances you will not be saved, since you came not in by the door. And as for this coat that is on my back, it was given me by the Lord of the place whither I go; and that, as you say, to cover my nakedness with. And I take it as a token of His kindness to me; for I had nothing but rags before. And besides, thus I comfort myself as I go: Surely, think I, when I come to the gate of the city, the Lord thereof will know me for good, since I have His coat on my back; a coat that He gave me freely in the day that he stript me of my rags. I have, moreover, a mark in my forehead, of which perhaps you have taken no notice, which one of my Lord's most **intimate** associates fixed there in the day that my burden fell off my shoulders. I will tell you, moreover, that I had then given me a roll sealed, to comfort me by reading as I go on the way; I was also bid to give it in at the celestial gate, in token of my certain going in after it; all which things I doubt you want, and want them because you came not in at the gate.

To these things they gave him no answer; only they looked upon each other, and laughed. Then I saw that they went on all, save that Christian kept before, who had no more talk but with himself, and that sometimes sighingly, and sometimes comfortably: also he would be often reading in the roll that one of the Shining Ones gave him, by which he was refreshed.

Meditating for Meaning

1. What metaphor does Bunyan borrow from Isaiah 26:1?

2. At last Christian can be relieved of his burden.
   a. What happened on Christ's cross that makes freedom from guilt possible?
   b. Explain the meaning of the fact that not only does the burden fall off, but it rolls into the sepulchre.
   c. How does this experience affect Christian?

3. The three Shining Ones probably represent the Trinity—the Father, Son, and Holy Spirit. Each gives something to Christian.
   a. If the rags of Christian represent his past unrighteous deeds, what does the new clothing represent (Romans 5:18, 29)?
   b. According to Ephesians 1:13, 14, what is the mark on the forehead in every Christian's life?
   c. After studying Hebrews 10:16, 17, define what the sealed roll likely represents in every Christian's life.

4. At the very bottom of the hill on which the cross stands, Christian meets three unconcerned pilgrims. They are like many who become complacent after the relief of conversion. In their three short replies to Christian's warning, Bunyan skillfully reveals the character of each—characters quite consistent with their names.
   a. What is simpleminded about Simple's reply?
   b. What is slothful about Slothful's reply?
   c. What is presumptuous about Presumption's reply?

5. Bunyan is also skillful in making proverbs. Choose one of the following statements which interprets his proverb "every fat must stand upon his own bottom."
   a. It is useless to try to help others.
   b. Everyone has what it takes to care for himself.
   c. A man should expect help from others.
   d. A man has no business meddling in the affairs of others.

6. Formalist and Hypocrisy are also well-named.
   a. Formalism is not the same thing as legalism, which Christian tried to follow earlier at Mr. Worldly Wiseman's advice. A legalist puts stress on winning the favor of God by obedience to the _____ . A formalist puts stress on impressing God by strict adherence to _____ .
   b. What fault does 2 Timothy 3:5 say that a formalist has?
   c. Judging by the name of the land from which these two men came, what is the motivation of a formalist and a hypocrite?
   d. The fact that both Formalist and Hypocrisy got in the way (professed Christianity) without entering the Wicket-gate means that they never (choose two):
      (a) knew the plan of salvation.   (c) were converted.
      (b) repented of their sins.   (d) were baptized.

7. A formalist and a hypocrite are greatly deceived.
   a. What do Formalist and Hypocrisy think makes a custom acceptable with God?
   b. What additional false grounds of confidence do these men have that they will come out well at the end of their journey?
   c. What three things does Christian inform them they are missing?

Chapter 7: Christian Climbs the Hill Difficulty

Defining for Comprehension	Choose the word or phrase below which most nearly defines each word at the left as it is used in this allegory.		
1 clambering	a. talking noisily	b. scrambling	c. ringing
2 arbour (arbor)	a. enthusiasm	b. shady place	c. boat dock
3 review	a. close study	b. introduction	c. regret
4 apace	a. spread apart	b. rapidly	c. determinedly
5 timorous	a. fearful; timid	b. quivering	c. well-scheduled

6	**mistrust**	a. doubt; suspicion	b. false confidence	c. false belief
7	**settle**	a. doorsill	b. thorn; burr	c. high-backed bench
8	**doleful**	a. forbidden	b. careless	c. sad; gloomy

I beheld then, that they all went on till they came to the foot of the Hill Difficulty, at the bottom of which was a spring. There were also in the same place two other ways, besides that which came straight from the gate: one turned to the left hand, and the other to the right, at the bottom of the hill; but the narrow way lay right up the hill and the name of the going up the side of the hill is called Difficulty. Christian now went to the spring, and drank thereof to refresh himself, and then began to go up the hill, saying,

> The hill, though high, I covet to ascend;
> The difficulty will not me offend;
> For I perceive the way to life lies here:
> Come, pluck up heart, let's neither faint nor
>   fear.
> Better, though difficult, the right way to go,
> Than wrong, though easy, where the end is
>   woe.

The other two also came to the foot of the hill. But when they saw that the hill was steep and high, and that there were two other ways to go; and supposing also that these two ways might meet again with that up which Christian went, on the other side of the hill; therefore they were resolved to go in those ways. Now the name of one of those ways was Danger, and the name of the other Destruction. So the one took the way which is called Danger, which did lead him into a great wood, and the other took directly up the way to Destruction, which led into a wide field, full of dark mountains, where he stumbled and fell, and rose no more.

I looked then after Christian to see him go up the hill, where I perceived he fell from running

to *going*[1] and from going to **clambering** upon his hands and his knees, because of the steepness of the place. Now about the mid-way to the top of hill was a pleasant **arbour**, made by the Lord of the hill for the refreshing of weary travellers. Thither, therefore, Christian got, where also he sat down to rest him: then he pulled his roll out of his bosom, and read therein to his comfort; he also now began afresh to take a **review** of the coat or garment that was given him as he stood by the cross. Thus pleasing himself awhile, he at last fell into a slumber,

Climbing the Hill Difficulty

---

1. going: walking.

and thence into a fast sleep, which detained him in that place until it was almost night; and in his sleep his roll fell out of his hand. Now as he was sleeping, there came one to him and awaked him, saying, 'Go to the ant, thou sluggard; consider her ways, and be wise.' And with that Christian suddenly started up, and sped him on his way, and went **apace** till he came to the top of the hill.

Now when he was got up to the top of the hill, there came two men running against him *amain*;[2] the name of the one was **Timorous,** and of the other **Mistrust**: to whom Christian said, Sirs, what's the matter? you run the wrong way. Timorous answered, that they were going to the city of Zion, and had got up that difficult place: but, said he, the farther we go, the more danger we meet with; wherefore we turned, and are going back again.

Yes, said Mistrust, for just before us lies a couple of lions in the way, whether sleeping or waking we know not; and we could not think, if we came within reach, but they would presently pull us in pieces.

CHR. Then said Christian, You make me afraid; but whither shall I fly to be safe? If I go back to mine own country, that is prepared for fire and brimstone, and I shall certainly perish there; if I can get to the Celestial City, I am sure to be in safety there: I must venture. To go back is nothing but death: to go forward is fear of death, and life everlasting beyond it: I will yet go forward. So Mistrust and Timorous ran down the hill, and Christian went on his way. But thinking again of what he had heard from the men, he felt in his bosom for his roll, that he might read therein and be comforted; but he felt, and found it not. Then was Christian in great distress, and knew not what to do; for he wanted that which was used to relieve him, and that which should have been his pass into the Celestial City. Here, therefore, he began to be much perplexed, and knew not what to do. At last he bethought himself that he had slept in the arbour that is on the side of the hill; and,

falling down upon his knees, he asked God forgiveness for that his foolish act, and then went back to look for his roll. But all the way he went back, who can sufficiently set forth the sorrow of Christian's heart? Sometimes he sighed, sometimes he wept, and oftentimes he chid himself for being so foolish to fall asleep in that place, which was erected only for a little refreshment from his weariness. Thus, therefore, he went back, carefully looking on this side and on that, all the way as he went, if *happily*[3] he might find the roll that had been his comfort so many times in his journey. He went thus till he came again within sight of the arbour where he sat and slept; but that sight renewed his sorrow the more, by bringing again, even afresh, his evil of sleeping unto his mind. Thus, therefore, he now went on bewailing his sinful sleep, saying, O wretched man that I am, that I should sleep in the day-time! that I should sleep in the midst of difficulty! that I should so indulge the flesh, as to use that rest for ease to my flesh, which the Lord of the hill hath erected only for the relief of the spirits of pilgrims! How many steps have I took in vain! Thus it happened to Israel; for their sin they were sent back again by the way of the Red Sea; and I am made to tread those steps with sorrow, which I might have trod with delight, had it not been for this sinful sleep. How far might I have been on my way by this time! I am made to tread those steps thrice over, which I needed not to have trod but once: yea, now also I am like to be *benighted*,[4] for the day is almost spent. Oh, that I had not slept!

Now by this time he was come to the arbour again, where for a while he sat down and wept; but at last (as Christian would have it) looking sorrowfully down under the **settle**, there he espied his roll, the which he, with trembling and haste, catched up, and put into his bosom. But who can tell how joyful this man was when he had gotten his roll again! For this roll was the assurance of his life, and acceptance at the desired haven. Therefore he laid it up in his

_____

2. amain: at full speed.

3. happily: haply; possibly; by chance.

4. benighted: overtaken by darkness.

bosom, gave thanks to God for directing his eye to the place where it lay, and with joy and tears betook himself again to his journey. But oh how nimbly now did he go up the rest of the hill! Yet, before he got up, the sun went down upon Christian; and this made him again recall the vanity of his sleeping to his remembrance; and thus he again began to condole with himself. O thou sinful sleep! how for thy sake am I like to be benighted in my journey! I must walk without the sun, darkness must cover the path of my feet, and I must hear the noise of the **doleful** creatures, because of my sinful sleep! Now also he remembered the story that Mistrust and Timorous told him, how they were frighted with the sight of the lions. Then said Christian to himself again, These beasts range in the night for their prey, and if they should meet me in the dark, how should I *shift*[5] them? how should I escape being by them torn in pieces? Then he went on. But while he was bewailing his unhappy *miscarriage*,[6] he lift up his eyes, and behold there was a very stately palace before him, the name of which was Beautiful, and it stood by the highway-side.

---

5. shift: escape.
6. miscarriage: mistake; failure.

Meditating for Meaning

1. Bunyan does not specify what the difficulty of the hill is. But anyone who sincerely lives the Christian life *will* face problems and difficulties.
   a. Suggest a few difficulties a Christian faces that could be symbolized by a hill.
   b. What is there about Formalist and Hypocrisy's reason for not entering the Wicket-gate that will make them avoid going over the Hill Difficulty at any cost?
   c. What does it cost them to take other routes?

2. From Christian's song, why is he willing to face difficulty and make the climb?

3. God does not require us to face constant difficulty but gives periods of refreshment even in the midst of difficulty. These times of refreshment are symbolized by the arbor.
   a. Give several things in a Christian's life that would be pleasant arbors for refreshing.
   b. Although these are for our refreshment, they should never cause us, like Christian, to
   _____ .
   c. A clue to the reason for Christian's lack of watchfulness is given in the same sentence that says he fell asleep. What is that reason?
   d. Explain what it means to sleep spiritually (1 Thessalonians 5:6, 7).
   e. While he sleeps, Christian loses the roll which one of the Shining Ones gave him. According to Bunyan, what does this roll represent?

4. Why are Timorous and Mistrust running down the hill?

5. Christian too runs backward, but for a different reason.
   a. Why does Christian need to retrace his steps?
   b. What does this tell us about the consequence of giving in to the desire for fleshly ease?

6. What lessons have you learned from this chapter about facing difficulty successfully?

Chapter 8: Christian Visits Palace Beautiful

Defining for Comprehension

Choose the word or phrase below which most nearly defines each word at the left as it is used in this allegory.

1. **furlong**
   a. ditch
   b. ⅛ mile
   c. farewell

2. **porter**
   a. small carriage
   b. doorkeeper
   c. gray metal

3. **discretion**
   a. cautious judgment
   b. crumbling action
   c. secrecy

4. **prudence**
   a. extreme zeal
   b. wise, careful conduct
   c. strong nation

5. **piety**
   a. self-satisfaction
   b. poorness
   c. religious devotion

6. **disposed**
   a. dethroned
   b. inclined
   c. unkind

7. **venturous**
   a. twisting
   b. tormenting
   c. courageous

8. **detestation**
   a. time of trial
   b. hatred
   c. summer hiding

9. **cogitations**
   a. meditations
   b. quarrels
   c. bargainings

10. **fain**
    a. eagerly desirous
    b. fictitious
    c. pale

11. **averse**
    a. backwards
    b. opposed to
    c. awkward

12. **implacable**
    a. hard to please
    b. out of place
    c. unskilled

13. **attested**
    a. aggravated
    b. gave witness
    c. challenged

14. **affirmed**
    a. declared to be true
    b. packed together
    c. argued

15. **rarities**
    a. uncommon things
    b. jumbled items
    c. difficulties

16. **antiquity**
    a. silence
    b. opposition to tradition
    c. state of being ancient

17. **pedigree**
    a. footman
    b. record of ancestry
    c. small amount

18. **aliens**
    a. foreigners
    b. nicknames
    c. supporters

19. **affronts**
    a. aspects
    b. insults
    c. tries

20. **solace**
    a. loneliness
    b. soothing comfort
    c. gloom

21. **delectable**
    a. likely
    b. decaying
    c. delightful

22. **assaults**
    a. humiliations
    b. efforts
    c. attacks

23. **accoutred (accoutered)**
    a. equipped; armed
    b. met with
    c. attacked

24. **reiterating**
    a. repeating
    b. backtracking
    c. reassuring

So I saw in my dream, that he made haste, and went forward, that if possible he might get lodging there. Now before he had gone far, he entered into a very narrow passage, which was about a **furlong** off the **Porter**'s lodge: and looking very narrowly before him as he went, he espied two lions in the way. Now, thought he, I see the dangers that Mistrust and Timorous were driven back by. (The lions were chained, but he saw not the chains.) Then he was afraid, and thought also himself to go back after them; for he thought nothing but death was before him. But the Porter at the lodge, whose name is Watchful, perceiving that Christian made a halt, as if he would go back, cried unto him, saying, Is thy strength so small? Fear not the lions, for they are chained, and are placed there for trial of faith where it is, and for discovery of those that have none: Keep in the midst of the path, and no hurt shall come unto thee.

Then I saw that he went on, trembling for fear of the lions; but taking good heed to the directions of the porter, he heard them roar, but they did him no harm. Then he clapped his hands, and went on till he came and stood before the gate where the Porter was. Then said Christian to the Porter, Sir, what house is this? and may I lodge here to-night? The Porter answered, This house was built by the Lord of the hill, and He built it for the relief and security of pilgrims. The Porter also asked whence he was, and whither he was going.

CHR. I am come from the City of Destruction, and am going to Mount Zion; but because the sun is now set, I desire, if I may, to lodge here tonight.

PORT. What is your name?

CHR. My name is now Christian, but my name at the first was Graceless: I came of the race of Japheth, whom God will persuade to dwell in the tents of Shem.

PORT. But how doth it happen that you come so late? The sun is set.

CHR. I had been here sooner, but that, wretched man that I am, I slept in the arbour that stands on the hill-side! Nay, I had, notwithstanding that, been here much sooner, but that in my sleep I lost my evidence and came with-out it to the brow of the hill; and then feeling for it, and finding it not, I was forced with sorrow of heart to go back to the place where I slept my sleep, where I found it; and now I am come.

PORT. Well, I will call out one of the virgins of this place, who will, if she likes your talk, bring you in to the rest of the family, according to the rules of the house. So Watchful the Porter rang a bell, at the sound of which came out at the door of the house a grave and beautiful damsel, named **Discretion**, and asked why she was called.

The Porter answered, This man is in a journey from the City of Destruction to Mount Zion; but being weary and benighted, he asked me if he might lodge here tonight: so I told him I would call for thee, who, after discourse had with him, mayest do as seemeth thee good, even according to the law of the house.

Then she asked him whence he was, and whither he was going; and he told her. She asked him also how he got into the way; and he told her. Then she asked him what he had seen and met with in the way; and he told her. And last she asked his name. So he said, It is Christian; and I have so much the more a desire to lodge here to-night, because, by what I perceive, this place was built by the Lord of the hill for the relief and security of pilgrims. So she smiled, but the water stood in her eyes; and after a little pause she said, I will call forth two or three more of the family. So she ran to the door and called out **Prudence, Piety,** and Charity, who after a little more discourse with him had him in to the family; and many of them meeting him at the threshold of the house, said, Come in, thou blessed of the Lord; this house was built by the Lord of the hill, on purpose to entertain such pilgrims in. Then he bowed his head, and followed them into the house. So when he was come in and sat down, they gave him something to drink, and consented together that, until supper was ready, some of them should have some particular discourse with Christian, for the best improvement of time; and they appointed Piety, Prudence, and Charity to discourse with him; and thus they began.

PIETY. Come, good Christian, since we have been so loving to you, to receive you in to our house this night, let us, if perhaps we may better ourselves thereby, talk with you of all things that have happened to you in your pilgrimage.

CHR. With a very good will, and I am glad that you are so well **disposed.**

PIETY. What moved you at first to *betake*[1] yourself to a pilgrim's life?

CHR. I was driven out of my native country by a dreadful sound that was in mine ears; to wit, that unavoidable destruction did attend me, if I abode in that place where I was.

PIETY. But how did it happen that you came out of your country this way?

CHR. It was as God would have it; for when I was under the fears of destruction, I did not know whither to go; but by chance there came a man, even to me, as I was trembling and weeping, whose name is Evangelist, and he directed me to the Wicket-gate, which else I should never have found, and so set me into the way that hath led me directly to this house.

PIETY. But did you not come by the house of the Interpreter?

CHR. Yes, and did see such things there, the remembrance of which will stick by me as long as I live, especially three things; *to wit,*[2] how Christ, in despite of Satan, maintains His work of grace in the heart; how the man had sinned himself quite out of hopes of God's mercy; and also the dream of him that thought in his sleep the day of judgment was come.

PIETY. Why, did you hear him tell his dream?

CHR. Yes, and a dreadful one it was, I thought it made my heart ache as he was telling of it; but yet I am glad I heard it.

PIETY. Was that all that you saw at the house of the Interpreter?

CHR. No; he took me, and had me where he showed me a stately palace, and how the people were clad in gold that were in it; and how there came a **venturous** man, and cut his way through the armed men that stood in the door to keep him out and how he was bid to come in, and win eternal glory. Methought those things did ravish my heart. I would have stayed at that good man's house a twelve-month, but that I knew I had farther to go.

PIETY. And what saw you else in the way?

CHR. Saw! Why, I went but a little farther, and I saw one, as I thought in my mind, hang bleeding upon the tree; and the very sight of Him made my burden fall off my back; for I groaned under a very heavy burden, but then it fell down from off me. 'Twas a strange thing to me, for I never saw such a thing before: yea, and while I stood looking up (for then I could not forbear looking), three Shining Ones came to me. One of them testified that my sins were forgiven me; another stripped me of my rags and gave me this broidered coat which you see; and the third set the mark which you see in my forehead, and gave me this sealed roll (and with that he plucked it out of his bosom.)

PIETY. But you saw more than this, did you not?

CHR. The things that I have told you were the best; yet some other matter I saw, as namely, I saw three men, Simple, Sloth, and Presumption, lie asleep a little out of the way as I came, with irons upon their heels; but do you think I could awake them? I also saw Formality and Hypocrisy come tumbling over the wall, to go, as they pretended, to Zion; but they were quickly lost, even as myself did tell them, but they would not believe. But, above all, I found it hard work to get up this hill, and as hard to come by the lions' mouth; and truly, if it had not been for the good man the Porter, that stands at the gate, I do not know but that, after all, I might have gone back again; but now I thank God I am here, and I thank you for receiving of me.

Then Prudence thought good to ask him a few questions, and desired his answer to them.

PR. Do you not think sometimes of the country from whence you came?

CHR. Yes; but with much shame and **detestation**. Truly, if I had been mindful of that coun-

---

1. betake: commit; devote.

2. to wit: namely; that is.

try from whence I came out, I might have had opportunity to have returned; but now I desire a better country, that is, an heavenly.

PR. Do you not yet bear away with you some of the things that then you were *conversant withal*?[3]

CHR. Yes, but greatly against my will; especially my inward and carnal **cogitations**, with which all my countrymen, as well as myself, were delighted. But, now, all those things are my grief; and might I but choose mine own things, I would choose never to think of those things more; but when I would be adoing of that which is best, that which is worst is with me.

PR. Do you not find sometimes as if those things were vanquished, which at other times are your perplexity?

CHR. Yes, but that is but seldom; but they are to me golden hours in which such things happen to me.

PR. Can you remember by what means you find your annoyances at times as if they were vanquished?

CHR. Yes; when I think what I saw at the cross, that will do it; and when I look upon my broidered coat, that will do it; also when I look into the roll that I carry in my bosom, that will do it; and when my thoughts wax warm about whither I am going, that will do it.

PR. And what is it that makes you so desirous to go to Mount Zion?

CHR. Why, there I hope to see Him alive that did hang dead on the cross; and there I hope to be rid of all those things that to this day are in me an annoyance to me: there they say there is no death: and there I shall dwell with such company as I like best. For, to tell you truth, I love Him, because I was by Him eased of my burden; and I am weary of my inward sickness. I would **fain** be where I shall die no more, and with the company that shall continually cry, Holy, holy, holy.

Then said Charity to Christian, Have you a family? are you a married man?

CHR. I have a wife and four small children.

CHAR. And why did you not bring them along with you?

CHR. Then Christian wept, and said, Oh, how willingly would I have done it! but they were all of them utterly **averse** to my going on pilgrimage.

CHAR. But you should have talked to them, and have endeavoured to have shown them the danger of being behind.

CHR. So I did; and told them also what God had showed to me of the destruction of our city; but I seemed to them as one that mocked, and they believed me not.

CHAR. And did you pray to God that He would bless your counsel to them?

CHR. Yes, and that with much affection; for you must think that my wife and poor children were very dear unto me.

CHAR. But did you tell them of your own sorrow, and fear of destruction? for I suppose that destruction was visible enough to you.

CHR. Yes, over, and over, and over. They might also see my fears in my countenance, in my tears, and also in my trembling under the apprehension of the judgment that did hang over our heads; but all was not sufficient to prevail with them to come with me.

CHAR. But what could they say for themselves why they came not?

CHR. Why, my wife was afraid of losing this world, and my children were given to the foolish delights of youth; so what by one thing, and what by another, they left me to wander in this manner alone.

CHAR. But did you not with your vain life damp all that you, by words, used by way of persuasion to bring them away with you?

CHR. Indeed, I cannot commend my life, for I am conscious to myself of many failings, therein. I know also, that a man, by his *conversation*,[4] may soon overthrow what by argument or persuasion he doth labour to fasten upon others for their good. Yet, this I can say, I was very wary of giving them occasion, by any unseemly action, to make them averse to going on pilgrimage. Yea, for this very thing, they

---

3. conversant withal: acquainted with.

4. conversation: conduct.

would tell me I was too precise, and that I denied myself of things (for their sakes) in which they saw no evil. Nay, I think I may say, that if what they saw in me did hinder them, it was my great tenderness in sinning against God, or of doing any wrong to my neighbour.

CHAR. Indeed, Cain hated his brother, because his own works were evil, and his brother's righteous; and if thy wife and children have been offended with thee for this, they thereby show themselves to be **implacable** to good; and thou hast delivered thy soul from their blood.

Now I saw in my dream, that thus they sat talking together until supper was ready. So when they had made ready, they sat down to meat. Now the table was furnished with fat things, and with wine that was well refined; and all their talk at the table was about the LORD of the hill; as, namely, about that He had done, and whereof He did what He did, and why He had builded that house; and by what they said, I perceived that He had been a great warrior, and had fought with and slain him that had the power of death, but not without great danger to Himself, which made me love Him the more.

For, as they said, and as I believe, said Christian, He did it with the loss of much blood. But that which put glory of grace into all He did, was, that He did it out of pure love to his country. And besides, there were some of them of the household that said they had been and spoke with Him since He did die on the cross; and they have **attested**, that they had it from His own lips, that He is such a lover of poor pilgrims, that the like is not to be found from the east to the west. They, moreover, gave an instance of what they **affirmed**; and that was, He had stripped Himself of His glory, that He might do this for the poor; and that they heard Him say and affirm, that He would not dwell in the mountain of Zion alone. They said, moreover, that He had made many pilgrims princes, though by nature they were beggars born, and their original had been the dunghill.

Thus they discoursed together till late at night; and after they had committed themselves to their Lord for protection, they betook them-

selves to rest. The pilgrim they laid in a large upper chamber, whose window opened towards the sun-rising. The name of the chamber was Peace, where he slept till break of day, and then he awoke and sang,

> Where am I now? Is this the love and care
> Of Jesus, for the men that pilgrims are,
> Thus to provide! that I should be forgiven,
> And dwell already the next door to heaven!

So in the morning they all got up; and, after some more discourse, they told him that he should not depart till they had showed him the **rarities** of that place. And first they had him into the study, where they showed him the records of the greatest **antiquity**; in which, as I remember my dream, they showed him first the **pedigree** of the Lord of that hill, that He was the Son of the Ancient of Days, and came by that eternal generation. Here also was more fully recorded the acts that He had done, and the names of many hundreds that He had taken into His service; and how He had placed them in such habitations, that could neither by length of days nor decays of nature, be dissolved.

Then they read to him some of the worthy acts that some of His servants had done; as how they had subdued kingdoms, wrought righteousness, obtained promises, stopped the mouths of lions, quenched the violence of fire, escaped the edge of the sword, out of weakness were made strong, waxed valiant in fight, and turned to flight the armies of the **aliens.**

Then they read again in another part of the records of the house, where it was showed how willing their Lord was to receive into His favour any, even any, though they in time past had offered great **affronts** to His person and proceedings. Here also were several other histories of many other famous things, of all which Christian had a view; as of things both ancient and modern, together with prophecies and predictions of things that have their certain accomplishment, both to the dread and amazement of enemies, and the comfort and **solace** of pilgrims.

The next day they took him, and had him into the armoury, where they showed him all manner of *furniture*[5] which their Lord had provided for pilgrims, as sword, shield, helmet, breastplate, all-prayer, and shoes that would not wear out. And there was here enough of this to harness out as many men for the service of their Lord, as there be stars in heaven for multitude.

They also showed him some of the *engines*[6] with which some of His servants had done wonderful things. They showed him Moses's rod; the hammer and nail with which Jael slew Sisera; the pitchers, trumpets, and lamps too, with which Gideon put to flight the armies of Midian. Then they showed him the ox's goad wherewith Shamgar slew six hundred men. They showed him also the jawbone with which Samson did such mighty feats. They showed him moreover the sling and stone with which David slew Goliath of Gath, and the sword also with which their Lord will kill the man of sin, in the day that He shall rise up to the prey. They showed him besides many excellent things, with which Christian was much delighted. This done, they went to their rest again.

Then I saw in my dream, that on the morrow he got up to go forwards, but they desired him to stay till the next day also; and then, said they, we will, if the day be clear, show you the **Delectable** Mountains; which, they said, would yet further add to his comfort, because they were nearer the desired haven than the place where at present he was; so he consented and stayed. When the morning was up, they had him to the top of the house, and bade him look south. So he did, and behold at a great distance, he saw a most pleasant, mountainous country, beautified with woods, vineyards, fruits of all sorts, flowers also, with springs and fountains, very delectable to behold. Then he asked the name of the country. They said it was Immanuel's Land; and it is as *common*,[7] said they, as this hill is, to and for all the pilgrims. And when thou comest there, from thence, said

they, thou mayest see to the gate of the Celestial City, as the shepherds that live there will make appear.

Now he bethought himself of setting forward, and they were willing he should. But first, said they, let us go again into the armoury. So they did, and when he came there, they harnessed him from head to foot with what was *of proof*;[8] lest perhaps he should meet with **assaults** in the way. He being therefore thus **accoutred,** walked out with his friends to the gate; and there he asked the Porter if he saw any pilgrims pass by. Then the porter answered, Yes.

CHR. Pray, did you know him? said he.

PORT. I asked his name, and he told me it was Faithful.

CHR. Oh, said Christian, I know him; he is my townsman, my near neighbour, he comes from the place where I was born. How far do you think he may be before?

PORT. He is got by this time below the hill.

CHR. Well, said Christian, good Porter, the

---

5. furniture: equipment.

6. engines: weapons.

7. common: for public use.

8. of proof: tested and proved worthy of use.

Lord be with thee, and add to all thy blessings much increase, of the kindness that thou hast showed to me.

Then he began to go forward; but Discretion, Piety, Charity, and Prudence would accompany him down to the foot of the hill. So they went on together, **reiterating** their former discourses, till they came to go down the hill. Then said Christian, As it was difficult coming up so, so far as I can see, it is dangerous going down. Yes, said Prudence, so it is; for it is a hard matter for a man to go down into the Valley of Humiliation, as thou art now, and to catch no slip by the way; therefore, said they, are we come out to accompany thee down the hill. So he began to go down, but very warily; yet he caught a slip or two.

Then I saw in my dream that these good companions, when Christian was gone to the bottom of the hill, gave him a loaf of bread, a bottle of wine, and a cluster of raisins; and then he went his way.

Meditating for Meaning

1. Bunyan probably intends for Palace Beautiful to be the church, the family of believers. Look for evidences of this symbolism.
   a. What does Christian meet as he approaches Palace Beautiful?
   b. Why is there no real danger?
   c. What is the purpose of this fearful situation?
   d. In what way can a pilgrim avoid being harmed?

2. Shem and Japheth were sons of Noah. Check a Bible dictionary to discover what two races of people descended from these two men and what special place the descendants of Shem held in Bible times. You will find that Bunyan has Scriptural basis for his comment about Christian's ancestry (Genesis 9:27). Christian was really a converted _____ who was to be brought into the _____ .

3. What does Christian call his roll at this point?

4. All true Christians must enter Palace Beautiful.
   a. Who built Palace Beautiful?
   b. For what purpose?

5. Christian is not accepted as a full guest yet. How does Discretion's questioning relate to the way the church receives new members?

6. Piety questions Christian about his past life.
   a. What major events in Christian's past does Piety lead Christian to recall?
   b. How does the review of past mercies help us maintain piety?

7. Prudence questions Christian about his present life in relation to his past.
   a. Christian's memory of the country from which he came can best be described as
      having little or no effect on his present life.
      an unwanted source of temptation.
      almost forgotten.
      evidence that he has secret longings to go back.
   b. What four things does Christian say give him more prudence and therefore help him conquer temptation?

8. Charity speaks to Christian about his witness to lost souls.
   a. Explain how the subject of Charity's conversation is related to her name.
   b. What three things does Charity point out as necessary for Christians to do to win the lost?
   c. Will a very conscientious life always make lost sinners inclined to become Christians? Explain.

9. The supper may symbolize the general spiritual fellowship in the church or it may more specifically stand for the Communion or Lord's Supper.
   a. What do they discuss at supper?
   b. How is their conversation very suitable for the observance of the Lord's Supper?

10. Next Christian goes to sleep for the second time since he began his pilgrimage.
   a. The first sleep is called a _____ sleep because he became careless in his Christian life by yielding to his flesh.
   b. But his second sleep is very much in order for the Christian; it is the sleep of _____ , one of the fruits of the Spirit.

11. The study probably symbolizes the Bible. List five subjects found in this study and match each with the part of Scripture to which it refers.

12. After visiting the study, Christian is taken to the armoury.
   a. From Ephesians 6:13-18 interpret the articles of clothing in the armoury.
   b. What piece of armour mentioned in Ephesians 6:13-18 does Bunyan miss?
   c. What piece of armour does he mention that cannot be worn?

13. Considering the Bible stories surrounding Moses' rod, Shamgar's ox goad, David's sling, etc., of what value is it to Christian to be familiar with these?

14. Before Christian leaves Palace Beautiful, he is given some last minute helps for the way.
   a. From the housetop he is given a view of _____ which shows him blessings to come in the latter part of the Christian life.
   b. In the armoury they provide him with _____ .
   c. At the gate the Porter informs him of _____ .

Chapter 9: Christian Battles With Apollyon in the Valley of Humiliation

But now, in this Valley of Humiliation, poor Christian was hard put to it; for he had gone but a little way before he espied a foul **fiend** coming over the field to meet him: his name is Apollyon. Then did Christian begin to be afraid, and to cast in his mind whether to go back or to stand his ground. But he considered again that he had no armour for his back, and therefore thought that to turn the back to him might give him greater advantage with ease to pierce him with his darts; therefore he resolved to venture and stand his ground; for, thought he, had I no more in mine eye than the saving of my life, 'twould be the best way to stand.

So he went on, and Apollyon met him. Now the monster was hideous to behold; he was clothed with scales like a fish, and they are his pride, he had wings like a dragon, feet like a bear, and out of his belly came fire and smoke; and his mouth was as the mouth of a lion. When he was come up to Christian, he beheld him with a **disdainful** countenance, and thus began to question him.

APOLLYON. Whence come you, and whither are you bound?

CHR. I am come from the City of Destruction, which is the place of all evil, and am going to the City of Zion.

APOL. By this I perceive thou art one of my subjects; for all that country is mine, and I am the prince and god of it. How is it, then, that thou hast run away from thy king? Were it not that I hope thou mayest do me more service, I would strike thee now at one blow to the ground.

CHR. I was born indeed in your dominions, but your service was hard, and your wages such as a man could not live on, "for the wages of sin is death," therefore when I was come to years, I did as other considerate persons do, look out if perhaps I might mend myself.

APOL. There is no prince that will thus lightly lose his subjects, neither will I as yet lose thee; but since thou complainest of thy service and wages, be content to go back, and what our country will afford, I do here promise to give thee.

CHR. But I have *left*[1] myself to another, even to the King of princes; and how can I with fairness go back with thee?

APOL. Thou hast done in this according to the proverb, changed a bad for a worse; but it is ordinary for those that have professed themselves His servants, after a while to *give Him the*

---

1. left: committed

slip,[2] and return again to me. Do thou so too, and all shall be well.

CHR. I have given Him my faith, and sworn my allegiance to Him; how then can I go back from this, and not be hanged as a traitor?

APOL. Thou didst the same to me, and yet I am willing to pass by all, if now thou wilt yet turn again and go back.

CHR. What I promised thee was in my *nonage*:[3] and besides, I count that the Prince, under whose banner now I stand, is able to **absolve** me, yea, and to pardon also what I did as to my **compliance** with thee. And besides, O thou destroying Apollyon, to speak truth, I like His service, His wages, His servants, His government, His company and country better than thine; therefore leave off to persuade me further; I am His servant, and I will follow Him.

APOL. Consider again when thou art in *cool blood*,[4] what thou art like to meet with in the way that thou goest. Thou knowest that for the most part His servants come to an ill end, because they are transgressors against me and my way. How many of them have been put to shameful death! And besides, thou countest His service better than mine; whereas He never came yet from the place where He is, to deliver any that served Him out of their hands; but as for me, how many times, as all the world very well knows, have I delivered, either by power or fraud, those that have faithfully served me from Him and His, though taken by them! And so I will deliver thee.

CHR. His forbearing at present to deliver them, is on purpose to try their love, whether they will cleave to Him to the end; and as for the ill end thou sayest they come to, that is the most glorious in their account. For, for present deliverance, they do not much expect it; for they stay for their glory; and then they shall have it, when their Prince comes in His, and the glory of the angels.

APOL. Thou hast already been unfaithful in thy service to Him; and how dost thou think to receive wages of Him?

CHR. Wherein, O Apollyon, have I been unfaithful to Him?

APOL. Thou didst faint at first setting out, when thou wast almost choked in the Gulf of Despond. Thou didst attempt wrong ways to be rid of thy burden, whereas thou shouldest have stayed till thy Prince had taken it off. Thou didst sinfully sleep, and lose thy choice things. Thou wast also almost persuaded to go back at the sight of the lions. And when thou talkest of thy journey, and of what thou hast heard and seen, thou art inwardly desirous of vain-glory in all that thou sayest or doest.

CHR. All this is true, and much more which thou hast left out; but the Prince whom I serve and honour is merciful and ready to forgive. But besides, these infirmities possessed me in thy country; for there I sucked them in, and I have groaned under them, been sorry for them, and have obtained pardon of my Prince.

APOL. Then Apollyon broke out into a grievous rage, saying, I am an enemy to this Prince; I

2. give him the slip: defect in allegiance
3. nonage: youth
4. cool blood: calm state of mind

Artist: J.D. Watson

hate His person, His laws, and people; I am come out on purpose to withstand thee.

CHR. Apollyon, beware what you do, for I am in the King's highway, the way of holiness; therefore take heed to yourself.

APOL. Then Apollyon straddled quite over the whole breadth of the way, and said, I am void of fear in this matter. Prepare thyself to die; for I swear by my **infernal** den, that thou shalt go no farther: here will I spill thy soul.

And with that he threw a flaming dart at his breast; but Christian had a shield in his hand, with which he caught it, and so prevented the danger of that.

Then did Christian draw, for he saw 'twas time to bestir him; and Apollyon as fast made at him, throwing darts as thick as hail; by the which, notwithstanding all that Christian could do to avoid it, Apollyon wounded him in *his head, his hand, and foot*.[5] This made Christian give a little back; Apollyon, therefore, followed his work amain, and Christian again took courage, and resisted as manfully as he could. This sore combat lasted for above half a day, even till Christian was almost quite spent. For you must know, that Christian, by reason of his wounds, must needs grow weaker and weaker.

Then Apollyon, espying his opportunity, began to gather up close to Christian, and wrestling with him, gave him a dreadful fall; and with that Christian's sword flew out of his hand. Then said Apollyon, I am sure of thee now. And with that he had almost pressed him to death; so that Christian began to despair of life. But as God would have it, while Apollyon was fetching his last blow, thereby to make a full end of this good man, Christian nimbly stretched out his hand for his sword, and caught it, saying, Rejoice not against me, O mine enemy: when I fall, I shall arise; and with that gave him a deadly thrust, which made him give back, as one that had received his mortal wound. Christian perceiving that, made at him again, saying, Nay, in all these things we are more than conquerors through Him that loved us. And with that Apollyon spread forth his

dragon's wings, and sped him away, that Christian saw him no more.

In this combat no man can imagine, unless he had seen and heard as I did, what yelling and hideous roaring Apollyon made all the time of the fight; he spake like a dragon: and on the other side what sighs and groans burst from Christian's heart. I never saw him all the while give so much as one pleasant look, till he perceived he had wounded Apollyon with his two-edged sword; then, indeed, he did smile and look upward; but 'twas the dreadfullest fight that ever I saw.

So when the battle was over, Christian said, I will here give thanks to Him that hath delivered me out of the mouth of the lion; to Him that did help me against Apollyon. And so he did, saying,

Great Beelzebub, the captain of this fiend,
Designed my ruin; therefore to this end
He sent him harnessed out, and he with rage,
That hellish was, did fiercely me engage:
But blessed Michael helped me, and I,
By **dint** of sword, did quickly make him fly:
Therefore to Him let me give lasting praise,
And thank and bless His holy name always.

5. from Ephesians 6; head: loss of assurance (helmet of salvation);
     hand: doubt of the authority of God's word (Sword in hand);
     foot: loss of peace with God (feet shod with the preparation of the Gospel of peace).

Artist: J.D. Watson

Then there came to him an hand with some of the leaves of the tree of life, the which Christian took, and applied to the wounds that he had received in the battle, and was healed immediately. He also sat down in that place to eat bread, and to drink of the bottle that was given him a little before; so being refreshed, he addressed himself to his journey, with his sword drawn in his hand; for, he said, I know not but some other enemy may be at hand. But he met with no other affront from Apollyon quite through this valley.

Meditating for Meaning

Jesus went down into the "Valley of Humiliation" when He came to earth to conquer Satan at Calvary. Every Christian, like Christ, will meet with the attack of Satan. This attack is symbolized by the confrontation of Christian with Apollyon.

1. Why does Christian know it will be useless to try to run away from Apollyon?

2. Bunyan describes Apollyon as a monster with animal features which represent Apollyon's characteristics. For instance, the fish scales represent pride (Job 41:15). Considering the characteristics of each wild beast and force, and with the help of the Scriptures given, interpret the remaining features.
   a. dragon wings (Revelation 13:2)
   b. bear feet (Revelation 13:2)
   c. fire and smoke (1 Peter 1:7; 4:12)
   d. lion's mouth (Revelation 13:2; 1 Peter 5:8)

3. Apollyon first torments Christian with words.
   a. What claim does Apollyon say he has on Christian?
   b. Why does he not strike Christian dead at once?
   c. What two reasons does Christian give for not remaining in Apollyon's dominions?

4. Notice carefully the tactics Satan uses.
   a. First Satan tries to lure Christian back with a promise that _____ .
   b. Next he calls Christian's attention to the many professors who _____ .
   c. Apollyon tries to discourage and frighten Christian by reminding him that many faithful Christians have been _____ and have not been _____ from evil hands.

5. But what reason does Christian see for Christ not delivering the saints from a martyr's death?

6. Next Apollyon tries to discourage Christian by accusing him of being unfaithful in the past.
   a. What five accusations does Apollyon bring against Christian?
   b. In reference to this work of Satan, what does Revelation 12:10 call him?
   c. How might some Christians be overcome by this tactic of Satan's?
   d. What knowledge helps Christian to successfully meet his attack?

7. Satan will not give up when arguments fail. He left Christ after the temptations in the wilderness and entered into the hearts of wicked men to destroy Jesus. The fire of Satan's wrath may take the form of severe temptation to commit sin. Whatever the form, Satan's blows are just as real as those Apollyon gave Christian.
   a. At first Christian's strong _____ is able to shield him.
   b. But he eventually draws his sword which is _____ .
   c. In actual practice what does this mean a Christian does with his "sword"?

8. Eventually the wounds Christian receives begin to weaken him.
   a. Interpret this as it applies to a Christian's conflict.
   b. The conflict represents temptation, but eventually Apollyon gives Christian "a dreadful fall." Explain the meaning of this fall.
   c. By what means does Christian rally from his fall and gain the victory?

9. Note the reassurance of the context of Christian's victory cry in Micah 7:8. The other victory cry is from Romans 8:37. In fact, the quoting of Bible verses is the use of the Sword. You would do well to collect a number of such victory verses in your mind.
   Here are some others for a start:

Joshua 23:10	1 Corinthians 15:57
Psalm 34:7	Philippians 4:13
Proverbs 24:16	

   Memorize at least three victory verses and use them.

10. Again Christian breaks out in a hymn poem. This makes six hymn poems that Christian sang.
    a. List the six occasions up to this point of his journey where he spoke poems.
    b. From this list give a general observation as to the kinds of events that call forth singing in the life of a Christian.

Chapter 10: Christian Passes Through the Valley of the Shadow

Defining for Comprehension

Choose the word or phrase below which most nearly defines each word at the left as it is used in this allegory.

1. **sequel**
   a. glass bead
   b. comrade
   c. following part of a story

2. **quag**
   a. swamp
   b. sharp cliff
   c. fear; doubt

3. **anon**
   a. unknown
   b. swiftly; suddenly
   c. soon

4. **muse**
   a. think; ponder
   b. complain
   c. refuse to speak

5. **blasphemies**
   a. disasters
   b. irreverent language
   c. hot, dry winds

6. **impediment**
   a. weight
   b. hindrance
   c. speed

7. **conspicuous**
   a. very noticeable
   b. variable
   c. rare

8. **tyranny**
   a. oppressive rule
   b. strange practice
   c. wearisome work

9. **pagan**
   a. sinner
   b. heathen
   c. god

Now at the end of this valley was another, called the Valley of the Shadow of Death; and Christian must needs go through it, because the way to the Celestial City lay through the midst of it. Now this valley is a very solitary place: the prophet Jeremiah thus describes it: A wilderness, a land of deserts and of pits, a land of drought, and of the Shadow of Death, a land that no man but a Christian passeth through, and where no man dwelt.

Now here Christian was worse put to it than in his fight with Apollyon, as by the **sequel** you shall see.

I saw then in my dream that when Christian was got on the borders of the Shadow of Death, there met him two men, children of them that brought up an evil report of the good land, making haste to go back; to whom Christian spake as follows:

CHR. Whither are you going?

MEN. They said, Back, back, and we would have you to do so too, if either life or peace is prized by you.

CHR. Why, what's the matter? said Christian.

MEN. Matter! said they; we were going that way as you are going, and went as far as we durst: and indeed we were almost past coming back; for had we gone a little farther, we had not been here to bring the news to thee.

CHR. But what have you met with? said Christian.

MEN: Why, we were almost in the Valley of the Shadow of Death, but that by good hap we looked before us, and saw the danger before we came to it.

CHR. But what have you seen? said Christian.

MEN. Seen! why, the valley itself, which is as dark as pitch: we also saw there the *hobgoblins*,[1] *satyrs*,[2] and dragons of the pit; we heard also in that valley a continual howling and yelling, as of a people under unutterable misery, who there sat bound in affliction and irons; and over that valley hangs the discouraging clouds of confusion: death also doth always spread his wings over it. In a word, it is *every whit*[3] dreadful, being utterly without order.

CHR. Then, said Christian, I perceive not yet, by what you have said, but that this is my way to the desired haven.

MEN. Be it thy way; we will not choose it for ours.

So they parted, and Christian went on his way, but still with his sword drawn in his hand, for fear lest he should be assaulted.

I saw then in my dream, so far as this valley reached, there was on the right hand a very deep ditch; that ditch is it, into which the blind hath led the blind in all ages, and have both there miserably perished. Again, behold, on the left hand there was a very dangerous **quag**, into which, if even a good man falls, he finds no bottom for his foot to stand on: into this quag King David once did fall, and had no doubt there been smothered, had not He that is able plucked him out.

The pathway was here also exceeding narrow, and therefore good Christian was the more put to it; for when he sought, in the dark, to shun the ditch on the one hand, he was ready to tip over into the mire on the other: also when he sought to escape the mire, without great carefulness he would be ready to fall into the ditch. Thus he went on, and I heard him here sigh bitterly; for besides the danger mentioned above, the pathway was here so dark, that ofttimes, when he lift up his foot to go forward, he knew not where, or upon what he should set it next.

About the midst of this valley I perceived the mouth of hell to be, and it stood also hard by the way-side. Now, thought Christian, what shall I do? And ever and **anon** the flame and smoke would come out in such abundance, with sparks and hideous noises (things that cared not for Christian's sword, as did Apollyon before), that he was forced to put up his sword, and betake himself to another weapon, called All-prayer, so he cried in my hearing, O Lord, I beseech Thee, deliver my soul. Thus he went on a great while, yet still the flames

1. hobgoblins: terrifying, elflike creatures.
2. satyr: mythical creature, part human and part goat or horse.
3. every whit: completely.

would be reaching towards him; also he heard doleful voices, and rushings to and fro, so that sometimes he thought he should be torn in pieces, or trodden down like mire in the streets. This frightful sight was seen, and these dreadful noises were heard by him, for several miles together; and coming to a place where he thought he heard a company of fiends coming forward to meet him, he stopped, and began to **muse** what he had best to do. Sometimes he had half a thought to go back; then again he thought he might be half way through the valley. He remembered also, how he had already vanquished many a danger; and that the danger of going back might be much more than for to go forward. So he resolved to go on; yet the fiends seemed to come nearer and nearer. But when they were come even almost at him, he cried out with a most vehement voice, I will walk in the strength of the Lord God. So they gave back, and came no farther.

One thing I would not let slip. I took notice that now poor Christian was so confounded, that he did not know his own voice; and thus I perceived it. Just when he was come over against the mouth of the burning pit, one of the wicked ones got behind him, and stepped up softly to him, and whisperingly, suggested many grievous **blasphemies** to him, which he verily thought had proceeded from his own mind. This put Christian more to it than anything that he met with before; even to think that he should now blaspheme Him that he loved so much before. Yet if he could have helped, he would not have done it; but he had not the discretion either to stop his ears, nor to know from whence these blasphemies came.

When Christian had travelled in this disconsolate condition some considerable time, he thought he heard the voice of a man, going before him, saying, Though I walk through the Valley of the Shadow of Death, I will fear none evil, for Thou art with me."

Then was he glad, and that for these reasons:

First, because he gathered from thence, that some who feared God were in this valley as well as himself.

Secondly, For that he perceived God was with them, though in that dark and dismal

state. And why not, thought he, with me? though by reason of the **impediment** that attends this place, I cannot perceive it.

Thirdly, For that he hoped (could he overtake them) to have company by and by. So he went on, and called to him that was before; but he knew not what to answer, for that he also thought himself to be alone. And by and by the day broke: then said Christian, He hath turned the shadow of death into the morning.

Now morning being come, he looked back, not of desire to return, but to see, by the light of the day, what hazards he had gone through in the dark. So he saw more perfectly the ditch that was on the one hand, and the quag that was on the other; also how narrow the way was which led betwixt them both. Also now he saw the hobgoblins, and satyrs, and dragons of the pit, but all afar off; (for after break of day they came not nigh) yet they were discovered to him, according to that which is written, He discovereth deep things out of darkness, and bringeth out to light the shadow of death.

Now was Christian much affected with his deliverance from all the dangers of his solitary way; which dangers, though he feared them more before, yet he saw them more clearly

Artist: J.D. Watson

now, because the light of the day made them **conspicuous** to him. And about this time the sun was rising, and this was another mercy to Christian; for you must note that though the first part of the Valley of the Shadow of Death was dangerous, yet this second part, which he was yet to go, was, if possible, far more dangerous; for, from the place where he now stood, even to the end of the valley, the way was all along set so full of snares, traps, *gins*,[4] and nets here, and so full of pits, pitfalls, deep holes, and *shelvings*[5] down there, that had it now been dark, as it was when he came the first part of the way, had he had a thousand souls, they had in reason been cast away; but, as I said, just now, the sun was rising. Then said he, His candle shineth on my head, and by His light I go through darkness.

In this light, therefore, he came to the end of the valley. Now I saw in my dream that at the end of this valley lay blood, bones, ashes, and mangled bodies of men, even of pilgrims that had gone this way formerly; and while I was musing what should be the reason, I espied a little before me a cave, where two giants, Pope and Pagan, dwelt in old time; by whose power and **tyranny** the men; whose bones, blood, ashes, etc., lay there, were cruelly put to death. But by this place Christian went without much danger, whereat I somewhat wondered; but I have learnt since that **Pagan** has been dead many a day; and as for the other, though he be yet alive, he is, by reason of age, and also of the many *shrewd*[6] *brushes*[7] that he met with in his younger days, grown so crazy and stiff in his joints, that he can now do little more than sit in his cave's mouth, grinning at pilgrims as they go by, and biting his nails because he cannot come at them.

So I saw that Christian went on his way; yet, at the sight of the old man that sat in the mouth of the cave, he could not tell what to think, especially because he spake to him, though he could not go after him, saying, You will never mend till more of you be burned. But he held his peace, and *set a good face on't*,[8] and so went by, and catched no hurt. Then sang Christian:

O world of wonders! (I can say no less),
That I should be preserved in that distress
That I have met with here! O blessed be
That hand that from it hath delivered me!
Dangers in darkness, devils, hell, and sin,
Did compass me, while I this vale was in;
Yea, snares and pits, and traps, and nets did lie
My path about, that worthless, silly I
Might have been catched, entangled, and cast down:
But since I live, let JESUS wear the crown.

4. gins: traps; snares.
5. shelvings: uneven, raised places in the ground surface.
6. shrewd: severe; rough
7. brushes: rough experiences
8. set a good face on't: approached with courage

Meditating for Meaning

1. Why must Christian go through the valley in spite of its dangers?

2. Bunyan says that the men who turned back are "children of them that brought up an evil report of the good land." This refers to the ten spies that brought back an evil report of the promised land (Numbers 13:25-33). What did the two men lack that made them fear to go on?

3. The two sides of the path represent opposite yet equally destructive dangers in the Christian life.
   a. The ditch on the one side could represent the danger of wrong _____ . Check the context of the "blind lead the blind" in Matthew 15:14. Also look at Matthew 16:12.
   b. The quag on the other side could represent the danger of yielding to _____ . This one is mentioned in Luke 8:13.
   c. What aspect of the pathway itself makes it treacherous?
   d. What further hindrance of the hour makes it difficult for Christian to stay on the way?
   e. What place which the path passes contributes to making this a fearful valley?

4. Christian must resort to another weapon in this valley.
   a. What is the only weapon that Christian can use here?
   b. Why are the sword and the shield ineffective? Consider the nature of these weapons in light of the nature of the foes Christian meets.

5. One of the horrors of this valley is the confusion that it brings into Christian's mind.
   a. What evil thoughts does Satan bring that Christian thinks are his own?
   b. For what three reasons does Christian not turn back?

6. Yet one other trial of this valley is the fact that Christian is alone.
   a. What three things give Christian encouragement when he hears the voice of a man in the valley?
   b. What does this suggest about how we can help others through their valley experiences?

7. As Christian enters the second part of this valley, the morning light dawns. Considering what connotations accompany morning in our everyday life, what does the light represent that helps Christian through this second part of the valley?

8. Bunyan lived during the 1600s. The two giants in the cave at the end of this valley represent two enemies to true Christianity prior to Bunyan's day.
   a. What happened to the men whose mangled bodies lay at the end of the valley?
   b. What threat to Christianity in the times of the early church does Pagan represent?
   c. What threat to Christianity just prior to Bunyan's day does Pope represent?
   d. What was the state of "Pope" in Bunyan's day?

Chapter 11: Christian Meets Faithful

Defining for Comprehension

Choose the word or phrase below which most nearly defines each word at the left as it is used in this allegory.

1. tempered	a. became angry	b. cooled	c. made harmonious
2. wanton	a. impure; unrestrained	b. accustomed	c. desirous
3. bewitched	a. overpowered as if by magic	b. begged	c. disappointed
4. arrogancy (arrogance)	a. close questioning	b. proud superiority	c. reckless spending
5. self-conceit	a. smug pride	b. stubbornness	c. laziness
6. lineage	a. ancestry	b. interior	c. descendants
7. haughty	a. mischievous	b. difficult	c. proud
8. hectoring	a. confusing	b. bullying	c. constructing
9. petty	a. fine-feathered	b. insignificant	c. annoying
10. fraternity	a. indefinite time span	b. motherhood	c. brotherhood
11. abomination	a. destruction	b. end goal	c. abhorrence
12. villain	a. hero	b. townsman	c. scoundrel
13. importunate	a. convenient	b. prominent	c. annoyingly persistent
14. audacious	a. greatly aged	b. rudely bold	c. brightly colored
15. bravados	a. boastful courage	b. heroes	c. warriors

Now as Christian went on his way, he came to a little ascent, which was cast up on purpose that pilgrims might see before them: up there, therefore, Christian went, and looking forward, he saw Faithful before him upon his journey. Then said Christian aloud, Ho, ho; so-ho; stay, and I will be your companion. At that Faithful looked behind him; to whom Christian cried, Stay, stay, till I come up to you.

But Faithful answered, No, I am upon my life, and the avenger of blood is behind me.

At this Christian was somewhat moved, and putting to all his strength, he quickly got up with Faithful, and did also overrun him; so the last was first. Then did Christian vaingloriously smile, because he had gotten the start of his brother; but not taking good heed to his feet, he suddenly stumbled and fell, and could not rise again until Faithful came up to help him.

Then I saw in my dream they went very lovingly on together, and had sweet discourse of all things that had happened to them in their pilgrimage; and thus Christian began.

CHR. My honoured and well-beloved brother Faithful, I am glad that I have overtaken you, and that God has so **tempered** our spirits, that we can walk as companions in this so pleasant a path.

FAITH. I had thought, dear friend, to have had your company quite from our town; but you did get the start of me wherefore I was forced to come thus much of the way alone.

CHR. How long did you stay in the City of Destruction, before you set out after me on your pilgrimage?

FAITH. Till I could stay no longer; for there was great talk presently after you were gone out, that our city would, in short time, with fire from heaven be burned down to the ground.

CHR. What! Did your neighbours talk so?

FAITH. Yes, 'twas for a while in everybody's mouth.

CHR. What? and did no more of them but you come out to escape the danger?

FAITH. Though there was, as I said, a great talk thereabout, yet I do not think they did firmly believe it. For in the heat of the discourse, I heard some of them deridingly speak of you, and of your desperate journey; for so they called this your pilgrimage. But I did believe, and so still, that the end of our city will be with fire and brimstone from above; and therefore I have made my escape.

CHR. Did you hear no talk of neighbour Pliable?

FAITH. Yes, Christian, I heard that he followed you till he came at the Slough of Despond, where, as some said, he fell in; but he would not be known to have so done; but I am sure he was soundly *bedabbled*[1] with that kind of dirt.

CHR. And what said the neighbors to him?

FAITH. He hath, since his going back, been

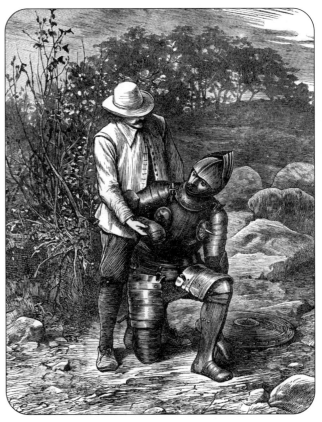

had greatly in derision, and that among all sorts of people: some do mock and despise him, and scarce will any set him on work. He is now seven times worse than if he had never gone out of the city.

CHR. But why should they be so set against him, since they also despise the way that he forsook?

FAITH. Oh, they say, Hang him; he is a *turn-coat*;[2] he was not true to his profession! I think God has stirred up even his enemies to hiss at him, and make him a proverb, because he hath forsaken the way.

CHR. Had you no talk with him before you came out?

FAITH. I met him once in the streets, but he *leered*[3] away on the other side, as one ashamed of what he had done; so I spake not to him.

CHR. Well, at my first setting out I had hopes of that man; but now I fear he will perish in the overthrow of the city. For it is happened to him according to the true proverb, The dog is turned to his vomit again, and the sow that was

---

1. bedabbled: smeared.

2. turn-coat: traitor.

3. leered: walked slyly so as not to be seen.

Artist: Townley Green

washed to her wallowing in the mire.

FAITH. They are my fears of him too; but who can hinder that which will be?

CHR. Well, neighbour Faithful, said Christian, let us leave him, and talk of things that more immediately concern ourselves. Tell me now what you have met with in the way as you came; for I know you have met with some things, or else it may be *writ*[4] for a wonder.

FAITH. I escaped the slough that I perceived you fell into, and got up to the gate without that danger; only I met with one whose name was **Wanton**, who had like to have done me a mischief.

CHR. 'Twas well you escaped her net; Joseph was hard put to it by her, and he escaped her as you did; but it had like to have cost him his life. But what did she do to you?

FAITH. You cannot think (but that you know something) what a flattering tongue she had; she *lay at me hard*[5] to turn aside with her, promising me all manner of content.

CHR. Nay, she did not promise you the content of a good conscience.

FAITH. You know that I mean all carnal and fleshly content.

CHR. Thank God you have escaped her; the abhorred of the Lord shall fall into her ditch.

FAITH. Nay, I know not whether I did wholly escape her or no.

CHR. Why, I trow, you did not consent to her desires?

FAITH. No, not to defile myself; for I remembered an old writing that I had seen, which said, Her steps take hold of hell. So I shut mine eyes, because I would not be **bewitched** with her looks. Then she railed on me, and I went my way.

CHR. Did you meet with no other assault as you came?

FAITH. When I came to the foot of the hill called Difficulty, I met with a very aged man, who asked me what I was, and *whither*[6] bound. I told him that I was a pilgrim, going to the Celestial City. Then said the old man, Thou lookest like an honest fellow; will thou be content to dwell with me, for the wages that I shall give thee? Then I asked him his name and where he dwelt. He said his name was Adam the First, and that he dwelt in the town of Deceit. I asked him then, what was his work, and what the wages that he would give. He told me, that his work was many delights; and his wages, that I should be his heir at last. I further asked him, what house he kept, and what other servants he had. So he told me, that his house was maintained with all the dainties in the world, and that his servants were those of his own begetting. Then I asked how many children he had. He said that he had but three daughters, the Lust of the Flesh, the Lust of the Eyes, and the Pride of Life, and that I should marry them, if I would. Then I asked how long time he would have me live with him, and he told me, as long as he lived himself.

CHR. Well, and what conclusion came the old man and you to at last?

FAITH. Why, at first I found myself somewhat inclinable to go with the man, for I thought he spake very fair; but looking in his forehead, as I talked with him, I saw there written, Put off the old man with his deeds.

CHR. And how then?

FAITH. Then it came burning hot into my mind, whatever he said, and however he flattered, when he got me home to his house, he would sell me for a slave. So I bid him forbear to talk, for I would not come near the door of his house. Then he reviled me, and told me that he would send such a one after me that should make my way bitter to my soul. So I turned to go away from him; but just as I turned myself to go thence, I felt him take hold of my flesh and give me such a deadly twitch back, that I thought he had pulled part of me after himself: this made me cry, O wretched man! So I went on my way up hill.

Now when I had got about half way up, I looked behind me, and saw one coming after me, swift as the wind; so he overtook me just

---

4. writ: recorded.

5. lay at me hard: tried hard to tempt me.

6. whither: to what place.

about the place where the settle stands.

CHR. Just there, said Christian, did I sit down to rest me; but being overcome with sleep, I there lost this roll out of my bosom.

FAITH. But, good brother, hear me out. So soon as the man overtook me, he was but a word and a blow; for down he knocked me, and laid me for dead. But when I was a little come to myself again, I asked him wherefore he served me so. He said, because of my secret inclining to Adam the first. And with that he *strook*[7] me another deadly blow on the breast, and beat me down backward; so I lay at his foot as dead as before. So when I came to myself again, I cried him mercy; but he said, I know not how to show mercy; and with that knocked me down again. He had doubtless made an end of me, but that One came by, and bid him forbear.

CHR. Who was that that bid him forbear?

FAITH. I did not know Him at first; but as He went by I perceived the holes in His hands and His side; then I concluded that He was our Lord. So I went up the hill.

CHR. That man that overtook you was Moses. He spareth none; neither knoweth he how to show mercy to those that transgress his law.

FAITH. I know it very well; it was not the first time that he has met with me. 'Twas he that came to me when I dwelt securely at home, and that told me he would burn my house over my head if I stayed there.

CHR. But did you not see the house that stood there, on the top of the hill on the side of which Moses met you?

FAITH. Yes, and the lions too, before I came at it. But for the lions, I think they were asleep, for it was about noon; and because I had so much of the day before me, I passed by the Porter, and came down the hill.

CHR. He told me, indeed, that he saw you go by; but I wish you had called at the house, for they would have showed you so many rarities, that you would scarce have forgot them to the day of your death. But pray tell me, did you meet nobody in the Valley of Humility?

FAITH. Yes, I met with one Discontent, who would willingly have persuaded me to go back again with him: his reason was, for that the valley was altogether without honour. He told me, moreover, that there to go was the way to disobey all my friends, as Pride, **Arrogancy, Self-Conceit,** Worldly Glory, with others, who he knew, as he said, would be very much offended if I made such a fool of myself as to wade through this valley.

CHR. Well, and how did you answer him?

FAITH. I told him, that although all these that he named might claim kindred of men, and that rightly (for indeed they were my relations according to the flesh), yet since I became a pilgrim, they have disowned me, and I also have rejected them; and therefore they were to me now no more than if they had never been of my **lineage.** I told him, moreover, that as to this valley, he had quite misrepresented the thing; for before honour is humility, and a **haughty** spirit before a fall. Therefore, said I, I had rather go through this valley to the honour that was so accounted by the wisest, than choose that which he esteemed most worth our affections.

CHR. Met you with nothing else in that valley?

FAITH. Yes, I met with Shame; but of all the men that I met with in my pilgrimage, he, I think, bears the wrong name. The other would be said nay, after a little argumentation, and somewhat else; but this bold-faced Shame would never have done.

CHR. Why, what did he say to you?

FAITH. What? why he objected against religion itself. He said it was a pitiful, low, sneaking business for a man to mind religion. He said that a tender conscience was an unmanly thing; and that for a man to watch over his words and ways, so as to tie up himself from that **hectoring** liberty that the brave spirits of the times accustom themselves unto, would make him the ridicule of the times. He objected also, that but few of the mighty, rich, or wise were ever of my opinion; nor any of them neither, before they were persuaded to be fools, and to be of a voluntary fondness to venture

---

7. strook: struck.

the loss of all, for nobody else knows what. He, moreover, objected the base and low estate and condition of those that were chiefly the pilgrims of the times in which they lived; also their ignorance and want of understanding in all natural science. Yea, he did hold me to it at that rate also about a great many more things than here I relate; as, that it was a *shame* to sit whining and mourning under a sermon, and a *shame* to come sighing and groaning home; that it was a *shame* to ask my neighbor forgiveness for **petty** faults, or to make restitution where I have taken from any. He said also, that religion made a man grow strange to the great, because of a few vices (which he called by finer names), and made him own and respect the base because of the same religious **fraternity**: and is not this, said he, a *shame*?

CHR. And what did you say to him?

FAITH. Say? I could not tell what to say at first. Yea, he put me so to it, that my blood came up in my face; even this Shame fetched it up, and had almost beat me quite off. But at last I began to consider, that that which is highly esteemed among men, is had in **abomination** with God. And I thought again, This Shame tells me what men are; but it tells me nothing what God, or the Word of God, is. And I thought, moreover, that at the day of doom we shall not be doomed to death or life, according to the hectoring spirits of the world, but according to the wisdom and law of the Highest. Therefore, thought I, what God says is best, is best, though all the men in the world are against it. Seeing then that God prefers His religion; seeing God prefers a tender conscience; seeing they that make themselves fools for the kingdom of heaven are wisest, and that the poor man that loveth Christ is richer than the greatest man in the world that hates Him; Shame, depart, thou art an enemy to my salvation! Shall I entertain thee against my sovereign Lord? how then shall I look Him in the face at His coming? Should I now be ashamed of His ways and servants, how can I expect the blessing? But indeed this Shame was a bold **villain;** I could scarce shake him out of my company;

yea, he would be haunting of me and continually whispering me in the ear with some one or other of the infirmities that attend religion. But at last I told him 'twas but in vain to attempt further in this business; for those things that he disdained, in those did I see most glory: and so at last I got past this **importunate** one. And when I had shaken him off, then I began to sing:

The trials that those men do meet withal,
That are obedient to the heavenly call,
Are manifold, and suited to the flesh,
And come, and come, and come again afresh;
That now, or sometimes else, we by them may
Be taken, overcome, and cast away.
O, let the pilgrims, let the pilgrims then,
Be vigilant, and *quit themselves like men!*[8]

CHR. I am glad, my brother, that thou didst withstand this villain so bravely; for of all, as thou sayest, I think he has the wrong name; for he is so bold as to follow us in the streets, and to attempt to put us to shame before all men; that is, to make us ashamed of that which is good. But if he was not himself **audacious**, he would never attempt to do as he does. But let us still resist him; for notwithstanding all his **bravados**, he promoteth the fool, and none else. The wise shall inherit glory, said Solomon; but shame shall be the promotion of fools.

FAITH. I think we must cry to Him for help against Shame, that would have us be valiant for truth upon the earth.

CHR. You say true; but did you meet nobody else in that valley?

FAITH. No, not I; for I had sunshine all the rest of the way through that, and also through the Valley of the Shadow of Death.

CHR. 'Twas well for you; I am sure it fared far otherwise with me. I had for a long season, as soon almost as I entered into that valley, a dreadful combat with that foul fiend Apollyon; yea, I thought verily he would have killed me, especially when he got me down, and crushed me under him, as if he would have crushed me to pieces. For as he threw me, my sword flew out of my hand; nay, he told me he was sure of

8. quit themselves like men: behave bravely.

me; but I cried to God, and He heard me, and delivered me out of all my troubles. Then I entered into the Valley of the Shadow of Death, and had no light for almost half the way through it. I thought I should have been killed there, over and over; but at last day broke and the sun rose, and I went through that which was behind with far more ease and quiet.

Meditating for Meaning

1. What is the cause of Christian's fall when he meets Faithful?

2. Faithful escaped the early peril of the _____ , which Christian encountered, but he was grievously tempted by a wicked _____ named _____ .

3. Faithful met Adam the First at the foot of the Hill Difficulty. What does this old man represent? (Colossians 3:9)

4. Moses overtook Faithful as he went up the hill.
   a. Considering what came by Moses in Scripture, explain the meaning of Faithful being struck down by Moses.
   b. What would the Law do to us if no one intervened?
   c. Who keeps the Law from doing all to us that it would?

5. While Christian's more introspective nature subjected him to inner struggles and doubts, Faithful's more society-loving temperament presented the temptation to be ashamed of living the Christian life. Discontent and Shame represent this temptation.
   a. What two reasons did Discontent use as a basis for trying to persuade Faithful to turn back?
   b. What knowledge of truth made Faithful willing to face a humiliating experience?
   c. List ten objections Shame had to being a Christian.
   d. Faithful recognized that these objections were only according to _____ and were not according to _____ .

6. Faithful had light all through the Valley of the Shadow of Death. He avoided other dangers Christian faced but met with some dangers that Christian avoided. What does this tell us about individual Christian lives?

Chapter 12: Christian and Faithful Meet Talkative

Defining for Comprehension

Choose the word or phrase below which most nearly defines each word at the left as it is used in this allegory.

1 **refute**
   a. oppose; contradict
   b. begin again
   c. renew a quarrel

2 **vindicate**
   a. defend from guilt
   b. weaken
   c. speak abusively

3 **evangelical**
   a. heavenly
   b. of the Gospel
   c. of missionary efforts

4 **circumstantial**
   a. coincidental
   b. secret
   c. minor; non-essential

5 **jest**
   a. scorn
   b. joke
   c. fit with clothing

6 **savour (savor)**
   a. flavor
   b. one who rescues
   c. stench

7 **brute**
   a. animal
   b. step hill
   c. impact

8 **churl**
   a. runaway
   b. young lad
   c. rude fellow

9 **expounds**
   a. gives off
   b. explains
   c. swells

10 **antipathy**
    a. dislike; hatred
    b. kindred feeling
    c. unhappiness

11 **propound**
    a. multiply
    b. to set forth for consideration
    c. insist

12 **peevish**
    a. immature
    b. irritable
    c. inexpensive

13 **melancholy**
    a. gloomy
    b. provoked
    c. sorrowing

14 **adieu**
    a. good-bye
    b. be quiet
    c. best wishes

15 **debauched**
    a. proud
    b. corrupt; immoral
    c. confused

16 **conformable**
    a. unyielding
    b. ready to submit
    c. pleasant

17 **wane**
    a. increase
    b. decrease
    c. bright shining

Moreover I saw in my dream, that as they went on, Faithful, as he chanced to look on one side, saw a man whose name is Talkative, walking at a distance besides them, for in this place there was room enough for them all to walk. He was a tall man, and something more comely at a distance than at hand. To this man Faithful addressed himself in this manner.

FAITH. Friend, whither away? Are you going to the heavenly country?

TALK. I am going to the same place.

FAITH. That is well; then I hope we shall

have your good company?

TALK. With a very good will will I be your companion.

FAITH. Come on, then, and let us go together, and let us spend our time in discoursing of things that are profitable.

TALK. To talk of things that are good, to me is very acceptable, with you, or with any other; and I am glad that I have met with those that incline to so good a work; for, to speak the truth, there are but few who care thus to spend their time as they are in their travels, but choose much rather to be speaking of things to no profit; and this hath been a trouble to me.

FAITH. That is, indeed, a thing to be lamented; for what thing so worthy of the use of the tongue and mouth of men on earth, as are the things of the God of heaven?

TALK. I like you wonderful well, for your sayings are full of conviction; and I will add, What thing is so pleasant, and what so profitable, as to talk of the things of God? What things so pleasant? that is, if a man hath any delight in things that are wonderful. For instance: if a man doth delight to talk of the history, or the mystery of things; or if a man doth love to talk of miracles, wonders, or signs, where shall he find things recorded so delightful, and so sweetly penned, as in the Holy Scripture?

FAITH. That is true; but to be profited by such things in our talk, should be our chief design.

TALK. That is it that I said; for to talk of such things is most profitable: for by so doing, a man may get knowledge of many things; as of the vanity of earthly things, and the benefit of things above. Thus in general; but more particular, by this a man may learn the necessity of the new birth, the insufficiency of our works, the need of Christ's righteousness, etc. Besides, by this a man may learn what it is to repent, to believe, to pray, to suffer, or the like; by this also, a man may learn what are the great promises and consolations of the gospel, to his own comfort. Further, by this a man may learn to **refute** false opinions, to **vindicate** the truth,

and also to instruct the ignorant.

FAITH. All this is true; and glad am I to hear these things from you.

TALK. Alas! the want of this is the cause that so few understand the need of faith, and the necessity of a work of grace in their soul, in order to eternal life; but ignorantly live in the works of the law, by which a man can by no means obtain the kingdom of heaven.

FAITH. But, by your leave, heavenly knowledge of these is the gift of God; no man attaineth to them by human industry, or only by the talk of them.

TALK. All that I know very well, for a man can receive nothing, except it be given him from heaven; all is of grace, not of works. I could give you a hundred Scriptures for the confirmation of this.

FAITH. Well then, said Faithful, what is that one thing that we shall at this time found our discourse upon?

TALK. What you will. I will talk of things heavenly, or things earthly; things moral, or things **evangelical**; things sacred, or things *profane;*[1] things past, or things to come; things foreign, or things at home; things more essential, or things **circumstantial;** provided that all be done to our profit.

FAITH. Now did Faithful begin to wonder; and stepping to Christian (for he walked all this while by himself), he said to him but softly, What a brave companion have we got! Surely this man will make a very excellent pilgrim.

CHR. At this Christian smiled, and said, This man, with whom you are so taken, will beguile with this tongue of his twenty of them that know him not.

FAITH. Do you know him then?

CHR. Know him? Yes, better than he knows himself.

FAITH. Pray what is he?

CHR. His name is Talkative: he dwelleth in our town. I wonder that you should be a stranger to him; only I consider that our town is large.

FAITH. Whose son is he? And whereabouts doth he dwell?

---

1. profane: nonreligious.

CHR. He is the son of one Say-well. He dwelt in *Prating*[2] Row, and he is known of all that are acquainted with him by the name of Talkative, in Prating Row; and, notwithstanding his fine tongue, he is but a sorry fellow.

FAITH. Well, he seems to be a very pretty man.

CHR. That is, to them that have not thorough acquaintance with him, for he is best abroad; near home he is ugly enough. Your saying that he is a pretty man, brings to my mind what I have observed in the work of the painter, whose pictures show best at a distance, but very near more unpleasing.

FAITH. But I am ready to think you do but **jest**, because you smiled.

CHR. God forbid that I should jest (though I smiled) in this matter, or that I should accuse any falsely. I will give you a further discovery of him. This man is for any company, and for any talk; as he talketh now with you, so will he talk when he is on the *ale-bench*;[3] and the more drink he hath in his crown, the more of these things he hath in his mouth. Religion hath no place in his heart, or house, or conversation; all he hath lieth in his tongue, and his religion is to make a noise therewith.

FAITH. Say you so? Then am I in this man greatly deceived.

CHR. Deceived! you may be sure of it. Remember the proverb, They say and do not: but the kingdom of God is not in word, but in power. He talketh of prayer, of repentance, of faith, and of the new birth; but he knows but only to talk of them. I have been in his family, and have observed him both at home and abroad; and I know what I say of him is the truth. His house is as empty of religion, as the white of an egg is of **savour**. There is there neither prayer, nor sign of repentance for sin; yea, the **brute**, in his kind, serves God far better than he. He is the very stain, reproach, and shame of religion to all that know him, it can hardly have a good word in all that end of the town where he dwells, through him. Thus say the common people that know him, A saint abroad, and a devil at home. His poor family finds it so; he is such a **churl**, such a railer at, and so unreasonable with his servants, that they neither know how to do for nor speak to him. Men that have any dealings with him say, it is better to deal with a Turk than with him, for fairer dealing they shall have at their hands. This Talkative (if it be possible) will go beyond them, defraud, beguile, and *overreach*[4] them. Besides, he brings up his sons to follow his steps; and if he finds in any of them a foolish timorousness (for so he calls the first appearance of a tender conscience), he calls them fools and blockheads, and by no means will employ them in much, or speak to their commendation before others. For my part, I am of opinion, that he has, by his wicked life, caused many to stumble and fall; and will be, if God prevent not, the ruin of many more.

FAITH. Well, my brother, I am bound to believe you, not only because you say you know him, but also because, like a Christian, you make your reports of men. For I cannot think that you speak these things of ill-will, but because it is even so as you say.

CHR. Had I known him no more than you, I might, perhaps, have thought of him as at the first you did; yea, had I received this report at their hands only, that are enemies to religion, I should have thought it had been a slander, a lot that often falls from bad men's mouths upon good men's names and professions. But all these things, yea, and a great many more as bad, of my own knowledge, I can prove him guilty of. Besides, good men are ashamed of him; they can neither call him brother nor friend; the very naming of him among them makes them blush, if they know him.

FAITH. Well, I see that saying and doing are two things, and hereafter I shall better observe this distinction.

CHR. They are two things indeed, and are as diverse as are the soul and the body; for as the body without the soul is but a dead carcase, so

---

2. prating: talking in an empty, foolish way.

3. ale-bench: barstool; tavern lounge.

4. overreach: take advantage of by trickery.

saying, if it be alone, is but a dead carcase also. The soul of religion is the practical part: Pure religion and undefiled before God and the Father is this, to visit the fatherless and widows in their affliction, and to keep himself unspotted from the world. This Talkative is not aware of; he thinks that hearing and saying will make a good Christian, and thus he deceiveth his own soul. Hearing is but as the sowing of the seed; talking is not sufficient to prove that fruit is indeed in the heart and life. And let us assure ourselves, that at the day of doom, men shall be judged according to their fruit. It will not be said then, Did you believe? but, Were you doers, or talkers only? and accordingly shall they be judged. The end of the world is compared to our harvest, and you know men at harvest regard nothing but fruit. Not that anything can be accepted that is not of faith; but I speak this to show you how insignificant the profession of Talkative will be at that day.

FAITH. This brings to my mind that of Moses, by which he describeth the beast that is clean. He is such an one that parteth the hoof, and cheweth the cud; not that parteth the hoof only, or that cheweth the cud only. The hare cheweth the cud, but yet is unclean, because he parteth not the hoof. And this truly resembleth Talkative; he cheweth the cud, he seeketh knowledge, he cheweth upon the Word, but he divideth not the hoof. He parteth not with the way of sinners; but, as the hare, he retaineth the foot of a dog or bear, and therefore is unclean.

CHR. You have spoken, for aught I know, the true Gospel sense of those texts. And I will add another thing: Paul calleth some men, yea, and those great talkers too, sounding brass and tinkling cymbals; that is, as he **expounds** them in another place, things without life, giving sound. Things without life; that is, without the true faith and grace of the Gospel; and, consequently, things that shall never be placed in the kingdom of heaven among those that are the children of life, though their sound, by their talk, be as if it were the tongue or voice of an angel.

FAITH. Well, I was not so fond of his company at first, but I am as sick of it now. What shall we do to be rid of him?

CHR. Take my advice, and do as I bid you, and you shall find that he will soon be sick of your company too, except God shall touch his heart and turn it.

FAITH. What would you have me to do?

CHR. Why, go to him, and enter into some serious discourse about the power of religion, and ask him plainly (when he has approved of it, for that he will), whether this thing be set up in his heart, house, or conversation.

FAITH. Then Faithful stepped forward again, and said to Talkative, Come, what cheer? How is it now?

TALK. Thank you, well: I thought we should have had a great deal of talk by this time.

FAITH. Well, if you will, we will fall to it now; and since you left it with me to state the question, let it be this: How doth the saving grace of God discover itself, when it is in the heart of man?

TALK. I perceive, then, that our talk must be about the power of things. Well, 'tis a very good question, and I shall be willing to answer you. And take my answer in brief, thus. First, where the grace of God is in the heart, it causeth there a great outcry against sin. Secondly—

FAITH. Nay, hold, let us consider of one at once. I think you should rather say, It shows itself by inclining the soul to abhor its sin.

TALK. Why, what difference is there between crying out against, and abhorring of sin?

FAITH. Oh! a great deal. A man may cry out against sin, of *policy;*[5] but he cannot abhor it but by virtue of a godly **antipathy** against it. I have heard many cry out against sin in the pulpit, who yet can abide it well enough in the heart, house, and conversation. Joseph's mistress cried out with a loud voice, as if she had been very holy; but she would willingly, notwithstanding that, have committed uncleanness with him. Some cry out against sin, even as the mother cries out against her child in her lap, when she calleth it *slut*[6] and naughty girl,

_____

5. policy: good manners.
6. slut: a bold girl.

and then falls to hugging and kissing it.

TALK. You *lie at the catch*,[7] I perceive.

FAITH. No, not I; I am only for setting things right. But what is the second thing whereby you would prove a discovery of a work of grace in the heart?

TALK. Great knowledge of Gospel mysteries.

FAITH. This sign should have been first; but first or last, it is also false; for knowledge, great knowledge, may be obtained in the mysteries of the gospel, and yet no work of grace in the soul. Yea, if a man have all knowledge, he may yet be nothing, and so, consequently, be no child of God. When Christ said, Do you know all these things? and the disciples had answered, Yes; He added, Blessed are ye if ye do them. He doth not lay the blessing in the knowing of them, but in the doing of them. For there is a knowledge that is not attended with doing: He that knoweth his Master's will, and doth it not. A man may know like an angel, and yet be no Christian; therefore your sign of it is not true. Indeed, to know, is a thing that pleaseth talkers and boasters; but to do, is that which pleaseth God. Not that the heart can be good without knowledge, for without that the heart is *naught*.[8] There is, therefore, knowledge and knowledge;—knowledge that resteth in the bare speculation of things, and knowledge that is accompanied with the grace of faith and love, which puts a man upon doing even the will of God from the heart: the first of these will serve the talker; but without the other the true Christian is not content. Give me understanding, and I shall keep Thy law; yea, I shall observe it with my whole heart.

TALK. You lie at the catch again; this is not for edification.

FAITH. Well, if you please, propound another sign how this work of grace discovereth itself where it is.

TALK. Not I, for I see we shall not agree.

FAITH. Well, if you will not, will you give me leave to do it?

TALK. You may use your liberty.

FAITH. A work of grace in the soul discovereth itself, either to him that hath it, or to standers by.

To him that hath it, thus: It gives him conviction of sin, especially of the defilement of his nature, and the sin of unbelief, for the sake of which he is sure to be damned, if he findeth not mercy at God's hand by faith in Jesus Christ. This sight and sense of things worketh in him sorrow and shame for sin. He findeth, moreover, revealed in him the Saviour of the world, and the absolute necessity of closing with Him for life; at the which he findeth hungerings and thirstings after Him; to which hungerings, etc., the promise is made. Now, according to the strength or weakness of his faith in his Saviour, so is his joy and peace, so is his love to holiness, so are his desires to know Him more, and also to serve Him in this world. But though, I say, it discovereth itself thus unto him, yet it is but seldom that he is able to conclude that this is a work of grace; because his corruptions now,

---

7. lie at the catch: want for opportunity to disagree.

8. naught: nothing.

and his abused reason, make his mind to misjudge in this matter; therefore in him that hath this work there is required a very sound judgment, before he can with steadiness conclude that this is a work of grace.

To others, it is thus discovered:

1. By an *experimental confession*[9] of his faith in Christ. 2. By a life answerable to that confession: to wit, a life of holiness, heart-holiness; family-holiness (if he hath a family), and by conversation-holiness in the world; which in the general teacheth him inwardly to abhor his sin, and himself for that, in secret; to suppress it in his family, and to promote holiness in the world; not by talk only, as a hypocrite or talkative person may do, but by a practical subjection in faith and love to the power of the Word. And now, sir, as to this brief description of the work of grace, and also the discovery of it, if you have aught to object, object; if not, then give me leave to **propound** to you a second question.

TALK. Nay, my part is not now to object, but to hear; let me, therefore, have your second question.

FAITH. It is this: Do you experience this first part of this description of it? And doth your life and conversation testify the same? or standeth your religion in word or in tongue, and not in deed and truth? Pray, if you incline to answer me in this, say no more than you know the God above will say Amen to, and also nothing but what your conscience can justify you in; for not he that commendeth himself is approved, but whom the Lord commendeth. Besides, to say, I am thus and thus, when my conversation, and all my neighbours tell me I lie, is great wickedness.

TALK. Then Talkative at first began to blush; but, recovering himself, thus he replied: You come now to experience, to conscience, and God; and to appeal to Him for justification of what is spoken. This kind of discourse I did not expect; nor am I disposed to give an answer to such questions, because I count not myself bound thereto, unless you take upon you to be a *catechiser*;[10] and though you should so do, yet I may refuse to make you my judge. But I pray, will you tell me why you ask me such questions?

FAITH. Because I saw you forward to talk, and because I knew not that you had aught else but notion. Besides, to tell you all the truth, I have heard of you that you are a man whose religion lies in talk, and that your conversation gives this your mouth profession the lie. They say you are a spot among Christians, and that religion fareth the worse for your ungodly conversation; that some already have stumbled at your wicked ways, and that more are in danger of being destroyed thereby; your religion, and an ale-house, and covetousness, and uncleanness, and swearing, and lying, and vain company-keeping, etc., will stand together. The proverb is true of you which is said of a whore, to wit, that she is a shame to all women. So you are a shame to all professors.

TALK. Since you are ready to take up reports, and to judge so rashly as you do, I cannot but conclude you are some **peevish** or **melancholy** man, not fit to be discoursed with; and so, **adieu**.

CHR. Then came up Christian and said to his brother, I told you how it would happen; your words and his lusts could not agree. He had rather leave your company than reform his life. But he is gone, as I said: let him go; the loss is no man's but his own; he has saved us the trouble of going from him; for he continuing (as I suppose he will do) as he is, he would have been but a blot in our company. Besides, the apostle says, From such withdraw thyself.

FAITH. But I am glad we had this little discourse with him; it may happen that he will think of it again: however, I have dealt plainly with him, and so am clear of his blood, if he perisheth.

CHR. You did well to talk so plainly to him as you did. There is but little of this faithful dealing with men now-a-days, and that makes religion to stink so in the nostrils of many as it doth: for they are these talkative fools, whose

---

9. experimental confession: statement of belief based on experience.

10. catechiser: one who questions and reproves another.

religion is only in word, and are **debauched** and vain in their conversation, that (being so much admitted into the fellowship of the godly) do puzzle the world, blemish Christianity, and grieve the sincere. I wish that all men would deal with such as you have done; then should they either be made **conformable** to religion, or the company of saints would be too hot for them. Then did Faithful say,

> How Talkative at first lifts up his plumes!
> How bravely doth he speak! How he presumes
> To drive down all before him! But so soon
> As Faithful talks of heart-work, like the moon
> That's past the full, into the **wane** he goes.
> And so will all but he that heart-work knows.

Meditating for Meaning

1. Talkative is another example of Bunyan's skillfully named characters.
   a. What is Talkative very willing to do?
   b. What does Faithful say should be the chief aim in talking?
   c. What value does Talkative see in talking?
   d. What makes Faithful begin to wonder about Talkative's character?

2. In describing Talkative, Christian uses two vivid comparisons.
   a. How is Talkative like a painting?
   b. How is Talkative like the white of an egg?

3. From Christian's information about Talkative, tell about:
   a. Talkative's home
   b. his reputation
   c. his relationships with servants and family
   d. his dealing in business
   e. his influence

4. Talkative's religion lies basically in his speech.
   a. What important thing does Talkative not understand?
   b. Which mark of clean beasts does Talkative have?
   c. Which mark of clean beasts does Talkative lack?

5. At Christian's suggestion, Faithful talks to Talkative about the power of religion and the effect of grace in the heart.
   a. What does Talkative say is the first evidence of grace in the heart?
   b. How does Faithful correct him?
   c. What does Talkative say is the second evidence?
   d. How does Faithful again correct him?

6. Talkative now feels that he is being exposed, and therefore becomes cross and refuses to give Faithful any further answer to his question.
   a. What does Faithful say makes the grace in the soul known to the person who has it?
   b. What makes this grace known to others?

7. Talkative refuses to answer Faithful's final question as to whether he has experienced the work of grace in his heart and lives a life in accordance.
    a. Why does Faithful stress that Talkative consider God and his conscience before answering this question?
    b. What excuse does Talkative give for not answering?
8. According to Christian, why did Talkative leave their company?
9. According to Faithful, for what two reasons was the conversation with Talkative profitable?

Chapter 13: Christian and Faithful Enter the Town of Vanity

Defining for Comprehension

Choose the word or phrase below which most nearly defines each word at the left as it is used in this allegory.

1. tedious	a. intricate	b. laborious	c. inquisitive
2. preferments	a. choices	b. refusals	c. promotions
3. knaves	a. criminals	b. sailors	c. simple persons
4. rogues	a. mischievous persons	b. popular fashions	c. dialects
5. vended	a. bought	b. sold	c. fought
6. commodity	a. product	b. modern convenience	c. tradition
7. allure	a. convince	b. entice	c. become hardened
8. diverse	a. strongly opposed	b. many	c. different
9. taunting	a. stretching	b. showing off	c. teasing
10. confounded	a. confused	b. proven false	c. established
11. deputed	a. argued	b. appointed	c. transported
12. confederates	a. helpers in wrongdoing	b. republics	c. army generals
13. pillory	a. instrument of punishment	b. horse's saddle	c. marble column
14. divers	a. evil	b. various	c. extreme
15. ignominy	a. lack of education	b. disgrace	c. lack of importance
16. remanded	a. ordered to return	b. rebuked	c. repaired

17. **arraigned**	a. set in order	b. brought before court	c. harnessed
18. **indictment**	a. release	b. formal accusation	c. inclination
19. **plausible**	a. worthy of praise	b. easily satisfied	c. logical
20. **diametrically**	a. separately	b. exactly	c. sinfully
21. **dispatch**	a. put to death quickly	b. disagree	c. irritate
22. **pestilent**	a. troublesome	b. speechless	c. rude; impolite
23. **lechery**	a. thievery	b. unrestrained impurity	c. covetousness
24. **vilifying**	a. defending	b. raiding	c. slandering
25. **gentry**	a. friendly persons	b. high society	c. harsh speech
26. **heretic**	a. rebel	b. outcast person	c. ancestor
27. **amiss**	a. lost	b. wrong	c. friendship
28. **recantation**	a. forsaking of previous belief	b. repetition	c. renewal of courage
29. **supposition**	a. assignment	b. guess	c. deception
30. **unanimously**	a. agreeing totally	b. without identification	c. viciously

Thus they went on, talking of what they had seen by the way, and so made that way easy, which would otherwise no doubt have been **tedious** to them, for now they went through a wilderness.

Now when they were got almost quite out of this wilderness, Faithful chanced to cast his eye back, and espied one coming after them, and he knew him. Oh! said Faithful to his brother, who comes yonder? Then Christian looked, and said, It is my good friend Evangelist. Ay, and my good friend too, said Faithful, for 'twas he that set me the way to the gate. Now was Evan-

gelist come up to them, and thus saluted them.

EVAN. Peace be with you, dearly beloved, and peace be to your helpers.

CHR. Welcome, welcome, my good Evangelist, the sight of thy countenance brings to my remembrance thy ancient kindness and unwearied labouring for my eternal good.

FAITH. And a thousand times welcome, said good Faithful, thy company, O sweet Evangelist, how desirable is it to us poor pilgrims!

EVAN. Then said Evangelist, How hath it fared with you, my friends, since the time of our last parting? What have you met with, and how have you behaved yourselves?

Then Christian and Faithful told him of all things that had happened to them in the way; and how, and with what difficulty, they had arrived to that place.

EVAN. Right glad am I, said Evangelist, not that you have met with trials, but that you have been victors, and for that you have, notwithstanding many weaknesses, continued in the way to this very day.

I say, right glad am I of this thing, and that for mine own sake and yours; I have sowed, and you have reaped; and the day is coming when both he that soweth and they that reap shall rejoice together; that is, if you hold out; for in due time ye shall reap, if ye faint not. The crown is before you, and it is an incorruptible one; so run that you may obtain it. Some there be that set out for this crown, and after they have gone far for it, another comes in and takes it from them: hold fast, therefore, that you have; let no man take your crown. You are not yet out of the gun-shot of the devil; you have not yet resisted unto blood, striving against sin. Let the kingdom be always before you, and believe stedfastly concerning things that are invisible. Let nothing that is on this side the other world get within you. And, above all, look well to your own hearts and to the lusts thereof; for they are deceitful above all things, and desperately wicked. Set your faces like a flint; you have all power in heaven and earth on your side.

CHR. Then Christian thanked him for his exhortation; but told him withal, that they would have him speak further to them for their help the rest of the way; and the rather, for that they well knew that he was a prophet, and could tell them of things that might happen unto them, and also how they might resist and overcome them. To which request Faithful also consented. So Evangelist began as followeth.

EVAN. My sons, you have heard in the words of the truth of the Gospel, that you must through many tribulations enter into the kingdom of heaven; and again, that in every city, bonds and afflictions abide on you; and therefore you cannot expect that you should go long on your pilgrimage without them, in some sort or other. You have found something of the truth of these testimonies upon you already, and more will immediately follow; for now, as you see, you are almost out of this wilderness, and therefore you will soon come into a town that you will by and by see before you; and in that town you will be hardly beset with enemies, who will strain hard but they will kill you; and be you sure that one or both of you must seal the testimony which you hold with blood; but be you faithful unto death, and the King will give you a crown of life. He that shall die there, although his death will be unnatural, and his pain, perhaps great, he will yet have the better of his fellow; not only because he will be arrived at the Celestial City soonest, but because he will escape many miseries that the other will meet with in the rest of his journey. But when you are come to the town, and shall find fulfilled what I have here related, then remember your friend, and quit yourselves like men, and commit the keeping of your souls to your God in well-doing, as unto a faithful Creator.

Then I saw in my dream, that when they were got out of the wilderness, they presently saw a town before them, and the name of that town is Vanity; and at the town there is a fair kept, called Vanity Fair. It is kept all the year long. It beareth the name of Vanity Fair, because the town where it is kept, is lighter than vanity; and also, because all that is there sold, or that cometh thither, is vanity, as is the saying of the wise, All that cometh is vanity.

This fair is no new-erected business, but a thing of ancient standing. I will show you the original of it.

Almost five thousand years ago, there were pilgrims walking to the Celestial City, as these two honest persons are; and Beelzebub, Apollyon, and Legion, with their companions, perceiving by the path that the pilgrims made, that their way to the city lay through this town of Vanity, they contrived here to set up a fair; a fair wherein should be sold all sorts of vanity, and that it should last all the year long. Therefore at this fair are all such merchandise sold as houses, lands, trades, places, honours, **preferments**, titles, countries, kingdoms, lusts, pleasures, and delights of all sorts, as whores, *bawds*,[1] wives, husbands, children, masters, servants, lives, blood, bodies, souls, silver, gold, pearls, precious stones, and what not.

And moreover, at this fair there is at all times to be seen jugglings, cheats, games, plays, fools, apes, **knaves**, and **rogues**, and that of every kind.

Here are to be seen too, and that for nothing, thefts, murders, adulteries, false swearers, and that of a blood-red colour.

And as, in other fairs of less moment, there are the several rows and streets under their proper names, where such and such wares are **vended**; so here likewise you have the proper places, rows, streets (*viz.*[2] countries and kingdoms), where the wares of this fair are soonest to be found. Here is the Britain Row, the French Row, the Italian Row, the Spanish Row, the German Row, where several sorts of vanities are to be sold. But as in other fairs some one **commodity** is as the chief of all the fair, so the ware of Rome and her merchandise is greatly promoted in this fair; only our English nation, with some others, have taken a dislike thereat.

Now, as I said, the way to the Celestial City lies just through this town where this lusty fair is kept; and he that will go to the city, and yet not go through this town, must needs go out of the world. The Prince of princes Himself, when here, went through this town to His own country, and that upon a fair-day too; yea, and as I think, it was Beelzebub, the chief lord of this fair, that invited Him to buy of his vanities; yea, would have made Him lord of the fair, would He but have done him reverence as He went through the town. Yea, because He was such a person of honour, Beelzebub had Him from street to street, and showed Him all the kingdoms of the world in a little time, that he might,

---

1. bawd: immoral woman.
2. viz.: Latin (videlicet)—namely, that is.

THE PILGRIM'S PROGRESS   **539**

if possible, **allure** that Blessed One to *cheapen*[3] and buy some of his vanities; but He had no mind to the merchandise, and, therefore, left the town without laying out so much as one farthing upon these vanities. This fair, therefore, is an ancient thing, of long standing, and a very great fair.

Now these pilgrims, as I said, must needs go through this fair. Well, so they did; but, behold, even as they entered into the fair, all the people in the fair were moved, and the town itself, as it were, in a hubbub about them: and that for several reasons: For,

First, The pilgrims were clothed with such kind of raiment as was **diverse** from the raiment of any that traded in that fair. The people, therefore, of the fair made a great gazing upon them; some said they were fools; some they were *bedlams*;[4] and some they are *outlandish*[5] men.

Secondly, And as they wondered at their apparel, so they did likewise at their speech; for few could understand what they said. They naturally spoke the language of Canaan; but they that kept the fair were the men of this world. So that from one end of the fair to the other they seemed *barbarians*[6] each to the other.

Thirdly, But that which did not a little amuse the merchandizers was, that these pilgrims set very light by all their wares. They cared not so much as to look upon them; and if they called upon them to buy, they would put their fingers in their ears, and cry, Turn away mine eyes from beholding vanity, and look upwards, signifying that their trade and traffic was in heaven.

One chanced mockingly, beholding the carriage of the men, to say unto them, What will ye buy? But they, looking gravely upon him, said, We buy the truth. At that, there was an occasion taken to despise the men the more; some mocking, some **taunting,** some speaking reproachfully, and some calling upon others to smite them. At last things came to a hubbub, and great stir in the fair, insomuch that all order was **confounded**. Now was word presently brought to the great one of the fair, who quickly came down and **deputed** some of his trusty friends to take those men into examination, about whom the fair was almost overturned. So the men were brought to examination; and they that sat upon them asked whence they came, whither they went, and what they did there in such an unusual garb. The men told them that they were pilgrims and strangers in the world, and that they were going to their own country, which was the heavenly Jerusalem, and that they had given no occasion to the men of the town, nor yet to the merchandizers, thus to abuse them, and to *let*[7] them in their journey, except it was for that, when one asked them what they would buy, they said they would buy the truth. But they that were appointed to examine them, did not believe them to be any other than bedlams and mad, or else such as came to put all things into a confusion in the fair. Therefore they took them and beat them, and besmeared them with dirt, and then put them into the cage, that they might be made a spectacle to all the men of the fair.

There, therefore, they lay for some time, and were made the object of any man's sport, or malice, or revenge; the great one of the fair laughing still at all that befell them. But the men being patient, and not rendering railing for railing, but contrariwise blessing, and giving good words for bad, and kindness for injuries done, some men in the fair, that were more observing and less prejudiced than the rest, began to *check*[8] and blame the baser sort for their continual abuses done by them to the men. They, therefore, in angry manner let fly at them again, counting them as bad as the men in the cage, and telling them, that they seemed

3. cheapen: to lower one's spiritual standards.
4. bedlams: insane persons.
5. outlandish: foreign, strange.
6. barbarians: foreigners.
7. let: hinder.
8. check: rebuke.

confederates, and should be made partakers of their misfortunes. The others replied, that, for aught they could see, the men were quiet and sober, and intended nobody any harm; and that there were many that traded in their fair, that were more worthy to be put into the cage, yea, and **pillory** too, than were the men that they had abused. Thus, after **divers** words had passed on both sides (the men behaving themselves all the while very wisely and soberly before them), they fell to some blows, and did harm one to another. Then were these two poor men brought before their examiners again, and there charged as being guilty of the late hubbub that had been in the fair. So they beat them pitifully, and hanged irons upon them, and led them in chains up and down the fair, for an example and a terror to others, lest any should speak in their behalf, or join themselves unto them. But Christian and Faithful behaved themselves yet more wisely, and received the **ignominy** and shame that was cast upon them, with so much meekness and patience, that it won to their side (though but few in comparison of the rest) several of the men in the fair. This put the other party yet into a greater rage, insomuch that they concluded the death of these two men. Wherefore they threatened, that the cage nor irons should serve their turn, but that they should die for the abuse they had done, and for deluding the men of the fair.

Then were they **remanded** to the cage again, until further order should be taken with them. So they put them in, and made their feet fast in the stocks.

Here, therefore, they called again to mind what they had heard from their faithful friend Evangelist, and were the more confirmed in their way and sufferings, by what he told them would happen to them. They also now comforted each other, that whose lot it was to suffer, even he should have the best of it; therefore each man secretly wished that he might have that preferment. But committing themselves to the all-wise disposal of Him that ruleth all things, with much content they abode in the condition in which they were, until they should be otherwise disposed of.

Then, a convenient time being appointed, they brought them forth to their trial, in order to their condemnation. When the time was come, they were brought before their enemies and **arraigned.** The judge's name was Lord Hategood; their **indictment** was one and the same in substance, though somewhat varying in form; the contents whereof was this: That they were enemies to, and disturbers of, their trade; that they had made commotions and divisions in the town, and had won a party to their own most dangerous opinions, in contempt of the law of their prince.

Then Faithful began to answer, that he had only set himself against that which hath set itself against Him that is higher than the highest. And, said he, as for disturbance, I make none, being myself a man of peace: the parties that were won to us, were won by beholding our truth and innocence, and they are only turned from the worse to the better. And as to the king you talk of, since he is Beelzebub, the enemy of our Lord, I defy him and all his angels.

Then proclamation was made, that they that had aught to say for their lord the king against the prisoner at the bar, should forthwith appear, and give in their evidence. So there came in three witnesses, to wit, Envy, Superstition, and Pickthank. They were then asked, if they knew the prisoner at the bar; and what they had to say for their lord the king against him.

Then stood forth Envy, and said to this effect: My lord, I have known this man a long time, and will attest upon my oath before this honourable bench, that he is—

JUDGE. Hold—give him his oath.

So they sware him. Then he said, My lord, this man, notwithstanding his **plausible** name, is one of the vilest men in our country; he neither regardeth prince nor people, law nor custom, but doth all that he can to possess all men with certain of his disloyal notions, which he in the general calls principles of faith and holiness. And, in particular, I heard him once myself affirm, that Christianity and the customs of our town of Vanity were **diametrically** opposite, and could not be reconciled. By which saying, my lord, he doth at once not only condemn all our laudable doings, but us in the doing of them.

JUDGE. Then did the judge say to him, Hast thou any more to say?

ENVY. My Lord, I could say much more, only I would not be tedious to the court. Yet if need be, when the other gentlemen have given in their evidence, rather than any thing shall be wanting that will **dispatch** him, I will enlarge my testimony against him. So he was bid stand by.

Then they called Superstition, and bid him look upon the prisoner. They also asked, what he could say for their lord the king against him. Then they sware him; so he began.

SUPER. My Lord, I have no great acquaintance with this man, nor do I desire to have further knowledge of him. However, this I know, that he is a very **pestilent** fellow, from some discourse that the other day I had with him in this town; for then, talking with him, I heard him say, that our religion was nought, and such by which a man could by no means please God. Which sayings of his, my lord, your lordship very well knows what necessarily thence will follow, to wit, that we still do worship in vain, are yet in our sins, and finally shall be damned: and this is that which I have to say.

Then was Pickthank sworn, and bid say what he knew in behalf of their lord and king against the prisoner at the bar.

PICK. My lord, and you gentlemen all, this fellow I have known of a long time, and have heard him speak things that ought not to be spoken; for he hath railed on our noble prince Beelzebub, and hath spoken contemptibly of his honourable friends, whose names are, the Lord Old Man, the Lord Carnal Delight, the Lord Luxurious, the Lord Desire of Vain Glory, my old Lord **Lechery**, Sir Having Greedy, with all the rest of our nobility: and he hath said, moreover, that if all men were of his mind, if possible, there is not one of these noblemen should have any longer a being in this town. Besides, he hath not been afraid to rail on you, my lord, who are now appointed to be his judge, calling you an ungodly villain, with many other such

like **vilifying** terms, with which he hath bespattered most of the **gentry** of our town.

When this Pickthank had told his tale, the judge directed his speech to the prisoner at the bar, saying, Thou *runagate*,[9] **heretic**, and traitor, hast thou heard what these honest gentlemen have witnessed against thee?

FAITH. May I speak a few words in my own defence?

JUDGE. Sirrah, Sirrah, thou deservest to live no longer, but to be slain immediately upon the place; yet, that all men may see our gentleness towards thee, let us hear what thou vile runagate, hast to say.

FAITH. 1. I say, then, in answer to what Mr. Envy hath spoken, I never said aught but this, that what rule, or laws, or custom, or people, were flat against the Word of God, are diametrically opposite to Christianity. If I have said **amiss** in this, convince me of my error, and I am ready here before you to make my **recantation.**

2. As to the second, to wit, Mr. Superstition and his charge against me, I said only this, that in the worship of God there is required a divine faith; but there can be no divine faith without a divine revelation of the will of God. Therefore whatever is thrust into the worship of God, that is not agreeable to divine revelation, cannot be done but by a human faith, which faith will not be profitable to eternal life.

3. As to what Mr. Pickthank hath said, I say (avoiding terms, as that I am said to rail and the like), that the prince of this town, with all the *rabblement*[10] his attendants by this gentleman named, are more fit for a being in hell than in this town and country. And so the Lord have mercy upon me.

Then the Judge called to the jury (who all this while stood by to hear and observe), Gentlemen of the jury, you see this man about whom so great an uproar hath been made in this town; you have also heard what these worthy gentlemen have witnessed against him; also you have heard his reply and confession: it lieth now in your breasts to hang him, or save his life; but

_____

9. runagate: apostate, rebel.
10. rabblement: noisy mob.

yet I think meet to instruct you in our law.

There was an act made in the days of Pharaoh the great, servant to our prince, that, lest those of a contrary religion should multiply, and grow too strong for him, their males should be thrown into the river. There was also an act made in the days of Nebuchadnezzar the great, another of his servants, that whoever would not fall down and worship his golden image, should be thrown into a fiery furnace. There was also an act made in the days of Darius, that whoso for some time called upon any God but him, should be cast into the lions' den. Now the substance of these laws this rebel has broken, not only in thought (which is not to be borne), but also in word and deed; which must, therefore, needs be intolerable.

For that of Pharaoh, his law was made upon **supposition**, to prevent mischief, no crime yet being apparent; but here is a crime apparent. For the second and third, you see he disputeth against our religion; and for the treason he hath confessed, he deserveth to die the death.

Then went the jury out, whose names were Mr. Blindman, Mr. No-good, Mr. Malice, Mr. Love-lust, Mr. Live-loose, Mr. Heady, Mr. High-mind, Mr. Enmity, Mr. Liar, Mr. Cruelty, Mr. Hate-light, and Mr. Implacable; who every one gave in his private verdict against him among themselves, and afterwards **unanimously** concluded to bring him in guilty before the judge. And first among themselves, Mr. Blindman, the foreman, said, I see clearly that this man is a heretic. Then said Mr. No-good, Away with such a fellow from the earth. Ay, said Mr. Malice, for I hate the very looks of him. Then said Mr. Love-lust, I could never endure him. Nor I, said Mr. Live-loose, for he would always be condemning my way. Hang him, hang him, said Mr. Heady. A sorry scrub, said Mr. High-mind. My heart riseth against him, said Mr. Enmity. He is a rogue, said Mr. Liar. Hanging is too good for him, said Mr. Cruelty. Let's dispatch him out of the way, said Mr. Hate-light. Then said Mr. Implacable, Might I have all the world given me, I could not be reconciled to him; therefore let us forthwith bring him in guilty of death.

And so they did; therefore he was presently condemned to be had from the place where he was, to the place from whence he came, and there to be put to the most cruel death that could be invented.

They, therefore, brought him out, to do with him according to their law; and first they scourged him, then they buffeted him, then they lanced his flesh with knives; after that they stoned him with stones, then pricked him with their swords; and last of all they burned him to ashes at the stake. Thus came Faithful to his end.

Now I saw, that there stood behind the multitude a chariot and a couple of horses, waiting for Faithful, who (so soon as his adversaries had dispatched him) was taken up into it, and straightway was carried up through the clouds with sound of trumpet, the nearest way to the celestial gate.

But as for Christian, he had some respite, and was remanded back to prison; so he there remained for a space. But He that overrules all things, having the power of their rage in His own hand, so wrought it about that Christian for that time escaped them, and went his way.

And as he went he sang, saying,

Well, Faithful, thou hast faithfully profest
Unto thy Lord; with whom thou shalt be
    blest,
When faithless ones, with all their vain
    delights,
Are crying out under their hellish plights:
Sing, Faithful, sing, and let thy name survive.
For though they killed thee, thou art yet
    alive.

Meditating for Meaning

Often before a time of severe trial and hardship, the Lord brings special comfort and strength to Christians. Evangelist's visit with the pilgrims represents such preparation of the heart for suffering.

1. Bunyan had a great working knowledge of Scripture and was able to weave its exact phraseology into his writings. All but three of the following phrases from Evangelist's sermon are from Scripture. Test your own Bible background by first trying to pick out those three items that are not from the Bible. Then match the others with the references from which they come.

   a. tribulation enter into the kingdom
   b. bonds and afflictions abide
   c. the truth of these testimonies   1 Samuel 4:9
   d. hardly beset with enemies   Acts 14:22
   e. seal the testimony   Acts 20:23
   f. faithful unto death   1 Peter 4:19
   g. a crown of life   Revelation 2:10 (2)
   h. quit yourselves like men   1 Corinthians 16:13
   i. commit the keeping of your souls

2. What, according to Evangelist's prediction, will happen in the town they are approaching?

3. Vanity Fair is nearly as old as the world.
    a. Who set up Vanity Fair?
    b. Why was it set up?
    c. All the merchandise sold at Vanity Fair can be classed into what three categories? (1 John 2:16)

4. Why must the pilgrims go through this town?

5. To which of Jesus' three temptations does Bunyan refer soon after he says Beelzebub would have made him lord of the fair? (Matthew 4:3-10)

6. The pilgrims find Vanity Fair in a hubbub soon after they enter.
    a. What three peculiarities of the pilgrims cause this?
    b. What are their two answers to those who would sell them vanities?

7. True to Evangelist's prophesy, the pilgrims meet with suffering at the fair.
    a. How do Christian and Faithful respond to persecution?
    b. What effect does their response to persecution have on the people of the fair?

8. When the pilgrims are finally brought to trial, the judge brings three accusations against them. List the three accusations and give Faithful's answer to each.

9. Set up a chart to show the witnesses against Faithful.

Name of witness	Testimony of witness	Faithful's reply

10. What does Superstition say that is very characteristic of him?

11. What irony do you see in the judge's concern to have Envy properly sworn?

12. The Judge informs the jury of three former laws by which they can condemn Faithful. But he does not tell them that God had overturned these laws. Give each law and tell how God made them of none effect.

13. Bunyan does a masterful job of characterization with the twelve jurors. Each juror's comment is in keeping with his name. "Out of the abundance of the heart the mouth speaketh" (Matthew 12:34). Select four jurors and show how their comments fit their characters.

14. Faithful receives the preferment which Evangelist prophesied.
    a. Describe Faithful's death.
    b. What reality can the crowd not see?

15. What happens to Christian?

Chapter 14: Hopeful Joins Christian

Now I saw in my dream, that Christian went not forth alone; for there was one whose name was Hopeful (being so made by the beholding of Christian and Faithful in their words and behaviour, in their sufferings at the fair), who joined himself unto him, and entering into a brotherly covenant, told him that he would be his companion. Thus one died to bear testimony to the truth, and another rises out of his ashes to be a companion with Christian in his pilgrimage. This Hopeful also told Christian, that there were many more of the men in the fair that would take their time and follow after.

So I saw, that quickly after they were got out of the fair they overtook one that was going before them, whose name was By-ends; so they said to him, What countryman, sir? and how far go you this way? He told them, that he came from the town of Fair-speech, and he was going to the Celestial City; but told them not his name.

From Fair-speech? said Christian; is there any good that lives there?

BY-ENDS. Yes, said By-ends, I hope.

CHR. Pray, sir, what may I call you? said Christian.

BY-ENDS. I am a stranger to you, and you to me: if you be going this way, I shall be glad of your company; if not, I must be content.

CHR. This town of Fair-speech, said Christian, I have heard of it; and, as I remember, they say it's a wealthy place.

BY-ENDS. Yes, I will assure you that it is; and I have very many rich kindred there.

CHR. Pray who are your kindred there, if a man may be so bold?

BY-ENDS. Almost the whole town; and in particular, my Lord Turn-about, my Lord Time-server, my Lord Fair-speech from whose ancestors that town first took its name; also Mr. Smooth-man, Mr. Facing-both-ways, Mr. Anything; and the parson of our parish, Mr. Two-tongues, was my mother's own brother, by father's side; and to tell you the truth, I am become a gentleman of good quality; yet my great-grandfather was but a waterman, looking one way and rowing another, and I got most of my estate by the same occupation.

CHR. Are you a married man?

BY-ENDS. Yes, and my wife is a very virtuous woman, the daughter of a virtuous woman; she was my Lady **Feigning's** daughter, therefore she came of a very honourable family, and is arrived to such a pitch of breeding, that she knows how to carry it to all, even to prince and peasant. 'Tis true, we somewhat differ in religion from those of the stricter sort, yet but in two small points: First, we never strive against wind and tide. Secondly, we are always most zealous when Religion goes in his silver slippers; we love much to walk with him in the street, if the sun shines, and the people **applaud** him.

Then Christian stepped a little aside to his fellow Hopeful, saying, It runs in my mind that this is one By-ends, of Fair-speech; and if it be he, we have as very a knave in our company as dwelleth in all these parts. Then said Hopeful,

Ask him; methinks he should not be ashamed of his name. So Christian came up with him again, and said, Sir, you talk as if you knew something more than all the world doth; and, if I take not my mark amiss, I deem I have half a guess of you. Is not your name Mr. By-ends, of Fair-speech?

BY-ENDS. This is not my name, but indeed, it is a nickname that is given me by some that cannot abide me, and I must be content to bear it as a reproach, as other good men have borne theirs before me.

CHR. But did you never give an occasion to men to call you by this name?

BY-ENDS. Never, never! The worst that ever I did to give them an occasion to give me this name was, that I had always the luck to jump in my judgment with the present way of the times, whatever it was, and my chance was to get thereby; but if things are thus cast upon me, let me count them a blessing; but let not the malicious load me, therefore, with reproach.

CHR. I thought, indeed, that you were the man that I heard of; and to tell you what I think, I fear this name belongs to you more properly than you are willing we should think it doth.

BY-ENDS. Well, if you will thus imagine, I cannot help it; you shall find me a fair company-keeper, if you will still admit me your associate.

CHR. If you will go with us, you must go against the wind and tide; the which, I perceive, is against your opinion: you must also own Religion in his rags, as well as when in his silver slippers; and stand by him, too, when bound in irons, as well as when he walketh the streets with applause.

BY-ENDS. You must not **impose**, nor lord it over my faith; leave me to my liberty, and let me go with you.

CHR. Not a step farther, unless you will do in what I propound as we.

Then said By-ends, I shall never desert my old principles, since they are harmless and profitable. If I may not go with you, I must do as I did before you overtook me, even go by myself, until some overtake me that will be glad of my company.

Now I saw in my dream, that Christian and Hopeful forsook him, and kept their distance before him; but one of them, looking back, saw three men following Mr. By-ends; and behold, as they came up with him, he made them a very low *congee*;[1] and they also gave him a compliment. The men's names were Mr. Hold-the-world, Mr. Money-love, and Mr. Save-all; men that Mr. By-ends had formerly been acquainted with, for in their minority they were schoolfellows, and were taught by one Mr. Grip-man, a schoolmaster in Love-gain, which is a market-town in the county of Coveting, in the North. This schoolmaster taught them the art of getting, either by violence, *cozenage*,[2] flattery, lying, or by putting on a **guise** of religion; and these four gentlemen had attained much of the art of their master, so that they could each of them have kept such a school themselves.

Well, when they had, as I said, thus saluted each other, Mr. Money-love said to Mr. By-ends, Who are they upon the road before us? (for Christian and Hopeful were yet within view).

BY-ENDS. They are a couple of far country-men, that, after their **mode**, are going on pilgrimage.

MONEY-LOVE. Alas! why did they not stay, that we might have had their good company? for they, and we, and you, sir, I hope are all going on a pilgrimage.

BY-ENDS. We are so, indeed; but the men before us are so rigid, and love so much their own notions, and do also lightly esteem the opinions of others, that let a man be ever so godly, yet if he jumps not with them in all things, they thrust him quite out of their company.

SAVE-ALL. That's bad; but we read of some that are righteous overmuch, and such men's rigidness prevails with them to judge and condemn all but themselves. But I pray, what, and how many, were the things wherein you differed?

BY-ENDS. Why they, after their headstrong manner, conclude that it is duty to rush on their journey all weathers; and I am for waiting for wind and tide. They are for hazarding all for God at a *clap*;[3] and I am for taking all advantages to secure my life and estate. They are for holding their notions, though all other men are against them; but I am for religion in what, and so far as, the times and my safety will bear it. They are for Religion when in rags and contempt; but I am for him when he walks in his golden slippers, in the sunshine, and with applause.

MR. HOLD-THE-WORLD. Ay, and hold you there still, good Mr. By-ends; for my part, I can count him but a fool, that having the liberty to keep what he has, shall be so unwise to lose it. Let us be wise as serpents. It's best to make hay when the sun shines. You see how the bee lieth still all winter, and bestirs her only when she can have profit with pleasure. God sends sometimes rain, and sometimes sunshine; if they be such fools to go through the first, yet let us be content to take fair weather along with us. For my part, I like that religion best that will stand with the security of God's good blessings unto us; for who can imagine, that is ruled by his reason, since God has bestowed upon us the good things of this life, but that He would have us keep them for His sake? Abraham and Solomon grew rich in religion; and Job says, that a good man shall lay up gold as dust; but he must not be such as the men before us, if they be as you have described them.

MR. SAVE-ALL. I think that we are all agreed in this matter and therefore there needs no more words about it.

MR. MONEY-LOVE. No, there needs no more words about this matter indeed; for he that believes neither Scripture nor reason (and you see we have both on our side), neither knows his own liberty nor seeks his own safety.

MR. BY-ENDS. My brethren, we are, as you see, going all on pilgrimage; and for our better diversion from things that are bad, give me

---

1. congee: bow (usually spelled *congé*).
2. cozenage: cheating; deceiving by coaxing or shrewd trickery.
3. clap: sudden misfortune.

leave to propound unto you this question.

Suppose a man, a minister or a tradesman, etc., should have an advantage lie before him to get the good blessings of this life, yet so as that he can by no means come by them, except, in appearance at least, he becomes extraordinary zealous in some points of religion that he meddled not with before, may he not use this means to attain his end, and yet be a right honest man?

MR. MONEY. I see the bottom of your question; and, with these gentlemen's good leave, I will endeavour to shape you an answer. And first, to speak to your question as it concerns a minister himself: suppose a minister, a worthy man, possessed but of a very small benefice, and has in his eye a greater, more fat and plump by far; he has also now an opportunity of getting of it, yet so as by being more studious, by preaching more frequently and zealously, and, because the temper of the people requires it, by altering of some of his principles; for my part, I see no reason but a man may do this, provided he has a call, ay, and more a great deal besides, and yet be an honest man. For why?

1. His desire of a greater benefice is lawful (this cannot be contradicted), since 'tis set before him by Providence; so then he may get it if he can, making no question for conscience sake.

2. Besides, his desire after that benefice makes him more studious, a more zealous preacher, etc., and so makes him a better man, yea, makes him better improve his parts, which is according to the mind of God.

3. Now, as for his complying with the temper of his people, by dissenting, to serve them, some of his principles, this argueth, 1. That he is of a self-denying temper. 2. Of a sweet and winning deportment. 3. And so more fit for the ministerial function.

4. I conclude, then, that a minister that changes a small for a great, should not, for so doing, be judged as covetous; but rather, since he is improved in his parts and industry thereby, be counted as one that pursues his call, and the opportunity put into his hand to do good.

And now to the second part of the question, which concerns the tradesman you mentioned. Suppose such an one to have but a poor employ in the world, but by becoming religious, he may mend his market, perhaps get a rich wife, or more and far better customers to his shop; for my part, I see no reason but that this may be lawfully done. For why?

1. To become religious is a virtue, by what means soever a man becomes so.

2. Nor is it unlawful to get a rich wife, or more custom to my shop.

3. Besides, the man that gets these by becoming religious, gets that which is good of them that are good, by becoming good himself; so then here is a good wife, and good customers, and good gain, and all these by becoming religious, which is good; therefore, to become religious to get all these is a good and profitable design.

This answer thus made by Mr. Money-love to Mr. By-ends' question, was highly applauded by them all; wherefore they concluded upon the whole, that it was most wholesome and advantageous. And because, as they thought, no man was able to contradict it, and because Christian and Hopeful were yet within call, they jointly agreed to assault them with the question as soon as they overtook them; and the rather, because they had opposed Mr. By-ends before. So they called after them and they stopped and stood still till they came up to them; but they concluded as they went, that not Mr. By-ends, but old Mr. Hold-the-World, should propound the question to them, because, as they supposed, their answer to him would be without the remainder of that heat that was kindled betwixt Mr. By-ends and them at their parting a little before.

So they came up to each other, and after a short salutation, Mr. Hold-the-World propounded the question to Christian and his fellow, and bid them to answer it if they could.

CHR. Then said Christian, Even a babe in religion may answer ten thousand such questions. For if it be unlawful to follow Christ for loaves, as it is; how much more is it abominable to make of Him and religion a stalkinghorse to get and enjoy the world! Nor do we find any other than heathens, hypocrites, devils, and witches, that are of this opinion.

1. Heathens: for when Hamor and Shechem had a mind to the daughter and cattle of Jacob, and saw that there was no way for them to come at them but by becoming circumcised, they say to their companions, If every male of us be circumcised, as they are circumcised, shall not their cattle, and their substance, and every beast of theirs be ours? Their daughters and their cattle were that which they sought to obtain, and their religion the stalking-horse they made use of to come at them. Read the whole story.

2. The hypocritical Pharisees were also of this religion: long prayers were their pretence; but to get widows' houses was their intent, and greater damnation was from God their judgment.

3. Judas the devil was also of this religion: he was religious for the bag, that he might be possessed of what was therein; but he was lost, cast away, and the very son of perdition.

4. Simon the witch was of this religion too; for he would have had the Holy Ghost, that he might have got money therewith; and his sentence from Peter's mouth was according.

5. Neither will it out of my mind, but that that man that takes up religion for the world, will throw away religion for the world; for so surely as Judas *designed*[4] the world in becoming religious, so surely did he also sell religion and his Master for the same. To answer the question, therefore, affirmatively, as I perceive you have done, and to accept of, as authentic, such answer, is heathenish, hypocritical, and devilish; and your reward will he according to your works.

Then they stood staring one upon another, but had not wherewith to answer Christian. Hopeful also approved of the soundness of Christian's answer; so there was a great silence among them. Mr. By-ends and his company also staggered, and kept behind, that Christian and Hopeful might outgo them. Then said Christian to his fellow, If these men cannot stand before the sentence of men, what will they do with the sentence of God? And if they are mute when dealt with by vessels of clay, what will they do when they shall be rebuked by the flames of a devouring fire!

Then Christian and Hopeful outwent them again, and went till they came at a delicate plain, called Ease, where they went with much content; but that plain was but narrow, so they were quickly got over it. Now at the farther side of that plain was a little hill, called Lucre, and in that hill a silver mine, which some of them that had formerly gone that way, because of the rarity of it, had turned aside to see; but going too near the brim of the pit, the ground, being deceitful under them broke, and they were slain: some also had been maimed there, and could not, to their dying day, be their own men again.

Then I saw in my dream, that a little off the road, over against the silver mine, stood *Demas*[5] (gentleman-like) to call passengers to come and see; who said to Christian and his fellow, Ho! turn aside hither, and I will show you a thing.

CHR. What thing so deserving as to turn us out of the way to see it?

DEMAS. Here is a silver mine, and some digging in it for treasure; if you will come, with a little pains you may richly provide for yourselves.

HOPE. Then said Hopeful, Let us go see.

CHR. Not I, said Christian, I have heard of this place before now, and how many there have been slain; and, besides, that treasure is a snare to those that seek it, for it hindereth them in their pilgrimage.

Then Christian called to Demas, saying, Is not the place dangerous? Hath it not hindered many in their pilgrimage?

DEMAS. Not very dangerous, except to those that are careless; but withal, he blushed as he spake.

CHR. Then said Christian to Hopeful, Let us not stir a step, but still keep on our way.

HOPE. I will warrant you, when By-ends comes up, if he hath the same invitation as we, he will turn in thither to see.

---

4. designed: had intent concerning.

5. 2 Timothy 4:10.

CHR. No doubt thereof, for his principles lead him that way, and a hundred to one but he dies there.

DEMAS. Then Demas called again, saying, But will you not come over and see?

CHR. Then Christian roundly answered, saying, Demas, thou art an enemy to the right ways of the Lord of this way, and hast been already condemned for thine own turning aside, by one of His Majesty's judges, and why seekest thou to bring us into the like condemnation? Besides, if we at all turn aside, our Lord the King will certainly hear thereof, and will there put us to shame, where we would stand with boldness before Him.

Demas cried again, that he also was one of their fraternity; and that if they would tarry a little, he also himself would walk with them.

CHR. Then said Christian, What is thy name? Is it not the same by the which I have called thee?

DEMAS. Yes, my name is Demas; I am the son of Abraham.

CHR. I know you; *Gehazi*[6] was your great-grandfather and Judas your father, and you have trod their steps; it is but a devilish prank that thou usest; thy father was hanged for a traitor, and thou deservest no better reward. Assure thyself that when we come to the King, we will do Him word of this thy behaviour. Thus they went their way.

By this time By-ends and his companions were come again within sight, and they at the first **beck** went over to Demas. Now whether they fell into the pit by looking over the brink thereof, or whether they went down to dig, or whether they were smothered in the bottom by the **damps** that commonly arise, of these things I am not certain; but this I observed, that they never were seen again in the way. Then sang Christian:

> By-ends and silver Demas both agree;
> One calls, the other runs, that he may be
> A sharer in his lucre: so these do
> Take up in this world, and no farther go.

Now I saw, that just on the other side of this plain, the pilgrims came to a place where stood an old monument hard by the highway-side, at the sight of which they were both concerned, because of the strangeness of the form thereof; for it seemed to them as if it had been a woman transformed into the shape of a pillar. Here therefore, they stood looking and looking upon it, but could not for a time tell what they should make thereof. At last Hopeful espied written above upon the head thereof a writing in an unusual hand; but he being no scholar, called to Christian (for he was learned) to see if he could pick out the meaning: so he came, and after a little laying of letters together, he found the same to be this, Remember Lot's wife. So he read it to his fellow; after which they both concluded that that was the pillar of salt into which Lot's wife was turned, for her looking back with a covetous heart, when she was going from Sodom for safety, which sudden and amazing sight gave them occasion of this discourse.

CHR. Ah, my brother! this is a seasonable sight, it came **opportunely** to us after the invitation which Demas gave us to come over to view the Hill Lucre; and had we gone over, as he desired us, and as thou wast inclining to do, my brother, we had, for aught I know, been made like this woman a **spectacle** for those that shall come after, to behold.

HOPE. I am sorry that I was so foolish, and am made to wonder that I am not now as Lot's wife; for wherein was the difference 'twixt her sin and mine? She only looked back, and I had a desire to go see. Let grace be adored; and let me be ashamed that ever such a thing should be in mine heart.

CHR. Let us take notice of what we see here, for our help for time to come. This woman escaped one judgment, for she fell not by the destruction of Sodom; yet she was destroyed by another, as we see; she is turned into a pillar of salt.

HOPE. True, and she may be to us both caution and example; caution, that we should shun her sin, or a sign of what judgment will overtake such as shall not be prevented by this cau-

---

6. 2 Kings 5:20-27.

tion; so Korah, Dathan, and Abiram, with the two hundred and fifty men that perished in their sin, did also become a sign or example to beware. But above all, I muse at one thing, to wit, how Demas and his fellows can stand so confidently yonder to look for that treasure, which this woman but for looking behind her after (for we read not that she stepped one foot out of the way) was turned into a pillar of salt; specially since the judgment which overtook her did but make her an example within sight of where they are; for they cannot choose but see her, did they but lift up their eyes.

CHR. It is a thing to be wondered at, and it argueth that their hearts are grown desperate in that case; and I cannot tell who to compare them to so fitly, as to them that pick pockets in the presence of the judge, or that will cut purses under the gallows. It is said of the men of Sodom, that they were sinners exceedingly, because they were sinners 'before the Lord,' that is, in His eye-sight, and notwithstanding the kindnesses that He had showed them; for the land of Sodom was now like the garden of Eden heretofore. This, therefore, provoked Him the more to jealousy, and made their plague as hot as the fire of the Lord out of heaven could make it. And it is most rationally to be concluded, that such, even such as these are, they that shall sin in the sight, yea, and that too in despite of such examples that are set continually before them to caution them to the contrary, must be partakers of severest judgments.

HOPE. Doubtless thou hast said the truth; but what a mercy is it that neither thou, but especially I, am not made myself this example! This ministereth occasion to us to thank God, to fear before Him, and always to remember Lot's wife.

Meditating for Meaning

1. If Bunyan would have been entirely consistent with his symbolism, Hopeful could not join Christian at this point in the pilgrimage without having experienced something else first. What is lacking at the opening of this chapter about what Hopeful experienced?

2. By-ends is a man who will use any means in order to get *his* ends accomplished. He will be careful to conceal his selfish reason for doing something and will try to make his actions appear virtuous.
   a. Why would such a man be careful not to tell his name?
   b. Explain how the occupation of his great-grandfather very well describes By-ends' character.
   c. How is By-ends' character related to the town he is from?

3. List By-ends' seven relatives and after each name write a short phrase describing what kind of person he would be.

4. Explain By-ends' attitude toward religion by interpreting these expressions:
   a. "We never strike against wind and tide."
   b. "We are most zealous when religion goes in his silver slippers."

5. By-ends shrewdly denies Christian's accusation.
   a. What defence does By-ends give for his name?
   b. He sees no reason to give up his ways since, so far as he is concerned, his ways are both _____ and _____ .
   c. What is wrong with his ways?
6. By-ends is not alone in these characteristics.
   a. Name By-ends' schoolfellows.
   b. Who had been their teacher?
   c. Where was the school?
   d. What had they been taught?
7. In describing the pilgrims to his friends, By-ends says they are rigid and headstrong. In what four ways do the pilgrims approach life, which By-ends gives as a basis for this description?
8. The pilgrims now come to the Plain of Ease. What is symbolized by the fact that the plain is narrow?
9. Considering the meaning of *lucre*, why does the Hill Lucre naturally follow the Plain of Ease?
10. Demas is the advertising agent for the silver mine.
    a. Why is he so named? (2 Timothy 4:10)
    b. What warning is there in God's Word against the dangers of the silver mine? (1 Timothy 6:9-11)
    c. What might be some "silver mines" in the life of a present-day Christian?
    d. How is Gehazi a great-grandfather and Judas a father to Demas? Consider what was the downfall of each.
11. Why do By-ends and his companions hearken to Demas so readily?
12. On the other side of the plain the pilgrims come to a pillar of salt, a monument of Lot's wife.
    a. What did Lot's wife and Demas have in common?
    b. Why does Hopeful have a good reason to adore grace?
    c. How is a person who pursues money after he knows about Lot's wife like a man who would "pick pockets in the presence of the judge"?

Chapter 15: Christian and Hopeful Meet Giant Despair at Doubting Castle

Defining for Comprehension

Choose the word or phrase below which most nearly defines each word at the left as it is used in this allegory.

1. **surfeits**
   a. sickness from overeating
   b. denials of pleasure
   c. white-capped waves

2. **incident**
   a. likely
   b. accompanying
   c. surprising

3. **stile**
   a. steps over fence
   b. mannerism
   c. eye sore

4. **diffidence**
   a. rebellion
   b. lack of confidence
   c. result

5. **rating**
   a. stacking up
   b. reproving angrily
   c. improving

6. **moderate**
   a. rebuild
   b. make less severe
   c. encourage

7. **valiant**
   a. vicious
   b. dependent
   c. brave

8. **passionate**
   a. full of emotion
   b. impatient
   c. remorseful

9. **jurisdiction**
   a. sentence
   b. conversation
   c. range of control

10. **contrive**
    a. endeavor
    b. plan
    c. quarrel

I saw then that they went on their way to a pleasant river, which David the king called the river of God, but John, the river of the water of life. Now their way lay just upon the bank of the river: here, therefore, Christian and his companion walked with great delight; they drank also of the water of the river, which was pleasant and enlivening to their weary spirits. Besides, on the banks of this river, on either side, were green trees for all manner of fruit; and the leaves to prevent **surfeits**, and other diseases that are **incident** to those that heat their blood by travels. On either side of the river was also a meadow, curiously beautified with lilies; and it was green all the year long. In this meadow they lay down and slept, for here they might lie down safely. When they awoke, they gathered again of the fruit of the trees, and drank again of the water of the river, and then lay down again to sleep. Thus they did several days and nights. Then they sang:

> Behold ye how these crystal streams do glide,
> To comfort pilgrims by the highway-side.
> The meadows green, besides their fragrant smell,
> Yield dainties for them; and he that can tell
> What pleasant fruit, yea, leaves, these trees do yield,
> Will soon sell all, that he may buy this field.

So when they were disposed to go on (for they were not as yet at their journey's end), they ate and drank, and departed.

Now I beheld in my dream, that they had not journeyed far, but the river and the way for a time parted, at which they were not a little sorry; yet they durst not go out of the way.

Now the way from the river was rough, and their feet tender by reason of their travels; so the souls of the pilgrims were much discouraged because of the way. Wherefore still as they went on, they wished for better way. Now a little before them, there was on the left hand of the road a meadow and a **stile** to go over into it, and that meadow is called By-path Meadow. Then said Christian to his fellow, If this Meadow lieth along by our way-side, let's go over into it. Then he went to the stile to see, and behold a path lay along by the way on the other side of the fence. 'Tis according to my wish, said Christian; here is the easiest going; come, good Hopeful, and let us go over.

HOPE. But, how if this path should lead us out of the way?

CHR. That's not like, said the other. Look, doth it not go along by the way-side? So Hopeful, being persuaded by his fellow, went after him over the stile. When they were gone over, and were got into the path, they found it very easy for their feet; and withal, they, looking before them, espied a man walking as they did, and his name was Vain-Confidence: so they called after him, and asked him whither that way led. He said, To the celestial gate. Look, said Christian, did not I tell you so? by this you may see we are right. So they followed, and he went before them. But behold the night came on, and it grew very dark; so that they that were behind lost the sight of him that went before.

He therefore that went before (Vain-Confidence by name), not seeing the way before him, fell into a deep pit, which was on purpose there made by the prince of those grounds to catch vain-glorious fools withal, and was dashed to pieces with his fall.

Now Christian and his fellow heard him fall. So they called to know the matter, but there was none to answer, only they heard a groaning. Then said Hopeful, Where are we now? Then was his fellow silent, as mistrusting that he had led him out of the way; and now it began to rain, and thunder and lighten in a very dreadful manner, and the water rose amain.

Then Hopeful groaned in himself, saying, Oh that I had kept on my way!

CHR. Who could have thought that this path should have led us out of the way?

HOPE. I was afraid on't at very first, and therefore gave you that gentle caution. I would have spoke plainer, but that you are older than I.

CHR. Good brother, be not offended; I am sorry I have brought thee out of the way, and that I have put thee into such imminent danger. Pray, my brother, forgive me; I did not do it of an evil intent.

HOPE. Be comforted, my brother, for I forgive thee; and believe, too, that this shall be for our good.

CHR. I am glad I have with me a merciful brother; but we must not stand thus: let's try to go back again.

HOPE. But, good brother, let me go before.

CHR. No, if you please, let me go first, that if there be any danger, I may be first therein, because by my means we are both gone out of the way.

HOPE. No, said Hopeful, you shall not go first, for your mind being troubled may lead you out of the way again. Then for their encouragement they heard the voice of one saying, Let thine heart be towards the highway, even the way that thou wentest; turn again. But by this time the waters were greatly risen, by reason of which the way of going back was very dangerous. (Then I thought that it is easier going out of the way when we are in, than going in when we are out). Yet they adventured to go back; but it was so dark, and the flood was so high, that in their going back they had like to have been drowned nine or ten times.

Neither could they, with all the skill they had, get again to the stile that night. Wherefore, at last, lighting under a little shelter, they sat down there till the day brake; but, being weary, they fell asleep. Now there was, not far from the place where they lay, a castle, called Doubting Castle, the owner whereof was Giant Despair, and it was in his grounds they were now sleeping: wherefore he, getting up in the morning early, and walking up and down in his fields, caught Christian and Hopeful asleep in his grounds. Then with a grim and surly voice he bid them awake, and asked them whence they were, and what they did in his

grounds. They told him they were pilgrims, and that they had lost their way. Then said the giant, You have this night trespassed on me by trampling in and lying on my ground, and therefore you must go along with me. So they were forced to go, because he was stronger than they. They also had but little to say, for they knew themselves in a fault. The giant, therefore, drove them before him, and put them into his castle, into a very dark dungeon, nasty, and stinking to the spirits of these two men. Here, then, they lay from Wednesday morning till Saturday night, without one bit of bread or drop of drink, or light, or any to ask how they did: they were, therefore, here in evil case, and were far from friends and acquaintance. Now in this place Christian had double sorrow, because 'twas through his unadvised haste that they were brought into this distress.

Now Giant Despair had a wife, and her name was **Diffidence**: so when he was gone to bed, he told his wife what he had done, to wit, that he had taken a couple of prisoners, and cast them into his dungeon for trespassing on his grounds. Then he asked her also what he had best to do further to them. So she asked him what they were, whence they came, and whither they were bound, and he told her. Then she counselled him that when he arose in the morning he should beat them without any mercy. So when he arose, he getteth him a grievous crab-tree *cudgel*,[1] and goes down into

the dungeon to them, and there first falls to **rating** of them as if they were dogs, although they gave him never a word of distaste. Then he falls upon them, and beats them fearfully, in such sort that they were not able to help themselves, or to turn them upon the floor. This done, he withdraws and leaves them there to condole their misery, and to mourn under their distress: so all that day they spent the time in nothing but sighs and bitter lamentations. The next night she, talking with her husband about them further, and understanding they were yet alive, did advise him to counsel them to make away themselves. So when morning was come, he goes to them in a surly manner, as before, and perceiving them to be very sore with the stripes that he had given them the day before, he told them, that since they were never like to come out of that place, their only way would be forthwith to make an end of themselves, either with knife, halter, or poison: for why, said he, should you choose life, seeing it is attended with so much bitterness? But they desired him to let them go. With that he looked ugly upon them, and rushing to them, had doubtless made an end of them himself, but that he fell into one of his fits (for he sometimes, in sunshiny weather, fell into fits), and lost for a time the use of his hand; wherefore he withdrew, and left them as before to consider what to do. Then did the prisoners consult between themselves, whether 'twas best to take his counsel or no; and thus they began to discourse:

CHR. Brother, said Christian, what shall we do? The life that we now live is miserable. For my part, I know not whether is best to live thus, or to die out of hand. My soul chooseth strangling rather than life, and the grave is more easy for me than this dungeon. Shall we be ruled by the giant?

HOPE. Indeed our present condition is dreadful, and death would be far more welcome to me than thus for ever to abide; but yet

---

1. cudgel: stout club.

let us consider, the Lord of the country to which we are going hath said, Thou shalt do no murder, no, not to another man's person; much more then are we forbidden to take his counsel to kill ourselves. Besides, he that kills another, can but commit murder upon his body; but for one to kill himself, is to kill body and soul at once. And, moreover, my brother, thou talkest of ease in the grave; but hast thou forgotten the hell, whither for certain the murderers go? For no murderer hath eternal life, etc. And let us consider again, that all the law is not in the hand of Giant Despair; others, so far as I can understand, have been taken by him as well as we, and yet have escaped out of his hand. Who knows but that God, that made the world, may cause that Giant Despair may die; or that at some time or other he may forget to lock us in; or but he may, in short time, have another of his fits before us, and may lose the use of his limbs? And if ever that should come to pass again, for my part, I am resolved to pluck up the heart of a man, and to try my utmost to get from under his hand. I was a fool that I did not try to do it before. But, however, my brother, let's be patient, and endure a while; the time may come that may give us a happy release; but let us not be our own murderers. With these words Hopeful at present did **moderate** the mind of his brother; so they continued together in the dark that day, in their sad and doleful condition.

Well, towards evening the giant goes down into the dungeon again, to see if his prisoners had taken his counsel. But when he came there he found them alive; and truly, alive was all; for now, what for want of bread and water, and by reason of the wounds they received when he beat them, they could do little but breathe. But, I say, he found them alive; at which he fell into a grievous rage, and told them, that seeing they had disobeyed his counsel, it should be worse with them than if they had never been born.

At this they trembled greatly, and I think that Christian fell into a *swoon*,[2] but coming a little to himself again, they renewed their discourse about the giant's counsel; and whether yet they had best to take it or no. Now Christian again seemed to be for doing it, but Hopeful made his second reply as followeth:

HOPE. My brother, said he, rememberest thou not how **valiant** thou hast been heretofore? Apollyon could not crush thee, nor could all that thou didst hear, or see, or feel in the Valley of the Shadow of Death. What hardship, terror, and amazement hast thou already gone through! and art thou now nothing but fears? Thou seest that I am in the dungeon with thee, a far weaker man by nature than thou art. Also this giant has wounded me as well as thee, and hath also cut off the bread and water from my mouth: and with that I mourn without the light. But let's exercise a little more patience. Remember how thou *playedst the man*[3] at Vanity Fair, and wast neither afraid of the chain nor cage, nor yet of bloody death: wherefore let us (at least to avoid the shame that becomes not a Christian to be found in) bear up with patience as well as we can.

Now night being come again, and the giant and his wife being in bed, she asked him concerning the prisoners, and if they had taken his counsel: to which he replied, They are sturdy rogues, they choose rather to bear all hardship, than to make away themselves. Then said she, Take them into the castle-yard to-morrow, and show them the bones and skulls of those that thou hast already dispatched, and make them believe, ere a week comes to an end, thou also wilt tear them in pieces, as thou hast done their fellows before them.

So when the morning was come, the giant goes to them again, and takes them into the castle-yard, and shows them as his wife had bidden him. These, said he, were pilgrims as you are, once, and they trespassed in my grounds as you have done; and when I thought fit I tore them in pieces, and so within ten days I will do you; get you down into your den again. And with that he beat them all the way thither. They lay, therefore, all day on Saturday in a lamentable case, as before. Now when

---

2. swoon: faint.

3. playedst the man: acted bravely.

night was come, and when Mrs. Diffidence and her husband, the Giant, were got to bed, they began to renew their discourse of their prisoners; and withal the old giant wondered, that he could neither by his blows nor counsel bring them to an end. And with that his wife replied, I fear, said she, that they live in hopes that some will come to relieve them or that they have *picklocks*[4] about them, by the means of which they hope to escape. And sayest thou so, my dear? said the giant; I will therefore search them in the morning.

Well, on Saturday, about midnight, they began to pray, and continued in prayer till almost break of day.

Now, a little before it was day, good Christian, as one half amazed, brake out in this **passionate** speech; What a fool, quoth he, am I, thus to lie in a stinking dungeon, when I may as well walk at liberty! I have a key in my bosom called Promise, that will, I am persuaded, open any lock in Doubting Castle. Then said Hopeful, That's good news, good brother, pluck it out of thy bosom, and try.

Then Christian pulled it out of his bosom, and began to try at the dungeon door, whose bolt, as he turned the key gave back, and the door flew open with ease, and Christian and Hopeful both came out. Then he went to the outward door that leads into the castle-yard, and with his key opened that door also. After

he went to the iron gate, for that must be opened too; but that lock went hard, yet the key did open it. Then they thrust open the gate to make their escape with speed; but that gate, as it opened, made such a cracking, that it waked Giant Despair, who hastily rising to pursue his prisoners, felt his limbs to fail; for his fits took him again, so that he could by no means go after them. Then they went on, and came to the King's highway, and so were safe, because they were out of his **jurisdiction**.

Now when they were gone over the stile, they began to **contrive** with themselves what they should do at that stile, to prevent those that shall come after from falling into the hands of Giant Despair. So they consented to erect there a pillar, and to engrave upon the side thereof this sentence: OVER THIS STILE IS THE WAY TO DOUBTING CASTLE, WHICH IS KEPT BY GIANT DESPAIR, WHO DESPISETH THE KING OF THE CELESTIAL COUNTRY, AND SEEKS TO DESTROY HIS HOLY PILGRIMS. Many, therefore, that followed after, read what was written, and escaped the danger. This done, they sang as follows:

Out of the way we went, and then we found
What 'twas to tread upon forbidden ground:
And let them that come after have a care,
Lest heedlessness makes them, as we, to fare.
Lest they for trespassing his pris'ners are,
Whose castle's Doubting, and whose name's
  Despair.

---

4. picklocks: devices to open the door without a key.

Meditating for Meaning

1. Name three comforts provided for the pilgrims along the banks of the river.

2. Although we know what characteristics distinguish the narrow way, it is not always easy to make the right choice when faced with the decision.
   a. Why do the pilgrims leave the narrow way?
   b. Why are they not fearful that this other path will cause them to fail in their Christian life?
   c. What does this tell us about how sincere Christians may be most easily led astray?

3. Throughout the allegory when Bunyan says the pilgrims meet a certain man, he may mean that another individual meets them. But he may also mean that a specific spirit enters into them as in the case of meeting Vain-Confidence.
   a. What warning does the Bible give against being vainly confident? (1 Corinthians 10:12)
   b. What circumstance leads them to become vainly confident?

4. When the pilgrims lose their vain confidence, some very disagreeable things come into their experience. What two things hinder the pilgrims in returning to the right road? Note that night often comes quickly when Christian yields to the temptation to dwell at ease (e.g. when he slept at the arbor).

5. For a logical reason they now come under the influence of Giant Despair.
   a. What aspects of their present situation lead them to despair?
   b. What reason does Giant Despair give for demanding that they go with him?
   c. Why are they forced to go with him?

6. An evil spirit often leads one into the whirlpool of a vicious cycle; that is, one bad feeling leads to another, which then makes the first feeling worse; and so round and round, worse and worse. When Giant Despair leads the pilgrims to Doubting Castle, they are caught in one of these cycles. Explain how despair can lead to doubt and doubt would bring on more despair.

7. The name of Giant Despair's wife is Diffidence. Why is a person in the clutches of despair likely to be also diffident?

8. What three things does Diffidence suggest Giant Despair should do to the prisoners? Note that these represent things that come upon a person in deep despair.

9. Despair is a state of hopelessness. It is fitting that Hopeful is the one who is able to offer hope. What three rays of hope does he give to encourage them?

10. The pilgrims now reach a turning point in their prison experience.
    a. What do the pilgrims do just prior to thinking of a way to escape?
    b. What does this key called Promise represent?
    c. What is the significance of the pilgrims' escaping on Sunday?

11. The stile provides passage across the fence between the narrow way and By-path Meadow.
    a. What does the stile symbolize in actual life?
    b. In what practical way might we erect warning signs for others?

Chapter 16: Christian and Hopeful Pass Through the Delectable Mountains

Defining for Comprehension

Choose the word or phrase below which most nearly defines each word at the left as it is used in this allegory.

1. **wayfaring**   a. lost   b. successful   c. traveling

2. **dissemble**   a. tear apart   b. dissolve   c. hide motives
                                          partnership

3. **perspective**   a. view from   b. future; likely   c. backwards
                         a distance   look

4. **essayed**   a. assigned   b. attempted   c. intended

They went then till they came to the Delectable Mountains, which mountains belong to the Lord of that hill of which we have spoken before. So they went up to the mountains, to behold the gardens and orchards, the vineyards and fountains of water; where also they drank and washed themselves, and did freely eat of the vineyards. Now there were on the tops of these mountains shepherds feeding their flocks, and they stood by the highwayside. The pilgrims, therefore, went to them, and leaning upon their staves (as is common with weary pilgrims when they stand to talk with any by the way), they asked, Whose delectable mountains are these, and whose be the sheep that feed upon them?

SHEP. These mountains are Emmanuel's land, and they are within sight of His city; and the sheep also are His, and He laid down His life for them.

CHR. Is this the way to the Celestial City?

SHEP. You are just in your way.

CHR. How far is it thither?

SHEP. Too far for any but those that shall get thither indeed.

CHR. Is the way safe, or dangerous?

SHEP. Safe for those for whom it is to be safe; but transgressors shall fall therein.

CHR. Is there in this place any relief for pilgrims that are weary and faint in the way?

SHEP. The Lord of these mountains hath given us a charge, not to be forgetful to entertain strangers: therefore the good of the place is before you.

I also saw in my dream, that when the Shepherds perceived that they were **wayfaring** men, they also put questions to them (to which they made answer as in other places), as, Whence came you? and, How got you into the way? and, By what means have you so persevered therein? for but few of them that begin to come hither, do show their face on these mountains. But when the Shepherds heard their answers, being pleased therewith, they looked very lovingly upon them, and said, Welcome to the Delectable Mountains.

The Shepherds, I say, whose names were Knowledge, Experience, Watchful, and Sincere, took them by the hand, and had them to their tents, and made them partake of that which was ready at present. They said, moreover, We would that ye should stay here a while, to be acquainted with us; and yet more to solace yourselves with the good of these Delectable

Mountains. They then told them, that they were content to stay. And so they went to their rest that night, because it was very late.

Then I saw in my dream, that in the morning the Shepherds called up Christian and Hopeful to walk with them upon the mountains. So they went forth with them, and walked a while, having a pleasant prospect on every side. Then said the Shepherds one to another, Shall we show these pilgrims some wonders? So when they had concluded to do it, they had them first to the top of a hill, called Error, which was very steep on the farthest side, and bid them look down to the bottom. So Christian and Hopeful looked down, and saw at the bottom several men dashed all to pieces by a fall that they had from the top. Then said Christian, What meaneth this? The Shepherds answered, Have you not heard of them that were made to err, by hearkening to Hymenaeus and Philetus, as concerning the faith of the resurrection of the body? They answered, Yes. Then said the Shepherds, Those that you see lie dashed in pieces at the bottom of this mountain are they; and they have continued to this day unburied, as you see, for an example to others to take heed how they clamber too high, or how they come too near the brink of this mountain.

Then I saw that they had them to the top of another mountain, and the name of that is Caution, and bid them look afar off; which, when they did, they perceived, as they thought, several men walking up and down among the tombs that were there; and they perceived that the men were blind, because they stumbled sometimes upon the tombs, and because they could not get out from among them. Then said Christian, What meant this?

The Shepherds then answered, Did you not see a little below these mountains a stile that led into a meadow, on the left hand of this way?

They answered, Yes. Then said the Shepherds, From the stile there goes a path that leads directly to Doubting Castle, which is kept by Giant Despair, and these men (pointing to them among the tombs) came once on pilgrimage, as you do now, even till they came to that same stile. And because the right way was rough in that place, they chose to go out of it into that meadow, and there were taken by Giant Despair, and cast into Doubting Castle; where, after they had awhile been kept in the dungeon, he at last did put out their eyes, and led them among those tombs, where he has left them to wander to this very day, that the saying of the wise man might be fulfilled, He that wandereth out of the way of understanding shall remain in the congregation of the dead. Then Christian and Hopeful looked upon one another, with tears gushing out, but yet said nothing to the Shepherds.

Then I saw in my dream that the Shepherds had them to another place in a bottom, where was a door in the side of a hill; and they opened the door, and bid them look in. They looked in, therefore, and saw that within it was very dark and smoky; they also thought that they heard there a rumbling noise, as of fire, and a cry of

some tormented, and that they smelt the scent of brimstone. Then said Christian, What means this? The Shepherds told them, This is a by-way to hell, a way that hypocrites go in at; namely, such as sell their birthright, with Esau; such as sell their Master, with Judas; such as blaspheme the gospel, with Alexander; and that lie and **dissemble,** with Ananias and Sapphira his wife.

Then said Hopeful to the Shepherds, I perceive that these had on them, even every one, a show of pilgrimage, as we have now; had they not?

SHEP. Yea, and held it a long time too.

HOPE. How far might they go on pilgrimage in their day, since they, notwithstanding, were thus miserably cast away?

SHEP. Some farther, and some not so far as these mountains.

Then said the pilgrims one to another, We had need cry to the Strong for strength.

SHEP. Ay, and you will have need to use it, when you have it, too.

By this time the pilgrims had a desire to go forwards, and the Shepherds a desire they should; so they walked together towards the end of the mountains. Then said the Shepherds one to another, Let us here show to the pilgrims the gates of the Celestial City, if they have skill to look through our **perspective**-glass. The pilgrims then lovingly accepted the motion: so they had them to the top of a high hill, called Clear, and gave them the glass to look.

Then they **essayed** to look but the remembrance of that last thing that the Shepherds had shown them made their hands shake, by means of which impediment they could not look steadily through the glass, yet they thought they saw something like the gate, and also some of the glory of the place. Then they went away and sang this song:

Thus by the Shepherds secrets are revealed,
Which from all other men are kept concealed:
Come to the Shepherds then, if you would
see
Things deep, things hid, and that mysterious
be.

When they were about to depart, one of the Shepherds gave them a note of the way. Another of them bid them beware of the Flatterer. The third bid them take heed that they sleep not upon the Enchanted Ground. And the fourth bid them God-speed. So I awoke from my dream.

Meditating for Meaning

Commentaries do not always agree on the precise interpretation of the symbols in *The Pilgrim's Progress*. The Delectable Mountains are one such symbol whose meaning is doubtful. They may symbolize the Word of God with its comforts and warnings. They may symbolize approaching old age with release from the heat of youthful passions and a more calm and peaceful Christian experience. At least we can understand that these enjoyable and delightful (delectable) mountains are a season of refreshment after the bitter experience of Doubting Castle. You will remember that Christian was shown these mountains from Palace Beautiful, probably to encourage Christian in hard times that delightful seasons would come.

1. Shepherds are a common figure in Scripture.
   a. Whom might these shepherds represent in real life?
   b. What are the shepherds' names?
   c. How are these fitting names when applied to the shepherds of the church?

2. What warning do the pilgrims receive while on the top of the Hill Error?
3. The shepherds now take the pilgrims to the top of the Mountain Caution.
   a. What do the pilgrims learn finally happens to those who are overcome by despair and doubt?
   b. Why do they look at one another with tears in their eyes?
4. Consider the names of those who took the by-way to hell. What root of evil, present in each of their lives, leads people to foolishly give up their entire lives to Satan?
5. If you have ever looked through binoculars or a telescope while holding it with an unsteady hand, then you will understand why the pilgrims cannot get a clear view of the gates of the Celestial City. How is our view of heaven from earth similar?
6. Do you observe any relationship between the names of the shepherds and what parting helps and warnings they give? Bunyan may not have intended a one-to-one relationship between these, but knowing his literary skill, it is possible that he did intend such a relationship. Copy the names of the four shepherds on your paper. Then beside each, write the parting gift he possibly gave.

Chapter 17: Christian and Hopeful Reach the Enchanted Ground

Defining for Comprehension

Choose the word or phrase below which most nearly defines each word at the left as it is used in this allegory.

1. apostasy
   a. forsaking of right
   b. doubt
   c. prosperity

2. damnable
   a. salvageable
   b. fit for destruction
   c. worthy of memory

3. atheist
   a. one who believes many gods
   b. one who denies God's existence
   c. uncivilized person

4. rioting
   a. indulgence in noisy pleasure
   b. decaying
   c. extravagance

5. revelling
   a. delighting
   b. partying
   c. disclosing

6. toll
   a. decorate
   b. express gloom
   c. ring as a bell

7. amendments
   a. praise
   b. additions to buildings
   c. corrections

8. efficacy
   a. power to produce effect
   b. detailed construction
   c. truthfulness

9. imputed
   a. calculated
   b. credited to
   c. debated

10. mediator
    a. wrestler
    b. peacemaker
    c. collector

And I slept, and dreamed again, and saw the same two pilgrims going down the mountains along the highway towards the city. Now a little below these mountains on the left hand, lieth the country of Conceit; from which country there comes into the way in which the pilgrims walked, a little crooked lane. Here, therefore, they met with a very brisk lad, that came out of that country, and his name was Ignorance. So Christian asked him from what parts he came and whither he was going.

IGNOR. Sir, I was born in the country that lieth off there, a little on the left hand, and am going to the Celestial City.

CHR. But how do you think to get in at the gate, for you may find some difficulty there?

IGNOR. As other good people doth, said he.

CHR. But what have you to show at the gate, that may cause that the gate should be opened to you?

IGNOR. I know my Lord's will, and I have been a good liver: I pay every man his own; I pray, fast, pay tithes, and give alms, and have left my country for whither I am going.

CHR. But thou camest not in at the Wicket-gate that is at the head of this way; thou camest in hither through that same crooked lane, and therefore I fear, however thou mayest think of thyself, when the reckoning-day shall come, thou wilt have laid to thy charge that thou art a thief and a robber, instead of getting admittance into the city.

IGNOR. Gentlemen, ye be utter strangers to me; I know you not: be content to follow the religion of your country, and I will follow the religion of mine. I hope all will be well. And as for the gate that you talk of, all the world knows that that is a great way off of our country. I cannot think that any man in all our parts doth so much as know the way to it; nor need they matter whether they do or no, since we have, as you see, a fine, pleasant, green lane, that comes down from our country, the next way into the way.

When Christian saw that the man was wise in his own conceit, he said to Hopeful, whisperingly, There is more hopes of a fool than of him. And said, moreover, When he that is a fool walketh by the way, his wisdom faileth him, and he saith to every one that he is a fool. What, shall we talk further with him, or outgo him at present, and so leave him to think of what he hath heard already, and then stop again for him afterwards, and see if by degrees we can do any good by him? Then said Hopeful,

Let Ignorance a little while now muse
On what is said, and let him not refuse
Good counsel to embrace, lest he remain
Still ignorant of what's the chiefest gain.
God saith, those that no understanding have
(Although He made them), them he will not
    save.

HOPE. He further added, It is not good, I think, to say to him all at once; let us pass him by, if you will, and talk to him anon, even as he is able to bear it.

So they both went on, and Ignorance he came after. Now when they had passed him a little way, they entered into a very dark lane, where they met a man whom seven devils had bound with seven strong cords, and were carrying him back to the door that they saw on the side of the hill. Now good Christian began to tremble, and so did Hopeful, his companion; yet, as the devils led away the man, Christian looked to see if he knew him; and he thought it might be Turn-away, that dwelt in the town of **Apostasy**. But he did not perfectly see his face, for he did hang his head like a thief that is found; but being gone past, Hopeful looked after him, and espied on his back a paper with this inscription, Wanton professor, and **damnable** apostate.

* * * * * * *

So they went on, and Ignorance followed. They went then till they came at a place where they saw a way put itself into their way, and seemed withal to lie as straight as the way which they should go; and here they knew not which of the two to take, for both seemed straight before them; therefore here they stood still to consider. And as they were thinking about the way, behold, a man black of flesh, but covered with a very light robe, came to them, and asked them why they stood there. They answered, they were going to the Celestial City, but knew not which of these ways to take. Follow me, said the man; it is thither that I am going. So they followed him in the way that but now came into the road, which by degrees turned, and turned them so from the city that they desired to go to, that in little time their faces were turned away from it; yet they followed him. But by and by, before they were aware, he led them both within the compass of a net, in which they were both so entangled that they knew not what to do; and with that the white robe fell off the black man's back. Then they saw where they were. Wherefore there they lay crying some time, for they could not get themselves out.

CHR. Then said Christian to his fellow, Now do I see myself in error. Did not the Shepherds bid us beware of the Flatterers? As is the saying of the wise man, so we have found it this day: A man that flattereth his neighbour spreadeth a net for his foot.

HOPE. They also gave us a note of directions about the way, for our more sure finding thereof; but therein we have also forgotten to read, and have not kept ourselves from the paths of the destroyer. Here David was wiser than we; for, saith he, Concerning the works of men, by the word of Thy lips I have kept me from the paths of the destroyer. Thus they lay bewailing themselves in the net. At last they espied a Shining One coming toward them with a whip of small cord in his hand. When he was come to the place where they were, he asked them whence they came, and what they did there. They told him that they were poor pilgrims going to Zion, but were led out of their way by a black man clothed in white, who bid us, said they, follow him, for he was going thither too. Then said he with the whip, It is Flatterer, a false apostle, that hath transformed himself into an angel of light. So he rent the net, and let the men out. Then said he to them, Follow me, that I may set you in your way again. So he led them back to the way which they had left to follow the Flatterer. Then he asked them, saying, Where did you lie the last night? They said, With the Shepherds upon the Delectable Mountain. He asked them then if they had not a note of those Shepherds of direction for the way. They answered, Yes. But did

you, said he, when you were at a stand, pluck out and read your note? They answered, No. He asked them, Why? They said they forgot. He asked, moreover, if the Shepherds did not bid them beware of the Flatterer. They answered, Yes; but we did not imagine, said they, that this fine-spoken man had been he.

Then I saw in my dream, that he commanded them to lie down; which when they did, he chastised them sore, to teach them the good way wherein they should walk; and as he chastised them, he said, As many as I love I rebuke and chasten; be zealous, therefore, and repent. This done, he bid them go on their way, and take good heed to the other directions of the Shepherds. So they thanked him for all his kindness, and went softly along the right way, singing:

> Come hither, you that walk along the way,
> See how the pilgrims fare that go astray:
> They catched are in an entangling net,
> 'Cause they good counsel lightly did forget:
> 'Tis true they rescued were, but yet, you see,
> They're scourged *to boot.*[1] Let this your caution be.

Now after a while they perceived afar off one coming softly, and alone, all along the highway to meet them. Then said Christian to his fellow, Yonder is a man with his back towards Zion, and he is coming to meet us.

HOPE. I see him; let us take heed to ourselves now, lest he should prove a flatterer also. So he drew nearer and nearer, and at last came up unto them. His name was **Atheist**, and he asked them whither they were going.

CHR. We are going to Mount Zion.

Then Atheist fell into a very great laughter.

CHR. What is the meaning of your laughter?

ATHEIST. I laugh to see what ignorant persons you are, to take upon you so tedious a journey, and yet are like to have nothing but your travel for your pains.

CHR. Why, man, do you think we shall not be received?

ATHEIST. Received! There is not such place as you dream of in all this world.

CHR. But there is in the world to come.

---

1. to boot: in addition.

ATHEIST. When I was at home in mine own country, I heard as you now affirm, and from that hearing went out to see, and have been seeking this city twenty years, but find no more of it than I did the first day I set out.

CHR. We have both heard, and believe, that there is such a place to be found.

ATHEIST. Had not I, when at home, believed, I had not come thus far to seek; but finding none (and yet I should, had there been such a place to be found, for I have gone to seek it farther than you), I am going back again, and will seek to refresh myself with the things that I then cast away for hopes of that which I now see is not.

CHR. Then said Christian to Hopeful his companion, Is it true which this man hath said?

HOPE. Take heed, he is one of the flatterers; remember what it hath cost us once already for our hearkening to such kind of fellows. What! no Mount Zion? Did we not see from the Delectable Mountains the gate of the city? Also, are we not now to walk by faith? Let us go on, said Hopeful, lest the man with the whip overtake us again! You should have taught me that lesson, which I will *round you in the ears*[2] withal: Cease, my son, to hear the instruction that causeth to err from the words of knowledge," I say, my brother, cease to hear him, and let us believe to the saving of the soul.

CHR. My brother, I did not put the question to thee, for that I doubted of the truth of our belief myself, but to prove thee, and to fetch from thee a fruit of the honesty of thy heart. As for this man, I know that he is blinded by the god of this world. Let thee and I go on knowing that we have belief of the truth, and no lie is of the truth.

HOPE. Now do I rejoice in hope of the glory of God. So they turned away from the man, and he, laughing at them, went his way.

Atheist

I saw then in my dream, that they went till they came into a certain country, whose air naturally tended to make one drowsy, if he came a stranger into it. And here Hopeful began to be very dull, and heavy of sleep; wherefore he said unto Christian, I do now begin to grow so drowsy, that I can scarcely hold up mine eyes; let us lie down here, and take one nap.

CHR. By no means, said the other, lest sleeping we never awake more.

HOPE. Why, my brother? sleep is sweet to the labouring man; we may be refreshed if we take a nap.

CHR. Do you not remember that one of the Shepherds bid us beware of the Enchanted Ground? He meant by that, that we should beware of sleeping; wherefore let us not sleep as do others, but let us watch and be sober.

HOPE. I acknowledge myself in a fault; and had I been here alone, I had by sleeping run the danger of death. I see it is true that the wise

---

2. round you in the ears: tell you privately.

man saith, Two are better than one. Hitherto hath thy company been my mercy; and thou shalt have a good reward for thy labour.

CHR. Now, then, said Christian, to prevent drowsiness in this place, let us fall into good discourse.

HOPE. With all my heart, said the other.

CHR. Where shall we begin?

HOPE. Where God began with us. But do you begin, if you please.

CHR. I will sing you first this song.

When saints do sleepy grow, let them come hither,
And hear how these two pilgrims talk together:
Yea, let them learn of them in any wise,
Thus to keep ope their drowsy, slumb'ring eyes.
Saints' fellowship, if it be managed well,
Keeps them awake, and that in spite of hell.

CHR. Then Christian began, and said, I will ask you a question. How came you to think at first of doing what you do now?

HOPE. Do you mean, how came I at first to look after the good of my soul?

CHR. Yes, that is my meaning.

HOPE. I continued a great while in the delight of those things which were seen and sold at our fair; things which I believe now would have, had I continued in them still, drowned me in perdition and destruction.

CHR. What things are they?

HOPE. All the treasures and riches of the world. Also I delighted much in **rioting, revelling,** drinking, swearing, lying, uncleanness, sabbath-breaking, and what not, that tended to destroy the soul. But I found at last, by hearing and considering of things that are divine, which, indeed, I heard of you, as also of beloved Faithful, that was put to death for his faith and good living in Vanity Fair, that the end of these things is death; and that for these things' sake the wrath of God cometh upon the children of disobedience.

CHR. And did you presently fall under the power of this conviction?

HOPE. No, I was not willing presently to know the evil of sin, nor the damnation that follows upon the commission of it; but endeavoured, when my mind at first began to be shaken with the Word, to shut mine eyes against the light thereof.

CHR. But what was the cause of your carrying of it thus to the first workings of God's blessed Spirit upon you?

HOPE. The causes were,

1. I was ignorant that this was the work of God upon me. I never thought that by awakenings for sin, God at first begins the conversion of a sinner.

2. Sin was yet very sweet to my flesh, and I was loath to leave it.

3. I could not tell how to part with mine old companions, their presence and actions were so desirable unto me.

4. The hours in which convictions were upon me, were such troublesome and such heart-affrighting hours, that I could not bear, no, not so much as the remembrance of them upon my heart.

CHR. Then, as it seems, sometimes you got rid of your trouble?

HOPE. Yes, verily, but it would come into my mind again; and then I should be as bad, nay, worse, than I was before.

CHR. Why, what was it that brought your sins to mind again?

HOPE. Many things, as,

1. If I did but meet a good man in the street; or,

2. If I have heard any read in the Bible; or,

3. If mine head did begin to ache; or,

4. If I were told that some of my neighbours were sick; or,

5. If I heard the bell **toll** for some that were dead; or,

6. If I thought of dying myself; or,

7. If I heard that sudden death happened to others.

8. But especially when I thought of myself, that I must quickly come to judgment.

CHR. And could you at any time with ease get off the guilt of sin, when by any of these ways it came upon you?

HOPE. No, not I; for then they got faster hold of my conscience; and then, if I did but think of going back to sin (though my mind was turned against it), it would be double torment to me.

CHR. And how did you do then?

HOPE. I thought I must endeavour to amend my life; or else, thought I, I am sure to be damned.

CHR. And did you endeavour to amend?

HOPE. Yes; and fled from, not only my sins, but sinful company too, and betook me to religious duties; as prayer, reading, weeping for sin, speaking truth to my neighbours, etc. These things did I with many others, too much here to relate.

CHR. And did you think yourself well then?

HOPE. Yes, for a while; but at the last my trouble came tumbling upon me again, and that over the neck of all my reformations.

CHR. How came that about, since you were now reformed?

HOPE. There were several things brought it upon me, especially such sayings as these: All our righteousnesses are as filthy rags. By the works of the law shall no flesh be justified. When ye have done all those things, say, We are unprofitable, with many more such like. From whence I began to reason with myself thus: If all my righteousnesses are filthy rags; if by the deeds of the law no man can be justified, and if, when we have done all, we are yet unprofitable, then 'tis but a folly to think of heaven by the law. I further thought thus: If a man runs a hundred pounds into the shopkeeper's debt, and after that shall pay for all that he shall fetch; yet if this old debt stand still in the book uncrossed, the shopkeeper may sue him, and cast him into prison till he shall pay the debt.

CHR. Well, and how did you apply this to yourself?

HOPE: Why, I thought thus with myself; I have by my sins run a great way into God's book, and that my now reforming will not pay off that score. Therefore I should sink still under all my present **amendments.** But how shall I be freed from that damnation that I brought myself in danger of by my former transgressions?

CHR. A very good application: but pray go on.

HOPE. Another thing that hath troubled me,

even since my late amendments, is, that if I look narrowly into the best of what I do now, I still see sin, new sin, mixing itself with the best of that I do; so that now I am forced to conclude, that notwithstanding my former fond conceits of myself and duties, I have committed sin enough in one day to send me to hell, though my former life had been faultless.

CHR. And what did you do then?

HOPE. Do! I could not tell what to do, till I *brake my mind*[3] to Faithful; for he and I were well acquainted. And he told me that unless I could obtain the righteousness of a man that never had sinned, neither mine own, nor all the righteousness of the world, could save me.

CHR. And did you think he spake true?

HOPE. Had he told me so when I was pleased and satisfied with mine own amendment, I had called him fool for his pains; but now, since I see mine own infirmity, and the sin that cleaves to my best performance, I have been forced to be of his opinion.

CHR. But did you think, when at first he suggested it to you, that there was such a man to be found, of whom it might justly be said that he never committed sin?

HOPE. I must confess the words at first sounded strangely; but after a little more talk and company with him, I had full conviction about it.

CHR. And did you ask him what man this was, and how you must be justified by him?

HOPE. Yes, and he told me it was the Lord Jesus, that dwelleth on the right hand of the Most High. And thus, said he, you must be justified by Him, even by trusting to what He hath done by Himself in the days of His flesh, and suffered when He did hang on the tree. I asked him further, how that Man's righteousness could be of that **efficacy** to justify another before God. And he told me He was the mighty God, and did what He did, and died the death also not for Himself, but for me; to whom His doings, and the worthiness of them, should be **imputed**, if I believed on Him.

CHR. And what did you do then?

HOPE. I made my objections against my

3. brake my mind: revealed my thoughts.

believing, for that I thought He was not willing to save me.

CHR. And what said Faithful to you then?

HOPE. He bid me go to Him and see. Then I said it was presumption. He said, No; for I was invited to come. Then he gave me *a book of Jesus His inditing*,[4] to encourage me the more freely to come; and he said concerning that book, that every *jot and tittle*[5] thereof stood firmer than heaven and earth. Then I asked him what I must do when I came; and he told me, I must entreat upon my knees, with all my heart and soul, the Father to reveal Him to me. Then I asked him further, how I must make my supplication to Him; and he said, Go, and thou shalt find Him upon a mercy-seat, where He sits, all the year long, to give pardon and forgiveness to them that come. I told him, that I knew not what to say when I came; and he bid me say to this effect: God be merciful to me a sinner, and make me to know and believe in Jesus Christ; for I see, that if His righteousness had not been, or I have not faith in that righteousness, I am utterly cast away. Lord, I have heard that Thou art a merciful God, and hast ordained that Thy Son Jesus Christ should be the Saviour of the world; and moreover, that Thou art willing to bestow Him upon such a poor sinner as I am. And I am a sinner indeed. Lord, take therefore this opportunity, and magnify Thy grace in the salvation of my soul, through Thy Son Jesus Christ. Amen.

CHR. And did you do as you were bidden?

HOPE. Yes, over, and over, and over.

CHR. And did the Father reveal His Son to you?

HOPE. No, not at the first, nor second, nor third, nor fourth, nor fifth, no, nor at the sixth time neither.

CHR. What did you do then?

HOPE. What! why I could not tell what to do.

CHR. Had you not thoughts of leaving off praying?

HOPE. Yes; a hundred times twice told.

CHR. And what was the reason you did not?

HOPE. I believed that that was true which had been told me, to wit, that without the righteousness of this Christ, all the world could not save me; and therefore, thought I with myself, if I leave off, I die, and I can but die at the throne of grace. And withal this came into my mind, If it tarry, wait for it; because it will surely come, and will not tarry. So I continued praying until the Father showed me His Son.

CHR. And how was He revealed unto you?

HOPE. I did not see Him with my bodily eyes, but with the eyes of mine understanding, and thus it was. One day I was very sad, I think sadder than at any one time in my life; and this sadness was through a fresh sight of the greatness and vileness of my sins. And as I was then looking for nothing but hell, and the everlasting damnation of my soul, suddenly, as I thought, I saw the Lord Jesus Christ look down from heaven upon me, and saying, Believe on the Lord Jesus Christ, and thou shalt be saved.

But I replied, Lord, I am a great, a very great sinner: and he answered, My grace is sufficient for thee. Then I said, But, Lord, what is believing? And then I saw from that saying, He that cometh to Me shall never hunger, and he that believeth on Me shall never thirst, that believing and coming was all one; and that he that came, that is, ran out in his heart and affections after salvation by Christ, he indeed believed in Christ. Then the water stood in mine eyes, and I asked further, But, Lord, may such a great sinner as I am be indeed accepted of Thee, and be saved by thee? And I heard Him say, And him that cometh to Me I will in no wise cast out. Then I said, But how, Lord, must I consider of Thee in my coming to Thee, that my faith may be placed aright upon Thee? Then He said, "Christ Jesus came into the world to save sinners. He is the end of the law for righteousness to every one that believes. He died for our sins, and rose again for our justification. He loved us, and washed us from our sins in His own blood. He is **Mediator** betwixt God and us. He ever liveth to make intercession for us. From all which I gathered, that I must look for righteousness in His person, and for satisfaction for

---

4. a book of Jesus His inditing: a book dictated by Jesus.

5. jot and tittle: every word; smallest part—a jot is the same as iota, the smallest letter in the Greek alphabet; a tittle is a small diacritical mark.

my sins by His blood: that what He did in obedience to His Father's law, and in submitting to the penalty thereof, was not for Himself, but for him that will accept it for his salvation, and be thankful. And now was my heart full of joy, mine eyes full of tears, and mine affections running over with love to the name, people, and ways of Jesus Christ.

CHR. This was a revelation of Christ to your soul indeed. But tell me particularly what effect this had upon your spirit.

HOPE. It made me see that all the world, notwithstanding all the righteousness thereof, is in a state of condemnation. It made me see that God the Father, though He be just, can justly justify the coming sinner. It made me greatly ashamed of the vileness of my former life, and confounded me with the sense of mine own ignorance; for there never came thought into my heart before now that showed me so the beauty of Jesus Christ. It made me love a holy life, and long to do something for the honour and glory of the Lord Jesus. Yea, I thought that had I now a thousand gallons of blood in my body, I could spill it all for the sake of the Lord Jesus.

Meditating for Meaning

1. Here is another example of Bunyan's skillful choice of names.
   a. From the name of the lad who came from the country of Conceit, you can conclude that at the base of all conceit is a great deal of _____ .
   b. What irony do you see in Ignorance's answer about what he would have to show at the gate? Compare what he says with his name.

2. Ignorance's entrance by the way of a little crooked lane reminds us of the way Formalist and Hypocrisy entered.
   a. Interpret the meaning of this way of entering.
   b. How should Ignorance have entered?
   c. In Ignorance's mind, one _____ is as good as another.

3. What does the account of Turn-away show happens to one who turns back from the right way?

4. The pilgrims get off the way again.
   a. What is symbolized by a *black* man with a *white* robe?
   b. When the pilgrims are completely out of the way, what happens to them?

5. A Shining One appears to rescue them and reminds them that they could have avoided this sorrow.
   a. What two helps given earlier had they failed to use?
   b. What further kindness does the Shining One do for them?

6. Next the pilgrims meet Atheist.
   a. Why is Atheist walking with his back toward Zion?
   b. Why does he laugh?
   c. What sure proof does Hopeful present that there is a Mount Zion?
   d. What did Atheist lack that would guide the pilgrims in their journey?

7. The Enchanted Ground can have a twofold meaning. It can represent a period of time in which the church is free from persecution and oppression. Or it can be a period in a man's life when he is enjoying material prosperity. Often when the church is not experiencing persecution, the members do prosper in a material way. Such times tend to make Christians spiritually "sleepy." This is a time for much watchfulness.
   a. How does the air of the Enchanted Ground affect the pilgrims?
   b. What warning do they remember?
   c. Interpret the meaning of this forbidden sleep.

8. To help them "watch and be sober," the pilgrims discuss Hopeful's conversion experience.
   a. What was the first thing Hopeful tried to do when he became convinced that he could not shake off his guilt?
   b. For what two reasons was this not satisfactory?
   c. After going to Jesus for help, what new motivation did Hopeful have to live a holy life?

Chapter 18: Christian and Hopeful Attempt to Help Ignorance

Defining for Comprehension

Choose the word or phrase below which most nearly defines each word at the left as it is used in this allegory.

1. loitereth	a. scatters trash	b. tarries	c. gossips
2. warrant	a. guarantee	b. disappear	c. fasten
3. sluggard	a. lazy person	b. servant	c. taskmaster
4. attributes	a. regards	b. taxes	c. characteristics
5. shrouded	a. torn in pieces	b. clothed	c. announced
6. acquit	a. cleared of guilt	b. ceased	c. arrested
7. whimsies	a. notions	b. cheap items	c. cries
8. stifle	a. quiet; smother	b. make rigid	c. play with
9. verily	a. endlessly	b. truly	c. scarcely
10. curbing	a. annoying	b. restraining	c. encircling
11. launched	a. jerked	b. thrust	c. feasted

I saw then in my dream, that Hopeful looked back and saw Ignorance, whom they had left behind, coming after. Look, said he to Christian, how far yonder youngster **loitereth** behind.

CHR. Ay, ay, I see him; he careth not for our company.

HOPE. But I trow it would not have hurt him had he kept pace with us hitherto.

CHR. That's true; but I **warrant** you he thinketh otherwise.

HOPE. That I think he doth; but, however, let us tarry for him. So they did.

Then Christian said to him, Come away, man; why do you stay so behind?

IGNOR. I take my pleasure in walking alone, even more a great deal than in company, unless I like it the better.

Then said Christian to Hopeful (but softly), Did I not tell you he cared not for our company? But however, said he, come up, and let us talk away the time in this solitary place. Then, directing his speech to Ignorance, he said, Come, how do you do? How stands it between God and your soul now?

IGNOR. I hope well; for I am always full of good motions, that come into my mind to comfort me as I walk.

CHR. What good motions? pray tell us.

IGNOR. Why, I think of God and heaven.

CHR. So do the devils and damned souls.

IGNOR. But I think of them, and desire them.

CHR. So do many that are never like to come there. The soul of the **sluggard** desires, and hath nothing.

IGNOR. But I think of them, and leave all for them.

CHR. That I doubt; for leaving all is a hard matter; yea, a harder matter than many are aware of. But why, or by what, art thou persuaded that thou hast left all for God and heaven?

IGNOR. My heart tells me so.

CHR. The wise man says, He that trusts his own heart is a fool.

IGNOR. That is spoken of an evil heart; but mine is a good one.

CHR. But how dost thou prove that?

IGNOR. It comforts me in hopes of heaven.

CHR. That may be through its deceitfulness; for a man's heart may minister comfort to him in the hopes of that thing for which he has yet no ground to hope.

IGNOR. But my heart and life agree together; and therefore my hope is well grounded.

CHR. Who told thee that thy heart and life agree together?

IGNOR. My heart tells me so.

CHR. Ask my fellow if I be a thief. Thy heart tells thee so! Except the Word of God beareth witness in this matter, other testimony is of no value.

IGNOR. But is it not a good heart that has good thoughts? and is not that a good life that is according to God's commandments?

CHR. Yes, that is a good heart that hath good thoughts, and that is a good life that is according to God's commandments; but it is one thing indeed to have these, and another thing only to think so.

IGNOR. Pray, what count you good thoughts, and a life according to God's commandments?

CHR. There are good thoughts of divers kinds;—some respecting ourselves, some God, some Christ, and some other things.

IGNOR. What be good thoughts respecting ourselves?

CHR. Such as agree with the Word of God.

IGNOR. When do our thoughts of ourselves agree with the Word of God?

CHR. When we pass the same judgment upon ourselves which the Word passes. To explain myself: the Word of God saith of persons in a natural condition, There is none righteous, there is none that doeth good. It saith also, that every imagination of the heart of man is only evil, and that continually. And again, The imagination of man's heart is evil from his youth. Now, then, when we think thus of ourselves, having *sense*[1] thereof, then are our thoughts good ones, because according to the Word of God.

IGNOR. I will never believe that my heart is thus bad.

CHR. Therefore thou never hadst one good

---

1. sense: awareness.

thought concerning thyself in thy life.—But let me go on. As the Word passeth a judgment upon our hearts, so it passeth a judgment upon our ways; and when our thoughts of our hearts and ways agree with the judgment which the Word giveth of both, then are both good, because agreeing thereto.

IGNOR. Make out your meaning.

CHR. Why, the Word of God saith, that man's ways are crooked ways, not good, but perverse; it saith, they are naturally out of the good way, that they have not known it. Now when a man thus thinketh of his ways, I say when he doth sensibly, and with heart-humiliation, thus think, then hath he good thoughts of his own ways, because his thoughts now agree with the judgment of the Word of God.

IGNOR. What are good thoughts concerning God?

CHR. Even, as I have said concerning ourselves, when our thoughts of God do agree with what the Word saith of Him; and that is, when we think of His being and **attributes** as the Word hath taught; of which I cannot now discourse at large. But to speak of Him in reference to us: then we have right thoughts of God when we think that He knows us better than we know ourselves, and can see sin in us when and where we can see none in ourselves; when we think He knows our inmost thoughts, and that our heart, with all its depths, is always open unto His eyes; also when we think that all our righteousness stinks in His nostrils, and that therefore He cannot abide to see us stand before Him in any confidence, even in all our best performances.

IGNOR. Do you think that I am such a fool as to think God can see no further than I; or that I would come to God in the best of my performances?

CHR. Why, how dost thou think in this matter?

IGNOR. Why, to be short, I think I must believe in Christ for justification.

CHR. How! think thou must believe in Christ, when thou seest not thy need of Him! Thou neither seest thy original nor actual infirmities; but hast such an opinion of thyself, and of what thou doest, as plainly renders thee to be one that did never see a necessity of Christ's personal righteousness to justify thee before God. How, then, dost thou say, I believe in Christ?

IGNOR. I believe well enough for all that.

CHR. How dost thou believe?

IGNOR. I believe that Christ died for sinners; and that I shall be justified before God from the curse, through His gracious acceptance of my obedience to His Law. Or thus, Christ makes my duties, that are religious, acceptable to His Father by virtue of His merits, and so shall I be justified.

CHR. Let me give an answer to this confession of thy faith.

1. Thou believest with a fantastical faith; for this faith is nowhere described in the Word.

2. Thou believest with a false faith; because it taketh justification from the personal righteousness of Christ, and applies it to thy own.

3. This faith maketh not Christ a justifier of thy person, but of thy actions; and of thy person for thy actions' sake, which is false.

4. Therefore this faith is deceitful, even such as will leave thee under wrath in the day of God Almighty: for true justifying faith puts the soul, as sensible of its lost condition by the law, upon flying for refuge unto Christ's righteousness (which righteousness of His is not an act of grace by which He maketh, for justification, thy obedience accepted with God, but His personal obedience to the law in doing and suffering for us

what that required at our hands); this right-eousness, I say, true faith accepteth; under the skirt of which the soul being **shrouded**, and by it presented as spotless before God, it is accepted, and **acquit** from condemnation.

IGNOR. What! would you have us trust to what Christ in His own person has done with-out us? This conceit would loosen the reins of our lust, and tolerate us to live as we list: for what matter how we live, if we may be justified by Christ's personal righteousness from all, when we believe it?

CHR. Ignorance is thy name, and as thy name is, so art thou: even this thy answer demonstrateth what I say. Ignorant thou art of what justifying righteousness is, and as igno-rant how to secure thy soul through the faith of it, from the heavy wrath of God. Yea, thou also art ignorant of the true effects of saving faith in this righteousness of Christ, which is to bow and win over the heart to God in Christ, to love His name, His word, ways, and people, and not as thou ignorantly imaginest.

HOPE. Ask him if ever he had Christ revealed to him from heaven.

IGNOR. What! you are a man for revelations! I believe, that what both you and all the rest of you say about that matter, is but the fruit of dis-tracted brains.

HOPE. Why, man! Christ is so hid in God from the natural apprehensions of the flesh, that He cannot by any man be savingly known, unless God the Father reveals Him to them.

IGNOR. That is your faith but not mine; yet mine, I doubt not, is as good as yours, though I have not in my head so many **whimsies** as you.

CHR. Give me leave to put in a word. You ought not so slightly to speak of this matter: for this I will boldly affirm (even as my good com-panion hath done), that no man can know Jesus Christ but by the revelation of the Father: yea, and faith too, by which the soul layeth hold upon Christ (if it be right), must be wrought by the exceeding greatness of His mighty power; the working of which faith, I perceive, poor Ignorance, thou art ignorant of. Be awakened then, see thine own wretchedness, and fly to the Lord Jesus; and by His righteousness, which is the righteousness of God (for He Him-self is God), thou shalt be delivered from con-demnation.

IGNOR. You go so fast, I cannot keep pace with you; do you go on before: I must stay awhile behind.

Then they said—

Well, Ignorance, wilt thou yet foolish be,
To slight good counsel, ten times given thee?
And if thou yet refuse it, thou shalt know
Ere long the evil of thy doing so.
Remember, man, in time; stoop, do not fear;
Good counsel, taken well, saves; therefore
   hear.
But if thou yet shalt slight it, thou wilt be
The loser, Ignorance, I'll warrant thee.

Then Christian addressed thus himself to his fellow:—

CHR. Well, come, my good Hopeful, I per-ceive that thou and I must walk by ourselves again.

So I saw in my dream that they went on apace before, and Ignorance he came hobbling after. Then said Christian to his companion, It pities me much for this poor man: it will cer-tainly go ill with him at last.

HOPE. Alas! there are abundance in our town in this condition, whole families, yea, whole streets, and that of pilgrims too; and if there be so many in our parts, how many, think you, must there be in the place where he was born?

CHR. Indeed the Word saith, He hath blinded their eyes, lest they should see, etc.

But, now we are by ourselves, what do you think of such men? have they at no time, think you, convictions of sin, and so consequently fear that their state is dangerous?

HOPE. Nay, do you answer that question yourself, for you are the elder man.

CHR. Then I say, sometimes (as I think) they may; but they being naturally ignorant, under-stand not that such convictions tend to their good; and therefore they do desperately seek to **stifle** them, and presumptuously continue to flatter themselves in the way of their own hearts.

HOPE. I do believe, as you say, that fear tends much to men's good, and to make them right at their beginning to go on pilgrimage.

CHR. Without all doubt it doth, if it be right: for so says the Word, The fear of the Lord is the beginning of wisdom.

HOPE. How will you describe right fear?

CHR. True or right fear is discovered by three things:

1. By its rise: it is caused by saving convictions for sin.

2. It driveth the soul to lay fast hold of Christ for salvation.

3. It begetteth and continueth in the soul a great reverence of God, His Word, and ways; keeping it tender, and making it afraid to turn from them, to the right hand or to the left, to anything that may dishonour God, break its peace, grieve the Spirit, or cause the enemy to speak reproachfully.

HOPE. Well said; I believe you have said the truth. Are we now almost got past the Enchanted Ground?

CHR. Why? art thou weary of this discourse?

HOPE. No, **verily**, but that I would know where we are.

CHR. We have not now above two miles farther to go thereon.—But let us return to our matter.

Now the ignorant know not that such convictions as tend to put them in fear, are for their good, and therefore they seek to stifle them.

HOPE. How do they seek to stifle them?

CHR. 1. They think that those fears are wrought by the devil (though indeed they are wrought of God), and thinking so, they resist them, as things that directly tend to their overthrow.

2. They also think that these fears tend to the spoiling of their faith; when, alas for them, poor men that they are, they have none at all! and therefore they harden their hearts against them.

3. They presume they ought not to fear, and therefore, in despite of them, wax presumptuously confident.

4. They see that those fears tend to take away from them their pitiful old self-holiness, and therefore they resist them with all their might.

HOPE. I know something of this myself; for before I knew myself it was so with me.

CHR. Well, we will leave, at this time, our neighbour Ignorance by himself, and fall upon another profitable question.

HOPE. With all my heart, but you shall still begin.

CHR. Well, then, did you not know, about ten years ago, one Temporary in your parts, who was a forward man in religion then?

HOPE. Know him! yes; he dwelt in Graceless, a town about two miles off of Honesty, and he dwelt next door to one Turnback.

CHR. Right; he dwelt under the same roof with him. Well, that man was much awakened once; I believe that then he had some sight of his sins, and of the wages that were due thereto.

HOPE. I am of your mind, for (my house not being above three miles from him) he would ofttimes come to me, and that with many tears. Truly I pitied the man, and was not altogether without hope of him: but one may see, it is not every one that cries, Lord, Lord!

CHR. He told me once that he was resolved to go on pilgrimage, as we do now; but all of a sudden he grew acquainted with one Save-self, and then he became a stranger to me.

HOPE. Now, since we are talking about him, let us a little inquire into the reason of the sudden backsliding of him and such others.

CHR. It may be very profitable, but do you begin.

HOPE. Well, then, there are in my judgment, four reasons for it:

1. Though the consciences of such men are awakened, yet their minds are not changed; therefore, when the power of guilt weareth away, that which provoketh them to be religious ceaseth; wherefore they naturally return to their own course again; even as we see the dog that is sick of what he hath eaten, so long as his sickness prevails, he vomits and casts up all; not that he doth this of a free mind (if we may say a dog has a mind), but because it troubleth his stomach: but now, when his sickness is over, and so his stomach eased, his desires being not at all alienated from his vomit, he turns him about, and licks up all, and so it is true which is written, The dog is turned to his own vomit again. This I say, being hot for heaven, by virtue only of the sense and fear of the torments of hell, as their sense of hell and

the fears of damnation chills and cools, so their desires for heaven and salvation cool also. So then it comes to pass that when their guilt and fear is gone, their desires for heaven and happiness die, and they return to their course again.

2. Another reason is, they have slavish fears that do overmaster them; I speak now of the fears that they have of men: For the fear of man bringeth a snare. So then, though they seem to be hot for heaven so long as the flames of hell are about their ears, yet, when that terror is a little over, they betake themselves to second thoughts, namely, that 'tis good to be wise, and not to run (for they know not what) the hazard of losing all, or at least of bringing themselves into unavoidable and unnecessary troubles; and so they fall in with the world again.

3. The shame that attends religion lies also as a block in their way: they are proud and haughty, and religion in their eye is low and contemptible: therefore, when they have lost their sense of hell and wrath to come, they return again to their former course.

4. Guilt, and to meditate terror, are grievous to them; they like not to see their misery before they come into it; though perhaps the sight of it first, if they loved not that sight, might make them fly whither the righteous fly, and are safe; but because they do, as I hinted before, even shun the thoughts of guilt and terror; therefore, when once they are rid of their awakenings about the terrors and wrath of God, they harden their hearts gladly, and choose such ways as will harden them more and more.

CHR. You are pretty near the business, for the bottom of all is for want of a change in their mind and will. And therefore they are but like the *felon*[2] that standeth before the judge: he quakes and trembles, and seems to repent most heartily; but the bottom of all is the fear of the halter, not that he hath any detestation of the offences as is evident; because let but this man have his liberty, and he will be a thief, and so a rogue still; whereas, if his mind was changed, he would be otherwise.

HOPE. Now I have showed you the reasons of their going back, do you show me the manner thereof.

CHR. So I will willingly:

1. They draw off their thoughts, all that they may, from the remembrance of God, death, and judgment to come.

2. Then they cast off by degrees private duties, as closet prayer, **curbing** their lusts, watching, sorrow for sin, and the like.

3. Then they shun the company of lively and warm Christians.

4. After that they grow cold to public duty; as hearing, reading, godly conference, and the like.

5. Then they begin to pick holes, as we say, in the coats of some of the godly; and that devilishly, that they may have a seeming colour to throw religion (for the sake of some infirmity they have spied in them) behind their backs.

6. Then they begin to adhere to, and associate themselves with, carnal, loose, and wanton men.

7. Then they give way to carnal and wanton discourses in secret; and glad are they if they can see such things in any that are counted honest, that they may the more boldly do it through their example.

8. After this, they begin to play with little sins openly.

9. And then, being hardened, they show themselves as they are. Thus, being **launched** again into the gulf of misery, unless a miracle of grace prevent it, they everlastingly perish in their own deceivings.

---

2. felon: an evil person; criminal.

Meditating for Meaning

1. Why do you think Ignorance does not like the company of others?
2. Ignorance displays his ignorance in his speech.
   a. What answer does Ignorance twice give as evidence that he is on the right way?
   b. What does Christian inform him is the only proof of being right?
3. According to God's Word, what should we think about each of the following:
   a. our hearts
   b. our ways
   c. God's knowledge of us compared to our own
4. According to Ignorance's faith, Christ
   a. makes us acceptable to God in spite of our evil works.
   b. makes our good works outweigh the evil works.
   c. makes our good works acceptable with God.
   d. makes our evil works acceptable with God.
5. True "fear of the Lord" is known by its *rise* or beginning, its *expression*, and its *effect*. Explain each of these characteristics of true fear as Christian gives them.
6. In what way is Temporary like the plant growing in the stony soil of Matthew 13:20, 21?
7. What four reasons does Hopeful give for backsliding?
8. Give in your own words the nine steps of backsliding.

Chapter 19: Christian and Hopeful Enter the Land of Beulah and Cross the River

Defining for Comprehension	Choose the word or phrase below which most nearly defines each word at the left as it is used in this allegory.		
1. apparitions	a. dividers	b. unexpected appearances	c. written pleas
2. intimate	a. suggest	b. embarrass	c. become associated
3. ado	a. arrangement	b. trouble	c. farewell

Now I saw in my dream, that by this time the pilgrims were got over the Enchanted Ground, and entering into the country of Beulah, whose air was very sweet and pleasant; the way lying directly through it, they solaced themselves there for a season. Yea, here they heard continually the singing of birds, and saw every day the flowers appear in the earth, and heard the voice of the *turtle*[1] in the land. In this country the sun shineth night and day: wherefore this was beyond the Valley of the Shadow of Death, and also out of the reach of Giant Despair; neither could they from this place so much as see Doubting Castle. Here they were within sight of the City they were going to: also here met them some of the inhabitants thereof; for in this land the Shining Ones commonly walked, because it was upon the borders of heaven. In this land also the contract between the Bride and the Bridegroom was renewed; yea, here, as the Bridegroom rejoiceth over the Bride, so did their God rejoice over them. Here they had no want of corn and wine; for in this place they met with abundance of what they had sought for in all their pilgrimages. Here they heard voices from out of the City, loud voices, saying, Say ye to the daughter of Zion, Behold, thy salvation cometh! Behold, His reward is with him! Here all the inhabitants of the country called them: the holy people, the redeemed of the Lord, sought out, etc.

Now, as they walked this land, they had more rejoicing than in parts more remote from the kingdom to which they were bound; and drawing near to the City, they had yet a more perfect view thereof. It was builded of pearls and precious stones, also the street thereof was paved with gold; so that, by reason of the natural glory of the City, and the reflection of the sunbeams upon it, Christian with desire fell sick; Hopeful also had a fit or two of the same disease: wherefore here they lay by it awhile, crying out because of their pangs, If you see my Beloved, tell Him that I am sick of love.

But being a little strengthened, and better able to bear their sickness, they walked on their way, and came yet nearer and nearer, where were orchards, vineyards, and gardens, and their gates opened into the highway. Now, as they came up to these places, behold, the gardener stood in the way; to whom the pilgrims said, Whose goodly vineyards and gardens are these? He answered, They are the King's, and are planted here for His own delights, and also for the solace of pilgrims. So the gardener had them into the vineyards, and bid them refresh themselves with the dainties; he also showed them there the King's walks and the arbours where He delighted to be: and here they tarried and slept.

Now I beheld in my dream, that they talked more in their sleep at this time than ever they did in all their journey; and, being in a muse thereabout, the gardener said even to me, Wherefore musest thou at the matter? it is the nature of the fruit of the grapes of these vineyards to go down so sweetly as to cause the lips of them that are asleep to speak.

So I saw that when they awoke they addressed themselves to go up to the City. But, as I said, the reflection of the sun upon the City (for the City was pure gold), was so extremely glorious, that they could not as yet with open face behold it, but through an instrument made for that purpose. So I saw, that as they went on, there met them two men in raiment that shone like gold, also their faces shone as the light.

These men asked the pilgrims whence they came, and they told them. They also asked them where they had lodged, what difficulties and dangers, what comforts and pleasures, they had met in the way; and they told them. Then said the men that met them, You have but two difficulties more to meet with, and then you are in the City.

Christian then and his companion asked the men to go along with them: so they told them they would; But, said they, you must obtain it by your own faith. So I saw in my dream that they went on together till they came in sight of the gate.

Now I further saw that betwixt them and the gate was a river; but there was no bridge to go over; the river was very deep. At the sight

---

1. turtle: turtle dove.

therefore of this river the pilgrims were much stunned; but the men that went with them said, You must go through or you cannot come at the gate.

The pilgrims then began to inquire, if there was no other way to the gate. To which they answered, Yes; but there hath not any, save two, to wit, Enoch and Elijah, been permitted to tread that path, since the foundation of the world, nor shall until the last trumpet shall sound. The pilgrims then, especially Christian, began to despond in their minds, and looked this way and that, but no way could be found by them by which they might escape the river. Then they asked the men if the waters were all of a depth. They said, No; yet they could not help them in that case; For, said they, you shall find it deeper or shallower, as you believe in the King of the place.

They then addressed themselves to the water and entering, Christian began to sink, and, crying out to his good friend Hopeful, he said, I sink in deep waters; the billows go over my head, all His waves go over me! Selah.

Then said the other, Be of good cheer, my

brother: I feel the bottom, and it is good. Then said Christian, Ah! my friend, the sorrows of death have compassed me about, I shall not see the land that flows with milk and honey. And with that a great darkness and horror fell upon Christian, so that he could not see before him. Also here he in great measure lost his senses, so that he could neither remember nor orderly talk of any of those sweet refreshments that he had met with in the way of his pilgrimages. But all the words that he spake still tended to discover that he had horror of mind, and hearty fears that he should die in that river, and never obtain entrance in at the gate. Here also, as they that stood by perceived, he was much in the troublesome thoughts of the sins that he had committed, both since and before he began to be a pilgrim. 'Twas also observed, that he was troubled with **apparitions** of hobgoblins and evil spirits; for ever and anon he would **intimate** so much by words.

Hopeful therefore here had much **ado** to keep his brother's head above water; yea, sometimes he would be quite gone down, and then, ere awhile, he would rise up again half dead. Hopeful also would endeavour to comfort him, saying, Brother, I see the gate, and men standing by it to receive us; but Christian would answer, 'Tis you, 'tis you they wait for; you have been Hopeful ever since I knew you. And so have you, said he to Christian. Ah, brother, said he, surely if I was right He would now arise to help me; but for my sins He hath brought me into the snare, and hath left me. Then said Hopeful, My brother, you have quite forgot the text where it is said of the wicked, There is no band in their death, but their strength is firm; they are not troubled as other men, neither are they plagued like other men. These troubles and distresses that you go through in these waters, are no sign that God hath forsaken you; but are sent to try you, whether you will call to mind that which heretofore you have received of His goodness, and live upon Him in your distresses.

Then I saw in my dream, that Christian was as in a muse awhile. To whom also Hopeful added these words, Be of good cheer, Jesus Christ maketh thee whole. And with that Chris-

Artist: E. G. Dalziel

THE PILGRIM'S PROGRESS   **579**

tian brake out with a loud voice, Oh, I see Him again; and He tells me, When thou passest through the waters, I will be with thee; and through the rivers, they shall not overflow thee. Then they both took courage, and the enemy was after that as still as a stone, until they were gone over. Christian therefore presently found ground to stand upon, and so it followed that the rest of the river was but shallow. Thus they got over.

Meditating for Meaning

1. The Land of Beulah is the last scene before the river. Though there are many pleasures here, it is not yet heaven.
   a. What does the Land of Beulah represent?
   b. Look up the word *Beulah* in a Bible dictionary. How is it a fitting name for this land?
   c. What advantages do the pilgrims have in this land?

2. The pilgrims must cross the river before entering the Celestial City.
   a. What does the river, which only Enoch and Elijah escape, represent?
   b. Describe how the pilgrims react as they face the crossing of the river.

3. The river varies in depth for the two pilgrims.
   a. What helps to make the water shallower?
   b. From what you observed of Christian and Hopeful before this, why do you think Christian has more difficulty than Hopeful in crossing the river?
   c. Is a hard struggle at the time of death evidence that a person is not a Christian?
   d. What may be the purpose of such a struggle?

4. How does Hopeful strengthen Christian?

Chapter 20: Christian and Hopeful Reach Zion

Now upon the bank of the river, on the other side, they saw the two shining men again, who there waited for them. Wherefore being come out of the river, they saluted them, saying, We are ministering spirits, sent forth to minister for those that shall be heirs of salvation. Thus they went along towards the gate.

Now you must note, that the City stood upon a mighty hill; but the pilgrims went up that hill with ease, because they had these two men to lead them up by the arms; also they had left their mortal garments behind them in the river; for though they went in with them, they came out without them. They therefore went up here with much **agility** and speed, though the foundation upon which the City was framed was higher than the clouds; they therefore went up through the regions of the air, sweetly talking as they went, being comforted because they safely got over the river, and had such glorious companions to attend them.

The talk that they had with the Shining Ones was about the glory of the place; who told them that the beauty and glory of it was inexpressible. There, said they, is the Mount Zion, the heavenly Jerusalem, the innumerable company of angels, and the spirits of just men made perfect. You are going now, said they, to the paradise of God, wherein you shall see the tree of life, and eat of the never-fading fruits thereof: and when you come there you shall have white robes given you, and your walk and talk shall be every day with the King, even all the days of eternity. There you shall not see again such things as you saw when you were in the lower region upon the earth: to wit, sorrow, sickness, affliction, and death; For the former things are passed away. You are going now to Abraham, to Isaac, and Jacob, and to the prophets, men that God hath taken away from the evil to come, and that are now resting upon their beds, each one walking in his righteousness. The men then asked, What must we do in the holy place? To whom it was answered, You must there receive the comfort of all your toil, and have joy for all your sorrow; you must reap what you have sown, even the fruit of all your prayers, and tears, and sufferings for the King by the way. In that place you must wear crowns of gold, and enjoy the perpetual sight and visions of the Holy One; for there you shall see Him as He is. There also you shall serve Him continually with praise, with shouting and thanksgiving, whom you desired to serve in the world, though with much difficulty, because of the infirmity of your flesh. There your eyes shall be delighted with seeing, and your ears with hearing the pleasant voice of the Mighty One. There you shall enjoy your friends again that are gone thither before you; and there you shall with joy receive even every one that follows into the holy place after you. There also you shall be clothed with glory and majesty, and put into an *equipage*[1] fit to ride out with the King of glory.

---

1. equipage: horse-drawn carriage.

When He shall come with sound of trumpet in the clouds, as upon the wings of the wind, you shall come with Him; and when He shall sit upon the throne of judgment, you shall sit by Him; yea, and when He shall pass sentence upon all the workers of iniquity, let them be angels or men, you also shall have a voice in that judgment because they were His and your enemies. Also, when He shall again return to the City, you shall go too with sound of trumpet, and be ever with Him.

Now while they were thus drawing towards the gate, behold a company of the heavenly host came out to meet them; to whom it was said by the other two Shining Ones, These are the men that have loved our Lord, when they were in the world, and that have left all for His holy name; and He hath sent us to fetch them, and we have brought them thus far on their desired journey, that they may go in and look their Redeemer in the face with joy. Then the heavenly host gave a great shout, saying, Blessed are they that are called to the marriage-supper of the Lamb. There came out also at this

time to meet them several of the King's trumpeters, clothed in white and shining raiment, who with melodious noises and loud made even the heavens to echo with their sound. These trumpeters saluted Christian and his fellow with ten thousand welcomes from the world; and this they did with shouting and sound of trumpet.

This done, they compassed them round on every side; some went before, some behind, and some on the right hand, some on the left (as 'twere to guard them through the upper regions), continually sounding as they went, with melodious noise, in notes on high: so that the very sight was to them that could behold it as if heaven itself was come down to meet them. Thus therefore they walked on together; and, as they walked, ever and anon these trumpeters, even with joyful sound, would, by mixing their music with looks and **gestures**, still signify to Christian and his brother how welcome they were into their company, and with what gladness they came to meet them. And now were these two men, as 'twere, in heaven, before they came at it, being, swallowed up with the sight of angels, and with hearing of their melodious notes. Here also they had the City itself in view; and they thought they heard all the bells therein to ring, to welcome them thereto. But, above all, the warm and joyful thoughts that they had about their own dwelling there, with such company, and that for ever and ever, oh, by what tongue or pen can their glorious joy be expressed! Thus they came up to the gate.

Now when they were come up to the gate, there was written over it in letters of gold, BLESSED ARE THEY THAT DO HIS COMMANDMENTS, THAT THEY MAY HAVE RIGHT TO THE TREE OF LIFE, AND MAY ENTER IN THROUGH THE GATES INTO THE CITY.

Then I saw in my dream that the Shining Men bid them call at the gate: the which when they did, some looked from above over the gate, to wit, Enoch, Moses, and Elijah, etc., to whom it was said, These pilgrims are come from the City of Destruction, for the love that they bear to the King of this place: and then the pilgrims gave in unto them each man his certificate, which they had received in the beginning; those therefore were carried in to the King, who when He had read them, said, Where are the men? To whom it was answered, They are standing without the gate. The King then commanded to open the gate, That the righteous nation, said He, that keepeth truth may enter in.

Now I saw in my dream that these two men went in at the gate; and lo! as they entered, they were transfigured; and they had raiment put on that shone like gold. There were also that met them with harps and crowns, and gave them to them; the harps to praise withal, and the crowns in token of honour. Then I heard in my dream that all the bells in the City rang again for joy, and that it was said unto them, Enter ye into the joy of our Lord. I also heard the men themselves, that they sang with a loud voice, saying, "Blessing, honour, glory, and power, be to Him that sitteth upon the throne, and to the Lamb for ever and ever.

Now, just as the gates were opened to let in the men, I looked in after them, and behold, the City shone like the sun, the streets also were paved with gold; and in them walked many men, with crowns on their heads, palms in their hands, and golden harps, to sing praises withal.

There were also of them that had wings, and they answered one another without intermission, saying, Holy, holy, holy is the Lord. And after that they shut up the gates: which when I had seen, I wished myself among them.

Now, while I was gazing upon all these things, I turned my head to look back, and saw Ignorance come up to the river side; but he soon got over, and that without half the difficulty which the other two men met with. For it happened that there was then in the place one Vain-Hope, a ferryman, that with his boat helped him over; so he, as the other I saw, did ascend the hill, to come up to the gate; only he came alone; neither did any man meet him with the least encouragement. When he was come up to the gate, he looked up to the writing that was above, and then began to knock, supposing that entrance should have been quickly administered to him; but he was asked by the men that looked over the top of the gate, Whence came you? and what he would have? He answered, I have ate and drank in the presence of the King, and He has taught in our streets. Then they asked him for his certificate, that they might go in and show it to the King: so he fumbled in his bosom for one, and found none. Then said they, Have you none? but the man answered never a word. So they told the King, but He would not come down to see him, but commanded the two Shining Ones that conducted Christian and Hopeful to the City, to go out and take Ignorance, and bind him hand and foot, and have him away. Then they took him up, and carried him through the air, to the door that I saw in the side of the hill, and put him in there. Then I saw that there was a way to hell, even from the gates of heaven, as well as from the City of Destruction. So I awoke, and behold it was a dream.

Meditating for Meaning

1. Two shining men meet the pilgrims on the other side of the river. Whom do they represent? (Hebrews 1:13, 14)

2. What does the hill up to Zion represent? Note that it comes after the river and goes higher than the clouds.

3. List four of the pilgrims' activities in Zion.

4. Describe the pilgrims' reception into Zion.

5. Ignorance crosses the river easily.
   a. What means does he use?
   b. Why do you think the unbeliever sometimes has an easier death than the true Christian? (Psalm 73:4)

6. Though death was easy for Ignorance, he is not yet in the Celestial City.
   a. Why is Ignorance not received into Zion?
   b. Why do you think he is speechless?

7. Why do you suppose Bunyan closes his allegory with the unhappy end of Ignorance rather than with the joys of Christian and Hopeful?

The Celestial Railroad

by Nathaniel Hawthorne

Like a modern-day Jotham, Nathaniel Hawthorne stood on the hill of his literary reputation and shouted an allegory to the liberal theologians of his day. They had elected to follow the false doctrines of Unitarianism. That is the big name for the religion that teaches that there is only one person in the Godhead instead of three as the Bible teaches. Therefore Unitarians deny that Christ is divine and to them there is no Holy Spirit. They deny the existence of hell and do not believe that man has a sinful nature. They optimistically believe that man can improve himself and make the world a better place to live, all by himself.

It is really no wonder that Unitarians believe these wrong things because they do not depend on revelation for their ideas but put much stress on human reasoning as a way to arrive at truth. They do believe in a spirit world. They believe there is reality beyond the physical world that can be seen and felt. But they think that spiritual truth can be discovered by reasoning aside from a special communication from God. The Bible to them is no more authoritative than other ancient religious books. This philosophy of the Unitarians for arriving at absolute truth through reasoning is called transcendentalism. It is represented in Hawthorne's allegory as Giant Transcendentalist.

Unitarians would pride themselves in their ability to gain insights from the religious writings of all ages and beliefs. Therefore they react to accepting the straight and narrow way of the Bible as the only way to God. They scorn the idea of carrying a burden of guilt for one's sins. With their emphasis on the ability of man to solve his own problems, Unitarians are much too proud to grovel along in a Valley of Humiliation or to pick their way through the Valley of the Shadow of Death. The Unitarian way is almost completely opposite to the hard road of Christian in **The Pilgrim's Progress.**

So to expose their errors, what better literary form could Hawthorne use than a modern imitation version of Bunyan's **Pilgrim's Progress?** *When a writer copies the style of another author for the purpose of ridicule, the result is a* **parody.** *It will not be difficult for you to recognize that "The Celestial Railroad" is a parody on* **The Pilgrim's Progress.** *Parodies are usually written with a satirical tone; that is, the author is ridiculing or making light of something that others take very* seriously. In "The Celestial Railroad" Hawthorne is belittling the ideas of the Unitarians. The Unitarians themselves were generally well-educated aristocrats. They included such prominent men as John Adams and Ralph Waldo Emerson. Although Thomas Jefferson was not a member of any religious group, he favored the Unitarians. To these men, Unitarianism was a respectable religion. But to the Christian, their doctrines are as foolish as the superstitious ideas of the heathen. "The Celestial Railroad" is so skillfully satirical that it would cause even a Unitarian to lift his eyebrows. Emerson himself gave this parody special commendation as a piece of literature.

While Hawthorne had Unitarianism in mind when he wrote "The Celestial Railroad," the liberal religious ideas of many modern Christians are similar enough to make this allegory applicable to our present time. Wrong ideas from science (falsely so-called) are often included in what is proclaimed to be the gospel message. With insights from psychology and sociology, modern preachers and philosophers promise their guilt-ridden adherents an easier way than repentance and the Cross. They in effect become modern Mr. Smooth-it-Aways (a prominent character in the parody you are about to read). Be on the alert for further applications to our day.

The Celestial Railroad – Part 1

Defining for Comprehension

Choose the word or phrase below which most nearly defines each word at the left as it is used in this allegory.

1. **populous**
   a. famous
   b. proud; rich
   c. densely inhabited

2. **gratify**
   a. satisfy
   b. make thankful
   c. enact

3. **statistics**
   a. social positions
   b. facts
   c. clever plans

4. **enterprise**
   a. reward
   b. business
   c. beginning

5. **immemorial**
   a. not worthy of remembrance
   b. beyond memory
   c. forgetful

6. **ingenious**
   a. clever
   b. frank; outspoken
   c. disgraceful

7. **formidable**
   a. threatening
   b. denied
   c. out of sight

8. **loth (loath)**
   a. lazy
   b. envious
   c. reluctant

9. **edifice**
   a. grand speech
   b. grand structure
   c. profit

10. **mystic**
    a. mysterious
    b. foggy
    c. antique

11. **reputable**
    a. subject to argument
    b. honorable
    c. replaceable

12. **competent**
    a. rivaling
    b. skillful
    c. spiteful

13. **imposture**
    a. intruder
    b. slouching position
    c. false identity

14. **eminence**
    a. fame
    b. nearness
    c. threatening character

15. **indubitably**
    a. unquestionably
    b. without energy
    c. traitorously

16. **infidel**	a. fortress	b. unbeliever	c. insane person
17. **respective**	a. honorable	b. corresponding	c. polite
18. **benevolent**	a. vicious	b. brave	c. good; kind
19. **feud**	a. medieval lord	b. tangle	c. quarrel
20. **adherents**	a. loners	b. followers	c. hindrances
21. **illustrious**	a. famous	b. shiny	c. well-described
22. **potentate**	a. sovereign	b. helper	c. president
23. **pacifically**	a. exactly	b. peaceably	c. formally
24. **congenial**	a. agreeable	b. from childhood	c. hot
25. **preposterously**	a. ridiculously	b. reasonably	c. tardily
26. **embroiled**	a. cooked	b. depressed	c. involved in quarrel
27. **irrepressible**	a. uninspiring	b. uncontrollable	c. rebellious
28. **obliterated**	a. made clumsy	b. schooled	c. erased

Not a great while ago, passing through the gate of dreams, I visited that region of the earth in which lies the famous City of Destruction. It interested me much to learn that by the public spirit of some of the inhabitants a railroad has recently been established between this **populous** and flourishing town and the Celestial City. Having a little time upon my hands, I resolved to **gratify** a liberal curiosity to make a trip thither. Accordingly, one fine morning, after paying my bill at the hotel, and directing the porter to stow my luggage behind a coach, I took my seat in the vehicle and set out for the station-house. It was my good fortune to enjoy the company of a gentleman—one Mr. Smooth-it-Away—who, though he had never actually visited the Celestial City, yet seemed as well acquainted with its laws, customs, policy and **statistics** as with those of the City of Destruction, of which he was a native townsman. Being, moreover, a director of the railroad corporation and one of its largest stockholders, he had it in his power to give me all the desirable information respecting the praiseworthy **enterprise**.

Our coach rattled out of the city, and, at a short distance from its outskirts, passed over a bridge of elegant construction, but somewhat too slight, as I imagined, to sustain any considerable weight. On both sides lay an extensive quagmire which could not have been more disagreeable either to sight or smell had all the kennels of the earth emptied their pollution there.

"This," remarked Mr. Smooth-it-Away, "is the famous Slough of Despond—a disgrace to all the neighborhood, and the greater that it might so easily be converted into firm ground."

"I have understood," said I, "that efforts have been made for that purpose from time **immemorial**. Bunyan mentions that above twenty-thousand cart-loads of wholesome instructions had been thrown in here without effect."

"Very probably! And what effect could be anticipated from such unsubstantial stuff?" cried Mr. Smooth-it-Away. "You observe this convenient bridge? We obtained a sufficient foundation for it by throwing into the slough some editions of books of morality, volumes of French philosophy and German rationalism, tracts, sermons and essays of modern clergymen, extracts from Plato, Confucius and various Hindu sages, together with a few **ingenious** commentaries upon texts of Scripture—all of which, by some scientific process, have been converted into a mass like granite. The whole bog might be filled up with similar matter."

It really seemed to me, however, that the bridge vibrated and heaved up and in a very **formidable** manner; and, in spite of Mr. Smooth-it-Away's testimony to the solidity of its foundation, I should be **loth** to cross it in a crowded omnibus, especially if each passenger were encumbered with as heavy luggage as that gentleman and myself. Nevertheless, we got over without accident, and soon found ourselves at the station house. This very neat and spacious **edifice** is erected on the site of the little wicket-gate which formerly, as all old pilgrims will recollect, stood directly across the highway, and by its inconvenient narrowness was a great objection to the traveler of liberal mind and expansive stomach. The reader of John Bunyan will be glad to know that Christian's old friend Evangelist, who was accustomed to supply each pilgrim with a **mystic** roll, now presides at the ticket-office. Some malicious persons, it is true, deny the identity of this **reputable** character with the Evangelist of old times, and even pretend to bring **competent** evidences of an **imposture**. Without involving myself into a dispute, I shall merely observe that, as far as my experience goes, the square pieces of pasteboard now delivered to passengers are much more convenient and useful along the road than the antique roll of parchment. Whether they will be as readily received at the gate of the Celestial City, I decline giving an opinion.

A large number of passengers were already at the station house awaiting the departure of the cars. By the aspect and demeanor of these persons, it is easy to judge that the feelings of the community had undergone a very favorable change in reference to the celestial pilgrimage. It would have done Bunyan's heart good to see it. Instead of a lonely and ragged man with a huge burden on his back, plodding along sorrowfully on foot, while the whole city hooted after him, here were parties of the first gentry and most respectable people in the neighborhood setting forth towards the Celestial City as cheerfully as if the pilgrimage were merely a summer tour. Among the gentlemen were characters of deserved **eminence**—magistrates, politicians and men of wealth by whose example religion could not but be greatly recommended to their meaner brethren. In the ladies' apartment, too, I rejoiced to distinguish some of those *flowers*[1] of fashionable society who are so well fitted to adorn the most elevated circles of the Celestial City. There was much pleasant conversation about the news of the day, topics of business, politics or the lighter matters of amusement, while religion, though **indubitably** the main thing at heart, was thrown tastefully into the background. Even an **infidel** would have heard little or nothing to shock his sensibility.

One great convenience of the new method of going on pilgrimage I must not forget to mention. Our enormous burdens, instead of being carried on our shoulders, as had been the custom of old, were all snugly deposited in the baggage-car, and, as I was assured, would be delivered to their **respective** owners at the journey's end. Another thing, likewise, the **benevolent** reader will be delighted to understand. It may be remembered that there was an ancient **feud** between Prince Beelzebub and the keeper of the wicket-gate, and that the **adherents** of the former distinguished personage were accustomed to shoot deadly arrows at honest pilgrims while knocking at the door. This dispute, much to the credit as well of the **illustrious potentate** above mentioned as of the worthy and enlightened directors of the railroad, has been **pacifically** arranged on the principle of mutual compromise. The prince's subjects are now pretty numerously employed about the station house—some in taking care of the baggage, others in collecting fuel, feeding the engines, and such **congenial** occupations—and I can conscientiously affirm that persons more attentive to their business, more willing to accommodate or more generally agreeable to the passengers are not to be found on any railroad. Every good heart must surely exult at so satisfactory an arrangement of an immemorial difficulty.

"Where is Mr. Greatheart?" inquired I. "Beyond a doubt, the directors have engaged that famous old champion to be chief conductor on the railroad?"

"Why no," said Mr. Smooth-it-Away, with a dry cough. "He was offered the situation of brakeman, but, to tell you the truth, our friend Greatheart has grown **preposterously** stiff and narrow in his old age. He has so often guided pilgrims over the road on foot that he considers it a sin to travel in any other fashion. Besides, the old fellow had entered so heartily into the ancient feud with Prince Beelzebub that he would have been perpetually at blows or ill-language with some of the prince's subjects, and thus have **embroiled** us anew. So, on the whole, we were not sorry when honest Greatheart went off to the Celestial City in a huff and left us at liberty to choose a more suitable and accommodating man. Yonder comes the conductor of the train. You will probably recognize him at once."

The engine at this moment took its station in advance of the cars, looking, I must confess, much more like a sort of mechanical demon that would hurry us to the infernal regions than a laudable contrivance for smoothing our way to the Celestial City. On its top sat a personage almost enveloped in smoke and flame which—not to startle the reader—appeared to gush from his own mouth and stomach, as well as from the engine's brazen abdomen.

"Do my eyes deceive me?" cried I. "What on earth is this? A living creature? If so, he is own brother to the engine he rides upon?"

"Poh, poh! you are *abtuse!*[2]" said Mr. Smooth-it-Away, with a hearty laugh. "Don't you know Apollyon, Christian's old enemy, with whom he fought so fierce a battle in the Valley of Humiliation? He was the very fellow to manage the engine, and so we have reconciled him to the custom of going on pilgrimage, and engaged him as chief conductor."

"Bravo, bravo!" exclaimed I, with **irrepressible** enthusiasm. "This shows the liberality of the age; this proves, if anything can, that all musty prejudices are in a fair way to be **obliterated.** And how will Christian rejoice to hear of this happy transformation of his old antagonist! I promise myself great pleasure in informing him of it when we reach the Celestial City."

---

1. flowers: prominent, highly cultivated ladies.
2. abtuse: obtuse; dull-witted.

Meditating for Meaning

1. "The Celestial Railroad" is a parody of *The Pilgrim's Progress*.
   a. Define *parody*. Use a dictionary.
   b. From the first paragraph of this allegory, what similarities do you see to *The Pilgrim's Progress*?
   c. Both *The Pilgrim's Progress* and its parody contain a first person "I." But what difference is there in point of view?

2. There is also a difference in tone.
   a. While *The Pilgrim's Progress* has a very serious and sympathetic tone, this parody has a _____ tone.
   b. What evidences of this different tone can you detect in the opening paragraph of "The Celestial Railroad"?

3. A parody presents contrasts as well as similarities.
   a. Who is taking Evangelist's place in helping the pilgrim find the way?
   b. What does Hawthorne wish to suggest by this replacement?

4. The Celestial Railroad has "improved" on many inconveniences that Christian encountered.
   a. How does the modern pilgrim get over the Slough of Despond?
   b. What book in the foundation is notably missing?
   c. How could "ingenious commentaries upon texts of Scripture" contribute to making a shaky foundation? (1 Cor. 3:11, 2 Peter 3:16)

5. What outstanding differences exist between the station house and the former Wicket-gate?

6. The tickets are intended to be quite handy.
   a. Who is the ticket seller? Read carefully before you answer this.
   b. What do the pasteboard tickets replace?

7. Explain the irony of the statement: "It would have done Bunyan's heart good to see it."

8. The passengers differ from the pilgrims in *The Pilgrim's Progress*.
   a. Describe the kind of passengers who are going to travel on the Celestial Railroad.
   b. What are the subjects of conversation among the passengers? Note that the name *passengers* really fits these people better than *pilgrims*.

9. The modern pilgrim's and Mr. Smooth-it-Away's luggage is the same as Christian's in *The Pilgrim's Progress*.
   a. What is this luggage?
   b. How do the modern pilgrims transport their luggage?
   c. How does the final end of their luggage compare with the end of Christian's burden?

10. Prince Beelzebub no longer shoots arrows at pilgrims that enter the Wicket-gate.
    a. How has this danger been eliminated?
    b. Why are the station workers so helpful and friendly?

11. Mr. Greatheart is a character from Part 2 of *The Pilgrim's Progress,* which is not included in your text. He is a very stable and aggressive Christian who is quite helpful in conducting Christiana (Christian's wife) to the Celestial City. What has happened to Mr. Greatheart in the modern times of this allegory?

12. A steam locomotive is the basic symbol for this allegory.
    a. How do the involvements of a steam engine, such as the type of energy used to produce the steam, make it a suitable symbol for the agency of a false religion?

b. Who is the conductor?

c. Why would he agree to be an engineer on the Celestial Railroad?

The Celestial Railroad – Part 2

Defining for Comprehension

Choose the word or phrase below which most nearly defines each word at the left as it is used in this allegory.

1. **gibes**
   - a. smooth words
   - b. mocking remarks
   - c. lies

2. **obstreperous**
   - a. boisterous
   - b. apparent
   - c. uncertain

3. **inestimable**
   - a. precious
   - b. evident
   - c. insignificant

4. **unanimity**
   - a. calmness
   - b. liveliness
   - c. complete harmony

5. **incidental**
   - a. tragic
   - b. chance
   - c. tremendous

6. **obviating**
   - a. preventing
   - b. making apparent
   - c. erasing

7. **prodigious**
   - a. native
   - b. enormous
   - c. shameful

8. **reminiscences**
   - a. fragrances
   - b. memories
   - c. repeated services

9. **palpitations**
   - a. accusations
   - b. appointments
   - c. vibrations

10. **encomiums**
    - a. expressions of praise
    - b. fancy buildings
    - c. ugly names

11. **conception**
    - a. formal dinner
    - b. refusal
    - c. idea for beginning

12. **ingenuity**
    - a. inventiveness
    - b. reality
    - c. frankness

13. **exudes**
    - a. closes out
    - b. gives off
    - c. departs

14. **quadrupled**
    - a. enormous
    - b. dilapidated
    - c. multiplied by four

15. **reverberating**
    - a. scolding
    - b. increasing
    - c. echoing

16. **unprecedented**
    - a. unexpected
    - b. unremoved
    - c. new; unique

17. **lurid**
    - a. horrible; flaming
    - b. clear
    - c. black and blue

18. **obscurity**
    - a. safety
    - b. hiding
    - c. unpleasant-ness

19.	grotesque	a. distorted; ugly	b. cavern	c. statue
20.	articulate	a. revolving	b. understandable	c. ridged
21.	propensity	a. ascent	b. offer	c. inclination
22.	contortion	a. twisted deformity	b. extreme effort	c. waste
23.	indolent	a. mournful	b. poor	c. lazy
24.	impede	a. block	b. hasten	c. declare
25.	appalled	a. horrified	b. attacked	c. entreated
26.	delusions	a. removals	b. false beliefs	c. endings
27.	miscreant	a. mistaken	b. freak	c. scoundrel

The passengers being all comfortably seated, we now rattled away merrily, accomplishing a greater distance in ten minutes than Christian probably trudged over in a day. It was laughable while we glanced along, as it were, at the tail of a thunderbolt, to observe two dusty foot-travelers in the old pilgrim guise, with *cockle-shell*[1] and staff, their mystic rolls of parchment in their hands and their intolerable burdens on their backs. The preposterous obstinacy of these honest people in persisting to groan and stumble along the difficult pathway rather than take advantage of modern improvements excited great mirth among our wiser brotherhood. We greeted the two pilgrims with many pleasant **gibes** and a roar of laughter; whereupon they gazed at us with such woeful and absurdly compassionate visages that our merriment grew tenfold more **obstreperous**. Apollyon, also, entered heartily into the fun, and contrived to *flirt*[2] the smoke and flame of the engine or of his own breath into their faces, and envelop them in an atmosphere of scalding steam. These little practical jokes amused us mightily, and doubtless afforded the pilgrims the gratification of considering themselves martyrs.

At some distance from the railroad Mr. Smooth-it-Away pointed to a large, antique edifice which, he observed, was a tavern of long

1. cockle-shell: ornamentation usually in the collar imitating the shell of a scallop. The cockle shell became the pilgrim's badge because pilgrims often picked them up from the shore of Spain when visiting St. James' shrine.

2. flirt: toss suddenly.

standing, and had formerly been a noted stopping-place for pilgrims. In Bunyan's road-book it is mentioned as the Interpreter's House.

"I have long had a curiosity to visit that old mansion," remarked I.

"It is not one of our stations, as you perceive," said my companion. "The keeper was violently opposed to the railroad, and well he might be, as the track left his house of entertainment on one side, and thus was pretty certain to deprive him of all his reputable customers. But the footpath still passes his door, and the old gentleman now and then receives a call from some simple traveler and entertains him with fare as old-fashioned as himself."

Before our talk on this subject came to a conclusion we were rushing by the place where Christian's burden fell from his shoulders at the sight of the cross. This served as a theme for Mr. Smooth-it-Away, Mr. Live-for-the-World, Mr. Hide-Sin-in-the-Heart, Mr. Scaly-Conscience and a knot of gentlemen from the town of Shun-Repentance to *descant*[3] upon the **inestimable** advantages resulting from the safety of our baggage. Myself—and all the passengers indeed—joined with great **unanimity** in this view of the matter, for our burdens were rich in many things esteemed precious throughout the world, and especially we each of us possessed a great variety of favorite habits which we trusted would not be out of fashion even in the polite circles of the Celestial City. It would have been a sad spectacle to see such an assortment of valuable articles tumbling into the sepulcher.

Thus pleasantly conversing on the favorable circumstances of our position as compared with those of past pilgrims and of narrowminded ones at the present day, we soon found ourselves at the foot of the Hill Difficulty. Through the very heart of this rocky mountain a tunnel had been constructed, of most admirable architecture, with a lofty arch and a spacious double track; so that, unless the earth and rocks should chance to crumble down, it will remain an eternal monument of the builder's skill and enterprise. It is a great though **incidental** advantage that the materials from the heart of the Hill Difficulty have been employed in filling up the Valley of Humiliation, thus **obviating** the necessity of descending into that disagreeable and unwholesome hollow.

"This is a wonderful improvement, indeed," said I. "Yet I should have been glad of an opportunity to visit the Palace Beautiful and be introduced to the charming young ladies—Miss Prudence, Miss Piety, Miss Charity, and the rest—who had the kindness to entertain pilgrims there."

"'Young ladies'!" cried Mr. Smooth-it-Away, as soon as he could speak for laughing. "And charming young ladies! Why, my dear fellow, they are old maids, every soul of them—*prim*,[4] starched, dry, and *angular*[5]—and not one of them, I will venture to say, has altered so much as the fashion of her gown since the days of Christian's pilgrimage."

"Ah, well!" said I, much comforted; "then I can very readily *dispense with*[6] their acquaintance."

The respectable Apollyon was now putting on the steam at a **prodigious** rate—anxious, perhaps, to get rid of the unpleasant **reminiscences** connected with the spot where he had so disastrously encountered Christian.

Consulting Mr. Bunyan's road-book, I perceived that we must now be within a few miles of the Valley of the Shadow of Death, into which doleful region, at our present speed, we should plunge much sooner than seemed at all desirable. In truth, I expected nothing better than to find myself in the ditch on one side or the quag on the other. But on my communicating my apprehensions to Mr. Smooth-it-Away he assured me that the difficulties of this passage, even in its worse condition, had been vastly exaggerated, and that in its present state of improvement I might consider myself as safe as on any railroad in Christendom.

---

3. descant: comment at length.

4. prim: strictly proper.

5. angular: bony; sharp-featured.

6. dispense with: discard.

Even while we were speaking the train shot into the entrance of this dreaded valley. Though I plead guilty to some foolish **palpitations** of the heart during our headlong rush over the causeway here constructed, yet it were unjust to withhold the highest **encomiums** on the boldness of its original **conception** and the **ingenuity** of those who executed it. It was gratifying, likewise, to observe how much care had been taken to dispel the everlasting gloom and supply the defect of cheerful sunshine, not a ray of which has ever penetrated among these awful shadows. For this purpose the inflammable gas which **exudes** plentifully from the soil is collected by means of pipes, and thence communicated to a **quadrupled** row of lamps along the whole extent of the passage. Thus a radiance has been created even out of the fiery and sulphurous curse that rests forever upon the Valley—a radiance hurtful, however, to the eyes, and somewhat bewildering, as I discovered by the changes which it wrought in the visages of my companions. In this respect, as compared with natural daylight, there is the same difference as between truth and falsehood; but if the reader have ever traveled through the dark valley, he will have learned to be thankful for any light that he could get—if not from the sky above, then from the blasted soil beneath. Such was the red brilliancy of these lamps that they appeared to build walls of fire on both sides of the track, between which we held our course at lightning speed, while a **reverberating** thunder filled the valley with its echoes. Had the engine run off the track—a catastrophe, it is whispered, by no means **unprecedented**—the bottomless pit, if there be any such place, would undoubtedly have received us. Just as some dismal fooleries of this nature had made my heart quake there came a tremendous shriek *careering*[7] along the Valley as if a thousand devils had burst their lungs to utter it, but which proved to be merely the whistle of the engine on arriving at a stopping-place.

The spot where we had now paused is the same that our friend Bunyan—truthful man, but infected with many fantastic notions—has designated in terms plainer than I like to repeat as the mouth of the infernal region. This, however, must be a mistake, inasmuch as Mr. Smooth-it-Away, while we remained in the smoky and **lurid** cavern, took occasion to prove that Tophet has not even a metaphorical existence. The place, he assured us, is not other than the crater of a half-extinct volcano in which the directors had caused forges to be set up for the manufacture of railroad iron. Hence, also, is obtained a plentiful supply of fuel for the use of the engines. Whoever had gazed into the dismal **obscurity** of the broad cavern-mouth, whence ever and anon darted huge tongues of dusky flame, and had seen the strange, half-shaped monsters and visions of faces horribly **grotesque** into which the smoke seemed to wreathe itself, and had heard the awful murmurs and shrieks and deep shuddering whispers of the blast, sometimes forming themselves into words almost **articulate**, would have seized upon Mr. Smooth-it-Away's comfortable explanation as greedily as we did. The inhabitants of the cavern, moreover, were unlovely personages, dark, smoke-begrimed, generally deformed, with misshapen feet and a glow of dusky redness in their eyes, as if their hearts had caught fire and were blazing out of the upper windows. It struck me as a peculiarity that the laborers at the forge and those who brought fuel to the engine, when they began to draw short breath, positively emitted smoke from their mouths and nostrils.

Among the idlers about the train, most of whom were puffing cigars which they had lighted at the flame of the crater, I was perplexed to notice several who to my certain knowledge had heretofore set forth by railroad for the Celestial City. They looked dark, wild and smoky, with a *singular*[8] resemblance, indeed, to the native inhabitants, like whom, also, they had a disagreeable **propensity** to ill-natured gibes and sneers, the habit of which had wrought a settled **contortion** of their vis-

---

7. careering: rushing headlong.
8. singular: unusual; unique.

ages. Having been on speaking terms with one of these persons—an **indolent,** good-for-nothing fellow who went by the name of Take-it-Easy—I called him and inquired what was his business there.

"Did you not start," said I, "for the Celestial City?"

"That's a fact," said Mr. Take-it-Easy, carelessly puffing some smoke into my eyes; "but I heard such bad accounts that I never took pains to climb the hill on which the city stands—no business doing, no fun going on, nothing to drink and no smoking allowed, and a thrumming of church music from morning till night. I would not stay in such a place if they offered me house-room and living free."

"But, my good Mr. Take-it-Easy," cried I, "why take up your residence here of all places in the world?"

"Oh," said the loafer, with a grin, "it is very warm hereabouts, and I meet with plenty of old acquaintances, and altogether the place suits me. I hope to see you back again some day soon. A pleasant journey to you!"

While he was speaking the bell of the engine rang, and we dashed away after dropping a few passengers, but receiving no new ones.

Rattling onward through the valley, we were dazzled with the fiercely gleaming gas-lamps, as before, but sometimes, in the dark of intense rightness, grim faces that bore the aspect and expression of individual sins or evil passions seemed to thrust themselves through the veil of light glaring upon us and stretching forth a great dusky hand as if to **impede** our progress. I almost thought that they were my own sins that **appalled** me there. These were freaks of imagination—nothing more, certainly; mere **delusions** which I ought to be heartily ashamed of—but all through the dark valley I was tormented and pestered and dolefully bewildered with the same kind of waking dreams. The *mephitic*[9] gases of that region intoxicate the brain. As the light of natural day, however, began to struggle with the glow of the lanterns, these vain imaginations lost their vividness, and finally vanished with the first ray of sunshine that greeted our escape from the Valley of the Shadow of Death. Ere we had gone a mile beyond it, I could well-nigh have taken my oath that this whole gloomy passage was a dream.

At the end of the valley, as John Bunyan mentions, is a cavern where in his days dwelt two cruel giants, Pope and Pagan, who had strewn the ground about their residence with the bones of slaughtered pilgrims. These vile old *troglodytes*[10] are no longer there, but in their deserted cave another terrible giant has thrust himself, and makes it his business to

---

9. mephitic: foul-smelling and poisonous.
10. troglodytes: prehistoric cave dwellers.

seize upon honest travelers and fat them for his table with plentiful meals of smoke, mist, *moonshine*,[11] raw potatoes, and sawdust. He is a German by birth, and is called Giant Transcendentalist; but as to his form, his features, his substance, and his nature generally, it is the chief peculiarity of this huge **miscreant** that neither he for himself nor anybody for him has ever been able to describe them. As we rushed by the cavern's mouth we caught a hasty glimpse of him, looking somewhat like an ill-proportioned figure, but considerably more like a heap of fog and duskiness. He shouted after us, but in so strange a phraseology that we knew not what he meant, nor whether to be encouraged or affrighted.

---

11. moonshine: empty talk; nonsense.

Meditating for Meaning

1. What evidence do we have that Christian's old footpath is still in existence?

2. Mr. Smooth-it-Away disdains the Interpreter's House as old-fashioned. Considering Unitarian beliefs as explained on page 585 and what this house represented in *The Pilgrim's Progress*, what is the reason for such an attitude?

3. Why would the passengers of the Celestial Railroad not want to stop at the Cross?

4. Most of Christian's sources of conflict and trial have disappeared.
    a. What has been done to avoid (the Hill of) difficulty?
    b. What has been done to avoid (the Valley of) humiliation?
    c. What do you think this represents in the lives of false "Christians?"

5. What is Mr. Smooth-it-Away's attitude toward the occupants of Palace Beautiful?

6. Has the Celestial Railroad been successful in removing the horrors of evil in the Valley of the Shadow of Death? Explain your answer.

7. What is Mr. Smooth-it-Away's explanation for hell?

8. From the testimony of Mr. Take-it-Easy, why would sinners not be happy in heaven even if they could get there?

9. Another giant has replaced Pope and Pagan.
    a. Use an encyclopedia to find out why Hawthorne says Giant Transcendentalist is a German by birth.
    b. Explain how a philosophy could be "like a heap of fog and duskiness."
    c. Interpret Hawthorne's attitude toward the philosophy of transcendentalism as revealed by his characterization of Giant Transcendentalist.

The Celestial Railroad – Part 3

Defining for Comprehension

Choose the word or phrase below which most nearly defines each word at the left as it is used in this allegory.

1. epitome
   a. type; ideal
   b. tombstone inscription
   c. large book

2. patron
   a. father
   b. customer
   c. signal

3. effervescent
   a. long-lived
   b. lively
   c. fragrant

4. reverend
   a. fearful
   b. sorrowful
   c. worthy of respect

5. maxims
   a. greatest amount
   b. commands
   c. wise sayings

6. sagest
   a. oldest
   b. wisest
   c. sweetest

7. diffuse
   a. disturb
   b. spread
   c. include

8. erudition
   a. complete ruin
   b. extensive learning
   c. printing

9. quota
   a. proverb
   b. portion
   c. information

10. aggregate
    a. combined
    b. tremendous
    c. awesome

11. exorbitant
    a. excessive
    b. off track
    c. unearthly

12. paltry
    a. hot and humid
    b. insignificant
    c. needy

13. lucrative
    a. private
    b. profitable
    c. greedy

14. speculations
    a. views
    b. business risks
    c. introductions

15. recruited
    a. filled up
    b. met
    c. grew

16. constituents
    a. laws
    b. represented persons
    c. agreements

17. adage
    a. wise saying
    b. addition
    c. repair

18. tenements
    a. long arms
    b. rented dwellings
    c. beliefs

19. deportment
    a. portion
    b. rented room
    c. conduct

20. commencement
    a. completion
    b. beginning
    c. restoration

21. ogling
    a. jittering
    b. staring rudely
    c. teasing

22. askance
    a. scornfully
    b. crooked
    c. questioning

23. repudiation
    a. submission
    b. establishment
    c. rejection

24. pragmatic
    a. irritable
    b. listless
    c. practical

25. appellation
    a. title
    b. summit
    c. criticism

26. incorporation
    a. act of merging
    b. training
    c. unruly conduct

27. indicted
    a. foretold
    b. charged
    c. pardoned

28.	**libel**	a. danger	b. collar	c. slander
29.	**commodiously**	a. comfortably	b. repulsively	c. skillfully
30.	**rigorously**	a. harshly	b. energetically	c. hopefully
31.	**relinquished**	a. enjoyed	b. disappeared	c. surrendered; given up
32.	**ponderous**	a. thoughtful	b. heavy	c. wondering
33.	**propagated**	a. reproduced	b. watered	c. given entrance
34.	**ascertain**	a. determine	b. reassure	c. get
35.	**emitting**	a. recognizing	b. giving off	c. allowing entrance
36.	**perturbation**	a. anger	b. distress	c. time of testing
37.	**impudent**	a. unwise	b. rude	c. imported

It was late in the day when the train thundered into the ancient City of Vanity, where Vanity Fair is still at the height of prosperity and exhibits an **epitome** of whatever is brilliant, gay and fascinating beneath the sun. As I purposed to make a considerable stay here, it gratified me to learn that there is no longer the want of harmony between the towns-people and pilgrims which impelled the former to such lamentably mistaken measures as the persecution of Christian and the fiery martyrdom of Faithful. On the contrary, as the new railroad brings with it great trade and a constant influx of strangers, the lord of Vanity Fair is its chief **patron** and the *capitalists*[1] of the city are among the largest stockholders. Many passengers stop to take their pleasure or make their profit in the fair, instead of going onward to the Celestial City. Indeed, such are the charms of the place that people often affirm it to be the true and only heaven, stoutly contending that there is no other, that those who seek further are mere dreamers, and that if the fabled brightness of the Celestial City lay but a bare mile beyond the gates of Vanity they would not be fools enough to go thither. Without *subscribing to*[2] those perhaps exaggerated *encomiums*,[3] I can truly say that my abode in the city was mainly agreeable and my intercourse with the inhabitants productive of much amusement and instruction.

Being naturally of a serious turn, my attention was directed to the solid advantages derivable from a residence here, rather than to the **effervescent** pleasures which are the grand object with too many visitants. The Christian reader, if he have had no accounts of the city later than Bunyan's time, will be surprised to hear that almost every street has its church, and that the **reverend** clergy are nowhere held in higher respect than at Vanity Fair. And well do they deserve such honorable estimation, for the **maxims** of wisdom and virtue which fall from their lips come from as deep a spiritual source and tend to as lofty a religious aim as those of

---

1. capitalists: people whose wealth is invested in business ventures.
2. subscribing to: accepting as true.
3. encomium: warmly enthusiastic praise.

the **sagest** philosophers of old. In justification of this high praise I need only mention the names of the Rev. Mr. Shallow-Deep, the Rev. Mr. Stumble-at-Truth, that fine old *clerical*[4] character the Rev. Mr. This-to-Day, who expects shortly to resign his pulpit to the Rev. Mr. That-to-Morrow, together with the Rev. Mr. Bewilderment, the Rev. Mr. Clog-the-Spirit, and, last and greatest, the Rev. Dr. Wind-of-Doctrine. The labors of these eminent divines are aided by those of innumerable lecturers, who **diffuse** such a various *profundity*[5] in all subjects of human or celestial science that any man may acquire an *omnigenous*[6] **erudition** without the trouble of even learning to read. Thus literature is *etherealized*[7] by assuming for its medium the human voice, and knowledge, depositing all its heavier particles—except, doubtless, its gold—becomes exhaled into a sound which forthwith steals into the ever-open ear of the community. These ingenious methods constitute a sort of machinery by which thought and study are done to every person's hand without his putting himself to the slightest inconvenience in the matter. There is another species of machine for the wholesale manufacture of individual morality. This excellent result is effected by societies for all manner of virtuous purposes, and with which a man has merely to connect himself, throwing, as it were, his **quota** of virtue into the common stock, and the president and directors will take care that the **aggregate** amount be well applied. All these, and other wonderful improvements in ethics, religion and literature, being made plain to my comprehension by the ingenious Mr. Smooth-it-Away, inspired me with a vast admiration of Vanity Fair.

It would fill a volume in an age of pamphlets were I to record all my observations in this great capital of human business and pleasure. There was an unlimited range of society—the powerful, the wise, the witty and the famous in every walk of life, princes, presidents, poets, generals, artists, actors and *philanthropists*[8]—all making their own market at the fair and deeming no price too **exorbitant** for such commodities as hit their fancy. It was well worth one's while, even if he had no idea of buying or selling, to loiter through the *bazaars*[9] and observe the various sorts of traffic that were going forward.

Some of the purchasers, I thought, made very foolish bargains. For instance, a young man having inherited a splendid fortune laid out a considerable portion of it in the purchase of diseases, and finally spent all the rest for a heavy lot of repentance and a suit of rags. A very pretty girl bartered a heart as clear as crystal, and which seemed her most valuable possession, for another jewel of the same kind, but so worn and defaced as to be utterly worthless. In one shop there were a great many crowns of laurel and myrtle which soldiers, authors, statesmen and various other people pressed eagerly to buy. Some purchased these **paltry** wreaths with their lives, others by a toilsome servitude of years, and many sacrificed whatever was most valuable, yet finally slunk away without the crown. There was a sort of stock or scrip called Conscience which seemed to be in great demand, and would purchase almost anything. Indeed, few rich commodities were to be obtained without paying a heavy sum in this particular stock, and a man's business was seldom very **lucrative** unless he knew precisely when and how to throw his hoard of Conscience into the market. Yet, as this stock was the only thing of permanent value, whoever parted with it was sure to find himself a loser in the long run. Several of the **speculations** were of a questionable character. Occasionally a member of Congress **recruited** his pocket by the sale of his **constituents**, and I was assured that public officers have often sold their country at very moderate prices. Thousands sold

---

4. clerical: pertaining to clergymen or ministers.
5. profundity: depth of intellect.
6. omnigenous: of all kinds; various.
7. etherealized: made spiritual or heavenly.
8. philanthropists: men who work for the good of mankind.
9. bazaars: markets.

their happiness for a whim. Gilded chains were in great demand and purchased with almost any sacrifice. In truth, those who desired, according to the old **adage**, to sell anything valuable for a song, might find customers all over the fair, and there were innumerable messes of pottage, piping hot, for such as chose to buy them with their birthrights. A few articles, however, could not be found genuine at Vanity Fair. If a customer wished to renew his stock of youth, the dealers offered him a set of false teeth and an auburn wig; if he demanded peace of mind, they recommended *opium*[10] or a brandy bottle.

Tracts of land and golden mansions situate in the Celestial City were often exchanged at very disadvantageous rates for a few years' lease of small, dismal, inconvenient **tenements** in Vanity Fair. Prince Beelzebub himself took great interest in this sort of traffic, and sometimes condescended to meddle with smaller matters. I once had the pleasure to see him bargaining with a miser for his soul, which, after much ingenious skirmishing on both sides, His Highness succeeded in obtaining at about the value of sixpence. The prince remarked with a smile that he was a loser by the transaction.

Day after day, as I walked the streets of Vanity, my manners and **deportment** became more and more like those of the inhabitants. The place began to seem like home; the idea of pursuing my travels to the Celestial City was almost obliterated from my mind. I was reminded of it, however, by the sight of the same pair of simple pilgrims at whom we had laughed so heartily when Apollyon puffed smoke and steam into their faces at the **commencement** of our journey. There they stood amid the densest bustle of Vanity, the dealers offering them their purple and fine linen and jewels, the men of wit and humor gibing at them, a pair of *buxom*[11] ladies **ogling** them **askance**, while the benevolent Mr. Smooth-it-Away whispered some of his wisdom at their elbows and pointed to a newly erected temple; but there were these worthy simpletons making the scene look wild and monstrous merely by

their sturdy **repudiation** of all part in its business or pleasures.

One of them—his name was Stick-to-the-Right—perceived in my face, I suppose, a species of sympathy and almost admiration, which, to my own great surprise, I could not help feeling for this **pragmatic** couple. It promoted him to address me.

"Sir," inquired he, with a sad yet mild and kindly voice, "do you call yourself a pilgrim?"

"Yes," I replied; "my right to that **appellation** is indubitable. I am merely a sojourner here in Vanity Fair, being bound to the Celestial City by the new railroad."

"Alas, friend!" rejoined Mr. Stick-to-the-Right; "I do assure you and beseech you to receive the truth of my words, that the whole concern is a bubble. You may travel on it all your lifetime, were you to live thousands of years, and yet never get beyond the limits of Vanity Fair. Yea, though you should deem yourself entering the gate of the blessed city, it will be nothing but a miserable delusion."

"The Lord of the Celestial City," began the other pilgrim, whose name was Mr. Foot-it-to-Heaven, "has refused, and will ever refuse, to grant an act of **incorporation** for this railroad, and unless that be obtained no passenger can ever hope to enter his dominions; wherefore every man who buys a ticket must lay his account with losing the purchase money, which is the value of his own soul."

"Poh! nonsense!" said Mr. Smooth-it-Away, taking my arm and leading me away; "these fellows ought to be **indicted** for a **libel**. If the law stood as it once did in Vanity Fair we should see them grinning through the iron bars of the prison window."

This incident made a considerable impression on my mind and contributed with other circumstances to indispose me to a permanent residence in the City of Vanity, although, of course, I was not simple enough to give up my original plan of gliding along easily and **commodiously** by railroad. Still, I grew anxious to be gone. There was one strange thing that troubled me; amid the occupations or amusements

---

10. opium: a narcotic drug prepared from the seeds of one type of poppy plant.

11. buxom: full of gaiety (archaic).

of the fair, nothing was more common than for a person—whether at a feast, theater or church, or trafficking for wealth and honors or whatever he might be doing, and, however unreasonable the interruption—suddenly to vanish like a soap-bubble and be nevermore seen of his fellows; and so accustomed were the latter to such little incidents that they went on with their business as quietly as if nothing had happened. But it was otherwise with me.

Finally, after a pretty long residence at the fair, I resumed my journey toward the Celestial City, still with Mr. Smooth-it-Away at my side. At a short distance beyond the suburbs of Vanity we passed the ancient silver mine of which Demas was the first discoverer and which is now wrought to great advantage, supplying nearly all the coined currency of the world. A little farther onward was the spot where Lot's wife had stood for ages under the semblance of a pillar of salt. Curious travelers have long since carried it away piecemeal. Had all regrets been punished as **rigorously** as this poor dame's were, my yearning for the **relinquished** delights of Vanity Fair might have produced a similar change in my own *corporeal*[12] substance and left me a warning to future pilgrims.

The next remarkable object was a large edifice constructed of moss-grown stone, but in a modern and airy style of architecture. The engine came to a pause in its vicinity with the usual tremendous shriek.

"This was formerly the castle of the *redoubted*[13] Giant Despair," observed Mr. Smooth-it-Away, "but since his death Mr. Flimsy Faith has repaired it and now keeps an excellent house of entertainment here. It is one of our stopping-places."

"It seems but slightly put together," remarked I, looking at the frail yet **ponderous** walls. "I do not envy Mr. Flimsy-Faith his habitation. Some day it will thunder down upon the heads of the occupants."

"We shall escape, at all events," said Mr. Smooth-it-Away, "for Apollyon is putting on the steam again."

The road now plunged into a gorge of the Delectable Mountains, and traversed the field where, in former ages, the blind men wandered and stumbled among the tombs. One of these ancient tombstones had been thrust across the track by some malicious person and gave the train of cars a terrible jolt. Far up the rugged side of a mountain I perceived a rusty iron door half overgrown with bushes and creeping plants, but with smoke issuing from its crevices.

"Is that," inquired I, "the very door in the hillside which the shepherds assured Christian was a by-way to hell?"

"That was a joke on the part of the shep-

12. corporeal: bodily.
13. redoubted: awesome; formidable.

herds," said Mr. Smooth-it-Away, with a smile. "It is neither more nor less than the door of a cavern which they use as a smoke-house for the preparation of mutton-hams."

My recollections of the journey are now for a little space dim and confused, inasmuch as a singular drowsiness here overcame me, owing to the fact that we were passing over the Enchanted Ground, the air of which encourages a disposition to sleep. I awoke, however, as soon as we crossed the borders of the pleasant Land of Beulah. All the passengers were rubbing their eyes, comparing watches and congratulating one another on the prospect of arriving so seasonably at the journey's end. The sweet breezes of this happy clime came refreshingly to our nostrils; we beheld the glimmering gush of silver fountains overhung by trees of beautiful foliage and delicious fruit, which were **propagated** by grafts from the celestial gardens. Once, as we dashed onward like a hurricane, there was a flutter of wings and the bright appearance of an angel in the air speeding forth on some heavenly mission.

The engine now announced the close vicinity of the final station house by one last and horrible scream in which there seemed to be distinguishable every kind of wailing and woe and bitter fierceness of wrath, all mixed up with the wild laughter of a devil or a madman. Throughout our journey, at every stoppingplace, Apollyon had exercised his ingenuity in screwing the most abominable sounds out of the whistle of the steam engine, but in this closing effort he outdid himself, and created an infernal uproar which, besides disturbing the peaceful inhabitants of Beulah, must have sent its discord even through the celestial gates.

While the horrid clamor was still ringing in our ears we heard an exulting strain, as if a thousand instruments of music with height and depth and sweetness in their tones, at once tender and triumphant, were struck in unison to greet the approach of some illustrious hero who had fought the good fight and won a glorious victory, and was come to lay aside his battered arms forever. Looking to **ascertain** what

might be the occasion of this glad harmony, I perceived on alighting from the cars, that a multitude of shining ones had assembled on the other side of the river to welcome two poor pilgrims who were just emerging from its depths. They were the same whom Apollyon and ourselves had persecuted with taunts and gibes and scalding steam at the commencement of our journey—the same whose unworldly aspect and impressive words had stirred my conscience amid the wild revellers at Vanity Fair.

"How amazingly well those men have got on!" cried I to Mr. Smooth-it-Away. "I wish we were secure of as good a reception."

"Never fear! Never fear!" answered my friend. "Come! make haste. The ferryboat will be off directly, and in three minutes you will be on the other side of the river. No doubt you will find coaches to carry you up to the city gates."

A steam ferryboat—the last improvement on this important route—lay at the riverside puffing, snorting, and **emitting** all those other disagreeable utterances which betoken the departure to be immediate. I hurried on board with the rest of the passengers, most of whom were in great **perturbation**, some bawling out for their baggage, some tearing their hair and exclaiming that the boat would explode or sink, some already pale with the heaving of the stream, some gazing affrighted at the ugly aspect of the steersman, and some still dizzy with the slumberous influences of the Enchanted Ground.

Looking back to the shore, I was amazed to discern Mr. Smooth-it-Away waving his hand in token of farewell.

"Don't you go over to the Celestial City?" exclaimed I.

"Oh, no!" answered he, with a queer smile and that same disagreeable contortion of visage which I had remarked in the inhabitants of the dark valley, "oh, no! I have come thus far only for the sake of your pleasant company. Goodbye! We shall meet again."

And then did my excellent friend, Mr. Smooth-it-Away laugh outright; in the midst of which *cachinnation*[14] a smoke-wreath issued

---

14. cachinnation: loud laughter.

from his mouth and nostrils, while a twinkle of lurid flame darted out of either eye, proving indubitably that his heart was all of a red blaze. The **impudent** fiend! To deny the existence of Tophet when he felt its fiery tortures raging within his breast! I rushed to the side of the boat, intending to fling myself on shore, but the wheels, as they began their revolutions, threw a dash of spray over me, so cold—so deadly cold with the chill that will never leave those waters until Death be drowned in his own river—that with a shiver and a heartquake I awoke.

Thank Heaven! it was a dream.

Meditating for Meaning

1. Vanity Fair, too, has changed but not so much as the relation of modern pilgrims to it.
   a. What relation does Vanity Fair have to the Celestial Railroad?
   b. How do you account for the many churches in Vanity Fair?
   c. What is meant by spending a fortune for the purchase of disease or using conscience to purchase almost anything?
   d. What inferior substitutes are sold at Vanity Fair?

2. What two things induced the modern pilgrim to leave Vanity Fair?

3. The pillar of salt may be applied to the many biblical accounts of people who, like Lot's wife, were brought to judgment for loving the present world more than the kingdom of God. What do you think is meant by the sentence: "Curious travelers have long since carried it away piecemeal"?

4. Mr. Flimsy Faith has repaired Giant Despair's Doubting Castle and made it a house of entertainment. How would this be more successful in keeping pilgrims from the Celestial City than doubt and despair?

5. What do modern pilgrims do in the Enchanted Ground that Christian and Hopeful tried to avoid?

6. How do the Celestial Railroad passengers plan to cross the river?

7. Often men recognize the realities of life too late.
   a. What reality about Mr. Smooth-it-Away and the Celestial Railroad does the modern pilgrim discover at the river?
   b. Why is this discovery too late?
   8. To Hawthorne, his allegory was like a bad dream that one is glad to discover is not reality. Explain how some will "awake" to find the "dream" is only too true.

Writing an Allegory

Now that you have studied five allegories, try to write an allegory yourself. Write an original allegory or write a parody on an existing allegory such as "Wheelbarrows" or "A Plea for Fishing."

If you choose either "Wheelbarrows" or "A Plea for Fishing," write a parody with a serious undertone showing a proper Christian response to the problems presented in the original allegories. Write your allegory as a sequel: that is, write it as a continuation to the story, telling what happens next. Have the White Vantress chickens or the fishermen awake to their inconsistencies. Then by a series of allegorical events, show what we as modern Christians should be doing.

You may borrow objects and events from the original allegory but you will likely want to introduce some new symbols. You have Hawthorne's "Celestial Railroad" to serve as a good model for the way an effective parody can be written.

But for your parody to be effective, you will need to do some good thinking before you write. Be sure you have clearly in mind what Christians really should be doing about their extravagant cars or lack of soul-winning.

INDEX OF AUTHORS, TITLES, AND FIRST LINES OF POETRY

"A little bird I am," 239
Acres of Diamonds, 354
Addison, Joseph, 210
"Am I a stone, and not a sheep," 246
Apostrophe to the Ocean, 212
"And what is so rare as a day in June," 209

Bad Times, 223
Baker, Robert, 22, 67
Baldwin, Hanson, 370
Battle of Blenheim, The, 196
Beaumont, Joseph, 223
Berg, Viola Jacobson, 169
Betrayal, 232
Bible, The, 170
Bigot, 248
"Blessed is the man that walketh not in the counsel of the ungodly," 182
Blind But Happy, 234
Boat, The, 243
"Bowed by the weight of centuries he leans," 159
Braganca, Nadejda de, 175
Brainerd, David, 400
Browning, Robert, 145
Bryant, William Cullen, 225
Building, 224
Bunyan, John, 155, 268, 472
"But Thee, but Thee, O sovereign Seer of Time," 241
Byron, George Gordon, 212

Cache of Honor, 55
Calvary, 244
Celestial Railroad, The, 585
Chappell, Clovis G., 435
Chariots of God, The, 339
Cholmondeley, Hester H., 232
Conscience and Remorse, 230
Conventionality, 249
Conwell, Russell H., 354
Crosby, Fanny, 234
Crystal Christ, The, 241
Cushman, Ralph Spaulding, 150

"Defeat may serve as well as victory," 229
Diary of David Brainerd, The, 400
Discipline, 334
Discipline of Deformity, The, 347
Doctor of Afternoon Arm, The, 118
Drescher, John, 467
Dunbar, Paul Laurence, 230, 238
Duncan, Norman, 118

Edman, V. Raymond, 347
Edwards, Jonathan, 406
Elegy Written in a Country Churchyard, 215
Emerson, Ralph Waldo, 199

Fable, A, 199
Fool's Prayer, The, 194
Forgiveness, 176
Fretz, Clarence Y., 286
"Friendless and faint, with martyred steps and slow," 244
Frost, Robert, 250

Garber, Faustina Martin, 171
George Wagner, 191
George Wagner, A.D. 1527, 193
Giono, Jean, 361
Good Friday, 246
"Good-bye, I said to my conscience—," 230
Grace Abounding to the Chief of Sinners, 268
Gray, Thomas, 215
Great Stone Face, The, 100
Grizzard, Lewis, 3
Guyon, Madame, 239

Hackett, Eloise, 249
"Happy the men who always goodness find," 170
Hawthorne, Nathaniel, 100, 585
Hayes, John F., 55
Hobbs, Ruth Kurtz, 132
Horse, The, 11

"I asked the Lord that I might grow," 200
"I know the road to Jericho," 162
"I know what the caged bird feels, alas!" 238
"I owned a little boat a while ago," 243
"I watched them tearing a building down," 224
Infinity, 169
"Into the future time stretches its arms," 169
"It was a summer evening," 196

Jericho Road, The, 162
"Judge me, O God, and plead my cause against an ungodly nation," 183
Julius Caesar, 207

Key to Happiness, A, 170
Kraybill, Don, 463
Kulski, Julian E., 407

Lament, 165
Lanier, Sydney, 241
Last Night of Sodom, The, 424
Letters of Herman Stohr, 407
Little Bird I Am, A, 239
Longfellow, Henry Wadsworth, 152
"Lord, what a change within us one short hour," 173
Lowell, James Russell, 208

Macbeth, 205
MacDonald, George, 243

Mac Donald, William, 334
Mackay, Charles, 231
"Make a joyful noise unto God, all ye lands," 184
Mama and the Garfield Boys, 3
Man Who Planted Hope and Grew Happiness, The, 361
Man With the Hoe, The, 159
March, Daniel, 424
Markham, Edwin, 159, 229
McNeely, Marian Hurd, 11
"Men wrap themselves in smug cocoons," 248
Mending Wall, 250
Menno Simons, 1496-1561, 260
Merchant of Venice, The, 204
Milton, John, 236
Mote and the Beam, The, 67
"My heart was heavy, for its trust had been," 176

No Enemies, 231

"O God, I love Thee in the stars at night," 175
"O what a happy soul am I!" 234
"Oh the sheer joy of it," 150
On His Blindness, 236
Overholt, John J. (translator), 191

Parable of the Ten Virgins, The, 459
Paterson, Evangeline, 165
Pippa's Song, 145
Pilgrim, The, 155
Pilgrim's Progress, The 472
Plea for Fishing, A, 467
Poet, The, 225
Pooler, James, 35
Poteat, Edwin McNeill, 162
Prayer Answered By Crosses, 200
Psalm of Life, A, 152
Psalm 1, 182
Psalm 43, 183
Psalm 66, 184
Psalm 119:9-16, 186
Psalm 126, 188

RMS Titanic, 370
Robinson, Edwin Arlington, 244
"Roll on, thou deep and dark blue ocean, roll!" 212
Rossetti, Christina, 246
Ruth, the Moabitess, 445

Second Chance, 22
Self-Made Fool—Saul, The, 435
Shago, 35
Shakespeare, William, 204, 205, 207
Sheer Joy, 150
Showalter, Lester E., 169, 170, 170, 171
Sill, Edward Rowland, 194
Slater, Eleanor, 248
Smith, Hannah Whitall, 339

"Something there is which doesn't love a wall," 250
Southey, Robert, 196
Spacious Firmament, The, 210
Spark Neglected, A, 43
Spring, 171
"Still as of old," 232
Stohr, Herman, 407
Stoll, Joseph, 86
Swalm, E. J., 413
"Sweet spring speaks gentle words," 171
Sympathy, 238

"Tell me not, in mournful numbers," 152
"The curfew tolls the knell of parting day," 215
"The mountain and the squirrel," 199
"The royal feast was done; the King," 194
"The spacious firmament on high," 210
"The triolet is comely," 169
"The year's at the spring," 145
"Thou who wouldst wear the name," 225
Though He Slay Me, 413
"Though you be scholarly, beware," 247
Thy Brother, 252
Tolstoy, Leo, 43, 74
Too Dark, 132
Top Man, 383
Trench, Richard Chenevix, 173
Triolet, The, 169
True…Till Death—The Story of Clayton Kratz, 286

Ullman, James Ramsey, 383

Victory in Defeat, 229

Walker, F. Deaville, 312
"Weep, weep for those," 165
Wenger, John C., 260
What Is So Rare as a Day in June? 208
Wheelbarrows, 463
"When I consider how my light is spent," 236
"When the LORD turned again the captivity of Zion," 188
"When thy heart, with joy o'erflowing," 252
Where Love Is, There Is God Also, 74
"Wherewithal shall a young man cleanse his way?" 186
Whittier, John Greenleaf, 176
"Who Christ will follow now, new-born," 191
"Who would true valor see," 155
Whom Shall I Fear? 86
"Why slander we the times? 223
William Carey, 1761-1834, 312
Williams, Theodore Chickering, 252
"Winter whistles warily," 171
Winter's Coming, 171
"Within God's book," 170

"You have no enemies, you say? 231

INDEX OF LITERARY TERMS

Abercrombie, 157
Acrostic, 168
Alliteration, 153, 352
Allusion, 166, 346
Anecdote, 346
Anapest, 147
Apostrophe, 211
Assonance, 153
Autobiography, 258
Ballad, 190
    Literary, 194
Blank Verse, 158
Bound Verse, 162
Character, 20
Characterization, 20, 54
Climax, 9, 29
Conflict, 9, 29
Common Meter, 158
Connotation, 64, 73
Dactyl, 147
Didactic Poetry, 222
Dimeter, 147
Drama, 202
Elegy, 214
Fable, 199
Flashback, 30
Foreshadowing, 62, 381, 382
Free Verse, 164
Hebrew Poetry, 177-180
Hyperbole, 186
Iambus, 146
Irony, 65
Lament, 157
Long Meter, 158
Lyric Poetry, 208
Metaphor, 41, 154
Monometer, 147
Narrative Poetry, 190
    Satirical, 196
Ode, 209
Onomatopoeia, 41, 154

Outline, 443
Parallelism, 177-180, 452
    Antithetic, 178
    Climactic, 179, 180
    Synonymous, 177
    Synthetic, 179
Parody, 585
Pentameter, 147
Personification, 41
Plot, 29
    Complication, 29
    Loose, 29
Point of View, 84, 85
    All-knowing, 84
    First Person, 84, 442
    Third Person, 85
    Objective, 84
    Subjective, 84
Rhyme, 148, 149
    Feminine, 148
Rhythm, 146, 147
Satire, 65
Scansion, 147
Setting, 30, 31
Short Meter, 158
Simile, 41
Songs of Degrees, 188
Sonnet, 172-176
    Italian, 173
    Miltonic, 176, 236
    Shakespearian, 174
Symbolism, 32-34
Synecdoche, 369
Tetrameter, 147
Theme, 9, 95
Tone, 64-66
Trimeter, 147
Triolet, 169-172
Trochee, 147
Unity, 96, 98, 99, 117, 131, 139
Zanze, 157

INDEX OF BIBLE REFERENCES   Those with asterisks (*) are referred to in the study exercises only.

Genesis
1, p. 359*
1:11, p. 455
1:27, p. 159
1:28, p. 222*
3:6, p. 233*
4:3-5, 8, 9, p. 20*
4:9, p. 70
6:5, p. 572
8:21, p. 572
9:27, p. 512*
13:13, p. 552
18:16-33, p. 433*
19, p. 433*
27:29, p. 178
37:28, p. 233*
41:17-21, p. 456
43, p. 29

Exodus
3, p. 317*
15:16, p. 179
20:13, pp. 5, 8*

Leviticus
19:9, 10, p. 451*
19:34, p. 19*

Numbers
13:25-33, p. 522*
23:9, p. 272

Deuteronomy
6:10-12, p. 346*
8, p. 433*
19:14, p. 251*
25:5, 6, p. 451*
25:9, 10, p. 452*
27:17, p. 251*
27:19, p. 19*
33:26, p. 342

Joshua
23:10, p. 518*

Judges
5:12, p. 181*
9:8-15, pp. 66*, 456

Ruth, pp. 446-449

1 Samuel
4:9, p. 544*
15:11, 13, p. 437
15:14, 15, p. 233*
15:22, p. 62*
20:14-16, p. 349
23:18, p. 349
26:21, p. 436
31:4, p. 442*

2 Samuel
9:3, 13, p. 349
12:1-6, p. 457
21:7, p. 349
24:17, p. 458*

1 Kings
12:7, p. 40*
17, p. 62*

2 Kings
5:20-27, p. 551*
6:13-18, p. 346*

6:15, 17, p. 340
7, p. 349
14:9, p. 65
18:27, p. 65

1 Chronicles
26:27, p. 282

Nehemiah
13:23-25, p. 451*

Esther
1:10, p. 195*

Job
12:2, p. 66*
12:22, p. 520
13:15, pp. 283*, 421*
14:7-9, p. 32
14:14a, b, p. 33
28:1, p. 178
28:2, p. 181*
29:3, p. 521
41:15, p. 517*

Psalms
1, p. 182
1:3, p. 97*
8, p. 161*
17:4, p. 565
19:1, p. 177
19:1-6, p. 211*
21:1, 2, p. 178
22:1, p. 33
23, p. 177
23:1, p. 33
23:4, p. 520
24:3, p. 178
24:10, p. 181*
25, p. 187*
27:1, pp. 92, 310*
34, p. 187*
34:7, p. 518*
34:10b, p. 19*
38:4, p. 477*
40:2, pp. 342, 482*
41:1, p. 179
42, p. 184*
43, p. 183
44:11, p. 458*
44:12-26, p. 282
45:4, p. 341
46:1, p. 342
53:1, p. 442*
62:10b, p. 359*
66, pp. 184, 185
66:10, 11, p. 40*
68:17, p. 343
73:4, p. 584*
73:4, 5, p. 579
80, p. 184*
84:11, p. 310*
91:2, p. 305
96:7, 8, p. 179
100:3, p. 458*
103, p. 231*
104:3, p. 341
105:17, p. 233*
107, p. 184*

115:12, 13, p. 181*
118:8, p. 179
119, p. 168
119:9, p. 179
119:9-16, p. 186
119:34, p. 533
119:37, p. 540
119:105, p. 478*
120-134, p. 188*
121:7, p. 310*
121:7, 8, p. 180
123:1, 2, p. 180
123:3, p. 179
126, p. 188
127:3-5, p. 277
136, p. 184*
137:4, p. 126*
150, p. 180

Proverbs
1:22, p. 442*
4:7, p. 2
5:5, p. 525
6:6, p. 504
9:10, p. 575
10:18, p. 442*
11:31, p. 310*
13:1, p. 181*
13:2, p. 178
13:3, p. 181*
13:6, p. 178
13:7, p. 359*
13:11, p. 359*
13:19, p. 442*
14:9, p. 442*
15:1, p. 178
15:5, p. 442*
15:17, p. 181*
16:18, p. 526
17:5, p. 19*
18:6, p. 442*
18:9, p. 466*
18:12, p. 526
19:17, p. 83*
19:27, p. 566
20:3, p. 442*
21:4, p. 166*
21:16, p. 561
22:3, p. 331
22:28, p. 251*
23:10, p. 251*
24:16, p. 518*
25, p. 88
26:12, p. 564
26:20b, p. 53*
27:1, p. 181*
27:8, p. 181*
28:13, p. 325
28:26, p. 572
29:5, p. 565
29:22, p. 53*
29:25, pp. 28*, 71*, 95*

Ecclesiastes
4:9, p. 567
5:13, p. 359*
7:8, p. 328*

7:9, p. 442*
7:18, p. 86
10:3, p. 564
11:1, p. 309*
12:9, p. 417

Song of Solomon
2:12, p. 578
3:10, p. 340

Isaiah
5:7, p. 34*
26:1, p. 501*
26:2, p. 583
28:10, p. 325
33:23, p. 349
35:3-6, p. 348
38:8-20, p. 188*
42:1-3, p. 166*
43:2, p. 580
53:6, p. 458*
53:7, p. 458*
54:2, 3, p. 319
55:10, 11, p. 455
62:11, p. 578
64:6, pp. 477*, 568

Jeremiah
2:21, pp. 34*, 455
2:25, p. 270
9:23, p. 359*
17:8, p. 97*
17:11, p. 442*
18:12, p. 270
31:21, p. 555
38:6, p. 97*

Lamentations, p. 168
1-4, p. 187*
3:27, p. 333

Daniel
5:2, p. 195*

Hosea
10:1, p. 34*

Amos
5:8, p. 520
7:14, 15, p. 315

Micah
7:8, p. 518

Habakkuk, p. 186*
2:3, p. 569
3:8, p. 341

Malachi
3:6, p. 62*
3:10, p. 349

Matthew
1:5, p. 451*
4:3-10, p. 545*
5:15, p. 248*
5:16, p. 361
5:21-26, p. 407
5:29, p. 235*
5:33-37, p. 407
5:38-48, p. 407
5:40, p. 309*
5:44, pp. 5, 8*
5:46, 47, p. 9*

6:9, 12, p. 408
6:12, p. 242*
6:15, p. 71*
6:33, p. 411*
6:34, p. 433*
6:46, 47, p. 9*
7:3-5, p. 72*
7:7, p. 488
7:13, 14, p. 478*
7:14, p. 273
7:15, p. 458*
7:21-23, p. 165
10:9, 10, p. 309*
10:39, p. 55
12:19, 20, p. 166*
12:34, p. 545*
13:3-9, p. 455
13:11, p. 457
13:15, p. 351*
13:20, 21, p. 577*
13:45, 46, p. 456
15:14, p. 522*
16:12, p. 522*
16:26, p. 233*
18:12-14, p. 456
18:13, p. 458*
18:23, p. 461*
20:1, p. 461*
21:33-41, p. 34*
22:1-14, p. 461*
22:2, p. 461*
23, p. 166*
23:3, p. 531
23:11, 12, p. 77
23:14-17, p. 64
23:29-35, p. 245*
25:1-13, pp. 459, 460
25:14, p. 461*
25:14-30, p. 237*
25:32, p. 458*
25:40, p. 80
26:52, p. 413
28:19, 20, pp. 321*, 329

Mark
4:33, p. 457
7:7-9, p. 249*
7:11-13, p. 249*
8:17b, 18, p. 66

Luke
1:46, 47, p. 181*
1:53, p. 178
3:8, 11, p. 83*
6:29-31, pp. 76, 81*
6:34, p. 62*
6:46-49, pp. 76, 81*
7:6, p. 488*
7:44-46, p. 76
8:13, p. 522*
10, p. 317*
10:25-37, p. 98
10:29, p. 252
13:3, p. 417
13:24, p. 498*
14:12-14, p. 249*
14:26, 33, p. 478*
15:11-32, pp. 328*, 456
16:19, 25, p. 466*
16:19-23, p. 497*

16:19-31, p. 498*
17:10, p. 568
17:32, pp. 488*, 551
18:12, p. 488*
18:13, pp. 488*, 569
18:21, p. 488*
19:8, p. 97*
22:19, p. 275
23:2, p. 266

John
3:1-21, p. 351*
6:6, p. 98
6:35, 37, p. 569
6:53, p. 32
6:66, p. 32
8:33, p. 488*
9:28, p. 488*
14:6, p. 273
14:26, p. 496*
15:13, pp. 81*, 308
16:33, p. 487*
17:15, p. 433*
20:31, p. 258
21:16, p. 458*
21:25, p. 258

Acts
2:37, p. 477*
5:29, pp. 233*, 407
7:56, p. 97*
10:38, p. 266
14:22, p. 544*
16:9, p. 317*
16:30, p. 477*
16:31, p. 569

Romans
3:10, 12, p. 572
3:24, p. 275
4:25, p. 569
5:18, 19, p. 501*
7:7-10, p. 498*
7:24, p. 504
8:17, p. 276
8:28, p. 62*
8:28, 29, p. 19*
8:31, p. 150
8:37, p. 516, 518*
10:4, p. 569
11:33-36, p. 164*
12, p. 88
13:10, p. 81*
14:19, p. 224*
14:21, p. 71*

1 Corinthians
1:21b, p. 202
3:11, p. 590*
3:12, 13, p. 166*
9:14, 16, 19, p. 279*
10:11, p. 423
10:12, p. 559*
12:8, 9, p. 272
13:1, p. 278
14:1, 12, p. 353
15:32, p. 156*
15:55, p. 276
15:57, p. 518*

2 Corinthians
1:9, p. 281

1:12, p. 202
2:14, p. 154*
3:18, p. 116*
4:2, p. 308
4:4, p. 235*
4:7-10, p. 154*
4:18, p. 281
4:18b, p. 32
9:6, p. 309*
11:24-27, p. 487*
12:7, p. 279*
12:7-9, p. 278
12:7, 10, p. 342
12:9, pp. 154*, p. 569
12:9, 10, pp. 349, 498*

Galatians
2:16, p. 568
3:10, p. 486
4:22-26, p. 456

Ephesians
1:13, 14, p. 501*
2:6, p. 340
4, 5, p. 337*
4:19, p. 231*
5:6, p. 567
5:18, p. 98
5:26, p. 498*
6, p. 516
6:13-18, p. 513*
6:24, p. 202

Philippians
3:7, 8, p. 342
4:4, p. 151*
4:11, p. 235*
4:13, p. 518*

Colossians
1:11, p. 280*
2:8, p. 248*
3, p. 337*
3:9, p. 528*

1 Thessalonians
5:6, 7, p. 505*
5:19, p. 141*
5:22, p. 202

1 Timothy
1:15, pp. 273*, 569
2:5, p. 569
2:9, p. 466*
3:1-13, p. 498*
4:2, p. 231*
6:8, p. 235*
6:9, p. 359*
6:12, p. 498*
6:9-11, p. 533*

2 Timothy
1:9, p. 276
1:11, 13, p. 498*
2:19, p. 462*
3:1-5, p. 433*
3:5, p. 502*
4:2, 3, p. 232*
4:10, pp. 550, 553*
4:16, 17, p. 156*

Titus
3:5, p. 276

Hebrews
1:13, 14, p. 584*
3:13, p. 231*

4:2, p. 321*
6:4-8, p. 498*
6:6, p. 245*
7:25, p. 570
10:16, 17, p. 501*
10:26-29, p. 498*
11:14-16, p. 155
11:33, 34, p.510
12:1, p. 399
12:2, p. 478*
12:11, p. 340
12:17, p. 459
12:22, 23, p. 581
12:22-24, p. 276
13:2, p. 560
13:5, p. 235*

James
1:2-4, p. 83*
1:22-25, p. 116*
1:27, p. 532
2:6, p. 359*
2:19, p. 245*
5:1-6, p. 161*
5:12, p. 407
5:13, p. 145

1 Peter
1:7, p. 517*
1:21, p. 280
2:21, p. 53*
2:22, pp. 524, 525
3:10, 11, p. 223*
4:12, p. 517*
4:13-16, p. 409
4:15, p. 232*
4:19, p. 544*
5:8, pp. 156*, 517

2 Peter
1:16, p. 280
1:19, p. 478*
2:22, p. 524
3:16, p. 590*

1 John
1:9, p. 231*
2:9, p. 71*
2:11, p. 53*
2:16, pp. 235*, 545*
3:15, p. 557
3:17, pp. 83*, 252*
4:16, p. 81*
5:3, p. 81*
5:20, p. ix

Revelation
1:5, p. 119
2:9, p. 354
2:10, pp. 408, 544*
3:17, 18, p. 359*
3:19, pp. 9*, 565
5:13, p. 583
12:10, p. 517*
13:1, p. 97*
13:2, p. 517*
19:9, p. 582
20:11-15, p. 498*
22:14, p. 582
22:18, 19, p. 62*

ACKNOWLEDGEMENTS

Cover Designers: Elmore Byler and David W. Miller
Reviewers: Howard Bean, John Coblentz, and Gerald Hiebert

TEXT:

*Illustration

A Plea for Fishing	By John M. Drescher. Reprinted by permission of the author.
A Spark Neglected	Leo Tolstoy, translated by Louise Maude.
Bigot	From *Why Hold the Hand?* by Eleanor Slater © 1941, by Henry Harrison, Poetry Publisher.
Cache of Honor	By John F. Hayes, from *All Sails Set,* by J. Ranton McIntosh.
*Christian and Hopeful meeting a man, Atheist, laughing as he talks to them	F. Barnard
*Christian and Hopeful wading through the river; Christian nearly going under	E. G. Dalziel
*Christian and Hopeful walking and talking with a boy	F. Barnard
*Christian and Faithful enter the town of Vanity	F. Barnard
*Christian and Faithful meet Talkative	F. Barnard
*Christian and Hopeful meet Giant Despair at Doubting Castle	J. D. Watson
*Christian and Hopeful pass through the Delectable Mountains	J. D. Watson
*Christian and Hopeful reach Zion	J. D. Watson
*Christian Battles with Apollyon in the Valley of Humiliation	J. D. Watson
*Christian climbing hill of difficulty	J. D. Watson
*Christian falls in the Slough of Despond	W. Small
*Christian knocking at the Wicket Gate	J. D. Watson
*Christian meets Faithful	Townley Green
*Christian meets Worldly Wiseman	F. Barnard
*Christian passes through the Valley of Shadow	J. D. Watson
*Christian reaches the cross	Townley Green
*Christian reading the Bible, burdened and dressed in rags	J. D. Watson
*Christian reasoning with Obstinate and Pliable; Obstinate turning back	J. D. Watson
*Christian visits Palace Beautiful	J. D. Watson
*Christian visits the Interpreter's house	
1. Passion and Patience	J. D. Watson
2. Man in iron cage	E. F. Brewtnall
Discipline	From *Seek Ye First,* by William MacDonald. Used by permission.
George Wagner	From the *Ausbund.* Translated by John J. Overholt. Copyright 1972, The Christian Hymnary Publishers, Sarasota, FL. All rights reserved. Used by permission.
Hark, the Herald Angels Sing	Charles Wesley
Hebrew for Psalm 119:9-16	From the *Biblia Hebraica Stuttgartensia* (a Hebrew Old Testament), © 1967/177 by the German Bible Society, Stuttgart.
*Hopeful joins Christian	Townley Green
*John Bunyan asleep in prison	F. Barnard
John Styaerts, and Peter, A.D. 1538	From Thieleman J. Van Braght, *Martyr's Mirror,* translated by Joseph F. Sohm (Scottdale, Pennsylvania: Mennonite Publishing House), p.449, 450.
Joy to the World	Isaac Watts
*Jury Scene	F. Barnard
Letters of Hermann Stohr	From *Dying We Live* by Julian E. Kulski. Copyright © 1979 by Julian Eugeniusz Kulski. Reprinted by permission of Henry Holt and Company, Inc.
Mama and the Garfield Boys	Reprinted and edited with permission from *Don't Forget to Call Your Mama—I Wish I Could Call Mine,* by Lewis Grizzard, published 1991 by Longstreet Press, a subsidiary of Cox Newspapers.
*Mending Wall	David W. Miller. Copyright 1996 Christian Light Publications, Inc.
My Jesus I Love Thee	London Hymn Book, 1864.
*Ruth, the Moabitess	David W. Miller. Copyright 1996 Christian Light Publications, Inc.

Second Chance	Used by permission of Robert J. Baker and Herald Press.
Shago	By James S. Pooler, from *Story Magazine*. Copyright, 1941, by Story Magazine, Inc.
*Shago	David W. Miller. Copyright 1996 Christian Light Publications, Inc.
"Standing up to his chest in . . . ."	From "You've Got to Learn," by Robert Murphy. Copyright by the Curtis Publishing Company.
*The Chariots of God	David W. Miller. Copyright 1996 Christian Light Publications, Inc.
*The Discipline of Deformity	David W. Miller. Copyright 1996 Christian Light Publications, Inc.
"The Flier Fell . . . ."	From "The Flying Machine," by Ray Bradury.
The Horse	From *The Way to Glory and Other Stories* by Mary Hurd McNeely, Copyright 1932, 1960.
The Man Who Planted Hope and Grew Happiness	Jean Giono
The Mote and the Beam	Used by permission of Robert J. Baker and Herald Press.
*The Pilgrim	David W. Miller. Copyright 1996 Christian Light Publications, Inc.
The Triolet; The Bible; A Key to Happiness; Spring	Lester E. Showalter. Used by permission.
Though He Slay Me	By E. J. Swalm, from *My Beloved Brethren*. Courtesy of Evangel Publishing House.
*Though He Slay Me	David W. Miller. Copyright 1996 Christian Light Publications, Inc.
Too Dark	Ruth K. Hobbs. Used by permission.
True . . . Till Death—The Story of Clayton Kratz	By Clarence Y. Fretz, from *Youth Messenger* 1965. Used by permission.
What Is So Rare as a Day in June?	From "Vision of Sir Launfal," by James Russell Lowell.
Wheelbarrows	© 1969 by Donald Kraybill. Used by permission.
"When the hearse . . . ."	From "The Sculpter's Funeral," from *Youth and Bright Medusa*. Copyright 1904, 1932 by Willa Cather.
When I Survey the Wondrous Cross	Isaac Watts.
Where Love is, There is God Also	Leo Tolstoy, translated by Nathan Haskel Dole, Copyright 1925.
Whom Shall I Fear?	From *The Drummer's Wife* by Joseph Stoll. Copyright 1968 by Pathway Publishers. Used by permission.
Winter's Coming	Faustina Martin Garber. Used by permission.
Zion's Glad Morning; Hail the Blest Morn	Reginald Heber

Attempt has been made to secure permission for the use of all copyrighted material. If further information is received, the publisher will be glad to properly credit this material in future printings.